SOIL AND WATER CONSERVATION

for Productivity
and Environmental
Protection

SOIL AND WATER CONSERVATION

for Productivity and Environmental Protection

Frederick R. Troeh

*Professor of Agronomy
Iowa State University*

J. Arthur Hobbs

*Professor of Agronomy
Kansas State University*

Roy L. Donahue

*Professor Emeritus of Soil Science
Michigan State University*

Editorial assistance
Miriam R. Troeh

Prentice-Hall, Inc., Englewood Cliffs, New Jersey 07632

Library of Congress Cataloging in Publication Data

Troeh, Frederick R. (date)
    Soil and water conservation for productivity and
environmental protection.

    Bibliography: p.
    Includes index.
    1. Soil conservation. 2. Water conservation.
3. Soil erosion. I. Hobbs, James Arthur, (date)
joint author. II. Donahue, Roy L., joint author.
III. Title.
S623.T76 1980   333.7'2   80-364
ISBN 0-13-822-155-3

Editorial/production supervision by Leslie Nadell
Interior design by Kim McNeily Davis and Leslie Nadell
Cover design by Jorge Hernandez
Manufacturing buyers: Edmund Leone and John Hall

Printed in the United States of America

10 9 8 7 6 5

Prentice-Hall International, Inc., *London*
Prentice-Hall of Australia Pty. Limited, *Sydney*
Prentice-Hall of Canada, Ltd., *Toronto*
Prentice-Hall of India Private Limited, *New Delhi*
Prentice-Hall of Japan, Inc., *Tokyo*
Prentice-Hall of Southeast Asia Pte. Ltd., *Singapore*
Whitehall Books Limited, *Wellington, New Zealand*

Contents

6 PREDICTING SOIL LOSS, 147

7 SOIL SURVEYS AND LAND USE PLANNING, 201

8 CROPPING SYSTEMS, 233

9 TILLAGE PRACTICES FOR CONSERVATION, 274

Preface

Soil and water conservation deals with the wise use of these important resources. Wise use requires knowledge, understanding, and value judgment. The hazards posed by erosion, sedimentation, and pollution, and the techniques needed to conserve soil and maintain environmental quality are all treated in this book. Situations and examples are drawn from many places constituting a cross-section of the soils, climates, and cultures of the world. The scope includes agricultural, engineering, mining, and other uses of land. Soil and water are recognized as essentials for everyone's life.

Soil and water have always been vital for sustaining life, and these resources are becoming more limited and crucial as population increases. The importance of conserving soil productivity and protecting the quality of both soil and water is becoming clear to more people than ever before. Declining productivity and increasing pollution could spell disaster for all residents of the earth. The soil and water resources of the planet are finite and are already under intensive use and misuse.

Much of this book can be read and understood by anyone with a good general education. Some parts, however, necessarily assume an acquaintance with basic soil properties such as texture, structure, water-holding capacity, and cation exchange capacity. These topics are covered in any introductory soil science textbook and one of these should be consulted if the reader lacks this background. The system of soil taxonomy used in the United States is followed in this book. An explanation of that system can also be found in modern introductory soils textbooks.

The authors have a broad collective background in soil science and soil conservation in the United States and abroad. This experience has been supplemented by extensive use of the available literature, through excellent libraries plus many publications from government agencies. Many colleagues have also contributed valuable suggestions and have thoughtfully reviewed the manuscript. The helpful assistance of the following persons is gratefully acknowledged:

Gustave Fairbanks, Professor of Agricultural Engineering, Kansas State University

George R. Foster, SEA-USDA, Purdue University

Harold R. Godown, SCS-USDA, Nevada, Iowa

Walter E. Jeske, SCS-USDA, Washington, D.C.

John M. Laflen, Associate Professor of Agricultural Engineering, Iowa State University

Rattan Lal, Soil Physicist, International Institute of Tropical Agriculture, Ibadan, Nigeria

Leon Lyles, SEA-USDA, Kansas State University

John Malcolm, USAID, Washington, D.C.

Harry L. Manges, Associate Professor of Agricultural Engineering, Kansas State University

Jerry V. Mannering, Professor of Agronomy, Purdue University

Gerald A. Miller, Associate Professor of Agronomy, Iowa State University

John A. Miranowsky, Assistant Professor of Economics, Iowa State University

Basil Moussouros, former Minister for Agriculture, Government of Greece

Gerald W. Olson, Professor of Soil Science, Cornell University

G. Stuart Pettygrove, Department of Land, Air, and Water Resources, University of California at Davis

William L. Powers, Professor of Agronomy, Kansas State University

Frank W. Schaller, SEA Extension, Iowa State University

Homer E. Socolofsky, Professor of History, Kansas State University

E. L. Skidmore, SEA-USDA, Kansas State University

Gene Taylor, U.S. Congress from 7th District of Missouri

D. Keith Whigham, Associate Professor of Agronomy, Iowa State University

C. M. Woodruff, Professor Emeritus, Department of Agronomy, University of Missouri

Frederick R. Troeh
Ames, Iowa

J. Arthur Hobbs
Manhattan, Kansas

Roy L. Donahue
Forsyth, Missouri

1

Conserving
Soil Productivity

Soil is a vital resource for the production of food, fiber, and other necessities of life. The food and fiber are renewable resources—a fresh crop can be grown to replace what is consumed. The soil that produces these renewable resources is formed so slowly that it is essentially nonrenewable.

Great concern is expressed when there is a shortage of a food product or some other renewable resource. Prices of coffee and sugar, for example, have increased suddenly and dramatically when a significant part of the world's crop was damaged, temporarily decreasing the supply. Other prices respond similarly to the economics of supply and demand. Such situations attract attention because they arise suddenly and require an adjustment in the lives of many people. The more gradual changes resulting from persistent processes such as soil erosion may escape attention in spite of their fundamental importance. The long-term loss of productivity caused by soil erosion should be of greater concern than temporary shortages.

Soil conservation objectives include both using the soil and maintaining its productive capacity. Soil can be preserved by being covered with concrete, but its use to produce crops is lost in the process. Intensive cropping uses the soil but often causes the soil on sloping land to be lost by erosion. Type and intensity of land use and management must be chosen for long-term usefulness of the land as well as for current needs. Scarred landscapes, as shown in Figure 1-1, tell a sad story of waste and ruin where long-term principles have been sacrificed for short-term gain.

High rates, or even what many consider moderate rates, of soil loss are more detrimental than might be supposed from the actual

Figure 1-1 The amount of soil eroded by gullies eating their way into a landscape is spectacular but is often exceeded by sheet erosion around the gullies. (Courtesy USDA—Soil Conservation Service.)

amount of soil lost. The sorting action of either water or wind removes a high proportion of the clay and humus from the soil and leaves the less productive coarse sand, gravel, and stones behind. Most of the soil fertility is associated with the clay and humus. These components also are important in microbial activity, soil structure, permeability, and water-holding capacity. Thus, an eroded soil is degraded chemically, physically, and biologically.

1-1 NEEDS INCREASING WITH TIME

The demand for plant and animal products increases with time as population increases and standards of living are raised. The human population has multiplied to a point where people now consume more food than all other land animals combined (Deevey, 1960). The increased demand for products places an increasing load on soil productivity. Plants can be grown without soil by hydroponics and sand or gravel culture (McCall and Nakagawa, 1972), but the expense is high and the scale is small. Even seafood is used on a relatively small scale compared to soil products.

Until recent decades, production increases came mostly by bringing new land into use. New frontiers were opened, forests were cut, prairies were plowed, and deserts were irrigated, thereby maintaining the average cultivated area per person. Some people suggested that a minimum area of one hectare per person was needed to maintain a satisfactory standard of living. Approximately that much area was maintained for a long time by continually expanding the land base being used. Of course, the best land is chosen first, so the average suitability of the land declines even if the area per person is maintained. The results of using poorly suited land as intensively as the better land are often devastating.

The one-hectare-per-person rule is no longer supported. Many countries now have more people than hectares of land. Production depends not only on land area but also on soil, crop, climate, and management. One hectare per person may not be enough in some places, but it is more than adequate in others.

The land base in recent decades has been relatively constant. Most of the good cropland is already in use. Irrigation has been increasing and may continue to increase (Doorenbos, 1975), but much of this increase is on land that was already being cropped without irrigation. The small areas of new cropland being added each year are offset by the construction of roads, homes, factories, and other structures on former cropland. Ryabchikov (1976) estimates that people already are using 56% of earth's land surface, 15% of it intensively. Much of the rest is not suitable for human use.

Increased production is now obtained mostly by increasing yields and intensifying the use of present cropland. New crop varieties and increased fertilization are important factors producing higher yields. More intensive crop rotations increase the amount of row crops and grain crops at the expense of forage crops. Other adjustments have also been made, such as multiple cropping and the reduction or elimination of the rest period in the slash-and-burn system of some tropical areas. The effect of these changes on soil erosion has been mixed. Fertilization and multiple cropping increase plant cover on land and reduce erosion. The replacement of forage crops with row crops and grain crops and the shortening of rest periods in slash-and-burn tend to increase erosion.

1-2 EROSION PROBLEMS

Erosion occurs in many forms as a result of several causes. Anything that moves, including water, wind, glaciers, animals, and vehicles, can be a causative agent. Gravity tends to move soil downslope—either very slowly as in soil creep or very rapidly as in landslides.

1-2.1 Intermittent Erosion

Erosion can be uniform and subtle. Sheet erosion, for example, removes layer after layer a little at a time until 10, 20, or 30 cm of soil or more are gone without anyone having paid much attention. More often, though, erosion is intermittent and spotty. Irregularities in the land surface concentrate the erosive effect of either wind or water in certain spots. Cavities may be blown out by wind or gullies cut by water—gullies that may eventually be enlarged into valleys. The pattern is usually spotty, as shown in Figure 1-2.

Most of the erosion at any one place typically occurs during relatively short periods. Weeks, months, or even years may pass without much soil being lost. When a ferocious storm strikes and tears away the soil, the loss in a single day may exceed that of an entire century. The soil loss in most places is intermittent enough that half of the annual loss occurs in only a few days. These few days often occur during a season when rain and wind are especially intense and plant cover is at a minimum.

The spotty and intermittent nature of erosion complicates the interpretation of erosion measurements. A field with an average soil loss of 5 metric tons per hectare (mt/ha) annually is within the accepted tolerable rate for most deep soils, if the loss is evenly distributed. But, if the average consists of 50 mt/ha from part of the field and little or none from the rest, part of the field is being ruined by erosion. Furthermore, crops on adjoining areas may be suffering damage from sedimentation, as shown in Figure 1-3. An average over time is equally deceptive. All benefits of having only small soil losses for nine years are wiped out if severe loss the tenth year completely destroys a crop.

1-2.2 Accelerated Erosion

The normal rate of erosion under natural vegetation is in approximate equilibrium with the rate of soil formation, thereby maintaining a nearly constant soil depth at any one place. The stable soil depth for a particular set of conditions insulates the underlying parent material from weathering just enough so that soil is formed as

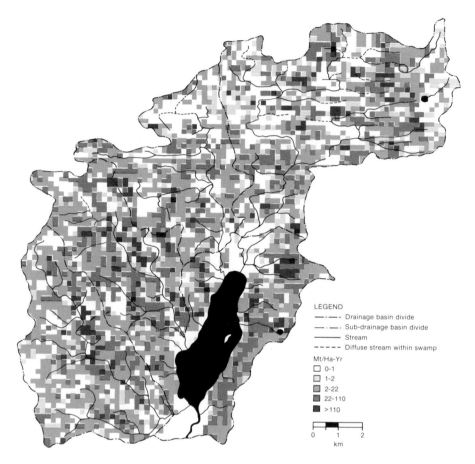

Figure 1-2 Estimated annual soil-loss rates by 4-ha cells in the Lake Canadarago drainage basin, New York. (Modified from Kling and Olson, 1975.)

fast as it is lost. Deviations from equilibrium cause the soil to get either thicker or thinner until a new equilibrium is established. Precise data on the average rates of geologic (natural) erosion and soil formation are difficult to obtain but are thought to be less than 1 mt/ha annually (Smith and Stamey, 1965).

Removal of vegetation by tilling cropland, by grazing pasture or rangeland, or by cutting trees nearly always increases the rate of soil erosion. The soil has less protection against the detaching action of raindrop impact and the transporting action of runoff water and wind. Loss of soil cover may accelerate soil loss by a factor of 10, 20, 50, or 100 times. Formation of new soil cannot keep pace with

Figure 1-3 Sediment from the higher areas covered and killed the crop in the foreground in this Iowa field. (Courtesy USDA— Soil Conservation Service.)

such accelerated erosion rates, so the soil becomes progressively thinner until a new equilibrium is established or all the soil is lost.

Accelerated erosion reduces the amount of plant growth a soil is able to support. Sometimes the actual production is maintained or even increased by the use of fertilizer and other management techniques but the potential production is still reduced. The shallower soil, with its reduced capacity for storing water and plant nutrients and its generally poorer structure and aeration, has less productive potential than the uneroded soil. The significance of reduced potential productivity becomes greater as the actual yields come closer to the potential.

1-2.3 An Old Problem in a New Setting

Erosion has been a problem since the dawn of civilization. Cultivated fields, overgrazed pastures, and cut-over forest lands have always suffered from erosion. The eroded soil becomes sediment that pollutes streams, covers bottomlands, and sometimes becomes so thick that it buries both fields and cities. The result becomes an archaeologist's treasure when a famous city such as Babylon is uncovered centuries after its inhabitants lost a frustrating battle with sediment eroded from the nearby hills.

Gullies, sand dunes, and other obvious signs of erosion have undoubtedly caused concern from the beginning of agriculture. Impressive terrace systems were built thousands of years ago to stop erosion. Even so, erosive forces are so widespread and persistent that entire soil profiles have been lost by sheet erosion, gullies have cut hillsides to pieces, and sand dunes have drifted across anything in their path as, for example, the sidewalk shown in Figure 1-4. Many millions of hectares of formerly productive land have been abandoned because of erosion damage.

A new concern has been added in recent years in addition to the age-old problems of erosion and deposition. Eroded soil is now recognized as a major cause of air and water pollution. Soil erosion produces dust clouds and muddy water, and the eroded soil particles carry plant nutrients and other chemicals that contaminate water. Eroded soil has become an environmental problem that must be remedied for the sake of clean air and water. This new concern has added an urgency to erosion control that should have been recognized earlier.

Figure 1-4 Sand from a nearby beach drifted into the city and blocked this sidewalk in Montevideo, Uruguay. (Courtesy F. R. Troeh.)

Conserving soil is important for the sake of the land threatened by erosion, but its direct impact is felt mostly by people who actually work with the land. Pollution, however, affects everyone. Soil conservation practices must be used along with other pollution controls to protect the environment. The early stages of pollution control concentrated on point sources such as sewage systems and smokestacks. Current efforts are beginning to include nonpoint sources such as soil erosion. An increasing part of the impetus for soil conservation, especially that which is legally mandated, stems from environmental concerns.

1-2.4 A Concern for All People

Eroded soil and the chemicals it carries are matters of concern because a degraded environment can be detrimental to everyone's health and enjoyment. Polluted water, for example, is unsafe for drinking, swimming, and many other uses. It can cause fish kills; moreover, the surviving fish may impair the health and reproductive capacity of birds that eat them. Both the fish and the birds may be made unfit for human food.

Erosion adds to the cost of producing food and other soil products. These costs ultimately increase the prices of harvested crops and thereby add to the cost of living. Taking ruined land out of production places a greater load on the remaining land and drives up production costs. Installing expensive erosion control practices also adds to production costs, but these practices help assure that production will continue.

The importance of soil conservation and pollution control has led to the passage of many laws, especially in recent years. Proposed legislation should be of concern to all voters, even those not directly affected by it. Government may provide too little, too much, or the wrong kind of control to bring about effective soil conservation. Tax funds are used to pay the public's share of conservation costs. Everyone is affected; the public needs to understand and support the principles of soil and water conservation and environmental protection.

1-3 OBSTACLES TO CONSERVATION

Conservation is difficult to oppose in principle, yet easy to overlook or ignore in practice. Too many people give lip service to conservation but leave the application to someone else. Reasons for inaction include economic and aesthetic obstacles, insecurity and uncertainty, ignorance, and apathy.

1-3.1 Economic Obstacles

Major decisions are usually based largely on economic considerations. How much will it cost? What returns can be expected? Will the cost be repaid in a short time, in a long time, or not at all?

Conservation practices vary greatly in costs, returns, and effectiveness. The easiest practices to promote are those that will return a profit within a short time. For example, a good fertilizer program returns a profit as soon as the crop is harvested and helps conserve soil at the same time. Longer-term practices such as liming and soil drainage may be recognized as desirable for some time before the necessary financing can be arranged. The time lag is still longer for terracing and other practices that have high investment costs requiring many years to repay. Least popular of all are practices such as changing to a less intensive land use with lower probable returns.

1-3.2 Aesthetic and Cultural Obstacles

A great deal of pride can be involved in certain agricultural traditions. Straight rows, for example, are considered a mark of skill. Years ago young persons learning to handle horses were instructed "Don't look back!" because a tug on the reins would turn the horses and make a crooked row. Straight rows are appealing but they also cause erosion. Straight rows on hilly land provide cultivated channels for runoff water to erode. Contour tillage is often the solution, but it must overcome tradition.

Many farmers take pride in plowing so that none of last year's crop residues remain on the soil surface. The uniform dark color of a residue-free surface is highly regarded, but this practice causes erosion by exposing the soil to the impact of rain, runoff, and wind. Conservation tillage reduces erosion by leaving residues on the surface, but it must overcome tradition before its advantages and disadvantages will be fairly considered.

1-3.3 Insecurity and Uncertainty

Many people in developing countries are barely able to eke out a living from their land by hard work such as the hand tillage shown in Figure 1-5. They know that their traditional management has kept them and their predecessors alive. They also know that they have no margin for error to gamble on a new method. It is difficult for them to change their techniques even if they would benefit immediately by higher yields and/or less soil loss. It is even more difficult for them to adopt a practice that requires an investment, especially if the

Figure 1-5 Much hand labor is used in areas where people are barely able to subsist by tilling the land. (Courtesy F. Botts, Food and Agriculture Organization of the United Nations.)

benefits are delayed or distributed over several years. The establishment of conservation practices under such conditions requires financing and a reliable guarantee that these people will not starve to death if the new practice fails.

Short-term tenancy promotes another form of insecurity that prevents the adoption of many desirable practices. A one-year contract, or even a five-year contract, does not give the renter enough time to benefit from the sizable investment of money and labor required to install many long-term conservation practices. Theoretically, the land owners should be willing to invest in sound long-term practices, but many owners are too far removed from the land to realize what practices are needed. Short-term tenancy makes it easy for both tenants and owners to overlook problems even when those problems reach critical stages.

1-3.4 Ignorance and Apathy

Most erosion occurs so gradually and subtly that its effects are easily overlooked until long after preventive action should have been taken.

Even the presence of rills (small erosion channels) in a field is often ignored because tillage operations can smooth the surface again. Unproductive subsoil exposed on a knob or on the shoulder of a hill is overlooked if the rest of the field remains productive. Even people who work with the land are unaware of how many tons of soil are being lost each year, of how costly these losses are, and of how short the useful life expectancy may be for a rapidly eroding soil.

Too many people have short-term viewpoints regarding the use of soil and other resources. Short-term outlooks are apathetic about future needs. Land that was ruined by past generations is unavailable now, and land that is ruined now is lost to the future population. The decline in productivity of eroded but usable land is even more important because it is more widespread. Erosion adds to the cost of production or reduces the amount of production or both.

Erosion control practices needed to prevent environmental pollution often are not installed or are long postponed because of indifference. Some land owners feel that they have the right to use their land as they please even if it is being ruined and even if the sediment is being deposited on other people's property. Public opinion has been swinging against such extreme views, and several states have passed laws restricting the rate of soil erosion allowable under specific conditions. Environmental considerations have provided much of the impetus for such laws.

Much reluctance to protect the environment is based on economics. The people who must spend money to conserve their soil are not the only ones who suffer if the soil is eroded or benefit if it is conserved. Often the persons most affected live someplace downstream or downwind or will live at a later time. People are commonly reluctant to spend their money for unknown beneficiaries. In fact, many people are unwilling to spend money to conserve soil for their own future benefit.

1-4 CONSERVATION VIEWPOINT

Erosion problems call for solutions. Obstacles must be overcome. The need for soil conservation has been clear enough to catch the attention of many people. The conservation viewpoint has had advocates for thousands of years. For example, ancient people of Rome, India, Peru, and several other places valued soil highly enough to build terraces such as those shown in Figure 1-6 that still stand today. Terrace walls were built of stones left on eroded hillsides; the laborers then carried soil in baskets on their backs from the foot of

Figure 1-6 These terraces in Bolivia were built hundreds, or perhaps thousands, of years ago and are still protecting the soil from erosion. (Courtesy F. R. Troeh.)

the hill up to the terraces to make level benches. The Chinese still carry out similar laborious projects, but most modern conservation structures are built with the aid of machines.

The labor investment in hand-built terraces is very high and indicates a great devotion to the land. A concern for the land is actually the most important characteristic of a soil conservationist. Those who have such a concern will find a way to conserve their soil; those who lack it often neglect to use even the most obvious and inexpensive means of conserving soil. Conservation efforts therefore include a large measure of education and persuasion aimed at convincing more people to care for their land.

There are now well-organized groups whose primary function is to promote soil and water conservation. The U.S. Department of Agriculture has the Soil Conservation Service to help people install conservation practices; several other agencies work with them and support their efforts. The Soil Conservation Service works in cooperation with local Soil Conservation Districts that also have their own national association. Interested individuals can become members of the Soil Conservation Society of America, and there are many other groups at national, state, and local levels that advocate conservation of soil, water, and other resources.

Conservationists normally take a long-term view regarding the use of resources. Some land is still productive after several thousand years of use. All land needs to be used in ways that will maintain its usefulness. The objective of soil conservation has been stated as "the use of each acre of agricultural land within its capabilities and the treatment of each acre of agricultural land in accordance with its needs for protection and improvement."

1–5 CONSERVATION TECHNIQUES

The practices used for conserving soil and water are many and varied. Some practices are expensive and some require only a change in habits; some are permanent and some are temporary; some are limited to very restricted conditions while others are widely useful, though none have universal application. The amount of erosion reduction varies from one practice to another and from one set of circumstances to another.

1–5.1 Land Use and Management

One of the first considerations of a soil conservationist is the use of land within its capabilities. Some land is suited for intensive cropping—especially where the soil is deep, level, fertile, and well drained and has favorable texture and structure. Other land is so steep, shallow, stony, or otherwise limited that it is suitable only for wildlife, recreation, or other uses that cause no erosion. Many gradations exist between these two extremes. Most land is suitable for some uses but unsuitable for others.

Land use can be broadly classified into cropland, pastureland, woodland, wildlife and recreational land, and miscellaneous use. Each broad class can be subdivided several times. For example, cropland includes land used for cultivated row crops, small grain crops, and hay crops. The soil exposure to erosive forces declines from row crops to small grain crops to hay crops because of differing growth habits and management techniques. The exposure to erosive forces continues to decline from cropland to pasture and woodland and then to wildlife land. These latter uses are therefore considered to be of progressively lower intensity.

Land use is a complex factor that fits approximately into a

simple classification system such as that in the preceding paragraph. A more complete system would provide nonagricultural classes paralleling the agricultural ones. For example, lawn grasses, as shown in Figure 1-7, might be roughly equivalent to a similar growth of pasture grasses.

Management can alter the effect of a single type of land use on a wide range of erosive tendencies. Row crops, for example, can be grown in wide or narrow rows that may or may not follow contour lines. There may or may not be a lengthy exposure to the elements between the harvesting of one crop and the protective growth of the next. The soil may or may not be protected by crop residues or by special cover crops during periods when the main crop is not on the land. Each of these variables has a considerable effect on the amount of erosion that is likely to occur.

Variations also occur with other types of land use. Pasture, for example, may have grasses and legumes that were specially selected to provide ground cover and forage, or it may have whatever happens to grow. The number of livestock per hectare may be limited to what the pasture can readily support, or it may be so large that overgrazing kills part of the vegetation. Both extremes may occur in the same

Figure 1-7 A dense growth of bluegrass in this lawn provides excellent protection against erosion. (Courtesy F. R. Troeh.)

pasture if the livestock are permitted to spend too much time in one area. Also, both soil and vegetation may be damaged by trampling if livestock are allowed to graze when the soil is too wet.

1–5.2 Vegetative and Mechanical Practices

Conservation techniques are often divided into vegetative and mechanical practices. There is no good reason for always favoring one type over the other; both include a wide variety of methods of protecting soil against erosive forces. The best approach in many situations requires a combination of vegetative and mechanical practices.

Vegetative practices include techniques that provide denser vegetative cover for a larger percentage of the time. Changing to less intensive land use is usually a very effective means of reducing erosion. The problem with less intensive land use is that it usually is less profitable. A compromise using a series of different crops with some providing more income and some giving more soil protection is known as a crop rotation. Crops grown for the sole purpose of protecting soil between other crops are known as cover crops.

Choices of land use, crop rotations, and cover crops are all vegetative means of erosion control. They need to be accompanied by good management techniques that help each crop grow well. Good seed planted at the right time in a proper seedbed helps get the crop off to a good start. Adequate fertilizer and lime where needed promote vigorous growth. Narrow row spacing allows a row crop to provide better soil cover sooner. These management techniques generally improve both yield and erosion control.

Placement of special vegetation in critical places also is important. Grassed waterways can prevent the formation of gullies. Windbreaks can direct the wind stream away from erodible land. Various forms of strip cropping reduce water erosion, wind erosion, and pollution. Appropriate plantings in odd corners, steep slopes, or other problem areas provide food and cover for wildlife as well as erosion control. Special plantings are needed also for disturbed areas such as roadbanks and mine spoils.

Vegetative methods can limit erosion to geologic rates. Grasses, trees, and other plants are nature's tools for controlling erosion; the rate of erosion that native vegetation allows defines the geologic rate for a particular setting. Though geologic rates are usually quite slow, they occasionally are as sudden and rapid as a landslide. Sometimes the rate of erosion should be reduced below the geologic rate by providing more than the natural amount of protection. More often, some increase above the geologic rate is allowable.

Mechanical methods broaden the choice of vegetation and allow a higher-income crop to be grown even though the crop provides less soil protection. Contour tillage, for example, can often reduce erosion to half that resulting from random orientation to the slope. Leaving most of the crop residues on the soil surface by reducing the amount of tillage reduces erosion markedly. Further reductions can be achieved by building a terrace system such as that shown in Figure 1-8 to prevent eroded soil from leaving the field. Soil movement may occur between terraces, but the soil is deposited in terrace channels rather than being allowed to pollute a stream. Of course, the channels must be cleaned periodically as a part of terrace maintenance.

Various structures made of concrete, wood, metal, or some other sturdy material are used to control erosion by controlling water flow. Critical points occur where water must be dropped from a higher elevation to a lower one. The soil may be protected by conducting the water through a pipeline, down a flume or chute, or over a drop structure. Pilings, riprap, or other bank protection may be used to keep a stream from meandering to a new location.

Figure 1-8 A set of terraces such as these holds the soil on the field rather than letting it erode away. (Courtesy USDA—Soil Conservation Service.)

Mechanical methods of erosion control tend to be either very inexpensive or very expensive. Conservation tillage practices save fuel, time, and money by reducing the total amount of work done on the soil. Also, conservation tillage often combines two or three operations into one and therefore requires fewer trips across the field. Reorienting the direction of tillage to a contour system may require more planning and layout and add the inconvenience of many short rows, but it normally costs no more than conventional tillage. The fuel requirement for working across the slope is usually slightly less than that for up and down the slope.

Tillage changes require no new investments unless new equipment is needed. On the other hand, these inexpensive or money-saving practices are short-lived and must be repeated with each new crop. Most longer-lived, mechanical methods of erosion control involve expensive structures such as terraces, dams, and drop structures. The earth moving and concrete work required are costly. Expensive structures are usually justified by their many years of usefulness and increased flexibility of land use.

1-5.3 Conserving Soil and Water Together

Soil and water conservation are so interrelated that they can only be accomplished together. There are relatively few techniques for conserving soil that do not also conserve water and still fewer techniques for conserving water that do not also conserve soil.

Both soil and water can be conserved by protecting the soil from raindrops that would puddle the surface and cause a crust to form. Plant material intercepting raindrops helps maintain a permeable condition that allows water to infiltrate instead of running off. The soil acts as a reservoir that conserves water; soil is conserved by reducing both splash and runoff.

Contouring, contour strip cropping, rough surfaces created by tillage, and terracing all increase infiltration by holding water on the land longer. Some runoff occurs, but it is slower and carries less soil. Streams fed by slow runoff and seepage water have longer-lasting flow and lower flood peaks than they would have if their watersheds were unprotected.

Reducing erosion keeps streams, ponds, and lakes from filling as rapidly with sediment. Reservoir capacities are thus maintained for their intended purposes of recreation, flood control, power generation, and irrigation. Keeping sediment out of the water also avoids the buildup of plant nutrients in the water and thereby reduces unwanted growth of algae and other vegetation. Pollutants attached to soil particles are best kept out of water by keeping the soil on the land. The control of nonpoint sources of water pollution therefore centers on conserving soil.

Wind erosion control is more closely related to water conservation than it might seem. Soil detachment by raindrop impact leaves loose particles that are subject to wind erosion when the soil dries. Plants and plant residues that protect the soil surface from raindrops also prevent wind erosion.

Water conservation becomes very important for plant growth in dry climates. Anything that helps get more water into the soil or keeps it there by reducing evaporation provides more water for plant growth. Improved plant growth in turn helps reduce wind erosion as well as water erosion.

1-6 CHOOSING CONSERVATION PRACTICES

No single land use is appropriate everywhere, nor is any single conservation practice needed everywhere. Soil and water conservation is too complex to be solved by only one approach. Each situation needs to be analyzed to determine what problems and potentials exist and what alternatives are available. Such an analysis provides the basis for making intelligent decisions.

1-6.1 Soil Properties Basic to Conservation

Many soil properties influence soil and water conservation, but a few deserve special emphasis because they strongly influence erosion control. Soil topography, depth, permeability, texture, structure, and fertility are worth consideration in relation to conservation.

Soil topography includes the gradient, length, shape, and aspect (direction) of slopes. These features control the concentration or dispersion of erosive forces such as runoff water and wind. Topography also influences the practicality of erosion control practices such as contouring, strip cropping, and terracing. These practices may be very helpful on long, smooth slopes but impractical on rolling topography with short, steep slopes.

Soil depth, the nature and thickness of the soil horizons, and the underlying rock material greatly affect the rate of soil formation and the tolerable rate of erosion. The erosion tolerance is much lower for shallow soils over hard bedrock than it is for deep soils underlain by unconsolidated material such as loess. Subsoils with high clay contents or other unfavorable properties also need to be covered with topsoil to support plant growth. Deep soil is favorable for water storage and plant growth. Where the soil is shallow, it may be impossible to smooth the land for drainage and irrigation or to move soil for building terraces and ponds.

Soil permeability and the rate of rainfall or irrigation determine how much water will run off and cause erosion. Conditions that most commonly limit soil permeability are a soil surface puddled by raindrops or traffic, plowsoles or other highly compacted layers, heavy subsoils with only small pores for water passages, frozen soil, and bedrock or cemented layers. The closer a restrictive layer is to the soil surface, the less water is required to saturate the soil above it and cause runoff to begin. Soil permeability also influences the functioning of subsurface drainage systems and of septic tank drain fields.

Soil texture and structure both influence soil permeability and erodibility. The clay in a soil helps it cohere either into a solid mass or into structural units with pore space between them. Individual clay particles are difficult to detach from a soil but can easily be moved long distances after they are detached. Sand particles are easily detached from sandy soils, but a high velocity of water is required to move them very far. Silty soils are often the most erodible by water, because the silt particles are too large to stick together well and are small enough to be transported readily. Silt particles are small enough, however, to resist detachment by wind unless they are knocked loose by something else, such as moving sand particles.

Soil fertility is important to soil conservation because plant growth helps protect the soil. The more vigorous growth produced on a fertile soil provides better protection and is less likely to leave bare spots vulnerable to erosion. Fertilizer and lime are therefore important for soil conservation.

1-6.2 Maps for Conservation Planning

Most of the soil properties discussed in the preceding section can be mapped. Topographic shapes and elevations are shown by contour lines. Soil depth, texture, structure, and many other properties are considered in naming the soil series shown on soil maps along with slope gradient and past erosion.

Soil maps are prepared by the Soil Conservation Service and by other agencies that have responsibilities for certain areas of land. The maps are used as a basis for conservation planning. The various soil areas are classified on the basis of the intensity of land use for which they are suited, their limitations, and the treatment they need. Soil maps are often colored to make their important features stand out for use in planning. The soil maps are published along with descriptions of the various soils and interpretations for various uses in soil survey reports such as those shown in Figure 1-9.

1-6.3 Considering Alternatives

Any piece of land could be used and managed in a variety of ways. Some ways would cause disastrous damage to the land or monetary loss from the operation. Several satisfactory ways usually remain after the disastrous and other unsatisfactory ways are eliminated. For example, a field might be used for pasture or hay production without any special practices, or it might be used for a crop rotation without excessive erosion if contour strip cropping and conservation tillage were used, or it might be used for intensive row crops if terraces were built and conservation tillage used. Economic factors and personal preference are usually considered when a choice must be made from alternatives such as these.

Many choices depend on the basic intent of the land owner or operator. Producing hay or pasture on part or on all of one's land

Figure 1-9 Soil survey reports such as these contain soil maps, descriptions, and interpretations for various uses such as soil and water conservation. (Courtesy F. R. Troeh.)

implies an operation that includes livestock. Building terraces to permit more row crops fits a cash-crop operation. Cover crops can be used to protect the soil between the trees in an orchard. Irrigation makes it possible to grow a wide variety of crops in arid climates, and soil drainage permits the use of otherwise wet areas. Each increase in the intensity of use requires additional conservation practices to protect the land.

1-7 CARING FOR THE LAND

Conservationists see land as a stewardship. The same land that is now in one person's care was previously in someone else's and will soon pass to others. Its condition when passed on should be as good as when it was received. The owner also has a responsibility to society for the way the land is used and the care it receives. The authority of governmental units to tax land, to restrict its use in certain ways, and to require that access and some other rights be granted to others indicates that ownership is not absolute.

Soil and water conservation attitudes and practices are needed everywhere. Even the best land is subject to damage if it is abused. Good land, fair land, and poor land are all useful if they receive proper care. People need constant reminders not to choose short-term exploitation over long-term productivity.

The use and care of agricultural land are stressed throughout this book, but the need for conservation on nonagricultural land must not be overlooked. Erosion is often more rapid on a construction site than in any nearby field. Excess traffic in a park area can wear paths that may become gullies. Modified versions of agricultural practices may serve to control erosion in these and many other circumstances. Vegetation and mechanical structures can be adapted to a wide variety of situations.

Population growth is making good land stewardship more crucial. Soil productivity must be conserved and enhanced to avert mass starvation. "How many people can the earth support?" has become a very pertinent question. The increasing pressure on the land from higher population densities makes the conservation task both more important and more difficult. The need for population control has become sufficiently obvious to cause many programs to be developed for that purpose, such as the family planning center shown in Figure 1-10. These programs and soil conservation practices are both needed, literally, for the salvation of the world.

Figure 1-10 Family planning centers such as this one on Mauritius, an island in the Indian Ocean, are helping reduce birth rates and control population. This island has 850,000 people living in an area of 1,865 km². (Courtesy P. Morin, Food and Agriculture Organization of the United Nations.)

SUMMARY

Soil is a basic resource that can be lost through gradual erosion that may go unnoticed. The loss in productive capacity is usually worse than the tonnage indicates because erosion sorts the soil and removes the most fertile part. Soil conservation seeks ways to use the soil without losing it.

Population growth increases the load on soil productivity. Production increases formerly came mostly by increasing the cultivated land area. Now, increased production must be obtained by increasing yields and intensity of land use because new land is hard to find.

Erosion is so intermittent and spotty that averages fail to reveal the serious damage done to soil and crops. Accelerated erosion reduces the soil depth because soil is lost much more quickly than it is formed.

Cultivated fields, overgrazed pastures, and cut-over forest lands have suffered from erosion since the dawn of civilization, and sediment has been polluting streams and burying fields and cities. Erosion control efforts such as terrace systems have been in use for thousands of years but have been inadequate to prevent the loss of millions of hectares of land. The contribution of erosion to air and water pollution has become a major concern in recent years. Erosion, pollution, and soil conservation are costly to everyone.

The installation of conservation practices is delayed by the cost and the reluctance to abandon traditional methods. Subsistence agriculture, short-term tenancy, ignorance of erosion problems, and apathy are additional obstacles, but people who care about the land find ways to conserve their soil.

Many different techniques are available for conserving soil and water. The first requirement is to select an appropriate use within the land capability. Good management and conservation practices come next. Protective practices may be vegetative, mechanical, or a combination of the two. The effectiveness of vegetative practices depends on the density of the vegetation and the percentage of time it covers the land. Special permanent vegetation, such as grassed waterways, windbreaks, or other plantings, can be placed where more protection is needed. Mechanical methods such as conservation tillage and water-control structures permit the growth of higher-income crops.

Soil and water conservation are interrelated and must be accomplished together. Contouring, terracing, and protecting the soil surface against crusting all increase infiltration and reduce runoff and erosion. Keeping sediment out of water lengthens the life of reservoirs and reduces pollution. Water conservation in dry climates increases plant growth and reduces wind erosion.

Soil properties such as topography, depth, permeability, texture, structure, and fertility influence the erodibility of soil and the types of conservation practices that can be used successfully. Topographic maps and soil maps identify many of these properties and are useful for conservation planning.

Good stewardship of land requires that it be passed on to others in good condition for continued productivity. Soil and water conservation are needed for managing both agricultural and nonagricultural land. Population growth makes land stewardship increasingly important.

QUESTIONS

1. In what ways can average rates of erosion be misinterpreted?
2. Why should a factory worker living in an apartment house be concerned about erosion?
3. Why do people fail to adopt new methods of erosion control?
4. Why would one build expensive terraces to control runoff and erosion that could be controlled by inexpensive vegetative methods?
5. What influence has increased environmental concern had on soil conservation?
6. Why are different techniques needed to conserve soils of sandy, silty, and clayey textures?
7. What information useful for conservation planning can be shown on maps?
8. Why do some people do a much better job of soil and water conservation than others?

REFERENCES

BARNETT, A. P., 1972. Agriculture and a quality environment. *J. Soil Water Cons.* 27:104-108.

BRINK, R. A., J. W. DENSMORE, and G. A. HILL, 1977. Soil deterioration and the growing world demand for food. *Science* 197:625-630.

BROWN, L. R., 1968. World food problems. In R. I. MATELES and S. R. TANNENBAUM (eds.), *Single Cell Protein.* MIT Press, Cambridge, Mass., p. 11-26.

DEEVEY, E. S., JR., 1960. The human population. *Scientific American* 203(3): 195-204.

DOORENBOS, J., 1975. The role of irrigation in food production. *Agr. and Environ.* 2:39-54.

HARLAN, J. R., 1975. *Crops and Man.* American Society of Agronomy and Crop Science Society of America, Madison, Wisc., 295 p.

KLING, G. F., and G. W. OLSON, 1975. *Role of Computers in Land Use Planning.* Information Bull. 88, Cornell Univ., Ithaca, N.Y., 12 p.

LOEHR, R. C. (ed.), 1977. *Food, Fertilizer, and Agricultural Residue,* Proc. 9th Annual Cornell Agr. Waste Mgmt. Conf., 1977. Ann Arbor Science Pub., Inc., Ann Arbor, Mich., 727 p.

MANSFIELD, T. A., 1976. *Effects of Air Pollutants on Plants.* Society for Experimental Biology Seminar Series I. Cambridge Univ. Press, New York, 217 p.

McCALL, W. W., and YUKIO NAKAGAWA, 1972. *Growing Plants Without Soil.* Univ. of Hawaii Coop. Ext. Ser. Circular 440, 20 p.

OWENS, H. B., 1973. The public's responsibility to the American landscape. *J. Soil Water Cons.* 28:195-196.

RITCHIE, J. C., 1972: Sediment, fish, and fish habitat. *J. Soil Water Cons.* 27:124-125.

ROSENBERRY, P. E., and W. C. MOLDENHAUER, 1971. Economic implications of soil conservation. *J. Soil Water Cons.* 26:220-224.

RYABCHIKOV, A. M., 1976. Problems of the environment in a global aspect. *Geoforum* 7:107-113.

SMITH, R. M., and W. L. STAMEY, 1965. Determining the range of tolerable erosion. *Soil Sci.* 100:414-424.

STAMEY, W. L., and R. M. SMITH, 1964. A conservation definition of erosion tolerance. *Soil Sci.* 97:183-186.

U.S. DEPARTMENT OF AGRICULTURE, 1974. *Our Land and Water Resources.* Misc. Pub. No. 1290, 54 p.

WADLEIGH, C. H., and R. S. DYAL, 1970. Soils and pollution. In *Agronomy and Health,* American Society of Agronomy, Madison, Wisc., p. 9-19.

WISCHMEIER, W. H., and J. V. MANNERING, 1969. Relation of soil properties to its erodibility. *Soil Sci. Soc. Amer. Proc.* 33:131-137.

2
Soil Erosion
and Civilization

Fields were probably small when cultivated agriculture began thousands of years ago, and cultivation was likely restricted to the more level, more productive soils. Shifting cultivation was probably employed. Under these conditions it is unlikely that erosion losses from these cultivated fields were serious. As population increased, demand for food increased. The cropping period was extended and cultivation spread to steeper, less productive, more erodible sites. Erosion became a significant menace, and soil productivity decreased over time because of soil loss. In some cases the land was destroyed by erosion.

2-1 ORIGIN OF AGRICULTURE

People have cultivated crops only relatively recently; originally they were hunters and gatherers. It is impossible to determine where the first crop was cultivated, but archaeologists can find relics in early agricultural villages that indicate the origins of tillage.

A party of archaeologists from the Oriental Institute of the University of Chicago uncovered an ancient village at Jarmo in the Chemchemal Valley in northern Iraq in 1946. One relic found in the "dig" was a stone hand sickle. Presumably this implement was used to harvest grain, and use of such a tool in harvest operation implies that the grain was domesticated, not just growing wild. Other stone implements found at the village site could have been used for tilling the soil and for cultivating (weeding) the growing crops. This is regarded as the earliest evidence of cultivated agriculture. The date of the occupation of the village is now believed to be about 11,000 B.C. (Braidwood and Howe, 1960). Other prehistoric villages were found in the same general area. These also date from 11,000 to 9,500 B.C.

These villages in northern Iraq were located on upland sites which had friable, fertile, easily tilled, silt loam soils. Native vegetation consisted mainly of grasses with associated forbs, including legumes. The progenitors of modern domestic wheats and barleys are believed to have been among these grasses. The legumes included wild beans, lentils, and vetches. Rains probably fell mainly in the winter with 450 to 500 mm annually; however, the winters were warm enough that there was little snow.

Villages were also excavated in the southern part of Iraq, near the Tigris and Euphrates rivers. These villages apparently were established during the period 9500 to 8800 B.C. They were found mostly on lowland sites. The climate of this area is considerably drier than that farther north. Present rainfall in the lowland area is only about 125 mm per year and is insufficient for rain-fed crop production. Accordingly, the people had to import food grains from more humid areas or they had to develop a new type of agriculture. Probably importations were made initially, but the record is clear that water from the rivers was used to produce irrigated crops. Irrigation made the production of abundant food possible, and in time large cities were built. One of these cities was Babylon.

The early inhabitants of this area, Sumerians, contributed greatly to human development. Not only were they the first to cultivate the soil, but they also invented the wheel and developed a system of counting based on cycles of 60 which we still use in measuring time. Civilization spread from this region east to India and China and west to the lands around the Mediterranean Sea.

2-2 EROSION IN THE CRADLE OF CIVILIZATION

The population of Mesopotamia at the peak of its power and prestige was about 25 million. How long the agriculture of the area prospered is not known with certainty, but by the 1930s Iraq, the major part of ancient Mesopotamia, had a population of only about four million. Many of these people were nomadic tribesmen depending not on crops but on their flocks for sustenance. It is obvious that the area lost its ability to support its one-time large population. What happened to cause agricultural productivity to decline? All of the prehistoric village sites so far discovered were excavated from beneath several to many meters of erosional debris. This evidence suggests that soil erosion was at least partly responsible for the deterioration.

Water erosion on the sites of the upland villages began as soon as relatively large fields were opened on sloping land and farmed continuously. The soils are now badly gullied, and much of the original soil is gone. Food production declined even on ungullied sites, and a large population could no longer be fed.

The irrigated fields of the southern lowland region did not lose soil by erosion, but still it was erosion that ruined the land. Demand for food forced cultivation ever higher up the steep slopes in the hilly and mountainous watershed to the north, sheep and goats overgrazed the hill pastures, and trees were felled indiscriminately for lumber and fuel. These practices denuded the watershed, causing severe erosion and erratic river flow. Large sediment loads were carried by the rivers in the sloping areas where flow was rapid, but the sediment was dropped where flow rate decreased on the level areas. Sediment was deposited in the river bed and, more importantly, in the irrigation canals and ditches. This sediment had to be removed for irrigation to continue. In time, human labor was insufficient to cope with removal, so sections of irrigated land were abandoned. No plant cover grew on the abandoned land because the area was arid. Without vegetative cover, wind eroded the fields, and drifting soil filled the remaining irrigation structures. Eventually the whole irrigated area was abandoned. The large population, much of it in the larger cities, could not be supported. Cities were abandoned, and the area became a desert of shifting sand.

Lowdermilk (1953) insists it was the sediment from the eroding uplands rather than nomadic invasions that caused the downfall of eleven empires and the destruction of a people. Irrigation had to be abandoned when the sediment clogging canals and ditches could no longer be cleared. Agricultural production then declined and eventually ceased. This marks the first, though not the last, failure to develop a permanent, productive cropland agriculture.

2-3 EROSION IN MEDITERRANEAN LANDS

Shortly after tillage was initiated in Mesopotamia, Egypt and other areas on the trade routes between Mesopotamia and Egypt began to develop a system of arable agriculture. It is probable that the knowledge of cultivation and irrigation was carried from the Sumerians to these countries by traders and other travellers.

2-3.1 Soil Productivity in Egypt

Egypt had a dry climate. Only the narrow strip of land along the Nile River, which was flooded annually, was cultivated. A type of irrigated crop production developed, but canals were not constructed. Water was obtained only by natural flooding. Accordingly, only level lands were cultivated in Egypt, so little soil was lost from the tilled fields.

The headwaters of the Nile River are in the mountains and tablelands of Ethiopia about 3000 km south of the irrigated flood plain. Considerable erosion occurred there as a result of extensive forest cutting and cultivation of steep slopes brought on by population pressure. The coarser sediments were deposited mostly in the Sudan where the river left the high country and entered the more level plain. The sediment carried into Egypt was fine textured and fertile; the annual deposit helped maintain soil productivity over the years. Erosion occurred on the arid uplands but did not seriously affect the population. The Nile valley was the site of the first successful attempt to develop a permanent, productive, cultivated agriculture.

2-3.2 Erosion in Israel, Lebanon, Jordan, and Syria

The ancient lands of Palestine, Phoenicia, and Syria have long been the home of sedentary peoples. They have had a long-established cultivated agriculture. Cultivation was restricted to gently sloping lowland areas, with the flocks and herds utilizing the steeper-sloping lands as range. Cultivation gradually encroached on the steeper lands, however, as the population increased and overgrazing and lumbering reduced the cover on the steeper uncultivated slopes. Without the protective native cover, runoff and erosion increased.

The Phoenicians were probably the first people to experience severe erosion from steep slopes. They built bench terraces by constructing stone walls on the contour and leveling the soil behind them. These reduced water erosion and made irrigation on steeply sloping land possible. The land is still being cultivated with some success where this system was used in both Phoenicia and the surrounding countries. Much sloping land, however,. was not terraced, and large soil losses have occurred through the years.

Half of the upland soil area east of the Jordan River and around the Sea of Galilee has been eroded down to bedrock. Much of the eroded material has been deposited in the valleys, where it it still being cultivated. But even the deposited material is subject to repeated erosion every time it rains, and gullies are cutting these more level lands more deeply with each storm. Archaeologists have found as much as 10 m of erosional sediment covering many former cities and villages in bottomland areas. North of Antskye (Antioch), now in Turkey, there are about a half million hectares from which one to two meters of soil have been eroded.

Some arid regions, such as the Sinai Peninsula, have been over-grazed to the extent that the land is crossed by extremely large gullies in spite of the low rainfall of the area. Wind erosion severely damaged the soil between the gullies, but as stones of various sizes were exposed, a closely fitted desert pavement formed which now prevents further wind damage.

The productive capacity of the soil has greatly deteriorated as a result of this erosion. Population in many sections is greatly reduced from what it was in earlier times. Some areas which formerly produced food for export in the days of the Roman and Greek empires now cannot even produce enough to feed the population that once lived there.

Some authorities have claimed that declining productivity, particularly in the drier sections, is the result of a change of climate. Agricultural scientists who have studied the matter seriously feel that the climate has not changed sufficiently over the centuries to account for the decline in production. They are almost unanimously of the opinion that soil loss due to water and wind erosion is the root of the problem (Le Houérou, 1976).

2-3.3 Erosion in Southern Europe and in Northern Africa

Civilization spread westward from Egypt and the Middle East to Greece, Italy, and northern Africa and from there to other parts of Europe.

Erosion in Greece and Italy. Originally the Greeks were a pastoral people. The upland areas of their country were covered with forests and the lowlands contained productive soils suitable for grazing. But farming gradually superseded the care of flocks and herds. Cultivation was restricted initially to the productive valley soils, but as population increased, food demands made necessary the cultivation of land higher and higher up the hillsides. Forests were cut down and grain was grown instead. Still the demand for food grains increased. This demand eventually could be met only by importing food grains from overseas. Actually the Greeks acquired agricultural (grain-producing) colonies in Italy, in northern Africa, and on islands in the Mediterranean. The cheap grain imported from these colonies caused a shift in the types of crops raised in Greece itself. Olives, grapes, and vegetables replaced grains in many areas. Declining fertility of Greek soils made crops unprofitable and had an influence on this production shift also. The imported grains, however, were often intercepted by warlike acts and piracy, and shipments were sometimes lost to storms. Accordingly, some areas inside Greece which had not been too seriously impoverished continued to be used for food grain production.

Greek literature does not mention soil erosion or soil deterioration in any detail, but does include a few special soil-improvement practices which would help to maintain productivity or at least reduce the rate of its decline. Frequent cultivation for the production of a single crop, the use of fallow for one to several years, and deep plowing are all described as means of increasing crop yields. Erosion and soil deterioration, however, must have been serious. Over the centuries more than a meter of soil was washed from the surface of extensive areas; in places the soil was removed to bedrock; severe gullying occurred on the steeper slopes; and lower-lying fields were buried under unproductive erosion debris.

Italy was a colony of Greece for several centuries before the Romans gained independence and set out to establish their own empire. Little of the land was cultivated when the Greeks first conquered parts of Italy about the eighth century B.C. The hills were forest covered and the lowlands were surprisingly productive. Cultivation was introduced and Italy became one of Greece's granaries. Dryland farming methods and irrigation played a large part in crop production because the climate of the southern lowlands was relatively dry.

When Rome first became independent of Greece, all the food needed for the population was provided locally. The principal profession was agriculture; leading Romans were land owners and farmers, and they were proud of this fact. Many important Roman authors had searched for and assembled all the available knowledge of successful farming methods, both those developed by earlier people and those worked out by the Romans themselves. Widespread use was made of fallow; the legume crop, alfalfa (lucerne), was highly recommended, not only as a valuable forage but also for its soil-fertility-improving properties. Other legumes, such as vetch and beans, were also recommended and used.

As the Roman population increased, demands for food also increased, and the more level bottomland areas were not sufficient to produce what was needed. Here, too, cultivation moved farther and farther up the hillsides. Erosion in the uplands became increasingly serious as forests were felled to supply timber for ships and other uses. Soils were denuded and huge gullies developed. Sediment washed into streams and was deposited in irrigation works, making regular removal necessary. As the strength of the empire deteriorated and as invasions and wars occurred, the task of sediment removal became difficult or impossible and the irrigated fields were progressively abandoned. Sediment in the major rivers caused frequent and destructive floods. Swamps developed close to the streams as the water level rose. Malaria and other diseases increased in severity and caused the people to move to higher ground. Intensive farming of the steeper lands at higher elevations caused severe soil erosion. The dedicated and industrious Roman farmers terraced and contoured much of their land to reduce erosion. Figure 2-1 shows some terraces currently in use in northern Italy.

With deteriorating soils, growing populations, and smaller yields Rome came to depend on imported grain from other countries, particularly Carthage, Libya, and Egypt. Roman farms could not compete with cheap imported grains and were forced to switch to the production of olives, vegetables, and vines, as shown in Figure 2-2. Declining productivity also contributed to the shift in crops. The soils of Italy, however, were more durable than those of Greece, so that despite severe damage, the soils recuperated over the years

Figure 2-1 Numerous terraces help to control erosion on this cropland near Miniato in northern Italy. (Courtesy F. R. Troeh.)

Figure 2-2 This vineyard near Florence, Italy has widely spaced rows that allow room for soil-conserving grain and hay crops. Hillside ditches provide drainage below each row of grapes. (Courtesy F. R. Troeh.)

after the fields were abandoned. At present, reasonable yields can be produced with modern techniques on most soils, but erosion is a continual threat.

Erosion in Northern Africa. Northern Africa (Tunisia and Algeria) was a very productive land in the early Roman era, not only along the coast of the Mediterranean Sea where the rainfall was approximately 1000 mm annually, but inland for a considerable distance.

The inhabitants of Carthage and the surrounding area were excellent farmers. Cultivation techniques were advanced for the times, and yields were good. Relics of grain-storage structures and olive-oil presses attest to the region's thriving agricultural history. Much of the grain produced was transported to Rome. Successful crop production, except very close to the sea, depended on dryland farming methods and on extensive irrigation works. Water conservation was a key to agricultural production. Water-spreading techniques were employed in many of the drier regions.

Serious deterioration took place over the centuries in spite of the initially high productivity of the soils of northern Africa. Winter rainfall caused water erosion on soils laid bare at that season, and wind erosion was often destructive when soils were left bare during drier parts of the year. In addition, settlements in northern Africa suffered attacks by desert dwellers from the south after the decline of Rome. These new conquerors were not farmers but raised animals for their livelihood. The clash between cultivators and herders was easily won by the newcomers. The vegetation deteriorated and erosion, mainly by wind, reduced soil productivity still further as grazing increased. Much formerly productive land lost all of its topsoil as it was eroded down to a stony desert pavement.

Overgrazing and erosion caused the desert to encroach on formerly productive cultivated fields. The potential for feeding a large human population was drastically reduced. The soil in many areas that once supported famous Roman cities with many thousands of inhabitants now supports only a few hundred. Lowdermilk (1953) mentions the ruins of the city of El Jem on the plains of Tunisia. El Jem must have been a large city. Its amphitheater could accommodate 60,000 people. Lowdermilk states that when he visited the area in the late 1930s there were fewer than 5000 inhabitants in the whole district surrounding the city's ruins. El Jem's cultivation agriculture had been destroyed after only a short period of successful production. Invasion played a part in the destruction of a civilization, but soil erosion caused the deterioration and ultimate death of the system.

2-4 EROSION IN EUROPE

Western Europe north of the major mountain ranges (Alps, Jura, and Pyrennes) has a humid climate and, in most places, its climax vegetation is forest. Its agriculture is based on natural rainfall, unlike southern Europe where irrigation is used. The local agriculture was generally improved after the Roman legions conquered the various parts of Europe and Roman methods of farming were introduced.

2-4.1 Erosion in the British Isles

The pre-Roman inhabitants of Britain, known as Celts, had a well-developed arable agriculture. They farmed a system of rectangular fields with boundaries parallel and perpendicular to the slope. The downhill side of each field was gradually built up by sediment washed down by sheet erosion and by soil moved downhill during seedbed preparation (Bennett, 1939). Gully erosion was not a serious problem because the rainfall was gentle. The Celtic agricultural methods were altered but not replaced by Roman ones during the Roman occupation.

The Saxons from mainland Europe later introduced a system of long, narrow, cultivated fields, mainly on the more level lowlands. Most of the old Celtic fields were then abandoned, and many have not been cultivated since that time.

Soil erosion was more severe in Scotland than in England because a shortage of level land caused more steeply sloping soils to be cultivated. The detrimental effects of erosion were recognized in Scotland, and conservation practices were developed. Contour ridges were recommended and used, and a predecessor of the graded terrace was developed.

2-4.2 Erosion in France, Germany, and Switzerland

Steep slopes were cleared of forest cover and cultivated in hilly areas of central Europe, and erosion was so severe that something had to be done. The farmers in what is now France developed bench terraces and returned some of the land to forest over a thousand years ago. Lowdermilk (1953) suggests that the Phoenicians were responsible for this development. Some terraces were constructed on land as steep as 100% slope (45°). The soils on the benched areas were improved every fifteen to thirty years by being turned as deep as a meter. These terraces are still being used.

Water-erosion control over most of the region involved mainly a suitable choice of land use and careful husbandry. The steep land at high elevations is now used only for forest and pasture, as shown in Figure 2-3, but crops are grown on moderate slopes at lower elevations, as in Figure 2-4. Level bottomlands are likely to be used for truck crops, as shown in Figure 2-5.

At times, wind erosion has been a serious menace in Europe. Sandy soils subject to wind damage are found along seacoasts and inland where water-laid or glaciated coarse deposits occur. Systems of revegetation have been developed to hold the sands and prevent drifting in most areas where wind erosion poses a threat. These sandy soils are generally used for pasture or forest and are rarely cultivated.

2-4.3 Erosion in Eastern Europe

Considerable sheet erosion occurred in Hungary, Czechoslovakia, and Poland, but gully erosion usually was not severe. Most of the rains

Figure 2-3 Steep areas in the Swiss Alps are either left in forest or grazed judiciously. (Courtesy F. R. Troeh.)

Figure 2-4 Upland areas in Switzerland are cropped where the soils are favorable and the slopes are not too steep. Pasture- and woodland are interspersed with the cropland. (Courtesy F. R. Troeh.)

Figure 2-5 Level alluvial soils in Swiss valleys are used for vegetables such as the lettuce in this field and other high-value crops. (Courtesy F. R. Troeh.)

were gentle, and a type of agriculture was developed which was uniquely adapted to forest soils and which improved rather than depleted soil productivity (Jacks and Whyte, 1939). Here, as in western Europe, the use of adapted crop rotations, the return of animal manure and crop residues to the soils, and more recently, the judicious application of lime and fertilizers improved many of these formerly forested soils. Cultivated crops in much of the area are produced only on gentle slopes. Grain and other agricultural products are imported when local production is not sufficient to meet national food and feed needs. Actually, the main conservation needs of these soils are the maintenance of soil fertility and the improvement of drainage.

Erosion in the Soviet Union has been severe and has had a long history. Excessive tree cutting on forested slopes and overgrazing and cultivation of steep and semiarid lands caused serious water and wind erosion in both European and Asian regions. The cultivation of "new lands" in southern Siberia following World War II increased the extent of submarginal, cold, and dry farming area. Wind erosion increased and some of these areas proved so erodible that cultivation was abandoned.

2-4.4 Soil Reclamation in the Low Countries

The Netherlands and a part of Belgium occupy a generally flat plain with little land more than 50 m above sea level. Instead of losing land because of soil deterioration, these countries have increased the arable area by reclaiming land from the sea. The new land was obtained by building dikes such as that shown in Figure 2-6, pumping the salt water out, originally with windmills such as the one in Figure 2-7, and using river water for irrigation and reclamation (Note 2-1). Much of the land above sea level, both on the sea coast and inland, is sandy. There are also extensive areas of clayey soils and considerable peat. Water erosion was never serious on these lands, and wind erosion has been well controlled on sandy sites by protective vegetation. The soils in this area are generally more productive now than they were when first reclaimed.

NOTE 2-1 RECLAMATION OF THE POLDERS

The people of The Netherlands and Belgium have been reclaiming land from the sea for hundreds of years to help meet the needs of dense populations. Most of the reclaimed land was near sea level and much of it was reclaimed in relatively small tracts. The polders con-

Figure 2-6 A dike protecting lowlands in the southern part of the Netherlands. (Courtesy F. R. Troeh.)

Figure 2-7 A windmill near Kapelle, Netherlands. Windmills were the original power source for pumping water to reclaim the polders. (Courtesy F. R. Troeh.)

stitute a much larger and better-known reclamation project than any of the others.

The general plans for the polder reclamation project were drafted about 1890 by Cornelius Lely, but the project did not begin to reach fruition until the 1930s. The project involved cutting off the Zuider Zee, an arm of the sea that reached deep into The Netherlands, and converting it into a body of fresh water called Lake Eissel. Five polders covering 220,000 ha have been reclaimed within Lake Eissel by the following procedures:

1. The *Afluijdijk* barrier dam, 30 km long and nearly 100 m wide, was completed in 1932 to form Lake Eissel. River inflow gradually converted it to a fresh-water lake (excess water is emptied into the ocean by sluices).

2. An area within Lake Eissel was surrounded by an inner dike, and the water was pumped out to form a polder. The lake next to the polder made a convenient place to pump the water.

3. Rushes were planted in the freshly drained polder to control weeds, use up water, and help aerate the soil.

4. Trenches, ditches, and canals were dug for drainage and irrigation. The reeds were burned and a crop of rape was planted the

first year and wheat the second year. Both rape and wheat tolerate the initial saline conditions and are good soil conditioners.
5. After three to five years the land was dry enough to replace the trenches with drain tile, farmsteads were built, and the land was leased to farmers.

2-5 EROSION IN ASIA

China and the countries of south-central Asia (India, Pakistan, Bangladesh, and Sri Lanka) have suffered catastrophic soil erosion. Southeast Asian countries also have suffered from erosion.

Cultivation began in China and India soon after the Sumerians developed it in Mesopotamia. This long history of land utilization, rather than excessive exploitation, is responsible for the very severe erosion damage, although extreme population pressure recently has caused severe exploitation and considerably increased soil losses.

2-5.1 Erosion in China

High east-west mountains in central China interfere with the northward passage of moisture-laden winds, so that rainfall irregularity plagues the north and plays a major role in both water and wind erosion. Erratic but intense rainfall and relatively steep land slopes in northern China combine to cause severe sheet and gully erosion when cultivation moves farther and farther upslope to produce food for the ever-increasing population. Gullies as deep as 200 m have eaten back into the deep loess hills of Shansi and surrounding provinces. Erosion has so damaged the soils of the area that only isolated patches of more level land are now fit for cultivation. Because population density per hectare of cultivated land is higher in this gullied area than anywhere else in China, the population is forced to continue cultivating the land for food production.

The potential for water erosion is greater in southern China than in the north because the terrain is more rugged and rainfall is greater (up to 2000 mm annually). Actual water erosion has been less in the southern part than farther north because of less pressure on the land for food production, better protection by native forest vegetation, more assured crop cover on cultivated fields, and less erodible soils. Bench terraces are used extensively on the steeper cultivated slopes; contouring is employed on less steeply sloping land.

Although erosion threatens the existence of the Chinese in the hilly lands, the millions of people on the plains of China suffer more severely from it. A number of major river systems traverse China from west to east. They collect water and vast quantities of eroded sediment and carry it eastward. In the west, the river headwaters have relatively steep gradients; in the east, they level out and sediment is deposited. The sediment elevates the streambed, reducing channel capacity and causing periodic flooding. This is particularly true of the Hwang (Yellow) River. About 4000 years ago, the Chinese started constructing levees along the river to reduce the flood potential. A system of double dikes about 600 km long has been built. The inner dikes are close to the river channel and the outer ones are about 10 km on each side of the inner levee system. Sediment has built up the river channel within the levees, in many places making the river flow more than 15 m above the flood plain and delta. Floodwater still breaks through the levees occasionally and rampages across the unprotected plain, laying waste to cultivated fields and homes, drowning thousands, and causing hundreds of thousands more to die of starvation. The sediment deposited by a flood may be a long-time benefit to soil fertility, but it is a short-time disaster. In one dike break, 50 cm of sediment covered the soil 100 km south of the river channel.

Wind erosion has also been severe in many sections of northern and western China where semiarid and arid climates prevail. Soil drifting has been most severe in desert areas and on cultivated fields during droughts in semiarid areas.

2-5.2 Erosion in South-Central Asia

South-central Asia contains a wide range of topography from very steep slopes in the mountains and hills to the level alluvial plains. It is very old and stable geologically and has a mantle of very diverse soils. Most are Oxisols and Ultisols in the higher rainfall sections, but a large belt of Vertisols on the Deccan Plateau has developed from basalt rock. It is a tropical and subtropical region with rainfall ranging from less than 100 mm in the northwestern desert to over 10,000 mm annually in the western Ghats and along the border between Bangladesh and Assam. The region has wet summers and dry winters because monsoons control the rainfall.

Native vegetation of the region, except in the desert and some semiarid areas, controlled erosion well. The vegetative cover under cultivation is less protective, and the soils tend to become less permeable, making erosion common.

Early agriculture in this region involved shifting cultivation. The recuperative period was often ten or more times as long as the period of cultivation. Soil erosion and deterioration were negligible with this system. As population has increased, especially over the last 150 years or so, the fallow periods have been shortened until continuous cropping has become normal, giving the soil little chance to recuperate. The resulting larger contiguous areas of cultivated land also increase the potential for erosion.

Probably the worst erosion in south-central Asia occurred on the steep slopes of the range of hills south of the Himalaya Mountains, in what is now Pakistan. Here the livestock herder, the woodcutter, and the farmer combined to denude the land. As a result, torrents of water rushed downhill during the rainy season, causing severe sheet erosion and forming deep gullies. Here, as elsewhere, the damage was not restricted to land from which soil was removed; flooding and sedimentation caused havoc in lower-lying fields. Floods inundated farms and villages, causing death and destruction; transported sediments deposited on good soil caused severe crop and soil damage.

Many fields on more level plains and alluvial soils have not eroded seriously. Plantation crops such as tea and coffee also have produced little erosion. Major obstacles to erosion control in this region are the high and increasing human population to be fed, the large number of livestock, and the great difficulty of getting information on effective conservation measures into the hands of the millions of farmers.

2-6 EROSION IN THE AMERICAS

There are two major areas in the Americas with long histories of sustained, continuous cultivation. The remainder of the two continents has not, until relatively recent times, been subjected to continuous cultivation and serious soil depletion.

2-6.1 Erosion Under Prehistoric Civilizations

In Peru, the Incas and their predecessors were wonderfully ingenious agriculturists and expert soil and water conservationists. They developed bench terraces to control water and soil loss on more sloping sites when the population became too large for adequate support from the level bottomlands alone. Relatively large areas were covered with these terraces. The face of each bench was a stone wall generally 1 to 5 m high, as shown in Figure 2–8. Rocks, gravel, and other nonsoil materials were placed behind the stone face to within a meter of the level surface of the bench. This last meter was filled

Figure 2-8 Rock-faced bench terraces constructed by the Incas at Machu Picchu, Peru (the "Lost City of the Incas"). The dark channel in the foreground carried irrigation water to the terrace. (Courtesy F. R. Troeh.)

with good soil, which was carried from the level bottomland, or more frequently from a considerable distance. Many of these terraces are still being cultivated.

The Incas also installed terraces in the stream valleys to prevent flooding and soil erosion. These were much broader than those on the sloping hillsides. The Incas produced probably the world's most effective erosion-control structures. It is unlikely that any modern civilization will be willing to pay the price in money, energy, and labor to duplicate them.

Native Peruvian farmers presently cultivate the steep slopes of the mountains without the meticulous care of the ancient Incas. They have cut down the forests, overgrazed the range, and greatly reduced the length of the recuperative fallow between periods of cultivation. They are now farming exceedingly steep slopes, as shown in Figure 2-9. Not only do they use manure as a fuel rather than a soil builder, they also dig up tree roots for their fires. The system

Figure 2-9 Peruvian fields on a steep mountainside south of Cuzco. Hand tillage is used to raise grain crops on these steep slopes (Courtesy F. R. Troeh.)

currently used has caused severe erosion over a relatively short period, whereas the Incan system was successful over millennia.

The Mayas of Central America depended chiefly on corn for their food. This crop originally was grown with a great deal of expertise on the level lowlands. Eventually it became necessary to cultivate the forested slopes also. Recent examination of some of these sites shows that very severe erosion occurred on the sloping lands. Damage was so severe that the soil lost much of its ability to produce, and the sediment from the sloping fields filled the streams which were necessary to the continued existence of the population. The modern-day Maya has gone back to shifting cultivation, taking two or three crops, then abandoning the field for long periods of recuperation. If an abandoned field is recultivated too soon, yields are not satisfactory; if erosion is severe during the first cultivation period, crop yields are unsatisfactory even after very long abandonment, and the land may be permanently ruined for further agricultural use. The population supported by this system is, of necessity, far smaller than that of the

Mayan civilization at its peak. Here again a system of continuous cultivation failed largely because of erosion.[1]

2-6.2 Erosion in the United States

In most other areas of the Americas, population pressure did not force the people to use continuous cultivation until after the European settlers arrived on these continents. Gradually at first, then with greater rapidity, field sizes and numbers were increased. Farm implements, imported or made locally, and animal power were used to cultivate larger fields and to incorporate crop residues thoroughly into the soil.

Details on the nature and extent of erosion damage in the United States will be presented here because they are better documented than for any of the other countries.

The influx of new settlers from all over Europe and the population buildup in the United States provided the labor and the market for expanded cultivation. The crops raised, both native and introduced, were grown as monocultures, not as mixtures. These crops left the fields open to the beating action of the rain and to unrestricted movement of runoff water for long periods each year. Cotton and tobacco production in the southern states caused extensive erosion. Corn grown continuously in northern states was nearly as destructive. Rainfall was much more intense in the new land than it was in Europe, and far greater erosion damage was done to the lands than the settlers had previously experienced. They knew of no way to reduce the losses.

The productivity losses resulting from deterioration and erosion didn't seem to bother many of the new settlers. There was an abundance of new land farther west. When they "wore out" a farm, they simply moved to a new area and started again. Some of the farmers that stayed in the eastern area tried to cope with land deterioration, but without much success.

By the early 1900s, there was no longer a western frontier in the United States. The productive capacity of many of the eastern farms was greatly depleted, primarily by erosion, but also by declining

---

[1] Recent archaeological studies show that Preclassic Period Mayas in southeastern Mexico had perfected a complex system of bench terraces, dams and other water-diverting devices, and underground water-storage cisterns and walk-in-wells before the Christian Era and that, where used, these practices and structures apparently were effective in reducing soil and water losses. See Matheny, R. T. and D. L. Gurr, 1979. Ancient hydraulic techniques in the Chiapas Highlands. *American Scientist* 64(4):441–449.

fertility resulting from intensive use of row crops. Soil deterioration was also becoming severe on many of the "new" farms in the central part of the country. Drought and wind erosion were hazards which had to be faced where the climate was drier. Probably in no continent or country in the world had such a short period of farming caused such tremendous soil wastage. Approximately 170 million hectares of land were cultivated in the United States in 1930. Erosion surveys in the middle 1930s by the newly formed Soil Conservation Service showed that of the total cropland (including all harvested areas, crop-failure land, idle land, and fallow) 12% was essentially ruined, another 12% was severely damaged, 24% had lost one-half to all of its topsoil, and 24% had suffered measurable erosion loss, leaving only 18% unaffected by erosion.

Loss of fertility was also a serious factor. Crops were harvested and sold off the farm with little thought of replacing the fertility shipped away. Limited applications of nutrients were made in the most humid areas; essentially no fertilizer or manure was applied in the drier regions. The use of summer fallow increased and helped to stabilize crop production in semiarid areas, but it also increased soil exposure to erosive winds, and in later years contributed to soil salinity in the form of saline seeps.

Sheet, rill, gully, and streambank erosion were common. The erosion survey of the 1930s indicated that 3.6 billion metric tons of soil were washed off the fields, pastures, and forests of the United States annually, about three-fourths of it (2.7 billion mt) from cropland. Severe dust storms transported vast quantities of soil also. The storm of May 12, 1934, in the panhandles of Texas and Oklahoma, southeastern Colorado, and southwestern Kansas, carried dust 2500 km to New York City and Washington, D.C., and several hundred kilometers out to sea. It carried an estimated 185 million metric tons of soil. Spectacular events of this sort and the steady relentless loss of soil by water erosion finally prompted the U.S. Congress in the late 1920s and early 1930s to pass legislation setting up government agencies to combat erosion. These agencies are discussed in Chapter 19.

2-7 EROSION IN AUSTRALIA

Australia had a relatively small population before the immigration of European settlers. The original inhabitants were mainly hunters and gatherers, so land was cultivated only in scattered small patches and there was little accelerated erosion. Soil drifting occurred in the desert and on the semiarid fringes during drought periods. Water erosion also occurred in more humid regions when natural disasters bared the sloping hillsides.

Sizable tracts of land began to be cultivated when the settlers arrived with their agricultural implements and draft animals. Soil erosion increased as the size of cultivated fields increased and as the land was cropped more continuously. Water erosion became especially severe in southeastern Australia (New South Wales). The rainfall there comes mostly in the summer and includes occasional intense thunderstorms. Farther west the rainstorms occur in the winter period and are more gentle.

Large flocks and herds in the states of South Australia and Western Australia overgrazed the dryland vegetation. An excessively large rabbit population caused still greater grazing pressure. Depletion of vegetative cover increased the soil's susceptibility to wind erosion. Sandy soils, especially in the drier sections of the country south of the desert, also have been seriously damaged by wind erosion.

Overcutting of the forests in Queensland has influenced the conservation of water and soil, and threatens to reduce markedly the longtime profitability of lumbering in the country.

2-8 EROSION IN SOUTHERN AFRICA

Erosion was not a serious problem in southern Africa as long as low population pressure allowed sufficiently long recuperative (fallow) periods for shifting cultivation, and as long as livestock numbers were moderate and native forage plants remained. Even in the deserts and on the desert fringes, wind erosion was only intermittently serious. The discovery of gold accelerated immigration from Europe. This increased the need for cultivated land, and erosion rapidly became severe on many soils.

Rainfall is generally erratic over the southern half of Africa, and this adds to the erosion problem. At the end of the nineteenth century, many government officials and observant farmers realized that erosion was a real problem in many countries. It was generally believed that the root cause of the problem was a change in climate, because erosion was accompanied by the drying of the streams, the lowering of the groundwater table, and increasing damage from both drought and floods. The report of the Union of South Africa's Drought Investigation Committee in 1923 pointed out clearly that there was no basis for the assumption that climate had changed markedly. The Committee stated that the damage was the direct result of vegetative deterioration and subsequent erosion. Because of overgrazing, rains rapidly ran off the land and entered streams, causing floods instead of percolating into the soil. Groundwater recharge became minimal.

Only about 5% of the land area was cultivated in the early 1930s. Accordingly, soil erosion at that time resulted mainly from improper pasture utilization and annual burning rather than from intensive cultivation. Water erosion of cultivated land often was serious, though, wherever soil and slope characteristics were conducive to erosion. The best and longest-cultivated soils in southern Rhodesia suffered such severe erosion that a government-sponsored conservation program was started in that country in the 1930s.

The number of European settlers was still small in northern Rhodesia (Zambia) and Nyasaland (Malawi) in the 1930s, and no great expansion of cultivated area had occurred. The soils were still largely protected by forest vegetation, and erosion was not a major problem. Nonetheless, the ministries of agriculture of these two countries promoted conservation practices in order to keep erosion from developing and becoming serious.

2-9 EROSION IN THE TROPICS

Much of the uncultivated arable land of the world is located in tropical countries. This mass of potentially productive land has often been considered tillable with no problem except that of clearing cost. This is not true; there is real danger of soil deterioration from loss of fertility and by erosion. Until relatively recently, the populations of most tropical countries have remained in balance with the food produced by a system of shifting cultivation. This system was permanently productive if the rest period (fallow) was long enough (ten or more times as long as the cultivation period) for soil recuperation. Over the last half century, however, populations throughout the tropics have increased as a result of reductions in the occurrence and severity of intertribal wars, improvement of health services, the control of diseases, and more accessible world markets. Pressure for food production has reduced the fallow period in many areas. This has caused soil deterioration by fertility decline and increased erosion on the larger cultivated fields.

Development of large cities has compounded the production problem. With inadequate transport systems, especially farm-to-market and village-to-city roads, these cities depend on the land in their immediate vicinity for the bulk of their staple food needs. There is no way that local farmers can let land lie idle long enough to replenish its productive capacity in this situation. Soil fertility is quickly reduced unless extreme care is taken in land management. Manures must be used as much as possible, and commercial fertilizers containing N, P, and perhaps K must be applied. Even these practices will solve only some of the problems and may actually cause new ones. Nitrogen fertilizers cause soil acidification. This may necessitate the use of lime, often a scarce commodity in the tropics. Removing fertility from the soil in harvested crops means that fertilizer nutrients in addition to N, P, and K will be needed eventually.

Soil productivity and soil erosion in moist, tropical regions occur partly as a result of the irreversible dehydration of hydrous iron oxides in some soils of these areas. When forest cover is removed for extended periods, the temperature and moisture regimes of the soils change and the plinthite in some Oxisol subsoils hardens into an ironstone (crystallized iron oxide) that largely prevents water and root penetration. The poor plant cover that usually results allows erosion. The friable soil above the ironstone is often eroded away, as shown in Figure 2-10, because of poor plant cover.

Figure 2-10 Ironstone (hardened plinthite) in a tropical soil in Ghana exposed by the erosion of about 15 cm of overlying soil. (Courtesy Henry Obeng.)

Large cultivated fields are much more subject to erosion than are small isolated tracts, but a large number of small land holdings makes the initiation of erosion-control measures difficult because the operators must be persuaded individually to accept unfamiliar erosion-control practices. Even when they are persuaded that a cooperative control measure such as terracing is necessary, each farmer probably will want the structure built on someone else's property.

Water erosion has increased in eastern Africa in both Kenya and Uganda as a result of increased cultivation. Much of the additional erosion in Uganda is the result of the remarkable increase in area of cotton, a profitable but highly erosive crop. Both cotton and corn production, along with cultivation of more sloping soils, overgrazing, and the unrestricted felling of trees in the forests have caused erosion to increase in Kenya. Advance of the desert in both these countries was noted in the early 1930s. This advance resulted from expanded cultivation in the semiarid desert fringe and overgrazing due to enlarged herds of livestock maintained as a bank account, not primarily as a source of meat.

Water from Ethiopian highlands fed the Nile River over the centuries. The highland area was not devastated by erosion over the whole of this period because a forest cover protected much of the land. Deforestation of the upland regions of Ethiopia, resulting from forest cutting and overgrazing, has occurred over the last several hundred years. Whereas 75% of Ethiopia was forest covered, now only about 4% is protected in this way. This has caused rapid runoff and soil loss; the highland, particularly the Amhara Plateau, is now severely eroded.

Erosion and soil deterioration have increased in western Africa also. Water erosion increased as population increased in the humid areas near the Gulf of Guinea and the Atlantic Ocean. Both water and wind erosion are prominent in the drier areas farther inland. The world became aware of the remarkable destitution brought about by the drought in the Sahel region in the 1970s. Too many cattle, camels, sheep, and goats overgrazed the range. Cultivation in areas too drought-susceptible for regular farming removed the native cover and left the soil open to severe wind erosion during the drought years. Desert expansion (desertification) is taking place both north and south of the Sahara and also around other deserts in Africa and the rest of the world. The desert spreads not because of irreversible climatic change, but because of abuse.

In Brazil, deforestation by logging, by fires to improve pastureland, and by clearing for cultivation has opened the way for water erosion. The same is true in many countries of central America and in many of the islands of the West Indies.

SUMMARY

Accelerated erosion is older than recorded history. It has been a common cause of soil deterioration all over the world. Soil erosion has been severe from the earliest civilizations in the Middle East to the most recently cultivated lands in the Americas, Australia, and southern Africa. Soil deterioration has often been so great that the land has been abandoned because it is no longer productive.

Mankind has frequently failed to develop effective cultivation systems that maintain soil productivity over long periods. Soil deterioration resulting from erosion has caused the decline of many civilizations. A few civilizations have developed and used conservation measures that reduced soil deterioration and maintained soil productivity at satisfactory levels for many centuries. In many "new" lands, colossal productivity losses occurred in very short periods and emphasized the urgency for conservation measures.

QUESTIONS

1. Point out where soil deterioration and sedimentation have played a major role in the decline of early civilizations.
2. What positive and negative effects did the Romans have on soil-conservation methods in Europe?
3. How and why have people reclaimed land from the sea?
4. Explain why most European settlers in the United States failed to take adequate precautions to reduce soil erosion and deterioration as they moved into and across the country.
5. Describe the forces that have impinged on the stable farming systems found in many tropical countries and caused the systems to break down.

REFERENCES

BALDWIN, Mark, J. L. BUCK, HERBERT GREENE, A. B. LEWIS, T. C. TSIANG, S. B. SHOW, T. B. CHAMBERS, J. G. STEELE, C. E. KELLOGG, and R. L. PENDLETON, 1948. *Soil Conservation: An International Study.* FAO Agric. Studies No. 4, Food and Agriculture Organization of the United Nations, Washington, D.C.

BEASLEY, R. P., 1972. *Erosion and Sediment Pollution Control.* Iowa State Univ. Press, Ames, Iowa, 320 p.

BEAUMONT, P., and K. ATKINSON, 1969. Soil erosion and conservation in northern Jordan. *J. Soil Water Cons.* 24:144–147.

BENNETT, H. H., 1939. *Soil Conservation.* McGraw-Hill, New York, 993 p.

BLOOMFIELD, N. J. T., 1977. *An Evaluation of Soil Erosion in Southern Brazil, and a Proposal for an Integrated National Program of Soil Conservation and Soil Survey.* M. S. Thesis, University of Wisconsin, Madison.

BRAIDWOOD, R. J., and BRUCE HOWE, 1960. *Prehistoric Investigation in Iraqi Kurdistan.* University of Chicago Press, Chicago, 184 p.

BUIE, T. S., 1964. After thirty years. *J. Soil Water Cons.* 19:93–102, p. 147–152.

HUBERT, P., 1970. The soils of Cyrenaica (Libya). *Pedologie* 20:285–338.

JACKS, G. V., and R. O. Whyte, 1939. *Vanishing Lands.* Doubleday, New York, 332 p.

KELLOGG, C. E., 1957. We seek: We learn. In *Soil,* U.S. Yearbook of Agriculture, Washington, D.C., p. 1–11.

KORELESKI, K., 1975. Types of soil degradation on loess near Krakow. *J. Soil Sci.* 26:44–52.

LAL, RATTAN, 1974. Soil erosion and shifting agriculture. In *Shifting Cultivation and Soil Conservation in Africa,* Soils Bulletin 24, Food and Agriculture Organization of the United Nations, Rome, Italy, p. 48–71.

LE HOUÉROU, H. N., 1976. Can desertization be halted? In *Conservation in Arid and Semiarid Zones.* FAO Conservation Guide 3, Food and Agriculture Organization of the United Nations, Rome, Italy, p. 1–15.

LOWDERMILK, W. C., 1953. *Conquest of the Land Through Seven Thousand Years.* USDA, SCS Agric. Inform. Bull. 99.

3

Geologic Erosion
and Sedimentation

Geologic erosion takes place without human influence. This term excludes the accelerated erosion that occurs when soil exposure is increased by land use such as tillage, overgrazing by livestock, cutting of trees, or heavy traffic, but naturally caused catastrophic events such as glaciation, landslides, and large floods are included. Understanding geologic erosion improves one's comprehension of the impact of erosion processes and underscores the importance of controlling accelerated erosion.

3-1 THE GREAT LEVELER

Erosion is known as the "great leveler" because it wears down high places and produces sediment that fills up low places. Valleys are created and the hills between them are eroded. The end result of long-continued erosion theoretically is a rather featureless plain.

Geologic erosion is very old and very persistent. It has worn mighty mountain systems down to stubs. Entire sea basins have been filled by materials eroded from the land. The shapes of the earth's landscapes have been determined by the combined action of erosion and sedimentation.

Geologists are able to interpret much of what has happened to the land by studying sediment and rock layers. The nature of sedimentary deposits depends on many factors including the source of the material, the transporting agent, and the environment of deposition. Proper interpretation of sediment layers can reveal much about the conditions of climate, vegetation, and landscapes of ages past.

3-2 ROCK TYPES

The earth's original crust was formed of igneous rocks that solidified as the earth cooled from an earlier molten state. Weathering forces caused the surface of the early rocks to disintegrate into small particles. The leveling action of erosive forces followed immediately and has been active ever since. Sedimentary and metamorphic rocks now cover about 85% of the land surface, but the underlying "basement" rocks are igneous (Note 3-1).

NOTE 3-1 ROCK TYPES

Rocks are broadly classified as igneous, sedimentary, or metamorphic depending on how they were formed. They are further classified according to mineral composition and grain size. Igneous rocks form by solidification when a magma (molten rock material) cools. The rate of cooling determines the grain size. Magma that erupts to the surface becomes a lava flow and forms a fine-grained rock because it cools quickly. Lava rocks are called extrusive in contrast to the slower-cooling, coarser-grained intrusive rocks. A simple classification of four important igneous rock types is as follows:

	Extrusive (fine-grained)	Intrusive (coarse-grained)
Rocks containing quartz crystals	Rhyolite	Granite
Rocks lacking quartz crystals	Basalt	Gabbro

Basalt and granite are the most common igneous rocks. Several other types are often defined as intermediates or extremes of the above types or as having special mineral contents.

Sedimentary rocks are formed where transported material is deposited. Soft sedimentary rocks are classified by transporting agent and grain size. Some important examples are:

Alluvium—material deposited by water
Colluvium—material moved downslope by gravity
Glacial till—material deposited by glaciers
Loess—silty material deposited by wind

Hard sedimentary rocks include a cementing agent or process in their formation. Some important examples are:

Sandstone—cemented sandy alluvium
Shale—clayey material compressed enough to bond together
Limestone—primarily precipitated calcium carbonate

Metamorphic rocks form when other rocks are subjected to enough heat and pressure to make them recrystallize and form new, usually larger, crystals. The material does not melt—that would form a magma and result in an igneous rock. Metamorphism may be either low grade (relatively small changes produced) or high grade. While some low-grade metamorphic rocks are easily related to a specific earlier rock type, others are more general. The metamorphosed rock is often harder than the original:

Marble—metamorphosed limestone
Slate—metamorphosed shale
Quartzite—metamorphosed sandstone with a high quartz content
Schist—low-grade metamorphic rock high in small flakes of mica
Gneiss—high-grade metamorphic rock with elongated grains and a general banded appearance

Many sedimentary deposits have accumulated to thicknesses of several kilometers. The pressure and heat of deep burial eventually change their form, producing metamorphic rocks. Even rocks that have been deeply buried may be reexposed at the surface by uplift and erosion.

3-3 PROCESSES THAT ELEVATE LAND

Erosion has worked long and persistently. It has moved enough material from the land to the ocean to have eliminated all dry land if there were no counteracting processes. Fortunately, these forces are as potent and persistent as erosion. The net result is a balance that maintains a nearly constant amount of land.

The processes that elevate land masses can be classified into three groups—deposition, lava flows, and uplift. Deposition usually occurs at a lower elevation than the source of the material, but not necessarily below sea level. Wind deposits are an exception; they often occur on hills at a higher elevation than their source areas.

3-3.1 Deposition

Sediments that gradually fill a pond, lake, or other basin often produce fertile level land in the process. Gray colors are common in sediments deposited in water. Some of these sediments include organic layers where the residues of lush vegetation fall into shallow water and are preserved. Bogs are formed where thick layers of organic materials fill a low area. Lakes and other depressions are considered to be temporary landscape features because, with time, they are either filled with mineral and organic deposits or drained through an outlet cut by erosion. Low, wet areas can become part of a smooth valley floor by the combined action of erosion and deposition.

Much of the material removed by young, actively eroding streams is deposited downstream where the river floods across its broad flat valley. Small tributary streams entering the side of a large valley often deposit their sediment in alluvial fans that slope down to merge with the valley floor, as the one shown in Figure 3-1.

Sediments deposited in valleys usually accumulate to thicknesses of a few meters. Some deposits keep accumulating until they are hundreds or even thousands of meters thick. A thick deposit over a large area can cause the area to sink under its weight and remain low enough to continue receiving sediment.

3-3.2 Lava Flows

Molten rock flowing out on the land as in Figure 3-2 is an obvious way to increase elevation. Lava flows from one to a few meters thick are common. Most lava areas have multiple flows resulting in cumula-

Figure 3-1 An alluvial fan is formed where a small stream flowing on a steep gradient enters a large valley and slows down on the flatter slope. Orchards are grown on alluvial fans in this Idaho scene because the fan soils are well-drained but the bottomland soils are wet. (Courtesy F. R. Troeh.)

Figure 3-2 The edge of a basalt lava flow in Oregon. This flow is about 20 m thick. (Courtesy F. R. Troeh.)

tive thicknesses ranging up to several hundred meters. Sometimes the lava rock is covered by or layered with volcanic ash that was spewed out of a volcano and carried across large areas by wind. Loess layers and alluvial deposits may also occur on or between lava flows.

The ocean basins are lined with basalt (the most common type of lava rock). Undersea lava flows have built up mountains that reach thousands of meters above the sea floor. The upper parts of such mountains form islands where they protrude above sea level. Islands surrounded by deep ocean are composed mostly of lava accumulations. The Hawaiian Islands are an outstanding example where active volcanoes still exist.

The largest area of lava rock on land is the Columbia River Basalt which covers large areas of Washington, Oregon, and Idaho in northwestern United States. Many areas of basalt, rhyolite, and other lava-formed rocks exist in various parts of the world.

3-3.3 Uplift

Uplift is as slow and persistent as erosion and is the principal process that elevates land masses. Actually, both upward and downward movements occur, resulting in the warping and twisting evidenced by contorted rock layers. The net effect of these shifts is an upward movement that offsets erosion.

Uplift is an expression of *isostasy* (the tendency to equalize pressure). Even solid rock is able to flex and move across dimensions of many kilometers. Pressure inequalities produced by erosion are thereby balanced by internal shifts in the earth's crust. Eroded areas are lifted up again, and areas that receive sediments gradually sink. Sometimes the stresses produced by unequal pressures become so strong that they are released suddenly in the form of an earthquake.

Equal pressures require unequal elevations because different rock types have different densities. The dominant rock in ocean basins, basalt, has an average density of about 3.0 g/cm^3. The dominant rock in the cores of large mountain ranges, granite, has an average density of about 2.7 g/cm^3. The 10% difference in density permits the lighter-weight rocks in the mountains to "float" above the denser rocks much as an iceberg floats in the sea. Like the iceberg, the mountain exposes only about 10% of its total mass. The other 90% is submerged, providing the buoyancy that supports the exposed part, as shown in Figure 3-3.

Uplift and erosion are opposing processes that continually reactivate each other. They are influenced by other processes that influence the pressures on and positions of materials in the earth's crust. For example, the gradual cooling of the earth causes a slight shrinkage that produces stress in the crust.

The theory that continental masses slowly move around the globe has gained wide acceptance in recent times. The process,

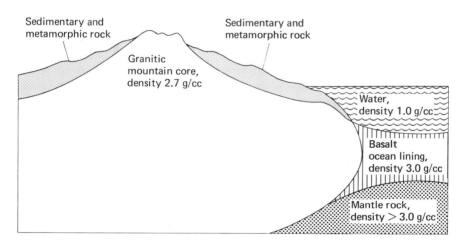

Figure 3-3 Land areas, especially mountains, protrude above sea level because they are formed of rock with a lower density than that lining the oceans.

known as plate tectonics, is believed to be widening the Atlantic Ocean at the expense of the Pacific. A dramatic type of uplift deduced within this framework is illustrated by the action of the sub-continent of India. India appears to have split from Africa and moved across the ocean to its present position. The "collision" of India with Asia pushed up the highest mountains in the world, the Himalayas.

3-4 LANDSCAPE DEVELOPMENT

Erosion, deposition, lava flows, and uplift play major roles in shaping landscapes. The results are seen all over the globe in the forms of hills and valleys, mountains, plateaus, and plains. All landscapes, whether simple or picturesque, have been affected by one or more of these age-old forces. While the geologic history of some landscapes is fairly easily interpreted, that of others is very complex.

Some landforms are controlled by single agents of erosion or deposition in ways that produce close approximations of geometric shapes. River floodplains, for example, come close to being plane surfaces. Alluvial fans formed where small streams enter a main valley provide a more complex example. The flow of water produces a nearly uniform slope profile in every direction it moves. The result is a fan-shaped area with contour lines approximating segments of concentric circles. The effect continues even though the slope gradient decreases with distance.

Erosional surfaces resembling alluvial fans are called *pediments*. A classic example of a pediment, located in the area of Gila Butte, Arizona, is shown in Figure 3-4. The pediment surface comes close to fitting a mathematical equation. The floodplain and other adjoining landforms have shapes that differ from the pediment equation.

3-4.1 Geomorphology

"The study of the Earth's surface forms, and of the processes that shape them, constitutes the field of geomorphology" (Butzer, 1976, p. 7). Geomorphology and soil science are so interrelated that neither can be understood without some consideration of the other. As Butzer says (p. 56), "Soils modify the gradational process and, in turn, the external agents of erosion and deposition affect the soil mantle and its development." Some principles of geomorphology are included in this section to help clarify the subject of landscape development.

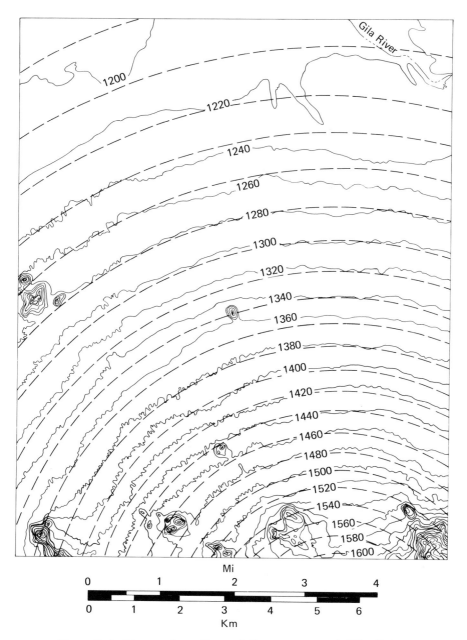

Figure 3-4 The contour lines of the area around Gila Butte, Arizona are closely approximated by a series of concentric circles. The elevations shown are in feet above mean sea level. (Courtesy F. R. Troeh.)

3-4.2 Uniformitarianism

Credit for the early development of modern geomorphic principles is given to James Hutton. Hutton's ideas were presented in a paper in 1785 and in his book, *Theory of the Earth,* in 1795. The underlying theory that Hutton developed and used as a basis for his explanation of how the earth received its form is called the principle of uniformitarianism. Previous theories had supposed that landscapes were shaped primarily by sudden nonrecurrent events. Hutton argued that the processes acting now are the same as those that acted in the past. Uniformitarianism permits an understanding of the processes now at work to be used to explain past events. The meaning of uniformitarianism is summed up in the statement, "The present is the key to the past." Due allowance must be made for variations in rates and importance of various processes, but strange and unknown processes need not be invoked.

3-4.3 Structure, Process, and Stage

The principles of geomorphology were further clarified by W. M. Davis in the 1890s. Davis theorized that erosion phenomena resulted in a cycle of landform development which he called the geographical cycle. According to Davis, the nature of any landform was a function of structure, process, and stage of development in the geographical cycle.

Structure. Structure includes all aspects of the physical nature and arrangement of the rocks in which the landscape formed. The hardness of each rock material, the presence or absence of layers, and any tilting, folding, or faulting of the layers are part of structure. Grain size, degree of cementation, and permeability are also included because they influence the rate and pattern of erosion. Structural factors determine which rocks are most erodible and thereby help guide the erosion process. The shape of erosional landscapes depends largely on the rock structure.

Process. Process refers to the combined action of the agents building and eroding a landscape. Various forms of water erosion, wind erosion, and mass movement remove material from some areas and deposit it elsewhere. Glaciers add their own dramatic touch. The soil-moving action of plant and animal activity should not be overlooked. Human activity, however, causes accelerated erosion and is excluded from geologic erosion.

Rock weathering and soil formation are vital predecessors of the erosion process because they help produce fragments small enough to be moved. Erosion rates are limited in many places by the rate of production of loose material.

Erosive agents are often identifiable by the distinctive impressions they leave on the landscape. Landslides leave scars on the hillside and debris in the valley long after the event. Scratches left thousands of years ago on the bedrock of central Canada can be read today as evidence of glacial scour. The moraines and other glacial features in northern United States show how far the glaciers reached. Bison trails of centuries past show conspicuously on aerial photos of certain areas in midwestern United States (Clayton, 1975).

Climate. Climate exerts a strong influence on the geomorphic process. Arid regions typically have angular topography resulting from the type of weathering, erosion, and deposition at work on the landscapes (Note 3-2). Humid regions usually have rounded topographic features because of the combination of erosive agents working on their landscapes. Very cold climates with heavy snowfall produce glaciers and glacial landscapes. A trained observer can learn much about the climate simply by observing landscapes, such as those shown in Figure 3-5.

NOTE 3-2 ARID LANDSCAPES

It is often assumed that arid landscapes are shaped by wind. It is true that wind is an active agent in arid regions, but other factors should not be overlooked. Among these are the relative sparsity of vegetation and the distribution of water in both time and space.

The bunchgrasses, shrubs, cacti, and other native plants of arid regions cover only a fraction of the soil surface, leaving bare areas exposed to the direct impact of rainfall. Also, the relatively low organic matter content resulting from limited vegetation provides less resistance to erosion than a higher content would. The soil aggregates are weaker and the permeability slower than would be likely under more humid conditions.

Arid regions occasionally have heavy runoff because their rainfall, though infrequent, can be locally intense. Runoff can quickly accumulate and cause a "flash flood" because there is not enough vegetation to slow the water flow. A literal wall of water comes rushing down a streambed that was dry only a moment before. The stream may empty onto a broad flat area where the water spreads out and infiltrates. Such flat areas are composed of the alluvium deposited by the countless flash floods of ages past. Their flatness is a marked

Figure 3-5 The shape of a landscape tells much about the climate of the area. (a) An angular arid landscape in Arizona. (Courtesy F. R. Troeh.) (b) A semiarid landscape on the island of Kauai, Hawaii. (Courtesy USDA—Soil Conservation Service.) (c) A rounded humid-region landscape in New York. (Courtesy F. R. Troeh.)

contrast to the adjacent steep angular hills. Some flat areas completely surround one or more hills.

Because low areas receive runoff water from higher areas, the flats have more water than adjacent low hills (higher hills or nearby mountains may receive more precipitation than the lower areas). Rock material within a few meters of the flats is often moist enough to weather and erode faster than the drier rock above. This softening of the lower rock layers works with flash floods and wind erosion to produce angular topography and unusual landforms such as natural bridges and balanced rocks. Wind erosion abrades such landforms, particularly at low levels because the wind carries more and heavier particles at low levels than it lifts to high levels.

Stage. Landscapes pass through stages of *youth, maturity,* and *old age.* When water erosion in an upland area, for example, first cuts a pattern of steep, narrow valleys, the landscape is said to be in youth even though the relatively undisturbed areas between the valleys represent an older stage of a preceding geomorphic process. Maturity is reached when the new cycle has spread its molding influence to the entire area. Maturity is a long stage that is often divided into early and late substages. A mature landscape is typically cut by many valleys, making it very hilly. Old age is reached when the hills are nearly worn away and the erosion rate has slowed.

Multiple Cycles. Landscape development through stages of youth and maturity to old age is often interrupted by environmental changes. Davis included cycle changes in his discussion of the geographical cycle. Since then, the concept of changes producing multiple cycles of landscape development has been widely accepted. Any of several factors such as climatic change, uplift, and the cutting of a barrier by erosion may cause significant changes in landscape development. A landscape may show the effects of two or more cycles of development long after such changes occur.

Climatic changes have caused glaciers to come and go several times during the last million years across the vast areas of North America, Europe, and Asia shown in Figure 3–6. Each glacial and interglacial stage had marked effects on landscapes both within and beyond the glacier-covered areas. Glacial deposits have been cut by valleys, filled by a later glacier, and then cut by new valleys in different directions. Very complex landscapes can result from such processes, especially when the associated water and wind deposits are considered along with the glacial deposits.

Climatic changes can produce dramatic differences in landscape

Figure 3-6 Glacial ice still covers major areas between 60° and 90° North and South latitude and once covered much more extensive areas in Europe, Asia, and the Americas. (Courtesy F. R. Troeh.)

development even without glaciation. A small change in precipitation or temperature might alter the vegetation and thereby influence the rate and pattern of erosion. Major climatic changes may cause an angular topography to shift toward roundness or vice versa.

Renewed uplift rejuvenates old landscapes. Greater elevation differences result in faster erosion and deeper valleys with steeper slopes. Uplift in one area may be accompanied by downwarp (sinking) in another, making the downwarped area more likely to receive deposits. The intervening area is tilted to a new angle that shifts the position of streams and their erosional and depositional areas. The record of such changes is often preserved in buried surfaces, sloping and dissected terraces, and other variations in slope gradient.

3-4.4 Stream Systems

Streams occur in all but the most arid landscapes. Most streams are integrated into river systems that eventually carry the runoff water to the ocean. Exceptions occur where the water reaches an area porous enough to absorb it or where the water accumulates in a low area such as the Dead Sea or the Great Salt Lake and escapes by evaporation. Such exceptions are called closed drainage systems in contrast to open systems that drain to the ocean.

Some streams appear to have resulted from water flowing down the original slope of an area when it was first exposed to erosion. An area recently lifted above sea level is a good example. Such streams are called *consequent streams* because they are a consequence of the original slope.

Tributaries flowing into consequent streams are called *subsequent streams* because they developed later. Subsequent streams flow down the sides of consequent valleys and erode back from there as they cut their valleys across the original slope of the area.

Tributaries to subsequent streams are called *secondary consequent* if they flow in the same direction as the consequent stream and *obsequent* if they flow in the opposite direction.

The preceding terminology works well on *rectangular* stream patterns where all streams tend to meet each other at right angles. Tilted rock layers of varying erodibility can produce such a pattern. Most of the streams are subsequent streams flowing in valleys cut into the most erodible rock strata and are parallel to each other. The connecting links are consequent streams that flow down the tilt-produced slope in a direction perpendicular to the others. Parallel fault lines are a less common cause of a rectangular pattern. Rectangular patterns are called *trellis* patterns when there is a large preponderance of parallel streams in one direction with few cross links.

Dendritic stream patterns are the most common type. Directional terminology is not very useful in describing the development of a dendritic system because the branching streams may flow in any direction. Dendritic stream patterns on a map resemble the branching of a tree as they reach into all parts of the area drained by the stream, as illustrated in Figure 3-7. They develop where there are thick rock masses either without any layering or with horizontal layers.

Figure 3–7 A dendritic stream pattern is one that "branches like a tree" and has streams flowing in all directions. (Courtesy F. R. Troeh.)

Other patterns also occur. For example, a mass of rock may be pushed up in the form of a dome and develop a *radial* drainage pattern from the water running off on all sides. *Complex* patterns include elements of several patterns and are not readily describable.

Streams are also classified into orders. *First-order streams* are the first identifiable channels formed where thin layers of rain water begin to concentrate into streams. A *second-order stream* is formed where two first-order streams meet, a *third-order stream* is formed by the union of two second-order streams, and so on.

3–4.5 Development of Valleys

Stream erosion produces valleys. It should be recognized that valleys are the growing parts of a landscape, whereas hills are remnants that have not yet been worn away. Observers may see the hills, but they need to study the valleys to understand the formation of the landscape.

A valley begins where water collects from a large enough area to form a stream. The stream develops a channel in a position determined by the shape of the topography, the erodibility of the soil and rock material, and the source of the water. The early development is often so rapid that a gully forms.

The stream is a dynamic entity that does three things as it forms its valley. (1) It erodes downward toward a *base level* determined by the elevation of the stream or area into which it empties. (2) It erodes headward toward the source of its main flow of water. Headward erosion causes the largest change in valley dimensions. (3) It picks up tributaries resulting from smaller flows of water coming in from the sides of the main valley and producing their own smaller valleys.

3-4.6 Mass Wasting

Much material that a stream removes from its valley reaches the stream by mass wasting. This broad term includes several processes by which gravity moves soil downslope. The movement may be rapid and dramatic as in landslides and mudflows or it may be measured in fractions of millimeters per year as in soil creep (Troeh, 1975). Water acts as a lubricant promoting movement by weakening the mass but is not the actual transporting agent. The slope need not be very steep, because soils on gentle slopes can become saturated and almost fluid during some seasons. Saturated soil is especially common where wet springs follow winters that freeze the soil to a significant depth.

Two different theories, often called downwearing and backwearing, describe how mass wasting progresses with time.

3-4.7 Downwearing

W. M. Davis developed the downwearing theory in the 1890s as part of his geographical cycle idea discussed in Section 3-4.3. Davis suggested that the hills in a landscape are gradually worn down by erosion and valley slopes gradually change from steep during youthful stages to gentle in old landscapes. The end result, if the landscape remained stable long enough, would be such gentle slopes that erosion would cease. The landscape would then be a nearly featureless, poorly drained surface called a *peneplain.* There has been much debate about whether any present-day landscapes are old enough to be called peneplains, but surfaces such as the Pampas of Argentina are certainly close to the concept (the meaning is "almost a plain" rather than an absolutely flat plain).

3-4.8 Backwearing

Walther Penck challenged many of the ideas of W. M. Davis in his book *Die Morphologische Analyse,* published in 1927. The book was written after Davis had challenged the concepts of Walther's father, Albrecht Penck. Walther's untimely death prevented him from seeing his book in print and from developing his concepts further.

Penck's lengthy development of the concept of backwearing

made geomorphologists realize that the subject of slope retreat had not received the study it deserved. Penck argued that a valley develops two kinds of slopes as shown in Figure 3–8—a relatively steep backslope called the valley wall and a flatter footslope between the backslope and the bottomland along the stream.

Backwearing is also called *parallel retreat of slopes.* Penck reasoned that after an equilibrium is reached, the slope gradients should remain constant while the hill gradually wastes away. Flat hilltops would not wear down as Davis had suggested but would be worn away from the sides. The difference between the two theories is at a maximum during the mature stage of landscape development. The end result is similar to the peneplain concept but is called a *pediment* to distinguish between the two theories. The term pediment can be used to describe a smaller area than is appropriate for peneplain and is useful at an earlier stage.

The pediment surface begins as an enlarging footslope. It is normally covered with a mantle of soil material that is slowly moving from the backslope area across the pediment to the stream. The soil on the pediment is considered to be moving *en masse* as a form of mass wasting in addition to any water transport occurring at the soil surface.

Many efforts have been made to combine the ideas of Davis and Penck. It has often been suggested that the rounded topography of

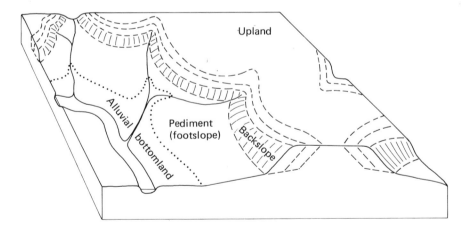

Figure 3–8 A backwearing landscape gradually erodes an upland as the backslope recedes in a manner described by Penck as "parallel retreat of slopes." A sloping pediment surface forms between the backslope and the bottomland. (Courtesy F. R. Troeh.)

humid regions may best fit Davis' downwearing concept whereas Penck's backwearing concept better explains the angular topography of arid regions.

3-4.9 Soils on Eroding Landscapes

The concepts of downwearing and backwearing have important implications for soil development. Downwearing implies constant erosion of all parts of the landscape. Gradual smoothing of the landscape requires that the highest areas erode fastest. The soils on hilltops should therefore be less developed than those in lower areas.

Because backwearing leaves the hilltops undisturbed until removed by eroding slopes, this theory predicts that hilltop soils should have stronger development than others. The shallowest and least-developed soils, apart from floodplains, should occur on the backwearing slopes. The footslope tends to accumulate material and produce deep, moderately developed soils.

Soil scientists usually favor the backwearing theory because the pattern of soil development predicted from it accurately depicts most landscapes. A composite theory dominated by backwearing but with some loss from the hilltops would probably have the most support. Most hilltops have enough slope for some water erosion to occur, and wind erosion is possible even on flat areas. Furthermore, chemical erosion by leaching removes dissolved material from hilltop soils in humid regions.

3-5 SEDIMENTARY LANDFORMS

Material eroded from one place must be deposited elsewhere, so the wearing away of one area is balanced by the building up of another. Buildup occurs both on dry land and below water level. Deposition sometimes converts water areas into land by filling lakes or ponds. Even a shallow sea may become land through deposition and uplift. The many gray-colored limestone, sandstone, and shale formations which accumulated on sea floors are evidence that vast amounts of erosion, deposition, and uplift have taken place.

Some authors use the term sedimentation to cover the combination of erosion, transportation, and depositional processes. Others emphasize the depositional process and include erosion and transportation only as they influence the nature of the deposited sediment. The latter meaning is used in this book.

3-5.1 Water Deposits

Water normally sorts materials by particle size as it transports sediment. The coarsest materials are either left in place or moved only occasionally and for short distances. For reasons explained more fully in Chapter 4, progressively finer particles are deposited as the water flow reaches lower, flatter areas and moves at slower velocities.

Alluvium. Material deposited by flowing water is called *alluvium*. Alluvial deposits occur in such landforms as floodplains, terraces, fans, piedmonts, and deltas. Alluvial land is desirable for many purposes because it tends to have smooth topography, deep, fertile, permeable soils, and more readily available water than most other land. Such land is in demand for farming, road building and other construction activities, and many other uses.

Floodplains are narrow or nonexistent in young valleys but become broader and flatter as the landscape ages. Water floods across these areas during periods of heavy runoff and deposits a fresh layer of alluvium. The deposition produces a nearly flat surface on floodplains except for places cut by stream channels. Of course, each flood may rearrange material deposited earlier and cut new channels while filling old ones. The stream channel itself is inclined to meander gradually across its floodplain, occasionally making sudden major shifts. Though natural, these shifts are distressing and costly to land owners.

Flood hazard should be taken into account whenever construction on floodplains is considered. Protective works such as levees and channel dredging may control small floods but are often inadequate to protect the land from major floods. In fact, flood-prevention efforts cause rivers to raise the level of their beds by depositing sediment that should have been deposited on their floodplains. The result is an ever-increasing flood hazard such as that experienced by the Chinese along the Yellow River and the Americans along the Mississippi River. There is no known way to control a major river permanently.

Alluvium in river valleys is usually only a few meters thick, although some very thick exceptions exist. Thick alluvium occurs mostly in downwarp areas. The weight of the sediment contributes to the sinking, but other forces causing shifts in the earth's crust are probably the decisive factors. Whatever the cause, the lowered position increases the likelihood that the area will trap more sediment. The magnitude such deposits can reach is illustrated in Note 3-3.

NOTE 3-3 SEDIMENTARY DEPOSITS

Some sedimentary deposits become very large. The Idaho Formation will serve as an example. This body of sand and silt occupies an area 150 km long and 50 km wide in southern Idaho and eastern Oregon. The sediments were washed out of the Rocky Mountains into a gradually sinking area that has been called the Snake River Downwarp. A well drilled to a depth of 1500 m failed to reach the bottom of the formation; in fact, it was far short of the formation's probable thickness of 5000 m estimated from the slope of its layers. Samples taken from the well indicated that the sediments were all deposited on dry land even though the bottom of the well is now about 700 m below sea level.

Sedimentary deposits are common in most parts of the world, though most are smaller than the Idaho Formation. Although some deposits remain loose, many are cemented into sandstone and shale. The depositional environment is indicated by the nature of the rock. Red colors are characteristic of land deposits where oxidizing conditions prevailed; gray colors and fossils of water creatures indicate that the sedimentation occurred in a body of water.

Terraces are formed when the base level of a stream changes and the channel is cut too deep for normal flooding to occur. The stream may have cut through a barrier to a lower outlet level, or uplift may have increased the stream's erosive potential. Either cause leaves the former floodplain at a level above the stream and its new floodplain. The old floodplain becomes a terrace, but its origin is recognizable by its flat surface bordered by a slope down to the new floodplain on one side and another slope up to another terrace or the upland above on the other side. Terraces are subject to erosion as the new floodplain enlarges. They are also gradually dissected by tributary streams flowing across them.

Alluvial fans, also called *alluvial cones* because of their shapes, line the sides of many valleys. An alluvial fan forms where a tributary stream flows into a larger main valley. Suddenly free to spread out, the stream slows down, loses energy, and deposits much of its load of sediment. The deposit builds up on the shape of a fan radiating downward from the point where the tributary enters the main valley. Fan deposits are usually quite permeable so the depositing stream often disappears by soaking into the fan. The upper part of the fan is normally the steepest and coarsest textured. The gradient decreases and the texture becomes finer with distance, until the fan blends into the terrace or floodplain below.

A *piedmont* is a plain formed at the base of some mountain ranges. It forms in a manner similar to that of alluvial fans but on a larger scale. Erosional effects and sediment from many streams blend together to form a smooth surface sloping away from the mountains. A piedmont surface resembles a pediment but includes depositional as well as erosional surfaces and often has a great thickness of accumulated sediment in contrast to the thin coating of soil characteristic of a pediment. Similar depositional surfaces in arid regions where the coalescing alluvial fans merge into the level area of an undrained basin are called *bajadas.*

Deltas form where streams empty into bodies of water instead of into larger valleys. The name comes from the resemblance of the shape, as seen on a map, to the Greek letter Δ. Deltas have nearly level surfaces that are partly above and partly below water level. The size is proportional to the size of the stream and the duration of deposition. A small delta may be only a few meters across, but some large ones continue for hundreds of kilometers. Small deltas formed in lakes are quite sandy because the finer sediments are carried farther into the lake. Rivers flowing into the ocean produce finer-textured deltas because salt water flocculates clay particles and makes them settle out. Such sediment represents the richest part of the soils from the source area and produces a relatively fertile soil. The internal drainage is quite poor because of the delta's low elevation. Much rice is grown on deltas in warm climates.

Bottom Deposits. Sand and gravel are seldom carried far into a body of water, but clay and dissolved material may cover the entire bottom. Slow settling and chemical precipitation gradually form deposits on most lake and seafloor bottoms. Sometimes the solid particles are dominant, but the chemical precipitates dominate at other times and places.

Lacustrine deposits, also called lake-laid clays, are composed mostly of the fine material carried beyond deltas into the main body of water. The texture of the material usually varies from silt or sand during seasons of high runoff to fine clay during cold or dry seasons, thus producing a layered effect such as that shown in Figure 3-9. These layers are called *varves* and are sometimes counted to estimate the age of the deposit. The depositional process usually levels the surface, so the varves lie horizontally.

Lacustrine deposits and deltas remain long after the lake or sea that formed them is gone. Glaciers crossing hilly topography pro-

Figure 3-9 A varved clay deposit in Michigan. Each varve is about 1 mm thick and is composed of a thin sandy layer deposited during the summer thaw and a coating of silt and clay deposited while the glacial lake was frozen. The scale is in centimeters. (Courtesy Roy L. Donahue.)

duced many small lakes that left deltaic deposits high on hillsides marking the former water level. Some of these deltas have been used as sources of gravel for road construction. The lacustrine deposits are at lower elevations and often are poorly drained because they contain clay that causes low permeability. They are erodible and, when wet, subject to small slips and even landslides.

Limestone is the most common bottom sediment. It normally contains some silt and clay sediments but is composed mostly of a consolidated chemical precipitate of calcium carbonate triggered by the growth of algae and other plant and animal life. Sea water and some lake water is nearly saturated with calcium carbonate so that minor changes in the carbon dioxide supply may cause precipitation. Conditions that result in the formation of limestone are common on the floor of shallow seas and have produced large formations of limestone. Uplift may later convert the area into dry land. Limestone rock is gradually dissolved away in humid regions but is quite resistant to weathering in arid regions. Chalk and marl are calcium carbonate deposits that are less consolidated (and less resistant to weathering) than limestone, chalk being a salt-water deposit and marl a fresh-water deposit.

Evaporite deposits form where a shallow body of water concentrates its salts by evaporation. An ideal situation for evaporites occurs where a bay in a warm climate with little rainfall is nearly cut off from the sea but still receives an input of salty sea water. Another evaporite situation occurs where rainfall in mountain areas seeps down into low, dry, closed basins such as Death Valley, Great Salt Lake, or the Dead Sea. Large deposits of sodium chloride have been formed as evaporites in both recent and older geologic periods. Other salts also precipitate, sometimes in mixed and sometimes in relatively pure form. Potassium chloride from evaporite deposits in western Canada, southwestern United States, and elsewhere is the principal source of potassium fertilizer. Borax deposits in Death Valley provide much of the world's commercial boron. Sodium nitrate from the Athabasca Desert in Chile was an early source of nitrogen fertilizer. All of these salts are too soluble for their deposits to form in humid environments.

3-5.2 Wind Deposits

Wind sorts materials by particle size even more effectively than water does. Wind deposits are relatively free of textural layering and are usually more uniform in particle size in any particular vicinity than are water deposits.

Wind deposits are widespread but much of their area is not very thick. A few deposits attain thicknesses of 100 to 200 m or more, but even these thin to less than 50 m thick within a short distance. The deposits generally become thinner with increasing distance from the source until they become too mixed with other materials to be identified separately. The thick parts of wind deposits bury the underlying landforms and have a steep topography of their own resulting from a combination of depositional and erosional effects. Most of the area is mantled with a layer of silty wind deposit averaging no more than 2 or 3 m thick and conforming approximately to the shape of the buried surface.

Aeolian Sands. Wind normally moves sand only a short distance. As it does so, it leaves behind any stone fragments that may be present. Desert areas eroded by wind often accumulate a surface layer of gravel one pebble thick as the wind carries away the finer soil particles. This gravel layer, called *desert pavement,* protects the area from continued wind erosion. The sand component of the soil is deposited nearby, often in the form of dunes. Sand dunes are unstable and subject to continued movement by the wind unless they are covered by vegetation. It is difficult to establish vegetative cover on sand dunes because of their droughtiness and their shifting tendencies.

The difference between a stable surface and one that can be blown into sand dunes is largely a matter of vegetative cover. Climate is also a factor because additional precipitation increases the likelihood of stabilizing vegetation being established. Thinner, smoother deposits of aeolian sands are easier to stabilize than sand dunes. Some nearly level deposits have a water table within reach of plant roots and are able to support a thick stand of vegetation.

Loess. Loess is wind-deposited material dominated by silt-size particles. Loess deposits are the most extensive form of wind deposits because silt particles are easier to detach from a mass than clay particles and easier to transport over long distances than sand particles. Most wind deposits change from aeolian sands to loess within one or a few kilometers of the source.

Guy Smith (1942), in his widely recognized study on Illinois loess, found three distinct trends in loess deposits: (1) the deposit is thickest near the source and becomes thinner with increasing distance from the source, (2) the average particle diameter decreases from coarse silt to fine silt and the clay percentage increases with increasing distance from the source, and (3) the mineral composition of the deposit gradually changes as the calcium carbonate percentage decreases with increasing distance from the source. The decreases in deposit thickness and in particle size are direct results of the additional energy required to transport particles longer distances. The decreased calcium carbonate content is attributed to leaching during the period of deposition. The thin portions were deposited so slowly that leaching removed much of the slightly soluble materials.

Soils formed in loess are fairly resistant to wind erosion because they lack the sand particles that would move first and knock the silt particles loose. But loess deposits and the soils formed in them are susceptible to both water erosion and mass movement. Either falling raindrops or flowing water can readily detach silt particles which are easily transported in runoff water. Gully erosion is relatively common in loess materials, and the gullies often cut straight down to the bottom of the deposit. The nearly vertical sides and flat bottoms of such gullies are described as U-shaped. The U-shaped gullies help to identify loess deposits because most other gullies are V-shaped.

When an exposed loess surface becomes saturated with water, it is subject to mass movement ranging from small soil slips or slumps to large landslides. Landslides were a common problem in loess roadbanks until road builders learned to make vertical banks in loess rather than the usual slopes. Loess has a natural tendency to cleave along nearly vertical planes, as shown in Figure 3-10. The resulting banks are more stable than sloping surfaces for reasons that have been much debated but not fully resolved. Friction between the flat silt particles and cementation by calcium carbonate have been suggested as factors. Also, while vertical surfaces absorb too little water to get wet in a storm, sloping surfaces may become saturated with water—a condition that makes loess weak and unstable.

Windblown Clay. Wind deposits contain less clay than silt and sand. Clay particles stick together and are hard to erode, but bounc-

Figure 3-10 A nearly vertical loess bank in western Iowa. (Courtesy F. R. Troeh.)

ing sand particles knock loose some clay, much of which is mixed with silt in the downwind portions of loess deposits. Clay also may be picked up and carried with drifting snow.

Extensive clay deposits formed by wind during the Pleistocene have been identified in southern Australia. More recent clay deposits occur near the gulf coast of Texas and Mexico, and in Senegal and Algeria (Bowler, 1973). In an arid environment, material containing 20% to 77% clay can become so strongly aggregated and so loose between aggregates that it can be moved by the wind as sand-size aggregates. Bowler (1973) indicates that clay dunes only form on the downwind side of seasonally exposed mud flats around shallow bodies of saline water.

Volcanic Ash. Volcanoes occasionally spew out large quantities of ash that cover the landscape like a blanket. The ash layer is deposited much like a thin layer of loess but has a higher clay content. Some such layers can be traced to a specific event and thus become a time marker in geologic strata. The explosion that formed Crater Lake in Oregon by blowing off the top of Mount Mazama is a prime example. The resulting layer of volcanic ash can be identified across much of the state of Oregon.

Volcanic ash produces soils with very high clay contents. They are very sticky when wet and hard when dry. Some of them crack open so wide during dry seasons that they have the self-swallowing action characteristic of Vertisols.

3-6 GLACIAL LANDSCAPES

Glaciers have dramatic effects on the landscapes they cross. Moving ice picks up soil and stones from much of the area it crosses, then deposits them far away from their source. Stony material held in the ice at the bottom of a glacier scratches and gouges into the bedrock. Areas such as central Canada were eroded in this manner. In places the glacial movement followed the length of valleys and deepened them. The Finger Lakes in New York have bottoms cut below sea level by the glaciers. The fjords of Norway, Greenland, Canada, and Alaska had a similar glacial origin in coastal areas and now hold sea water. The moving ice also eroded laterally and produced very steep valley walls near the lakes and fjords.

Much of the material picked up by glaciers is deposited near the end of their travel. The ice margin is marked by a very hilly area where the glacial debris was dumped in a *terminal moraine,* commonly forming an irregular ridge several meters above the adjacent landscape. A thinner *ground moraine* (also called a till plain) extends back over the area that was covered by the ice and is commonly marked by lines of small arcing hills representing end moraines formed by brief advances of the ice during its waning phase. Many former valleys were filled with glacial deposits, so the present landscapes may be quite different than the preglacial ones.

Glacial influence also extends beyond the area actually covered by ice. Valleys leading away from glaciers were often enlarged by torrents of meltwater. The meltwater was as full of debris as the ice and therefore deposited much sediment in broad, flat floodplains. Some of these floodplains remain today as oversize floodplains for the present streams; others are terraces or outwash plains on upland areas completely separated from major streams. The broad floodplains of major rivers such as the Missouri and Mississippi became source areas for some of the world's major loess deposits.

3-7 RATE OF GEOLOGIC EROSION

The geologic erosion rate is an important reference for understanding the significance of accelerated erosion, but even geologic erosion rates vary widely from one time and place to another. Some rates have been measured or estimated by various means. Ruhe (1969) gives some examples of Iowa landscapes that eroded at rates ranging from 2 mm to 222 mm per 1000 years before agricultural settlement entered the area. One of the areas changed from a pre-settlement rate of 150 mm per 1000 years to 1500 mm per 1000 years after settlement. Each millimeter of soil depth represents 13 metric tons per hectare (mt/ha) of soil with a bulk density of 1.3 g/cm^3. Thus, Ruhe's sample data can be converted to estimates of 0.03 mt to 2.9 mt of geologic erosion per year and 19 mt of accelerated erosion per year.

A rate of 1 mt/ha may be considered as an approximate average rate of geologic erosion from gently sloping soils. It must be realized that actual rates range from essentially zero for many thousand years in the most stable areas to catastrophic events such as a landslide that in a moment's time removes several meters of soil and rock from a hillside and deposits them in a valley. Water and wind have caused remarkable geologic erosion that is only slightly less sudden and sometimes much more puzzling than a landslide. For example, the origin of the "channeled scablands" in the state of Washington, as shown in Figure 3–11, was unknown for a long time. Finally it was

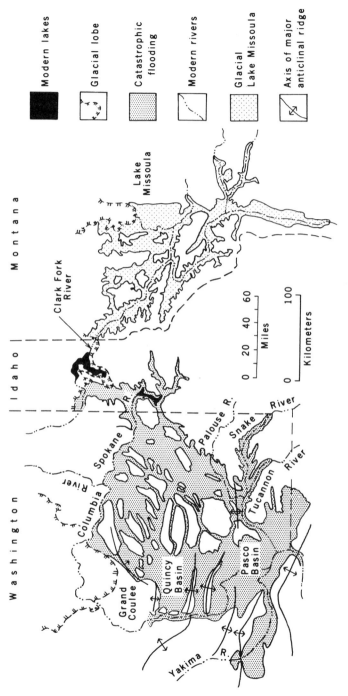

Figure 3-11 The channeled scablands were formed when an ice blockage broke in northern Idaho and released the water from Lake Missoula in Montana as a torrent that raged across eastern Washington. (Courtesy Victor R. Baker, *Science* 202: 1255, 22 December 1978. Copyright 1978 by the American Association for the Advancement of Science.)

explained on the basis of a sudden release of water from glacial Lake Missoula in northern Idaho and eastern Montana (Baker, 1978). Torrents of water crisscrossed hundreds of square kilometers of land, eroding channels to bedrock but leaving scattered islands of soil. The event was brief but its effects, including gravel bars 30 m high and soil islands surrounded by channels of bare rock, are still conspicuous.

Geologic erosion rates are occasionally influenced by catastrophic events such as those mentioned. More often, the rates are determined by such factors as climate, vegetation, slope, and soil material. The effect of precipitation is of interest because moderate amounts produce a minimum rate of geologic erosion. The rate is higher in very wet climates because of the greater erosive force of more precipitation. Relatively high rates also occur in dry climates because there is too little vegetation to protect the soil against wind erosion and the occasional heavy rains that occur in such areas.

SUMMARY

Erosion is known as "the great leveler" because it persistently removes material from high sloping areas and fills low areas with the resulting sediment. The end result, a featureless peneplain, is seldom reached because the process rarely continues uninterrupted for a long enough time. All land would have been worn down to sea level if not for the work of opposing forces—deposition, lava flows, and uplift. Uplift results from isostatic adjustments and is the most powerful rejuvenating force.

Geomorphology is the study of landforms and the processes that shape them. Geomorphologists apply the principle of *uniformitarianism* to landscapes and consider the effects of *structure, process,* and *stage.* Much landscape development occurs as streams cut downward, lengthen headward, and pick up tributaries. Valleys develop along with the streams and gradually enlarge as the hills erode. Two theories have been developed to explain how hills are eroded by mass wasting. The *downwearing* theory supposes that higher areas wear down and slopes become less steep until a *peneplain* is formed. According to the *backwearing* theory, a parallel retreat of slopes erodes the hillsides but not the hilltops. The surface formed as a slope retreats is called a *pediment.* Because older soils are usually found on hilltops and younger soils on hillsides, most soil scientists favor the backwearing theory.

Soil and rock material eroded from one area is deposited in another as sediment. Water deposits *alluvium* in alluvial fans and on floodplains; remnants of former floodplains become terraces when a new floodplain forms at a lower level. Sediments are normally sorted by particle size, the coarsest material being deposited near the source and the finer material being carried into quieter waters. *Deltas* form where a stream enters a lake or sea. *Lacustrine deposits* high in clay accumulate on lake bottoms. Calcium carbonate precipitates as limestone, chalk, or marl on the bottom of many bodies of water, especially on shallow sea floors. More soluble salts precipitate from briny lakes in arid regions.

Wind also sorts the material it erodes. Sand is deposited in nearby dunes, but silty *loess* deposits blanket larger areas. Volcanic ash also blankets large areas but in a much shorter time.

Glaciers scour soil and rock in their source areas and deposit the material where they melt. Glacial margins are marked by hilly *moraines* and valleys oriented in the direction of glacier movement may be deepened and left with steep walls. However, much of the area covered by glaciers is smoothed as the hills are eroded and the low places filled.

QUESTIONS

1. Discuss the relative importance of erosion and deposition in forming steep and level landscapes.
2. Why is the principle of uniformitarianism important to geomorphologists and soil scientists?
3. What combinations of structure, process, and stage produce hilly landscapes?
4. Why are some hills angular while others are rounded?
5. What difference does it make whether the dominant process of landscape development is downwearing or backwearing?
6. Why is an alluvial fan steepest near the top and flatter in its lower parts?
7. What evidence is there that wind is able to sort particles by size?
8. Why did glacial action deepen some valleys and fill others?

REFERENCES

ANDREWS, J. T., and W. E. LEMASURIER, 1973. Rates of quaternary glacial erosion and corrie formation, Marie Byrd Land, Antarctica. *Geology* 1:75-80.

BAKER, V. R., 1978. The Spokane flood controversy and the Martian outflow channels. *Science* 202:1249-1256.

BOWLER, J. M., 1973. Clay dunes: Their occurrence, formation, and environmental significance. *Earth Science Reviews* 9:315-338.

BULL, W. B., 1968. Alluvial fans. *J. Geol. Educ.* 16:101-106.

BUTZER, K. W., 1976. *Geomorphology from the Earth.* Harper & Row, Pub., New York, 463 p.

CLAYTON, LEE, 1975. Bison trails and their geologic significance. *Geology* 3:498-500.

DAVIS, W. M., 1922. Peneplains and the geographical cycle. *Geol. Soc. Am. Bull.* 23:587-598.

FEHRENBACHER, J. B., 1973. Loess stratigraphy, distribution, and time of deposition in Illinois. *Soil Sci.* 115:176–182.

FLINT, R. F., 1971. *Glacial and Quaternary Geology.* John Wiley, New York.

GARMER, H. F., 1974. *The Origin of Landscapes.* Oxford Univ. Press, New York, 734 p.

HAXBY, W. F., and D. L. TURCOTTE, 1976. Stresses induced by the addition or removal of overburden and associated thermal effects. *Geology* 4:181–184.

McKERROW, W. S., and R. ST. J. LAMBERT, 1973. Deep earthquakes, surface subsidence, and mantle phase changes. *J. Geol.* 81:157–175.

MIDDLETON, G. V., 1976. Hydraulic interpretation of sand size distributions. *J. Geol.* 84:405–426.

MILLS, H. H., 1976. Estimated erosion rates on Mount Rainier, Washington. *Geology* 4:401–406.

PENCK, WALTHER, 1927. *Die Morphologische Analyse.* Stuttgart. J. Engelhorns Nachf., 283 p.

ROY, R. N., and A. B. BISWAS, 1975. Use of grain-size parameters for identification of depositional processes and environments of sediments. *Indian J. Earth Sci.* 2:154–162.

RUHE, R. V., 1969. *Quaternary Landscapes in Iowa.* Iowa State University Press. 255 p.

RUHE, R. V., and P. H. WALKER, 1968. Hillslope models and soil formation. I. Open systems. Trans. 9th Int. Cong. of Soil Sci. 4:551–560. II. Closed systems. 4:561–568.

SMITH, G. D., 1942. *Illinois Loess: Variations in Its Properties and Distribution.* Illinois Agr. Exp. Sta. Bull. 490, p. 139–184.

SPARKS, B. W., 1972. *Geomorphology,* 2d ed. Longman, London. 530 p.

STURGUL, J. R., and ZVI GRINSHPAN, 1975. Finite-element model for possible isostatic rebound in the Grand Canyon. *Geology* 3:169–171.

TROEH, F. R., 1965. Landform equations fitted to contour maps. *Am. J. Sci.* 263:616–627.

TROEH, F. R., 1975. Measuring soil creep. *Soil Sci. Soc. Am. Proc.* 39:707–709.

4

Water Erosion and Sedimentation

Movement of soil by water occurs in three stages. First, individual grains (particles and small aggregates) are detached from the soil mass. Second, the detached grains are transported over the land surface. Third, the soil grains fall out of suspension and are deposited as sediment on a new site. Soil removal and deposition occur to some degree in nearly all locations but detachment and removal are of major concern on uplands, and deposition is most important on lowland sites and in streams and lakes.

Though of little significance in areas that are covered by a thick canopy of vegetation, erosion is often very severe when fire, cultivation, overgrazing, logging, mining, or construction activity destroys the vegetation. In arid regions, rare, intense rainstorms cause excessive runoff and severe erosion even when the soil is covered with its sparse native vegetation.

4-1 TYPES OF WATER EROSION

Soil erosion by water is classified as sheet erosion, rill erosion, gully erosion, and streambank erosion. The classification is based on the nature and extent of soil removal.

4-1.1 Sheet Erosion

Sheet erosion is the removal of thin layers of soil by water acting over the whole soil surface. Raindrop splash and surface flow cause sheet erosion, with splash providing most of the detaching energy and flow providing most of the transporting capacity. Soil loss by sheet erosion is insidious because it is so difficult to see or measure. A farmer is seldom aware of soil loss until farm fields begin to change color as subsoil becomes mixed with topsoil, as shown in Figure 4-1. Sheet erosion can occur on any part of a slope but becomes apparent first on the convex upper portions.

4-1.2 Rill Erosion

Rills are erosion channels small enough to be obliterated by normal tillage operations, as shown in Figure 4-2. Most rill erosion occurs on recently cultivated soils where runoff water concentrates in streamlets as it passes downhill. This water has greater scouring action than sheet flow and it removes soil from the edges and beds of the streamlets. Rills frequently occur in relatively straight lines between crop rows or along tillage marks. After smoothing by tillage, the long-term effect of rill erosion is similar to that of sheet erosion, but because it is more obvious, action is more likely to be taken to control it.

4-1.3 Gully Erosion

Erosion channels that are too large to be erased by ordinary tillage, such as the one in Figure 4-3, are called *gullies*. The slope of the gully

Figure 4-1 The hilltops in this Iowa field are light-colored because the dark-colored topsoil has been lost by sheet erosion. (Courtesy F. R. Troeh.)

Figure 4-2 Rills in a cultivated vertisol in India. (Courtesy Roy L. Donahue.)

walls depends on the angle of repose characteristic of the material. Deep, relatively straight-sided channels develop where the soil material is uniformly friable throughout the profile. In deep loess soils the walls are almost vertical, forming U-shaped channels, but most other soils have less steep side slopes. Broad V-shaped channels often develop where cohesive, tight subsoil that resists cutting underlies friable surface soil. Gullies are considered to be *active* as long as erosion keeps the sides bare of vegetation, and *inactive* when they have been stabilized by vegetation. Gullies are further described as small, medium, or large according to depth, with medium-sized gullies being between 1 and 5 m deep.

4-1.4 Streambank Erosion

Sheet, rill, and gully erosion are active only during or immediately after rainstorms. Erosion along the banks of perennial streams occurs both during and between rainstorms.

Although the actual area damaged by streambank erosion is small compared to the area affected by other types of water erosion, it is very important because bottomland soils damaged by this type of

Figure 4-3 A gully eroding uphill from a cultivated field into a grassed area near Bruxelles, Manitoba, Canada. The equipment in the background is smoothing the gully to make it into a grassed waterway. (Courtesy Manitoba Department of Agriculture.)

erosion are usually more productive than any other soils in the area, and because soil picked up by streams is carried completely away, with little or no chance for deposition close to the original site. Streambank erosion is usually most intense along the long shore (outside) of bends. Inside river meanders can be very intensively scoured during severe floods. Bank erosion often damages or destroys the approaches to bridges and culverts. Stream bed erosion also causes bridge failure by removing materials that serve as footings.

Streambank and bed erosion can be accentuated by removing sediments from the streams, either by use of conservation measures on the uplands or by catching the upstream sediments in reservoirs or other traps. Removal of sediments from the Nile River by the sediment storage capacity of the High Aswan Dam has caused increased scouring of the river bed below the dam.

4-2 EROSION DAMAGE

There are many ways in which water erosion causes damage. Soil is lost; plant nutrients are removed; texture is changed; structure deteriorates; productive capacity is reduced; and fields are dissected. The sediments produced pollute streams and lakes and pile up on bottomlands, in stream channels, and in reservoirs.

4–2.1 Soil Loss

The most apparent damage caused by water erosion is the removal of soil from eroding surfaces. While erosion from land covered with perennial vegetation, either grass or trees, amounts to only a fraction of a ton per hectare annually, that from bare cultivated fields may exceed 450 metric tons a year (Grant, 1975). Soil losses on annually cropped sloping land frequently exceed 50 metric tons per hectare (mt/ha). At this rate it would take only forty-five years to wash away the entire furrow slice 17 cm deep if the loss were uniform over the land.

Loss of any soil is cause for concern, but topsoil loss is most important. Topsoil is generally more friable and more permeable to water, air, and roots than deeper soil material and it contains more organic matter and fertility than the subsoil.

4–2.2 Plant Nutrient Losses

During the early years of the conservation movement in the United States emphasis was often placed on the tremendous loss of plant nutrients caused annually by erosion. In the publication "Soil Erosion a National Menace," Bennett and Chapline (1928) stated that over 20 million metric tons of the three major plant nutrients, nitrogen, phosphorus, and potassium, were lost in the 13 billion metric tons of soil washed each year from the fields and forests of the United States. They related these large nutrient losses to the much smaller amounts of nutrients taken up by crop plants. This gives the misleading impression that most nutrients lost by erosion are in a usable form. Actually, a high proportion of the nutrient elements in eroded soil is not immediately useful to crops. Some will not become available for many years.

4–2.3 Textural Change

Water erosion is selective. The coarser grains are left near their original location while the finer ones are transported some distance. This selective removal makes originally sandy soil even sandier. However, medium- or fine-textured soil may not be altered seriously because the water sorts aggregates, not individual soil particles. Both small and large aggregates are usually of similar textural composition.

Long-continued erosion removes the entire surface horizon. The new topsoil, really the exposed subsoil, is generally finer textured, and poses serious physical problems in preparing a seedbed and in other phases of crop production.

4-2.4 Structural Damage

Water erosion alters soil structure in three general ways. First, because underlying soil is generally less granular and porous than surface soil, erosion exposes a less friable and less permeable soil at the surface. Second, the beating action of raindrops disintegrates aggregates on the surface and compacts a thin layer into a surface crust. This compacted layer has been observed by soils investigators ever since Wollny mentioned it in 1879. Third, as rainwater percolates into the soil, it carries suspended soil particles and grains into the surface pores. These small grains and particles lodge in the pores, plug them, and thus reduce the soil's permeability and infiltration rate. All of these changes are usually accompanied by increased rates of runoff which lead to increased rates of erosion.

4-2.5 Productivity Loss

The loss of productive topsoil and of available nutrients, and the structural deterioration which accompany erosion reduce the productive capacity of the soil. The amount of crop yield reduction depends on the properties of the topsoil and subsoil. Yield loss is largest where the subsoil is shallow, infertile, or fine textured, compact, and intractible. Yield losses on artificially truncated profiles were 60% to 75% on several soil conservation stations where no fertilizer or manure was used. A later investigation started in 1941 and continued through the 1960s on Mexico silt loam, a claypan soil (Albaqualf) in central Missouri, showed that average corn yields were seriously reduced when the topsoil was removed, in spite of the use of sufficient fertilizer to provide adequate plant nutrients. In years with poor rainfall distribution, yields were reduced from between 45 and 60 quintals per hectare (q/ha) to less than 10 q/ha. On the other hand, when rains were well spaced and adequate, comparable yields were obtained on the truncated and normal soils.

A more natural indication of the effect of erosion on soil productivity was obtained by studies on farmers' fields which had undergone erosion of differing severity (Hays and others, 1949). Here, too, crop yields were distinctly superior where little or no erosion had occurred. Yields were reduced progressively as erosion was more severe (Table 4–1).

Table 4-1 Effect of erosion severity on crop yield

Crop	State	No. of farms	Crop yield (kg/ha)		
			Slight erosion	Moderate erosion	Severe erosion
Corn	Wisconsin	8	5018	4202	3763
Grain	Wisconsin	11	4234	3360	2890
Grain	Minnesota	5	2419	2016	1546

SOURCE: Hays and others, 1949.

4-2.6 Field Dissection

A farmer can continue to farm a field as a unit in the normal way as long as the channels formed by erosion are small. When the channels become gullies too large to be crossed with ordinary farm machinery, the field must be farmed in two or more smaller units, with shorter lands and much more turning. Net profits go down because of higher production costs as well as because of less cultivatable land and lower yields.

4-2.7 Engineering Structure Damage

Erosion causes great damage to buildings, roads, bridges, and other engineering structures. Foundations are undermined by washing and by landslides and soil creep. Approaches to bridges, footings, pilings, and supports near shore and in midstream are washed away, causing structural weakening and actual failure. Figure 4-4 shows erosion damage along a roadway. Erosion in road ditches and at culvert sites often causes gullies which cut through or under the road and necessitate its closing.

4-2.8 Water Pollution

The greatest single pollutant of surface water, on a volume basis, is soil sediment. The muddying of streams and lakes reduces their value for home and industrial use, for recreation, and as habitats for fish and wildlife. The greater the sediment load, the less suitable the water is for any of these uses.

Another problem of more recent concern involves the contaminants that are carried into the streams. Fertilizers and pesticides may be dissolved in running water or carried with the soil into streams

Figure 4-4 Erosion damage to the ditch along a roadway in Kansas. (Courtesy USDA—Soil Conservation Service.)

and rivers. In some instances these contaminants affect plants and aquatic animal life, and even land animals and man.

4-2.9 Sedimentation

Although the rich bottomland soils adjacent to small streams and major river systems result from deposition of soil material eroded from the uplands, these same soils can be harmed when eroded subsoil and other less productive material is deposited on them. Sedimentation damage also occurs on lower-lying areas in upland fields. Deposition of eroded soil at the foot of an upland slope is seen in Figure 4-5.

Sediment is also deposited in stream channels, lakes, and reservoirs, often changing the ecological conditions of the aquatic environment and affecting plant and animal life. For example, deposition of sediment in fish spawning areas may ruin these sites for fish propagation. Sedimentation raises streambeds, reducing the depth and capacity of the channels, causing severe flooding and navigational

Figure 4–5 Sediment deposited at the foot of a slope in a cultivated field near Alexander, Manitoba, Canada. Several rills and a small gully were subsequently eroded through the sediment. (Courtesy J. A. Hobbs.)

problems. Sedimentation of lakes and reservoirs reduces their capacity, value, and life expectancy. In extreme cases, sedimentation changes an aquatic habitat into a terrestrial one.

4–3 AGENTS ACTIVE IN WATER EROSION

Two major agents are active in water erosion: falling raindrops and running water. Both of these derive the energy needed to detach and transport soil grains from the force of gravity. In addition, water acts as a lubricant as gravity causes soil to roll or slide downhill. This type of movement, while spectacular and important when it occurs, in the aggregate is less important than the direct movement of soil by water.

4–3.1 Falling Raindrops

In the early years of erosion-control activity it was tacitly assumed that overland flow caused water erosion. As evidence of the importance of the energy of raindrops in the erosion process accumulated, thinking changed, and now a substantial part of soil movement is credited directly to raindrops.

Energy of Falling Raindrops. The kinetic energy of a falling body can be calculated from the equation

$$E = \frac{1}{2} m v^2$$

where E = kinetic energy, ergs
     m = mass of falling body, g
     v = velocity of fall, cm/sec.

Air friction slows the fall of water drops and prevents each drop from exceeding a *terminal velocity* that is related to its mass. Laws (1941) and Gunn and Kinzer (1949) studied the relationship between drop diameter and terminal velocity over a range of drop sizes from 0.2 to 6.0 mm. Figure 4-6 presents their data in graphic form. These data show that drop size affects kinetic energy because larger drops have both larger mass and faster fall. Laws (1941) found that smaller drops reached terminal velocity in a shorter distance but that all normal drops reach terminal velocity after falling 10 m or less.

Rainstorm Intensity and Energy. Laws and Parsons (1943) found that natural rain contains a range of drop diameters from less than 0.25 mm to 7 mm. In general, drop size increases as storm intensity increases up to 150 mm/hr, but a range of sizes is present in each storm. Hudson (1971) and McGregor and Mutchler (1976) corroborate the increase in drop size for low- and intermediate-intensity storms, but show that above about 75 mm/hr the median drop diameter decreases with increasing intensity.

Wischmeier and Smith (1958) used Laws and Parsons' data to develop an equation for predicting rainstorm energy:

$$e = 118.9 + 87.3 \log_{10} I$$

where e = total energy in units of 10^3 joules/ha for each millimeter of rainfall
    I = rainfall intensity, mm/hr.

Table 6-1, developed from this equation, is presented in Chapter 6.

Wind and Raindrop Energy. Strong winds add a horizontal velocity component to raindrop fall. Also, by moving the air horizontally away from the drop, the wind partially reduces air resistance. This reduced resistance and the actual force of the wind combine to accelerate the drop. Smith and Wischmeier (1962) found that the velocity of wind-driven rain can be estimated by multiplying the drop's terminal velocity in still air by the secant of the angle between vertical and the direction of fall in the wind. They calculated that a

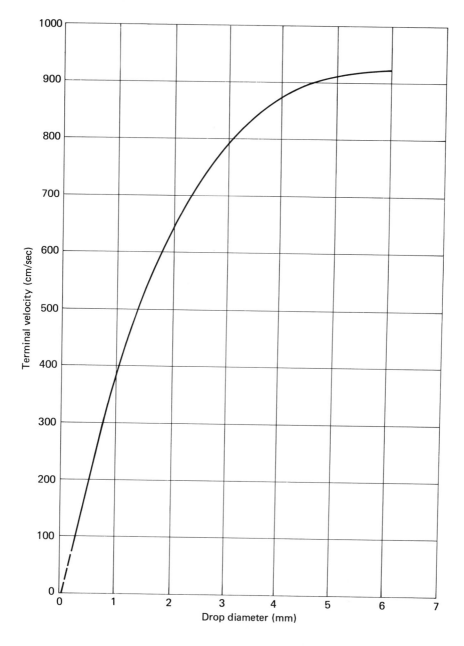

Figure 4-6 The relationship between drop diameter and terminal velocity of falling raindrops. [Based on data of Laws (1941) and Gunn and Kinzer (1949).]

3-mm median-drop-size rain falling in a wind at a 30-degree angle of inclination has a velocity 1.7% greater and kinetic energy 36% greater than the same rain falling vertically without a wind. Lyles (1977) calculated the kinetic energy of a 2-mm drop in a 32-km/hr wind was 2.75 times that of a similar drop falling in still air. A counteracting effect of wind is the breakdown of larger drops into smaller ones, but, overall, windblown drops are much more erosive than drops falling in still air.

Vegetation and Raindrop Energy. All raindrops do not strike the soil at terminal velocity and so do not always release maximum energy. Shaw (1959) showed that a growing corn crop intercepts and holds 3 to 5 mm of moisture from a storm that exceeds 7.5 mm total rainfall. This water never reaches the ground to beat the soil and cause erosion. Many drops that strike plants eventually reach the ground, but the short fall from the canopy reduces their velocity and energy level. Other drops strike vegetation and break into smaller drops that continue falling, but with reduced energy. The importance of vegetative cover in intercepting raindrops was first reported by Wollny in 1890 (Baver, 1939). His study showed that growing crops intercepted as much as 45% of the raindrops.

Work of Raindrops. Raindrops release energy when they strike the soil surface. This energy does three kinds of work, all of which are involved in the erosion process. First, it breaks aggregates and clods into smaller aggregates and individual particles. Second, it moves small soil grains (aggregates and individual particles) to new locations as water splashes back into the air. Third, it compacts and puddles the surface layer of soil. The first is the basis for the detaching capacity of the raindrops; the second is the source of the transporting capacity of rainfall; and the third reduces the soil's infiltration rate, causing more water to run off the soil surface.

Raindrops and the Erosion Process. Ellison (1944, 1947a, 1947b) probably did more than any other conservation research worker in the United States to clarify the mechanics of raindrops in the erosion process. His studies show that the main detaching agent in sheet erosion is the falling raindrop. It appears clear, in fact, that raindrops are more responsible for sheet erosion than is sheet flow (Roose, 1977). Ellison showed that raindrops break many aggregates into smaller aggregates and particles and detach them from the soil mass.

The fact that raindrops detach soil grains is readily seen in the field wherever a stone, a piece of straw, a root, or other object protects a highly erodible soil. The object absorbs the force of the falling drops, leaving the soil grains below it undisturbed. Unprotected soil grains are eroded away, lowering the soil level and leaving the undisturbed soil standing as a pedestal under its protecting cap.

A wide range of grain sizes is loosened by raindrop splash. Certainly all material 2 mm in diameter and smaller can be detached directly. Ellison (1944) found that pebbles as large as 10 mm in diameter were moved by raindrops when the pebbles were partly submerged in surface flow. He also found that splashed particles reach a maximum height of two-thirds of a meter or more and move horizontally as much as 1.5 m or more on level surfaces. More than 225 mt/ha are splashed by heavy rains beating on bare, highly detachable soil (Ellison, 1947a).

Raindrops falling on level, bare soil in the absence of wind tend to spatter equally in all directions. Therefore, soil movement out of an area is matched by soil movement into the area from other splashes. Thus, there may be a great deal of soil movement in splashes, but no net loss of soil and no measurable erosion from a particular unit of soil surface. Raindrops falling on sloping land, however, do not splash equally in all directions. The average angle of splash back from the soil is equal but opposite to the angle at which the drop hits the surface. Consequently, more water and soil splash downhill than uphill. It has been suggested that the proportion of splashed grains that move downhill from the point of raindrop impact is equal to 50% plus the percent slope of the land. According to this rule, 60% of the soil should be splashed downhill on a 10% slope, but Ellison (1944) found 75% of the splash was downhill on a 10% slope. Furthermore, the average splash distance downhill is greater than the movement uphill. This excess of downhill over uphill splash causes erosion even if no runoff takes place. Wind causes a similar directional splash movement even on level surfaces. Wind-driven raindrops hit the soil at an angle and water and soil are carried downwind by splash.

Duley and Kelly (1939) noted the development of a thin compacted layer at the surface of the soil where unimpeded raindrops beat on bare soil. Crop residues on the soil surface eliminated or greatly reduced the compacted layer. When compact layers developed, the soil's infiltration rate declined rapidly during the storm and runoff increased. Duley and Kelly found that each time they removed the thin compacted layer, infiltration immediately increased almost to its rate at the beginning of the storm, but declined with continued drop impacts.

4-3.2 Running Water

Overland flow or runoff was once considered the major, if not the only, cause of water erosion. It is still recognized as playing an important role, but now the contribution of falling raindrops to the erosion process is recognized. The most common cause of runoff is rain falling at a rate faster than the soil can absorb it. Other causes of surface flow are snow melt and irrigation.

Runoff can be divided into prechannel or sheet flow and channelized flow. The depth of unimpeded sheet flow seldom exceeds 3 or 4 mm. Vegetation lying on the land surface can dam up the flow and cause it to be deeper, though not markedly so. Channelized flow varies from about 5 mm deep in small rills to a few meters in large streams. The erosiveness of running water is influenced by several factors including depth, velocity, turbulence, and transported material.

Energy of Running Water. The kinetic energy, and consequently the erosive force, of running water is related to the quantity and velocity of flow by the same equation that relates energy of raindrops to their mass and velocity of fall. The velocity generally increases with the depth of the water layer but seldom exceeds 150 cm/sec even in a gully. Runoff water moving 150 cm/sec has only 1/28th of the energy of an equal mass of raindrops falling at 800 cm/sec; very slow flows have so little energy they are nonerosive.

Energy of Transported Material. The erosive energy of clear water is limited. Soil grains saltating (jumping along the bed) in the stream are about 2.65 times as dense and therefore carry about 2.65 times as much energy as an equal volume of water (assuming both have the same velocity). The energy differential is even larger when the grains move faster than the water in contact with the streambed (the common case). Thus a stream carrying abrasive material has greater power than clear water to break up aggregates and clods on the bed and put them into motion.

Stream Depth and Energy. The depth of water moving in sheet flow, in rills, and in smaller gullies is controlled by the intensity of the rainfall and the infiltration rate of the soil. There will be no runoff from a gentle rain of 2 to 3 mm/hr because almost any soil can absorb all the water. Runoff commences when rainfall intensity exceeds the soil infiltration rate. The thickness of the runoff films increases with the intensity of the rain. With greater depth of flow, velocity is higher and the erosive energy is greater.

Type of water movement, whether in sheet flow or in channelized flow, also influences water depth. Depth is minimal in sheet flow. Water films at the top of a slope are thin even in intense rainstorms because there is little water movement from above, and therefore little water accumulates. Water films are thicker farther down the slope because of extra water from above. However, with increasing thickness, the water moves at an increasing rate and thus limits the thickness of flow.

Water is more likely to flow in channels farther down the slope. Runoff from relatively broad areas is funneled into rills and gullies. This extra water causes appreciably thicker layers and higher velocities, giving it more energy to erode soil than sheet flow has.

Turbulence and Energy. Fast-flowing fluids move in an irregular manner with random oscillations in direction and with small to large changes in both horizontal and vertical velocity. This irregular motion is called *turbulence.* Water passing across the land in very thin films moves in laminar flow at relatively slow velocity. Its energy is restricted to that from horizontal velocity and is generally of little significance in initiating soil movement. Turbulence develops, however, as depth of flow and velocity increase. The turbulent areas gradually coalesce as flow depth continues to increase and the whole flow becomes turbulent. The kinetic energy of the stream and its erosive capacity are both increased dramatically by turbulence.

Slope and Runoff and Erosion. The slope of the land surface over which water flows influences runoff velocity and volume, and hence erosiveness. Four features of slope affect the velocity and amount of runoff—slope gradient, slope length, slope shape, and slope aspect.

Slope gradient (steepness) is described and measured in units of vertical fall either per single horizontal unit (decimal) or per hundred horizontal units (percent). Increasing slope gradient increases the speed of water moving downhill and therefore increases the erosive force of flowing water, as explained in Note 4-1. *Slope length* is the distance from the crest of a knoll or hill to the point where either slope steepness decreases enough so deposition of transported material starts, or the runoff enters a natural or prepared waterway. Slope length in a terraced field is the distance from the ridge top of one terrace to the center of the channel of the terrace immediately below. *Slope shape* can be straight, convex—with increasingly steeper slope downhill, or concave—with slopes progressively smaller downhill. Many slopes are convex at the top and concave at the bottom. *Slope aspect* is the direction the slope faces.

NOTE 4-1 SLOPE STEEPNESS AND FORCE OF RUNOFF

A body moving on a frictionless inclined plane has a downhill force, F, that is equal to its mass, m, times the acceleration of gravity, g, times the sine of the gradient angle, θ, or

$$F = m \cdot g \sin \theta$$

Increasing the gradient angle increases $\sin \theta$ and therefore increases the value of F.

If land slope is measured in units of vertical fall per unit of distance along the land surface, rather than along the true horizontal, the slope so determined is numerically equal to the sine of the gradient angle. In other words,

$$F = m \cdot g \cdot \text{gradient}$$

where "gradient" is a decimal fraction. Thus a unit volume of runoff water exerts twice the force on a 10% (0.10) frictionless slope as on a 5% (0.05) slope.

When friction is considered in calculating the force, F, of a volume of water with mass, m, as it flows downhill on a surface with a gradient, θ, it can be shown that

$$F = m \cdot g \sin \theta - f \cdot m \cdot g \cos \theta$$

where f is the coefficient of friction. $\sin \theta$ increases but $\cos \theta$ decreases as the gradient, θ, increases. Consequently, the force of the water, taking friction into account, increases proportionately faster than $\sin \theta$ increases, or faster than the gradient, expressed as a decimal fraction, increases.

Runoff is also influenced by the shape of the contour lines across the slope. Convex contours cause the water flow lines to diverge in the downhill direction. Concave contours cause them to converge and produce a deeper accumulation of water with a higher velocity than would occur with straight or convex contours.

Runoff from medium- and fine-textured soils usually increases with the *slope gradient*. Runoff from sandy soils, on the other hand, does not always increase with increasing slope. Erosion, however, always increases with *slope steepness*.

Slope length has a variable effect on runoff and erosion. Runoff losses per unit area are usually greatest on short slopes and decrease on longer ones. Increasing slope length on some soils, however, has either no effect or actually increases runoff rate. There is generally more erosion per unit area on longer slopes in spite of less total runoff. The soils on which erosion is less affected by slope length usually are permeable and consequently less erodible. Duley and Ackerman (1934) found that longer slopes increase the amount of erosion when rainfall intensity is high or the permeability of the soil is low or both.

The effect of *slope shape* on runoff and erosion is complex. Runoff velocity is slow and soil movement is minimal near the top of convex slopes because runoff volume is small and the slope is gentle. Water movement is faster lower on the slope where the gradient is steeper and more runoff water accumulates. Soils tend to be shallow on convex slopes because soil replacement from the flatter slope above is slower than the loss to the steeper slope below. Concave slopes usually suffer less from erosion and have deeper soils than convex slopes because the higher runoff volumes on the lower part flow more slowly where the gradient is flatter. Meyer and Kramer (1968) studied the effect of four slope types on erosion using a computerized program. The smallest predicted losses were from the concave slope and the greatest from the convex slope. Complex- and uniform-slope losses were intermediate, with the complex slope losing less than the uniform one. Nearly all natural slopes in humid regions are complex, having convex slopes at the top and concave ones at the bottom.

The effect of *slope aspect* on runoff and erosion has not been studied extensively. The major effect arises from its influence on microclimate, the result of the angle at which the sun's rays strike the soil. Aspect has minimal effect at the equator, but the influence increases toward the poles. A south- or west-facing slope in the northern hemisphere is warmer and has higher evaporation during the growing season. Water storage is reduced and there is less plant growth, especially in dry climates. The sparse vegetation often results in increased erosion. A north- or east-facing slope, on the other hand, is usually noticeably cooler, more moist, and better vegetated. Wollny and his associates in Germany studied the effect of slope aspect nearly a century ago. They found smaller runoff but greater erosion losses on south-facing slopes (Baver, 1939).

Surface Condition. The nature of the soil surface and vegetative cover also has a marked effect on the amount and velocity of runoff. A smooth, bare surface offers the least possible frictional resistance to the passage of water; a soil covered with dense vegetation presents the ultimate in resistance to water movement. Velocity of water flow is directly proportional to land slope and depth of flow, and inversely proportional to surface roughness (Note 4-2). Both microtopographical depressions and plant material, living or dead, reduce runoff volume and velocity. These in turn reduce the energy of runoff water and the amount of erosion. Water flow velocities are inversely proportional to the surface roughness factors shown in Table 4–2.

NOTE 4-2 MANNING'S FORMULA

The most common method for estimating flow velocity in an open channel employs *Manning's formula:*

$$V = \frac{R^{2/3}S^{1/2}}{\eta}$$

where V = average velocity of flow, m/sec
       R = hydraulic radius, m
       S = land slope, m/m
       η = coefficient of surface roughness.

The hydraulic radius (R) is related to depth of flow, but is not depth, not even average depth. It is defined as

$$R = \frac{A}{P}$$

where A = cross-sectional area of flow, m^2
      P = wetted perimeter, m.

The method for calculating the hydraulic radius is shown below:

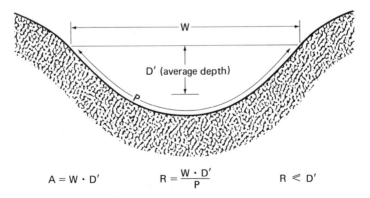

$$A = W \cdot D' \qquad R = \frac{W \cdot D'}{P} \qquad R \leqslant D'$$

The value of R is equal to the average depth in sheet flow but is less than the average depth in channel flow.

The surface roughness coefficient (η) ranges from 0.017 for a smooth, straight, bare, earthen ditch to 0.300 for a dense, uniform stand of grass such as bermudagrass more than 25 cm tall. Selected values of η are shown in Table 4-2.

Table 4-2 Selected values for coefficient of surface roughness (η) for use in Manning's formula

	Values of η		
Surface condition	*Minimum*	*Design*	*Maximum*
Ditches:			
Earth, straight and uniform	0.017	0.022	0.025
Winding, sluggish ditches and gullies	0.022	0.025	0.030
Ditches with rough, stony beds, and			
vegetated (weedy) banks	0.025	0.035	0.040
Earth bottom, rubble on sides	0.028	0.032	0.035
Natural stream channels:			
Clean, straight banks, no rifts or pools	0.025		0.033
Clean, straight banks, some weeds and			
stones	0.030		0.040
Winding, some pools, but clean	0.033		0.045
Winding, some pools, some weeds and			
stones	0.035		0.050
Sluggish river channels, either weedy			
or with deep pools	0.050		0.080
Very weedy channels	0.075		0.150
Vegetated waterways (prepared):			
Dense, uniform bermudagrass, 25 cm tall[a]	0.040	0.040	0.300
Dense, uniform bermudagrass, 6 cm tall	0.034		0.110

[a]Other sod grasses slightly less rough.

SOURCE: *SCS Engineers' Handbook.*

Runoff and the Erosion Process. Both the detaching and transporting capacity of runoff are small when the flow is in thin films and the velocity is low, but they increase as the runoff becomes channelized and depth and velocity increase. Prechannel flow by itself has little or no capacity to detach and transport soil particles. However, rain falls during most of the time prechannel flow is occurring, and the raindrops detach large numbers of soil grains. The falling drops also cause sheet flow to be turbulent, thus increasing its carrying capacity. Because the stirring action of the drops creates turbulent flow in the runoff water, soil grains detached by raindrops can be transported long distances by prechannel flow.

Raindrops cannot easily detach grains below the surface of running water, but the velocities of streams give them detaching and transporting powers of their own. The erosive energy of soil particles carried in the runoff must be added to the energy of the clear water. The erosiveness of the particles often exceeds that of the clear stream. The composition of the sediment load is constantly changing. Even though a stream is carrying as much sediment as it can (an amount directly related to the third power of its velocity and to its turbulence), gravity causes some soil particles to drop out of suspension while other particles are picked up. The larger and heavier grains drop out quickest; the smallest remain in suspension for long periods (Note 4–3).

NOTE 4-3 STOKES' LAW

Stokes' law predicts the velocity of fall of spherical bodies through a fluid. The rate of settling of soil particles between 0.1 and 0.001 mm in diameter can be estimated from the following equation:

$$v = \frac{2(d_s - d_f)}{9\eta} gr^2$$

where v = velocity of fall, cm/sec
d_s = density of the solid, g/cm^3
d_f = density of the fluid, g/cm^3
η = viscosity of fluid, poise
g = acceleration of gravity, cm/sec^2
r = radius of particle, cm.

If soil particles are suspended in water at 20°C, it can be assumed that d_s = 2.65 g/cm^3, d_f = 0.998 g/cm^3, η = 0.01005 poise, and g = 980 cm/sec^2. It follows, under these conditions, that

$$v = 35{,}800r^2 \text{ cm/sec}$$

Solving for a variety of "r's" gives their individual velocities of fall, and from these velocities it is possible to calculate, for example, how long it takes the various sizes to fall 20 cm:

$$\frac{20 \text{ cm}}{v \text{ (cm/sec)}} = t \text{ (sec)}$$

These values can be used to determine how far a stream with known velocity will travel in that period of time:

$$t \text{ (sec)} \cdot \text{stream velocity (cm/sec)} = L \text{ (cm)}$$

The results indicate how far the different-sized particles will move horizontally while dropping vertically 20 cm through the flowing water. For example, in a stream flowing at 100 cm/sec (neglecting turbulence), fine sand 0.1 mm in diameter will travel 22 m horizontally while dropping 20 cm vertically. Silt 0.02 mm in diameter travels 559 m, and a 0.002-mm clay particle is carried 56 km while settling the same 20 cm vertically.

Sand can be deposited on land from fast-moving waters; silt will settle out in quantity only as the stream's velocity is markedly reduced, such as when the stream gradient levels off; and clay settles out in quantity only when the water is still or when it is flocculated as the stream enters a body of salt water.

4-3.3 Gravity

Gravity works directly to move soil and soil material in addition to providing the energy contained in falling raindrops and flowing water. Movements caused directly by gravity are known by a variety of names, such as landslides, mud flows, slips, slumps, soil creep, and surface creep. The term avalanche applies strictly to a mass of snow, but moving snow may strip all soil and vegetation down to bedrock and deposit them in a heap at the bottom of the slope.

In most cases of gravity-induced movement the topography must be steeply sloping. Steeply sloping land is usually found in native vegetation rather than in cultivated fields. Soil creep is a notable exception. It occurs on slopes of only a few percent, especially in foot-slope positions.

Land in native vegetation, even on steep slopes, is ordinarily in equilibrium with its environment. Downward movement of soil masses is usually extremely slow. If, however, the equilibrium is destroyed or greatly upset by fire, overgrazing, logging, cultivation, surface mining, or construction, sudden mass movements may result. This usually happens when there is an excess of moisture due to heavy rains or rapid snow melt, making the soil almost a fluid. The moisture also acts as a lubricant below the surface, especially if a layer with slow permeability is located within reasonable depths. Normal friction between the semiviscous soil mass and the underlying material is reduced and the mass slowly or rapidly slides downhill. The soil often slumps down and out, forming a hump above the former surface at the bottom, and a depression at the top. This is the sort of movement that occurs on the north sides of hills in the steep cultivated fields in the Palouse region of eastern Washington and northern Idaho. There the saturating moisture is provided by snow melt.

Along the Pacific slopes of the Cascades and the Coastal Range, in the Intermountain Region, and in other hilly and mountainous regions of the United States and of other countries, a watery soil mass called a mud flow may progress down a valley like a very slowly moving river. Mud flows also occur in permafrost regions when the upper soil layers thaw and become saturated by rain or snow melt. There the mud flows move downslope or move vertically into solution caverns.

4-4 SOIL PROPERTIES AND SOIL ERODIBILITY

Differences in soil erodibility are obvious to most farmers and were noted by government scientists and others in the early years of the conservation movement. A great deal of work has been undertaken over the years to discover individual properties that make a soil erodible. The true erodibility of a soil is determined in the field by measuring the amount of soil lost during natural rainstorms or under carefully regulated artificial water applications. However, this is a costly and time-consuming exercise, so approximate methods are needed to serve as interim predictors.

In the early years of soil conservation activity, Middleton (1930), and Middleton, Slater, and Byers (1932, 1934) analyzed a number of soils from some of the newly established soil erosion stations and from other sites. Many chemical and physical analyses were made and the results compared to an assessment of erodibilities made by scientists in the field. Some properties and combinations of properties related to aggregate size, structural stability, and soil permeability appeared to be related to soil erodibility.

Wischmeier, Johnson, and Cross (1971) developed a method of predicting soil erodibility using the four soil properties—texture, organic-matter content, soil structure, and soil permeability. This method will be explained more fully in Chapter 6. The fact that these four soil properties can be used to predict soil erodibility means that they must account for a significant part of the soil's potential erodibility.

Erosion detaches individual soil grains from the soil mass and carries them away in raindrop splash or running water. Soil erodibility is therefore a combination of its detachability and its transportability. Any property that prevents or makes difficult soil detachment or soil transportation reduces the soil's erodibility. Runoff must occur for rapid erosion to take place. Accordingly, soil properties that affect infiltration rate and permeability to water also affect the amount of erosion that takes place. Texture and structure are two soil properties that affect permeability and soil erodibility.

4-4.1 Soil Texture

Sand particles are difficult to transport because of their size even though they are easily detached from the soil mass. Clay particles, at the other extreme, tend to stick together and are difficult to detach, but are easily carried great distances once separated from the soil mass. Silt soils are frequently well aggregated, but the aggregates break down readily when wetted, and the particles are easily detached and transported.

Infiltration rate and permeability to water are related in part to texture. Water moves rapidly through the macropores; it moves only slowly through the micropores. The large pores between sand particles permit rapid water movement. The fine to very fine pores common in medium- and fine-textured soils such as the loams, clay loams, and clays resist water movement. While total porosity of the fine-textured soils is nearly always greater than that of coarse-textured soils, the individual pores in the fine soils are usually much smaller, and both infiltration and permeability are slower. Therefore a moderate storm often produces more runoff and erosion from the finer-textured soils than from the sandy ones.

4-4.2 Soil Structure

Large, stable aggregates make a soil difficult to detach and transport. They also make it more permeable to water. While soils high in clay usually have low permeability and low infiltration rate, a well-aggregated clay soil permits faster water movement than a poorly aggregated soil of the same texture.

Factors that influence the size and stability of aggregates include texture, kind of ions on the cation-exchange complex, type of clay mineral, organic-matter content, cementing materials other than clay and organic matter, and cropping history.

Texture. Clay generally acts as a cementing and aggregating agent. If the soil's cation-exchange complex is occupied mainly by H^+ or di- or tri-valent cations, the colloid will be flocculated. Aggregation of individual soil particles, including the sands and silts as well as the clays, takes place. Large stable aggregates resist both detachment and transportation. The higher the clay content, up to a point, the larger the aggregate size and the greater the stability. Excessively high clay content (above 40%) promotes the development of very small aggregates that erode more easily, especially where surface soils freeze and thaw frequently during the winter. Soil colloids will be deflocculated if the exchange sites are occupied by large amounts of Na^+ and K^+ or by very large amounts of Mg^{++}. Deflocculated colloids prevent aggregate formation and cause low permeability.

Some soil aggregates are relatively unstable. This is particularly true of soils low in organic matter and high in silt and very fine sand. These aggregates are easily destroyed by the beating action of rain. Raindrop energy and the fine grains flowing into and plugging surface pores combine to produce a dense compact layer at the soil surface. Water infiltrates very slowly into this compacted layer because its pores are so small. Reduced infiltration results in increased runoff and erosion.

Type of Clay Mineral. Aggregation of soils is influenced by the type of clay mineral. Tropical and subtropical soils, which are high in hydrous oxides of iron and aluminum and in the 1:1-type lattice clay, kaolinite, tend to be better aggregated than soils high in 2:1-type lattice clays, montmorillonite and illite.

Organic-Matter Content. Structure development is also influenced by organic content. Soil structure improves and the individual aggregates become more stable as organic matter content increases. Soil aggregates very high in organic matter are quite small and have low densities. Improved structure invariably is accompanied by increased permeability and by decreased runoff and erosion. Where runoff is excessive in spite of good permeability (heavy rainfall or steeply sloping land), soils high in organic matter may be very erodible because of the small size and low bulk density of the granules.

Cementing Agents. Secondary lime sometimes acts as a cementing agent holding particles into aggregates, though there are other soil chemicals more effective than lime. Certain iron compounds in subsoils or topsoils bind clays and other soil grains together in quite stable forms in many strongly leached, temperate-region soils and in numerous tropical soils. These soils may be quite resistant to erosion.

Cropping History. Soils just plowed from native vegetation, cultivated pasture, or meadow resist erosion. They have excellent structure and relatively large, stable aggregates. Roots that permeate the aggregates, together with large amounts of incorporated crop residue, add to the stability. Freshly decomposing plant material helps to develop resistant structures, whereas humus, stabilized by long periods of decomposition, seems to be less effective. Consequently, initially resistant aggregates become less stable and more subject to breakdown and erosion as the native vegetation or pasture areas undergo repeated cultivation operations.

4-5 VEGETATION AND WATER EROSION

Above-ground vegetation limits the erosive action of raindrops on the soil and decreases the amount of erosion caused by surface runoff. Plant material either above or on the soil surface intercepts raindrops but it must be *on* the surface to slow down runoff. Perennial vegetation also develops erosion-resisting aggregates in soils.

One of the earliest soil erosion studies in the United States was at Columbia, Missouri. Results from these studies showed clearly that crops differ significantly in their effect on water erosion (Table 4-3). These results show that runoff and erosion are most severe on land without crop (fallow). Continuous corn, a row or intertilled crop, was the next most erosive cropping system, followed by continuous wheat, and then by the rotation of corn, wheat, and clover. Continuous bluegrass was the most protective cropping system tested.

Kramer and Weaver (1936) demonstrated conclusively that the top growth of plants was significantly more important than roots in reducing water erosion. Duley and Kelly (1939), in their classic study, showed that dead plant material on the soil surface is as effec-

Table 4-3 Effect of cropping system on runoff and erosion at Columbia, Missouri, 1918-1931

Cropping system	Average runoff		Average annual erosion (mt/ha)	Time to erode a 17-cm layer (yrs)
	Millimeters	Percent		
Continuous fallow	322	31.4	92.5	24
Continuous bluegrass	128	12.6	0.7	3214
Continuous wheat	246	24.1	22.6	100
Continuous corn	311	30.5	44.1	51
Corn, wheat, clover rotation	148	14.4	6.0	375

SOURCE: Modified from Miller and Krusekopf, 1932.

tive as thick perennial vegetation in maintaining infiltration rate and in reducing runoff and erosion. The concept of *stubble mulch tillage* (Ch. 9) developed from this early research finding.

4-6 WATER EROSION AND POLLUTION

The major concern about soil erosion, until recently, was the damage done to the soil itself—the loss of soil and of soil productivity. Recently, however, strong criticism has been leveled at the polluting effects erosion sediments have on land, water, and life downstream. Pollutants enter streams from definite, identifiable discharge outlets (*point source*) such as waste discharge pipes from factories or industry, or in a diffuse pattern over a wide area (*nonpoint source*), as does eroded soil from cultivated fields.

Sediment carried to streams and lakes is excessive in the view of many people even when erosion is reduced to the "tolerable level" of 2 to 11 mt/ha annually. Runoff water carries not only soil, but some of the fertilizers and pesticides applied to it, as well as animal wastes. Soil sediment, though, is the number-one pollutant on a volume basis. Water pollution and its control are discussed in Chapter 17.

4-7 WATER EROSION AND SEDIMENTATION

Deposition of transported soil material (sedimentation) is an essential component of the erosion process. Repeated detachment, transportation, and deposition move soil from the highest uplands to the bed of the sea.

Not all sediment comes from cultivated lands or upland sites. A stream will gouge and scour material from its own banks and bed if it is not already loaded to capacity. Using every practical means to control erosion on cultivated range, forest, and other land will reduce but not control sedimentation. For example, the Mississippi River in central United States was given the name "Big Muddy" by the western pioneers at a time when there was little or no cultivation along its banks. The word "Winnipeg," the name of the capital city of Manitoba, Canada, is from the Cree Indian dialect. It means "murky water" and referred to the river (the Red River of the North) that passes through that city. This name, too, was used long before there was any cultivation on the land in that area.

Sedimentation is both beneficial and harmful. Alluvial soils, built up over centuries by the deposition of rich topsoil along rivers and streams, are among the world's most productive soils. Accelerated erosion initially removes topsoil, but eventually carries less productive subsoil. The erosion sediments initially benefit the depositional sites, but eventually cause productivity declines. Serious floods, like those of Midwestern rivers in the United States in the early 1950s, buried highly productive alluvial soils under a half meter or more of coarse, unproductive sand. Denuded mountain slopes often deposit a meter or more of soil mixed with rocks and other coarse material on the formerly productive bottomland soil at the foot of the slopes.

Sedimentation also damages vegetation, both cultivated and native. The vegetation, even trees, may be killed. Highways, railroads, houses, and factories may be covered or inundated by flood-borne sediment.

Scouring and sedimentation is a continual process in all stream channels. Sediment carried from upland areas and the streambed is deposited on the bed as flow velocity decreases between periods of rapid runoff. This sediment raises the general level of the river bed and may reduce channel capacity enough to cause water to overtop the banks and cause increased flood damage to the land and structures in the flooded area when the next storm comes.

Levees have been built in many places to force rivers to remain in their channels. These are seldom permanently effective. Sedimentation fills the channels between the levees, raises the bed, and makes it necessary to raise the height of the levees to maintain channel capacity. River channels within levees in many river systems are so choked with sediment that the rivers flow above the level of much of the surrounding bottomland. Eventually a severe storm causes the river to overflow the levee, causing extreme losses on the alluvial land the levee was meant to protect.

Siltation of stream channels is important in navigable streams. Shallow areas and sandbars, formed by deposition, must be cleared away periodically to keep the channel deep enough for boat traffic. Dredging the sediments is very expensive and must be done at frequent intervals.

Gradual raising of streambeds has another serious consequence. Most alluvial soils have a water table not far below the soil surface. This water table rises as the river bed is raised. Initially a higher water table reduces crop growth because of the shallower depth of well-aerated soil. Eventually the soil is too wet for commercial crops, and many times even useful native vegetation will fail to thrive. The damaged areas then become swamps and their use may be limited to wildlife.

Siltation of reservoirs is another costly result of sedimentation.

The silt and the coarser clay carried by the stream drop out of suspension and accumulate on the reservoir bed; only the finest clay passes through the lake and out the lower end. The useful life of a storage structure is long where stream gradient is not too steep, where soils resist erosion, where the watershed area exceeds 250 square kilometers, and where the ratio of watershed area, in square kilometers, to the volume of storage, in hectare-centimeters, is greater than 200 to 1. Whatever the length of life of a reservoir, the site is gone forever when it is filled with sediments. Any other site in the area is likely to be far less suitable than the original one. Figure 4-7 shows a reservoir destroyed by sediment.

4-8 PRINCIPLES OF WATER EROSION CONTROL

Water erosion occurs when conditions are favorable for the detachment and transportation of soil material. Climate, soil erodibility, slope gradient and length, and surface and vegetative conditions in-

Figure 4-7 This reservoir in Kansas originally had a surface area of 8 ha, but has been filled with sediment that has changed most of the area into mud flats. The remaining water is only about 1 m deep. (Courtesy USDA—Soil Conservation Service.)

fluence how much erosion will take place. A method for predicting the effect variations of each of these factors has on erosion loss is presented in Chapter 6.

Many different practices have been developed to reduce water erosion. Not all practices are applicable in all regions. However, the *principles* of water erosion control are the same wherever serious water erosion occurs. These principles are:

1. Reduce raindrop impact on the soil.
2. Reduce runoff volume and velocity.
3. Increase the soil's resistance to erosion.

Management practices that effect one or more of these principles will help to control water erosion. These practices are discussed in later chapters.

SUMMARY

Water erosion occurs wherever rainfall strikes bare soil or runoff water flows over erodible and insufficiently protected soil. The principal forms of water erosion are sheet erosion, rill erosion, gully erosion, and streambank erosion. Erosion damages the upland areas from which soil and plant nutrients are removed and also the bottomlands on which sediments are deposited. It washes out crops on uplands, and buries them on depositional sites. It pollutes the waters, fills in river channels and reservoirs, and contributes to flooding. The erosiveness of rainfall is proportional to the energy of the falling drops and is influenced by the total amount of rain, the size of the drops, and their velocity of fall. The erosiveness of runoff is proportional to its energy and is influenced by both the volume and the velocity of flow. Flow volume is directly related to rainfall intensity and duration and inversely related to soil infiltration rate and permeability. Flow velocity is related to flow thickness, slope gradient, and surface condition.

Water also acts as a lubricant, aiding gravity in mass soil movement. Landslides and mud slides occur in some areas of steeper topography. Mud slides are most common in winter rainfall areas where cultivated soils are nearly saturated and lack adequate anchoring roots.

Soil properties, especially texture and structure, influence the ease or difficulty with which soil grains are detached and transported, and also influence infiltration and percolation rates. Vegetation, both living and dead, intercepts raindrops and reduces the energy they release at the soil surface. Vegetation also slows the passage of runoff water over the soil surface, reducing its energy.

Eroded soil is an important nonpoint-source water pollutant because of its large bulk and the chemicals it carries. Sedimentation is both beneficial and harmful, and part of it is natural. Sedimentation is most damaging when it raises the level of a stream channel or fills a reservoir with soil material. Water erosion and sedimentation can be controlled by reducing the energy of the erosive agents, usually rainfall and runoff water, or by increasing soil's resistance to erosion.

QUESTIONS

1. In what ways is water erosion important to the nonfarming segment of the world's population?
2. How do raindrops cause soil loss?
3. Describe briefly how runoff depth, land slope, and surface condition affect the erosiveness of running water.
4. How does soil structure influence the amount of soil lost by raindrop splash and runoff water?
5. How does vegetation reduce soil loss that is caused by water erosion?

REFERENCES

BAVER, L. D., 1939. Ewald Wollny—A pioneer in soil and water conservation research. *Soil Sci. Soc. Amer. Proc.* (1938) 3:330–333.

BENNETT, H. H., and W. R. CHAPLINE, 1928. *Soil Erosion a National Menace.* USDA Circ. 33.

DULEY, F. L., and F. G. ACKERMAN, 1934. Runoff and erosion from plots of different lengths. *J. Agr. Res.* 48:505–510.

DULEY, F. L., and L. L. KELLY, 1939. *Effect of Soil Type, Slope, and Surface Condition on Intake of Water.* Nebraska Ag. Exp. Sta. Res. Bull. 112.

ELLISON, W. D., 1944. Studies of raindrop erosion. *Agric. Eng.* 25:131–136, 181–182.

ELLISON, W. D., 1947a. Soil erosion studies: II. Soil detachment hazard by raindrop splash. *Agric. Eng.* 28:197–201.

ELLISON, W. D., 1947b. Soil erosion studies: V. Soil transportation in the splash process. *Agric. Eng.* 28:349–351.

ENVIRONMENTAL PROTECTION AGENCY, 1973. *Methods for Identifying and Evaluating the Nature and Extent of Nonpoint Sources of Pollutants.* EPA-430/9-73-014. Office of Air and Water Programs, Environmental Protection Agency, Washington, D.C., 261 p.

GRANT, K. E., 1975. Erosion in 1973–74: The record and the challenge. *J. Soil Water Cons.* 30:29–32.

GUNN, ROSS, and G. D. KINZER, 1949. The terminal velocity of fall for water droplets. *J. Meteor.* 6:243–248.

GUNTERMANN, K. L., M. T. LEE, and E. R. SWANSON, 1975. The off-site sediment damage function in selected Illinois watersheds. *J. Soil Water Cons.* 30:219-224.

HAYS, O. E., A. G. MCCALL, and F. G. BELL, 1949. *Investigations in Erosion Control and the Reclamation of Eroded Land at the Upper Mississippi Valley Conservation Experiment Station near LaCrosse, Wisconsin, 1933-43.* USDA Tech. Bull. 973.

HUDSON, NORMAN, 1971. *Soil Conservation.* Cornell Univ. Press, Ithaca, New York, 320 p.

KRAMER, J., and J. E. WEAVER, 1936. *Relative Efficiency of Roots and Tops of Plants in Protecting the Soil from Erosion.* Conservation Dept. Bull. 2, Univ. Nebraska, Lincoln.

LAL, R., 1977. Analysis of factors affecting rainfall erosivity and soil erodibility. In D. J. GREENLAND and R. LAL (eds.), *Soil Conservation and Management in the Humid Tropics.* John Wiley, New York, p. 49-56.

LAWS, J. O., 1941. Measurements of fall velocity of water drops and raindrops. *Trans. Amer. Geophys. Union* 22:709-721.

LAWS, J. O., and D. A. PARSONS, 1943. The relation of raindrop-size to intensity. *Trans. Amer. Geophys. Union.* 24:452-459.

LYLES, LEON, 1977. Soil detachment and aggregate disintegration by wind driven rain. In *Soil Erosion: Prediction and Control,* Soil Cons. Soc. Amer., Ankeny, Iowa, p. 152-159.

McGREGOR, K. C., and C. K. MUTCHLER, 1976. Status of the R factor in northern Mississippi. In *Soil Erosion: Prediction and Control,* Soil Cons. Soc. Amer., Ankeny, Iowa, p. 135-142.

MEYER, L. D., and L. A. KRAMER, 1968. Relation between land-slope and soil erosion. Paper No. 68-749. *Amer. Soc. Agric. Eng.,* St. Joseph, Mich. (abbreviated paper in *Agric. Eng.* 50:522-523).

MIDDLETON, H. E., 1930. *Properties of Soils Which Influence Soil Erosion.* USDA Tech. Bull. 178.

MIDDLETON, H. E., C. S. SLATER, AND H. G. BYERS, 1932. *Physical and Chemical Characteristics of the Soils from the Erosion Experiment Stations.* USDA Tech. Bull. 316.

MIDDLETON, H. E., C. S. SLATER, and H. G. BYERS, 1934. *The Physical and Chemical Characteristics of the Soils from the Erosion Experiment Stations, Second Report.* USDA Tech. Bull. 430.

MILLER, M. F., and H. H. KRUSEKOPF, 1932. *The Influence of Systems of Cropping and Methods of Culture on Surface Runoff and Soil Erosion.* Missouri Ag. Exp. Sta. Res. Bull. 177.

ROOSE, E. J., 1977. Use of the universal soil loss equation to predict erosion in West Africa. In *Soil Erosion: Prediction and Control,* Soil Cons. Soc. Amer., Ankeny, Iowa, p. 60-74.

SHAW, R. H., 1959. Water use from plastic-covered and uncovered corn plots. *Agron. J.* 51:172-173.

SMITH, D. D., and W. H. WISCHMEIER, 1962. Rainfall erosion. In *Advances in Agronomy,* Vol. 14, Academic Press, New York, p. 109-148.

STEWARD, B. A. (Coordinator), D. A. WOOLHISER, W. H. WISCHMEIER, J. H. CARO, and M. H. FRERE, 1975. *Control of Water Pollution from Cropland.* Vol. 1. Report No. A.R.S.-H-5-1, USDA, Washington, D.C.

WISCHMEIER, W. H., C. B. JOHNSON, and B. V. CROSS, 1971. A soil erodibility nomograph for farmland and construction sites. *J. Soil Water Cons.* 26:189–193.

WISCHMEIER, W. H., and D. D. SMITH, 1958. Rainfall energy and its relations to soil loss. *Trans. Amer. Geophys. Union* 39:285–291.

WOLLNY, EWALD, 1890. Untersuchungen über das Verhalten der atmosphärischen Niederschläge zur Pflanze und zum Boden, *Forsch. Geb. Agriphys.* 13:316–356. (Quoted by Baver, 1939).

5

Wind Erosion and Deposition

Wind erosion is the process of detachment, transportation, and deposition of soil material by wind action. It occurs in all parts of the world and is a cause of serious soil deterioration. Chepil (1957) says,

> The basic causes of wind erosion are few and simple. Wherever (1) the soil is loose, finely divided, and dry, (2) the soil surface is smooth and bare, and (3) the wind is strong, erosion may be expected.
>
> By the same token, whenever (a) the soil is compacted, kept moist, or made up of stable aggregates or clods large enough to resist the force of the wind, (b) the soil surface is roughened or covered by vegetation or vegetative residue, or (c) the wind near the ground is somewhat reduced, erosion may be curtailed or eliminated.

Wind erosion is usually considered a major problem in dryland regions, but reports over the years show that sandy soils, particularly along sea coasts, suffer severely from wind erosion. It is serious on muck soils in humid areas and also occurs sporadically on medium- and fine-textured soils that are laid bare in humid regions. Wind erosion can also be a serious problem on irrigated land (Mech and Woodruff, 1967). It is a serious problem on all continents, particularly in the United States and Canada in North America; in the drier countries, such as Argentina and parts of Bolivia and Peru, in South America; in both European and Asiatic parts of U.S.S.R.; in the Middle East countries, and in China, India, and Pakistan in Asia; both north and south of the equator in Africa; and in Australia.

Wind erosion in the United States is most widespread in the Great Plains states, but it is also important in the Pacific Northwest, in southeastern coastal areas, along the Atlantic seaboard, and around the Great Lakes.

Serious and widespread wind erosion has occurred periodically in the United States with the most severe and widespread occurrence during the 1930s. Research has since provided a better understanding of this phenomenon, and better techniques for its control have been developed. Efforts of the Soil Conservation Service, agricultural universities, and local Conservation Districts have promoted use of conservation measures on the nation's farms and ranches, and the U.S. Government has subsidized certain conservation practices in an effort to promote their adoption. As a result, acceptance of conservation measures has increased and, despite severe droughts and equally strong winds, soil losses have not again reached the levels encountered in the 1930s. Still, the U.S. Department of Agriculture (1965) estimated that wind erosion is the dominant problem on over 28 million hectares of land in the United States. Of this total, approximately 22 million hectares are cropland, 3.6 million hectares are in range, and 2.4 million hectares are put to other uses. The area on which severe erosion occurs has ranged from one-half to 6 million hectares a year, with an overall average of about 2 million hectares.

5-1 TYPES OF SOIL MOVEMENT

Soil is moved by wind in one of three ways. Soil particles and aggregates less than 0.05 mm in diameter (silt size and smaller), once raised into the wind stream, are kept suspended by the turbulence of the air currents. They may be moved great distances in *suspension*. Suspended dust does not drop out of the air in quantity unless rain washes it out or the velocity of the wind is drastically reduced.

Intermediate-sized grains, approximately 0.05 to 0.5 mm in diameter (very fine to medium sand), move in the wind in a series of leaps, rising into the air and falling again after a relatively short flight. This type of motion is called *saltation*. The moving grains gain a great deal of energy and may knock other grains into the air or bounce back themselves.

Soil grains larger than 0.5 mm in diameter cannot be lifted into the wind stream, but those smaller than about 1 mm may be bumped along the soil surface by saltating grains and, to a lesser extent, by the direct force of the wind. This type of movement is called *surface creep*.

Aggregates, clods, and particles larger than 1 mm in diameter are too large to be moved by wind, even in surface creep. They remain in place on the eroding surface and form a covering called desert pavement or lag gravel, as shown in Figure 5-1, that protects the soil against further erosion.

Soil grains moving in saltation are the key to wind erosion. They are moved by the force of strong winds, and they drastically increase the number of both smaller and larger grains that move in suspension and by surface creep.

5-2 EROSION DAMAGE

Wind erosion causes a great deal of damage each year. This damage takes a variety of forms including loss of soil, textural changes, nutrient and productivity losses, abrasion, air pollution, and sedimentation.

5-2.1 Loss of Soil

Annual loss rates as high as 700 mt/ha have been estimated for highly erodible bare sandy soils under conditions favorable for wind erosion.

Figure 5-1 A desert pavement in New Mexico. The finer soil particles have been blown away, leaving a heavy continuous gravel cover (scale is in inches). (Courtesy F. R. Troeh.)

Annual losses from less erodible bare soils (noncalcareous silt loams with less than 20% clay) under erosive conditions range up to about 125 mt/ha (Lyles, 1977). A hectare-furrow-slice 17 cm deep (about 2250 mt) could be blown away in about three years at the 700 mt/yr rate and in eighteen years at 125 mt/yr if soil was removed uniformly from the entire surface. Actual losses are usually less than these figures because land is seldom left bare and unprotected for a whole year. Some losses, however, are even greater. Plowed layers from many farm fields in the Great Plains were blown away in a single dust storm in the 1930s. Some fields in western Canada, such as the area in Figure 5-2, lost 60 cm of soil in one year.

5-2.2 Textural Change

Wind winnows soil much as it winnows chaff from threshed grain. The finest soil grains are carried great distances in suspension. Saltating grains are usually moved to the fencerows or other barriers at the edges of the fields. Coarser grains stay where they are or move relatively short distances within the eroding field.

The winnowing action affects soil texture markedly in soils developed from glacial till, mixed residuum, and other materials having a wide range of particle sizes. Silt and clay are removed as suspended

Figure 5-2 More than 30 cm of soil was removed by wind erosion from this fine sandy loam soil in southwestern Manitoba. The concrete structure on the left is a geodetic survey marker. (Courtesy Canada-Manitoba Soil Survey.)

dust, but the coarser material remains, so the soils gradually become coarser-textured. A number of investigators showed such texture changes during the erosion period of the 1930s in the United States and Canada (Chepil, 1946; Daniel, 1936; Moss, 1935).

Soil aggregates erode from many medium- and fine-textured soils, particularly the many silt loams of the Plains regions. Coarser grains are left behind in the eroding fields, but these grains (aggregates rather than particles) consist of about the same proportions of fine and coarse particles as the whole soil had before erosion. Texture does not change as markedly in these soils as in coarse-textured and poorly aggregated ones. There are many farms in the Great Plains with well-aggregated soils where remnant dunes, formed around buildings during severe wind erosion from 1910 to 1914, have silt loam texture like those of the soil in nearby cultivated fields and uncultivated fencerows.

5–2.3 Nutrient Losses

The colloidal clay and organic matter are the seat of most of the soil's fertility. The loss of colloidal material in the clouds of dust blown from eroding fields causes considerable fertility loss. Fertility loss is particularly severe in coarse-textured soils that become coarser as erosion progresses, but it also occurs in medium-textured soils that lose soil but do not change texture with erosion. Topsoil, which contains higher concentrations of available nutrients than subsoil, is lost first. In this way, eroding soil becomes progressively less fertile.

5–2.4 Productivity Losses

Soils become less productive as winds erode them. Soils developed from glacial till and other mixed-textured material lose productivity mostly because of lowered nutrient contents and reduced water-holding capacities. Soils developed from loess or other relatively uniform material lose productivity because of loss of friable topsoil and the exposure of more clayey, less permeable, less fertile subsoil material containing less organic matter.

Productivity losses, as indicated by crop-yield declines, have been measured. Finnell (1951), for example, found that average wheat yields in the southern Great Plains were lowered progressively with increasingly severe wind erosion. Lyles (1977) suggested a method for estimating productivity decline from the prediction of surface soil loss and the known relationship between depth of surface soil and crop yield.

5-2.5 Abrasion

Flying soil particles do considerable damage by abrasion. Soil grains carried by wind have etched automobile windows so that they had to be replaced and have sandblasted paint on houses, cars, and machinery. Soil particles sift into bearing surfaces in machinery and accelerate wear. This type of damage is costly, but it is insignificant compared with the damage done to young, growing plants.

Plants seldom suffer permanent damage solely from the flogging action of high winds, but severe damage is done, especially to young plants, when the erosive wind carries abrasive soil material. Damage ranging from delayed growth and reduced yield to actual death has been inflicted on cotton, sorghum, wheat, soybeans, sunflower, alfalfa, a number of native grasses, and several vegetables. A relatively short exposure to soil blast lasting perhaps ten minutes will reduce final yields; plants are killed when the exposure is long enough. Figure 5-3 shows a field of wheat in southwestern Kansas destroyed by severe wind erosion.

Figure 5-3 The wheat crop in this field in southwestern Kansas was destroyed by a windstorm on February 10, 1976. (Courtesy USDA—Soil Conservation Service.)

5-2.6 Air Pollution

The presence of soil particles in the air has been noticed for centuries (Free, 1911). Early Greek writers nearly 3000 years ago mentioned dust storms which probably originated in the Sahara Desert. Airborne dust is common in sections of all continents. Most dust originates in deserts or in dryland areas that are temporarily bared of vegetative cover by overgrazing, cultivation, or fires. The dust clouds from the world's desert regions have been given a variety of names, depending on the country or area involved. Saharan dust that settles out in western Europe is called *Passatstaub* by the Germans and *Sirocco* by the English. The Saharan dust storm that blankets the west African countries at times during the dry season (Figure 5-4) is called *Harmattan.* Atmospheric dust causes discomfort even considerable distances from its source; near the source, discomfort is much greater and a duststorm can be fatal to travelers caught in it.

Dust from agricultural activities seldom is the direct cause of fatalities, but it can and does cause accidents and respiratory ail-

Figure 5-4 A dust storm (Harmattan) in northern Nigeria. Wind erosion in the Sahara Desert anytime during the months of November through March fills the air with dust that is carried south and west at least 1500 km, often as far as the Gulf of Guinea. (Courtesy J. A. Hobbs.)

ments that sometimes prove fatal. The dust may also carry pathogens that cause skin disorders. Hagen and Skidmore (1977) report that dust in the air reduces visibility and causes danger to highway and airfield traffic.

Hagen and Woodruff (1973) found that the number of hours of dust storms per year at various locations in the Great Plains ranged from 0 to 250, with an overall average of 45 hours. The average length of single dust storms was 6.6 hr, and the average dust concentration was 4.85 mg/m^3.

5-2.7 Deposition (Sedimentation)

Suspended dust is carried long distances and deposited as a thin film over everything, both outside and inside houses and other structures. This deposit does no great physical damage, but the all-pervasive dust can demoralize rural families during drought periods because the dust is seen as proof of the inexorable and overwhelming power of nature from which they are attempting to wrest a living.

Saltating soil material is not carried far but its deposition causes considerable physical damage. Many farm fences were buried during the 1930s by soil which settled behind tumbleweeds trapped by the fences. New fences had to be built on top of the buried ones to keep livestock confined and cropland protected. Figure 5-5 shows a site where two fences were buried and a third fence was being buried by drifting soil in a sandy area.

Drainage and irrigation ditches have also been plugged with blowing soil. Land leveled for irrigation as well as ordinary farm fields have been made hummocky by drifting soil. Blowing soil drifts into houses, barns, and granaries, contaminating everything.

Crops can be buried by drifting soil, particularly when they are planted in furrows. Young plants are most likely to be damaged, but even mature crop plants can be completely buried on the windward edges of fields next to eroding areas. Sand dunes can move into windbreaks and tree shelterbelts, eventually killing them if the drifts get too deep. Highways and other engineering works can be covered with blown soil also.

Sand dunes are expensive to remove. The Santa Fe Railway encountered this problem when the John Martin Dam was built in eastern Colorado and the mainline track had to be moved out of the river valley and relocated on the uplands south of the river. Much of the new route passed through very sandy soils. Blowouts were common during the drought of the 1930s and sand frequently covered the right-of-way, stopping trains and necessitating frequent and extensive

Figure 5-5 Wind erosion sediments have buried three snow fences erected to protect the road at the right in this picture. The surface of the dunes over the snow fences is 3 to 8 m above the former ground level. (Courtesy USDA—Soil Conservation Service.)

clean-up operations. The soil drifting was controlled only after live-stock numbers were reduced and the area was revegetated.

5-3 EROSIVENESS OF SURFACE WIND

Soil grains are moved by wind because moving airstreams have energy. The higher the velocity of the wind, the higher the energy and the more erosive the wind.

5-3.1 Velocity of Wind Near the Ground

The wind velocity most frequently mentioned is the velocity measured by weather observers at a fixed height above the ground, usually about 10 m. The height is important because the velocity of even a steady wind varies dramatically from the ground to several meters above the surface. The height of measurement therefore must be specified along with wind velocity. Table 5-1 shows a classification of wind velocities measured at a height of 10 m and their effects near the ground.

Table 5-1 The Beaufort scale of wind velocities (measured at a height of 10 m) and their effects on wind erosion

Beaufort number	Descriptive word	Velocity (km/hr)	Specifications for estimating velocities	Wind erosion hazard
0	Calm	<1.5	Smoke rises vertically	None
1	Light air	1.5–5	Smoke drifts in direction of wind	
2	Light breeze	5–12	Wind felt on face; leaves rustle;	
3	Gentle breeze	12–20	Leaves and small twigs in constant motion	Begins in muck
4	Moderate breeze	20–30	Raises dust and loose paper; small branches are moved	Slight on mineral soil
5	Fresh breeze	30–40	Small trees in leaf begin to sway	
6	Strong breeze	40–50	Large branches in motion; whistling heard in telegraph wires	Considerable
7	Moderate gale	50–62	Whole trees in motion; inconvenient to walk against the wind	
8	Fresh gale	62–75	Breaks twigs off trees; generally impedes progress	
9	Strong gale	75–88	Slight structural damage occurs	Severe
10	Whole gale	88–100	Trees uprooted; considerable structural damage occurs	
11	Storm	100–120	Rarely experienced; accompanied by widespread damage	
12	Hurricane	>120	Devastation	

Wind velocity over a bare surface is zero at a height (Z_0) slightly above the average height of a bare soil surface but below the tops of soil irregularities, as shown in Figure 5-6(a). The wind velocity profile over a soil covered by vegetation extrapolates to zero, as shown in Figure 5-6(b). That is, the wind velocity gradient behaves as if velocity was zero at $D + Z_0$, where D represents the zero plane displacement caused by the vegetative cover and Z_0 is the roughness parameter. Air still moves slowly and erratically through the crop below this point, however, as indicated by the velocity-height curve in Figure 5-6(c). The velocity gradients over all surfaces plot as straight lines on a semilog graph, as shown in Figure 5-6(d), if $(z - D)$ is used for height plotted on the log scale.

Measurement of wind velocity profiles shows that the height Z_0 where velocity becomes zero is the same for all wind speeds, from gentle to very strong, on a specific bare surface. Similarly, the height $(D + Z_0)$ is constant for a specific vegetated surface as long as the crop is not bent over by the stronger winds.

Friction Velocity and Erosive Power of Wind. The friction velocity (u_*) evaluates the erosive power of wind (Note 5-1). It is related to the velocity profile and to the drag exerted by wind on the soil surface. The friction velocity over a bare soil increases in direct proportion to the wind velocity measured at a specific height until the drag on the soil surface (surface shear stress) begins to cause erosion. As soil starts to erode, some of the wind's energy is used to transport soil grains; wind velocity is decreased because there is less energy left.

NOTE 5-1 FRICTION VELOCITY OF WIND

The friction velocity u_* is not an actual velocity, but it has the same units as velocity, cm/sec. It is defined by the equation:

$$u_* = \frac{\bar{\tau}_0^{1/2}}{\rho}$$

where $\bar{\tau}_0$ = surface shear stress, dynes/cm^2
  ρ = air density, g/cm^3.

Friction velocity is related to wind velocity by the equation:

$$\bar{u}_z = \frac{u_*}{\kappa} \ln \frac{z - D}{Z_0} + \phi_0$$

where $\bar{u}_z$ = mean wind velocity, cm/sec, at height z, cm
  κ = von Karman's constant $\cong 0.4$
  D = zero plane displacement, cm [Fig. 5-6b]
  Z_0 = effective roughness height (roughness parameter, cm [Fig. 5-6a])
  ϕ_0 = integral adiabatic influence function (usually zero for highly turbulent flow).

The above equation can be solved for u_* under conditions of fully turbulent wind (for which $\phi_0 = 0$):

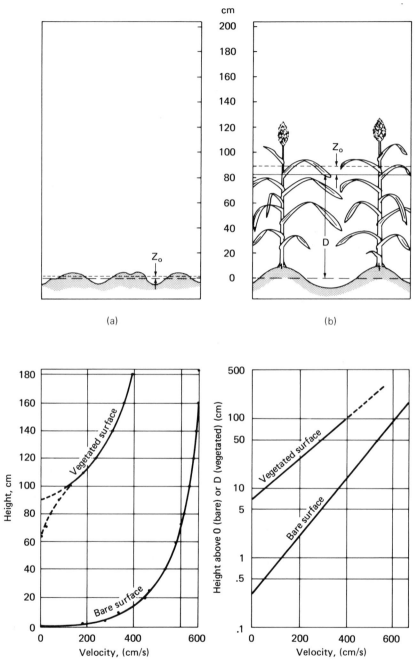

(a)   (b)

(c)   (d)

$$u_* = \kappa \, \frac{\bar{u}_z}{\ln \dfrac{z - D}{Z_0}}$$

The friction velocity u_* is proportional to the mean wind velocity $\bar{u}_z$ over a noneroding bare soil surface because D is zero, κ and Z_0 are constant under these conditions, and z can be made constant by always measuring wind velocity at the same height. Movement of soil changes the relationship by absorbing wind energy and the presence of vegetation changes it by influencing the values of Z_0 and D.

For a given friction velocity, the shear force is greater over rougher surfaces. Rougher surfaces would be more erodible than smoother ones if all surface grains were erodible, but the rougher surfaces usually result from nonerodible clods or surface plant material. These elements bear the brunt of the drag and leave only a small residual force to move erodible soil grains. Therefore, a rough surface usually helps the soil resist the erosive power of wind.

5-3.2 Wind Turbulence

Wind strong enough to cause erosion is always turbulent, with eddies moving in all directions at a variety of velocities. The frequency and velocity of the eddies are related to the wind velocity and to the roughness and temperature differences of the surface over which the wind moves. Turbulence increases in proportion to increases in friction velocity, is greater over a rough surface than over a smooth one, and is more pronounced where changes in surface temperature are great. It is also more pronounced close to the soil surface than higher in the wind stream (Chepil and Milne, 1941).

Figure 5-6 Wind velocity near a soil surface. (a) Zero wind velocity occurs at a height (Z_0) above the average height of the soil surface but below the high points. (b) A crop or other vegetative cover raises the level where wind velocity extrapolates to zero by a distance $D + Z_0$ equal to about 70% of the height of the vegetation. (c) Velocity profiles above a bare surface, as in (a), and above and within a vegetated surface, as in (b), under the influence of the same "free" velocity wind (same velocity at 500+ m). The velocity is higher at a given height above Z_0 over the bare surface than it is at the same height above $D + Z_0$ over the vegetated surface. (d) Velocity gradients plot as straight lines when a logarithmic scale is used for the height.

Air turbulence was once considered the major factor initiating movement of grains in saltation, but other factors are now known to play a more significant role. Turbulence is a major factor, however, in keeping soil grains suspended in air.

5-3.3 Wind Gustiness

Wind velocity fluctuates widely and frequently, often with rapid velocity increases (gusts) and equally rapid decreases (lulls). Wind tunnel studies show that soil composed of a mixture of erodible and nonerodible components will eventually cease moving if the wind velocity is constant. The nonerodible components blanket the surface and protect it from further loss at that wind velocity. Variable wind velocity in the field prevents the soil surface from stabilizing completely. Higher-velocity gusts cause a temporarily stabilized surface to begin eroding again. Erosive winds therefore tend to keep soil moving until the highest gust velocity drops below that required to cause erosion.

5-3.4 Prevailing Wind Direction

Erosive winds can come from any direction. Fluctuating wind direction affects the erosion process in two major ways. First, a change in the wind direction may cause a stabilized surface to erode again because the pattern of nonerosive clods and grains that induces surface stability is directionally effective. A shift in wind direction as little as 30° is likely to cause soil movement to start again.

Second, and probably more important, if erosive winds are predominantly from one or both of two opposite directions, it is possible to reduce soil losses by placing barriers, such as furrows, crop strips, and windbreaks, perpendicular to the prevailing wind direction. For example, the prevailing direction of the wind at Dodge City and Wichita, Kansas, is from the north for six months and from the south for six months. Each month, over twice as much erosive wind force occurs parallel to the prevailing direction as occurs perpendicular to it. East-west directional barriers are therefore quite effective. Douglas, Arizona, on the other hand, has prevailing winds from the east for three months, northwest or north-northwest for two months, southwest and south-southwest for six months, and south for one month, and in no month is much more than half the erosive wind from the prevailing direction. Barriers are not very effective against such variable winds.

5-4 INITIATION OF SOIL MOVEMENT BY WIND

Not all winds have high enough velocities to cause soil movement. Chepil (1945b) found that for each soil and surface condition there is a minimum wind velocity necessary to start soil movement. This minimum value is called the *threshold velocity* and varies from 575 to 1350 cm/sec, measured 30 cm above the soil surface.

5-4.1 Saltation

Serious soil drifting ordinarily does not start until medium-sized grains start moving in saltation. Geologists were familiar with the saltation process in the latter part of the nineteenth century. The first agricultural authors to discuss wind erosion (King, 1894; and Free, 1911) also mentioned saltation. Considerable study was required, however, to explain why saltation occurs.

Chepil watched sand grains on the smooth, wooden floor of his wind tunnel, and observed that sand particles started to roll along the bed. After a relatively short distance, often as little as 2 cm, without contacting other grains or striking any observable irregularity on the floor, the particles suddenly jumped almost vertically into the air. The angle of ascent generally ranged between 75° and 90°. By this time they had a very significant spin, later measured at 200 to 1000 revolutions per second (Chepil, 1945a). The ascending grains were carried downwind by the increasingly rapid velocity of the wind currents through which the grains rose. After reaching the zenith of the leap, they continued downwind with increasing velocity as they fell back toward the tunnel surface. The acceleration brought about by the wind seemed to match the acceleration of gravity, because the path back to the bed, as shown in Figure 5-7, was nearly a straight line with an impact angle generally between 6° and 12°.

Chepil observed that saltating grains ascended for about one-fourth to one-fifth of the total length of the leap. Grains leaping

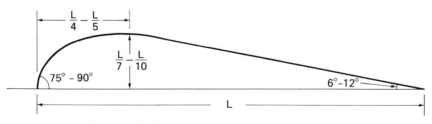

Figure 5-7 The path of a sand grain in saltation.

129

to a height of 5 cm or less traveled about seven times the height, but the distance factor increased progressively with increasing height. Grains leaping higher than 15 cm traveled about ten times the height of the leap. About 57% of the load carried in saltation by an erosive wind moves in leaps less than 5 cm high, 93% moves in leaps less than 30 cm, and less than 1% leaps higher than a meter above the soil surface.

Bagnold (1937) said that sand particles rise into the air in saltation for two reasons: (a) a stationary particle lying on the soil surface is knocked into the air by the impact of a descending particle, (b) the saltating particle returning to the soil surface caroms back into flight. Neither of these reasons, however, explains how particles first get into movement. Free (1911) suggested that the force responsible for starting soil grains moving in saltation was the turbulent currents in the air stream. Chepil also believed this at the beginning of his study of wind erosion (Chepil and Milne, 1939). His calculations showed that a velocity in excess of 465 cm/sec would be necessary for turbulence to lift a soil cube 0.5 mm on a side. His measurements showed, however, that sand grains larger than 0.5 mm diameter were saltating in a wind velocity of only about 200 cm/sec at 5 mm height. Consequently, he concluded that some other factor besides turbulence must be responsible for initiation of saltation.

Chepil (1945a) next considered the possibility that nonspherical soil grains might be bounced from the tunnel floor by irregular "facets" on their surfaces, but decided that such an action would not promote the near-vertical takeoffs he observed. He then considered that the rise in saltation might be due in some way to the spin of the particles and to the steep wind velocity gradient close to the surface. *Bernoulli's theorem* suggests that differences in velocity of fluid flow over the top and bottom surfaces of an object set up pressure differences on these surfaces. A zone of lower pressure develops where flow is more rapid; higher pressure develops where flow is slower.

The spin of sand particles rolling along the bed of a wind tunnel increases the flow velocity of the air on top of the grains and decreases it on the bottom. Also, the rapid increase in wind velocity with height close to the surface contributes to a large velocity differential between the top and bottom of the spinning grains, as shown in Figure 5-8. Chepil felt that the pressure differential was sufficient to force the particles steeply upward into the wind stream.

Bisal and Nielson (1962) claimed that soil grains do not roll on the soil surface prior to lifting into the air stream, but that they vibrate in place and then jump vertically. They showed that the air stream across a small vertical tube in a wind tunnel caused erodible

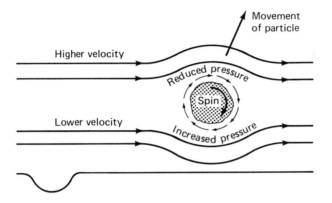

Figure 5-8 A spinning sand grain in a moving air stream is lifted by increased air pressure below and reduced pressure above.

soil grains inside the base of the tube to vibrate and leap upwards. This no doubt was the result of the *Venturi* effect producing a partial vacuum above the particles. The same forces could operate to initiate saltation of some particles from surface soil irregularities but would be ineffective over a smooth surface. Saltation in field conditions is probably a result of the combined effects of spinning particles, Venturi effect, and bouncing of irregularly shaped particles moving across rough surfaces. Chepil and Woodruff (1963) showed that the geometry of the placement of the topmost grains on the soil surface causes caroming grains to bounce back into the air again at a fairly sharp angle.

Soil particles and aggregates moving in saltation increase movement of all grain sizes. Grains less than 0.05 mm in diameter go into suspension in the air and may be carried long distances; those larger than 0.5 mm in diameter move in surface creep. Grains between 0.05 and 0.5 mm in diameter are likely to saltate along with the grains that knocked them loose. Therefore, the number of saltating grains and their erosive effects increase in the downwind part of open areas.

5-4.2 Avalanching

The increasing rate of erosion as the wind blows farther across a field is called *avalanching*. Chepil (1946) suggested three major reasons for avalanching:

1. Erosion often results from high winds coming from the same prevailing direction. The soil farther downwind in a field is

likely to be more erodible simply because it has been eroded previously and deposited there.

2. The farther leeward the wind moves, the more abrasive material it is likely to carry. Saltating particles constantly drop back to the soil surface and in the process detach new soil grains and abrade clods and aggregates. Abrasion, and consequently erosion, accelerates as these new materials are added to the wind stream.

3. Wind moving across a field smooths the surface by cutting and filling the humps and hollows. Wind flows more rapidly across a smooth surface, eroding it more easily than a rough one.

5-5 WIND AND THE EROSION PROCESS

Wind, like raindrops and running water, has power to detach and transport soil grains. Some particles and aggregates move short distances and some long distances before they settle out in a new location.

5-5.1 Detaching Capacity of Wind

The detaching capacity of wind is related solely to friction velocity or shear stress and to the size of the erodible grains.

$$D = f(u'_*)^2$$

where D = detaching capacity, g/cm^2-sec
      u'_* = friction velocity over an eroding surface, cm/sec.

The sharp velocity gradient near the soil causes grains that protrude higher into the wind stream to be struck by a stronger wind force. Larger particles stick up higher, but their larger mass requires more force to detach them. The maximum particle size that can be moved depends on the cross-sectional area of the particle (proportional to the radius squared) and its mass (proportional to radius cubed). Particles in the size range 0.1 to 0.15 mm are the easiest to detach of any grains that move in saltation, but any size from 0.05 to 0.5 mm in diameter can saltate if the wind is strong enough. Turbulent wind can detach particles less than 0.05 mm but even a wind with a velocity of 1650 cm/sec measured 15 cm above the soil surface cannot detach particles larger than 1 mm in diameter.

Airborne particles and grains greatly increase the wind's detaching capacity. As shown in Figure 5-9, these abrasive materials

Figure 5-9 Abrasion of soil cylinders 75 cm in diameter and 65 cm tall by dune sand carried in a wind blowing from left to right with a friction velocity of 61.5 cm/sec. Soils from left to right are fine sandy loam, loam, light silt loam, heavy silt loam, and silty clay. (Courtesy USDA, AES Soil Erosion Research Unit.)

not only detach erodible grains from the soil but also abrade non-erodible grains and clods, detach small erodible grains from them, and, if the wind continues long enough, abrade and disintegrate the whole clod.

5-5.2 Transporting Capacity of Wind

The capacity of wind to transport soil material is related mainly to wind velocity and seems not to vary with size of soil grains. A greater number of smaller-sized particles can be picked up, but the total weight of material the wind can carry remains relatively constant.

Early work by Chepil (1945a) showed that the proportion of material in suspension, saltation, and creep depended on the aggregate and particle size composition of the soil, not on the wind velocity. Whereas only minor quantities of suspended material are found over very coarse-textured soils and strongly aggregated, fine-textured soil, the quantity of creep is relatively large. Suspension is greater and creep noticeably lower over dusty, silty, and fine sandy soils. In every soil Chepil studied, the amount of material in saltation was always greater than that in suspension and creep combined. Amounts in suspension ranged from 3% to 38%, saltation from 55% to 72%, and creep from 7% to 25% of the moving soil.

Bagnold (1943) and Chepil (1945c) noted that the rate of dune sand and soil movement by wind, or the wind's transportation capacity, was related to the third power of the friction velocity:

$$q = f \; \frac{\rho}{g} \; u_*'^3$$

where q = rate of soil movement, g/cm width-sec

  ρ = air density, g/cm^3

g = gravitational constant, 980 cm/sec^2
u_*' = friction velocity over an eroding surface, cm/sec.

The relationship between the amount of soil removed from a unit area and the erosive force of the wind probably has greater significance than the rate of loss. Chepil and Woodruff (1963) suggest that

$$X = f(u_*')^5$$

when X = transportation capacity, g/cm^2.

This relationship is influenced by a number of factors, but the carrying capacity and the fifth power of the friction velocity appear to be closely related.

5-5.3 Soil Deposition

The distance soil is transported from its original site depends on the velocity of the wind and on the size and weight of particles and aggregates. Lag materials are not moved by the wind, but they may lose some of their bulk by abrasion. The saltating grains usually remain in the vicinity of the eroding field. They may be deposited as small dunes behind clumps of vegetation in the field, behind cultivation ridges, or in fencerows. In the deposition process, the coarser saltating grains are deposited on the windward sides of the dunes, the finer ones to the leeward ("leesands"). The dust, which is kicked up by saltating particles and carried in suspension by the wind, is moved far away from the original location. This cloud of dust, however spectacular it may be, does not contain nearly as much soil as is carried in saltation. It is, however, an important loss, because it contains the finer, more fertile elements from the soil—the clay and the humus.

5-6 FACTORS AFFECTING WIND EROSION

High-velocity winds do not always cause soil drifting, and erosive winds do not cause the same amount of erosion in all situations. The factors which influence the amount of erosion a wind will cause are the soil's resistance to erosion, surface ridges, rainfall, land slope (hummocks), length of exposed area, and vegetative cover.

5-6.1 Soil Resistance

The major factor that makes soil resist wind erosion is the mass (size) of the individual soil grains that are exposed to the wind. If the mass is sufficient, a grain (either a particle, an aggregate, or a larger soil mass) will not be moved by the force of the wind. These large grains not only resist movement, they also protect and stabilize erodible grains in their wind shadow. Chepil (1950) called this "the governing principle of surface roughness." This principle refers to roughness caused by soil cloddiness, not by mechanical ridging.

Dry Aggregate Size Distribution. Aggregates, clods, and particles larger than 1 mm in diameter are nonerodible; those between 1 and 0.5 mm are erodible only in very high velocity winds; grains less than 0.5 mm in effective diameter are highly erodible. The greater the proportion of nonerodible grains, the less erodible the soil, as shown in Figure 5–10.

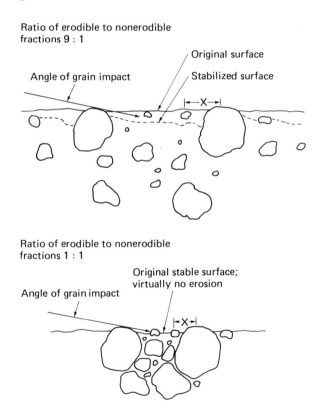

Figure 5-10 Diagrammatic representation of amounts of erosion with two different proportions, 9:1 and 1:1, of erodible to nonerodible fractions. Cross-sectional view through the soil. (Courtesy W. S. Chepil, *Soil Science,* Volume 69:155, 1950. © 1950 by The Williams & Wilkins Co., Baltimore, Maryland.)

The proportion of erodible to nonerodible grains present at and near the soil surface not only indicates the ease or difficulty with which the soil will start to move, but also influences how long erosion can continue before a blanket of nonerodible clods forms to halt it. A relatively smooth soil containing nonerodible clods may become rough as it erodes and thus reduce erosion losses. The likelihood of forming a protective surface condition can be assessed by determining the size-distribution of stable clods in the top 2.5 cm of soil. This determination is an essential part of assessing the erodibility of a soil for the soil-loss prediction equation for wind that will be discussed in Chapter 6. The relationship of the proportion of nonerodible clods to soil erodibility is indicated in Figure 5-11. A smooth, bare, infinitely wide field with 2% nonerodible clods would permit nearly 600 mt/ha to erode in a year whereas a similar field with 40% nonerodible clods would lose only a little over 100 mt/ha-yr under the same conditions.

Mechanical Stability of Structural Units. Having a specific mix of nonerodible structural units does not, by itself, prevent soil erosion. Aggregates and clods that are easily degraded by abrasion do not resist erosion. Accordingly, the stability of the nonerodible clods and aggregates has an important influence on soil erodibility.

Factors Affecting Aggregate Sizes and Stability. Soil properties such as texture, organic matter, exchangeable cations, and free calcium carbonate influence aggregate size and stability.

Soil texture greatly affects soil aggregation and clod size. Sandy soils and clays are generally the most erodible soils. The coarse-textured soils do not have enough clay in them to bind the sandy particles into structural units; the clayey soils develop aggregates and clods, but weathering, especially freezing and drying while frozen, breaks them down. Chepil (1953) claimed that a clay content of about 27% was best for clod development. Less than 15% clay almost precluded a good cloddy condition. The presence of large amounts of fine and very fine sand influences soil erodibility directly because these sizes can saltate. Very coarse sand and gravel help reduce soil erodibility because they are too large to be moved by most winds.

Soil organic matter is often associated with high levels of aggregation and with structural stability. Therefore, one of the most common recommendations for improving soil structure is to add organic residues to the soil. Observations and research, however, indicate that *high* organic-matter soils are often more erodible than those with moderate contents. Chepil (1955) found that additions of cereal

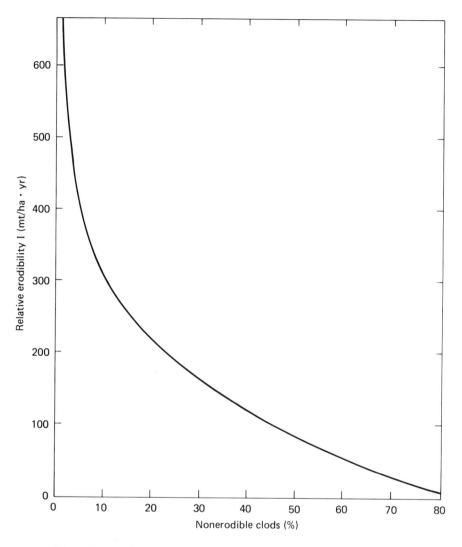

Figure 5-11 Relationship between percent nonerodible clods in a soil and its relative erodibility (*I*).

straw and leguminous hay to soils increased nonerodible dry clods and reduced erodibility while the materials were undergoing active decomposition (about six months). Nonerodible clods decreased after decomposition was almost complete, and soil erodibility increased, especially at high rates of residue addition. The favorable effects of the residues are closely related to microbial activity and the cemening materials microbes produce. The initial cementing materials change, lose their cementing ability, and become brittle when microbial activity diminishes. The microbial fibers also disintegrate in time and a high proportion of medium-sized water-stable aggregates develop. These are highly susceptible to wind erosion.

Another remedy often recommended for improving soil structure is to add calcium to the soil. Soils of arid and semiarid regions rarely are deficient in calcium. The surface soils have an abundance of calcium and the subsoil invariably contains free calcium carbonate. The shallow calcium carbonate horizons in the drier areas may be mixed with the surface soil by cultivation. Chepil (1954) showed that the presence of as little as 1% free calcium carbonate in a soil generally caused clod disintegration and increased erodibility. In spite of the relation between free calcium carbonate and erodibility, soils eroded to the B_{Ca} or C_{Ca} horizon develop surface crusts that effectively protect them from erosion.

5-6.2 Surface Ridges

Surface ridges produced by tillage also affect the amount of soil that is eroded. The effect of ridges depends on their height and lateral frequency, shape, and orientation relative to the direction of the wind.

Ridges affect erosion in two main ways. First, they reduce wind velocity near the ground and, second, soil grains that do start to move are trapped in the furrows between ridge crests. Armbrust and others (1964) studied ridges ranging in height from 1.3 to 20 cm. These ridges were constructed with a 1 : 4 side slope. Ridges from 5 to 10 cm high were effective in controlling wind erosion but shallower ridges were not as effective either in reducing wind velocity or in trapping soil grains. Ridges higher than 10 cm permitted extensive erosion by higher winds because the friction velocity increased over the crests of the ridges and there was more wind eddying.

The influence of specific field conditions on wind velocity and on soil trapping was evaluated with a portable wind tunnel because it was impossible to evaluate the effectiveness of ridges in the field directly. The results were compared to those with standard ridges of nonerodible gravel of various heights. If a specific field affects velocity and erosion to the same degree as 5-cm high gravel ridges do, a ridge roughness equivalent of 5 cm is used in the wind erosion equation (Ch. 6).

5–6.3 Rainfall

Rain moistens the surface soil, and moist soil is not eroded by wind. Studies have shown that soil erodibility decreases—slowly at first, then more rapidly—as a soil is moistened from the air-dry condition to the wilting point. Chepil (1956) worked with four Great Plains soils using wind velocities ranging from 894 to 1430 cm/sec at 15-cm height above the surface. He found that these soils became erodible at moisture contents ranging from 0.82 to 1.16 times the water content at 15-atm tension. Bisal and Hsieh (1966), in Canada, studied three soils with wind velocities ranging from 540 to 1250 cm/sec at 15-cm height. They found that moisture contents from 0.32 to 1.46 times that at 15-atm tension prevented soil drifting. Unfortunately, however, it takes only a very thin surface layer of dry soil to permit erosion to start, even if moisture is abundant immediately below. The wind soon reduces the moisture content of thin surface layers sufficiently for erosion to start in dryland regions. Erosion of some sandy soils can begin within 15 or 20 minutes after an intense shower.

Rain also reduces erosion by increasing plant growth. This is especially true in dryland regions, where lack of moisture is the most common cause of poor plant development. The response of crops to rainfall is extremely important, because plant cover is the best means of controlling wind erosion.

Rainfall can also increase wind erosion by breaking down exposed clods and aggregates, detaching erodible grains, and smoothing the soil surface so it does not resist erosion. Unprotected soils may start to erode as soon as the surface dries.

5–6.4 Knoll Slopes

Over long slopes, short slopes not exceeding 1.5%, and level land, the velocity gradient and friction velocity are reasonably constant for a given wind. Over hummocky topography, on the other hand, where slopes are relatively short, the layers of higher wind velocity move closer to the soil surface as they pass over the crests of the knolls, as shown in Figure 5–12. Since Z_0 is a relatively constant height above the surface, the shorter vertical distance to the higher-velocity flow makes the friction velocity greater over the knolls than elsewhere. Since the wind's erosive force is proportional to the square of the friction velocity, the erosive force is much greater on the crests than on level land or long sloping fields.

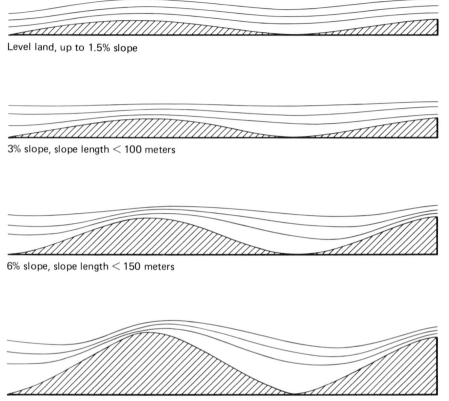

Level land, up to 1.5% slope

3% slope, slope length < 100 meters

6% slope, slope length < 150 meters

10% slope, slope length < 250 meters

Figure 5-12 Lines of equal wind velocity over different land slopes. If the top line in each diagram represents 625 cm/sec, this velocity is reached at approximately 30 cm above the soil surface on level land (up to 1.5% slope), at 18 cm above the knoll crest on the 3% slope, at 10 cm on the 6% slope, and at 6 cm on the 10% slope. (Modified from Chepil and others, 1964.)

Chepil and others (1964) calculated the likely increase in erosion on the crests and upper slopes of relatively short 3%, 6%, and 10% slopes, assuming that the zone of 625 cm/sec wind was found at 30.5, 18.3, 9.8, and 5.5 cm above the crests of knolls with side slopes of 1.5%, 3.0%, 6.0%, and 10% respectively. Their calculated values are presented in Table 5-2.

5-6.5 Length of Exposed Area

Many studies, as well as casual observations, show that soil drifting increases substantially with width of the eroding strip. In a wide un-

Table 5-2   Relative amounts of erosion from level (1.5% slopes) and short sloping (hummocky) land

Slope (%)	*Relative amounts of erosion*	
	Crests	*Upper slopes*
0–1.5 (level)	100	100
3.0	150	130
6.0	320	230
10.0	660	370

SOURCE: Chepil and others, 1964.

protected field, the wind starts to pick up soil grains close to the windward side. Its load increases as it passes over the field until it can carry no more. It may pick up other soil grains as it continues across the field, but it also must drop some of its load, because the carrying capacity is finite.

The maximum rate of transport of a wind with a specific friction velocity is very similar for all soils, but the distance the wind must travel across a field to pick up its full load depends on soil erodibility. The more erodible the soil, the shorter the distance required to reach its load capacity. The distance required for the maximum load to be picked up by a strong wind (about 1800 cm/sec at 10 m above the ground) varies from less than 55 m for a structureless fine sand to more than 1500 m for a cloddy medium-textured soil (Chepil and Woodruff, 1963). Many fields are not wide enough for the wind to pick up its maximum load.

The material carried in surface creep and saltation is dropped when wind passes from an erodible field into a protected area. Suspended material, however, is still carried, and more soil is picked up when the wind crosses another erodible area.

5-6.6 Vegetative Cover

The most effective way to reduce the erosiveness of wind is to cover the soil with a protective mantle of growing plants or with a thick mulch of crop residue. Barriers of plant material raise $(D + Z_0)$ farther from the soil and produce thick blankets of still air next to the soil.

The protection that plant cover provides is influenced by plant species (especially as they affect the amount of vegetative cover and time of year when cover is provided), plant geometry and population, and row orientation relative to prevailing wind direction. Crop residues left on the surface, especially if they are tall and dense, offer almost as much protection as growing plants.

A complete cover of growing plants offers maximum protection, but individual plants and rows of plants across the direction of the wind also reduce wind velocity and erosion. This effect is apparent where isolated weeds in fallow fields trap saltating grains by slowing the wind velocity. Similarly, blowing soil forms drifts around wind barriers such as field shelterbelts.

Barriers are effective in reducing velocity because air is a fluid. As air moves up to a porous barrier, part of it is pushed over or around the barrier. The air not deflected passes through the barrier at a fast rate (funneling effect), then immediately slows down as it spreads out to occupy all the space behind the barrier. Wind speed returns to normal only when the deflected air returns to its initial position in the wind stream.

Bates (1924) studied the effect of an artificial, porous barrier on wind velocity. He found that the wind velocity was reduced some eight times the barrier height ($8H$) to windward and 24 times the height ($24H$) to leeward. The greatest velocity reduction was not immediately behind the barrier, but was about $5H$ to leeward. He also found that wind swept around the ends of the barrier at increased velocities. More recent studies bear out these findings (Stoekeler, 1962; Woodruff, 1954; Woodruff and others, 1963). Hagen (1976) determined the relative wind speed and erosion for 20% and 40% porous windbreaks. His data are illustrated in Figure 5-13. They show that velocity and erosion were reduced from $6H$ windward to $24H$ leeward with the 20% porous windbreak and from $6H$ windward to $32H$ leeward with the 40% porous break. Erosion in the protected area was less than 50% of that in the open from $2H$ windward to $16H$ leeward, and from $2H$ windward to $17H$ leeward, respectively.

5-7 PRINCIPLES OF WIND EROSION CONTROL

Wind erosion occurs whenever conditions are favorable for detachment and transportation of soil material by wind. Five factors influence how much erosion will be experienced: soil erodibility, surface roughness (ridging), climatic conditions (wind velocity and humidity), length of exposed surface, and vegetative cover. Little can be done to change the climate of an area, but it is usually possible to alter one or more of the other factors to reduce erosion.

Many successful practices for reducing wind erosion have been

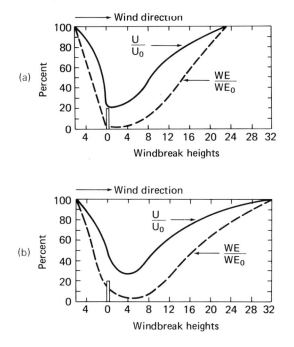

Figure 5-13 Ratio of sheltered to open field windspeed (U/U_o) and wind erosion (WE/WE_o) with all windspeeds above threshold velocity normal to (a) a 20% porous windbreak, and (b) a 40% porous windbreak. Wind speeds measured at $0.12H$ above the soil surface (where H = the height of the windbreak). (Hagen, 1976.)

developed by farmers as a result of their observations, and by research scientists as a result of their studies. These practices are not universally successful, but some work well in one region, while others are better in another. Regardless of the relative success of individual techniques, the aims or *principles* of soil drifting control are the same in all areas where wind erosion occurs. These are:

1. Reduce wind velocity near the ground level below the threshold velocity that will initiate soil movement.
2. Remove the abrasive material from the windstream.
3. Reduce the erodibility of the soil.

Any practice that accomplishes one or more of these objectives will reduce the severity of wind erosion.

SUMMARY

Wind erosion is a common phenomenon on most soils in dryland regions and on coarse-textured and high-organic-matter soils in humid areas. Wind erosion damages the land from which the soil is removed; it also damages the land on which sediment is deposited. Flying soil grains bury or abrade crops. Abrasive particles also damage buildings and equipment. In addition, dust in the air is a health and safety hazard.

Soil moves in the wind in three general forms: *suspension*—finest grains, *saltation*—intermediate-sized grains, and *surface creep*—coarsest erodible grains. The intermediate-sized grains are relatively easy for the wind to move, but the finer and coarser sizes are difficult for even strong winds to dislodge. Saltating particles, however, put fine grains into suspension and bump larger grains into surface creep.

Wind velocity, turbulence, gustiness, and direction all affect the severity of wind erosion. The forces that put particles into saltation include the velocity gradient near the soil and the irregular shapes of the soil grains and soil surface. These lift or bounce susceptible particles a short distance vertically, where they are accelerated by the wind. When they drop back to the soil surface, they rebound higher and faster, or they knock other particles into motion.

Friction velocity characterizes wind velocity and erosive power. The erosive force and detaching capacity of a wind are proportional to the square of the friction velocity; the carrying capacity is proportional to the cube of the friction velocity; and the amount of material eroded by wind from a unit area is proportional to the fifth power of the friction velocity.

Factors other than wind also affect wind erosion. Soil cloddiness, amount and nature of field ridging, amount of rainfall, knolly or hummocky topography, width of erodible area in the direction of the wind, and amount, nature, and distribution of vegetative cover all influence the amount of soil movement by wind.

There are three principal ways of reducing erosion: (1) reduce the velocity of the wind close to the soil, (2) remove abrasive material (saltating grains) from the wind stream, and (3) increase the soil's resistance to wind erosion.

QUESTIONS

1. Name and describe the three types of movement of soil particles in the wind.
2. Briefly describe the types of damage to soil, crops, and structures that can be caused by wind erosion.
3. List the characteristics of wind that influence the amount of soil that is eroded, and describe how each characteristic affects the erosion process.
4. What physical forces appear to be responsible for starting soil movement by wind?

5. Describe how each of the following soil properties affects the erodibility of soils: texture, structure, organic-matter content, lime content, and moisture content.
6. Describe each of the mechanisms by which vegetation reduces the amount of wind erosion.
7. What are the three principles of wind erosion control and why is each effective?

REFERENCES

ARMBRUST, D. V., W. S. CHEPIL, and F. H. SIDDOWAY, 1964. Effects of ridges on erosion of soil by wind. *Soil Sci. Soc. Amer. Proc.* 28:557-560.

BAGNOLD, R. A., 1937. The transport of sand by wind. *Geog. J.* 89:409-438.

BAGNOLD, R. A., 1941 (1973 reprint). *The Physics of Blown Sand and Desert Dunes.* Chapman and Hall Ltd., London, 265 p.

BATES, C. G., 1924. *The Windbreak as a Farm Asset.* USDA Farmers' Bull. 1405.

BISAL, F., and J. HSIEH, 1966. Influence of moisture on erodibility of soil by wind. *Soil Sci.* 102:143-146.

BISAL, F., and K. F. NIELSEN, 1962. Movement of soil particles in saltation. *Canadian J. Soil Sci.* 42:81-86.

CHEPIL, W. S., 1945a. Dynamics of wind erosion: I. Nature of movement of soil by wind. *Soil Sci.* 60:305-320.

CHEPIL, W. S., 1945b. Dynamics of wind erosion: II. Initiation of soil movement. *Soil Sci.* 60:397-411.

CHEPIL, W. S., 1945c. Dynamics of wind erosion: III. The transport capacity of the wind. *Soil Sci.* 60:475-480.

CHEPIL, W. S., 1946. Dynamics of wind erosion: V. Cumulative intensity of soil drifting across eroding fields. *Soil Sci.* 61:257-263.

CHEPIL, W. S., 1950. Properties of soil which influence wind erosion: I. The governing principle of surface roughness. *Soil Sci.* 69:149-162.

CHEPIL, W. S., 1953. Factors that influence clod structure and erodibility of soil by wind: I. Soil texture. *Soil Sci.* 75:473-483.

CHEPIL, W. S., 1954. Factors that influence clod structure and erodibility of soil by wind: III. Calcium carbonate and decomposed organic matter. *Soil Sci.* 77:473-480.

CHEPIL, W. S., 1955. Factors that influence clod structure and erodibility of soil by wind: V. Organic matter at varying stages of decomposition. *Soil Sci.* 80:413-421.

CHEPIL, W. S., 1956. Influence of moisture on erodibility of soil by wind. *Soil Sci. Soc. Amer. Proc.* 20:288-292.

CHEPIL, W. S., 1957. Dust bowl: Causes and effects. *J. Soil Water Cons.* 12:108-111.

CHEPIL, W. S., and R. A. MILNE, 1939. Comparative study of soil drifting in the field and in a wind tunnel. *Sci. Agric.* 19:249-257.

CHEPIL, W. S., and R. A. MILNE, 1941. Wind erosion of soil in relation to roughness of surface. *Soil Sci.* 52:417-431.

CHEPIL, W. S., F. H. SIDDOWAY, and D. V. ARMBRUST, 1964. Wind erodibility of knolly terrain. *J. Soil Water Cons.* 19:179-181.

CHEPIL, W. S., and N. P. WOODRUFF, 1963. The physics of wind erosion and its control. In *Advances in Agronomy*, Vol. 15. Academic Press, New York, p. 211-302.

DANIEL, H. A., 1936. The physical changes in soils of the southern high plains due to cropping and wind erosion and relation between sand plus silt over clay ratios in these soils. *J. Amer. Soc. Agron.* 28:570-580.

FINNELL, H. H., 1951. *Depletion of High Plains Wheatlands.* USDA Circ. 871.

FREE, E. E., 1911. *The Movement of Soil Material by the Wind.* USDA Bur. Soils Bull. 68.

HAGEN, L. J., 1976. Windbreak design for optimum wind erosion control. Proceedings, *Symposium on "Shelterbelts on the Great Plains,"* Denver, April 20-22, 1976.

HAGEN, L. J., and E. L. SKIDMORE, 1977. Wind erosion and visibility problems. *Trans. Amer. Soc. Agr. Eng.* 20:898-903.

HAGEN, L. J., and N. P. WOODRUFF, 1973. Air pollution from duststorms in the Great Plains. *Atmosph. Environ.* 7:323-332.

KING, F. H., 1894. *Destructive Effects of Winds on Sandy Soils.* Univ. of Wisc. Bull. 42.

LYLES, LEON, 1977. Wind erosion: Processes and effects on soil productivity. *Trans. Amer. Soc. Agr. Eng.* 20:880-884.

MECH, S. J., and N. P. WOODRUFF, 1967. Wind erosion on irrigated lands. In *Irrigation of Agricultural Lands*, Amer. Soc. Agron. Monograph No. 11. Madison, Wisc. p. 964-973.

MOSS, H. C., 1935. Some field and laboratory studies of soil drifting in Saskatchewan. *Sci. Agric.* 15:665-679.

STOEKELER, J. H., 1962. *Shelterbelt Influence on Great Plains Field Environment and Crops.* USDA Prod. Res. Rept. No. 62.

USDA, 1965. *Soil and Water Conservation Needs—A National Inventory.* Conservation Needs Inventory Committee of the U.S. Dept. Agric. USDA Publ. No. 971, 94 p.

WOODRUFF, N. P., 1954. *Shelterbelt and Surface Barrier Effects on Wind Velocities, Evaporation, House Heating, Snowdrifting.* Kansas Agri. Exp. Sta. Tech. Bull. 77.

WOODRUFF, N. P., D. W. FREYEAR, and LEON LYLES, 1963. *Reducing Wind Velocity with Field Shelterbelts.* Kansas Agri. Exp. Sta. Tech. Bull. 131.

WOODRUFF, N. P., and F. H. SIDDOWAY, 1965. A wind erosion equation. *Soil Sci. Soc. Amer. Proc.* 29:602-608.

6

Predicting Soil Loss

The need for methods of evaluating the effectiveness of erosion-control measures became apparent as the conservation movement took root, developed, and spread. A research section was established as an integral part of the Soil Conservation Service to study all aspects of erosion: to measure erosion losses from land, to assess the effects of soil properties, vegetation, slope, climate, and other factors on the erosion process, and to develop new and more effective techniques for erosion control.

Control programs called "farm plans" were devised for individual holdings. Conservationists used the best information available in drawing up these plans, but the information often was inadequate and the precise relationship between recommended control measures and erosion losses was not known. Accordingly, scientists worked to develop methods for predicting soil losses under a variety of conditions. Soil-loss prediction equations were developed for both water and wind erosion. Field technicians now have equations based on firm research data to predict soil loss under specific management conditions. These equations are still being refined as new information becomes available, as farming practices change, and as other applications requiring erosion prediction develop, such as nonpoint pollution.

6-1 SOIL-LOSS TOLERANCE

It is not possible to *prevent* erosion, but it is both possible and necessary to *reduce* erosion losses to tolerable rates. *Tolerable soil loss* is the maximum rate of soil erosion that will permit the indefinite maintenance of soil productivity. But how much is a tolerable rate of soil loss?

One metric ton of soil per hectare is equal to a depth of 0.075 millimeters. This much loss sounds insignificant, but if it occurs each year for approximately 133 years, a one-centimeter depth of soil is lost. If it continues for 2300 years, 17 centimeters, or the entire furrow slice, is lost. Kohnke and Bertrand (1959, p. 38) point out that the depth of soil development from fertile, glacial till in western Indiana can be predicted from the equation:

$$Y = 0.36t^{0.561}$$

where Y = depth of soil development, cm
        t = time, yr.

This equation can be manipulated as indicated in Note 6-1 so that the rate of soil development at any depth can be calculated:

$$\frac{dt}{dY} = 11Y^{0.783}$$

The value of dt/dY represents the number of years it would take to form 1 cm of new soil from glacial till covered by a specified depth of soil. The equation indicates that new soil develops at the rate of 1 cm/11 years at 1-cm depth, 1 cm/230 years at 50-cm depth, and 1 cm/405 years at a depth of 1 m. The rate, of course, varies with the nature of the parent material and the climatic conditions, as well as with the depth of overlying soil. It would, for example, take much more time to develop 1 cm of soil from granite rock than from glacial till.

NOTE 6-1 RATE OF SOIL DEVELOPMENT

Kohnke and Bertrand's equation relating soil development depth to time

$$Y = 0.36t^{0.561}$$

can be rearranged into the form

$$t = 6.18Y^{1.783}$$

where "t" and "Y" represent time in years and depth in centimeters. The first derivative of the latter equation is

$$\frac{dt}{dY} = 11Y^{0.783}$$

From this derivative, the rate of soil development can be calculated in years per centimeter (dt/dY) at any depth for the conditions existing in western Indiana.

Hallberg and others (1978) found in eastern Iowa that an A horizon 31 cm deep had developed in 100 to 125 years in a 64-cm deep fill of formerly B horizon material, with the top 10 cm indistinguishable in organic-matter and Bray-extractable P contents from the A horizon of a neighboring normal soil. The organic-matter content in the 10- to 20-cm layer was less than two-thirds of that in the normal soil. This is a faster rate of development than Kohnke and Bertrand found, but the material from which the topsoil developed had already been affected materially by soil-forming factors.

Even though soil is eroded off the top, new soil to maintain soil depth must develop at the bottom of the profile. Thus, loss at even the slow rate of 1 mt/ha annually (1 cm/133 yr) will not be fully replaced by annual soil development until the soil depth is reduced to approximately 25 cm. In addition, it must be recognized that all soil material is not as quickly converted into soil as is glacial till or loess, and all climates do not promote soil development as actively as those in Indiana and Iowa.

Four major factors affect the rate of erosion that can be tolerated without permanent loss of soil productivity: depth of soil, type of parent material, relative productivity of topsoil and subsoil, and amount of previous erosion. The deeper the soil (A + B horizons) and the greater the thickness of material permeable to plant roots, the faster erosion can occur without irreparable loss of productive capacity. Unconsolidated, fertile parent material such as glacial till or loess is more quickly converted into soil than is bedrock. Where topsoil is notably more fertile and productive than subsoil and parent material, the loss of even small quantities of surface soil will seriously reduce a soil's productive capacity. A soil that has already lost considerably from erosion cannot stand further erosion as well as a soil that has not.

The U.S. Soil Conservation Service has set up five levels of erosion tolerance based on the above factors. These levels are equal to annual losses of about 11, 9, 7, 5, and 2 mt/ha. The maximum tolerable loss, 11 mt/ha, is for deep, permeable, well-drained, productive soils. The minimum loss rate, 2 mt/ha, is for shallow soils having unfavorable subsoils and parent materials that severely restrict root penetration and soil development. Soils that previously have suffered severe erosion are usually placed one group lower than they would be otherwise.

These tolerable levels of soil loss are not maximum levels for each year in a farming system, but averages over a number of years. In a cropping system of meadow crops, small grains, and row crops, row-crop soil losses can exceed permissible values because the meadow crop, once established, will reduce losses far below the tolerable limit.

Soil losses from wind erosion of less than 34 mt/ha per year originally were considered "insignificant." This was partly because losses from a field were often offset by gains from neighboring fields, but mostly because smaller losses than this were impossible to see and difficult to measure. Eventually, however, uniform tolerable losses were accepted for both water and wind erosion.

Although deposition of eroded material on lower-lying portions of a field may reduce sediment yield from the field to a "tolerable" level, upslope erosion still may be excessive. When the major concern is pollution abatement, however, sediment yield becomes the limiting factor, and the movement of fine grains must be controlled. Installation of soil conservation practices within the watershed is the best way to keep silt- and clay-sized grains out of streams.

More stringent restrictions on erosion than those dictated by tolerable losses may need to be established to reduce pollution and sedimentation to acceptable levels in critical areas. Similarly, lower tolerable limits may be necessary to prevent damage to crops by wind-driven soil. For example, crops like carrots, lettuce, spinach, and table (red) beets are so sensitive to abrasion that they cannot survive any soil drifting. Tomatoes can tolerate about 1 mt/ha; asparagus, cabbage, soybeans, and sweet potatoes can tolerate 2 mt/ha; corn and sorghum can stand up to 5 mt/ha; and the small grains and buckwheat can tolerate up to 11 mt/ha or more and still produce fairly normal growth. Production of the more sensitive plants therefore requires that soil losses be kept lower than the usual tolerable limits.

6-2 DEVELOPMENT OF A WATER-EROSION PREDICTION EQUATION

An equation for predicting soil losses from water erosion (rainfall and runoff) was developed in the 1940s. Zingg (1940a and 1940b) developed an equation relating soil loss to percent slope and slope length. His immediate objective was to develop a scientific basis for terrace spacing. Smith (1941) incorporated crop and conservation management factors into Zingg's formula in order to apply conservation practices to the soils of the southern Corn Belt in the United States. Browning and others (1947) developed the system specifically for Iowa conditions, adding soil-erodibility factors and employing tables to facilitate field use of the method. Musgrave (1947) reported the results of a workshop in Cincinnati in 1946 at which conservation workers from all parts of the United States reviewed all previously used factors and systems and added a rainfall factor.

The National Runoff and Soil Loss Data Center was established at Purdue University, Lafayette, Indiana, by the Agricultural Research Service of the U.S. Department of Agriculture in 1954. This center made two important contributions to soil-loss prediction. The first was the establishment of a rainfall-erosion index that accounted for a greater proportion of the soil-loss variation from storm to storm than any other three rainstorm characteristics and interactions studied (Wischmeier, 1959). The second contribution was the development of a method for evaluating the cropping-management factor (Wischmeier, 1960).

6–3 WATER-EROSION PREDICTION EQUATION

Wischmeier and Smith (1965) proposed an equation for estimating sheet and rill erosion losses from cultivated fields. This has been called the Universal Soil Loss Equation (USLE). The equation was originally proposed for use on cropland in the area of the United States east of the Rocky Mountains. It has, however, been tested and used in other sections of the United States, in Europe, and in the tropics, especially in Hawaii and West Africa. It has also been tested for use on rangeland and in forest areas. The equation has been useful wherever tested, although some factors have occasionally had to be modified for effective prediction. The equation proposed by Wischmeier and Smith is:

$$A = R \cdot K \cdot LS \cdot C \cdot P$$

where A = estimated average annual soil loss, mt/ha
  R = rainfall and runoff factor, j/ha
  K = soil-erodibility factor, soil loss per unit of rainfall-erosivity index from bare fallow on a 9% slope 22.1 m long, mt/j
  LS = slope length and steepness factor, dimensionless
  C = cropping-management factor, dimensionless
  P = erosion-control-supporting-practice factor, dimensionless.

This equation predicts long-term average annual soil losses by sheet and rill erosion under specific physical conditions, land use, and management practices (Wischmeier, 1976). Losses represent the gross amount of soil detached and transported including soil redeposited in depressions, grassed waterways, or other parts of the field.

6-3.1 Rainfall Erosion Index (R)

Wischmeier (1959) found that the measurable characteristics of rainstorms most closely related to the amount of erosion produced were the total energy (E) and the maximum 30-minute intensity (I_{30}) of the storm. The rainfall erosion index, R, is the sum of the EI_{30} products for all the major storms in the area during an average year. The metric units for E are j/ha, representing either energy or work per unit area. I_{30} can be measured in mm/hr, but it is questionable whether rainfall intensity *per se* is directly responsible for erosion except through its effect on raindrop energy. The proper selection of units for rainfall erosiveness is important in the theoretical development of the soil loss prediction equation, but is relatively unimportant in the use of the equation in field predictions. Accordingly, the units have been omitted from I_{30} and its numerical value alone used as a scale factor. The units on the soil erodibility factor (K) are then chosen so that the product of R and K is mt/ha.

The rainfall erosivity factor used by Wischmeier (1959) was based on ft-tons/acre for energy and in./hr for intensity divided by 100 to obtain "convenient" sized numbers for individual storms and annual values. Wischmeier's "unit of R" (100 ft-ton/ac $\times$ in./hr) can be converted into the metric equivalent (10^7 j/ha $\times$ mm/hr) by multiplying the numerical value by 1.70. Calculations made using the metric system directly are divided by 10^7 mm/hr to produce "convenient" sized numbers with units of j/ha.

The EI_{30} value is calculated for each storm that exceeds 13 mm of rain. Recording rain gauge charts provide the data for dividing a storm into different energy periods, and the individual e values for each, as read from Table 6-1, then can be summed to give the E value for the storm. The maximum I_{30} value can also be read from the charts.

The energy values in Table 6-1 are based on the progressive increase in average drop size, velocity of fall, and kinetic energy that occur as rainfall intensity increases up to 75 mm/hr. At this point average drop size reaches a maximum and then declines slightly (Hudson, 1971; McGregor and Mutchler, 1976) so the e values for higher intensities remain near 283×10^3 j/ha.

Table 6-1 Kinetic energy, e values, in units of 10^3 j/ha, for each millimeter of rainfall on 1 ha as influenced by rainfall intensity (I) in mm/hr based on the equation: $e = 118.9 + 87.3 \log_{10} I$

Tens of mm/hr	Number of units of mm/hr added to tens column[a]									
	0	1	2	3	4	5	6	7	8	9
0	0	119	145	161	172	180	187	193	198	202
10	206	210	213	216	218	222	224	226	228	230
20	232	234	236	238	239	241	242	244	245	247
30	248	249	250	252	253	254	255	256	257	258
40	259	260	261	262	262	263	264	265	266	266
50	267	268	269	269	270	271	272	272	273	274
60	274	275	275	276	277	277	278	278	279	279
70	280	280	281	282	282	283 (all higher intensities have an e value of 283)				

[a]Reading the table row by row from left to right gives e values for rainfall intensities of 0, 1, 2, 3, . . . , 10, 11, 12 . . . , 70, 71, 72, 73, 74, 75 mm/hr.

Average annual EI_{30} values in the United States were calculated originally from data from over 2000 weather stations distributed over the eastern two-thirds of the country. These values were plotted on a map and lines called *iso-erodents* were drawn through points of equal rainfall erosivity (Wischmeier, 1962). A special estimating procedure was used in 1976 to enlarge the original iso-erodent map to include the entire conterminous part of the United States (Wischmeier and Smith, 1978). The iso-erodents in the western states are useful, though less precise than those in the eastern states.

All points along an iso-erodent have the same annual R value. The R values for points between lines must be approximated by interpolation. Interpolated values in the western area are not as accurate because of irregular changes in rainfall associated with rapid changes in elevation. An iso-erodent map of the conterminous United States is presented in Figure 6–1.

Erosion index values have been established for Hawaii (Wischmeier and Smith, 1978), for western Africa (Roose, 1977), and for parts of northern Africa and of France (Kalman, 1967; Masson, 1971; and Masson and Kalms, 1971).

The contribution of runoff from melting snow to erosion has not been thoroughly investigated, but it may be significant in the northern tier of states across the United States. As a temporary procedure, the effect of melting snow on R should be estimated by multiplying the December through March precipitation (measured in mm of water) by 0.1 and adding the product to the R value obtained in the conventional way.

The yearly distribution of erosive storms must be considered in assessing the erosiveness of the climate. Erosion is severe if the most erosive rains fall on bare soil, but mild if they fall when crops or other vegetation cover the soil. Accordingly, Wischmeier and Smith (1978) developed tables giving the R distribution pattern over the year for each of thirty-three geographic areas east of the Rocky Mountains, for selected areas in the three Pacific coast states, and for Hawaii and Puerto Rico. Figure 6–2 shows three distinctly different patterns representing the seasonal variations in erosion index in different locations.

6–3.2 Soil Erodibility Factor (K)

The soil erodibility factor, K, converts units of R to amounts of erosion. The original calculations were based on measurements made on standard plots with 9% slope 22.1 m long kept fallow by periodic tillage up-and-down the slope. The units of K are mt/j to make the

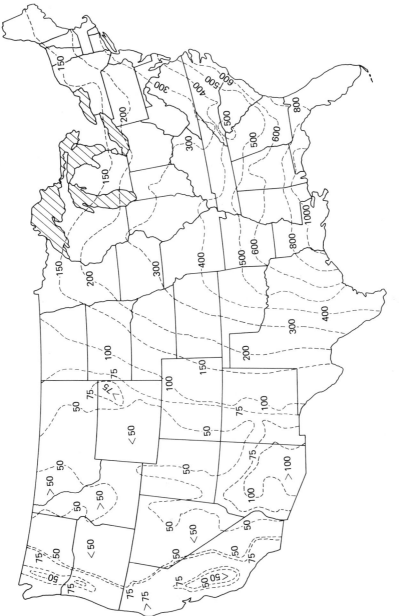

Figure 6-1 Rainfall erosion index (R) values in units of 10^7 j/ha for the conterminous United States. (Modified from Wischmeier and Smith, 1978.)

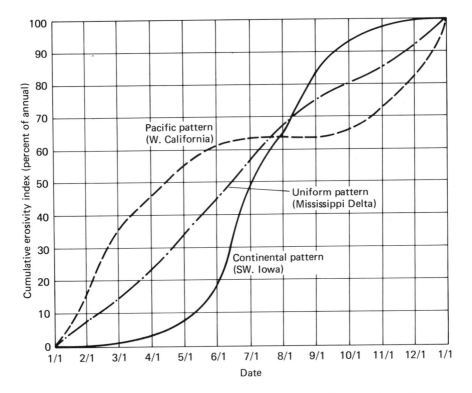

Figure 6-2 Cumulative erosion index curves for continental, Pacific, and uniform patterns of rainfall distribution. (Modified from Wischmeier and Smith, 1978.)

$R \cdot K$ product have units of mt/ha. Numerical values of K in the metric system are 1.3 times as large as those in Wischmeier's ton/ac system.

Several K values were obtained from long-time measurements on soil conservation experiment stations. More values were calculated from erosion measurements on row crop plots, making correction for the vegetative cover. Still more were determined by the use of a rainfall simulator on plots 3.7 m wide by 10.7 m long. Wischmeier and others (1971) studied the soil properties most intimately related to soil erodibility and developed a nomograph relating erodibility to easily measured or classified soil properties. These include percent silt plus very fine sand (0.002 to 0.1 mm), percent fine to very coarse sand (0.1 to 2.0 mm), organic-matter content, soil structure, and soil permeability. Information for the first three properties is obtained by laboratory analyses and that for the last two from normal field descriptions of soil or soil material. A modification of this nomo-graph is presented in Figure 6-3.

Using measured K values as guides, the SCS has assigned K values to many other soils on the basis of known soil properties and observed erodibility. These values may not be entirely accurate and will be changed when measured values are available. A few representative K values are presented in Table 6-2.

6-3.3 Slope Factor (*LS*)

Slope length is the horizontal distance downslope from the point where overland flow originates either to where the runoff water enters a defined waterway or to where the slope decreases and sediment deposition begins. For example, slope length on a terraced field is the distance from the top of one terrace ridge to the center of the terrace channel immediately below.

Erosion is proportional to the slope length raised to a power (L^m), where m has a value ranging from 0.2 to 0.5. A value for m of 0.2 is used for slopes less than 1%, a value of 0.3 for slopes from 1% to 3%, a value of 0.4 for slopes from 3.1% to 4.9%, and a value of 0.5 for all slopes 5% and steeper. For steeply sloping sites, particularly those subject to rill erosion, such as construction areas, m may have values considerably greater than 0.5.

The standard slope length used in determining K values is 22.1 m. Thus slope length factor L can be calculated from the identity:

$$L = \left(\frac{\text{field slope length}}{22.1} \right)^m$$

Slope steepness is defined as the gradient expressed in units of vertical rise or fall per unit of horizontal distance, or per 100 units of horizontal distance when the slope is expressed in percent. It is often more convenient in field work to determine slope on the basis of vertical fall per unit of distance along the land surface. The difference is negligible for gentle grades, but increases as slopes become steep.

The slope steepness (S) part of the LS factor is based on the percent slope as calculated by the land surface approach adjusted so the standard 9% slope has a value of 1.0. S can be calculated by means of the equation:

$$S = 0.065 + 0.045s + 0.0065s^2$$

where s is the vertical fall per 100 units along the land surface. The slope length and steepness are combined into a single LS factor

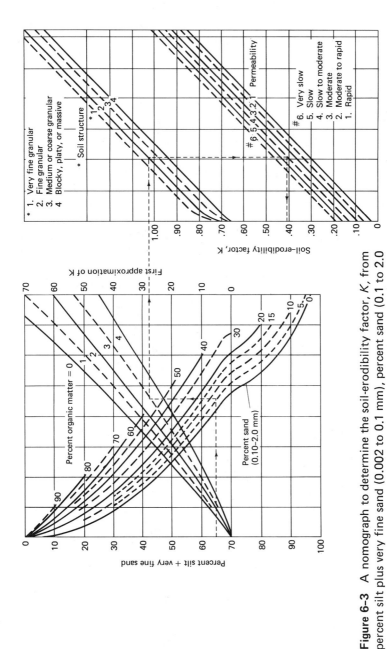

Figure 6-3 A nomograph to determine the soil-erodibility factor, *K*, from percent silt plus very fine sand (0.002 to 0.1 mm), percent sand (0.1 to 2.0 mm), percent organic matter, soil structure, and soil permeability. The dotted line shows how the nomograph is used to obtain a *K* value of 0.41 for a soil having 65% silt + very fine sand, 5% sand, 2.8% organic matter, fine granular structure, and slow to moderate permeability. This same sequence of properties must always be used to obtain *K* values from the nomograph. (Modified from Wischmeier and others, 1971.)

Table 6-2 Computed soil-erodibility values (K) and tolerable soil-loss values (T) for soils on erosion research stations

Soil	Location	K (mt/j)	T (mt/ha-yr)
Albia gravelly loam	Beemerville, N.J.	0.04	—
Austin clay	Temple, Tex.	0.38	4
Bath flaggy silt loam with surface stones > 5 cm removed	Arnot, N.Y.	0.07	7
Boswell fine sandy loam	Tyler, Tex.	0.33	11
Cecil clay loam	Watkinsville, Ga.	0.34	9
Cecil sandy clay loam	Watkinsville, Ga	0.47	7
Cecil sandy loam	Watkinsville, Ga.	0.30	7
Cecil sandy loam	Clemson, S.C.	0.37	7
Dunkirk silt loam	Geneva, N.Y.	0.91	7
Fayette silt loam	LaCrosse, Wis.	0.50	11
Freehold loamy sand	Marlboro, N.J.	0.11	9
Hagerstown silty clay loam	State College, Pa.	0.41	9
Honeoye silt loam	Marcellus, N.Y.	0.37	7
Ida silt loam	Castana, Iowa	0.43	11
Keene silt loam	Zanesville, Ohio	0.63	9
Lodi loam	Blacksburg, Va.	0.51	—
Mansic clay loam	Hays, Kans.	0.42	9
Marshall silt loam	Clarinda, Iowa	0.43	11
Mexico silt loam	McCredie, Mo.	0.37	7
Ontario loam	Geneva, N.Y.	0.36	—
Shelby loam	Bethany, Mo.	0.54	11
Tifton loamy sand	Tifton, Ga.	0.13	9
Zaneis fine sandy loam	Guthrie, Okla.	0.29	9

SOURCE: Modified from Wischmeier and Smith, 1978.

which is:

$$LS = \left(\frac{\text{field slope length}}{22.1 \text{ m}} \right)^m (0.065 + 0.045s + 0.0065s^2)$$

Calculated LS values for various slopes are shown in Table 6-3.

The LS equation used for Table 6-3 is based on research results from relatively short and simple slopes and works well for ordinary field conditions. Where slopes are complex or unusually long, values calculated from overall average slope steepness may not be very accurate. Meyer and Kramer (1968) showed that convex slopes lose more soil than concave slopes at the same length and average slope

Table 6-3 Values for topographic factor (LS) for various slope lengths and steepnesses[a]

Slope (%)	Slope length (m)									
	15	25	50	75	100	150	200	250	300	350
0.5	0.08	0.09	0.10	0.11	0.12	0.13	0.14	0.14	0.15	0.15
1	0.10	0.12	0.15	0.17	0.18	0.21	0.23	0.24	0.25	0.27
2	0.16	0.19	0.23	0.26	0.29	0.32	0.35	0.37	0.40	0.41
3	0.23	0.27	0.33	0.37	0.41	0.46	0.50	0.54	0.57	0.59
4	0.30	0.37	0.48	0.57	0.64	0.75	0.84	0.92	0.99	1.05
5	0.37	0.48	0.68	0.84	0.96	1.18	1.36	1.52	1.67	1.80
6	0.47	0.60	0.86	1.05	1.21	1.48	1.71	1.91	2.10	2.26
8	0.69	0.89	1.26	1.55	1.79	2.19	2.53	2.83	3.10	3.35
10	0.96	1.24	1.75	2.15	2.48	3.04	3.50	3.92	4.29	4.64
12	1.27	1.64	2.32	2.84	3.28	4.02	4.64	5.18	5.68	6.13
14	1.62	2.09	2.96	3.63	4.19	5.13	5.92	6.62	7.25	7.83
16	2.02	2.60	3.68	4.52	5.21	6.38	7.37	8.24	9.02	9.74
18	2.46	3.17	4.48	5.50	6.34	7.77	8.97	10.03	10.98	11.86
20	2.94	3.79	5.36	6.58	7.58	9.29	10.72	11.99	13.13	14.19

[a]Based on the equation $LS = (length/22.1)^m (0.065 + 0.045s + 0.0065s^2)$, where $m = 0.2$ for $s < 1\%$, $m = 0.3$ for $s = 1\%$ to 3%, $m = 0.4$ for $s = 3.1\%$ to 4.9%, and $m = 0.5$ for $s = > 5\%$.

SOURCE: Computed from Wischmeier and Smith, 1978.

gradient. Complex slopes (convex at the top and concave at the bottom) lose soil at slower rates than simple convex or uniform slopes, but faster than simple concave slopes. A method for evaluating long and complex slopes has been proposed by Foster and Wischmeier (1974), but other detailed relationships between shape of slope and the *LS* factor have not been fully worked out.

6-3.4 Crop-Management Factor (*C*)

Crop and management effects on erosion are complex and diverse. Crops intercept rainfall, reduce puddling of surface soil, help to maintain infiltration rate, and slow runoff. Crop roots produced in and residues returned to the soil influence soil structure, infiltration rate, and permeability. They also affect structural stability and soil erodibility. The type of crop, its stage of growth, and the way it is managed influence the amounts of soil improvement and erosion. Some crop sequences maintain a good soil cover, thus reducing erosion; others leave the land bare for extended periods and may permit extensive erosion damage. Canopy density, and therefore its effect on erosion, depends on planting method and on soil productivity. Tillage also has a tremendous influence on erosion, especially by its effect of either incorporating crop residue below the soil surface or leaving it on top.

The crop-management factor *C* is the ratio between the amount of soil lost under specific crop-cover-management conditions and that lost when the soil is fallow and cultivated up-and-down the slope at regular intervals. Soil loss from a continuously fallowed field is the product of *R, K,* and *LS.* Loss from a cropped field is usually far smaller.

Plant cover changes slowly but drastically during the life of a crop. The plant's protective cover must be assessed in order to calculate its effect on erosion. Wischmeier (1960) distinguished five *growth stage periods* for crops in order to evaluate the protection over a year:

PERIOD F: *Rough fallow.* From turn plowing (or similar inversion tillage) to seeding.

PERIOD 1: *Seedling.* From seeding to one month later.

PERIOD 2: *Establishment.* The second month after seeding for spring- or summer-planted crops. For fall-seeded cereals, this period extends over winter until active regrowth is well advanced the next spring—about April 1 in the southern United States and April 30 in the northern states.

PERIOD 3:   *Growing and maturing.* From the end of Period 2 to harvest.

PERIOD 4:   *Residue or stubble.* From harvest to turn plowing (or to new seeding if the residue is not buried by inversion tillage). Where small grains are overseeded with meadow, Period 4 extends for two months after small grain harvest. After that time, the meadow crop is considered established in its own Period 4. Period 4 is divided into three types according to whether the crop residue is left on the soil (4L), removed (4R), or left along with a winter cover crop (4L + WC).

Wischmeier and Smith (1978) developed a more detailed breakdown of cropping stages, but it is intended primarily for use by specialists; the accompanying explanations and tables are too complex to be included here.

Values for the different crop-stage periods of a variety of crops were developed in the United States from analyses of about 10,000 plot-years of runoff and soil-loss data. These values represent the ratios (percent) of soil losses from cropped plots to those from continuous fallow plots. In order to develop these values it was necessary to take into account all factors of crop production that affected crop growth and erosion reduction. Cropping sequence (particularly where meadow and green manure crops are grown) and crop yield had to be considered. Methods of residue management also had to be evaluated.

Selected soil-loss ratios for several crops and sequences developed by Wischmeier and Smith (1965) are presented in Table 6-4. The line numbers in the table are from the original publication. Line 120 shows the beneficial effect of meadow in reducing erosion losses. A comparison of lines 2, 61, and 93 + 115 reveals the effects of different cultivated crops on erosion. The influence of crop cover as indicated by crop yield is seen by comparing lines 2 and 5. The beneficial effect of reduced tillage is shown by the smaller erosion losses of lines 9 and 20 compared to lines 2 and 14.

An estimate of the cover-management factor C is obtained by summing the products of the soil-loss ratio and the percent of annual R for each growth stage period for a crop or cropping sequence. Specific steps in this procedure will be described in Section 6-3.6.

6-3.5 Erosion-Control Practice Factor (P)

Growing vegetation, residue cover, and normal crop and soil management practices are not always enough to prevent excessive soil loss.

Table 6-4 Ratio of soil loss from cropland to corresponding loss from continuous fallow

Line no.	Cover, sequence, and management	Productivity		Soil-loss ratio for crop-stage period						
		Hay yield (mt/ha)	Corn yield (q/ha)	F (%)	1 (%)	2 (%)	3 (%)	4L Residue left (%)	4R Residue removed (%)	4L + WC Winter cover (%)
	CORN IN ROTATION:									
	First-year corn after meadow									
2	Spring turn plowed, conv. tillage	4–7	>50	10	28	19	12	18	40	11
5	Spring turn plowed, conv. tillage	2–4	25–40	15	32	30	19	30	50	15
9	Spring turn plowed, min. tillage	4–7	>50	–	10	10	7	18	40	10
	Second-year corn after meadow									
14	Spring turn plowed, conv. tillage	4–7	>50	32	51	41	22	26	–	15
20	Spring turn plowed, min. tillage	4–7	>50	–	32	32	13	26	60	15
	Third- or fourth-year corn after meadow or second-year corn after grain or clover									
36	Spring turn plowed, conv. tillage	7–11	>50	36	63	50	26	30	–	–
	COTTON IN ROTATION:									
61	First-year cotton after meadow	7–11	–	8	25	30	20	22	–	15
	SMALL GRAIN IN ROTATION:									
	With meadow seed, after disked									
93	Second- or third-year corn after meadow	7–11	>50	–	32	19	5	3	–	–
	Without meadow seed, after disked									
93 + 115	Second- or third-year corn	7–11	>50	–	32	19	10	10	20	–
120	Grass and legume meadow	7+	–	–	–	–	–	0.4	–	–

Special practices are sometimes needed to provide more protection. The most common of these practices for cropland are contour culti- vation, contour strip cropping, and terracing with supporting vege- tated waterways. The P factor indicates the fractional amount of erosion that occurs with these special practices as compared to what it would be without them.

Contour Cultivation. Cultivating and planting on the contour, as opposed to farming up-and-down hill or parallel to the field border, is called contour cultivation or contouring. This practice successfully reduces erosion during low-to-moderate intensity rainstorms. It is seldom effective by itself against severe storms. Contouring is most effective on land slopes ranging from 2% to 8%. Wischmeier and Smith (1965) suggest P values for this practice ranging from 0.5 to 0.9, and maximum effective slope lengths of 15 to 120 m (Table 6–5). The P values in Table 6–5 assume that slope lengths employed do not exceed the recommended limit.

Contouring will not reduce erosion as much in fields containing gullies as in fields with no unvegetated depressions. The larger the ridges produced by tillage and planting on the contour, the less the soil loss will be. Consequently, lister planting of row crops on the contour is more effective in reducing soil loss than is surface planting.

Contour Strip Cropping. Contour strip cropping is the practice of interspersing contour strips of sod in cultivated fields. The sod

Table 6-5 Erosion-control practice (P) factor values for contouring on various slopes and recommended slope-length limits for contouring

Land slope (%)	P values	Maximum length[a] (m)
1 to 2	0.60	120
3 to 5	0.50	90
6 to 8	0.50	60
9 to 12	0.60	35
13 to 16	0.70	25
17 to 20	0.80	20
21 to 25	0.90	15

[a]Length limit may be increased by 25% if residue cover after crop seeding regularly ex- ceeds 50%.

SOURCE: Modified from Wischmeier and Smith, 1978.

strips reduce erosion on the areas they occupy, and collect the soil that moves from the cultivated strips. The greater the proportion of sod, the more effective the system. If 50% of the field is in sod, the *P* value for contour strip cropping is one-half that of the *P* value for contouring alone. With only 25% of the field in sod strips, the *P* value is reduced only 25% below the *P* value for contouring alone. Alternating different small grains and row crops without sod strips is much less effective. Some benefit is obtained on slopes less than 3% if the small grain strips are extra wide and include a winter cover seeding; otherwise no erosion-control credit can be taken other than that for contouring alone. Suggested strip widths are given in Chapter 8.

Terracing. Terraces (bunds) combined with contour cultivation are very effective in reducing erosion. The value of terraces, however, is not included in the *P* factor. Terracing is effective because it reduces slope length. Consequently, the effect of terracing is taken into account by evaluating the slope length between terraces.

6-3.6 Predicting Soil Loss for a Particular Field

The factors set forth in the preceding sections can be combined to predict the soil loss from a particular field. As an example, the average annual soil loss will be calculated for a field planted to a second crop of corn (maize) after a grass-legume meadow has been plowed down on a Marshall silt loam soil in southwestern Iowa. Assume that the field has an average slope of 8% and the slope length is 150 meters. Assume further that crop residues are all left on the field, that the land is turn plowed in early April, the seedbed prepared subsequently by disking and harrowing, and that fertilizer additions and other management practices are of a high order so that grain yield is about 65 q/ha. Also assume that planting and harvesting dates are May 15 and October 15, and that no special erosion-control practices are employed.

Values for *R*, *K*, and *LS* are obtained from Figure 6-1, Table 6-2, and Table 6-3, respectively.

$$R = 300 \text{ j/ha}$$

$$K = 0.43 \text{ mt/j}$$

$$LS = 2.19$$

The crop-management practice factor (*C*) value is calculated in Table 6-6 and is equal to 0.34.

Table 6-6   Calculations for crop-management factor *(C)* for the example cited in the text

Crop	Crop stage period	Crop stage dates	Curve values[a]	EI for crop period	Soil-loss ratio[b]	C value
Second-year corn	F	Apr. 1–May 15	0.03–0.12	0.09	0.32	0.0288
after meadow	1	May 15–June 15	0.12–0.33	0.21	0.51	0.1071
	2	June 15–July 15	0.33–0.57	0.24	0.41	0.0984
	3	July 15–Oct. 15	0.57–0.97	0.40	0.22	0.0880
	4	Oct. 15–Apr. 1	0.97–0.03	0.06	0.26	0.0156
				1.00		0.3379

[a]Values taken from curve for southwest Iowa in Figure 6–2.
[b]Line 14, Table 6–4.

The erosion-control practice factor *(P)* is 1.0 for this situation because no special practices are employed.

$$A = R \cdot K \cdot LS \cdot C \cdot P$$

$$= 300 \times 0.43 \times 2.19 \times 0.34 \times 1.0 = 96 \text{ mt/ha-yr}$$

This soil-loss rate is approximately nine times as rapid as the tolerable rate for Marshall silt loam (11 mt/ha-yr). Even when averaged with the other crops in the rotation, it is far too rapid. Accordingly, changes need to be made to reduce the rate of soil loss. There are several possibilities—minimum tillage could be used, the field could be contoured, terraces could be installed, or the crop rotation could be changed.

One appropriate combination to consider as a possible means of reducing erosion at minimum cost would be minimum tillage and contouring. The *C* factor would then drop to 0.24 (based on line 20 from Table 6–4 instead of line 14 as used in the calculations in Table 6–6) and a *P* factor of 0.5 would be introduced for contouring:

$$300 \times 0.43 \times 2.19 \times 0.24 \times 0.5 = 34 \text{ mt/ha-yr}$$

Though still excessive for one year, the rate must be averaged with the other years in the rotation. These can be calculated using lines 9, 93, and 120 from Table 6–4 to estimate soil losses of 12 mt/ha for first-year corn, 7 mt/ha from small grain with meadow seeding, and about 1 mt/ha from grass-legume meadow. Such a rotation including two years of corn, one of small grain, and two of meadow would reduce the soil-loss average to between 9 and 10 mt/ha-yr.

The soil loss on the Iowa field could also be markedly reduced by terracing. Terraces on a 30-m spacing would reduce the *LS* factor to about 1.0 and so reduce soil loss to less than half of that on the nonterraced field.

6-4 FIELD USE OF THE WATER-EROSION PREDICTION EQUATION

The water-erosion prediction equation was developed primarily to help field workers plan measures to control erosion on cultivated farm fields. Current levels of erosion can be calculated and alternative erosion-control packages evaluated by means of the equation. Several calculations need to be made for each field proposal developed.

In order to make the job easier and less time consuming, the Soil Conservation Service and other agency employees have developed calculation shortcuts. They have selected a single *R* value for each county and constructed tables of values for average *C* values for crops and cropping systems of various areas. Computer programs have been designed to solve parts of the equation and develop resource material.

Values for *R, K, LS,* and *T,* can be obtained easily and quickly from a knowledge of soil series, slope gradient, and length of slope. A table can be used to select *C* values that will keep soil loss below the tolerable limit, either with or without special erosion-control practices.

One system employed by the Soil Conservation Service uses a series of tables, each one developed for a specific set of *R, K,* and *P* values. Variables in the individual table include column headings of *LS* values and rows of *C* values that give the erosion (*A*) value immediately. Or, knowing the tolerable soil loss, the *A* value equal to *T* can be found in the table and the *C* value required to keep $A \leqslant T$ can be obtained. Average *C* values for the major crops in a variety of sequences and with a variety of management practices have been computed for each district and are contained in tables. Cropping-sequence and crop-management-system combinations with *C* values low enough to keep $A \leqslant T$ for each set of field conditions encountered can be selected in less than a minute by using values from the tables.

6–5 EXPANDED USE OF THE PREDICTION EQUATION

The water-erosion prediction equation was designed originally to estimate sheet and rill erosion from cultivated fields in the United States east of the Rocky Mountains (Wischmeier and Smith, 1965). Where the USLE is applied to situations for which it was not originally designed, it is the user's responsibility to insure that appropriate factor values are developed to fit the situations under examination; otherwise the application constitutes misuse of the equation (Wischmeier, 1976). Examples of legitimate use of the USLE in new areas and for new purposes follow.

6–5.1 Regions Adjacent to the Original Thirty-Seven States

McCool and others (1976) report on modifications needed in the prediction method and on research underway to include the effect of rapid snow melt on the erosion process on steeply sloping wheatlands in Washington, Oregon, and Idaho in northwestern United States. Studies also are underway concerning the usefulness of the equation in Hawaii. Singer and others (1976) in California and McGregor and Mutchler (1976) in Mississippi are studying climatic conditions to develop more suitable R values for using the equation in their areas.

6–5.2 Regions with Limited Factor Value Data

The problems posed by expanding the use of the prediction equation to new areas in North America or to other developed countries where considerable factor value data are available are usually fairly easy to overcome. More difficult problems must be solved in using the equation in countries lacking basic data.

It is not essential to have all the desirable detailed information before making a start at using the main concepts of the prediction equation. Most countries have some data available on at least some of the factors. In western Africa, for example, Roose (1977) has studied the limited climatic data available and outlined an iso-erodent map of the area between the desert and the South Atlantic from Senegal to Chad. He also believes that a rainfall-erosivity index can be developed for western Africa from the average annual rainfall in millimeters (H)

with an error of 5% or less from the equation:

$$R = 0.85H$$

Consequently, agricultural workers in western Africa should be able to generate a map showing rainfall regions and make a first approximation of the relative rainfall erosivity in each region.

Agricultural leaders should also clearly understand that only twenty-three soils in the United States were assigned K values on the basis of measured, long-time soil losses. The vast majority of the K values assigned are based on artificial rainstorm losses, measured soil properties, or the opinions developed as soil scientists and conservationists compared their ideas of the relative erodibility of soil series not tested extensively. Scientists in developing countries can do the same, keeping in mind the soil properties that appear to be related to erodibility. Values assigned may not be entirely accurate, but they can be modified when research results or field experience become available.

The equations relating slope length and gradient to soil loss have been extensively studied and seem to apply in many parts of the world. They should serve until local studies produce data indicating their need to be modified.

Data for the cropping factor C are likely to be the most difficult to obtain. The values assigned to the various growth stage periods in the revised handbook by Wischmeier and Smith (1978) are based on percentage soil cover. It should be possible to relate the protection of a wide variety of growing crops to these values and to assign growth stage periods to local crops and crop production techniques. Annual crops may offer less protection in developing countries than in developed countries where high rates of fertilizer and other inputs are used. Multiple cropping, as employed in the developing countries, should provide more complete soil cover and therefore more protection than single cropping. Plantation crops such as cocoa, coffee, tea, oil palm, and rubber permit extensive erosion in early stages unless seeded with a companion crop or heavily mulched. Once established, however, they offer fair to excellent protection. Knowledgeable agricultural officers should be able to make good initial estimates of C values for local crops.

Most erosion-control practice factor values initially have to be assigned with little or no local research substantiation. It seems likely, however, that the influence of contour cultivation, terraces, crop residue mulches, and other specific erosion-control practices will have the same or similar effects in other countries as in the United States.

6-5.3 Subsoil and Other Soil Material

The K values generally used are for soils with topsoils intact or only partly removed by erosion. Erosion prediction would be useful for construction sites where topsoil is removed and subsoil is exposed. These and other areas, such as strip-mined land, cannot be evaluated using normal K values. Sediment losses from these sites cause serious damage to properties below them, and the effectiveness of suggested erosion-control measures needs to be assessed. In order to do this with any degree of assurance, K values that apply specifically to these soil conditions must be found. The nomograph shown in Figure 6-3 was developed by Wischmeier and others (1971) to relate K values to soil properties in these situations.

6-5.4 Nonuniform Fields

The USLE, as described earlier, is for use on uniform fields. If soil, slope, or cover varies over a field but no soil deposition takes place within the field, appropriate values for K, LS, and C can be determined by a method developed by Foster and Wischmeier (1974).

Table 6-7 Relative soil losses from successive equal-length segments of a uniform slope

Number of segments in slope	Sequence number of segment	Fraction of soil loss from segment			
		$m = 0.5$ (slopes $\geqslant 5\%$)	$m = 0.4$ (slopes $3.1\%-4.9\%$)	$m = 0.3$ (slopes $1\%-3\%$)	$m = 0.2$ (slopes $<1\%$)
2	1	0.35	0.38	0.41	0.44
	2	0.65	0.62	0.59	0.56
3	1	0.19	0.22	0.24	0.27
	2	0.35	0.35	0.35	0.35
	3	0.46	0.43	0.41	0.38
4	1	0.12	0.14	0.17	0.19
	2	0.23	0.24	0.24	0.25
	3	0.30	0.29	0.28	0.27
	4	0.35	0.33	0.31	0.29
5	1	0.09	0.11	0.12	0.14
	2	0.16	0.17	0.18	0.19
	3	0.21	0.21	0.21	0.21
	4	0.25	0.24	0.23	0.22
	5	0.28	0.27	0.25	0.24

SOURCE: Modified from Wischmeier and Smith, 1978.

This method is based on the proportion of the total erosion from a uniform slope that is lost from each of two to five uniform length segments, as presented in Table 6-7. The field is divided into from two to five sections in which soil, slope, and cover are reasonably uniform. An *LS* value for each segment can be determined from Table 6-3 using the total slope length combined with the slope gradient for each segment. Each of these values is multiplied by an appropriate factor from Table 6-7 and by the *K* and *C* values for the segment. The overall values so obtained for the different segments are summed for a corrected *LS* × *K* × *C* value.

For example, if a complex, 150-m slope can be divided into three equal-length segments with 3%, 7%, and 2% gradients, *LS* values for 150-m slopes from Table 6-3 are 0.46, 1.84, and 0.32, respectively. These values multiplied by the appropriate values from the three-segment columns in Table 6-7 (0.22, 0.35, and 0.43) give products of 0.10, 0.64, and 0.13. The sum of these is the *LS* value 0.87.

This procedure also can include the effect of soil variation in the field. If the soil in the top segment in the former example has a *K* value of 0.48, the center segment a value of 0.54, and the bottom segment a value of 0.44, the *K·LS* for the site can be calculated as follows.

Segment no.	LS value (Table 6-3)	Proportional erosion (Table 6-7, 4% slope)	K value	K × LS
1	0.46	0.22	0.48	0.049
2	1.84	0.35	0.54	0.348
3	0.32	0.43	0.44	0.061
				K · LS = 0.458

The effects of moderate changes in cover coinciding with the borders set up for the slope and soil changes can be evaluated by adding a column for *C* to the table used for the foregoing calculations.

6-5.5 Cover Management (*C*) Values for Noncultivated Land

The USLE was designed for use on cultivated land. All *C* values were for cultivated crops—row crops, small grains, and planted meadow crops. Keen interest is developing in the use of the equation on soils in native vegetation and techniques are being developed for evaluating *C* for grass and trees (Singer and others, 1976; Wischmeier and Smith, 1978). Unfortunately, few long-term studies on erosion from native vegetation are available to check the accuracy of the values proposed.

6-6 DEVELOPMENT OF THE WIND-EROSION PREDICTION EQUATION

There are two main uses for an accurate wind-erosion prediction method: (1) to assess the erosion hazard in a particular field, and (2) to evaluate the protection offered by management alternatives. Attempts to use research results to predict wind erosion were made soon after information on the mechanics of wind erosion and the factors that influence the process began to accumulate.

Wind-erosion losses could be predicted easily and accurately if the soil were completely erodible. However, not only is soil not completely erodible, but the degree to which it can be eroded changes with different crops and crop management, with tillage, and from season to season. Accordingly, wind-erosion prediction generally is a matter of estimating what the erodibility of the soil will be at a future date.

Climate was the first factor shown to bear a quantitative relationship to wind erosion. The amount of erosion was found to vary directly with the cube of the average March–April wind velocity and inversely with the previous year's rainfall (Zingg and others, 1952). Preliminary relationships among percent erodible aggregates, quantity of surface crop residue, soil ridge roughness, and the amount of erosion taking place in a wind tunnel were developed as early as 1953. The original wind-tunnel equation was modified as new information developed and as new factors could be included. Much of the early work on wind-erosion prediction was done by W. S. Chepil. After Chepil's death in 1963, efforts continued in the Wind Erosion Laboratory of the Agricultural Research Service at Manhattan, Kansas. Woodruff and Siddoway (1965) published a prediction equation that had already undergone field testing. This equation is still being refined.

6-7 WIND-EROSION PREDICTION EQUATION

The wind-erosion prediction equation is

$$E = f(I', K', C', L', V)$$

where E = predicted annual soil loss, mt/ha
     I' = soil-erodibility factor, mt/ha-yr
     K' = soil ridge roughness factor
     C' = climatic factor
     L' = width-of-field factor, m
     V = vegetative-cover factor.

This equation, like the water-erosion equation, takes into account the principal factors that influence the amount of erosion that will occur; however, the individual factors in the wind-erosion equation often interact. Consequently, the solution to the equation involves more than finding values for the various factors and multiplying them together to obtain an overall product. Factor relationships are often so involved that complicated charts or complex equations are necessary to make the prediction.

6-7.1 Soil-Erodibility Factor (I')

Soil erodibility (I) is the potential annual soil loss in mt/ha from a wide, unsheltered, isolated field with a bare, smooth, noncrusted surface. Soil-erodibility (I) values are based on wind-tunnel relative erodibilities and on measured soil losses in the field in the vicinity of Garden City, Kansas, during 1954 to 1956, an excessively dry and windy period. Field soil losses were estimated by measuring depth of soil removal during individual storms and over the windy spring months each year. The smallest measurable removal was about 1.25 cm, amounting to about 165 mt/ha. Because of the great inaccuracies in measuring small soil losses, the conversion of relative erodibility to field loss must be considered an approximation only. The Wind Erosion Laboratory is currently using soil collecting traps that pivot so they always face into the wind to reevaluate field soil losses. This study should give a firmer basis for relating erosion losses to percent nonerodible clods.

Estimated erodibility (I) values are obtained from Table 6-8. These values are modified for knolly topography (slopes greater than 1.5% with slope lengths less than 150 m) because wind is more erosive over the tops of knolls. Figure 6-4 presents the effect of knoll steepness on soil loss (I_s). The values for I_s give the relationship, in percent, of the erodibility of a soil on a particular slope to its erodibility on level land. I_s for a short 4% slope is about 195% on the crest of the knoll and about 160% on the upper windward slopes.

Wind-erosion prediction literature states that surface crusts reduce soil erosion and should be considered in estimating potential

Table 6-8 Soil erodibility (I) values in mt/ha-yr for soils with various percentages of nonerodible clods ($>$ 0.84-mm diameter) determined by standard dry sieving

Percentages (tens)[a]	Percentages (units)[a]									
	0	1	2	3	4	5	6	7	8	9
0	–	694	560	493	437	403	378	356	335	315
10	300	292	285	278	270	262	254	245	236	228
20	220	213	206	200	195	190	185	180	175	170
30	166	162	158	154	150	146	142	138	134	130
40	126	122	118	114	111	108	104	99	94	89
50	84	79	74	69	65	61	57	54	52	49
60	47	45	43	41	39	37	35	33	31	29
70	27	25	22	19	16	13	10	7	6	5
80	4	–	–	–	–	–	–	–	–	–

[a]Reading the body of the table row by row from left to right gives I values for 0%, 1%, 2%, 3%, . . . 10%, 11%, 12%, . . . 80% nonerodible clods.

SOURCE: Reproduced from *Soil Science Society of America Proceedings*, Volume 29, pp. 602–608, 1965 (Woodruff and Siddoway), by permission of the Soil Science Society of America.

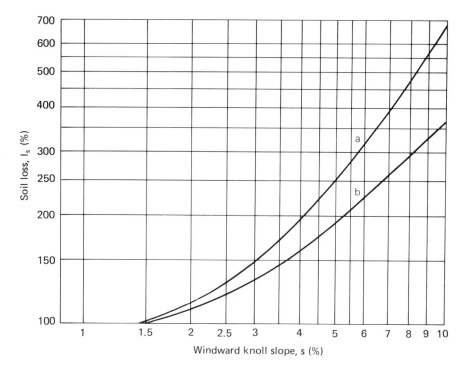

Figure 6-4 Potential soil loss, I_s, from the crest of knolls (a) and from the upper third of the windward side (b) of slopes < 150 m long as percentages of I_s on level land. (Reproduced from *Soil Science Society of America Proceedings,* Volume 29, pp. 602–608, 1965 [Woodruff and Siddoway], by permission of the Soil Science Society of America.)

erosion. As crusts are transitory and soon are disintegrated by weathering abrasion, however, they are seldom considered in the prediction exercise. Therefore the soil-erodibility factor (I') is generally taken to be the product of soil erodibility (I) and knoll-steepness factor (I_s).

6-7.2 Soil-Ridge-Roughness Factor (K')

Surface roughness results from three separate elements: cloddiness of the surface soil, which is considered in the soil-erodibility factor (I'); vegetative cover, which will be discussed in the vegetative factor (V); and ridges on the soil surface, which result mainly from the operation of tillage and planting equipment. This last element is the one involved in the soil ridge roughness factor (K').

Ridge roughness is the height of ridges composed of nonerodible gravel 2.0 to 6.4 mm in cross section, having a height-to-spacing ratio of 1 : 4, that affect the erosiveness of the wind in the same way as particular field ridges do. For example, if 10-cm gravel ridges spaced 40 cm apart perpendicular to wind direction resist the wind as much as a particular field condition, the ridge-roughness equivalent (K_r) for the field is 10 cm.

Precise evaluation of K_r can be made only with a wind tunnel, but Chepil devised a method of calculating values from measured field roughness in the field. Ridge height and ridge width are measured and ridge-height-to-spacing ratio $(1 : x)$ is calculated. These values are used along with the standard ratio $(1 : 4)$ to calculate K_r by means of the following equation:

$$K_r = \frac{\text{measured field ratio } (1 : x)}{\text{standard ratio } (1 : 4)} \cdot \text{measured ridge height}$$

For example, if measured ridge-roughness height is 15 cm and ridge spacing is 75 cm in a downwind direction, the calculated spacing ratio is 1 : 5 and

$$K_r = \frac{\frac{1}{5}}{\frac{1}{4}} \times 15 = 12 \text{ cm}$$

Calculated K_r values for fields average slightly higher than wind-tunnel calibrated values, but this appears to be the best way to estimate K_r unless a wind tunnel can be used. K_r is converted to the dimensionless soil-ridge-roughness factor (K') by means of Figure 6–5.

6–7.3 Climatic Factor (C')

Climate directly affects wind erosion through wind velocity and indirectly affects it through its influence on plant growth and surface soil moisture.

Wind Velocity. The detaching power of the wind is related to the square of the velocity (or friction velocity), and its transporting power is proportional to the fifth power of the velocity, as explained in Chapter 5. It is not surprising, therefore, that the amount of erosion is proportional to the cube of the wind velocity. In developing the wind-erosion equation, both the mean annual wind velocity and the mean monthly wind velocities at a height of 9 meters were studied. It was found that annual figures should be used in prediction where general propensity for wind erosion is the major concern;

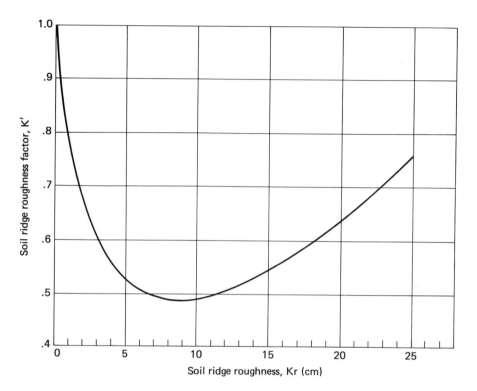

Figure 6-5 Relationship of equivalent soil ridge roughness in centimeters, K_r, to the soil ridge roughness factor, K'. (Reproduced from *Soil Science Society of America Proceedings*, Volume 29, pp. 602-608, 1965 [Woodruff and Siddoway], by permission of the Soil Science Society of America.)

specific monthly or seasonal velocities should be employed where erosion during a particular season is of greatest concern.

Moisture Content of Surface Soil. Soil moisture affects plant growth and plant material in turn reduces wind velocity close to the soil. The soil moisture regime also influences the state of soil aggregation. It is not these effects of soil moisture, however, that are evaluated by the moisture component of the overall climatic-erosiveness factor. Rather, it is the direct effect that soil moisture and atmospheric humidity have on the erodibility of the soil. The more frequently soils are moistened by rain, and the longer they remain moist after each rain, the less wind erosion is likely to occur.

Chepil and others (1962) suggested that the rate of soil movement varied directly as the cube of the wind velocity and inversely as the square of the surface soil moisture, as indicated by Thornthwaite's (1931) *P-E* Index, or

$$C = \frac{u^3}{(P\text{-}E)^2}$$

The method of calculating *P-E* is given in Note 6–2.

NOTE 6-2 CALCULATING HUMIDITY FACTOR

Thornthwaite (1931) suggested a complex rainfactor to characterize atmospheric humidity (*P-E* Index):

$$P\text{-}E = 115 \sum_{i=1}^{12} \left[\frac{P}{T-10} \right]_i^{10/9}$$

where *P* = monthly precipitation, in.
       T = mean monthly temperature, °F.

Thornthwaite did not use recorded temperature data for months with very low temperatures, rather he used 28.4°F as the minimum mean monthly temperature. Accordingly his minimum value for *T* –10 was 18.4. This modification becomes important in higher latitudes where several months each year will have mean temperatures considerably below freezing. Chepil realized that this *P-E* was not a satisfactory index of the effect of soil moisture on wind erosion in extremely dry regions because $u^3/(P\text{-}E)^2$ translates into an extremely large number wherever monthly precipitation is very small. In some U.S. locations calculated values for *C'* using actual precipitation data are as high as 1,000. These values invariably predict much higher amounts of wind erosion than are ever measured. To reduce these erroneously high values, Chepil used 0.5 in. (13 mm) as the minimum monthly precipitation figure. Where other methods of estimating soil moisture from climatic data are used, similar precautions will have to be taken.

The average value for the climatic-erosiveness factor for Garden City, Kansas, where soil-erodibility data were accumulated, was approximately 2.9. As the soil-erodibility factor (*I'*) is based on conditions at Garden City, the climatic-erosiveness factor for any location should be $u^3/(P\text{-}E)^2$ for that location divided by the 2.9 factor for Garden City, or in percent:

$$C' = \frac{u^3}{(P\text{-}E)^2} \cdot \frac{100}{2.9}$$

or

$$C' = 34 \, \frac{u^3}{(P\text{-}E)^2}$$

Chepil and others (1962) analyzed climatic data for 243 weather stations in southern Canada and the United States and prepared a map of the C' values, as shown in Figure 6-6. Skidmore and Woodruff (1968) prepared maps of monthly C' values for most of the United States. More detailed state and regional climatic-erosiveness maps were also prepared for use by the Soil Conservation Service and other agencies.

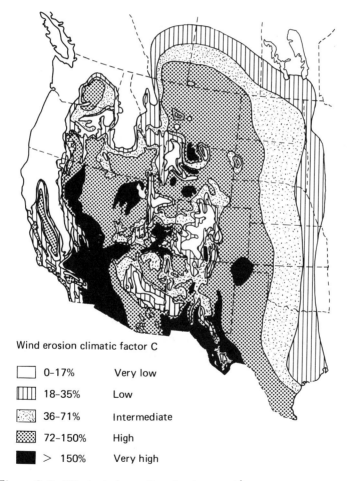

Wind erosion climatic factor C

□	0–17%	Very low
▥	18–35%	Low
▨	36–71%	Intermediate
▨	72–150%	High
■	> 150%	Very high

Figure 6-6 Wind-erosion climatic factor C' in percent of the value at Garden City, Kansas. (Courtesy Chepil et al., 1962.)

Values for C' are dimensionless; accordingly, methods other than the one proposed by Chepil and others (1962) can be used for estimating the C' factor. For example, wind velocity and the humidity factor can be measured in metric units using velocity in meters per second, precipitation in millimeters, and mean temperature in degrees Celsius. A rain factor that has been used in Europe is:

$$\frac{P}{T + 10}$$

Using Chepil's general form:

$$C = \frac{u^3}{\left(\dfrac{P}{T + 10}\right)^2}$$

This system gives C' values approximating the original method closely enough for predictive purposes. This C value for Garden City, Kansas, is 0.486, so C' for this method of characterization is:

$$C' = \frac{100}{0.486} \cdot \frac{u^3}{\left(\dfrac{P}{T + 10}\right)^2} = 206 \frac{u^3}{\left(\dfrac{P}{T + 10}\right)^2}$$

6-7.4 Width-of-Field Factor (L')

The width of a field (D) is the unsheltered distance across the field in meters in the downwind direction. D would be the same for all winds if all winds were from a prevailing direction. Some winds, however, travel longer or shorter distances across a field because winds come from different directions. Prevailing wind direction and the proportion of erosive forces from each wind direction are needed to assess the average downwind distances over which erosive winds travel (Note 6-3).

NOTE 6-3 EQUIVALENT FIELD WIDTH

Skidmore and Woodruff (1968) studied wind forces at 212 locations over the United States. They developed a method for estimating an equivalent field width (D_{50}) for these locations. This method is based on summing the erosive forces from all points of the compass. The preponderance of erosive forces, R_m, is obtained by summing, for each of the sixteen compass directions, the product of the cube of the mean wind speed and a duration factor for all wind speed groups. By vector analysis, these forces are calculated in terms of those parallel to and those perpendicular to the prevailing direction, or

$$R_m = \frac{\Sigma \text{ wind erosion forces parallel}}{\Sigma \text{ wind erosion forces perpendicular}}$$

Where R_m = 1.0, there is no prevailing wind-erosion direction. Where R_m = 2.0, there is a prevailing wind-erosion direction and erosion forces parallel to it are twice as great as those perpendicular to it. The information needed to make these calculations can be obtained from Skidmore and Woodruff (1968) or from local soil conservation offices.

It is possible from the vector data to calculate the percentage of wind-erosion forces that travel distances that are specific multiples (K) of the geometric field width. These percentages depend on the magnitude of R_m and on the orientation of the prevailing erosive forces relative to the field or field strip. A median condition (K_{50}) is one for which half the erosive forces travel farther and half not as far as the prevailing wind direction across the field.

Table 6-9 provides a means for determining the median field width factor (K_{50}) from the preponderance of erosion forces (R_m) and the deviation (A) of the direction of the prevailing wind-erosion forces from perpendicular to the field or field strip border. For example, R_m in April at Pensacola, Florida, is 1.6, and the prevailing wind direction is 135° (southeast). A field with an east-west bearing has A = 45° (180 – 135). K_{50} from Table 6-9 is 1.86. If the north-south dimension of the field is 300 meters, the equivalent field width (D_{50}) during April is 558 meters (300 × 1.86).

Any distances in the field that are sheltered by wind barriers must be subtracted from the equivalent field width. The sheltered distance for field hedges, tree shelterbelts, and similar barriers is ten times the height of the barrier (B). Thus the width of the field factor (L') is the difference between the equivalent field width (D_{50}) and the sheltered distance (10B) or

$$L' = D_{50} - 10B$$

Calculation of the effect of L' on soil loss is complex because it depends on the amount of soil being carried in the wind. The nomo-

Table 6-9 Chart to determine the multiplier (K_{50}) used to calculate the median travel distance of erosive forces across a field from the degrees of deviation of prevailing wind direction from perpendicular to field or strip border or barrier (A) and the preponderance of erosion forces in the prevailing direction (R_m)

R_m	*A (degrees)*				
	0	5	10	15	20
1.0	1.90	1.90	1.90	1.90	1.90
1.1	1.69	1.71	1.74	1.76	1.79
1.2	1.55	1.58	1.62	1.65	1.69
1.3	1.46	1.49	1.53	1.57	1.62
1.4	1.39	1.43	1.47	1.51	1.55
1.5	1.33	1.37	1.42	1.46	1.50
1.6	1.29	1.34	1.39	1.43	1.46
1.7	1.25	1.30	1.36	1.39	1.43
1.8	1.22	1.28	1.33	1.37	1.40
1.9	1.20	1.25	1.31	1.34	1.37
2.0	1.18	1.24	1.29	1.32	1.35
2.1	1.17	1.22	1.27	1.30	1.34
2.2	1.16	1.21	1.26	1.29	1.33
2.3	1.14	1.19	1.25	1.28	1.32
2.4	1.13	1.19	1.24	1.28	1.31
2.5	1.13	1.18	1.23	1.27	1.31
2.6	1.12	1.17	1.22	1.26	1.30
2.7	1.12	1.17	1.22	1.26	1.30
2.8	1.11	1.16	1.21	1.25	1.30
2.9	1.10	1.15	1.20	1.25	1.30
3.0	1.10	1.14	1.19	1.24	1.30
3.1	1.09	1.14	1.18	1.24	1.30
3.2	1.08	1.13	1.18	1.24	1.30
3.3	1.07	1.13	1.18	1.24	1.31
3.4	1.07	1.12	1.18	1.25	1.32
3.5	1.06	1.12	1.17	1.25	1.32
3.6	1.06	1.11	1.17	1.25	1.33
3.7	1.05	1.11	1.16	1.25	1.33
3.8	1.05	1.10	1.16	1.25	1.34
3.9	1.04	1.10	1.16	1.25	1.35
4.0	1.04	1.10	1.16	1.26	1.36

SOURCE: USDA—Soil Conservation Service.

Table 6-9 (Continued)

R_m	A (degrees)					
	25	30	35	40	45	50
1.0	1.90	1.90	1.90	1.90	1.90	1.90
1.1	1.81	1.84	1.85	1.87	1.89	1.92
1.2	1.73	1.77	1.80	1.84	1.88	1.93
1.3	1.66	1.70	1.76	1.83	1.88	1.94
1.4	1.59	1.64	1.71	1.79	1.87	1.95
1.5	1.55	1.60	1.68	1.77	1.86	1.96
1.6	1.51	1.56	1.65	1.75	1.86	1.97
1.7	1.47	1.52	1.62	1.73	1.86	1.99
1.8	1.44	1.49	1.60	1.71	1.86	2.01
1.9	1.41	1.46	1.57	1.69	1.86	2.03
2.0	1.40	1.44	1.56	1.68	1.86	2.04
2.1	1.38	1.43	1.55	1.67	1.86	2.06
2.2	1.37	1.41	1.54	1.67	1.87	2.07
2.3	1.36	1.40	1.53	1.66	1.87	2.09
2.4	1.36	1.40	1.53	1.66	1.89	2.11
2.5	1.35	1.40	1.53	1.67	1.90	2.13
2.6	1.35	1.40	1.54	1.68	1.92	2.16
2.7	1.35	1.41	1.55	1.70	1.94	2.19
2.8	1.36	1.42	1.57	1.72	1.97	2.22
2.9	1.36	1.43	1.59	1.74	2.00	2.26
3.0	1.37	1.44	1.60	1.77	2.03	2.30
3.1	1.37	1.45	1.62	1.80	2.07	2.33
3.2	1.38	1.46	1.64	1.83	2.10	2.37
3.3	1.39	1.47	1.67	1.86	2.14	2.41
3.4	1.40	1.49	1.69	1.90	2.17	2.45
3.5	1.42	1.51	1.73	1.95	2.22	2.49
3.6	1.43	1.53	1.76	2.00	2.27	2.54
3.7	1.44	1.55	1.80	2.05	2.32	2.58
3.8	1.45	1.57	1.83	2.10	2.36	2.63
3.9	1.47	1.60	1.88	2.16	2.42	2.68
4.0	1.49	1.63	1.93	2.23	2.48	2.73

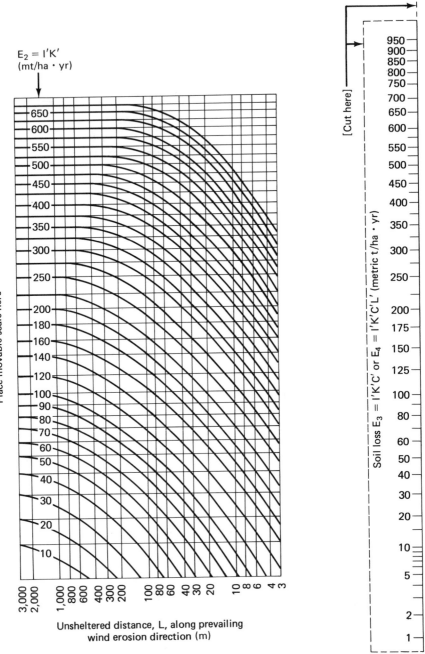

$E_2 = I'K'$
(mt/ha · yr)

Place movable scale here

Unsheltered distance, L, along prevailing
wind erosion direction (m)

[Cut here]

Soil loss $E_3 = I'K'C'$ or $E_4 = I'K'C'L'$ (metric t/ha · yr)

gram in Figure 6-7 is used to assess the effect of L' on erosion loss by incorporating it along with soil erodibility–soil-ridge-roughness erosion estimates (E_2) and soil-erodibility–soil-ridge-roughness-climatic-erosion estimates (E_3) in the prediction equation.

6-7.5 Vegetative Factor (V)

The amount of protection offered by vegetation depends on the amount of dry matter it contains, its relative texture, its height when standing, and whether it is living or dead, standing or flattened.

The original work on the effect of vegetative material was done with flattened wheat straw, and the standards for V in the erosion equation are based on those conditions. With growing crops or crop residues other than wheat straw, dry-matter amounts must be converted to equivalent quantities of flattened wheat straw. Weights of living or dead small grain (R') in the seedling and stooling (tillering) stages are converted into effective equivalents of flattened wheat straw (V) by using the curves in Figure 6-8.

Figure 6-9 is used to convert the mass of aboveground, standing or flat, anchored, small-grain stubble and straw (a), and of standing or flat sorghum stubble and stover (b) into effective equivalent mass V.

The effectiveness of the vegetative factor (V) in reducing soil loss depends on the level of erosion. Figure 6-10 provides the means of relating V to erosion.

Figure 6-7 Nomogram to determine soil loss, $E_4 = f(I', K', C', L')$, from soil loss $E_2 = I'K'$ and $E_3 = I'K'C'$ and the unsheltered distance L' across the field. In use, a copy of the movable scale is placed along the left side of the graph so that E_3 on the scale is aligned with E_2 on the graph. A line parallel to the curved lines is then followed to its intersection with the unsheltered distance line. The value of E_4 is located by following a horizontal line from the intersection back to the movable scale. For example, an E_3 value of 150 and an E_2 value of 120 combined with an unsheltered distance of 400 m give an E_4 value of 130. (Reproduced from *Soil Science Society of America Proceedings,* Volume 29, pp. 602-608, 1965 [Woodruff and Siddoway], by permission of the Soil Science Society of America.)

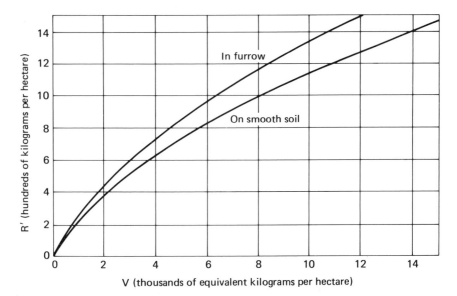

Figure 6-8 Curves to convert weights of living or dead small grain in seedling or stooling stages (R') into equivalent amounts of flattened wheat straw (V). (Reproduced from *Soil Science Society of America Proceedings,* Volume 29, pp. 602-608, 1965 [Woodruff and Siddoway], by permission of the Soil Science Society of America.)

6-7.6 Assessing Vegetative Cover

The best way to obtain an estimate of the amount of vegetative material on a field is to hand pick the living plants or the residue from a unit area, dry it, and weigh it. The amount of vegetation, living or dead, refers to that visible aboveground. An area of one square meter is probably sufficient for small grains, but two square meters is likely necessary for row crops. A minimum of three separate samples should be taken for a good estimate of a field or treatment. Soil, which may constitute up to 50% of the mass of a hand-picked sample of crop residue, must be removed before weighing. Washing is the preferred method of cleaning because it is two or three times quicker than cleaning a dry sample. Results should be calculated in kilograms per hectare (Whitfield and others, 1962).

Modifications of the range scientist's "line transect" method have also been employed to estimate residue cover. Hartwig and Laflen

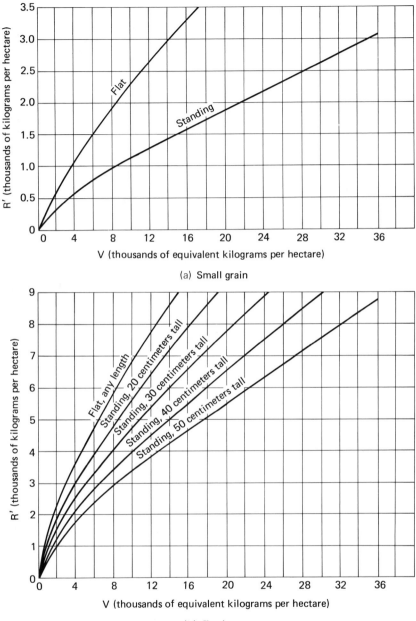

(a) Small grain

(b) Sorghum

Figure 6-9 Curves to convert weights of small grain or sorghum stubble (R') into equivalent amounts of flattened wheat straw (V). (Reproduced from *Soil Science Society of America Proceedings,* Volume 29, pp. 602-608, 1965 [Woodruff and Siddoway], by permission of the Soil Science Society of America.)

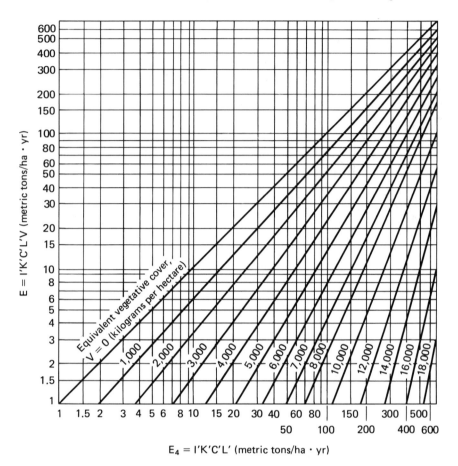

Figure 6-10 Graph to convert values of E_4 and V to predicted rates of wind erosion, $E = f(I', K', C', L', V)$. The E value is determined by entering the table at the E_4 value on the bottom scale, following upward to the V value, and then across to the E value. (Reproduced from *Soil Science Society of America Proceedings,* Volume 29, pp. 602-608, 1965 [Woodruff and Siddoway], by permission of the Soil Science Society of America.)

(1978) describe a meter-stick method where the total length of the various pieces of residue on one face of the stick is recorded. The meter stick is placed at random across the interrow area. The total length of contact per set is the percentage of residue cover. Sloneker and Moldenhauer (1977) describe a method in which fifty beads are strung every fifteen centimeters along a string. This beaded string is stretched across the area to be evaluated. Each bead that touches a "significant" piece of residue is counted as 2% soil cover. At least six separate counts should be made and averaged in each field. These investigators have found that the fraction of surface covered can be translated into weight of cover by using the following equations (metric equivalents of equations provided by L. L. Sloneker in a personal communication):

Corn: $X = -5,917 \log (1-Y)$ where X = residues in kg/ha

Small grain: $X = -17,398 \log (1-Y)$ where Y = cover as a decimal fraction

Soybeans: $X = -31,270 \log (1-Y)$

6-7.7 Predicting Soil Loss for a Particular Field

A large field 800 m long north and south on Ortello fine sandy loam in Ford County (Dodge City), Kansas will serve as an example. This soil has been sieved and contains 25% nonerodible clods (> 0.84 mm) in the surface 2.5 cm. Several knolls with 3% slopes less than 150 m are found within the field. A crop of dwarf sorghum was produced in 75-cm rows, and 1000 kg/ha of 40-cm tall stubble is standing in the field. The ridge-roughness equivalent produced by planting and cultivating machinery is 10 cm.

Calculation of expected soil loss from the knolls in the most erosive period (March) is as follows:

STEP 1. $E_1 = I' = I \cdot I_s \cdot F_s$

The value for I for 25% nonerodible clods is 190 mt/ha-yr (Table 6-8). The value for I_s on the knolls of a 3% slope is 148% (Figure 6-4).

$$E_1 = 190 \times \frac{148}{100} = 281 \text{ mt/ha-yr (from knolls)}$$

STEP 2. $E_2 = E_1 \cdot K'$

The soil-ridge-roughness condition, (K_r), observed in the field was equivalent to 10 cm. The appropriate value for K' is 0.49 (Figure 6-5).

$$E_2 = 281 \times 0.49 = 138 \text{ mt/ha-yr}$$

STEP 3. $E_3 = E_2 \times C'$

The value for C' assigned to Ford County, Kansas by the Soil

Conservation Service is 80. (This is a more detailed value than can be obtained from Figure 6–6.)

$$E_3 = 138 \times \frac{80}{100} = 110 \text{ mt/ha-yr}$$

STEP 4. $E_4 = E_3 \cdot f(L')$

Weather records at Dodge City show prevailing winds for March from due north ($A = 0°$ for this field) with $R_m = 2.4$ (Skidmore and Woodruff, 1968). The value of K_{50} from Table 6–9 is 1.13, so

$$D_{50} = K_{50} \times W \text{ (field dimension)} = 1.13 \times 800 = 904 \text{ m}$$

Since no wind barrier was described, $L' = 904$ m.

As mentioned earlier, determination of E_4 is not a simple multiplication because L', $I'K'C'$, and $I'K'$ are all interrelated. A graphical solution is obtained from Figure 6–7. Following the directions with the figure for $E_2 = 138$, $E_3 = 110$, and $L' = 904$ m gives $E_4 = 105$ mt/ha-yr.

STEP 5. $E = E_4 \cdot f(V)$

$V = R'$ for the growing crop $+ R'$ for surface crop residue. There is no growing crop, so only stover and straw need to be considered. V from Figure 6–9 is about 1700 kg for $R' = 1000$ kg of 40-cm tall sorghum stubble. The value for E is read from Figure 6–10 using $E_4 = 105$ mt/ha-yr and $V = 1700$ kg to give $E = 60$ mt/ha-yr.

The predicted 60 mt/ha-yr is an excessive soil-loss rate. A tolerable loss for this soil has been set as 11 mt/ha-yr. How can the loss be reduced to the tolerable limit? One obvious way is to reduce L'. With all other conditions the same as in the foregoing example and with $E = T = 11$ mt/ha-yr, it can be determined from Figure 6–10 that E_4 must be reduced to 23 mt/ha-yr. Figure 6–7 shows that an L value of 17 m is required to reduce an E_3 value of 110 mt/ha-yr to an E_4 value of 23 mt/ha-yr. An L value of 17 m divided by the 1.13 value of K_{50} determined in Step 4 gives a field width of 15 m. Strips 15 m wide are not very economical to operate with machinery, but strips 100 m wide could be used to reduce L' to 113 m.

With $E_2 = 137$ and $E_3 = 110$, and $L' = 113$ m, E_4 from Figure 6–7 is 68 mt/ha-yr. What amount of standing sorghum residue would be needed to reduce erosion to 11 mt/ha? Figure 6–10 shows a value of about 4300 kg of equivalent vegetative cover (V) for $E = T = 11$ and $E_4 = 68$. Figure 6–9 indicates that an R' of 2300 kg/ha of 40-cm standing sorghum stubble would reduce V to 4300. This amount of stubble can be provided by a crop that produces a grain yield of about 21 q/ha (fairly high for a dryland region). Figure 6–9 shows that small-grain straw is much more effective than sorghum straw for wind-erosion control. It would only take about 600 kg of standing wheat straw or 1100 kg of flattened wheat straw to have a V of 4300 kg/ha. A good wheat crop produces more than 3000 kg/ha of straw. Even if the straw were flattened and 50% incorporated, there would be enough residue left to reduce wind erosion to tolerable levels with strips 100 m wide across the prevailing winds.

6-8 FIELD USE OF THE WIND-EROSION PREDICTION EQUATION

The wind-erosion prediction equation was developed primarily to help conservation technicians and others assess wind-hazard conditions and to evaluate the changes in management needed to reduce the erosion hazard. Solving the equation for a specific set of conditions can be very time consuming. Consequently, conservation specialists and others have modified certain factor values and proposed shortcuts in calculations for specific regions to speed the evaluating process.

One modification involves the use of Wind Erodibility Groups (WEG). Nine such groups have been established, based primarily on soil texture and presence or absence of lime carbonate. The nine WEG are shown in Table 6–10. Each WEG except number 1 has been assigned a single soil-erodibility value. WEG 1 has four different values, depending on the sandiness of the texture. The WEG values permit I values to be estimated without requiring sieve data for nonerodible clods.

Another shortcut was made possible by the development of a Fortran computer program to solve the wind-erosion prediction equation (Fisher and Skidmore, 1970). The effect on erosion of several changes in each factor can be evaluated quickly with it. The program has been used to prepare tables of erosion prediction values for an area such as a county. Several different tables are prepared, each one having a fixed value for E_3 (a certain combination of I', K', and C'). The predicted E values for various combinations of L' and V are shown in the tables. Field inspection is still required to determine the soil texture, ridge roughness, field width, and crop residue present, but most of the calculations are eliminated by using the tables.

Table 6–10   Wind Erodibility Group (WEG) characteristics

WEG no.	Texture and other characteristics	Dry soil aggregates > 0.84 mm (%)	Soil erodibility factor (I) (mt/ha-yr)
1	Very fine, fine, and medium sands; dune sands	1–7	694–356
2	Loamy sands; loamy fine sands	10	300
3	Very fine sandy loams; fine sandy loams; sandy loams	25	190
4	Clays; silty clays; noncalcareous clay loams, silty clay loams with > 35% clay	25	190
4L	Calcareous loams, silt loams; noncalcareous clay loams and silty clay loams with < 35% clay	25	190
5	Noncalcareous loams and silt loams with < 20% clay; sandy clay loans; sandy clays	40	126
6	Noncalcareous loams and silt loams with > 20% clay; noncalcareous clay loams with < 35% clay	45	108
7	Silts; noncalcareous silty clay loams with < 25% clay	50	84
8	Very wet or stony soils, usually not erodible	—	—

SOURCE: USDA—Soil Conservation Service.

6-9 EXPANDED USE OF THE WIND-EROSION PREDICTION EQUATION

The wind-erosion prediction equation was originally developed for use in the Great Plains region of the United States. This is a semiarid to subhumid region. The required soil, climatic, and other data were collected from this region to assist in developing a practical and effective prediction tool. No sooner was the equation developed, however, than scientists and technicians in other regions in the United States showed an interest in it.

6-9.1 Use on Cultivated Soil in Humid Regions in the United States

The wind-erosion prediction equation has been used in many areas of the United States outside of the Great Plains. The portable wind tunnel of the Wind Erosion Laboratory was taken to some areas to check soils and results; in other areas the equation was used either without modification or with modifications based only on judgment of the field situation.

A wind-tunnel study in northwestern Ohio showed that those soils were more erodible than soils with the same percentages of nonerodible clods in the Great Plains. Accordingly, a special table relating the percent nonerodible clods to soil erodibility was set up for that area.

Carreker (1966), in a study on the sandy soils of the coastal plains of the southeastern United States, found a relationship between the percentage of coarse and very coarse sand in the soil (X) and its erodibility (I):

$$I = 174 - 4.64X + 0.03X^2$$

Hayes (1965) checked the efficacy of the wind-erosion equation using both the dry sieving results and the WEG to determine I. He found that the WEG values were not sufficiently accurate for conditions on very sandy soils in New Jersey. He used the calculations method for determining K_r. On the basis of predicted soil-loss values, Hayes pointed out the need to reduce wind-erosion losses to less than 11 mt/ha-yr to avoid damage to crops. Table beets and spinach were damaged by any amount of soil drift; asparagus and sweet potatoes could stand up to 2 mt/ha-yr.

In all of these studies on cultivated lands in the United States, satisfactory estimates of the climatic factor could be obtained from the publications of the Wind Erosion Laboratory, or local climatic data were sufficient to evaluate the effect of climate on erosiveness and erodibility. Accordingly, reasonable estimates of likely erosion losses were generally obtained.

6-9.2 Use on Rangeland in Western United States

The Bureau of Land Management and other agencies and individuals are concerned about wind erosion on range- and pasturelands in and to the west of the Great Plains. Predictions for these permanently vegetated lands can be made by estimating V factors for the range grass, living and dead, in terms of the amount of flattened wheat straw required to give equal protection. The other terms in the equation are obtained in the normal way, either from soil samples or WEG, and from maps and charts in Woodruff and Siddoway's (1965) publication or from local weather data. The staff of the Wind Erosion Laboratory at Manhattan is examining the effectiveness of residues from a variety of range plants on the erosion process, but no published results are available yet.

6-9.3 Use to Predict Air Pollution

Great concern has developed recently about air pollution. Suspended soil is one of the serious pollutants. Information is needed on the likelihood of dust storms because of the danger posed to highway and air traffic, and to human health.

The wind-erosion prediction equation evaluates soil movement of all kinds—surface creep, saltation, and suspension. Soil moving in surface creep and saltation is never a serious air pollutant because these particles seldom get farther than about 30 cm from the soil, and because even saltating particles are trapped completely by a 10-m wide band of close-growing vegetation. The only soil material that can be an important air pollutant is suspended dust. This constitutes a very small fraction of the total amount of soil moving on a field.

Efforts have been made to modify the equation to assess the amount of dust in the air under a variety of natural conditions. Wilson (1975) used I' values based on WEG, ranging from zero for stony land to 200 where the soil contained considerable sand, to predict dust emissions in New Mexico. Generally he used a K' value of 0.75 and C' values from Skidmore and Woodruff (1968). In this study, field length seemed to have little influence on dust production, so he assumed L' to be infinitely long. He used the conversion factor for changing standing wheat stubble to flattened wheat straw to transform range cover into V. The predicted erosion values he obtained were multiplied by 0.003 to change eroding soil to suspended dust. The equation was useful in this survey, but Wilson (1975) stressed that great care must be exercised in its use, and that the results obtained must be viewed with some caution.

6-9.4 Use of the Equation in Other Countries and Continents

Several factors in the wind-erosion prediction equation present problems when the equation is used in areas very different from the one for which it was developed. It has already been shown that the relationship between percent nonerodible clods and soil erodibility is not constant. Still the only possible initial assumption to make in a new area with little information available is that the relationship obtained in the Great Plains of the United States is approximately correct. Values for K_r in new areas should be approximated by the calculation method described in Section 6-7.2.

The equation's method of evaluating the erosiveness of the climate works well in the area for which it was designed and should give reasonable values in other areas with similar climatic conditions. A problem arises in very dry areas because the *P-E* value used in the denominator for calculating C' becomes very small and makes C' too large. A new way of evaluating C' is needed for such areas. A lack of long-term weather records, particularly wind records, from which the C' values can be obtained is likely to be another major problem. Climatic factor zones probably can be outlined and approximate relationships assigned on the basis of general knowledge. The boundaries of the zones and their C' values can be altered if local weather records show the need. The one unresolved limitation resulting from a lack of wind and other weather records is relating the local climatic erosiveness to that at Garden City, Kansas to evaluate the *I* factor.

Wind records are also used in the determination of L' values. Another technique is needed to determine the length of a field along the direction of the prevailing wind when wind records are inadequate. The general direction of the prevailing winds during the major wind-erosion periods must be estimated at least as close to the actual direction as the $22.5°$ difference between compass points. Field width (D) along with the prevailing wind direction is obtained from the perpendicular width (W) across the field and the angle (A) between the prevailing wind direction and the perpendicular direction:

$$D = W/\cos A$$

The sheltering effect of wind barriers must be considered in the usual way to obtain L'.

Values for R can be accurately obtained by picking, drying, and weighing the residues or growing crop, or by one of the line-transect methods. Surface residue is translated into standard residue by means of Figures 6-8, 6-9, and 6-10. Material other than small-grain or sorghum residues is translated to standard residue on the basis of the observed effectiveness of the specific material in relation to small-grain or sorghum residue.

Although predictions employing some of the less accurate techniques may not be entirely satisfactory, they are useful in assessing potential trouble and in instituting necessary erosion-control methods. Lack of some of the information required for full and best application is no justification for disregarding the prediction equation.

6–10 SLIDE RULES FOR PREDICTION CALCULATIONS

Slide rules designed cooperatively by the Soil Conservation Service and a commercial calculator company are available for calculating soil-loss predictions. The slide rule for water-erosion prediction has been used extensively by district conservationists. The wind-erosion prediction rule has been much less widely used. It is of recent design and is quite complicated.

Prediction workbooks and worksheets available to conservationists limit the need for slide rules, but field men without access to SCS worksheets find them helpful.

SUMMARY

Erosion cannot be prevented, but it must be limited to tolerable rates. Methods for predicting erosion rates are needed for two main reasons: to ascertain the erosion hazard with present management, and to evaluate alternative methods of crop and soil management. Erosion-predicting equations have been developed for estimating soil losses by both water and wind.

The water-erosion prediction equation was designed to predict soil movement by sheet and rill erosion in cultivated fields and has been widely and successfully used in the United States and in some other countries. The water erosion equation is:

$$A = R \cdot K \cdot LS \cdot C \cdot P$$

where A is the expected average annual rate of erosion in metric tons per hectare based on factors for rainfall erosivity, soil erodibility, slope length and steepness, cropping management, and special erosion-control practices. Techniques are available to calculate values for each factor from information obtained by field inspection and from tables, charts, and equations. The equation, or some modification of it, has been widely used by soil conservation technicians in working out effective alternative management practices for erosion control.

The water-erosion equation has been used in ways not originally contemplated and not always in keeping with the inherent reliability of the method. This is particularly true when attempts are made to predict sediment removal from fields, erosion losses in large gullies and along major stream channels, and the amount of sediment entering streams.

The wind-erosion prediction equation, originally intended to evaluate the erosion hazard of cultivated lands in the Great Plains region of the United States, is now widely used by conservationists and others in many areas. The wind-erosion equation is

$$E = f(I', K', C', L', V)$$

where E is the expected average annual rate of erosion in metric tons per hectare as a function of soil erodibility, soil-ridge roughness, climatic erosiveness, field length, and vegetative cover. Techniques are provided for calculating values for each factor using information obtained by field examination along with tables, graphs, and equations.

The wind-erosion equation has been successfully used in the Great Plains each fall and winter to predict the likelihood and extent of wind erosion the following spring. It has also been employed to determine the current erosion hazard and to evaluate the effectiveness of alternative management and erosion-control programs. Considerable interest has developed in using the equation on highly erodible soils (sands and mucks) in humid regions.

The wind-erosion equation has also been used in situations for which it was not originally designed such as predicting erosion on perennially vegetated areas and predicting airborne dust. Great care must be exercised if these special uses are to yield accurate estimates.

QUESTIONS

1. What needs prompted the development of the soil-loss prediction equations?
2. List the four major soil factors that affect the rate of erosion that can be tolerated, and point out why each factor is important.
3. What problems arise in applying the rainfall-erosivity index to a thinly populated developing country?
4. What is the water-erosion K factor? Describe three methods that have been used to establish specific K values in the United States.
5. Briefly describe the specific conditions for which the wind-erosion prediction equation was designed to estimate erosion losses accurately.
6. How does ridge roughness affect wind erosion? How was this effect evaluated initially?
7. (a) Describe a farm field and calculate the total erosion losses (water plus wind) predicted for it.
   (b) If the predicted losses exceed the tolerable amount, propose and justify control measures for reducing erosion.

REFERENCES

BROWNING, G. M., C. L. PARISH, and J. A. GLASS, 1947. A method for determining the use and limitations of soil erosion in Iowa. *J. Amer. Soc. Agron.* 39:65-73.

CARREKER, J. R., 1966. Wind erosion in the Southeast. *J. Soil Water Cons.* 21:86-88.

CHEPIL, W. S., 1960. Conversion of relative field erodibility to annual soil loss by wind. *Soil Sci. Soc. Amer. Proc.* 24:143-145.

CHEPIL, W. S., F. H. SIDDOWAY, and D. V. ARMBRUST, 1962. Climatic factor for estimating wind erodibility of farm fields. *J. Soil Water Cons.* 17: 162-165.

CHEPIL, W. S., and N. P. WOODRUFF, 1959. *Estimation of Wind Erodibility of Farm Fields.* USDA Prod. Res. Report No. 25.

FISHER, P. S., and E. L. SKIDMORE, 1970. *WEROS: A Fortran IV Program to Solve the Wind Erosion Equation.* USDA, ARS, 41-174.

FOSTER, G. R., and W. H. WISCHMEIER, 1974. Evaluating irregular slopes for soil loss prediction. *Trans. Amer. Soc. Agric. Eng.* 17:305-309.

HALLBERG, G. R., N. C. WOLLENHAUPT, and G. A. MILLER, 1978. A century of soil development in spoil derived from loess in Iowa. *Soil Sci. Soc. Amer. Jour.* 42:339-343.

HARTWIG, R. O., and J. M. LAFLEN, 1977. A meterstick method for measuring crop residue cover. *J. Soil Water Cons.* 33:90-91.

HAYES, W. A., 1965. Wind erosion equation useful in designing northeastern crop protection. *J. Soil Water Cons.* 20:153-155.

HUDSON, NORMAN, 1971. *Soil Conservation.* Cornell Univ. Press, Ithaca, New York, 320 p.

KALMAN, R., 1967. *Le Facteur Climatique de l'Erosion dans le Bassin du SEBOU (Maroc).* Project SEBOU, 32 p. (Quoted in ROOSE, E. J., 1977.)

KOHNKE, HELMUT, and A. R. BERTRAND, 1959. *Soil Conservation.* McGraw-Hill, New York, 298 p.

LAL, R., 1976. Soil erosion on Alfisols in western Nigeria. III. Effects of rainfall characteristics. *Geoderma* 16:389-401.

LAL, R., 1977. Analysis of factors affecting rainfall erosivity and soil erodibility. In D. J. GREENLAND and R. LAL (eds.), *Soil Conservation and Management in the Humid Tropics.* John Wiley, New York, p. 49-56.

MASSON, J. M., 1971. *L'Erosion des Sols par l'Eau en Climat Méditerranéen. Méthode Expérimentale pour l'Étude des Quantités de Terre Érodée a l'Échelle du Champ.* Thèse Doct. Ing. Univ. Sciences et techniques du Languedoc. CNRS No. AO 5445. 213 p. (Quoted in ROOSE, E. J., 1977.)

MASSON, J. M., and J. M. KALMS, 1971. *Analyse et Synthèse des Facteurs de l'Érosion sur le Bassin Versant de la TET à VINCA.* Note 14/71. EDF/Univ. Montpellier, 90 p. (Quoted in ROOSE, E. J., 1977.)

McCOOL, D. K., MYRON MOLNAU, R. I. PAPENDICK, and F. L. BROOKS, 1977. Erosion research in the dryland grain region of the Pacific Northwest: Recent developments and needs. In *Soil Erosion: Prediction and Control.* Soil Cons. Soc. Amer., Ankeny, Iowa, p. 50-59.

McGREGOR, K. C., and C. K. MUTCHLER, 1976. Status of the **R** Factor in northern Mississippi. In *Soil Erosion: Prediction and Control.* Soil Cons. Soc. Amer., Ankeny, Iowa, p. 135–142.

MEYER, G. J., P. J. SCHOENEBERGER, and J. H. HUDDLESTON, 1975. Sediment yields from roadsides: An application of the universal soil loss equation. *J. Soil Water Cons.* 30:289–291.

MEYER, L. D., and L. A. KRAMER, 1968. Relation Between Land-Slope and Soil Erosion. *Amer. Soc. Agric. Eng.* Paper No. 68-749 (abbreviated paper in *Agric. Eng.* 50:522–523).

MUSGRAVE, G. W., 1947. The quantitative evaluation of factors in water erosion—A first approximation. *J. Soil Water Cons.* 2:133–138.

ROOSE, E. J., 1977. Use of the universal soil loss equation to predict erosion in West Africa. In *Soil Erosion: Prediction and Control.* Soil Cons. Soc. Amer., Ankeny, Iowa, p. 60–74.

SINGER, M. J., G. L. HUNTINGTON, and H. R. SKETCHLEY, 1977. Erosion prediction on California rangeland: Research developments and needs. In *Soil Erosion: Prediction and Control.* Soil Cons. Soc. Amer., Ankeny, Iowa, p. 143–151.

SKIDMORE, E. L., P. S. FISHER, and N. P. WOODRUFF, 1970. Wind erosion equation: Computer solution and application. *Soil Sci. Soc. Amer. Proc.* 34: 931–935.

SKIDMORE, E. L., and N. P. WOODRUFF, 1968. *Wind Erosion Forces in the United States and Their Use in Predicting Soil Loss.* USDA Agric. Handbook No. 346.

SLONEKER, L. L., and W. C. MOLDENHAUER, 1977. Measuring the amounts of crop residue remaining after tillage. *J. Soil Water Cons.* 32:231–236.

SMITH, D. D., 1941. Interpretation of soil conservation data for field use. *Agric. Eng.* 22:173–175.

THORNTHWAITE, C. W., 1931. Climates of North America according to a new classification. *Geograph. Rev.* 21:633–655.

WHITFIELD, C. J., J. J. BOND, E. BURNETT, W. S. CHEPIL, B. W. GREB, T. M. McCALLA, J. S. ROBINS, F. H. SIDDOWAY, R. M. SMITH, and N. P. WOODRUFF, 1962. *A Standardized Procedure for Residue Sampling: A Committee Report.* USDA, ARS, 41-68.

WILLIAMS, J. R., and H. D. BERNDT, 1977. Determining the universal soil loss equation's length-slope factor for watersheds. In *Soil Erosion: Prediction and Control.* Soil Cons. Soc. Amer., Ankeny, Iowa, p. 217–225.

WILSON, LEE, 1975. Application of the wind erosion equation in air pollution surveys. *J. Soil Water Cons.* 30:215–219.

WISCHMEIER, W. H., 1959 A rainfall-erosion index for a universal soil-loss equation. *Soil Sci. Soc. Amer. Proc.* 23:246–249.

WISCHMEIER, W. H., 1960. Cropping-management factor evaluations for a universal soil-loss equation. *Soil Sci. Soc. Amer. Proc.* 24:322–326.

WISCHMEIER, W. H., 1962. Rainfall erosion potential. *Agric. Eng.* 43:212–215.

WISCHMEIER, W. H., 1974. New developments in estimating water erosion. In *Land Use: Persuasion or Regulation?* Proc. 29th Annual Meeting, Soil Cons. Soc. Amer., Aug. 11-14, 1974, Syracuse, New York.

WISCHMEIER, W. H., 1976. Use and misuse of the universal soil loss equation. *J. Soil Water Cons.* 31:5–9.

WISCHMEIER, W. H., C. B. JOHNSON, and B. V. CROSS, 1971. A soil erodibility nomograph for farmland and construction sites. *J. Soil Water Cons.* 26: 189–193.

WISCHMEIER, W. H., and D. D. SMITH, 1965. *Predicting Rainfall-Erosion Losses from Cropland East of the Rocky Mountains.* USDA Agric. Handbook No. 282.

WISCHMEIER, W. H., and D. D. SMITH, 1978. *Predicting Rainfall Erosion Losses: A Guide to Conservation Planning.* USDA Agric. Handbook No. 537.

WOODRUFF, N. P., and F. H. SIDDOWAY, 1965. A wind erosion equation. *Soil Sci. Soc. Amer. Proc.* 29:602–608.

ZINGG, A. W., 1940a. Degree and length of land slope as it affects soil loss in runoff. *Agric. Eng.* 21:59–64.

ZINGG, A. W., 1940b. An analysis of degree and length of slope data as applied to terracing. *Agric. Eng.* 21:99–101.

ZINGG, A. W., W. S. CHEPIL, and N. P. WOODRUFF, 1952. *Analysis of Wind Erosion Phenomena in Roosevelt and Currie Counties, New Mexico.* Region VI SCS Albuquerque, New Mexico M–436.

7

Soil Surveys and Land Use Planning

Soil surveys are a relatively recent means of recording information about land so that sound decisions can be made regarding its use and management. People have been using land for thousands of years and each user has learned much about particular parcels of land. Unfortunately, most have had no means of recording this knowledge for others. New users have had to learn about their land by experience because soil maps and soil survey reports were not available.

When European colonists arrived in America, they brought European customs and preferences with them. The cultivated lands in Europe were mostly on cleared lands that had been forested. The New England areas offered similar soils, so the settlers cleared areas that were most suited for cultivation as they knew it. They worked hard cutting trees and clearing stumps and stones from the land.

Pioneers seldom chose the best soils in the area for clearing. The best soils supported the most luxuriant growth of trees, and the early pioneers' tools and implements could not cope with them. The soils they did select would now be considered only moderately productive. Some, in fact, have since been abandoned or replanted to trees because they cannot compete with other land that is more productive with modern management.

The land and climate in the central United States were quite different from those of the East Coast and Europe, but adventuresome farmers moved westward following rumors of good soils free for the settling. The settlers in the tall-grass prairie region chose land that seemed to be most practical for farming, but the best soils were bypassed again. The fine-textured, humus-rich soils that are now the most productive in the corn belt were nearly impossible to plow with existing oxen, horses, and implements. Some of the pioneers continued westward into the Great Plains where it was easier to cultivate the land because the grasses were shorter and less dense. They discovered later that short grasses grow less dense because precipitation is more limited and more uncertain. Many pioneers lost everything in drought years and had to move back eastward or farther westward.

Many people settled in the Great Plains in response to the Homestead Law passed by the U.S. Congress in 1862. This act allowed a settler to claim 65 ha of "free land" by homesteading on it. A modern soil survey would have made it possible to create viable economic units for farming, ranching, and other uses with the area determined by the land and the use to be made of it. Such adjustments were not made because soil surveys were not available.

7-1 SOIL SURVEYS

Land-grant universities and state and federal agricultural research stations were founded in the last half of the nineteenth century and grew vigorously. The research stations obtained results from field plots, but there was no assurance that the new ideas could be transferred successfully from experimental plots to farms and ranches. Could technology be transferred freely from soil to soil, or was there a link missing? There *was* a missing link—soil classification—and soil surveys were initiated in 1899 so technology could be transferred. The surveys have changed in many details since 1899, but their objective remains the same—to help resource managers make the most efficient use of soil and land. A soil surveyor at work is shown in Figure 7-1.

Soil surveys proved to be so valuable that they are being made now throughout the world. The United States now has more than 1000 soil surveyors currently mapping 10,000 or more discrete soil series. There are about 100,000 mapping units, most of which are named for phases of soil series. Each series is divided into phases on the basis of slope, erosion, texture, or some other property significant to the use and management of the land.

7-1.1 Soil Surveys as Natural Resource Data

Soil surveys are used by many other people besides farmers and ranchers. The Council of State Governments (1977) sent questionnaires to 500 officials from all fifty state governments asking for the

Figure 7-1 This soil surveyor is showing the farmer how he uses 10% HC1 solution to detect the presence of calcium carbonate in soils and rocks. This information helps him classify the soil map that will help natural resource managers make efficient long-term use of the land. (Courtesy USDA—Soil Conservation Service.)

current level of use of natural resource data, including soil surveys. Table 7-1 details the frequency of use of ten types of natural resource data reported by thirteen state agencies. Results are shown where more than 50% of the states reported use of the data.

No one type of resource data is used universally, but soil surveys and topographic maps were generally used by eleven of the thirteen agencies. Even the two agencies that did not generally use soil surveys in 1977 may find them useful in the future. The passage of Public Law 95-87, "Surface Mining Control and Reclamation Act of 1977" (U.S. Congress, 1977), made stockpiling of surface soil (topsoil) mandatory. This surface soil must be replaced after completion of mining operations to facilitate the reestablishment of protective vegetation. The information needed to remove and replace the surface soil is readily obtained from a standard soil survey map and report.

Table 7-1 Percentage of state agencies in the fifty states using natural resource data

State agencies	Soil surveys	Aerial photos	Flood-plain maps	Hydro-logic reports	Geo-logic maps	Land use data	Topo-graphic maps	Vege-tation maps	Wet-land maps	Wildlife reports
				Type of natural resource data						
Agriculture	64	*	*	*	*	*	*	*	*	*
Coastal management zone	88	88	63	63	75	88	88	88	88	*
Environmental protection	91	77	81	77	82	77	96	*	52	*
Energy facilities siting	*	*	*	*	67	67	83	*	*	*
Fish and wildlife	90	79	62	52	*	83	100	83	83	86
Forestry	97	90	*	*	52	65	94	74	*	61
Land resources	70	*	*	*	*	*	*	*	*	*
Mine spoil reclamation	*	*	*	*	67	*	56	*	*	*
Natural resources	91	82	91	64	73	82	100	64	73	55
State land use planning	86	86	86	71	76	91	95	71	71	*
Transportation	83	88	83	71	75	88	100	67	71	79
Utilities	57	57	71	*	71	57	100	57	57	57
Water resources	91	73	91	82	91	77	96	55	55	57

*Less than 50% of agencies reported use.
SOURCE: Council of State Governments, 1977.

7-1.2 Soils and Agricultural Prosperity

The most prosperous farmers almost always farm the best soils. Olson (1977) presents evidence to support this statement in the environs of Syracuse, New York. He compared soil series, as mapped in standard soil surveys by the National Cooperative Soil Survey, with relative farm prosperity. The most prosperous farmers were farming Palmyra, Honeoye, and Lima soil series, all members of the Glossoboric Hapludalfs.* The least prosperous farmers were farming Worth series (Typic Fragiorthods) and Empeyville series (Aquic Fragiorthods). Coarse texture, low fertility, fragipans, droughtiness, and cold temperatures limit productive agriculture on these latter soils.

7-1.3 Types of Soil Surveys

Soil surveys are divided into two general types—detailed and reconnaissance. A *detailed soil survey* is one where sufficient field work is done to observe all soil mapping units and to trace all soil boundaries throughout their length. A *reconnaissance soil survey* has only intermittent field observations. Much of the information is interpreted from aerial photos or other maps of the area.

The current detailed surveys being made in the United States for publication under the National Cooperative Soil Survey are known as *Standard Soil Surveys*. The maps and accompanying reports must meet certain standards to serve the needs of their users.

7-1.4 Soil Survey Reports

Soil surveys in the United States are made by the National Cooperative Soil Survey. Leadership is by the USDA—Soil Conservation Service and the respective Land-grant University's Agricultural Experiment Station. In a few states the cooperating agency is another organization. The respective federal agency is the cooperator on federal lands. Information obtained by the National Cooperative Soil Survey is published in soil survey reports, usually on a county basis. By 1975, soil survey reports had been published for about one-fourth of the 3097 counties in the fifty states and territories.

Soil survey reports in the United States consist of two parts, the text and the soil maps. The text tells how the survey was made, describes the county and the soils, tells how the soils are classified, and discusses their use and management.

---

*Consult a modern introductory soils text for information on the U.S. Soil Taxonomy.

7-1.5 Base Maps

Base maps on which soil information is shown have experienced a genuine revolution. As late as the 1930s, some county soil maps were drawn on a base map made with a planetable for directions; distances were either paced or measured with an automobile tachometer. Topographic maps (made by the U.S. Geological Survey) were used when available. From about the 1930s to the 1950s, aerial photographs for most areas of the United States became available for use as base maps for soil surveys. These aerial photographs are updated periodically and continue to be the best base for drawing soil boundaries. The standard type is a black-and-white photograph with a matte (nonglossy) surface to facilitate marking soil boundaries and symbols in the field with a pencil.

Since the mid 1960s, infrared film has been used in some aerial photo mapping. These color photos are superior to black-and-white photos where land use and vegetation are to be interpreted. Color photos are seldom used as soil survey base maps.

At about the same time as infrared photography became available, scanners (multispectral photographic systems) were developed. This technique permits the separation on the map of wetlands, dark soils, and well-drained soils but is useful only when the soil is bare of vegetation.

Thermal infrared sensors in aircraft can measure relative soil temperatures. Scanners are most useful at the time of day when the temperatures of well-drained soil, poorly drained soil, surface rock, and types of vegetation are expected to be in greatest contrast, usually at about 3 P.M.

For most of the world, Earth Resources Technology Satellites (Landsats 1 and 2) have photographed four-spectral-band data at eighteen-day intervals from a height of 912 kilometers. Using Landsat maps at scales of 1:500,000 and 1:1,000,000, Klingebiel (1977) reports a technique for making a "good," "fair," and "poor" category map for food and fiber production in Mexico. This type of work has tremendous value for planning national development and identifying needs for more detailed soil surveys.

Although extremely useful as supporting and supplemental information, all air photo data require ground observations for full interpretation. Some reconnaissance-type soil surveys are made with minimal ground observations, but this diminishes the amount of information that can be mapped, and the accuracy is less than that of surveys made in the field.

7-1.6 Soil Maps

There are two kinds of soil maps in the Soil Survey Report:

1. General Soil Map, actually a Soil Association Map, made on a scale of 1 : 190,080. This map is especially useful in county-wide land use planning.
2. Detailed Soil Map, usually printed on a scale of 1 : 20,000 or 1 : 15,840 on an aerial photographic background.

Examples of mapping units on detailed soil maps are given along with land use capability interpretations in Section 7-2.1.

7-1.7 Soil Map Units

The individual soil map units are almost all named as phases of soil series. The principal exceptions are areas covered with mine spoils, made land in and around cities and developments, rough broken land, and intermixed soil series too small in area to map separately.

A soil surveyor, with the aid of a mapping legend, draws boundaries on the soil map to separate the soil map units. The soil surveyor maps as nearly as possible the taxonomic units known as *polypedons*. The map symbol designates the type of polypedons plus the slope and erosion classes.

Polypedons are composed of adjacent pedons of the same soil series. One soil series is differentiated from another by properties inherent in the constituent *pedons* (Greek, *pedon* = ground). The soil pedons are characterized by the color, texture, structure, porosity (permeability), consistence of structural units (peds or clods), pH, concretions, clay coatings, organic matter, and root abundance of each horizon and the depth to bedrock or other root-restricting layer. Laboratory analyses that supplement these field observations include X-ray mineralogy and other physical, chemical, and biological parameters.

Polypedon field characterizations also record the vegetation, surface drainage, slope class, erosion class, parent materials, stoniness, and land use (Soil Survey Staff, 1975; Olson, 1974b).

7-2 SOIL MAP UNIT INTERPRETATIONS

All mapping units in a modern soil survey report are interpreted for various uses in the text of the report (Kellogg, 1961). When the mapping units are used according to the limitations specified, the soils will remain productive, nonpolluting, and useful. Examples of soil map unit interpretations are included in the following sections.

7-2.1 Land Use Capability Groupings

The term *land* generally includes soil, mineral deposits, climate, water supply, location in relation to markets and transportation, vegetative cover, and improvements. However, in the definitions of the *land use capability groupings,* the word "soil" replaces "land" except in the name of each group and in the name of the subclass c for climate.

There are eight *Land Use Capability Classes,* as shown in Figure 7-2, differentiated and described on the basis of *limitations* (hazards) that restrict intensity of use or require special treatment.

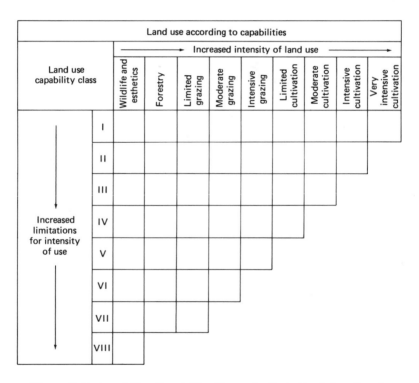

Figure 7-2 Land Use Capability Classes indicate the intensity of use for which soils are suited. Class I is suitable for any use, but other classes are restricted by various limitations and hazards. (Courtesy USDA—Soil Conservation Service.)

CLASS I: Soils that have few limitations for very intensive cultivation.

CLASS II: Soils that have moderate limitations that reduce the choice of adapted plants or that require moderate conservation practices.

CLASS III: Soils that have severe limitations that reduce the choice of plants, require intensive conservation practices, or both.

CLASS IV: Soils that have severe limitations that reduce the choice of plants, require very intensive management, or both.

CLASS V: Soils that are not likely to deteriorate but have other limitations, impractical to remove, that limit their use primarily to pasture grasses, range grasses, woodlands, wildlife, or aesthetics.

CLASS VI: Soils that have severe limitations that make them generally unsuited to cultivation and limit their use primarily to pasture grasses, range grasses, woodlands, wildlife, or aesthetics.

CLASS VII: Soils that have very severe limitations that make them unsuited to cultivation and that restrict their use primarily to pasture grasses, range grasses, woodlands, wildlife, or aesthetics; an example is shown in Figure 7–3.

CLASS VIII: Soils and landforms that have limitations that preclude their use for commercial plants and restrict their use to wildlife, aesthetics, recreation, and/or watersheds.

Class I land is suitable for all land uses, Class II land is suitable for all uses except "very intensive cultivation," and so on to Class VIII land, on which only wildlife, aesthetics, recreation, and/or watersheds are suited. Any land can be used for wildlife and other uses suitable for Class VIII, but the economics of land use usually dictate the selection of the most intensive use for which the land is adapted.

Land Use Capability Subclasses are groups within Land Use Capability Classes that designate the *dominant kind of limitation or hazard* restricting land use. The subclasses are designated by writing a lower-case letter following the Roman numeral that signifies the land capability class. The four subclasses are:

e = hazards of accelerated erosion and sedimentation.

w = hazards of excessive wetness.

s = hazards of plant root restrictions, including excessive shallowness, droughtiness, stoniness, salinity, or sodicity.

Figure 7-3 Fairmont flaggy silty clay loam in Kentucky on 25% slopes. The soil is a Typic Hapludoll. It is in land use capability Class VII and subclass **e** (eroded). Limited grazing is probably the most intensive use this soil can serve without excessive erosion. (Courtesy USDA—Soil Conservation Service.)

c = climatic hazards of excessive coldness or dryness for the normal growth of crop plants.

The relative abundance of these types of limitations in the United States is shown in Figure 7-4. Land Capability Class I, by definition, has no hazards limiting its use and therefore has no subclass. Each of the other seven classes is divided into subclasses. Soil map units are classified into subclasses according to which one of the four types of hazards limits the use of the land to its designated capability class. When two subclasses limit land use equally, only one is used, priority being assigned in the sequence **e**, **w**, **s**, and **c**.

Land Use Capability Units are divisions of land use capability subclasses into smaller, more homogeneous groups of soil map units having similar use potential and management requirements. They have also been called "soil management groups." Capability units are established because subclasses are too broad and soil map units more

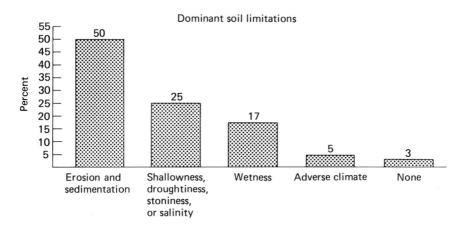

Figure 7-4 Dominant limitations (subclasses) that restrict the suitability of soils of the United States for more intensive use. Erosion and sedimentation limit the most intensive use of half of the soils of the nation. (Soil Conservation Service, 1971.)

specific than necessary for land management considerations. Therefore, soil map units with similar erosion hazards, degrees of wetness, stoniness, textural classes, and crop adaptations are grouped in the same land use capability unit.

Capability units are identified by Arabic numbers added to the symbols for land use capability class and subclass. An example is IIIe-1. However, the land capability units are so variable throughout the fifty states that separate systems of designations and interpretations are established for individual counties.

The following examples of soil map units and the land use capability classes, subclasses, and units into which they are classified are taken from soil survey reports from three states:

1. From the Soil Survey of Eastern Maricopa and Northern Pinal Counties area, Arizona (Soil Conservation Service, 1974a):
   Gm—Gilman loam. (The slope is less than 1%, so no slope class is indicated.)
   Irrigated capability class is I, meaning no limitations on intensity of use and therefore no *capability subclass*. The *capability unit* is I-1, indicating a deep friable soil.
   Nonirrigated capability class and *subclass* are VIIc, implying a servere dryness limitation for crop production. Wind and water erosion and sedimentation are not the principal hazards.
2. From the Soil Survey of Pitt County, North Carolina (Soil Conservation Service, 1974b):

NrB2—Norfolk sandy loam; B = slopes of 1% to 6%; 2 = eroded; land use capability class, subclass, and unit are IIe-1, meaning that the soil can be cultivated continuously with simple erosion- and sedimentation-control practices. The e implies that erosion and sedimentation are the principal hazards and that simple erosion-control practices such as contour tillage, minimum till- age, or sod-forming crops in the rotation should be employed. The 1 indicates a deep friable soil with no horizons or layers to restrict root growth of farm and ranch crops.

3.   From the Soil Survey of Lafayette County, Missouri (Soil Conser- vation Service, 1975):
     KnF3—Knox silt loam; F = 20% to 25% slopes; 3 = severely eroded. The capability class, subclass, and unit are VIIe-4. The VII means a soil unsuitable for cropland, with limited suitabil- ity for pastureland, but better suited to woodland, wildlife, and recreation. The e means erosion hazard and the 4 implies actual erosion so severe as to have removed all of the surface soil and, in gullies, all of the B and some of the C horizon. This unit must be managed very carefully, even when used for pasture- or woodland.

7-2.2 Predicting Crop Response

Soil survey reports published after 1965, and many published earlier, discuss general suitability of each soil map unit for the production of common farm crops, pasture, forage, and range grasses. Such discus- sions occur under "Descriptions of the Soils" and "Capability Groupings." In addition, under "Estimated Yields," all soil map units are rated for the average yields of their principal crops under two levels of management—average and high. Productivities for pasture-, range-, and woodland are included where appropriate. Field crop yields are indicated in bushels per acre, hay in tons per acre, and pasture in AUD (animal unit days). AUD are defined as the number of days that one cow or equivalent can be grazed on one acre (0.4 ha) without damage to the pasture.

In semiarid range country, the soil map units with similar char- acteristics are grouped and used as a basis for delineating various range sites and their relative productivity.

All soil survey maps and reports indicate the significant soil parameters of depth, slope, and surface texture. These three soil characteristics have been used from the irrigated San Diego area of California to the rainfed New York State to predict soil suitability for vegetable crops. The same principles are applied in each place even though details differ, as shown in Table 7-2.

Table 7-2 Relative suitability of soil map parameters for the production of vegetable crops in the irrigated San Diego area, California, and in the rainfed state of New York

Soil map parameter	Relative suitability			
	Well-suited	Moderately well-suited	Not suited	

San Diego area[a]

Soil map parameter	Well-suited	Moderately well-suited	Not suited
Soil depth	> 90 cm	50 to 90 cm	< 50 cm
Slope	< 5%	5% to 9%	> 9%
Surface texture	Fine sandy loam, very fine sandy loam, sandy loam, loamy sand, or loamy fine sand	Clay loam, loam, coarse sand, or gravelly loamy sand	Clay, silty clay, rocky, cobbly, stony, very gravelly, or rock outcrops

New York State[b]

Soil map parameter	Well-suited	Moderately well-suited	Not suited
Soil depth	> 50 cm	About 50 cm	< 50 cm
Slope	< 3%	3% to 8%	> 8%
Surface texture	Silt loam, loam, or sandy loams containing less than 5% coarse fragments; also Histosols	Silt loam, loam, or sandy loam with 5 to 35% coarse fragments; also loamy fine sand with up to 35% coarse fragments	Any soil texture with more than 35% coarse fragments; silty clay, clay, clay loam, silty clay loam, sandy clay loam, loamy sand, or sand with or without coarse fragments; cobbly or flaggy soil; or stony phases of any soil texture

[a]Bowman and others, 1973.
[b]Olson, 1974b.

7-2.3 Evaluating Rural Land

Soil map interpretations have been used in several states to evaluate rural land. For example, a study in Illinois compared the prices paid in 1509 rural land sales in thirty-three counties during 1966 to 1968 to soil productivity ratings of soil map units. The standard soil survey report and soil map can be used to evaluate rural land to help in equalization of taxes (Alexander, Carmer, and Fehrenbacher, 1978).

Taxes on farm- and ranchland should be based on the productive potential of the soils and not on the management skill of the farmers and ranchers. Neither should taxes on rural property being farmed be based on its potential value for urban developments.

An economic analysis of yield potential and costs of production permits calculation of the potential agricultural value of each soil. Assessors equipped with these data and soil maps can calculate the potential crop income of a farm or ranch. The procedures and the crops considered vary from state to state, but the essential steps are:

1. Calculate the weighting factor to be assigned to each soil map unit.
2. Measure the area of each kind of soil in each land ownership.
3. Sum the products of area × weighting factor.
4. Adjust for buildings, location, and other factors.

Several states now use the above procedure to determine all or part of the assessed valuation for property taxes.

7-2.4 Upgrading Soil Test Recommendations

The soil testing laboratory can make more precise lime and fertilizer recommendations for all soil samples that are collected and labeled on the basis of a soil map unit. For example, in the Soil Survey of Green County, Illinois (Soil Conservation Service, 1974c) a soil series is mapped as Clarksdale. With the words "Clarksdale Series" on the soil sample label, the soil testing laboratory can adjust the fertilizer and lime recommendations according to experimental data from Clarksdale and similar soil series.

The soil testing laboratory at Iowa State University, for example, requests the name of the soil series along with each soil sample so as to adjust the fertilizer recommendation based on known subsoil characteristics. Soil characteristics such as slope, depth of topsoil, and drainage can be supplied instead if the soil series is unknown.

7-2.5 Determining Need for Artificial Drainage

Soil surveys indicate soil series. One criterion for differentiating soil series is internal drainage. The natural internal drainage is classified as excessively drained, somewhat excessively drained, well drained, moderately well drained, *somewhat poorly drained, poorly drained,* or *very poorly drained.* The last three soil drainage classes usually require some type of artificial drainage for optimum yields of most upland farm crops.

7-2.6 Evaluating Woodland and Windbreak Sites

Tree species adaptation and relative growth rates depend on many factors, including soil depth through which roots may grow without physical or chemical hindrance, available water-holding capacity of the soil, soil texture, organic matter, aeration, and depth to the water table. Information about all these factors can be interpreted from the soil map unit. Such information for each county in which forest trees grow naturally, as well as for semiarid areas where windbreaks and shelterbelts are common, can be found in each county soil survey report. Examples are given in the following paragraph.

The Soil Survey Report for Brevard County, Florida (Soil Conservation Service, 1974d) has a section on "Woodland" that itemizes the soil map symbol, woodland group, potential productivity, seedling mortality, plant competition, equipment limitations, and preferred species for planting. The Soil Survey Report of Harlan County, Nebraska, where the annual precipitation is 550 mm (Soil Conservation Service, 1974e), discusses the suitability of the various soils for windbreak plantings. Tree species are recommended on a site basis. Similar information is presented in any modern soil survey report for an area where trees are adapted.

7-2.7 Selecting Sites for Wildlife Habitats

A table included in standard soil survey reports issued since 1965 rates all soil map units on suitability for "wildlife habitat elements," including grain and seed crops, grasses and legumes, wild herbaceous plants, hardwood trees and shrubs, coniferous trees, and wetland food and cover plants. Also, soil map units are rated for suitability to openland, woodland, and wetland wildlife.

7-2.8 Interpreting Engineering Uses

The most important soil characteristics for engineering uses are particle (grain) sizes, permeability to water, compressibility, shear strength, compaction, drainage, shrink-swell potential, plasticity, soil pH, depth to water table, depth to bedrock, and topography. Engineering test data are presented in tables in soil survey reports under the heading "Engineering Uses of the Soils." The interpretations are based on field testing, laboratory analyses, and estimations of soil properties.

The engineering test data can be used to predict the suitability of each soil map unit as a source of topsoil, sand, gravel, caliche, or road fill. They can also be used to evaluate the suitability of each soil map unit for constructing a sanitary landfill, a filter field for a septic tank, a sewage lagoon, a foundation for a house, a farm pond, a highway, or a playground. Other available information important to engineering uses of soils includes flooding hazard, relative wetness, erodibility, and stabilization of construction slopes with adapted vegetation.

7-3 MANAGING LAND

Land is used for many activities and purposes having a wide variety of soil requirements. Land managers can use soil survey information and interpretations to select soils and management best suited for particular uses.

7-3.1 Managing Agricultural Land

Farmers and ranchers need to be good land managers to make a profit without long-term soil deterioration. Soil survey reports provide information on which to base land-management decisions. They are useful for major decisions such as what land to purchase and what use to make of it. They are also useful for designing field layouts, planning conservation practices, and making general management decisions.

Selecting land for a particular enterprise is easier and more precise when soil survey information is used. For example, a rancher choosing land for a cattle ranch in the southern Great Plains would find that the Abilene soils shown in Figure 7–5 are known as Pachic Argiustolls to soil surveyors and deep hardland range soils to local ranchers. The native grasses are mid- and short-prairie grasses. Good grazing management is needed because overgrazing causes blue

Figure 7-5 A soil profile of the Abilene series (Pachic Argiustoll) in the 64-mm precipitation belt in Texas. This soil supports a good growth of nutritious range grasses. The root zone is nearly a meter deep to the whitish calcium carbonate zone at the bottom of the photo (Note: the arrow is at 1 meter). (Courtesy Texas Agricultural Experiment Station.)

gramagrass and buffalograss to increase at the expense of the taller grasses. Forage production then declines from its normal range of 700 to 100 kg/ha annually (Soil Conservation Service, 1974f).

Land usually returns the highest profit when it is used most intensively, but that use needs to be within its capabilities. For example, Class III land will produce more income when used to grow cultivated crops than when used for pasture- or woodland, but it needs to be managed according to the needs of Class III land. Soil survey reports contain use and management information for all the soils shown on their maps.

Adapted varieties can be selected for farms on the basis of experiment station results when soil survey maps show that the soils are similar. Also, needs for artificial drainage or for erosion-control practices can be identified and serious damage avoided. The general likelihood of needing lime and fertilizer may also be indicated in a soil survey report, but soil samples from the actual field should be tested when specific fertility recommendations are needed.

7-3.2 Mechanization in Developing Countries

Developing countries want to move rapidly from hand-hoe cultivation to animal-power cultivation to cultivation by tractors. These transitions sometimes succeed and sometimes fail. One reason for the failure of animal-powered farming in humid Africa is trypanosomiasis (African sleeping sickness) carried by several species of tsetse fly (*Glossina* species). In humid Africa, many governments want to lead their farmers from the use of the village-made hoes directly into the use of the most sophisticated tractors.

Rapid mechanization is feasible on some soils. For example, nearly level and fertile Vertisols occur in Ethiopia and Sudan (eastern Africa) and in Ghana and Nigeria (western Africa). Tractors are the most suitable farm power on Vertisols because animals cannot pull plows and other implements through such fine-textured soils.

By contrast, the ferruginous soils of Ghana in western Africa are so steep and irregular in topography, so low in fertility, and so high in plinthite (ironstone, laterite) that they cannot be cultivated with a tractor. Soils of the entire country of Ghana are currently being mapped so their capabilities will be known (Kline and others, 1969).

7-3.3 Delineating Nutritional Problem Areas

As early as 1878, President Welch of the Agricultural College at Ames, Iowa (now Iowa State University of Science and Technology) suggested that there should be a national study of soils in relation to animal and human nutrition. The Annual Report for 1898 of the USDA—Bureau of Animal Industry contained a section on the relationship between a bone disease of animals and the forage from pastures on the "noncalcareous" soils of the Gulf Coastal Plains. Later it was discovered that the soils were acid and low in calcium and phosphorus. The bone disease became known as osteomalacia. Extreme cases were reported in the 1930s in some northern states where animals ate only native prairie grasses and overwintered on prairie hay. Soils likely to supply only small amounts of phosphorus can be identified on soil maps and checked by nutrient tests. Phosphorus percentages in most forages can be increased by a soil application of phosphorus fertilizer or by liming acid soils. The phosphorus fertilizer will also increase forage production and reduce erosion on soils low in available phosphorus.

Forage plants growing on soils that are poorly drained, both on Histosols (peats and mucks) and on wet mineral soils, may contain concentrations of copper and molybdenum that are toxic to cattle and sheep (Kubota, 1975). These soils are readily identifiable on soil maps.

Some nutritional problems such as those mentioned relate to specific areas that can be mapped. People in most developed nations obtain food from a wide area and many soils. A balanced diet is therefore likely to contain adequate nutrients.

7-3.4 Cleansing the Environment

Pollution of the environment is a serious threat to human life. Pollutants discarded in oceans and other bodies of water may not degrade; water may preserve them. Soil is the only biodegrading medium for rational disposal of many kinds of polluting wastes (Ch. 17).

Soils vary in the kinds of pollutants each can absorb and the efficiency with which each is degraded. Soils that are ideal for use as septic tank drain fields are usually not ideal for sewage lagoons or

Table 7-3 Relative ratings and the reasons for the ratings of selected soil series in Kansas for use in waste disposal

| Soil Series | *Relative ratings* | | | | *Reason(s) for ratings* |
| | Septic tank drain field | Sewage lagoon | Sanitary landfill | | |
			Trench type	Area type	
Carwile	Poor	Good	Poor	Fair	Slow internal drainage
Goshen	Fair	Fair	Fair	Fair	Occasional flooding, rapid permeability
Grable	Fair	Fair	Fair	Fair	Rapid permeability, water table
Likes	Good	Poor	Poor	Poor	Rapid permeability, sandy
Lula	Fair	Fair	Poor	Good	Hard bedrock at 100 to 150 cm
McLain	Poor	Good	Fair	Fair	Fine-textured, slow permeability, occasional flooding
Riverton	Fair	Fair	Fair	Fair	Rapid permeability, coarse fragments

SOURCE: Olson, 1974a; Soil Survey Staff, 1972.

sanitary landfills. Even different types of landfills require different soil characteristics. Table 7-3 rates seven soil series in Kansas as "good," "fair," or "poor" for use as a disposal site for each of these kinds of polluting wastes. Similar tables can be found in other modern soil survey reports.

In general, a septic tank drain field requires a soil that is well drained, sandy-loam-to-loam textured, as deep as possible to a water table or a water-restricting layer, nearly level, pH 6.5 to 8.5, high in cation exchange capacity, high in organic matter, and free from coarse fragments. In contrast, the ideal soil for a sewage lagoon is fine-textured, poorly drained with no possibility of contaminating the surface or ground waters, structureless (puddled), level, any pH, low in organic matter, and free from coarse fragments. Soils for use as sanitary landfills should have properties intermediate between those ideal for drain fields and those ideal for sewage lagoons. However, since a trench-type landfill requires more soil manipulation under varying moisture conditions, its soil should be deep, medium-textured, and high in organic matter, and have stable structure.

7-3.5 Planning and Development

Soil survey reports and soil maps have been used in almost every conceivable type of land resource planning, zoning, and general development. The largest project is that for the entire 201-county watershed of the Tennessee Valley, comprising parts of seven states. To serve as a resource data base for continuing regional development, the Soil Conservation Service and the Tennessee Valley Authority are converting all soil maps of the Tennessee Valley to a computer retrievable form. This involves assembling all maps and converting them into 7½-minute quadrangle sheets of 14,580 hectares (Alden, Baxter, and Elder, 1978).

7-4 LAND USE PLANNING

Land use planning is often perceived as having three objectives: (1) to protect current land use, (2) to guide future developments, and (3) to reduce present and future conflicts.

Planning the use of government lands frequently evokes conflict. Even stronger dissension may erupt when government tries to restrict or direct land use on the two-thirds of the United States in private ownership.

A sampling of the attitude of local residents, mostly private land owners, toward land use was obtained in central southern North Dakota by Eshetu, Helgeson, and Dunn (1976). This survey showed 69% of the respondents agreed and only 17% disagreed with this statement: "Land use plans should be adopted only with the approval of the local citizens." More rural farm residents agreed (76%) than did urban residents (56%).

Scientists tend to believe that land use should be planned scientifically. Politicians, on the other hand, feel that political considerations should be given priority. The truth may lie in the "gray" zone between the two opposing views. To quote Starnes (1973) after working with land use planning in Florida: "We have had some difficulty in setting priorities and, frankly at this point, our way of determining priorities is about 50% political and about 50% pseudoscientific."

To assure environmental integrity in perpetuity, land use planning must have a rational scientific base related to soil characteristics. Modern soil surveys can provide this systematic base. For maximum use by planners, engineers, natural resource managers, and politicians, however, soil surveys should be interpreted by soil scientists for each proposed use.

Soil surveys are inventories of land surfaces to a depth of 1 to 2 meters. All uses of land are influenced by the physical, chemical, and biological properties of the soil. Soil surveys will therefore play an increasingly important role in planning land use as an increasing population becomes aware that there is not enough suitable land to satisfy all human needs and wants.

7-4.1 Land Use in the United States

Major uses of land in the United States are listed in Table 7-4. The 431 million hectares of "land in farms" is only slightly less than the 486 million hectares of "land not in farms." Each year about 1 million hectares of cropland are converted to other uses. At the same time, half this many hectares of new cropland is diverted from other uses such as pasture, range, and forest. The net result is an average annual loss of about 500,000 ha of cropland.

Contrary to popular opinion, only 10% of the diverted cropland (101,000 ha/yr) is used for urban developments. New roads use 1.4% (14,000 ha) of cropland a year, and new reservoirs 2% (20,000 ha). Miscellaneous uses of diverted cropland account for 8.7% (87,000 ha). The most surprising fact is that the largest part of the diverted cropland becomes pasture or forest. Each year 78% of the 1 million hectares of land shifted away from crops consists of soils too eroded,

Table 7-4 Land use in the fifty United States

Major land use	Million hectares	Percent of total
Land in Farms		
Cropland:		
Used for crops	135	14.7
Idle/cover crops	21	2.3
Total	156	17.0
Pastureland:		
Used for pasture	183	20.0
Cropland used only for pasture	36	3.9
Total	219	23.9
Woodland:		
Pastured	25	2.7
Not pastured	20	2.2
Total	45	4.9
Other uses (farmsteads, roads)	11	1.2
Total land in farms	431	47.0
Land Not in Farms		
Rangeland (humid, semiarid and arid woodland, shrubland, and grassland; all grazed)	117	12.8
Forestland not grazed	192	20.9
Other uses (cities, roads, railroads, barren lands)	177	19.3
Total land not in farms	486	53.0
Grand total land area of the 50 states	917	100.0
Inland water surfaces	20	

SOURCE: USDA-Agricultural Statistics, 1977.

too steep, too sloping, too irregular in topography, too stony, too infertile, too sandy, or too salty or sodic for efficient crop production. The chief problem is most often the limitations imposed by using modern farm machinery.

Of the 500,000 ha each year added as new cropland in the United States, 32% (162,000 ha) are irrigated with water from deep wells, reservoirs, or river diversions. These developments are limited by many crucial problems such as a scarce supply of water of suitable quality for irrigation, lowering of water tables, increasing salinity, and rising costs of energy to pump the water.

7-4.2 Land Use, Erosion, and Sedimentation

There is little doubt that a well-managed, fully stocked forest provides maximum protection against soil erosion and sediment loss. Next in rank of soil protection is a thick cover of grass, and least protective is bare soil. But how much does erosion increase when a forest is logged, burned, cleared and cropped, or when a pasture is plowed and cropped? Table 7-5 contains answers to these and other related questions.

Table 7-5 Relative erosion and sediment production rates resulting from disturbance in forestland, pastureland, and cropland

Land use before disturbance	Relative erosion and sedimentation rate before disturbance	Kind of disturbance	Relative erosion and sedimentation rate after disturbance	Reference
Forestland	1	Logging and skidding	1.6	Megahan, 1972
		Forest fire	7 to 1500	Ralston and Hatchell, 1971
		Clearing and row cropping	100 to 1000	Brown, 1960
		Logging road construction	220	Megahan, 1972
		General construction	2000	SCS, 1970
Pastureland	11	Row cropping	20 to 100	Brown, 1960
		General construction	200	SCS, 1970
Cropland	168	General construction	1000	SCS, 1970

The data in Table 7-5 are generalized for the entire United States and must be used only for relative comparisons of erosion or sedimentation rates. Nationwide reductions in total erosion and sedimentation could be achieved if only Class I land were used for the most intensive cropping and all other Land Use Capability classes were used within their designated limitations. Most land must be used as intensively as its limitations permit, and the country needs to reserve its best agricultural land for agricultural purposes. A new national concern for prime and unique agricultural lands recognizes this concept.

7-4.3 Prime and Unique Agricultural Lands

There has been increasing concern that the best lands for agricultural use were being irreversibly converted for such purposes as residential and business sites as shown in Figure 7-6. This concern has led to efforts to define and identify prime and unique agricultural lands. The following definitions come from a paper by Johnson (1975) delivered to a conference called to discuss these issues in Washington, D.C.

Prime farmland is land that has the best combination of physical and chemical characteristics for producing food, feed, forage, fiber, and oilseed crops. The land could be cropland, pastureland, rangeland, forestland, or other land, but not urban built-up land or water. It has the soil quality, growing season, and moisture supply needed to economically produce sustained high yields of crops when treated and managed, including water management, according to modern farming methods.

Prime agricultural lands are characterized by these eight parameters:

1. The soil must be on gentle slopes and not subject to excessive erosion.
2. Soil permeability must be at least 0.15 cm per hour in the upper 50 cm.
3. Gravel, cobbles, and stones must not be so common as to interfere with modern farm tractors and equipment.
4. Soil depth to hardpan or bedrock must be great enough to not interfere with adequate water storage or normal root extension.
5. Soil pH must be suitable for the crop to be grown and the salt and sodium contents must be acceptable.
6. The soil should not be subject to excess water from flooding or a high water table.
7. Soil moisture should be adequate and dependable from normal rainfall or from irrigation.

Figure 7-6 Most of the soil under this subdivision in Maryland would be classified in Land Use Capability Class I and would be considered as "prime agricultural land." Building costs were less than elsewhere because the area is nearly level and adequately drained. Who should determine whether it should be used for housing or reserved for agriculture? (Courtesy USDA—Soil Conservation Service.)

8. The mean annual soil temperature at a depth of 50 cm must be greater than 0°C and the mean summer soil temperature greater than 8°C for soils with an O (organic) horizon and 15°C for other soils.

Unique farmland is land other than prime farmland that is used for the production of specific high value food and fiber crops. It has the special combination of soil quality, location, growing season, and moisture supply needed to economically produce sustained high quality and/or high yields of a specific crop when treated and managed according to modern farming methods (Johnson, 1975).

Unique agricultural lands include cranberry bogs, citrus orchards, and rice fields, as examples. Three criteria characterize such lands:

1. Adequate soil moisture from whatever source.
2. Soil temperatures high enough and a growing season long enough to produce a satisfactory harvest of the selected crop.
3. A location that has the favorable attributes needed, such as nearness to market, good air drainage, the proper aspect (direction of slope), favorable relative humidity, and suitable soil temperature.

7-4.4 Soil Surveys for Planning and Zoning

Examples of specific uses of soil survey information for planning and zoning will be briefed for a city, two counties, and for "critical areas" in general.

Soil surveys were used in establishing subdivision regulations in Canfield, Ohio as early as 1966 (Soil Conservation Service, 1967). Canfield is a town in northeastern Ohio under 5000 in population. Based on those properties relevant to construction, public health, and erosion and sedimentation hazard, all soil series in Canfield were placed in one of five groups as follows (Soil Conservation Service, 1967):

I Favorable soils (well drained, 2% to 12% slopes)
II Steep soils (12% to 50% slopes)
III Seasonally wet soils (0% to 6% slopes)
IV Permanently wet soils with high shrink-swell potential (0% to 6% slopes)
V Restricted soils (flood hazard, nearly level)

Each of the first four soil groups had specific mandatory foundation construction specifications, whereas Group V was not to be used for buildings without very costly flood control structures approved in advance.

Black Hawk County in north central Iowa is a prosperous agricultural and industrial area with a population of 133,000 persons. Before zoning, pressures were tremendous to use prime agricultural lands for housing developments. Prime agricultural land was defined as any land that would produce 7735 kg/ha or more of corn. Based on this criterion, 68% of the county was rated as "prime."

After a soil survey of Black Hawk County was completed in 1973, a public hearing was held on a proposed county order to zone the county. One very controversial section of the order prohibited the use of prime agricultural lands for residential developments. The county board of supervisors passed the order and land developers moved to the surrounding counties. Within a year, however, the adjoining counties started passing similar orders (Vincent, 1977).

Walworth County, Wisconsin, using a 1966 soil survey as fundamental resource information, passed a sanitary code in 1968 and a shoreland and subdivision zoning order in 1971. Orders such as this help prevent disasters such as that shown in Figure 7-7.

Critical areas are those that either possess unique economic, recreational, historic, or cultural values to the nation, or that pose environmental hazards. Examples of national concern include floodplains, virgin redwood forests, Indian burial grounds, lakeshores, ocean beaches, groundwater recharge areas, unique wilderness areas, waterfowl flyways, prime agricultural land, and historic trails. Soil surveys are as important for delineating critical areas as in preparing

Figure 7-7 A zoning order based on soil maps would have prevented this house from being located on this area of Linside soil series. The soil is a Fluvaquentic Eutrochrept—the prefix "Fluv-" indicates the flooding hazard. (Courtesy H. C. Porter, Virginia Agricultural Experiment Station, Virginia Polytechnic Institute and State University.)

and enforcing city and county zoning ordinances and orders (Steinberg, 1974).

7-4.5 Environmental Impact Statements

Projects involving major soil disturbances such as starting a new housing development, building a new highway, opening a surface mine for coal, or siting a power plant must have prior approval based on an environmental impact statement submitted to the U.S. Council on Environmental Quality. This major innovation was mandated by Section 102(2)(c) of the National Environmental Protection Act (NEPA), passed by the U.S. Congress in 1969 and revised in 1973. By 1977, twenty-two states had passed laws requiring that an environmental impact statement also be filed with the designated state agency.

The essentials of an environmental impact statement include an inventory of air quality, water quality, aquatic life, terrestrial wildlife, people, jobs, transportation, and endangered plant and animal life. Another part of the report consists of predictions of the changes and disturbances that will be caused by the proposed activity. Soil considerations are usually crucial in environmental impact statements because of the wind and water erosion and sedimentation that result from land disturbance.

Teams set up to research and write an environmental impact statement should consist of subject-matter specialists trained in the various environmental areas involved. For example, a forester should be a member of a study team in a forested or potentially forested area, an urban planner in an urban or potentially urban area, and a dairy specialist where dairies exist or are being considered. Because several specialties are involved, the average environmental impact team consists of fifteen to twenty members. Any such team needs to have engineers, scientists, and planners concerned with soil, water, vegetation, and wildlife in addition to those dealing with construction of the proposed development. The team should be under the direction of an administrator who will assure that all pertinent factors are considered on their merits without bias.

SUMMARY

If the Pilgrims could have had soil surveys, they could have used them to guide the agricultural and other developments along the Atlantic Coast; such surveys could also have directed the scientific founding of roads, railroads, and new towns as the pioneers moved westward. Homestead Laws could have been written to permit the ownership of viable economic units rather than an equal area to everyone. But these events are all history, and soil surveys were not used because they were not available.

Soil surveys started in the United States in 1899 and are now used throughout the world. The first surveys in an area are sometimes reconnaissance type, but most others are detailed. Most map units on detailed soil surveys are named as phases of soil series. The surveys are published, usually on a county basis, as a bound volume containing explanatory text and the soil maps on a photographic base.

Land Use Capability Classes, Subclasses, and Units are interpreted from the soil map units. The objective is to place all map units into larger management groups and thereby facilitate maximum intensity of use without excessive erosion and sedimentation.

Each soil map unit can be interpreted for crop adaptations and predicted yields, land value, drainage needs, woodland sites, wildlife habitats, recreational sites, engineering qualities for construction, and other purposes. Soil surveys provide a sound basis for land management for farms and ranches, for mechanizing cultivation in developing countries, for identifying areas of nutritional deficiencies and toxicities for animals and people, for proper disposal of wastes, and for general land development.

Soil survey reports (texts and maps) are valuable as a scientific basis for land use planning. The concepts of *prime* and *unique* agricultural lands were developed to preserve productive soil for essential food, feed, and fiber crops. Such areas are delimited only with the help of a soil survey. Town and county planning and zoning agencies are now using soil surveys as a physical basis for their ordinances and orders.

Various construction projects that result in major soil disturbances now require environmental impact statements. Soil factors are important considerations in the preparation of environmental impact statements.

QUESTIONS

1. What is the principal purpose of a soil survey?
2. Soil surveys are one kind of natural resource data. What are the other principal kinds? Compare the relative use of soil surveys by natural resource and transportation agencies in relation to other kinds of natural resource data.
3. Describe the contents of any recent soil survey report.
4. Select two contrasting soil map unit interpretations and explain their significance to natural resource experts in these respective subjects.
5. Explain the use of soil surveys as a scientific basis for rational planning and zoning.

REFERENCES

ALEXANDER, J. D., S. G. CARMER, and J. B. FEHRENBACHER, 1978. Usefulness of detailed and general soil maps for rural land equalization. *Agronomy Abstracts*, American Society of Agronomy, Madison, Wisc., p. 165.

ALDEN, MILTON, F. P. BAXTER, and J. A. ELDER, 1978. Some considerations in the planning and development of computerized soil data bases for a large region. *Agronomy Abstracts*, American Society of Agronomy, Madison, Wisc., p. 165.

BEESON, K. C., and GENNARD MATRONE, 1976. *The Soil Factor in Nutrition: Animal and Human*, Marcel Dekker, New York, 152 p.

BOWMAN, R. H., and others, 1973. *Soil Survey of the San Diego Area, California. Part II.* USDA—Soil Conservation Service in cooperation with Univ. Cal. Agr. Expt. Sta., U.S. Bureau of Indian Affairs, and Dept. of the Navy— U.S. Marine Corps, 118 p.

BROWN, C. B., 1960. *Effect of Land Use and Treatment on Pollution.* Proceedings of the National Conference on Water Pollution, Dept. of Health, Education, and Welfare, Washington, D.C.

CONSTANTINESCO, I., 1976. *Soil Conservation for Developing Countries.* Soils Bull. 30. Food and Agriculture Organization of the United Nations, Rome, Italy.

COUNCIL OF STATE GOVERNMENTS, 1977. *General Description of Council of State Governments' Natural Resources Data Study.* Preliminary report, mimeographed, unnumbered. Lexington, Kentucky, 6 p.

ENVIRONMENTAL PROTECTION AGENCY, 1973. *Methods for Identifying and Evaluating the Nature and Extent of Nonpoint Sources of Pollutants.* EPA-430/9-73-014, Washington, D.C., p. 7.

ESHETU, TELAHOUN, D. L. HELGESON, and E. V. DUNN, 1976. Attitudes toward land use planning. *North Dakota Farm Research* 34(2):9-14.

JOHNSON, W. M., 1975. Classification and mapping of prime and unique farmlands. In *Recommendations on Prime Lands.* Prepared at the Seminar on Retention of Prime Lands, July 16-17, USDA, p. 189-198.

KELLOGG, C. E., 1961. *Soil Interpretation in the Soil Survey.* Soil Conservation Service USDA, Washington, D.C., 27 p.

KLINE, C. K., D. A. G. GREEN, R. L. DONAHUE, and B. A. STOUT, 1969. *Agricultural Mechanization in Equitorial Africa.* Research Report No. 6. Inst. International Agriculture. Michigan State University. Dec. 1969. p. 633.

KLINGEBIEL, A. A., 1977. Soil Survey Methodology—Use of landsat for determining soil potential. In *Soil Resource Inventories.* Proceedings of a workshop held at Cornell University, Ithaca, New York, April 4-7, p. 101-105.

KUBOTA, JOE, 1975. The poisoned cattle of Willow Creek. *Soil Conservation* 40(9):18-21.

MEGAHAN, W. F., 1972. Logging, erosion, sedimentation: Are they dirty words? *J. Forestry* 70(7), Washington, D.C.

OLSON, G. W., 1974a. *Using Soils of Kansas for Waste Disposal.* Univ. of Kansas, Bull. 208, Lawrence, Kansas.

OLSON, G. W., 1974b. Land classification. *Search Agriculture*, Vol. 4, No. 7, Agronomy No. 4, Cornell Univ. Ag. Exp. Sta., Ithaca, New York, p. 34.

OLSON, G. W., 1977. *Using Soils as Ecological Resources*. Information Bull. 6, Biological Sciences, Agronomy 1, 15 p. Cornell Univ., Ithaca, New York.

PRICE, V. J., 1974. Seventy-five years of the soil survey. *Soil Conservation* 40(4):4-7.

RALSTON, C. W., and G. E. HATCHELL, 1971. Effects of prescribed burning on physical properties of soil. *Proceedings, Prescribed Burning Symposium,* April 14-15, p. 68-85, USDA–Forest Service.

SCHNEPH, MAX, ed., 1977. *Land Use: Tough Choices in Today's World.* Soil Conservation Soc. of Amer., Ankeny, Iowa, 454 p.

SOIL CONSERVATION SERVICE, 1967. *Subdivision Regulations for Canfield, Ohio,* p. 20-35.

SOIL CONSERVATION SERVICE, 1970. *Controlling Erosion on Construction Sites.* Agr. Inform. Bull. 347, Washington, D.C.

SOIL CONSERVATION SERVICE, 1971. *Two Thirds of Our Land: A National Inventory.* Program Aid No. 984, USDA, Washington, D.C.

SOIL CONSERVATION SERVICE, 1974a. *Soil Survey, Eastern Maricopa and Northern Pinal Counties, Arizona.* USDA in cooperation with the Arizona Agr. Expt. Sta.

SOIL CONSERVATION SERVICE, 1974b. *Soil Survey, Pitt County, North Carolina,* in cooperation with the North Carolina Agr. Expt. Sta.

SOIL CONSERVATION SERVICE, 1974c. *Soil Survey of Green County, Illinois,* in cooperation with the Illinois Agr. Expt. Sta.

SOIL CONSERVATION SERVICE, 1974d. *Soil Survey of Brevard County, Florida,* in cooperation with the Univ. of Florida Agr. Expt. Sta.

SOIL CONSERVATION SERVICE, 1974e. *Soil Survey of Harlan County, Nebraska,* in cooperation with the Univ. of Nebraska Conservation and Survey Division.

SOIL CONSERVATION SERVICE, 1974f. *Soil Survey of Cottle County, Texas,* USDA in cooperation with the Texas Agr. Expt. Sta.

SOIL CONSERVATION SERVICE, 1975. *Soil Survey of Lafayette County, Missouri,* in cooperation with the Missouri Agr. Expt. Sta.

SOIL SCIENCE SOCIETY OF AMERICA, 1966. *Soil Surveys and Land Use Planning,* Madison, Wisc. 179 p.

SOIL SURVEY STAFF, 1972. *Soil Series of the United States, Puerto Rico, and the Virgin Islands: Their Taxonomic Classification.* Soil Conservation Service, USDA.

SOIL SURVEY STAFF, 1975. *Soil Taxonomy: A Basic System of Soil Classification for Making and Interpreting Soil Surveys.* Agriculture Handbook No. 436, Soil Conservation Service.

STARNES, EARL, 1973. Land use management. In *Proceedings of the National Symposium on Resource and Land Information,* The Council of State Governments in cooperation with the U.S. Geological Survey and the Office of Land Use and Water Planning, USDI, Reston, Virginia, Nov. 7-9, p. 38.

STEINBERG, ROGER, 1974. *Land Use Planning–Critical Areas.* South Dakota State University Circular FS 630.

U.S. CONGRESS, 1977. *Surface Mining Control and Reclamation Act of 1977.* Public Law 95-87, Washington, D.C.

USDA AGRICULTURAL STATISTICS, 1977. U.S. Government Printing Office, Washington, D.C., p. 420.

VINCENT, GARY, 1977. Land use control by law. *Successful Farming,* Oct., p. A6.

WHETZEL, JOSH, and CHARLES HOGELIN, 1977. Revegetation in the Rockies. *Soil Conservation* 43(5):4-5.

8

Cropping Systems

Native plant cover normally provides good erosion control. Trees, grasses, and other plants provide the protection by which nature limits soil loss to the rate of soil formation. Problems arise, though, when an area is converted to cropland. The crops grown are often much less effective than the native vegetation for controlling erosion. The resulting soil loss reduces soil productivity and increases environmental pollution.

Most cropping systems leave some or all of the soil surface exposed during part of the year. The impact of water or wind on the soil at such times can do serious damage. High rates of erosion can occur when plant cover is inadequate. The damage in many fields could be greatly reduced by adjusting the cropping systems to minimize exposure of the soil to the most erosive wind- and rainstorms. Vegetation can protect soil from excessive erosion if an adequate cover is maintained. Appropriate cropping systems are designed to protect both present and future productivity by controlling erosion.

8-1 PLANT COVER

The first requirement for a crop is that it be adapted to the environment in which it is to be grown. Tropical fruits are grown in warm climates and kept away from freezing conditions. Crops such as corn and soybeans that evade cold weather by growing in the summer are grown where summer moisture is available, whereas earlier maturing crops such as small grains are grown where the summers are dry. Every crop has its own limited range of climatic adaptation and needs to be grown under appropriate conditions.

Soil factors are also important for producing plant growth. A wet, puddled soil is good for paddy rice but bad for most other crops. Blueberries, strawberries, and other iron-loving crops do best in acid soils, but most other crops produce maximum growth in the slightly acid to nearly neutral range.

Poor crop growth can be a disaster to the soil and to the environment as well as to the grower. Poor growth exposes the soil to erosion by raindrop splash, runoff, and wind. The eroded soil is deposited elsewhere, often helping to bury plants under a layer of sediment, fill reservoirs, eutrophy streams, and cause other damage to the environment.

8-1.1 Amount of Plant Cover Needed

The amount of plant cover needed to protect a soil depends on the nature of the soil and the intensity of erosive forces at that time and place. Loose soil on steep slopes needs permanent vegetation to intercept raindrops and to limit the amount and velocity of runoff. Vegetation is also needed on land of any slope to keep high wind velocities away from the soil. However, some level soils of appropriate textures and structures are nearly immune to water erosion even without cover. Most soils have characteristics between these extremes and need to have an amount of plant cover that can be attained by proper use and management. Usually the need for cover is much greater at some seasons than at others. The soil loss equations discussed in Chapter 6 provide a means of estimating the adequacy of the cover produced by various cropping systems in a particular situation.

8-1.2 Types of Crops

There are many more kinds of crops grown in different parts of the world than can be discussed here. The best that can be done is to consider several groups or types of crops that cover large areas of land. Crops may be considered for this purpose to include any plants or parts of plants grown for agricultural production. Most crops are considered within the collective domains of agronomy, horticulture, and forestry. Usually some kind of management or culturing is needed to encourage crop growth so that a good yield can be harvested. The harvest may come after a few weeks or months or it may be delayed for years. Annual crops must be planted anew every year, but perennial crops may be planted once and harvested many times.

For discussion purposes, crops will be divided into row crops, small-grain crops, forage crops, and tree crops. Some characteristics of each group will be considered in this section; management factors will be discussed in later sections.

Row Crops. Many crops have traditionally been planted in rows far enough apart to permit cultivation to kill weeds. Often these are a farmer's most profitable crops and therefore receive the most attention. Cotton, corn, soybeans, sorghum, potatoes, sugar beets, sugar cane, and sunflowers are examples of field crops that are usually grown in rows. Truck crops such as most vegetables and small fruits are also grown in rows. The rows facilitate tillage to control weeds, spraying or dusting of pesticides, application of supplemental fertilizer as side-dressing after the crop is established, and finally the harvesting of the crop.

Row crops frequently create problems for soil conservationists. The area between the rows, as shown in Figure 8-1, is often unprotected long enough to be exposed to several erosive rainstorms. Cultivation keeps the soil loose and erodible. Rills form easily where the rows guide water down a slope. The result is usually more erosion while a soil is in row crop than would occur under closer-growing crops. The frequency of growing row crops in a rotation is often limited by the erosion hazard.

Figure 8-1 The soil between these young soybean rows was puddled by rain and crusted when it dried. (Courtesy F. R. Troeh.)

Small Grains. Rice, wheat, barley, oats, and rye are known as small grains or cereal crops. These crops are used to produce bread, cereals, and other foods for people and animals. They can be grown in nearly any climate where cropping is practiced. Rice is the main staple of many areas with warm climates and can be grown in wet conditions that preclude the growth of most other crops. Rye, wheat, barley, and oats are the cash crops and often the only crops grown in many areas with dry seasons because they produce most of their growth during cool fall and spring seasons and are ready for harvest during the warm dry summers. Summer fallow helps to extend their range into still drier climates. In more humid areas, the small grains may be grown in rotation with row crops and forage crops.

Small grains are usually drilled in rows about 15-cm apart or broadcast in the field. Their fast early growth and relatively close plant spacing provides much better erosion control than row crops but not as good as that of most forage crops.

Forage Crops. Crops grown to be fed to livestock as pasture or hay are known as forage or fodder crops. Many grasses and legumes are included either singly or in combination. Some are annuals, some are biennials, and some are perennials. Some are native plants, some are introduced from other parts of the world, and some have been improved by intensive plant breeding.

Forage crops are maintained as permanent cover on areas that are not cultivated because of the soil, climate, or some other reason. They are grown as part of the crop rotation in many fields. They may be kept on the land for only a few months in some fields, for a year in others, and for a few or many years in succession in still others.

Forage crops are grown with close spacing between plants except in areas too dry to support dense vegetation. A dense cover is attained whenever possible by planting crops that grow rapidly, by planting the forage crop along with a companion crop, or by maintaining established stands for a long time.

Forage crops are often considered to be "soil-building crops." This concept is true in some ways but false in other ways. Improved soil fertility is often inferred because many forage crops are legumes and nitrogen-fixing *Rhizobium* bacteria grow on their roots. Crops such as alfalfa or sweetclover have been extensively used to replenish the nitrogen supply of the soil before growing a corn or wheat crop. A large tonnage of plant material should be disked or plowed into the soil when a nitrogen-fertilizer effect is desired. Harvesting the forage crop shortly before disking or plowing results in little or no net addition of nitrogen to the soil and causes a significant net removal of all other nutrients. As shown in Table 8-1, forage crops are actually soil depleting because they remove much larger amounts of such nutrients as K, Ca, and Mg than most other crops. This soil-depleting effect can, however, be reduced by feeding the forage to livestock and returning the manure to the land.

The close spacing of plants in a forage crop coupled with the improved soil structure and permeability provide good protection against erosion. Forage crops are therefore regarded as soil conserving and are useful where the erosion hazard is too great for other crops.

Tree Crops. Trees are grown for many purposes ranging from wood and paper products to Christmas trees and other ornamental uses, to fruit products, to helping restore the fertility of tropical soils. Trees are planted in some places and allowed to spread naturally into other areas. Some trees are grown in pure stands, some are

Table 8-1 Nutrients contained in typical yields of various crops

	Yield *(mt/ha)*	*Nutrients (kg/ha)*					
		N	P	K	Ca	Mg	S
Forage crops:							
Alfalfa hay	9	216	22	177	132	28	26
Lespedeza hay	8	168	15	75	80	15	*a*
Red clover hay	5	95	10	82	57	19	7
Sweetclover hay	12	312	28	214	150	28	49
Timothy hay	4	44	6	64	14	7	5
Row crops:							
Corn grain	7	98	19	20	1	7	8
Peanuts	2.5	75	11	14	2	5	6
Potatoes	20	80	10	96	2	6	4
Soybeans	2.5	150	15	38	6	7	6
Sugar beets	40	104	16	100	16	12	4
Small grains:							
Barley	3	57	12	15	2	4	5
Oats	3	54	14	12	2	5	6
Rice	3	38	8	10	2	4	2
Rye	2	40	7	9	2	2	3
Wheat	3	63	12	13	1	4	6

[a] Data not available.

SOURCE: Calculated from percentage compositions in F. B. Morrison, *Feeds and Feeding,* 1956, Morrison Pub. Co., Ithaca, New York.

mixed with other species of trees, and some grow along with a wide variety of shrubs, grasses, and herbaceous plants.

There are hundreds of species of trees. Collectively, they are suited to a wide range of circumstances. Evergreen trees are most common in climates with dry summers whereas deciduous trees prevail in more humid conditions. Most trees need reasonably good drainage but certain species such as cypress and black spruce grow in swamps. Apple trees grow where the soil freezes in the winter, orange and other citrus fruit damaged by frost are grown in warmer climates, and bananas require tropical conditions. Trees grow in some of the warmest and wettest climates on earth and prevail far into the cold climates but give way to smaller plants such as grasses and herbaceous species in the drier climates.

Trees combined with undergrowth or a litter layer provide strong protection from erosion. Raindrops are intercepted by the leaves and branches, intercepted again by lower branches and undergrowth, and finally absorbed by the litter layer without having a chance to strike the soil surface. The protected soil surface retains a porous structure and the infiltration rate is much faster than it would be if a crust could form. Runoff volume is reduced because more water infiltrates. Runoff velocity is slowed as the water trickles through the litter layer and around the trees and other plants. Most soil loss from such settings is either by solution erosion in the percolating water or by sudden, rare, particularly intense rains that produce runoff concentrated enough to wash away the cover and cut a gully. Storms that may occur only once in thousands of years sometimes scour all the vegetation and soil away from an area and leave bare bedrock exposed. Even then, adjacent areas outside the main flow of runoff may be undamaged.

Not all trees provide as much protection as outlined in the preceding paragraph. Exposed soil in a clean-cultivated orchard, for example, is subject to erosion. Raindrop impact can be damaging even under the trees because drops falling off tree branches are often quite large. Erosion control requires cover to intercept these drops again nearer the soil surface.

8-1.3 Plant Population and Row Spacing

A bluegrass pasture should have millions of plants per hectare, while a few hundred trees may cover a nearby hectare. Most other plant populations fall somewhere between these extremes. The number of plants is, of course, likely to be inversely related to their size.

The number of plants grown per hectare of cropland can be quite important to both yields and erosion control. Newer varieties of some crops have been developed to be grown at higher populations than were formerly common. For example, top corn yields are likely to require 50,000 to 70,000 plants per hectare instead of the old standard of about 30,000 plants per hectare. The older varieties do not produce well at the higher densities because the crowding causes many barren stalks and reduced grain production.

Increased plant population in row crops is achieved by either narrower rows or closer spacing in the row or both. Although spacing plants equally in all directions helps minimize crowding and maximize protection of the soil against erosion, cultivation and harvesting practices often require that certain crops be grown in rows.

Field crops such as corn, soybeans, sorghum, sugar beets, potatoes, and cotton were often planted in rows 1 m apart so a horse could walk between the rows for cultivation. The 1-m spacing survived in many places long after tractors replaced horses. Narrower rows of 50- or 75-cm spacing have increased in popularity in recent years where tractors have become the rule and herbicides have eliminated much of the cultivation. The minimum row width is limited by tire width, driving precision, and equipment design. Some variable spacings are used with wider intervals for the wheel tracks than for other rows.

Narrow rows are often elected because they usually increase crop yields. The plants are better spaced to absorb sunlight, more water gets into the soil where the plants can use it, and the more complete crop canopy keeps the soil cooler so less water is lost by evaporation. Erosion control is also improved. Crops in 50-cm row spacing, for example, grow together and cover the space between the rows at an earlier date than those planted in 1-m rows. Fewer raindrops are able to strike the bare soil and cause erosion where the rows are narrow, more water infiltrates because the soil surface is less likely to crust, and less water accumulates in any one place to become erosive runoff. Mannering and Johnson (1969) found that infiltration was increased by 24% and soil loss was reduced by 35% where soybeans were grown in narrow rows (51cm) rather than wide rows (102 cm).

8-1.4 Soil Fertility and Fertilizers

Dramatic improvements in erosion control and reduced sedimentation can often be achieved through the proper use of fertilizers. Vigorous crops protect the soil much more effectively than weak ones, and vigorous crops require a high level of soil fertility. Fertilizers are therefore as important for conserving soil as they are for increasing yield.

A good soil fertility program combined with the best crop varieties and close plant spacing may reduce soil loss to less than half as much as would occur under the same crop with low fertility and wide row spacing (Whitaker, Jamison, and Thornton, 1961). Higher fertility produces a better stand and larger plants at all stages of growth including the critical early period when the soil is most exposed to erosion.

The proper amount and timing of fertilizer applications depends on soil, crop, and weather. The fertility status of the soil may be estimated if enough is known about the nature of the soil (depth, texture, organic-matter content, pH, drainage, and so on) and its cropping and fertilizer history. Rather than rely too heavily on such an estimate, however, it is usually better to have the soil tested at least once every four years. The cost of such tests is easily regained through more accurate fertilization. Excess fertilizer is expensive and can contribute to water pollution; too little fertilizer results in reduced yield.

Each crop has its own fertility needs and its own pattern of response to different levels of supply of the essential nutrients. A few examples will illustrate this point. Members of the legume family such as beans, peas, and clovers normally obtain nitrogen from their symbiotic relationship with *Rhizobium* bacteria and therefore do not need nitrogen fertilizer. They do need adequate supplies of all other nutrients, and many legumes, especially those used as forage crops, need enough lime to keep the soil pH near neutral. Most nonlegume crops, on the other hand, respond more dramatically to nitrogen than to any other plant nutrient. Large amounts of nitrogen fertilizer are used for members of the grass family such as corn, small grains, and the forage grasses.

The tonnage of growth produced and the part of the plant harvested influence the fertilizer needs of both the crop being considered and the next crop to be grown on the same land. As was shown in Table 8-1, a crop of twelve metric tons of sweetclover hay removes much larger quantities of nutrients than a three-ton crop of barley or oats grown on the same land. A large hay crop depends on a good supply of nutrients. And the large removal of potassium can leave the soil depleted and require extra amounts of potassium fertilizer for the next crop.

Weather influences fertilizer use in several ways including the choice of crop, the rate of crop growth, the loss of nutrients from the soil, the availability of nutrients that remain in the soil, and the ability of the soil to support a truck loaded with fertilizer. Even a crop adapted to the climate may suffer if the weather is cooler than usual in the spring or warmer than usual in the summer. Changes of a few degrees in soil temperature can make the difference between seeds rotting or germinating to produce a good stand. A few degrees can also make dramatic differences in the growth rate and nutrient requirements of seedlings.

Weather cool enough to retard growth is often wet enough for poor drainage to further limit growth on many soils and for leaching to deplete the supply of available nutrients in the soil solution. Intermittent wetness also leads to loss of much of the available nitrogen from the soil by denitrification, a microbial process by which nitrates formed by oxidation during dry periods are reduced to gaseous forms (N_2, N_2O, and NO) during wet periods. Nitrogen availability can also be limited by the effects of warm, dry weather. Capillary movement and evaporation at the soil surface combine to concentrate soluble salts such as nitrates in a surface crust where there is very little root activity. The nitrogen in such crusts is only temporarily unavailable because the next rain can wash it back down into the root zone.

Wet conditions often hamper plant absorption of potassium and, to a lesser extent, of other nutrients. The absorption process requires energy because nutrients are usually absorbed against a concentration gradient (the concentration in the plant roots may be several times higher than in the soil solution). Excessive wetness deprives the roots of oxygen and thereby restricts the oxidation processes that provide energy for root growth and nutrient absorption. More potassium is therefore needed in wet years and in poorly drained soils than in drier situations.

8-1.5 Seasonal Changes in Plant Cover

Seasonal variations occur in both the amount of plant cover produced by a crop and in the amount of protection the soil needs against erosive forces. A storm of large enough magnitude to cause disastrous erosion when there is little plant cover on the ground might cause very little damage later in the season.

The most hazardous periods occur when the soil is exposed by tillage for the planting of a new crop and during the early growth stages while the plants are too small to protect the soil, as shown in Figure 8-2. The erosion hazard diminishes as the percentage of bare ground remaining between plants decreases. Such changes are considered as components of the cropping factors in the soil-loss equations discussed in Chapter 6.

Figure 8-2 The erosion hazard is greatest while plants are small and diminishes as the growing plants cover the soil more completely. (Courtesy F. R. Troeh.)

Seasonal changes are most significant where annual crops are grown because new plants must be established every year and there is often a cold or a dry season between the harvesting of one crop and the planting of the next. Some soils suffer excessive erosion, for example, when the land is plowed after harvest in the fall and the bare ground is left exposed until a spring crop is planted. The exposure time is even longer where a year of summer fallow is used between crops. The practice of plowing land and leaving the bare soil exposed may sometimes have advantages for controlling weeds, insects, and plant diseases but it greatly increases the erosion hazard. Usually there are cropping and tillage alternatives that provide cover most of the time in the form of either plant residues or growing plants. Tillage practices that leave plant residues on the surface are especially useful where moisture must be conserved for the next crop and are discussed in Chapter 9.

Perennial crops also have seasonal changes that should not be overlooked. The cover in a hay field is greatly reduced for a time after the hay is cut. Even a pasture may be grazed heavily enough at some season to permit a heavy storm to cause erosion. Overgrazing is especially serious when it occurs along with trampling damage during a wet season or while the vegetation has stopped growing because of a drought.

Even tree crops have seasonal changes. Fortunately, the litter layer often provides adequate protection even under trees that lose their leaves for a season. The erosion hazard is greatly increased when someone rakes the leaves from beneath such trees or when the ground is bared partially by clear-cutting the trees.

8-2 MANAGING MONOCULTURES

Cropping systems in which the same crop is grown on the same land year after year are known as monocultures. The advantages and disadvantages of monocultures and crop rotations have been long debated without either system being eliminated. Each system is important in its own time and place. Monocultures will be discussed in this section and crop rotations in Section 8-3.

A monoculture permits a farmer to specialize in a particular crop and to handle the land strictly in accord with the needs of that crop. Usually the crop chosen is particularly suited to the soil and climate and to the economic opportunities for profit. Sometimes the soil and topography on a farm are variable enough to justify two or more monocultures rather than a rotation. For example, a farmer in a humid region might grow a row crop continuously on level land, hay on sloping land, and pasture on steep land. Another farmer in a drier climate might use large areas for rangeland, grow wheat on the most productive nonirrigated land, have an orchard on permeable sloping land in an irrigated valley, and perhaps use a crop rotation on the flatter terraces in the valley. Wet bottomland might be used for pasture. Each crop is grown where it fits best rather than trying to grow all the crops in rotation.

8-2.1 Annual Cash Crops

Arguments about monocultures usually center on the effects of growing annual crops such as wheat, corn, or cotton year after year on the same land. Farmers often grow these crops on as much land as possible because they provide a source of cash income. The monoculture system puts the most profitable crops on the available land every year rather than alternating them with other crops.

It was long assumed that certain monocultures such as continuous corn would ruin land. Indeed, yields from such systems soon dropped to low levels when they were tried without fertilizers. But after fertilizers became available it was found that well-fertilized continuous corn could produce yields as high as that grown in rotation. The yield results satisfied some people but others argued that the physical condition of the soil was deteriorating and the rate of erosion was excessive. The argument continues even now, partly because each side can choose situations that illustrate its point and partly because some people are more concerned than others about erosion and soil structure.

Corn can now be grown as a monoculture on certain soils without serious damage, but other soils are damaged by the same treatment. The damage is either soil loss by erosion on sloping land and sedimentation elsewhere or breakdown of soil structure producing poor drainage on level land. Persons using monocultures and other intensive-use cropping systems should be alert to such problems. Sometimes an intensive rotation is worse than a monoculture. For example, many farmers in the corn belt now grow corn and soybeans in rotation and suffer more erosion than they would with continuous corn. Soybeans are a legume but they are also a row crop that produces less cover than corn does.

Several things can be done to reduce the detrimental effects that may occur with intensive cropping systems such as cash-crop monocultures. The first thing is to limit such systems to suitable soils. The next thing is to plant the crop in narrow rows and make it grow as well as possible by providing all the lime, fertilizer, improved drainage, and other factors it needs. Then, tillage practices should be chosen to use the crop residues to protect the soil from erosion while there is no crop growing and to return as much organic matter to the soil as possible.

8-2.2 Forage Crop Monocultures

Land that is too steep for row crops and small grains is often used for hay or pasture. Close-growing perennial grasses and legumes provide excellent erosion control. Actually, combinations of grasses and a legume are commonly used for forage crops so they are not strictly monocultures. However, since the same crop remains on the land year after year, it is convenient to group these mixed forages with the true monocultures.

Management of land in forage crops is more often neglected than that of tilled land. Such neglect is unfortunate; good management can increase profit from this land and reduce soil loss at the same time. Three main factors are involved—soil fertility practices, good grazing or harvesting management, and occasional reseeding where feasible and needed. Some pastures in humid regions also need to be clipped (mowed) once or twice a year to keep weeds, trees, and brush from invading the pasture.

Fertilizer and lime can be used not only to increase forage production but also to help control the composition of mixed forages. Liming to near neutral pH combined with adequate phosphorus, potassium, and any other deficient nutrients will help maintain legumes in the stand. Nitrogen applications will favor the grasses and are often omitted where the grasses might crowd out the legumes.

Managing the livestock in a pasture and the haying equipment in a hay field are the most important means of controlling erosion on these lands. Enough plant growth should be left on the land to protect the soil and to maintain a thick growth of vigorous plants. The plants should be allowed to reseed themselves periodically, especially on land that is never tilled and reseeded. Late fall and early spring grazing should be avoided or limited to avoid weakening the plants.

Systems of rotation grazing usually result in more forage production and better utilization than uncontrolled grazing. Large pastures may be managed in the manner described for rangeland in Chapter 13. Smaller, more intensively managed pastures are sometimes grazed on a daily pasture basis by means of a movable electric fence. A fresh pasture is provided each day and enough livestock are placed in it to eat all the forage that day. This system often causes livestock to eat forage that they would leave untouched if they had more room to roam. Rotation grazing thereby achieves the rapid and complete utilization followed by a long regrowth period that is normally characteristic of a hay field.

Much land in forage crops has soil that is too shallow, stony, rough, wet, or otherwise limited to ever be tilled. Some land, however, is used to produce hay or pasture because of steep slope, dry climate, or some other reason that does not prevent occasional tillage. It is sometimes worthwhile to plow such land and reseed it to an improved type of forage. Often the legume component will be increased by reseeding, and the dominant grasses may be replaced with more desirable species. Usually a small-grain crop can be grown as a companion crop with the new seeding. Little erosion occurs because the sod from the previous forage crop helps hold the soil until the new crop becomes established. The fast-growing grain crop also helps control erosion, and the harvested grain helps defray the reseeding costs. Alternatively, a range or pasture may be renovated without plowing. A herbicide or perhaps shallow tillage with a disk may be used to kill part or all of the old vegetation before reseeding.

8-2.3 Tree Crops

Forest management is discussed in Chapter 13, but tree crops such as orchards and Christmas trees grown outside of forests are included here. These crops provide a good combination of income and erosion control in many places where other crops are less desirable. The scale of tree-crop enterprises ranges from a tree or two in a back yard to large orchards covering many hectares. Some growers devote all of their land to tree crops, whereas others use them only in odd corners or on steep slopes or other problem areas. The versatility of tree crops would undoubtedly make them useful to many more people than presently grow them.

Tree crops normally occupy land for years at a time. A few years growth is required before there is any harvest. The harvest usually extends over a period of years either in the form of annual fruit harvest or by selective tree-cutting. The time period may be extended indefinitely by planting new trees when old ones are removed.

Properly managed tree crops provide excellent erosion control even on steep erosive soils. Usually some kind of grass or other vegetation is needed for a cover crop between the trees. The cover crop must be considered when plans are made for applying lime, fertilizer, and irrigation water. A hay crop is sometimes removed from between the trees before pickers are sent in to harvest fruit. The cover crop helps protect the soil from erosion and from the traffic that passes through the orchard. The drastic amount of erosion that can occur where there is no cover crop shows in some orchards where the soil around each tree stands up like an island surrounded by eroded areas.

Trees are used in certain tropical areas as soil-improving crops in rotation with other crops. The slash-and-burn system of shifting cultivation (Section 20-3) has permitted agriculture to survive in places where soil fertility is difficult to maintain. The trees accumulate plant nutrients over a period of years. Burning the trees and scattering the ashes makes the nutrients available to other crops. Both soil fertility and soil physical condition deteriorate while annual crops are grown. The system works where there is enough land to permit two or three years of annual crops to be grown in rotation with extended periods of forest. Many areas that were once cropped by the slash-and-burn system can no longer be kept forested because of increased population pressure. Fertilizers help maintain the soil fertility but do little for the soil's physical condition.

8-3 CROP ROTATIONS

Two or more crops grown in a repetitive sequence on the same land constitute a crop rotation. Erosion, plant diseases, and other problems can often be controlled with a rotation on land where a monoculture of the most profitable crop might be disastrous. The soil-conserving crops in the rotation not only protect the soil while they are growing but also have a carryover effect that reduces erosion while the next crop is growing. The soil loss from a field of cotton, for example, might be only half as much when grown following a forage crop as it would be if the cotton followed another cotton crop. Rotations can also break insect and disease cycles and control persistent weeds resulting from monocultures.

A crop rotation often provides more continuous cover than is possible when the same annual crop is grown year after year. Many row crops are planted in the spring and harvested in the fall. Growing two such crops in succession leaves the soil without any crop during the winter. However, a forage crop might be grown during that time if the winter is not too severe. Forage crops are often included in rotations for their soil-conserving effects. Some are plowed under as a green manure crop in time for planting a row crop; others are left for one or more years of hay or pasture in the rotation.

Crop rotations necessarily differ from one part of the world to another in response to the climatic conditions, crops grown, the nature of the soil, and the kind and severity of erosion problems. The wet-dry seasons of some tropical areas, for example, require different crops and different management than the warm-cold seasons of the temperate regions. But both of these climates have a season when the soil is likely to be unprotected because the weather is unfavorable to the primary crops of the area. Rotations that provide cover during these dry or cold seasons help control erosion.

8-3.1 Planning a Rotation

The sequence of crops in many rotations is fixed and repetitive and can be projected as many years into the future as desired. Such rotations are designed to produce approximately the same amount of each crop each year and can be used as a basis for planning and managing crop production. Relatively constant production is achieved by dividing the land into as many parts as there are years in the rotation. A four-year rotation, for example, requires four fields or groups of fields of fairly equal productive capacity.

As an example of a fixed rotation, consider a farmer in the corn belt using a corn-corn-oats-meadow rotation (CCOM). This farm has six fields containing 18, 16, 15, 6, 6, and 5 ha, respectively. Though separated, the three small fields are equivalent to one field of 17 ha. The rotation can therefore be applied on the basis of four fields containing 18, 16, 15, and 17 ha. Each field can then be assigned to a specific crop each year, as shown in Table 8-2. With this arrangement there are always two fields in corn, one in oats, and one in meadow.

A farmer using a three-year rotation on the example farm could use the three small fields along with the three larger fields to form three pairs totaling 23, 22, and 21 ha, respectively. Or, two 33-ha field groups could be formed for a two-year rotation.

If two or more rotations are used on the same farm, each should have its own set of fields with balanced productive capacities. The total production of the farm is automatically balanced when the individual rotations are balanced.

Fixed rotations allow productivity and erosion control to be adjusted to the capability and needs of the land, but such scheduling is not always possible. Variable weather, for example, may require that plans be adjusted from year to year. Rotations can still be beneficial under such conditions, but their effects and benefits are less predictable than those of fixed rotations.

8-3.2 Companion Crops

A small-grain crop and a forage crop are often planted together as companion crops. The small-grain crop grows rapidly and is harvested within a few months. The forage crop is often alfalfa, a clover, or a slow-growing pasture grass that becomes well established about the time the small grain is harvested. The forage crop is then used for hay or pasture for one or more years (or it may be used for green manure as discussed in Section 8-3.4).

Table 8-2 The field plan for a corn-corn-oats-meadow crop rotation

	Years				
	1	*2*	*3*	*4*	*5[a]*
Field 1	C	C	O	M	C
Field 2	C	O	M	C	C
Field 3	O	M	C	C	O
Field 4	M	C	C	O	M

[a]The fifth year is the same as the first. Succeeding years are repetitions of the second and later years.

The small-grain member of companion crops has sometimes been called a "nurse crop." This erroneously implies that the tiny grass and legume plants need protection from the elements. Actually, the forage crop becomes established more rapidly and often produces a better stand if it is planted alone. Companion crops compete for water, plant nutrients, and sunlight, causing the small seedlings of the forage crop to develop slowly. If the small grain grows too vigorously, it may choke out the forage crop. It is usually wise to plant less small-grain seed per hectare when there is a companion crop than would be used for a maximum grain yield.

Fertilizer can be used to help control the growth of companion crops. Nitrogen should be used sparingly because it would favor the grain crop. Most other fertilizer elements and lime should be applied at rates determined by soil tests to encourage growth of the forage crop. Grass-type forages can be fertilized with nitrogen after the grain crop has been harvested.

Companion crops are very useful for controlling soil erosion and sedimentation. The small grain normally starts fast enough to provide reasonable protection within a short time. Thus the soil is covered rather than bare during the establishment period for the forage crop. Harvesting the small grain leaves both its residue and the growing forage crop to protect the soil. The close-growing nature of the forage crop provides excellent protection, and its soil-conserving effects normally carry over into the succeeding row crop.

8-3.3 Cover Crops

Cover crops are grown to protect the soil rather than for harvest. They fill gaps in either time or space when the other crops would leave the ground bare. Cover crops in a rotation are grown during cold or dry seasons unfavorable to the cash crops. Cover crops in an orchard are grown between and beneath the trees. In either case, their purpose is erosion control. Their use is limited in dry climates because they use soil water and leave the soil too dry for the next crop.

Hardy plants are needed to stand the cold or dry conditions under which cover crops are grown in rotations. They are either slow-starting plants that can be seeded along with the preceding crop or fast-growing plants that can become established rapidly after the previous crop is harvested. Several small-seeded legumes such as sweetclover, red clover, crimson clover, and vetch are examples of slow-starting cover crops. Fast-growing types include Austrian winter peas, rye, oats, and ryegrass. Timing is especially critical with the fast-growing types to allow them to grow large enough and thick enough between harvest and the cold or dry weather so they will protect the soil.

Cover crops in rotations normally do not mature. They are often plowed or disked into the soil as green manure. Young and succulent material has a lower carbon-to-nitrogen ratio and decomposes more readily than mature plant residues. The effect on soil fertility is good because decomposition releases plant nutrients rapidly. The effect on soil structure is also favorable because active microbes produce exudates that stabilize soil aggregates.

Cover crops may be killed or have their growth temporarily stopped by an appropriate herbicide. This method is used in no-tillage systems. Either a single main crop or a rotating sequence may be planted each year into the herbicide-treated cover crop.

Cover crops in orchards and vineyards are usually perennials that last for years without replanting. Forage crops such as alfalfa are often used. A mixture including one or more grass species may be used to produce a thicker stand and provide better erosion control. Legumes in the mixture help to reduce the nitrogen requirement of the crops.

A vigorous cover crop is desirable for erosion control in an orchard or vineyard but it may interfere with harvesting the fruit. Two alternatives are available: the forage crop may be harvested and removed or it may be beaten down into a mat before the fruit is harvested.

8-3.4 Green Manure

Plowing or disking a growth of forage into the soil as green manure benefits a soil's organic-matter content, structure, and permeability. Either the growth produced by a cover crop or the last growth of a forage crop may be used in this manner. The more growth there is the better, except that young succulent growth is best because it contains a higher concentration of plant nutrients and decomposes faster than older material.

Green manure can easily add more tons of organic matter per hectare to the soil than would likely be added in manure or other organic materials spread on the soil. The fresh organic matter decomposes readily and the population of soil microbes multiplies. This microbial activity produces cementing agents that have a strong positive effect on soil structure. Soil permeability is often increased by root channels produced by the crop, by channels held open by the plant residues, and by improved soil structure. The increased permeability improves soil aeration so that plant roots are better supplied with oxygen.

Green manure crops are often followed by impressive crop yields attained with little or no fertilizer. Part of this effect can be attributed to the nitrogen fixed when a legume is used for green manure. But the effect also occurs with nonlegume green manures and with nutrients other than nitrogen. The release of nutrients from the decomposition of the green manure is the key to this enhanced fertility. Nutrients that are normally released slowly from the soil can often be made available fairly rapidly by decomposition. The green manure crop thus serves to accumulate available nutrients for release to the next crop.

8-3.5 Crop Residue Utilization

Crop residues are much too valuable to be ignored. Sometimes they are used to feed livestock either by allowing them to graze in the field or by hauling the straw, stalks, or other residues to the livestock. Another type of utilization is sought by research aimed at making plastic or an energy source such as alcohol from the residues. But, to a soil conservationist, crop residue utilization means using the residues either as mulch to protect the soil or as raw material for soil organic matter. The effectiveness of residues for protecting the soil is important enough to be assigned first priority. There should always be enough residues left to control erosion and maintain satisfactory soil physical conditions.

Crop residues are usually available during the time between crops when the soil would otherwise be unprotected. This timeliness makes them an important factor in erosion control.

The soil protection afforded by crop residues is roughly proportional to the percentage of the soil surface that they cover. Residues that have been plowed under are no more effective as soil cover than those removed from the field. Bare, clean-tilled fields are very erodible. Leaving residues on the soil surface is an easy, cost-free means of conserving soil and water.

Different crops produce different kinds and amounts of residues. The stubble and straw from a small-grain crop usually provide adequate protection if they are simply left in place in the field; neither wind nor rain is able to exert much erosive power on the soil surface. The coarser residues left from a corn crop may need to be knocked down or chopped into small pieces to cover the soil between the rows.

Any tillage performed on the residues will affect their value as a mulch. Plowing will cover most of the residues and leave little or no soil protection. Disking covers about half of the residues but still leaves considerable protection. Chisel-type implements often leave about 80% of the residues on the surface. The practice of leaving significant amounts of residues on the surface during fallow periods, as shown in Figure 8-3, is known as *stubble mulching*.

Negative feelings toward stubble mulching and other crop-residue utilization practices arise when residues plug tillage implements. Plugging was common with many older implements, but machinery designers have since developed cutters and large open frameworks that work through the residues. The old practice of burning stubble or other crop residues has been mostly eliminated by these newer implements combined with the use of fertilizers that help decompose residues.

Plant residues mixed with soil decompose at rates depending on the nature of the residues, the supply of nutrients (especially nitrogen) available to the soil microbes, the soil temperature, and the water and air supply in the soil. Half or more of the residues will decompose during the first few months if conditions favor microbial activity. The remainder is more resistant than average, and the rate of decomposition becomes slower with time. The last remaining organic material is finely divided and resistant enough to be considered humus. Plant parts are no longer identifiable at this stage. Probably no more than 20% of the original residue weight remains, and most of that has been converted into microbial tissue. The time required for residues to reach this stage ranges from a few months in a well-drained soil in the tropics to several years in a cold climate or where the soil is permanently saturated with water.

Soil humus decomposes much more slowly than fresh plant residues, but it does decompose. Humus decomposition needs to be offset by humus formed from residues to maintain the organic-matter content of the soil. The residues and humus release plant nutrients as they decompose. The microbes that carry out decomposition produce exudates that help hold soil aggregates together and stabilize soil structure. Decomposing organic materials thus contribute to both soil fertility and to a desirable soil physical condition. Organic materials that are not in the process of decomposing contribute relatively little to soil fertility and soil structure but may increase permeability and reduce erosion and sedimentation.

Decomposition is often slowed by an inadequate supply of nitrogen. Many crop residues such as straw, stalks, and leaves are high in carbon but low in nitrogen. Microbes decomposing these residues

Figure 8-3 Stubble mulching protects the soil with both crop residues and clods. (Courtesy Washington State University.)

use available nitrogen from the soil. Inadequate soil nitrogen at this time results in slow decomposition and can severely retard crop growth. Under such conditions, crops respond dramatically to nitrogen fertilizer. Enough fertilizer should be applied to meet the needs of both the microbes and the crop.

Crop residues provide enough shade to keep a mulched soil cooler than a bare soil. The temperature difference can reach $10°$ to $20°C$ at a depth of 1 cm, during the heat of the day, though average differences are only $2°$ or $3°C$. The cooling effect of the mulch is generally beneficial in tropical climates and during the summer season in temperate regions. It can be detrimental, however, in the spring when a wet soil needs to dry out and warm up before it can be tilled and a crop planted. Mulching in temperate regions is therefore most desirable on well-drained soils. Fortunately, the well-drained soils usually coincide with the sloping areas that most need mulching for erosion control.

8-4 MULTIPLE CROPPING

Multiple cropping, also called sequential cropping (two or more crops a year in sequence) or intercropping (two or more crops on the

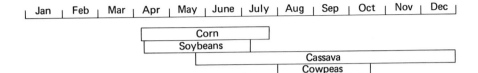

Figure 8-4 A multiple cropping schedule used in some fertility and row-spacing experiments in Peru. (After Soil Science Department, North Carolina State University, 1974.)

same field at the same time), is related to crop rotations in that the same land is used to produce more than one crop. Sequential cropping is essentially a crop rotation compressed into one year. Crop rotations that involve companion crops and monocultures such as orchards in which a cover crop is grown beneath the trees are closely related to intercropping. The difference is that intercropping overlaps the main growth phases of two or more harvestable crops. The crops involved include a variety of annual crops and tropical tree crops. At least one crop in the combination is planted in wide enough rows for another crop to be grown in between. An example of a schedule used in some experiments in Peru is shown in Figure 8-4.

Multiple cropping is most common in warm, humid tropical areas. Many such areas have small holdings that are intensively used, mostly to produce food for local consumption. Multiple cropping permits each family to produce a more varied and nutritious diet than monocultures or ordinary crop rotations would provide. Multiple cropping is similarly used in many gardens in various parts of the world.

Coffee, bananas, and several other tropical tree crops are intercropped with each other or with annual crops. Multiple benefits are obtained, for example, by growing bananas among coffee trees. The coffee trees need protection from both sun and wind. They are kept trimmed to a height of about three meters, a height easily exceeded by the fast-growing banana plants. The bananas also produce an abundance of leaves that cover the soil and protect it from erosion (Constantinesco, 1976).

Figure 8-5 illustrates an intercrop combination of upland rice growing between banana plants. The annual rice crop acts as a cover protecting the soil while the banana plants are young. The combination is said to protect against insects by confusing them as they try to locate their host plant by smell.

One objective of multiple cropping is to increase the total production from the land. Work done in densely populated areas in Costa Rica and El Salvador showed yields from each of the individual

Figure 8-5 Bananas and rice being grown together in inter-cropping in Gambia, West Africa. (Courtesy Roy L. Donahue.)

intercrops ranging from 30% to 107% of monoculture yields (Table 8-3). The reduced production from individual crops was more than offset by the presence of additional crops. The intercropping systems were considerably more profitable than the monocultures. Both multiple-crop yields and monoculture yields were improved by fertilization. The medium fertility level produced more profit than the low level in spite of relatively high fertilizer prices in the area.

Soil conservation is an important bonus from multiple cropping. Two or more crops growing on the same area almost always cover the ground better and longer than a single crop. More raindrops are intercepted, runoff is slowed, and erosion is markedly reduced. Erosion data are scarce, but the difference is often large enough to be obvious even without measurement, especially in comparison to a monoculture of the more open row crop included in the system.

8-5 STRIP CROPPING

Strip cropping divides a field into long narrow parcels that cross the path of the erosive force of water or wind. The individual strips are

Table 8-3 Relative yields of intercropped short-statured crops expressed as percent of monoculture yields

	Fertility level		
Crop	*Low*	*Medium*	*High*
Rice (January planting)	32	38	46
Rice (May planting)	44	30	39
Beans (bush-type)	87	91	78
Beans (climbing-type)	56	64	78
Soybeans (January planting)	107	70	84
Soybeans (May planting)	54	52	50
Sweet potatoes	93	92	86

SOURCE: Soil Science Department, North Carolina State University, 1974.

used to grow the various crops in a crop rotation so that the strips with the denser or taller vegetative cover can help provide protection for the more exposed soil in other strips. Thus the entire field receives enough protection to reduce the average soil loss to as little as one-fourth of what it would be in the same field with the same rotation but without the strips (see Section 6–3.5).

Some applications of strip cropping use permanent vegetation in designated protective strips and use the remaining area for either a crop rotation or a monoculture. More often, the protective vegetation is one of the crops in a rotation that shifts annually from one strip to the next. Such systems combine the favorable effects of crop rotations with contour tillage (Section 9–7), and often include the use of cover crops, green manures, and crop residues. Such a combination of practices is very effective for reducing erosion and sedimentation.

Strip cropping is an inexpensive means of reducing erosion and is usually very effective. Nevertheless, it is used less now than it once was. One reason for the decline is the shift of many farmers from crop rotations to monocultures. Other factors limiting its use are the inconvenience of farming long narrow parcels with large implements and the susceptibility of the long exposed edges to disease and insect attacks. Hot dry winds desiccating exposed edges are a negative factor in semiarid climates. Other erosion-control practices such as crop-residue utilization are more suitable than strip cropping under such conditions.

8-5.1 Contour Strip Cropping

Contour strip cropping is one of the most effective means of controlling water erosion while growing crops in a rotation. If necessary, terracing can be added for still better erosion control. Contour strip cropping is simple to apply where the slopes are long, smooth, and of uniform gradient, as shown in Figure 8–6. Variable slope gradients and rolling topography make it less practical to use contour practices of any kind.

One of the most important design factors of contour strip cropping is the width of the strips. Row crop strips must be limited in width to avoid excessive runoff and erosion. Forage crop strips must be at least wide enough to afford adequate protection and capacity to filter sediment from the runoff water. Recommended strip-width limits are given in Table 8–4. These limits assume a deep soil of average erodibility with slopes long enough to give a relief (elevation difference) of about five meters where the rainfall factor (as shown in Figure 6–1) is 400, or a relief of ten meters where the rainfall factor is 200. Soil-loss equation factors given in Chapter 6 can be used to adjust these strip widths where conditions differ markedly from those specified.

The strip widths chosen for a field should be exact multiples of the width of the row crop equipment to be used. Thus if a farmer is planting, cultivating, and harvesting six 75-cm rows at a time, the strip widths should be some multiple of 4.5 m. On a 4% slope, for example, widths of 9 m for the forage strips and 27 m for the row

Figure 8–6 Contour strip cropping divides the slope length into short segments to control erosion. (Courtesy F. R. Troeh.)

257

Table 8-4 Recommended limits for strip widths for contour strip cropping

Slope (%)	Forage crop strip minimum width (m)	Row crop strip maximum width (m)
2	8	40
5	10	25
8	12	20
12	15	15
18	30	8

crop strips might be chosen. These widths would be appropriate for a five-year rotation including three years of row crop, one year of small grain, and one year of hay. Each year in the rotation is assigned a 9-m strip and the three years of row crop together total 27 m. The small-grain strip would be included in the layout as shown in Figure 8-7 but is omitted from the calculations because its soil loss will be near the average of that for the other crops.

Contour strip cropping on slopes up to 2% or 3% may not always include forage strips. Instead, the small-grain strip may be relied upon to provide the needed protection. Such strips should be about three times as wide as a hay strip would need to be and should include a seeding for a winter-cover green-manure crop.

The row crop may be left out of a strip cropping system on very steep slopes. Strips of small grain may then be grown in rotation with a forage crop. The small-grain strips can be about as wide as are row crop strips on a slope only half as steep.

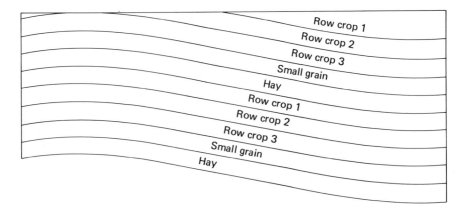

Figure 8-7 A contour strip cropping layout for a five-year rotation.

Contour strips necessarily deviate from the exact contour where-
ever there are irregularities in slope. Small deviations are acceptable
if the flow of water along the rows is slow enough to be nonerosive,
and if such flow is toward a swale rather than a ridge. An accumulation of water on a ridge will flow down the steepest slope in the
vicinity and probably cause a gully. Such flow can be avoided by
making the contour strips slightly straighter than the true contour
lines. This effect will usually result if an initial guideline is laid out
along a contour line near the top of the slope. Strip boundaries are
kept parallel to the initial guideline as long as the deviation from contour lines is small. The slope along a strip boundary should usually
be limited to less than 2%. Small filler areas of permanent vegetation
can be used to avoid excessive deviations, as shown in Figure 8-8.

Grassed waterways are needed where too much water accumulates in the swales of contour-stripped fields. The waterways catch

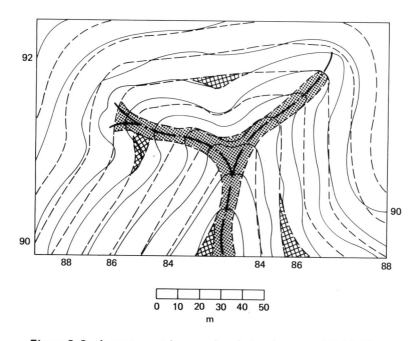

Figure 8-8 A contour strip cropping design for a small field. The
solid lines are contour lines with elevations shown in meters
above an arbitrary base level. The dashed lines are strip boundaries. The filler areas are crosshatched. The stippled area is grassed
waterway.

silt and tend to raise the elevations of the swales rather than allowing gullies to form.

Contour strip cropping may have little effect on the amount of runoff water from a field, but it does slow the velocity. Most of the soil lost from the row crop strips is caught in the adjacent forage crop strips and grassed waterways. However, the amount of water accumulation on the lower part of a very long slope may be too much for the forage strips to control. The effectiveness is reduced as the slopes get longer; those longer than 200 meters often need to have a diversion terrace to remove the excess water from the middle of the field.

Contour strip cropping usually results in more point rows and odd corners than do other cropping arrangements for the same field. Point rows occur where the strips meet field boundaries at angles such as those around the edges of the fields and at the waterways in Figure 8-8. Point rows reduce operational efficiency—more turning is required and small triangular areas may not be cropped at all. These uncropped areas may have permanent vegetation like the filler areas between strips.

Odd corners like the two upper ones in Figure 8-8 may also be planted to permanent vegetation or, since these are relatively flat, they can be planted to the same crop as the adjoining strips. Another possibility is to relocate the field boundaries to better match strip boundaries and thus minimize point rows and odd corners. The reverse has already been done on the right side of Figure 8-8, where strip boundaries were drawn parallel to the field boundaries that nearly followed contour lines.

The vegetation planted in filler areas may be chosen to be used as hay that can be harvested along with an adjoining strip. Another good alternative is to manage the filler areas and odd corners for wildlife purposes. Appropriate grasses, shrubs, and trees can be planted to provide both food and cover for animals and birds. Some such areas are used as sites for bee colonies or for growing Christmas trees. Any of these uses are preferable to annual crops in such locations. Crops are seldom profitable on small irregular areas and do not provide the erosion control that results from permanent vegetation.

8-5.2 Buffer Strip Cropping

Rolling topography with irregular slope gradients makes contour strip cropping impractical. Too many filler areas are needed to conform to boundary requirements. Buffer strip cropping is designed to work in such situations by lengthening the filler areas into continuous buffer strips that separate the crop strips. The crop strips are made uniform in width but the buffer strips are variable to allow for slope irregularities. The positioning of the buffer strips is arranged to include any rocky areas or other problem spots that occur in the field, as shown in Figure 8-9.

Buffer strips are planted to permanent vegetation to limit the velocity of runoff water and to catch any sediment that may have been eroded from the next higher crop strips. Perennial forage crops that can be used for hay or pasture are often used to vegetate buffer strips. Areas of trees and shrubs may also be included. The effectiveness of buffer strip cropping for reducing erosion depends on the nature of this vegetation, the widths of the buffer and crop strips, and on the topography, soil, and climate of the area.

The appropriateness of a particular crop or crop rotation to be grown in the crop strips can be tested by means of the soil-loss equa-

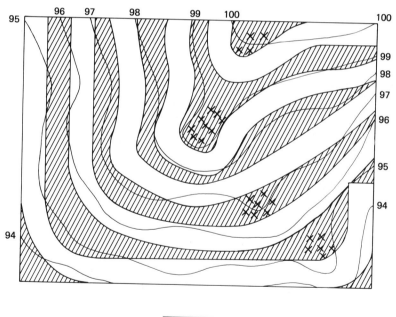

Figure 8-9 A buffer strip cropping design on a contour map. Elevations are shown in meters above an arbitrary base level. The X's represent rocky areas that are uncroppable.

tion presented in Chapter 6. The *P* factor for contour strip cropping can be used where the crop and buffer strip widths meet the requirements of Table 8-4.

8-5.3 Field Strip Cropping

Rectangular strips are sometimes laid out parallel to one side of a field in a pattern known as field strip cropping. The strips cross the general slope of the area but deviate too much from the contour to qualify as contour strip cropping. The system is managed like contour strip cropping but is less effective where the deviations from the contour are too large. These strips are easily cropped because they are straight and uniform in width.

The simplicity of layout and ease of cropping permit field strip cropping to be used in areas where the topography is too rolling for either contour or buffer strip cropping. Grassed waterways are usually needed in low areas because water flows along the sloping rows and accumulates in the swales.

8-5.4 Wind Strip Cropping

Strip cropping designed to control wind erosion crosses the path of the prevailing winds rather than following the contour. Wind strip cropping resembles field strip cropping in that both are laid out in straight lines. But wind strip cropping is typically used in areas such as the Great Plains of the United States and Canada that are drier than those in which strip cropping is used to control water erosion.

The soil-conserving vegetation in wind strip cropping needs to be dense enough to catch saltating particles and prevent them from jumping again. Also, the protective strips need to be wide enough to keep saltating particles from jumping completely across a strip. A few meters would suffice for stopping saltation, but cropping considerations make widths of 50 to 80 meters more practical. Because crops shift yearly from one strip to the next, each strip should be wide enough to be cropped conveniently. The chosen width is normally an exact multiple of the width of equipment used in farming operations. The maximum width is limited by the increasing amount of saltation that results from avalanching where exposed areas are too wide.

Close-growing vegetation such as a bluegrass pasture can stop saltation even when the grass is only a few centimeters tall. Bunchgrasses, however, are common in climates where wind erosion is most likely to be a problem. The open areas between clumps of grass need to be protected by vegetation that is at least as tall as the width of the open areas. The taller vegetation gives a windbreak effect in addition to its ability to catch and hold saltating particles. The deflection of wind away from exposed soil reduces the wind velocity downwind from the protecting strip. Saltation is greatly reduced for a distance of about ten times the height of the vegetation.

Wind strip cropping is often used with a wheat-fallow rotation. The wheat strips control saltation quite effectively after the wheat is 10 to 15 cm tall. The wheat stubble continues to offer protection after the wheat is harvested. In fact, the stubble can provide some protection during the fallow year if part of it is left on the surface as in stubble mulching.

Strips that catch soil particles in the summer can also catch snow during winter. Holding snow on the fields contributes to the soil moisture supply and increases productivity.

8-5.5 Barrier Strips

Narrow strips consisting of a few rows of small grains, grasses, or other crops can provide significant protection from wind erosion. These barrier strips must be spaced somewhat closer together to compensate for their narrowness. Even so, they occupy much less land than the protective strips in wind strip cropping.

Fryrear (1963) found that two rows of either sudangrass or grain sorghum made effective barriers for Texas conditions because they grew when protection was needed. He recommended spacing strips about 7 m apart for sudangrass or 4 m for grain sorghum to protect against winds up to 65 km/hr. Even after harvest, the highest-cut stubble afforded winter protection.

Hagan, Skidmore, and Dickerson (1972) also recommended two-row barrier strips on the basis of their work in Kansas. Single-row barriers used the land most efficiently but sometimes broke and failed when wind speeds exceeded 50 km/hr. They found that winter wheat barriers 10-cm tall were 20% effective for trapping soil particles from a 50 km/hr wind. Sudangrass barriers 30-cm tall were 60% effective under the same conditions. They calculated that a two-row rye barrier 20-cm tall could protect a strip about 32 m wide against a 50-km/hr wind.

8-5.6 Border Strips

Single strips of grass or other close-growing vegetation help keep soil from being carried into streams and ponds, living areas, or other sites that need protection. Border strips may be used to control movement of soil by wind after the manner of wind strip cropping, or they may be designed to restrict water transport. Their main purpose is often to control air and water pollution; preventing erosion may be secondary.

A strip of lush grass growing between a field and a body of water is very effective for catching sediment and reducing eutrophication (Ch. 17). The grass filters soil particles from the runoff water and absorbs dissolved nutrients from the water. The low nutrient content in the purified water reduces the growth of algae and other plants in ponds and streams. The water, nutrients, and fertile soil caught in the border strip help produce a lush growth that helps catch even more sediment and nutrients.

The dimensions of border strips vary with the situation but should usually be at least as wide as strips serving a similar purpose in fields. Most strips controlling water purity should be at least 10 m wide and need to be wider where the water flow is large or where the channel has a steep gradient. Wind-erosion control usually requires wider borders to keep the air clean—often 50 to 100 m across, with exact dimensions depending on topography and wind direction and velocity. These areas are often large enough to be used for pasture or hay production.

8-6 EVALUATING CROPPING SYSTEMS

A satisfactory cropping system must meet several standards. Economics, erosion control, pest control, the physical and chemical condition of the soil, and environmental concerns are all important. Accurate evaluation of all these factors is difficult, partly because several estimates and extrapolation of long-term trends are involved.

Economic considerations require that a desirable cropping system must produce a profit for the user. Adequate crop yields must be attainable on a long-term basis. Some aspects of the economics of soil conservation are discussed in Chapter 18, but much of the economics of cropping systems lies outside the scope of this book.

8-6.1 Cropping Systems and Soil Loss

The soil-loss prediction equations discussed in Chapter 6 are good tools for selecting appropriate cropping systems. Several possibilities can be analyzed and their results predicted without doing any damage to the land. The more intensive cropping systems usually give larger profits but also result in larger soil losses. Continuous row crops and other intensive cropping systems are therefore likely to be chosen where conditions are favorable but should be avoided where excessive erosion would occur.

Erosion naturally varies from one site to another according to soil and topographic conditions. A decision must therefore be made regarding the conditions where a particular cropping system is suitable. Average conditions of slope gradient and length combined with other average factors might give a fair basis for estimating the total soil loss from the field; however, the most erodible part of the field needs to be checked before the system can be classed as satisfactory. The hazards of averaging can be illustrated by an example wherein the annual soil loss from a 20-ha field might be 4 metric tons per hectare from most of the field, but 84 metric tons from one hectare. The average for the field is 8 metric tons per hectare and would be within the specified tolerable rate for many soils. The system would nevertheless be unsatisfactory because it would rapidly ruin the one hectare of highly erodible land. Such damage has already happened to too much land.

Adjusting land use and cropping systems to the most erodible land is usually impractical. Rather, these calculations are used to identify problem areas that need to be treated differently from the rest of the field. Perhaps the erodible hectare in the example could be transferred into an adjoining pasture, allowing the remaining 19 ha to be managed with an appropriate and much more productive cropping system.

Changing field boundaries solves some problems but does not help where the erodible land is surrounded by land suitable for intensive use. Terracing helps where the erosion hazard results from a steep slope. Another approach is to use a dual cropping system. For example, a farmer's best land might be used for continuous row crops, while the part needing protection has a rotation of row crops, small grain, and hay. The grain and hay crops require separate management, but the row crops can be handled along with the surrounding area. Such systems permit different parts of the field to be used in accordance with their potential and their need for protection as indicated by the soil-loss prediction equations.

8-6.2 Maintaining Soil Productive Potential

Maintaining the productive potential of soil over the long term is a fundamental purpose of soil conservation. Evaluation of the productive potential, however, is difficult. Crop yields are influenced by weather and management as well as by the soil potential. New crop varieties coupled with improved management practices and increased use of fertilizer and lime have often produced larger yields even though the soil was becoming shallower and harder to work. Thus the productivity can be increasing while the productive potential is decreasing.

Some items that influence productive potential are much easier to measure than the potential itself. Soil depth is one such item. Not only is the total soil thickness significant, but also the thickness of the topsoil (the "A" horizon for present purposes) is likely to have an important effect on soil productivity. Yield differences also depend on the nature of the subsoil—subsoil that is too compact or otherwise unsuitable for root development increases the importance of the topsoil thickness.

Another negative effect of erosion on soil productivity occurs through the reduction of soil fertility. Erosion has sometimes been called "the great robber" because small mineral and organic particles are carried away while the coarser particles are left behind. The available nutrient supply in the soil is closely associated with the finer particles; the remaining soil is less fertile than the eroded material. The largest differences occur when fertilizers are left on the soil surface and are eroded away with the soil. Additional fertilizer to compensate for the nutrient losses may maintain nearly equal yields but the costs are considerable. The profit from crops grown on eroding land therefore declines even if the yield is held constant by fertilization.

The removal of fine particles by erosion makes many soils gradually become more sandy, gravelly, or stony. The increased percentage of coarse material makes these soils more droughty and lowers the productive potential of many of them.

8-6.3 Maintaining Soil Structure

Tillage, erosion, and reduced organic-matter content weaken the structure of intensively cropped soils. Destruction of soil structure is favorable for paddy rice production but is undesirable for other crops.

Significance of Soil Structure. As the structure weakens, the soil tilth becomes poorer, the likelihood of crusting increases, and the soil permeability decreases. Soil *tilth* refers to how easily the soil can be tilled and cropped. Tilth is most important in soils high in clay because clay soils with poor tilth form hard clods when they dry, especially if they are tilled when wet. Poor tilth increases the amount of power required to till the soil and sometimes increases the required number of tillage operations to prepare a desirable seedbed.

Stable structure within the various soil horizons is important for maintaining permeability in all but the very coarse textured soils. Permeability depends on pore space between the soil peds. New pores are constantly being formed by roots and other living things forcing their way through the soil. Shrinking and swelling caused by moisture and temperature changes help form new aggregates and soil peds with natural surfaces between them. But tillage breaks aggregates and peds and blocks pores if the soil structure is weak. Permeability then declines, aeration and pore space are reduced, and the soil becomes less favorable for root growth.

Crusts form where raindrops beat on the soil surface and break down its structure. Loose particles from broken soil aggregates plug soil pores and often reduce the water infiltration rate to a fraction of its initial value. Runoff, erosion, sedimentation, and pollution increase. A continuous dense crust hardens on the soil surface as it dries after the rain. Some soil crusts markedly reduce the stand of a crop because they are too strong for seedlings to break through. Crust formation and reduced seedling emergence are the most readily observed problems resulting from weak soil structure.

NOTE 8-1 MEASURING STRUCTURAL STABILITY

Several methods can be used to measure the structural stability of soils. The two outlined here involve little equipment and can be used to compare structural stability differences resulting from contrasting treatments such as cropland versus pastureland or fencerows.

The percentage of water-stable aggregates in a soil can be determined by placing a weighed sample on a sieve with 0.25-mm openings. The sieve is then dipped repeatedly (fifty times or some other standard number) in a container of water. The material remaining on the sieve is then dried, weighed, and corrected for sand content to calculate the percentage of water-stable aggregates.

The structural stability of soil clods can be compared by letting water drip onto them from a buret as shown in the sketch on page 268. The volume of water required to wash the soil through the screen and into the beaker is an indication of structural stability.

Strength of Soil Structure. The qualitative terms weak, moderate, and strong are often used to indicate the distinctness of soil structure, although the actual strength is difficult to measure quantitatively. Aggregate stability is a related property that can be measured as described in Note 8-1. Such procedures can be used to measure changes produced in a soil by different cropping systems

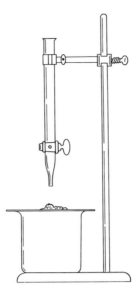

and various management practices. The soil in one field might be compared with nearby soil that has had different crops or with the less disturbed soil in a fencerow. Such comparisons often reveal large differences in aggregate stability accompanied by observable differences in porosity and crusting, as shown in Figure 8-10.

Effect of Crops on Soil Structure. A fine fibrous root system such as that produced by a dense growth of grass helps produce stable aggregates in soil. Deep taproots such as those of alfalfa help open channels in the lower soil horizons. These improvements in soil structure are important reasons why an alfalfa-grass mixture is widely regarded as a soil-improving crop. Most forage crops have similar effects but to different degrees.

Row crops such as sugar beets, cotton, corn, and beans usually cause the soil structure to deteriorate and contribute to erosion and sedimentation. Narrow rows and high yields cause these crops to cover the soil faster and permit their root systems to penetrate more uniformly through the entire soil volume, thus minimizing but not eliminating the soil deterioration. Actually, each combination of soil, cropping system, and management practices has an equilibrium of structural stability and of many other properties as well. As time passes, the soil shifts toward its equilibrium. The rate of change is

Figure 8-10 Soil structure differences resulting from a corn-wheat-hay rotation (left) and two years of corn-soybeans (right). (Courtesy Maryland Agricultural Experiment Station.)

roughly proportional to the difference between the present condition and its equilibrium.

Small-grain crops produce more cover and generally stronger soil structure than row crops but less cover and weaker structure than forage crops. Tree crops are much like row crops in their effect on soil structure unless there is a cover crop or other vegetation between the trees.

Most crops can be related to one or another of the groups already discussed. A good first approximation is that the effect of a crop on soil structure is closely related to how well it covers the soil and how thoroughly its roots permeate the soil. The effect of two crops grown together as companion crops is often more favorable to soil structure than either crop grown by itself. The effect of a crop rotation is an integration of the effects of all crops in the rotation. Some properties such as aggregate stability change fast enough to exhibit noticeable differences from one crop to another during a rotation.

Weakened soil structure is sometimes a reason to modify an intensive cropping system. The resulting low permeability causes runoff and erosion problems on slopes and drainage and sedimentation problems on flat lands. The remedy is usually to shift toward a system that includes more close-growing vegetation.

8-6.4 Environmental Effects of Cropping Systems

Most cropping systems expose the soil to accelerated erosion by wind and water. The eroded soil contaminates the air with dust particles and the water with sediment. The sheer mass of the eroded soil and the chemical and biological entities carried with it are significant. For example, soil particles carry plant nutrients that are important factors in eutrophication (Ch. 17).

The soil conservation program began primarily as an effort to control erosion for the sake of the land being eroded. Environmental concerns have made water and air pollution strong additional reasons to control erosion. Pollution caused by soil erosion extends far beyond the eroding area, making it a public rather than a private concern. Several states have responded to the environmental concerns by passing laws requiring the use of soil-conserving practices under certain conditions, as discussed in Chapter 19.

Environmental considerations have caused some cropping system changes that would not have been made for the sake of the eroding land. Border strips to keep sediment out of streams and ponds are a good example of adjustments made for the sake of the water rather than the land.

Most soil-conserving practices benefit both the land where erosion is reduced and the environment where the eroded soil would go. Cropping practices such as rotations, cover crops, and strip cropping are valuable for reducing air and water pollution as well as for protecting soil productivity. Mechanical practices such as terraces and conservation tillage also protect both soil productivity and the environment. Practices such as these have long been advocated to protect the land. Recognizing their environmental values increases the incentive to apply them.

Reducing erosion and its polluting effects to minimal values would be relatively simple if land were not needed for growing crops. However, the world's population needs to be fed, clothed, and housed largely with products from the land. Cropping systems therefore need to be carefully designed to meet needs without causing excessive erosion and sedimentation.

SUMMARY

Native vegetation normally provides enough cover to control erosion, but most crops leave the soil surface exposed periodically. Poor crop growth can allow disastrous erosion to ruin the land and pollute both air and water. Properly adapted crops and well-planned cropping systems can limit erosion and sedimentation to acceptable rates.

Most crops can be classified into four groups. Row crops usually produce the most profit and the least protection against erosion. Small-grain crops give better protection because the plants grow fast and close together. Forage crops produce still thicker cover and provide excellent erosion control. Tree crops with undergrowth and a litter layer on the soil surface almost eliminate erosion.

The spacing between plants and the resulting plant population influence both yield and erosion. Narrower rows permit crops to cover the soil sooner and protect it better. High soil fertility also helps by increasing crop growth.

Monocultures permit farmers to specialize and grow each crop where it is best suited. Fertilizers and lime make it possible to maintain yields under continuous cash crops, but the soil structure may deteriorate and erosion, sedimentation, and pollution increase. Land that is too steep for row crops and grain crops may be used for hay, pasture, or tree crops because these crops can provide excellent erosion control.

Crop rotations often provide more continuous soil cover than monocultures and help control erosion, plant diseases, and insects. Companion crops and cover crops in rotations help to keep the soil covered almost continuously; some crops offer carry-over effects that reduce erosion while the next crop is growing. Crop residues can be used for soil cover when no crop is growing. Their effectiveness depends on how well they cover the soil surface.

Multiple cropping is used in many gardens and in tropical areas to increase variety and total amount of production. Overlapping the growth periods of two or more crops provides an important soil conservation bonus.

Contour strip cropping is effective for controlling water erosion; buffer strip cropping and field strip cropping are useful where the land includes small uncroppable areas or the topography is too rolling for contour cropping. Wind strip cropping is laid out in straight lines across the prevailing wind to catch saltating particles. Barrier strips consisting of one, two, or a few rows of tall close-growing crops are also effective for reducing wind erosion if the exposed area between them is only a few meters wide. Border strips are single strips of close-growing vegetation used to reduce pollution by keeping soil particles out of the air or filtering sediment out of water.

The soil-loss prediction equations are useful for selecting appropriate cropping systems and for identifying areas that need special treatment to avoid excessive erosion. Appropriate cropping systems maintain adequate soil depth, fertility, and water-holding capacity to realize the productive potential of the soil. Soil structure needs to be stable enough to resist crusting and maintain adequate permeability. Forage crops usually have favorable effects on soil structure, whereas most row crops expose the soil to structure deterioration. The effect of any crop on soil structure is related to how well it covers the soil and how thoroughly its roots penetrate the soil.

Cropping systems need to protect the environment as well as the soil. Pollution resulting from soil erosion contaminates air and water far beyond the eroding area. Well-designed cropping systems are needed to produce food and fiber for the world's population without causing excessive erosion and sedimentation.

QUESTIONS

1. How is a forage crop both a "soil-building crop" and a "soil-depleting crop"?
2. Why are some crops grown in rows rather than equally spaced in all directions? What effects do rows and row spacings have on soil and water conservation?
3. Why do many farmers grow crops as monocultures rather than using crop rotations?
4. Under what conditions would the use of a companion crop for the establishment of a forage crop increase erosion? When would it reduce erosion?
5. Why do many farmers prefer to plow crop residues under rather than leave them on the soil surface?
6. Explain the differences between crop rotations, sequential cropping, and intercropping.
7. List five different types of strip cropping and distinguish them from one another.
8. How can fertilizer be used to reduce water pollution?

REFERENCES

BARNETT, A. P., J. R. CARREKER, FERNANDAO ABRUNA, W. A. JACKSON, A. E. DOOLEY, and J. H. HOLLADAY, 1972. Soil and nutrient losses in runoff with selected cropping treatments on tropical soils. *Agron. J.* 64:391–395.

BENOIT, R. E., N. A. WILLITS, and W. J. HANNA, 1962. Effect of rye winter cover crop on soil structure. *Agron. J.* 54:419–420.

BLACK, A. L., and F. H. SIDDOWAY, 1976. Dryland cropping sequences within a tall wheatgrass barrier system. *J. Soil Water Cons.* 31:101–105.

CARREKER, J. R., A. R. BERTRAND, C. B. ELKINS, Jr., and W. E. ADAMS, 1968. Effect of cropping systems on soil physical properties and irrigation requirements. *Agron. J.* 60:299–302.

CONSTANTINESCO, I., 1976. *Soil Conservation for Developing Countries.* Soils Bull. 30, Food and Agriculture Organization of the United Nations, Rome, Italy, 92 p.

DAVIDSON, J. M., FENTON GRAY, and D. I. PINSON, 1967. Changes in organic matter and bulk density with depth under two cropping systems. *Agron. J.* 59:375–378.

DRULLINGER, R. H., and B. L. SCHMIDT, 1968. Wind erosion problems and controls in the Great Lakes region. *J. Soil Water Cons.* 23:58–59.

FRYREAR, D. W., 1963. Annual Crops as Wind Barriers. *Trans. Am. Soc. Agr. Engr.* 6:340–342, 352.

HAGEN, L. J., E. L. SKIDMORE, and J. D. DICKERSON, 1972. Designing narrow strip barrier systems to control wind erosion. *J. Soil Water Cons.* 27: 269–272.

MANNERING, J. V., and C. B. JOHNSON, 1969. Effect of crop row spacing on erosion and infiltration. *Agron. J.* 61:902–905.

MANNERING, J. V., L. D. MEYER, and C. B. JOHNSON, 1968. Effect of cropping intensity on erosion and infiltration. *Agron. J.* 60:206–209.

MILLER, D. E., and W. D. KEMPER, 1962. Water stability of aggregates of two soils as influenced by incorporation of alfalfa. *Agron. J.* 54:494–496.

OLSON, T. C., 1977. Restoring the productivity of a glacial till soil after topsoil removal. *J. Soil Water Cons.* 32:130–132.

PAPENDICK, R. I., P. A. SANCHEZ, and G. B. TRIPLETT (eds.), 1976. *Multiple Cropping.* ASA Special Publication No. 27, American Society of Agronomy, Crop Science Society of America and Soil Science Society of America, 378 p.

SKIDMORE, E. L., W. A. CARSTENSON, and E. E. BANBURY, 1975. Soil changes resulting from cropping. *Soil Sci. Soc. Am. Proc.* 39:964–967.

SOIL SCIENCE DEPARTMENT, North Carolina State University, 1974. *Agronomic-Economic Research on Tropical Soils.* Annual Report for 1974, Raleigh, N.C., 230 p.

VAN DOREN, D. M., Jr., G. B. TRIPLETT, Jr., and J. E. HENRY, 1976. Influence of long-term tillage, crop rotation, and soil type combinations on corn yield. *Soil Sci. Soc. Am. J.* 40:100–105.

WHITAKER, F. D., V. C. JAMISON, and J. F. THORNTON, 1961. Runoff and erosion losses from Mexico silt loam in relation to fertilization and other management practices. *Soil Sci. Soc. Am. Proc.* 25:401–403.

9

Tillage Practices for Conservation

Vegetative cover provides the most effective erosion control known. But, effective year-round vegetative cover is impossible when soil is used to produce cultivated crops, especially annual crops, and other means of controlling erosion must be employed. Certain tillage practices can be used to assist in erosion control.

9-1 OBJECTIVES OF TILLAGE

Three generally accepted reasons for cultivating soils are: (1) preparation of a seed and root bed, (2) control of weeds, and (3) establishment of surface soil conditions that favor water infiltration and erosion control.

9-1.1 Preparation of Seed and Root Bed

Seed and root bed preparations are employed to prepare the surface soil for easy and effective seed placement, germination, and early emergence and to improve soil physical conditions that might otherwise restrict plant growth and development. Preparation ranges from simply stirring with the planter or grain drill to many operations with a variety of implements.

9-1.2 Control of Weeds

Weeds compete with crop plants for moisture, nutrients, space, and light. Tillage may bury weed seeds and kill seedling and mature weeds. Chemical herbicides control many weeds, but there are often some weeds that a specific chemical or chemical combination does not control. Some tillage is usually needed to control such weeds so they will not reduce crop yields.

Tillage in excess of that needed to control weeds does not benefit crops on most friable medium- and coarse-textured soils. On these soils, weed control by scraping the soil surface or by applying chemicals is generally as effective as tillage. Crop growth does benefit from more tillage than needed for weed control on some soils that have low permeability and low organic-matter contents.

9-1.3 Soil and Water Conservation

One of the earliest tillage techniques recommended for moisture conservation was dust mulch tillage. The soil was stirred after every rain to form a dry soil mulch that broke the water columns in the capillary pores at the soil surface. This practice soon lost favor because field tests failed to show increased moisture storage or improved crop growth and the smooth, dry surface increased susceptibility to wind erosion.

Cultivation to increase infiltration by roughening a crusted soil surface appeals to many practical farmers. Freshly plowed or cultivated soil absorbs water faster than crusted soil, but the increased infiltration rate of the cultivated soil does not last long. Roughening the soil surface by tillage to reduce soil erodibility has also been recommended and used widely. This beneficial effect of tillage is also short-lived because rain and wind soon smooth the surface.

Crop residues on the soil surface reduce both water and wind erosion. Accordingly, tillage that leaves straw and stubble on the soil surface instead of turning it under has much to recommend it.

9-2 TYPES OF TILLAGE IMPLEMENTS

Hand tillage and power equipment generally perform the same tasks, but the power equipment works faster and often is used to stir or mix the soil deeper and to bury more vegetative cover and plant residues. A family can cultivate about 1.5 to 3 ha of land with hand labor, whereas a farmer using bullock power can farm 5 to 8 ha. A farmer with a large tractor and suitable implements can cultivate, plant, and harvest 200 ha or more without additional human help.

Tillage implements are limited in many countries to hoes of different shapes and sizes. Hoes such as those shown in Figure 9-1 are used to "plow" the land, to prepare a seedbed, to open the furrow

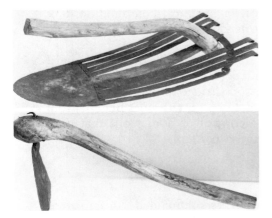

Figure 9-1 Hoes are the traditional tillage tools where hand labor is used for agriculture. The large hoe (upper photograph) is called a *garma* in West Africa and its blade is approximately 30 cm wide by 60-75 cm long. The small hoe is a general purpose tool called a *lalanya* in West Africa. It is used to control weeds, rebuild ridges, and harvest root crops. The blade is roughly triangular with a cutting edge about 15 cm wide. (Courtesy J. A. Hobbs.)

or hole for seed placement, to weed the growing crops, and even to harvest some crops. Many farmers own and use several types of hoes although some types are used for many purposes. Nearly all of these hoes are made of scrap iron by local blacksmiths, fitted with short wooden handles, and used from a stooped position only. A long-handled hoe is awkward and cumbersome to the operator familiar with these short-handled hoes. These hoes are effective agricultural tools in developing countries where capital is scarce and labor is plentiful and cheap.

Farm implement company brochures are replete with distinctive trade-marked names for specific tillage implements such as crust buster, duckfoot cultivator, flex-sweeps, Miller rod, offset disk, sidewinder, skew treader, spade-toothed cultivator, TNT plow, vibra-shank cultivator, and many others. There are, however, relatively few distinctly different types of tillage tools.

9-2.1 Plows

The original plow, and the type still used by farmers in many developing nations, was a sharpened spike drawn through the soil. This implement killed few weeds and did not invert the soil until it underwent modification in Europe. Then it was given a soil penetrating part, usually metal, and a soil turning part, originally of wood, that made it into the *moldboard plow*. Later the wooden moldboard was changed to iron, and then steel, as shown in Figure 9-2, to turn the furrows cleanly and use less power. Even so, plowing a field takes considerably more power than most other types of tillage.

Figure 9-2 A roll-over (two-way) moldboard plow. The plow share or cutting edge, the curved moldboard, and the landside are clearly visible on the units in the air. Also visible is the cutting, inverting, and crumbling action on the soil. The "two-way" feature makes it possible to turn all furrows in one direction, an excellent feature in a soil conservation program. (Courtesy Massey-Ferguson, Inc.)

Implements with very large sloping disks were developed for use on stony land and on soils that did not scour cleanly off moldboards. This implement, called the *disk plow*, has largely been replaced by the heavy offset disk. Moldboard and disk plows invert the plowed furrow and actually lift and move all soil in the plow layer (usually between 10 and 20 cm deep). They leave the soil rough and cloddy, but not ridged.

A *lister* or *lister plow* is an implement which loosens and moves soil into ridges on each side of the working unit. The soil under the ridges is buried but not cultivated. Thus the power requirement per unit of area cultivated is less than for the true plows. The lister uses either small back-to-back moldboards or disks to excavate the furrow and build the ridges.

9-2.2 Disk Cultivators

Implements with a number of saucer-shaped metal components mounted on axles are called disks. Two sets (gangs) of disks are usually connected so they face in opposite directions to each other to eliminate sidedraft. The angle between the axles and the line of travel is adjustable; in operation the axles are canted so that the disks cut and move the soil. A *tandem disk* is shown in Figure 9-3. It has two gangs of disks mounted in front and two behind. The leading sets of disks turn the soil out from the center and the following sets move it back.

Figure 9-3 A tandem disk. The front disks turn the furrows out from the center, the rear disks toward the center. Such disks produce a relatively smooth surface and cover part of the crop residues. This large unit is hinged so that the "wings" can be raised for transport through gates and on roads. (Courtesy Krause Plow Corporation.)

A heavy implement consisting of a series of large disks (approximately 50 cm in diameter) all saucered in the same direction was developed in the late 1920s. This implement is called a *one-way-disk plow.* It replaced the moldboard plow as the primary tillage tool on vast areas of the Great Plains because it required considerably less power than the plow and it cultivated more land in a unit of time.

An *offset disk,* shown in Figure 9-4, is an implement with disks that may be as large as or larger than those on one-ways, but with tandem single gangs. The leading and the following gangs move the soil in opposite directions.

9-2.3 Tine Cultivators

Some primary (initial) and much secondary tillage is performed by implements with points or blades mounted on a frame or else on curved shanks fastened on the frame. The simplest is the *drag harrow,* which has rectangular individual frames carrying fixed spikes about 20 cm long. These spikes break clods and smooth the soil surface. Individual frames are mounted in series across the direction of travel so that units many meters wide can be pulled across a field in a single pass. Twenty or thirty years ago, a humid area field was seldom seeded unless it had been harrowed first. The implement is less commonly used today, and almost never used in dryland regions.

Figure 9-4 An offset disk—a heavy-framed, large-disk implement that has replaced the moldboard plow and disk plow as an initial tillage tool on many farms. The smaller-diameter disk on the left of the rear bank levels out the soil surface and leaves a less conspicuous furrow. (Courtesy Royal Industries, Inc.)

Figure 9-5 A chisel plow equipped with narrow points. This model has three tiers of shanks on the frame and special shank supports that allow limited lateral movement (vibration). It is hinged, and the wings are folded for easier transport. (Courtesy International Harvester Company.)

A *chisel plow* is a ripping implement that can be used with narrow points (5 cm), wider points (7.5 cm), or blades up to 30 cm wide. The implement has several tiers of shanks on the frame, as shown in Figure 9-5. It is usually set to penetrate 20 to 30 cm deep when narrow points are used. Wider blades are set to the depth needed to cut the roots of weeds. They are spaced laterally so that the wings of succeeding banks overlap about 5 cm for complete undercutting of the soil surface. This implement has replaced "stiff toothed" and "spring toothed" cultivators unsuited for use with more powerful tractors and higher speeds.

A *heavy-duty chisel,* as shown in Figure 9-6, is a rugged implement. It is used only for soil ripping and is designed to penetrate 30 to 40 cm deep. A *subsoiler* is a still more rugged ripping implement designed to penetrate the soil 60 cm or more.

Sweep and *blade cultivators* are implements with individual cutting surfaces wider than 50 cm. Some have blades more than 2 m

Figure 9-6 A heavy-duty chisel. The very heavy shanks and narrow points are mounted on a V-shaped frame, so the center shank is ahead of those on each side. (Courtesy Allis-Chalmers Corporation.)

wide. Most have V-shaped blades mounted on very rugged shanks at the point of the V, as shown in Figure 9-7, but some are equipped with straight blades with shanks at each end. Gangs of these cultivators can be mounted behind a single tractor.

9-2.4 Miscellaneous Cultivators

A *rotary tillage machine* has a shaft, transverse to the direction of travel, on which is mounted a series of knives or blades, as shown in Figure 9-8. The machine is powered by its own engine or by a take-off from the tractor. The shaft and blades revolve at high speed and cut the soil as the machine passes across the field.

The *rotary hoe* has a multitude of curved-spoke, rimless wheels mounted on an axle transverse to the direction of travel. The wheels are spaced about 10 cm apart. The spokes penetrate easily into the soil as the implement is pulled forward, but as they are pulled out, they lift or throw the soil, crop residues, and small weeds. A *treader,* really a rotary hoe pulled backwards, has spokes curved so that as they first contact the ground, they press onto the surface and force

Figure 9-7 A blade implement with very rugged construction and large clearance between adjacent shanks and between blade and frame. This model has seven 1.5-m V blades for a total working width of 10 m. (Courtesy Sunflower Manufacturing Co.)

Figure 9-8 A rotary tillage implement. This is a front view of a 5-m-wide power-takeoff model. The rotor blades do the actual cultivating. (Courtesy FMC Corporation.)

residues and the surface soil into the soil. The spokes leave the soil cleanly without disturbance. Figure 9–9 shows the spoke shapes of rotary hoes and treaders. A *skew treader* is a treader on which the axle and the spoked devices are mounted at an angle to the direction of forward movement. Two treaders can be hooked up in tandem with a long chain or bar on one side and a short one on the other, thus forming a *tandem skew treader.*

The *rod weeder* is an implement with a backward-rotating bar or rod that is drawn below the ground surface. The revolving bar cuts

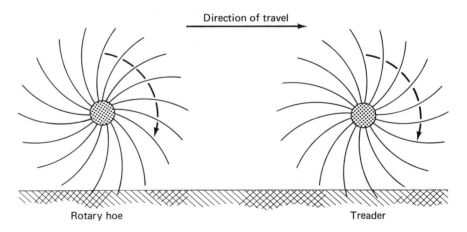

Figure 9-9 Diagram of spoke tines of the rotary hoe and treader. The angle of entry into and exit from the soil determines whether the curved tines lift the soil or press it down.

off and twists weeds and firms the soil. This type of implement cannot be used successfully in soils that contain stones or large gravel pieces, or in previously unstirred soil. The rod weeder can be made to penetrate uncultivated land, even to depths of 15 cm or more, if the bar is equipped with cultivator points or teeth (Miller rod).

9-3 TILLAGE, CROP RESIDUE, AND SOIL PROPERTIES

Tillage influences soil and water conservation through its effects on surface crop residues, surface soil roughness, both cloddiness and ridging, and on soil infiltration rate and permeability. Tillage generally buries at least part of a former crop's residue. Moldboard and disk plows which invert the furrow, and rotary tillers which mix the cultivated layers, bury or cover nearly all crop residue. A lister also covers nearly all crop residue in spite of the fact that it inverts only half of the surface soil. Implements that cultivate below the surface leave 75% to 90% of the residue on top; the wider sweeps and blades leave 85% to 90%. Other implements bury intermediate amounts of residue as indicated in Table 9-1.

Plows leave the soil surface cloddy and somewhat rough. Listers prepare a very ridged surface. Rotary tillers make the surface smooth, loose, and fluffy unless they are used when the soil is moist. Disk

Table 9-1 Effect of a single operation with various tillage implements on the amount of crop residue left on the soil surface

Implement	*Proportion of original residue remaining on surface (%)*
Sweeps > 1.0 meter	90
Sweeps < 1.0 meter	85
Duckfoot cultivator	75
Rod weeder	90
Rod weeder with small shovels or sweeps	85
Skew treader	90
Chisel	75
One-way disk plow	50
Tandem disk	50
Moldboard plow	0

SOURCE: Modified from Woodruff and others, 1966.

implements break the soil into smaller pieces than plows, so the surface tends to be smoother and less cloddy than plowed land. Chisels, especially when worked deep, leave the surface cloddy and rough. Tine implements with smaller blades usually leave the surface somewhat cloddy and rough, but wide-blade cultivators leave a smoother and less cloddy surface.

The effect of tillage on residue cover, cloddiness, and ridging depends on the speed and depth of operation as well as on the type of implement (Woodruff and Chepil, 1958). Higher speeds tend to bury more trash, rip stubble free from the soil, make larger ridges, and break down aggregates and clods more completely. A speed of about 3 km/hr produces the most cloddy surface but produces little ridging except with the lister. The best compromise speed for a cloddy, ridged surface appears to be about 6 km/hr. Deep tillage (15 cm or more), regardless of implement used in seedbed preparation, produces more nonerodible clods of higher stability than shallow tillage (5 to 10 cm).

The angle between a horizontal line through the axis of an individual disk of a one-way-disk plow and the direction of machine travel influences soil cloddiness, soil roughness, and the amount of crop residue left on the surface. The wider this angle, the more residue will be buried, the finer the clods will be, and the smaller will be the ridges. The angle of attack seems to be less important during the second and subsequent operations.

In general, tillage operations that leave the most crop residue on the soil surface maintain the highest infiltration rate, even though plowed land has a very high initial infiltration rate and permeability. This high initial rate declines rapidly because plowed soil has little protective cover.

9-4 FLAT VERSUS RIDGED TILLAGE AND PLANTING

Farmers generally use systems of seedbed preparation and planting that experience and tradition indicate are best for their local conditions. Often the land is prepared flat and is seeded with no attempt to ridge the soil, especially in the production of the small cereal grains, wheat, oats, barley, and rye. Row crops such as corn, sorghum, cotton, and sugar beets also have been grown without ridges in some areas.

Row crops are often grown on ridges by placing seed in the bottom of a furrow between two ridges. Cultivation breaks down the initial ridges and builds new ones over the crop rows. This practice buries seedling weeds in the crop row and cuts off the weeds between the rows. It also mounds soil around the base of the plants and is conducive to the growth and development of adventitious (brace) roots in corn. In mechanized, dryland farming, the furrow planter can be adjusted to sweep aside dry surface soil, placing seed in moist soil at normal planting depth.

Ridging is often employed when row crop land is prepared, seeded, and cultivated by hand. Crop seeds are generally planted on top of the ridges in this system, and postplanting cultivation both controls weeds and rebuilds the ridges as rain washes them down. There are a number of reasons why hand-hoe farmers ridge their land rather than prepare it flat. First, the initial ridge cultivation takes less labor than flat cultivation because only half the surface soil is turned—new ridges are made by inverting half of the soil from a pair of adjacent old ridges onto the old furrow bottom, which is not cultivated at that time. Second, ridged soil is better aerated than flat-cultivated soil. Third, ridges on the contour reduce soil erosion.

Seeds are placed on ridge tops rather than in the furrows for a number of reasons. First, planting is easier in the loosened soil of the ridge than in the more compact furrow bottoms. Second, seeds germinate and emerge better and seedlings grow faster in the aerated soil of the ridges. Third, less labor is required to maintain ridges than to move the entire ridge from the interrow area to the row area. Fourth, control of water erosion is more effective if ridges are maintained in one location during the entire growing season.

A relatively new form of seedbed has been developed for use in some mechanized, humid, or irrigated regions. Flat beds wide enough to accommodate two crop rows are constructed above the general soil level. These beds are separated by deep furrows that provide better surface drainage and early season aeration than regular flat planting. Specially designed tillage tools are needed to build these beds. The growing crops must be cultivated very carefully to insure that the beds are maintained as long as necessary. The furrows are used for water application on some irrigated land, but this alternate-row irrigation is less effective on slowly permeable soils than every-row irrigation.

9-5 CONSERVATION TILLAGE

Systems of cultivating the soil that form ridges and leave crop residues and clods on the surface of the soil are known collectively as *conservation tillage* systems. Conservation tillage increases infiltration and reduces runoff and erosion. A variety of names have been applied to individual tillage systems that provide for erosion protection.

9-5.1 Stubble Mulch Tillage

The main purpose of stubble mulch tillage is to keep enough residue on the surface to protect both crops and soils from damage by water and wind erosion. To be effective, crop residue must be handled carefully from harvest through planting time. Straw choppers and spreaders on combines, especially on modern, wide combines, are essential.

Alternate uses of crop residue as livestock feed, a source of energy, and a constituent of a building product are receiving considerable attention. These may provide additional sources of farm income, but the importance of the residues for soil erosion control and soil productivity maintenance must be considered carefully before any disposition of residue is made (Allamaras and others, 1979; Campbell and others, 1979; Larson, 1979; Lindstrom and others, 1979; Skidmore and others, 1979).

In 1938 Duley and Russell started to develop a tillage system that purposely retained crop residues on the soil surface for erosion control (Russell, 1976). Their cultivator consisted of two 55-cm sweeps mounted on a modified 105-cm corn cultivator. The original name for this system, *stubble mulch tillage,* is descriptive and is still used. The system was developed in eastern Nebraska, a subhumid area, but was tested, recommended, and used to some extent in almost all climatic regions in the United States, Canada, and U.S.S.R. Stubble mulch tillage was developed for the control of wind erosion in drier areas, but research workers and conservation specialists have adapted it to water-erosion control in more humid regions.

Implements for Stubble Mulch Tillage. Although undercutting tools such as sweep and blade machines and rod weeders are most useful in a stubble mulch system, other implements are also used. No individual cultivation implement meets all the needs of stubble mulch tillage, nor does a single tool work equally well under all conditions to produce or retain surface cover, cloddiness, and roughness.

Selection of specific tools with the right features for the soil conditions is essential. Concavity of disk affects the amount of residue buried, as well as the efficiency of weed kill and cloddiness and roughness produced. The "lift" of a blade affects the amount of clod disintegration and the size of ridges left by tillage. Shape of chisel points affects ridging and cloddiness produced. Implements should be adjustable for depth of cultivation, tilt of working surface, and, in disk implements, angle of attack.

The vertical distance between the implement frame and the soil surface needs to be at least 45 cm, and horizontal distance between adjacent shanks must be sufficient to allow bunched residue to slide through and clear the machine. With wide sweep and blade implements this is not a problem, but narrow bladed instruments need several banks of shanks, one behind the other, with tines offset so that crop residue can pass through. Machines that have upright shanks, particularly fairly straight ones, often "rake" enough residue to plug the machine. Rolling coulters or knives are needed in front of each shank, especially when working through fresh, heavy residues.

Planting equipment must be capable of working through surface residue if it is to be effective in stubble mulch tillage. Row crop planters have been improved so that some commercial planters do a good job of seeding through heavy trash, as shown in Figure 9-10,

Figure 9-10 A row crop planter working in untilled row crop residue. The planter is equipped to open the furrow, push crop residue to the side, fertilize, and apply herbicides. This type of implement can be modified to work equally well in untilled wheat stubble. (Courtesy Fleischer Manufacturing, Inc.)

but grain drills generally are not as satisfactory. Heavy disk and shoe drills as shown in Figure 9–11 have been developed that will work through limited amounts of residue. Figure 9–12 shows a commercial hoe drill that takes a lot of power but will work through 3000 kg/ha of wheat stubble.

Choosing Implements. Stubble mulch farming has to be flexible. Every effort must be made to keep all residue on the soil surface when little vegetation is produced; part of the residue may need to be incorporated when crop production is high. The amount of flattened wheat straw needed to control wind erosion on soils is illustrated in Figure 9–13. Standing wheat stubble is about twice as effective an an equal weight of flattened stubble. Sorghum stover is about half as effective for controlling wind erosion as wheat straw is. The amount and type of tillage which can be used without causing excessive wind erosion can be assessed if the amount of residue needed to control erosion and the amount of residue present after harvest are known (Note 9–1). Amounts of straw and stover needed to control water erosion are not known with the same precision as for wind erosion.

NOTE 9-1 REGULATING RESIDUE INCORPORATED

The proper choice of tillage implements to dispose of or retain crop residues for optimum erosion control and crop production

Figure 9-11 A heavy disk grain drill designed to seed small grain through reasonable quantities of crop residue (less than 1250 kg/ha). (Courtesy International Harvester Company.)

Figure 9-12 A high clearance, rugged hoe drill that can be obtained in single- or multiple-hitch units. This seven-unit implement seeds a swath 14.5 m wide. The hoe openers are mounted in three banks and can be adjusted to place seed in rows from 23 to 34 cm apart. This drill works well through as much as 3000 kg/ha of wheat straw. (Courtesy Noble Cultivators Limited.)

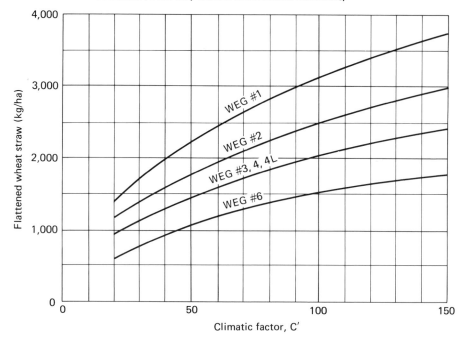

Figure 9-13 Graph showing the relationship between soil erodibility (WEG), climatic factor C' (Ch. 6), and the amount of flattened wheat stubble needed to keep soil loss by wind erosion below 11 mt/ha-yr. (Modified from Skidmore and Siddoway, 1978.)

requires a knowledge of the residues needed to control erosion (Figure 9-13), the amount of residue on the soil at harvest time (Section 6-7.6), and the proportion of residue incorporated by each tillage implement (Table 9-1).

Assume that 3000 kg/ha of stubble and straw are left on a silt loam soil (WEG #6) after wheat harvest, that three tillage operations are needed to control weeds and prepare a seedbed for the next wheat crop, that the one-way disk buries 50% of the residue and a sweep or blade machine or a rod weeder buries 10% each tillage operation, and that the climatic factor (C') for the area is 100. What combination of three tillage operations with disk or undercutting equipment or both will leave on the soil surface the minimum amount of residue (1500 kg/ha flat as shown in Figure 9-13 or 750 kg/ha standing) needed for wind-erosion protection?

Three undercutting operations will leave 2187 kg/ha.

$$3000 \times 0.9 \times 0.9 \times 0.9 = 2187$$

This is more than enough residue, whether it is standing or flat. A single one-way-disk cultivation and two undercutting operations will leave 1215 kg/ha.

$$3000 \times 0.5 \times 0.9 \times 0.9 = 1215$$

This is enough if the residue is standing (or partly standing and partly flat) but not if it is all knocked flat, as it probably would be with a one-way disk operation.

Field Experience with Stubble Mulch Tillage. The first experience a farmer has with stubble mulch tillage is nearly always bad. The tillage tools plug up with straw; weed control is often inadequate; planting, particularly with disk-type grain drills, is not always successful; and crop yields are reduced. Zingg and Whitfield (1957) reviewed the results of much of the early research with this practice in the western half of the United States. They found that yields were maintained or increased on stubble mulched land in semiarid regions, but were reduced in subhumid and humid areas. A review of investigations with stubble mulch tillage in eastern United States shows almost universal reductions in yield. However, stubble mulch tillage does reduce erosion markedly, often bringing it down to a tolerable limit. The practice has much to commend it, and efforts should be made to learn how to use it effectively.

Causes of Lowered Crop Yields. Several reasons have been suggested for poorer crop growth on stubble mulched soil. These reasons include the available nitrogen supply, weed control, seedbed quality, and soil temperature.

The top 90 cm of soil under stubble mulch tillage contains less nitrate nitrogen than similar depths under plowed land. Although plants on stubble mulched plots often appear nitrogen deficient, applications of extra nitrogen fertilizer have not always brought yields up to those on plowed plots. Dryland crop yields are not always reduced by lower available nitrogen content because the soil may still contain enough nitrogen to produce the amount of crop that the soil moisture is capable of supporting.

Weeds are usually a serious problem when noninverting tillage is used without chemical herbicides, because a weed that is cut off below the ground surface, but not buried, must be killed by desiccation. The weed may recover if rain comes soon after tillage. The more humid the area, the greater is the chance of rain shortly after cultivation, and the greater is the chance for weed survival. Also, weed seeds remain on the soil surface ready to germinate if the soil is not inverted during tillage.

Implements other than disks tend to gather residue into clumps when it is present on the surface in large amounts. The compacted residue eventually lifts the implement and causes it to ride over the surface. Weed control is unsatisfactory under these conditions, and a poor seedbed of variable firmness is produced. Poor planter operation in heavy residues results in a poor stand with many skips and misses, and yields are reduced.

Surface mulch insulates the soil from temperature changes. Soil stays warm longer in the fall; warming is delayed in the spring and the mulched plots are 1° to 2°C cooler than unmulched plots at 7 cm below the surface. Soil temperature below 30°C reduces early corn growth and subsequent yields. Above 32°C lowered temperatures are beneficial (van Wijk and others, 1959; Larson and others, 1960; Allamaras and others, 1964). Studies in the central Great Plains show that soil temperature in stubble-mulched land in the early spring is as much as 4°C lower than that in soil without mulch cover. Temperatures cooler than 10°C were noted in mulched plots as long as forty days after wheat regrowth started. Field and growth chamber studies show that spring regrowth of wheat is seriously reduced by temperatures below 10°C lasting for as short a period as eighteen days (personal communications from D. E. Smika to J. A. Hobbs).

Duley and Russell warned that insects and crop diseases might be a problem where residues are not buried, but to date there is little evidence that these pests are more serious on stubble mulch tilled land than on plowed land in either the winter wheat area or in the corn belt. Some insects have been more troublesome on mulch tilled land in spring wheat areas.

Current Use and Future of Stubble Mulch Tillage. Stubble mulch tillage, as shown in Figure 9–14, has been used extensively in the United States for small grain and row crop production where moisture limits crop growth and where danger of wind erosion is high (in the summer-fallow area of the Great Plains, the dryland sections of the Pacific Northwest, and in intermountain valleys). At least a few farmers in nearly every region have seen the conservation potential of stubble mulch tillage and have been sufficiently dedicated to erosion control to work with the system. They have learned how to gain the conservation advantages without incurring the losses in effective weed control and in yield, and the practice has slowly spread to some of their neighbors. Systems using less tillage increased dramatically when the price of petroleum products rose sharply in the early 1970s. Stubble mulch tillage did not, because it is not a reduced tillage system; in fact, it may require one or more additional tillage operations to control weeds effectively when chemicals are not used.

9–5.2 Minimum and No Tillage

Immediately after World War II, research scientists and some farmers in the summer-fallow areas of the United States used 2,4-D, a selec-

Figure 9–14 Undercutting wheat stubble with a four-blade implement (6.9 m wide) leaves abundant stubble standing on the soil surface. (Courtesy Noble Cultivators Limited.)

tive herbicide, as a substitute for mechanical weed control in the fallow operation. Unfortunately, the chemical did not kill all kinds of weeds. Grasses particularly, but some other weeds also, were immune. Grassy weeds increased until wheat yields became so low where 2,4-D was used without tillage that the idea of chemical fallow was abandoned.

Concern developed over soil deterioration in the early 1950s because soil organic-matter content had declined, soil structure had deteriorated, and compact layers were becoming common. These conditions were blamed on excessive tillage, so concerned farmers and scientists devised ways to reduce the number of tillage operations used, especially in row crop production. The main reductions developed were in the preplant period. No chemical herbicides were involved.

Reduced Preplant Tillage. These reduced tillage systems dispensed with moldboard plowing or with one or more subsequent cultivations. Crops were produced successfully where land was prepared and seeded in one or two passes across the field as long as weeds were controlled. The methods involving plowing were given a variety of names, among them *plow-plant* and *wheel-track-plant*. The once-over tillage and planting system was called *till-plant*. A commercial till-plant machine manufactured at that time had front-mounted sweeps and rotary hoe sections and rear-mounted planters and fertilizer attachments. Farmers developed their own till-planters by adding units to tractors, or by pulling implements in sequence behind a single tractor. These hookups did a good job, but they were difficult to turn at the end of the field. Less traffic across the fields caused less soil compaction. The looser condition between the rows permitted more rapid infiltration, so less water ran off and erosion was reduced. Plow-plant systems still buried all crop residues but till-plant systems did not. Satisfactory crop stands were obtained, and yields approximated those from conventional tillage. Weeds were often less of a problem in the plow-plant and wheel-track-plant systems, and less post-planting cultivation was needed. In the till-plant system weeds became a severe problem before wide-spectrum herbicides were available.

The success of till-plant systems showed that there are two zones in a row crop field: the seed zone in the row area, and the moisture storage zone between the rows. There is no need to compact the moisture storage zone; in fact, better infiltration and less runoff and erosion occur when this zone is left loose. Some packing of the seed zone is usually necessary to get uniform planting and good seed-soil contact.

While results with corn and soybeans were satisfactory with these techniques, sorghum, a crop that requires a warmer seedbed and therefore a later planting date, did not do as well. Weed stands often were dense, and individual weeds grew so large before planting time that they were hard to control. Consequently, plow-plant and till-plant systems were seldom successful with sorghum.

In spite of some success with these systems and acceptance by a limited number of farmers, the techniques never really became popular until chemical herbicides more effective than 2,4-D were developed. One of the main reasons farmers were reluctant to use these techniques, apart from weed buildup, was that the speed of planting the crop was reduced to the speed of preparing the seedbed. Farmers with large acreages to seed to row crops want to plant rapidly when conditions are right.

Reduced Pre- and Postplanting Tillage. Additional incentive to reduce tillage came in the early 1970s with the drastic increase in price of tractor fuel and the possibility of severely curtailed supplies for agriculture. Increasing numbers of farmers all over the United States reduced cultivation and some even omitted it entirely, as shown in Figure 9–15. Weed control in these *no-till* systems is accomplished wholly with chemicals. Benefits are obtained from no-till systems, but there are also dangers. The major benefits are lower fuel and machinery costs, considerably less soil compaction, and better runoff and erosion control. An intangible benefit, but one that can be very important, is that the farm operator has more time to think, plan, and supervise his operations because he is not spending so much time cultivating.

The major disadvantage of no-tillage is that not all weeds are controlled even when chemicals are used. Chemicals restrict cropping choices and may damage crops. Herbicide results are not precisely predictable. Soil properties such as soil reaction, organic-matter content, clay content, and drainage characteristics, the amount of crop residue on the soil surface, and the climate all affect the activity and longevity of the chemicals. Options for fertilizer placement are seriously reduced with no-tillage, but this is not as serious a disadvantage as originally feared. Experience shows that plants can satisfactorily absorb even immobile phosphorus from surface-applied fertilizer if the residue cover keeps the surface soil reasonably moist and if crop roots are not pruned by postplanting cultivation. Other types of reduced tillage do not restrict fertilizer placement as severely as no-tillage.

Figure 9-15 Row crops can be seeded in untilled soil with a no-till planter. This model is equipped to apply liquid starter fertilizer but not herbicides. Attachments are available for this and other makes and models to apply dry fertilizer and either dry or liquid herbicides. The fluted coulter below the hydraulic cylinder loosens a 7.5-cm-wide slot for the planter opener to run in. (Courtesy Allis-Chalmers Corporation.)

Cost and Energy Requirements of Reduced Tillage. Fuel and machinery costs are less if less tillage is performed. Research results from the Southwest Great Plains Research Station at Bushland, Texas, show that reduced tillage systems can save up to half the normal fuel costs. Lower fuel and machinery costs, however, do not guarantee less farming expenses. The cost of buying and applying chemicals used to replace tillage operations must be deducted from the fuel savings. Some of the newer herbicides cost over $50/ha. Costs have been reduced by judicious selection of the most effective and economical combinations of tillage and chemical treatments. One study in North Dakota showed that using herbicides for weed control usually takes less energy than mechanical cultivation (Nalewaja, 1974). In a specific program of flax seed production, the use of chemical weed control reduced total energy use from 898,406 Kcal/ha for conventional tillage to 285,680 Kcal with chemicals, a reduction of nearly 70%, and increased the energy ratio output/input from 4.9 to 15.4.

Reduced Tillage and Soil Compaction. Reduced tillage systems in which plowing is eliminated can be expected to produce less soil compaction, both in the furrow slice and at the plowsole. During the first few years, however, the top 17 cm of soil may be denser under reduced tillage than it was when plowed regularly. This is especially true in no-till systems. Soil permeability and infiltration rate may therefore be slower in the no-till system land than in conventionally tilled land. Some but not all studies have shown that the surface soil becomes less dense as the reduced or no-till systems are continued.

Reduced Tillage and Erosion Losses. Infiltration rates should be higher and runoff lower with less compacted soils and with more surface residue on the reduced tillage soils. Erosion by water and wind should be lower also.

Data from a three-year study in Mississippi comparing no-till with conventional tillage are shown in Table 9–2. Average rainfall for the three years was 1320 mm. Conventional tillage, which included moldboard plowing, caused significantly more erosion than no-till in all cropping systems studied. Erosion losses were not significantly different on the various no-till cropping systems.

A six-year Wisconsin study compared conventional cultivation, stubble mulch tillage, till-plant up-and-down hill, and till-plant on the contour (Table 9–3). Results showed that both runoff and soil loss during the period April through October were less where residue remained on the soil surface, but all the soil losses were below tolerable limits (Onstad, 1972).

Investigations of the way reduced tillage affects wind erosion

Table 9–2 Effect of tillage system on runoff and soil loss at Biloxi, Mississippi, 1970, 1971, 1972

Tillage and crop system	Runoff (%)	Soil loss (mt/ha-yr)
No-till, soybean-wheat doublecrop	23	1.8
No-till, corn after soybeans	33	5.2
No-till, soybeans after corn	24[a]	1.3[a]
No-till, continuous soybeans	23	2.5
Conventional tillage, continuous soybeans	29	17.5

[a]Only two-year average results.
SOURCE: McGregor and others, 1975.

Table 9-3   Effect of method of tillage on six-year average runoff and soil losses in Wisconsin

| Parameter | Fallow | Tillage system | | | |
		Conven-tional	Mulch tillage	Till-plant up-down	Till-plant contour
Runoff (mm)	50.3	29.5	24.4	20.8	9.7
Runoff (%)	12.0	7.0	5.8	5.0	2.3
Erosion (mt/ha)	17.5	6.0	3.7	3.5	0.9

SOURCE: Onstad, 1972.

have been conducted both in the drylands of the Great Plains and on sandy soils in more humid regions. Black and Power (1965) found that chemically fallowed soil had a higher percentage of nonerodible clods in the surface soil and more surface crop residues than even stubble mulched fallow soil. Potential erodibility of the chemical fallow soil is therefore even lower than that of stubble mulched land.

The no-till method of seedbed preparation was compared to conventional tillage including moldboard plowing on sandy soils in northwestern Ohio. The no-till technique left 4 to 7 mt/ha of corn residue on the soil surface, while the surface with conventional tillage was nearly bare. The conventionally treated area lost 291 mt/ha of soil during one severe windstorm, whereas the no-till area lost only 4 mt/ha. Corn yields over the two years of the study averaged 4265 kg/ha on the conventionally treated land and 5833 kg/ha on the no-till area (Schmidt and Triplett, 1967).

Reduced tillage does not always increase infiltration rate and reduce runoff and soil erosion. Whitaker and others (1973) studied the effect of chemical weed control on Mexico silt loam (a claypan soil—an Albaqualf—in central Missouri). An immediate and striking reduction of runoff and erosion was noted when this soil was cultivated. A significant increase in runoff and erosion and a significant decrease in crop yield were measured when this soil was cropped using chemical treatment without tillage (Table 9-4). The mechanical treatment was better because tillage broke a pronounced crust on this soil and permitted better infiltration of rainwater.

Adapting Reduced Tillage Systems to Soils. Experience with reduced tillage systems has shown that successful systems are soil-specific. Poorly drained, high organic-matter soils do not respond

Table 9-4   Effect of chemical and mechanical weed control on runoff, soil
erosion, and corn yield on Mexico silt loam at the Midwest
Claypan Experiment Farm near McCredie, Missouri (four-year
average, 1966–1969)

		Runoff			
Treatments	*Precipitation* *(mm)*	*(mm)*	*(%)*	*Erosion* *(mt/ha-yr)*	*Corn yield* *(q/ha)*
Chemical	1016	241	23.7	23.5	66
Mechanical	1016	221	21.8	15.0	71

SOURCE: Whitaker and others, 1973.

well to the same chemical-tillage combinations that better-drained,
lower organic-matter soils do. Different responses also come from
sandy soils, medium-textured soils, and fine-textured soils.

As an example, a very successful reduced tillage-chemical herbicide system for sorghum production in a wheat-sorghum-fallow rotation has been devised for the Harney silt loam (an Argiustoll) and
similar soils in a 525- to 675-mm rainfall area in west central Kansas
(Nilson and others, 1973). This system has two tillage operations
between wheat harvest in early July and sorghum planting the following year: (1) cultivation with a blade implement in July or early
August, coincident with spraying the wheat stubble with herbicide,
(2) cultivation with a disk, duckfoot, or sweep implement no more
than 10 cm deep preceding sorghum planting in mid-May. Another
herbicide application may be used in the spring if grassy weeds become prevalent. Yields have been higher with this system than with
the traditional mechanical method of seedbed preparation. This
system cannot be used safely on sorghum on sandy soils in the same
rainfall region because of herbicide damage to the crop, nor can it
be used for sorghum in the same rotation father west in Kansas
where the climate is a little drier. The rates of herbicide application
must be cut back by 20% in the drier area.

Galloway and others (1977) grouped the soils of Indiana on the
basis of topographic position, drainage, color, texture, permeability,
and slope, and evaluated the usefulness of various forms of tillage
deeper than 15 cm (plowing and chiseling), and of tillage less than 15
cm deep (disking, tillplant, ridge-plant, and no-till) on the individual
soils. In general they rated reduced shallow tillage poorly on muck
soils. Reduced tillage, especially no-till, rated highly on sloping, well-
drained, permeable, coarse- and medium-textured soils. Moldboard
plowing, as an initial tillage technique, rated best on poorly drained,

slowly permeable soils with less than 4% organic matter and is quite satisfactory on somewhat poorly drained, permeable soils with 2% to 4% organic matter. An effort is required to find the right system of reduced tillage for a particular soil, but the possibilities of reduced costs, improved erosion control, and reduced compaction make the extra effort worthwhile.

9-6 DEEP TILLAGE

Farmers have been interested in stirring the soil to great depth much longer than they have had the power to do so. Their interest apparently stemmed from the belief that crop roots will develop more satisfactorily in soil that is disturbed by tillage. Early agricultural scientists evidently had the same belief. Many, if not most, U.S. experiment stations conducted studies that compared the effects on crop growth and yield of different depths of plowing, subsoiling, and dynamiting.

Sewell (1919) summarized the results of much of the early experimental work and concluded that plowing deeper than 18 to 20 cm had no special merit. Plowing as shallow as 7 to 8 cm generally produced lower yields, but there was no indication that any plowing depth between 8 and 18 cm was better than 18. Early crop root studies by Weaver (1926) at the University of Nebraska and moisture utilization studies at many dryland experiment stations in the Great Plains proved beyond doubt that crop roots go far below the cultivated zone, to depths of 1.5 to 2 m or more in most instances. These results should have ended the idea that deep tillage is better. It must be recognized that these early studies were conducted on soils that had no particularly serious compaction or other problem below the depth of conventional plowing. Deep tillage may improve crop performance on soils that have physical or chemical problems in their subsoils.

9-6.1 Deep Chiseling and Subsoiling

Deep chiseling is the practice of stirring the soil 30 to 40 cm deep with a heavy-duty chisel or chisel-plow that penetrates and rips the soil without inverting the ripped layer, as shown in Figure 9-16. *Subsoiling* involves ripping the soil 50 cm or more without inversion. Power requirements for deep chiseling and subsoiling are high. Chiseling the soil every 55 cm to a depth of 40 cm, or subsoiling 55 to 60 cm deep every 110 cm, takes more power than plowing 17 cm deep.

Figure 9-16 Deep-chiseling a field leaves clods on the surface and deep chisel marks in the soil. (Courtesy Allis-Chalmers Corporation.)

Water moves readily into soil as long as the cracks and slots made by tillage implements remain open to the soil surface. As the tillage marks are covered over or are filled by subsequent tillage or by normal weathering processes, water infiltration is limited by the small pores at the surface. Subsurface cracks that are not connected to the surface can drain off excess water from saturated soil, but they cannot help water infiltrate. Consequently, deep chiseling usually has no direct effect on the control of runoff and erosion except immediately after the tillage operation.

Deep chiseling can destroy or disrupt the continuity of a pan formed by tillage or soil development. Shattering such pans makes it possible for roots to penetrate better into the subsoil. Larger root systems absorb more nutrients and moisture, so the crop grows better and produces a denser ground cover that may help to reduce erosion.

Campbell and others (1974) found that chiseling to a depth of 38 cm loosened two Ultisols (Norfolk sandy loam and Varina sandy loam) enough to improve root penetration. The larger root systems collected enough extra moisture to permit the growing crop to evade damage during short drought periods, but the deep chiseling did not increase crop yields either in years of adequate and timely rainfall or in years of long droughts. Other similar investigations in both humid and dryland areas generally have failed to show consistent profitable crop responses to deep tillage (Hobbs and others, 1961; Jamison and others, 1952; Laws, 1953).

9-6.2 Vertical Mulching

Deep chiseling and subsoiling fail to reduce runoff and erosion mainly because the tillage marks do not stay open for continued rapid infiltration. Spain and McCune (1956) suggested a practice they called *vertical mulching*. They stuffed plant residues into subsoiler marks in an attempt to keep the slots open and effective longer. Surface water flows down the wicks in the subsoiler marks and moves into the soil through the sides of the slots as well as through the aboveground surface. These marks may remain effective for several years if sufficient crop residue is employed and tillage does not cover the slots. Thorough cultivation erases the tillage marks with their crop stuffing. A lot of crop residue is needed to do a good job of vertical mulching. At Bushland, Texas, a crop of sudangrass was grown instead of a year's cash crop production to fill the experimental slots.

There is little evidence that vertical mulching has an appreciable effect on runoff when done on the contour. No yield increases have been credited to it. In Indiana, where the idea was developed, the vertical mulch slots appeared to be more effective as drains to remove excess water from the subsoil than as channels to increase infiltration and crop production.

9-6.3 Deep Plowing

The methods of deep tillage mentioned so far involve only stirring the soil or cracking it open. Deep plowing involves inversion of the cultivated layer by very large disk plows (disks up to a meter or more in diameter) or with large moldboard plows. Some of the latter are capable of turning a furrow slice nearly two meters deep.

Early deep plowing did not go deeper than 30 to 50 cm. Investigations of this depth of plowing were undertaken to determine crop response to deep soil loosening. No instance of substantial benefit has been noted from this type of deep tillage except in a few soils containing pans that seriously restricted root penetration below normal plowing depth (Fehrenbacher and others, 1958). Deep plowing has been employed successfully where a productive soil has been buried by unproductive erosion sediments or where an infertile or a highly erodible surface layer is underlain by more productive or less erodible material. Deep plowing of this sort was apparently first used successfully in California where deep zones of mixed and rocky material from eroding hilly land were deposited on productive bottomland soils. Deep plowing proved a successful and an economical practice where the layer of sediment could be turned under and the old topsoil returned to the surface. The soil had to have a high productive capacity initially in order to make it worthwhile. Large areas of bottomland covered by relatively sterile, sandy, flood deposits also have been restored to something like their original productivity by deep plowing.

Deep plowing has been used successfully where highly erodible sandy surface layers of soil overlie finer-textured subsoils. These soils usually had sandy surface horizons initially, but wind erosion over the years had winnowed out still more of the clay and organic matter and left them structureless and extremely susceptible to wind erosion. The soils can be rendered less erodible and more productive if the finer-textured material is brought to the surface by deep plowing. The new surface tends to be cloddier and often contains more organic matter than the former surface material.

Thousands of hectares of very sandy surface soils are found in the southern Great Plains and elsewhere. Many hectares were deep-plowed in the late 1940s and especially in the 1950s. Results of studies in Oklahoma, Texas, and Kansas showed that *some* plowed soils were indeed less erodible and more productive, but some plowed land was not improved. Crop yields did not remain high unless greatly improved crop and soil management practices were used after the deep plowing.

Deep plowing should be restricted to soils that have the following properties:

1. A surface texture of sand or loamy sand with generally less than 10% clay.
2. A subsoil within reasonable depth (30 to 40 cm usually) with between 20% and 40% clay. Soils with more than 40% clay in the subsoil should not be deep-plowed because too much clay at the surface reduces infiltration rate.
3. A relatively level surface, without frequent hummocks, which indicate areas of deep sand.

If a sandy soil is to be deep-plowed, the following precautions should be taken:

1. Plow deep enough to turn up at least 1 cm of the finer-textured subsoil for each 2 cm of sandy surface soil present.

2. Plow in large solid blocks to minimize the proportion of the area of the deeply ridged, plowed land affected by drifting sand originating from nonplowed areas.
3. Fields with small areas of soils which have less than 20% clay in the subsoil can be deep-plowed if the extent of the sandy subsoil is less than 10% of the field area.
4. Furrows must be turned completely over so the subsoil is on top rather than mixed with the topsoil. Moldboard plows invert best with minimal mixing; if a disk plow is used, the disks should have a diameter at least twice the expected depth of plowing.

Deep plowing of appropriate sandy soils has brought about favorable changes in surface texture, structure, and organic-matter content. Soil erodibility has been reduced and crop yields increased.

Soil Texture. Surface clay content is increased by appropriate deep plowing. Clay increased from an original 4% to more than 12% in soils studied by Harper and Brensing (1950). Clay increased from 5% to 14% in some Texas soils but decreased again to 6% (Chepil and others, 1962) after only five years of subsequent cultivation. Clay increased from 6% to 12% in some Kansas surface soils.

Soil Organic-Matter Content. Changes in organic-matter content of surface soils were studied in both Texas and Kansas. Organic matter was increased from 0.3% to 0.5% in Texas, but was down to 0.4% after five years. The increase in Kansas was from 0.5% to 0.7%.

Structural Change. Clod-size distribution in surface soils was studied in Kansas. Deep plowing doubled the proportion of nonerodible clods from 25% to 50%. The cloddiness decreased over six and a half years to 32%.

Soil Erodibility. In the Kansas study soil erodibility was estimated from the proportion of nonerodible clods. Potential erodibility was 940 mt/ha-yr on the original unplowed soil. Erodibility averaged 360 mt/ha-yr immediately after deep plowing but was back up to 730 mt/ha-yr after six and a half years. These data show that supplementary erosion-control practices are essential even immediately after deep plowing in order to reduce soil drifting to a tolerable level and prevent subsequent damage to the deep-plowed land. The presence of a dense growing crop or of a thick plant mulch on the soil surface is the best assurance for controlling wind erosion.

These sandy soils require either 1250 kg/ha of standing wheat stubble or 2500 kg/ha of standing sorghum residue, or double these amounts of flattened residues in an area with a C' value of 100.

Crop Yields. Harper and Brensing (1950) showed that crop yields were increased by deep plowing alone, but that other improved soil and crop management practices such as better crop rotations and the use of fertilizer increased yields even more. Sorghum yields in Kansas were also higher after deep plowing, but yields declined with continued cultivation even where no serious wind erosion occurred. It appears likely that yield increases resulted from increased nitrogen released by oxidation of the higher organic-matter contents in the surface soils after deep plowing.

9-7 CONTOUR CULTIVATION

Contour cultivation, also known as *contouring,* is tillage and planting of crops across the slope along contour lines rather than up and down hill or parallel to field boundaries. Contour cultivation in humid and moist subhumid regions is used mainly to reduce soil erosion. It is used in semiarid and drier portions of subhumid regions primarily to increase soil moisture by reducing runoff losses. It also reduces water erosion, but this is often a secondary concern. Contouring as a soil conservation practice is discussed in the following pages. Contouring as a moisture conservation activity is discussed in Chapter 14.

Contour ridges produced by tillage, planting, and crop rows such as those in Figure 9-17, form barriers that slow or stop downhill movement of water. Temporary water-storage capacity for a given surface roughness is greatest on nearly level land and decreases as land slope increases. Thus more water is held in the contour furrows on nearly level land and less will run off than on steeper slopes. Contouring may prevent water erosion on gentle slopes, but its effect is much less on steep slopes.

The larger the ridges made by tillage, the more effective contour cultivation becomes. Lister ridges are larger and more effective than those made by cultivators. Where contoured lister furrows are blocked (dammed) at intervals along their length, rain is held where it falls and runoff control is improved. This practice is rather common in parts of Africa and Asia, where it is called tie-ridging. This practice is seldom used where agriculture is mechanized because the ridges and ties make the land too rough to be comfortably cultivated by tractors.

Figure 9-17 Contour cultivation on 1% to 3% slopes in Kansas. The ridges reduce soil erosion by acting as barriers to the flow of water. (Courtesy USDA—Soil Conservation Service.)

Contour cultivation has long been practiced in many parts of the world. In older lands with a long history of cultivation, it is rare to find sloping cultivated lands in a good state of productivity that have not been contour cultivated. Contouring in the United States was used first and most extensively in the southeast. Even there, however, relatively few farmers employed the practice until the 1940s, after the soil conservation movement was well started. Adoption of the practice has been slow and resistance to acceptance is still very strong, even though contouring is an inexpensive practice to install.

9-7.1 Contour Cultivation, Erosion, and Crop Yields

Most of the studies of contouring for erosion control appeared in the literature of the 1930s and early 1940s. A summary of results from various state and federal sources as compiled and mimeographed for the Soil Conservation Service by J. H. Stallings showed 25% to 76% reductions in water erosion resulting from contour cultivation compared to farming up and down hill. Smith (1946) quotes experimental results that showed contouring reduced soil erosion losses by 40% to 80%. A study near Ottawa, Canada, on Rideau clay soil showed that contour cultivation of land in corn reduced erosion from 17.5 to 5.8 mt/ha-yr (Ripley and others, 1961).

Most of the early studies on contour cultivation were conducted on small plots, and the tillage was nearer the exact contour than is possible in farm fields. Tillage lengthwise of the plots was almost exactly up and down hill. Two points should be kept in mind when viewing the experimental results. (1) The rows in the contoured plots were short and had little row grade to carry water to a low spot, so there was little water buildup behind the ridges. Contouring in fields usually has some gradient along the rows and is therefore less effective in reducing runoff and erosion than it is in the plots. (2) Farmers usually farm parallel to a field boundary rather than directly up and down hill. Thus farm field erosion is likely to be less severe than on plots farmed up and down hill. For these two reasons, the actual percentage erosion reduction a farmer achieves by changing to contour cultivation is usually less than that obtained in experimental plots.

Studies generally have shown that in addition to reducing runoff and erosion, farming across the slope increases crop yields. Summaries compiled by the Soil Conservation Service in the early 1940s showed only seven sets of comparisons, out of over 600, where the contour-treated land failed to outyield the noncontoured land. Average corn yields increased about 10%, average wheat yields about 29%, soybeans 11%, and sorghum about 28%. Reasons for these increases include more available moisture and a more productive soil on the contoured treatment. Also, there was less washing out of seeds and less burying of seedlings on the contour treatments.

9-7.2 Drawbacks of Contour Cultivation

There is much land that could benefit from contouring but is still being farmed parallel to a fence line. The most common reasons given for continuing to "farm with the fence" is that working a field on the contour is inconvenient, causes many short rows and much more turning, and increases labor and machinery time and cost. These objections become stronger as farm equipment gets bigger. It is known, though, that tractors operated on the level are more efficient than when operated up and down hill. Also, contouring produces longer rows as well as shorter ones. An old study in Kansas (Barger, 1938) showed that average tractor speed and area covered per hour were slightly higher and that fuel consumption was slightly lower with contouring than with up- and down-hill farming. Accordingly, costs in time, fuel, and convenience of contouring may not offset the benefits of erosion control and higher yields.

9-7.3 When and Where to Use Contour Cultivation

Contouring is most efficient in reducing runoff and erosion on gentle slopes. Intense rainstorms on steeper slopes cause water to accumulate behind the ridges until it breaks over, rushes downhill, and erodes rills and gullies. Erosion becomes progressively more severe on longer slopes until more erosion actually occurs in the gullies on the contoured land than in the rills between crop rows on the noncontoured land. Limits on slope gradient and length therefore have been set beyond which contouring alone is not sufficient for erosion control.

The slope-length data for successful contouring presented in Table 9-5 are average values. These change with soil characteristics (length can be greater on more permeable soils), with type of crop grown (longer for more protective crops, such as small grains), and with the area's rainfall characteristics (longer with less intense storms). Experience with no-till and other reduced tillage systems that leave the soil surface well protected with crop residue show that field lengths far in excess of those given in Table 9-5 can be used safely. The soil must be adequately protected by residue *every* year if field lengths are to be increased safely beyond these limits. Terracing (Ch. 10) is the only convenient way to reduce longer slope lengths to the limits indicated.

9-7.4 Farming a Contoured Field

Wherever possible, the upper and lower field boundaries should be changed to follow the contour. This reduces the number of short

Table 9-5 Slope-length limits for successful contouring

Land slope (%)	Maximum slope length (m)
1–2	120
3–5	90
6–8	60
9–12	35
13–16	25
17–20	18
20–25	15

SOURCE: Wischmeier and Smith, 1978.

(point) rows in the field and makes it more convenient to farm. Next, natural drainageways in a field should be prepared to handle the water that will be guided onto them by tillage marks and crop rows. Waterways that are to serve as paths or access roadways for implements may have to be extra-wide, as regular travel up and down the center of the waterway will severely damage the grass cover.

Any water flowing onto the field from higher land should be intercepted by a diversion built along the upper field boundary to catch the foreign water and carry it away from the field. A new waterway may have to be installed or an existing one widened and reshaped to accommodate the diverted water.

Farm fields generally contain complex slopes so that contour lines are crooked and adjacent lines are seldom parallel. A number of master lines (guidelines) are therefore necessary to lay out a field for contouring, as shown in Figure 9–18. The best guidelines are terrace ridges, but if a field is to be contour-cultivated without terraces, the guidelines must be laid out and marked permanently in some way. Guidelines need to be located so that the grade of tillage marks and crop rows falls toward the field edges and waterways and is within tolerable limits. It is seldom advisable to have these marks and rows exactly on the contour. They must not grade away from field edges or waterways because water would pond behind them, break over, and cause damage. Grades between 0.1% and 2% can be used on permeable soils. Less permeable soils should have gradients between 0.2% and 0.6% toward field edges or waterways (Carter and Carreker, 1969; Harris and Watson, 1971).

Some fields have such simple, uniform slopes that it is possible to farm the whole field parallel to a single guideline. Most fields have complex slopes, so several guidelines are usually necessary. The top guideline ordinarily is laid out about one terrace interval below the upper side of the field. Other guidelines are established wherever needed to keep row gradients from exceeding the permissible limits.

Guidelines should be laid out by engineers or conservation workers who have the necessary equipment (engineer's level and surveyor's rod) and experience. In the United States this service is provided free to all cooperators of Soil Conservation Districts (Ch. 19). The farmer should mark the guidelines by plowing or other suitable means before the layout crew leaves the field. Permanent stakes must be set in fencerows or elsewhere to mark the ends of guidelines that do not coincide with terraces.

All cultivating and planting operations are started along a guideline. Slopes remain the same along all tillage marks or plant rows where the guidelines are parallel but change with distance above or

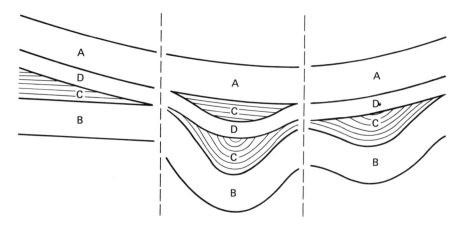

Figure 9-18 Diagram showing techniques for cultivating non-uniform width contour strips for most efficient field management and erosion control. The areas are planted in the sequence ABCD as explained in Note 9-2. D is the turn-row strip. (Courtesy USDA—Soil Conservation Service.)

below the nonparallel guidelines required where slopes are not uniform. Two situations arise: (1) The width between an adjacent pair of guidelines is greater in the center of the field than at the edges. In this case, successive rows parallel to and below a guideline carry water toward the field edges along progressively steeper gradients. Rows above and parallel to a guideline move water toward the field center. (2) The width between guidelines is narrower in the center and rows above a guideline direct water toward the field boundaries; those below a guideline direct water toward the center.

All cultivation and planting operations should be performed so that each furrow leads excess water to the sides of fields or to other vegetated areas established to carry the water safely to the foot of the slope. Unfortunately, such rigid water control is seldom practical because of the inconvenience of farming many areas of short (point) rows. Consequently, systems have been developed that keep the number of furrows that lead water away from field borders and other vegetated areas to a practical minimum, but which reduce the size of point-row areas considerably (Note 9-2).

NOTE 9-2 FARMING CONTOURED FIELDS

Fieldwork between parallel contour guidelines is commonly performed halfway up and halfway down from adjacent guidelines. It

is advisable to work the areas between adjacent nonparallel guidelines (on irregular slopes) in the following sequence:

A. Cultivate or plant full-length rows about halfway down at the
   narrowest width from the upper guideline.
B. Cultivate or plant the same number of rounds up from the
   lower guidelines, leaving an unworked strip wide enough to
   turn at the narrowest point.
C. Fill the intervening spaces with short rows according to field
   conditions as shown in Figure 9–18, leaving a uniform turn-
   row strip wide enough for the equipment used across the
   entire field length. Usually the area of short rows is below
   the turn-row strip. Field work here is done so that the ridges
   and plant rows grade down toward the field edges or to a
   waterway. Short rows should be worked out both above and
   below the turn-row strip where there are more short rows in
   C than full-length rows in B.
D. Cultivate or plant the turn-row area. This area can be seeded
   to the crop planted in the field, to another annual crop, or to
   a perennial grass or grass-legume mixture.

It is especially important to follow these instructions when planting a contoured field to row crops; the sequence is less critical when
planting small grains. Water will flow toward the center of the field
in some strips in area A of each section of Figure 9–18. Maximum
permissible slope lengths have therefore been established and terraces are recommended to help control runoff where the slopes are
too long.

9–7.5 Contour Furrows for Range- and Pastureland

Overgrazed or otherwise depleted rangeland may suffer from erosion
that would not occur on well-managed range or pasture. Contour
furrows and pits have been recommended as ways of reducing runoff,
increasing plant growth, and reducing erosion. Contour furrows are
not likely to be effective on sandy or rocky soils, on claypan areas,
or on steep slopes. Best results are obtained if the range includes
grass species that spread by rhizomes or by stolons. Bunchgrasses
that spread by seed or by tillering only are slow to respond.

Design and Construction of Range Furrows. Rangeland furrows should be laid out on the exact contour for best results. The simplest way to insure this is to lay out key contour lines as on cropland, about one terrace interval apart. The furrowing implement is worked halfway up and halfway down from the contour guidelines, with the odd-shaped lands filled in afterward.

Furrows are most commonly constructed with small shovels mounted on tractor tool bars. Sturdy equipment is needed to withstand the heavy pull through the sod and the fast speed required to scatter the turned sod. The tool bar should be capable of a fast lift so that furrows can be stopped short of rills, gullies, and roadways. Furrows may be from 7.5 to 30 cm wide and from 7.5 to 15 cm deep. Furrows that expose subsoil may reduce or prevent improvement and spread of vegetation. Furrows should be broken at intervals by lifting the shovels out of the ground. This reduces the danger of water concentrating at breakover sites where the furrows are not on the exact contour.

Range Pitting. Range pitting involves working the soil surface with specially prepared, large disk implements that have alternate disks removed. The remaining disks are either mounted eccentrically or have one-third of the circumference cut away so that each disk bites into the soil only part of the time. The irregular bites leave pits in the soil. Range pitting is less expensive than furrowing but is also less effective. Contour lines to guide the pitting operation should be laid out in the usual way at about normal terrace intervals.

9-8 EMERGENCY TILLAGE FOR WIND-EROSION CONTROL

It is not uncommon for wind erosion to start in some fields in spite of precautions taken to reduce the erosion hazard. Some soils are naturally very erodible, but the predominant factor that sets the stage for soil drifting is the lack of sufficient vegetative cover. Drought is a common cause of reduced vegetation. Winter killing of vegetation, insect depredations, and diseases can affect the amount of top growth produced and the protective cover on the land. Whatever the cause of poor cover, strong winds striking bare soil can cause drifting. Once movement starts, it usually spreads across the field, pasture, or range, and may also spread to neighboring areas. Emergency tillage is used to stabilize the drifting soil as quickly as possible and to prevent the spread of erosion.

9-8.1 Emergency Wind-Erosion Control

There are two general methods of emergency soil-drifting control. One is to spread a protective cover on the soil. Straw, manure, and other vegetative mulches have been employed successfully as have asphalt and other similar sprays. A cover of inert material such as very coarse sand and fine gravel also can be used. The second method is to roughen the surface of the soil by tillage to reduce wind velocity at the soil surface and trap flying soil particles.

Mulching. There is seldom enough vegetative mulching material available for emergency use on commercial agricultural fields. The nonvegetative organic mulches and the coarse aggregates are too expensive for widespread agricultural use, so tillage is the main method of emergency control.

Emergency Tillage. Implements that have been used in emergencies to control soil drifting include rotary hoes, disks, cultivators, chisels, listers, sweep and blade machines, and rod weeders. The main requirement for emergency control on fallow or other bare fields is an implement that will roughen the soil surface rapidly over a large area, as shown in Figure 9-19.

9-8.2 Controlling Active Soil Drifting

A strip of soil is roughened across the direction of the wind starting at the windward side of the field. The implement is then moved downwind to where soil is being picked up again by the wind and another pass is made parallel to the first. Successive passes are made across the field at intervals narrow enough to trap all saltating soil grains in the roughened soil; the wind passes on relatively free of abrasive material.

Spacing the passes across the field rather than tilling the whole field accomplishes three things: (1) It speeds up the emergency operation, permitting a much greater area to be controlled in a period of time. (2) It reduces the cost of the operation. (3) It leaves uncultivated strips that can be tilled in a second emergency action if the clods turned up by the first tillage break down under the wind. The space between tilled strips should be narrower than the immediate need if it appears that the wind velocity may increase later.

9-8.3 Emergency Tillage and Crop Damage

Emergency tillage destroys some plants if there is a crop on the land. A speedy decision therefore has to be made when erosion starts on

Figure 9-19 Emergency tillage to control soil drifting in a wheat field in Kansas. A chisel with wide spacing was used to produce ridges and furrows across the path of the wind where the cover provided by the wheat crop was inadequate. A large part of the crop was not damaged by the chisel operation. (Courtesy USDA—Soil Conservation Service.)

a cropped field: shall emergency tillage be performed, or shall erosion be permitted to continue in the hope that movement will not be serious and will stop before much damage is done? Knowing how much crop damage is done by tillage is helpful in making this decision.

A study near Dodge City in southwestern Kansas compared the effects of three emergency tillage operations:

1. Plots were cultivated every six meters with a two-row lister. This damaged the crop on about one-sixth of the soil surface.
2. Plots were cultivated every three meters with the lister. This damaged the crop on about one-third of the soil surface.
3. Plots were cultivated with an instrument equipped with chisel points spaced every meter. This damaged the crop on about one-fourth of the soil surface.

The yield results from each of these treatments on wheat after summer fallow and wheat after wheat are shown in Table 9-6. As wind erosion was never allowed to occur on the experimental field, this trial measured only the damage done by the tillage operations; it did not measure the benefits of erosion control. Yield reductions

Table 9-6 Effect of emergency tillage on wheat yields in southwest Kansas

	Wheat after summer fallow		Wheat after wheat	
Treatment	*Yield (q/ha)*	*Reduction (q/ha)*	*Yield (q/ha)*	*Reduction (q/ha)*
No emergency tillage	16.2	—	11.7	—
List every 6 m	15.4	0.8	9.8	1.9
List every 3 m	13.6	2.6	8.9	2.8
Chisel every 1 m	15.3	0.9	9.2	2.5

SOURCE: 1959 Annual Report of Southwest Kansas Experimental Field, Minneola, Kansas.

were greatest where the lister was used every three meters and were least where the lister passes were six meters apart. Actual yield reductions were less in the fallow wheat (wheat on summer-fallowed land), even though crop yields were higher in that system.

The crop yield decreases shown in Table 9-6 closely paralleled tillage damage on wheat after wheat. Fallow wheat crop damage was proportionately much less than the area of crop damaged by tillage. These data indicate that strip tillage on land in crop damages the crop but not excessively. The control of erosion and the lowered damage to the remaining crop more than compensate for tillage in a severe soil drifting period.

9-8.4 Implement Operation

Many different kinds of implements have been used for emergency tillage, but some work better than others. Woodruff and others (1957) studied the effect of speed and depth of tillage, spacing of points on a variable spacing machine such as a chisel, and the type of points (narrow, heavy-duty, and shovels) on the effectiveness of the operation and on the power requirements. They found that speed of implement travel had little effect on soil cloddiness, but increased speed made larger ridges. Depth of tillage seemed not to have much effect on erodibility. Spacing chisel points farther apart reduced the amount of surface roughness produced and gave less satisfactory erosion control. Narrow and heavy-duty points increased cloddiness more than shovels did, but the shovels produced bigger ridges. The heavy-duty points were most effective in reducing erodibility, with the narrow points more effective than the shovels at spacing about 0.7 m, and the shovels more effective at wider spacings.

Both deeper and faster operations increased the power requirement. On the basis of these results, the following recommendations for emergency tillage can be made.

1. Speeds in excess of 6 km/hr give the most effective immediate results on compact soils. A larger area can be covered more quickly and at lower cost with these high speeds. Slightly slower speeds, 2.5 to 6 km/hr, are better for longer-term effectiveness.
2. Close spacing, 0.7 m, of chisel points is more effective for erosion control. Chisel spacings of 1.0 to 1.5 m may permit control with less crop damage if soil drifting is not too intense.
3. Narrow-pointed implements work best for compacted soils, and shovel points are best for looser, medium-textured soils. Very loose soils, such as sands and loamy sands, usually cannot be prevented from drifting by tillage except by deep listing. Even listing works only for brief periods.

SUMMARY

There are three generally accepted objectives of tillage: to prepare a seed and root bed, to control weeds, and to prepare the soil to absorb water and resist erosion. Many tillage instruments are used in soil management and crop production. Some of these make the soil more erodible under certain conditions; some generally reduce erodibility. The tools that reduce erosion the most are those that increase soil cloddiness, produce surface roughness, and leave crop residue on the soil surface. Planting through a trashy surface and leaving the soil in a ridged and cloddy condition reduce erosion.

Conservation tillage is a term that is applied to a variety of systems that leave the soil surface trashy, cloddy, and ridged. Water and wind erosion are reduced by tillage systems that leave more crop residue on the soil surface and that make the soil more permeable. Two good examples of conservation tillage are stubble mulch tillage and minimum tillage.

Stubble mulch tillage is a method of farming with undercutting implements and associated equipment so that crop residue remains on the soil surface at seeding time to control erosion until the new crop provides its own protection. Stubble mulch tillage has been widely accepted in dryland regions but not generally adopted in humid areas.

Minimum tillage dispenses with some or all of the preplant and postplant tillage operations. At first tillage operations were omitted to reduce soil damage by implement traffic. Now they are omitted mainly to reduce operating costs. Systems of reduced tillage generally require the use of chemical weed control.

Tillage deeper than 17 or 18 cm has seldom proved beneficial or economical in the past. Powerful modern tractors and huge implements have provided the potential for very deep tillage. *Deep chiseling* or *subsoiling* may help where there is a subsoil condition that interferes with root penetration or with nutrient or moisture uptake, especially in years when the rainfall is insufficient for normal crop growth and development. *Deep plowing* has been used to bury infertile surface material and bring up productive soil from below.

Contour cultivation reduces erosion on gentle slopes. Contouring combined with terraces has wide adaptability and great potential for erosion control. Contouring used on cropland and contour furrows on rangeland help conserve water and soil.

Emergency tillage with a chisel implement reduces active wind erosion by bringing clods to the surface and forming ridges that trap the drifting soil. The implement must be pulled across the direction of the wind in passes close enough together to trap the abrasive material. Emergency tillage can be used both on fallowed land and on land in crop.

QUESTIONS

1. Is any tillage implement (for example, the plow) really indispensible now? Explain.
2. Under what specific conditions would a one-way-disk plow be a useful instrument on a dryland farm?
3. What can a subsistence farmer in western Africa do to conserve soil while growing grain sorghum, when little if any crop residue remains on the land at the beginning of the rains when seedbed preparation starts? (What the farmer has not removed for his own use is harvested by nomadic cattle herds or by termites.)
4. State the soil conditions that would be necessary for deep tillage with a 65-cm subsoiler to be a profitable practice.
5. Diagram the proper layout of contour guidelines on a real or hypothetical field and describe how to prepare the seedbed and plant a row crop on the field.
6. Tell what kind of implement is best and how it should be used for emergency tillage to control wind erosion.

REFERENCES

ALLAMARAS, R. R., S. C. GUPTA, J. L. PIKUL, and C. E. JOHNSON, 1979. Tillage and plant residue management for water erosion control on agricultural land in easter Oregon. *J. Soil Water Cons.* 34:85–90.

ALLAMARAS, R. R., W. C. BURROWS, and W. E. LARSON, 1964. Early growth of corn as affected by soil temperature. *Soil Sci. Soc. Amer. Proc.* 28:271–275.

AMEMIYA, MINORU, 1977. Conservation tillage in the western Cornbelt. *J. Soil Water Cons.* 32:29–36.

BARGER, E. L., 1938. Power, fuel, and time requirements of contour farming. *Agric. Eng.* 19:153–157.

BENNETT, O. L., 1977. Conservation tillage in the Northeast. *J. Soil Water Cons.* 32:9–12.

BLACK, A. L., and J. F. POWER, 1965. Effect of chemical and mulch fallow methods on moisture storage, wheat yields, and soil erodibility. *Soil Sci. Soc. Amer. Proc.* 29:465–468.

CAMPBELL, R. B., T. A. MATHENY, P. G. HUNT, and S. C. GUPTA, 1979. Crop residue requirement for water erosion control in six southeastern states. *J. Soil Water Cons.* 34:83–85.

CAMPBELL, R. B., D. C. REICOSKY, and C. W. DOTY, 1974. Physical properties and tillage of Paleudults in the southwestern Coastal Plains. *J. Soil Water Cons.* 29:220–224.

CARTER, C. E., and J. R. CARREKER, 1969. Controlling water erosion with graded rows. *Trans. Amer. Soc. Agric. Eng.* 12:677–680.

CHEPIL, W. S., W. C. MOLDENHAUER, J. A. HOBBS, N. L. NOSSAMAN, and H. M. TAYLOR, 1962. *Deep Plowing of Sandy Soil.* USDA Prod. Res. Rpt. No. 64.

DULEY, F. L., and J. C. RUSSELL, 1943. Effect of stubble mulching on soil erosion and runoff. *Soil Sci. Soc. Amer. Proc.* (1942) 7:77–81.

FEHRENBACHER, J. B., J. P. VAVRA, and A. L. LANG, 1958. Deep tillage and deep fertilization experiments on a claypan soil. *Soil Sci. Soc. Amer. Proc.* 22:553–557.

FENSTER, C. R., 1977. Conservation tillage in the northern plains. *J. Soil Water Cons.* 32:37–42.

FENSTER, C. R., H. I. OWENS, and R. H. FOLLETT, 1977. *Conservation Tillage for Wheat in the Great Plains.* USDA Extension Service PA-1190.

GALLOWAY, H. M., D. R. GRIFFITH, and J. V. MANNERING, 1977. *Adaptability of Various Tillage-Planting Systems to Indiana Soils.* Purdue Univ. Coop. Ext. Serv. Bull. A.V. 210.

GRIFFITH, D. R., J. V. MANNERING, and W. C. MOLDENHAUER, 1977. Conservation tillage in the eastern Corn Belt. *J. Soil Water Cons.* 32:20–28.

HARPER, H. J., and O. H. BRENSING, 1950. *Deep Plowing to Improve Sandy Land.* Okla. Ag. Exp. Sta. Bull. B-362.

HARRIS, W. S., and W. S. WATSON, Jr., 1971. Graded rows for the control of rill erosion. *Trans. Amer. Soc. Agric. Eng.* 14:577–581.

HOBBS, J. A., R. B. HERRING, D. E. PEASLEE, W. W. HARRIS, and G. E. FAIRBANKS, 1961. Deep tillage effects on soils and crops. *Agron. J.* 53:313–316.

JAMISON, V. C., I. F. REED, C. M. STOKES, and T. E. CORLEY, 1952. Effect of tillage depth on soil conditions and cotton plant growth for two Alabama soils. *Soil Sci.* 73:203–210.

JOHNSON, W. E., 1977. Conservation tillage in western Canada. *J. Soil Water Cons.* 32:61–65.

KETCHESON, JOHN, 1977. Conservation tillage in eastern Canada. *J. Soil Water Cons.* 32:57–60.

LARSON, W. E., 1979. Crop residues: Energy production or erosion control? *J. Soil Water Cons.* 34:74–76.

LARSON, W. E., W. C. BURROWS, and W. O. WILLIS, 1960. Soil temperature, soil moisture, and corn growth as influenced by mulches of crop residue. *Trans. 7th Int. Cong. Soil Sci., Madison, Wisconsin,* Vol. 1, p. 629–637.

LAWS, W. D., 1953. Tillage tests on Texas Blacklands. *Soil Sci.* 75:131–136.

LINDSTROM, M. J., S. C. GUPTA, C. A. ONSTAD, W. E. LARSON, and R. F. HOLT, 1979. Tillage and crop residue effects on soil erosion in the corn belt. *J. Soil Water Cons.* 34:80–82.

McGREGOR, K. C., J. D. GREER, and G. E. GURLEY, 1975. Erosion control with no-till cropping practice. *Trans. Amer. Soc. Agric. Eng.* 18:918–920.

NALEWAJA, J. D., 1974. Energy requirements of various weed control practices. *Proc. North Central Weed Cont. Conf.* 29:19–23.

NILSON, E. B., H. E. JONES, and W. H. PHILLIPS, 1973. *Grain Sorghum Production with Minimum Tillage.* Kans. State Univ. Coop. Ext. Circ. C–477.

ONSTAD, C. A., 1972. Soil and water losses as affected by tillage practices. *Trans. Amer. Soc. Agr. Eng.* 15:287–289.

PAPENDICK, R. I., and D. E. MILLER, 1977. Conservation tillage in the Pacific Northwest. *J. Soil Water Cons.* 32:49–56.

REICOSKY, D. C., D. K. CASSEL, R. L. BLEVINS, W. R. GILL, and G. C. NADERMAN, 1977. Conservation tillage in the Southeast. *J. Soil Water Cons.* 32:13–19.

RIPLEY, P. O., WILLIAM KABBFLEISCH, S. J. BOURGET, and D. J. COOPER, 1961. *Soil Erosion by Water.* Canada Dept. Agric. Publ. 1083.

RUSSELL, J. C., 1976. Some historical aspects of stubble mulch tillage. In *Conservation Tillage, Great Plains Workshop,* August 12–14, 1976. Ft. Collins, Colo., Great Plains Agric. Council Publ. 77, p. 1–12.

SCHMIDT, B. L., and G. B. TRIPLETT, Jr., 1967. Controlling wind erosion. *Ohio Report on Research and Devel.* 52:35–37.

SELBY, W. E., 1974. *Contour Farming Pays.* Kans. State Univ. Coop. Ext. Service R–14.

SEWELL, M. C., 1919. Tillage: A review of literature. *J. Amer. Soc. Agron.* 11:269–290.

SKIDMORE, E. L., M. KUMAR, and W. E. LARSON, 1979. Crop residue management for wind erosion control in the Great Plains. *J. Soil Water Cons.* 34:90–94.

SKIDMORE, E. L., and F. H. SIDDOWAY, 1978. Crop residue requirements to control wind erosion. In *Crop Residue Management Systems,* Amer. Soc. Agron., Madison, Wisc., p. 17–33.

SMITH, D. D., 1946. The effect of contour planting on crop yield and erosion losses in Missouri. *J. Amer. Soc. Agron.* 38:810–819.

SPAIN, J. M., and D. L. McCUNE, 1956. Something new in subsoiling. *Agron. J.* 48:192–193.

UNGER, P. W., A. F. WIESE, and D. R. ALLEN, 1977. Conservation tillage in the southern plains. *J. Soil Water Cons.* 32:43–48.

VAN WIJK, W. R., W. E. LARSON, and W. C. BURROWS, 1959. Soil temperature and the early growth of corn from mulched and unmulched soil. *Soil Sci. Soc. Amer. Proc.* 23:428–434.

WEAVER, J. E., 1926. *Root Development of Field Crops.* McGraw-Hill, New York, 291 p.

WHITAKER, F. D., H. G. HEINEMANN, and W. H. WISCHMEIER, 1973. Chemical weed controls affect runoff, erosion, and corn yields. *J. Soil Water Cons.* 28:174–176.

WISCHMEIER, W. H., and D. D. SMITH, 1978. *Predicting Rainfall Erosion Losses—A Guide to Conservation Planning,* UDSA Agric. Handbook No. 537.

WOODRUFF, N. P., and W. S. CHEPIL, 1958. Influence of one-way-disk and subsurface-sweep tillage on factors affecting wind erosion. *Trans. Amer. Soc. Agric. Eng.* 1:81–85.

WOODRUFF, N. P., W. S. CHEPIL, and R. D. LYNCH, 1957. *Emergency Chiselling to Control Wind Erosion.* Kans. Ag. Exp. Sta. Tech. Bull. 90.

WOODRUFF, N. P., C. R. FENSTER, W. S. CHEPIL, and F. H. SIDDOWAY, 1965. Performance of tillage implements in a stubble mulch system. I. Residue conservation. *Agron. J.* 57:45–51.

WOODRUFF, N. P., C. R. FENSTER, W. W. HARRIS, and MARVIN LUNDQUIST, 1966. Stubble-mulch tillage and planting in crop residues in the Great Plains. *Trans. Amer. Soc. Agric. Eng.* 9:849–853.

ZINGG, A. W., and C. J. WHITFIELD, 1957. *Stubble Mulch Farming in the Western States.* USDA Tech. Bull. 1166.

10

Conservation
Structures

The effects of crops, cropping systems, and tillage on the control of erosion were pointed out in the preceding two chapters. Nothing else need be done to control water and wind erosion where these practices work successfully. Sometimes, however, general crop and soil management techniques do not reduce erosion and sedimentation to tolerable levels. Conservation structures such as terraces and diversions, terrace outlets, waterway and gully control devices, streambank protectors, several types of dams, and artificial wind barriers are useful in many such situations.

10–1 TERRACES AND DIVERSIONS

Terraces have been used for centuries in parts of Africa, Asia, and Europe to reduce water-erosion losses from cultivated, erodible soils. The oldest terraces were mostly *bench terraces* consisting of a narrow leveled area bounded on the lower side by an almost vertical bank. Terraces were used in Central and South America before the Spanish discovered these areas. Generally, terraces were employed where the supply of good, level, agricultural land was limited and where population pressure forced the cultivation of steeply sloping soils. Field terraces and hillside ditches have been used since colonial times in North America to reduce soil loss and prevent gully formation. The early structures did not have enough capacity to carry off the water that ran into them during intense storms. Water frequently overtopped them, destroying the terraces and gullying the fields. These terraces were also narrow and steep-sided, so that cultivation with conventional farm implements was difficult or impossible and weeds were a serious problem.

The first really "farmable" terraces were constructed in 1885 by Priestly H. Mangum of Wake Forest, North Carolina. He made the channels and ridges wide enough to be cultivated, seeded, and harvested with ordinary machinery. The "Mangum" or broad-based terrace is now widely used around the world for erosion control on mechanically cultivated, moderately sloping soil. A narrower type called the *steep-backslope terrace* is used on steeper land where the terrace backslope becomes too steep for farming.

Most modern terraces are designed to intercept runoff water in a channel bordered by a ridge on the lower side. One type of ridge terrace has a graded channel that allows runoff water to flow slowly along the channel and be discharged onto stable, vegetated areas or into specially prepared outlets. This is a *graded terrace*. The other type of ridge terrace is a *level terrace* built with no grade in the channel so that accumulated water is held behind the ridge until it is absorbed by the soil. This terrace helps to reduce water erosion but its main function is to conserve water for dryland crop production. Its design and use will be discussed in Chapter 14.

Terraces cannot be used effectively on sandy soils because the ridges cannot be maintained. They are not useful on stony soils or on soils that are shallow over bedrock or over fine-textured, impermeable subsoils. They are not practical on fields with complex rolling topography and become very expensive and impractical for mechanized agriculture on fields with slopes in excess of 8% to 12%.

10-1.1 Bench Terraces

The early bench terraces were laboriously constructed by laying out strips across the slope and carrying soil from the uphill side of a strip to a lower side so that a level step or bench was formed. A second leveled bench was formed below the first, a third below the second, and so on. Because bench terraces were usually constructed only on steeply sloping land, the level benches were invariably narrow. A part of the original steep slope was sometimes left between terraces. The nearly vertical lower sides of terraces were stabilized by vegetation or by neatly fitted stonework.

Another even more laborious method of terrace construction was used where erosion had left only a shallow stony soil. The stones were gathered and carefully fitted into stone walls across the slope. Baskets were then used to carry soil from where it had been deposited in the valley back up the hill to where it was used to fill the area above the stone wall.

Some bench terraces built in ancient times are still being used successfully as shown in Figure 10-1. Many bench terraces are so expertly leveled that they can be irrigated by adding a small ridge at the downhill side to prevent water from flowing over the edge. New bench terraces are still constructed in developing areas where rapidly increasing population forces the cultivation of ever more steeply sloping land. The tremendous amount of labor or of machine time that is necessary to construct this kind of terrace prevents its use in areas of commercial agriculture except in some cases for irrigation. In the United States, for example, this type of terrace is used almost exclusively for landscaping steep urban and suburban properties.

10-1.2 Graded Terraces

Graded terraces such as the one shown in Figure 10-2 are designed to intercept runoff and carry it to a protected outlet. Some do not reduce runoff losses, but they reduce soil erosion and sedimentation by shortening slope length and slowing velocity of runoff. Some terraces empty water on a grass pasture or wooded area or in a natural waterway. More often, a specially shaped waterway of

Figure 10-1 Bench terraces on a steep mountain slope in the Punjab, India. (Courtesy Dr. G.S. Sekhon.)

Figure 10-2 A graded terrace carrying excess water from the terrace interval to a grassed waterway. (Courtesy USDA—Soil Conservation Service.)

the type described in Chapter 12 must be prepared to carry runoff safely from the field.

Advantages and Disadvantages. Graded terraces reduce effective slope length and thus reduce runoff accumulation and flow velocity. Soil erosion, particularly rill and gully formation, is reduced as volume and velocity of runoff decrease. Crop yields over a period of years are higher on terraced land than on unterraced soil in spite of the yield reductions that often follow immediately after construction. Long-time yields are increased because soil loss is reduced, soil productivity is maintained, and runoff water does less damage to seeds, seedlings, and growing plants. Greatest benefits are obtained when contouring accompanies terracing, but many farmers farm parallel to the field boundaries even on terraced land. Although non-contour cultivation always means more rapid terrace deterioration, farmers using large implements often prefer to reconstruct terraces rather than maintain them by contour cultivation.

Many farmers refuse to install terraces on their farms until bad gullying forces them to do so. Terraces roughen an otherwise smooth field. Also, there is danger that sections of the channel will stay wet long enough to cause delays in cultivation, planting, and harvesting, and often reduce crop yield. On shallow soils or on soils with less productive or impermeable subsoils, excavation seriously reduces the productive capacity in the channel area (Phillips and Kamprath, 1973). Low productivity often can be improved by applications of animal manure and extra fertilizer and amendments.

Most graded terraces are the broad-based type. Construction of ordinary broad-based terraces *increases land slope* because the ridge crest is above the former land surface and the center of the channel is below former ground level. The vertical fall from one terrace to the next is increased by the height of the ridge crest above the channel bottom, and the horizontal distance over which water moves is reduced by the length of the reverse slope from the ridge to the channel. On 4% sloping land, the average slope from terrace crest to the center of the terrace channel immediately below is increased to just over 5%.

10–1.3 Steep-Backslope Terraces

A newly constructed steep-backslope terrace is shown in Figure 10-3. These terraces are structures with relatively flat front slopes and nar-

Figure 10-3 A newly-constructed steep-backslope terrace in Iowa. This terrace is straight and parallel to the fence line. The near end of the channel is blocked and the water drains through the vertical white pipe at the bottom of the channel into an underground pipeline. (Courtesy F. R. Troeh.)

row, steeply sloping (2 : 1 or steeper) backslopes. Because the back-slope is generally seeded to grass, the structures are sometimes called "grass-backed terraces" or "seeded-backslope terraces." They are invariably designed as a series of parallel terraces, because the back-slopes are too hazardous to cross with farm equipment and it is impractical or impossible to move from one terrace interval to an-other except at field ends. Where feasible the terraces are constructed from the bottom side only, but where the channel must be cut below ground level in order to have the proper grade, or where taking soil from one side only involves too much earth moving, the excavated material from the terrace channel is added to the terrace ridge and the ridge is built from both sides. The ridge may be built from the upper side only in unusual cases where very deep channels must be excavated to maintain the proper gradient.

Advantages and Disadvantages of Steep-Backslope Terraces. Steep-backslope terraces reduce the field gradient between terraces by the amount of excavation below the terrace. Field gradient be-comes even lower as terraces are farmed and soil washes into the terrace channel. This type of terrace can therefore be used on land too steep to farm with broad-based terraces.

A disadvantage of this system of terracing is that the backslopes are too steep for equipment to cross; all up- and down-field move-ment must be at the field edges, and across-the-slope travel must be between the terraces. Part of the field is removed from crop produc-tion because the very steep backslopes cannot be farmed. These steep uncropped backslopes can contribute to accidents and pose problems of pest control and general management. Rodents burrow-ing through the ridges have caused terraces to fail when impounded water washed through their burrows.

10-1.4 Terrace Design

Terraces are usually designed to handle the runoff from a ten-year storm (the most intense storm likely to occur on an average of once in ten years). The U.S. national requirements for cross-sectional area of terrace channels specify a minimum of 0.75 m^2 on slopes less than 5%, 0.65 m^2 on 5% to 8% slopes, and 0.55 m^2 on slopes steeper than 8%. This usually requires channels at least 30 to 45 cm deep, and sometimes considerably deeper. Steep-backslope terraces often have much deeper channels and larger cross sections than these. Broad-based terraces should also have larger cross sections where farming operations angle across the terraces rather than being parallel to them.

The front slope of a steep-backslope terrace and both slopes of a broad-based terrace must be wide enough to accommodate the equipment that will be used in the field, generally not less than 4.5 m. The flatter these slopes are, the easier they are to farm but the more expensive they are to build. Cropped slopes should be no steeper than 10:1 (10%), but they must be steeper on steeply sloping land. Any slopes steeper than 4:1 (25%) should be seeded to perennial grasses.

The terrace channel gradient should be the minimum required to avoid wet spots and dispose of the runoff water fast enough to prevent overtopping. Maximum permissible gradient is about 0.4% for most soils to avoid serious erosion of unprotected channels. Steeper channels should be protected by perennial grasses. The minimum gradient to move water along the channel without ponding in microdepressions is about 0.1% on permeable soils and about 0.2% on less permeable soils. Steeper gradients are permissible at the upper ends of terraces where less water is carried than at the outlet end.

Parallel terrace systems with straight terraces are more convenient to farm. Variable channel gradients help make terraces straight and parallel but usually must be accompanied by cuts and fills during construction. These *cut-and-fill* terraces are the most expensive kind to build because soil must be hauled from ridges to swales along the length of the terraces. Straight parallel terraces are convenient enough to be preferred by many farmers in spite of the expense.

Failures sometimes occur on long terraces because water built up over excessive distance causes overtopping during intense storms. All the accumulated water rushes down to the terrace below, over it, and on down the field. Large gullies can thus be cut in a single storm. Terrace length must be restricted to reduce this danger. Terraces rarely should be longer than 600 m. Terraces should not be longer than 375 m on already gullied land. Longer terraces need to be subdivided with an outlet provided for each segment.

The best interval between terraces must make the land farmable as well as control erosion. The more permeable the soil, the less intense the rainfall, and the more erosion-resisting the crops that are raised, the wider the safe terrace interval on a particular slope gradient. Because terraces are nearly always laid out with an engineer's level, it is common to define terrace spacing in terms of the vertical interval (VI) between two adjacent terraces. The U.S. Soil Conservation Service devised a formula for estimating the best vertical interval (VI). In general form it is

$$VI = xS + y$$

where x = rainfall factor

S = slope, percent

y = soil and cropping factor.

Where *VI* is expressed in meters, x carries values from 0.12 to 0.24 and y values are from 0.3 to 0.6. The values of x, as shown in Figure 10-4, reflect climatic conditions, especially rainfall. The value of x is 0.12 in southeastern United States and 0.24 in north-central and western United States. If a soil is particularly impermeable and a crop provides little cover, the value of 0.3 is used for y; 0.45 is selected if *either* the soil *or* the crop is favorable for erosion control; 1.2 is used for permeable soil combined with good crop cover. For northeastern United States (x = 0.21), the vertical interval for a permeable soil producing a row crop (y = 0.45) on a 7% slope is $VI = (0.21 \times 7) + 0.45 = 1.92$ m.

Other empirical methods for determining vertical interval have been worked out in other countries. Hudson (1971) mentions those devised in the former Federation of Rhodesia and Nyasaland, in South Africa, and Israel. The former two give values similar to those obtained with the SCS formula, but the Israeli equation values for

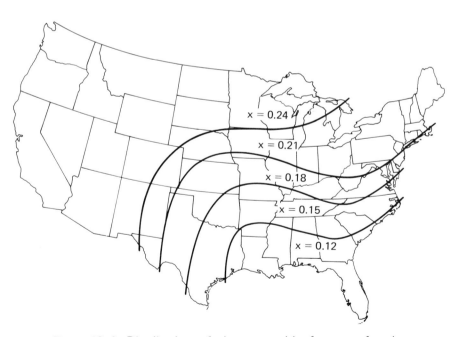

Figure 10-4 Distribution of the geographic factor x for the vertical-interval equation in mainland United States.

lower slopes are considerably larger. Bensalem (1977) gives equations used in Algeria, Morocco, and Tunisia. These also give values similar to those from the SCS equation.

The horizontal interval (*HI*) between terraces can be calculated by means of the formula

$$HI = \frac{VI}{\% \text{ slope}} \times 100$$

For the former example, the horizontal interval is calculated to be

$$HI = \frac{1.92}{7} \times 100 = 27.4 \text{ m}$$

HI is actually the *horizontal* interval, not the distance between terraces measured *across the surface* of the land. There is little difference between the two measurements, however, for gradients commonly encountered in fields to be terraced. For example, the distance across the land surface between terrace lines on the 7% slope mentioned previously is 27.5 m rather than the 27.4 m calculated from the equations.

The terrace spacings calculated for steep slopes are too narrow for convenient farming with modern large-scale agricultural implements. In practice, the SCS in the United States does not recommend intervals narrower than 30 m. Whatever the calculated spacing may be, it is usually adjusted to the nearest multiple of the width of the equipment to be used to farm the terraced area. The horizontal interval on hand-cultivated land can be considerably narrower than would be used for mechanical agriculture.

Terrace Layout. Designing terrace systems and staking terrace lines involves finding the appropriate sites for the terraces, selecting a suitable channel gradient, and "shooting" the terrace lines. Some terrace systems are sited on the basis of a complete topographic survey with readings on a grid every 15 to 30 m. Such a survey provides excellent information for design decisions, but a great deal of time is required to prepare the topographic map. Installation of terraces would have been very slow if such a map had always been required, because sufficient technical assistance was never available.

Terrace system design usually begins with a technician evaluating the water regime of the field from observations, soil surveys, and other information. The next decision is whether waterways should follow natural draws or be constructed on new sites. These decisions need to be made and vegetated waterways or tile lines laid before terraces are constructed. If waterways and terraces are constructed simultaneously, the waterways must be isolated from the terraces by *berms* (earth ridges) until the waterways are adequately vegetated to handle the water. The berms can then be removed and the soil used to fill the gullies that will surely have developed where the terrace water flowed outside the berm.

Terrace layout begins from the high point of the field. The vertical fall and slope gradient from the high point to the approximate site of the top terrace, usually 30 to 50 m downslope (depending on gradient), are determined with an engineering level. Several readings should be taken around the hill to determine an average gradient where the slope is complex. The recommended vertical interval is then determined using the observed slope gradient and the *VI* formula. The calculated interval is used if the high area is a long ridge. If the slope converges to a single high point, the *VI* determined from the formula can be increased by 50% for the top terrace.

The site of the terrace channel outlet is then located and marked by a stake where the vertical drop from the hill crest is correct. The location of the terrace is surveyed by giving the channel its proper gradient (based on soil permeability) across the slope. The outlet onto a waterway or other grassy area should usually be given the maximum permissible channel gradient (about 0.4% for most soils) so the water will escape readily. Allowance must also be made for the depth of fall from the bottom of the waterway to the soil surface at the outlet by adding about 15 cm to the elevation of the second stake point. The second stake is set 30 m from the outlet at the site where the surveyed elevation indicates the required channel gradient. Third and successive stakes are set at 30-m intervals on uniform slopes, but at 20 m on more complex slopes and at 10 m on curves and through draws.

It is usually preferable to begin staking a terrace at the waterway and work up to the top end, especially if the waterway is to collect water from terraces on both sides. Beginning at the upper end would place the outlet end too low on the hill unless a proper adjustment was made in the elevation of the beginning point. The line of stakes should be examined after all the stakes are set. Usually some stakes need to be reset to avoid short, sharp curves and to make field work parallel to the terrace easier. Adjustments upslope must be limited so that extra cutting depth for channel construction is reasonable. Downslope adjustments should also be restricted and precautions taken to raise the terrace ridge so water will not overtop the low spots.

Successive terraces are sited by measuring the appropriate vertical interval downslope and staking the terrace line as before. The first layout of a terrace system seldom achieves the most satisfactory design. Some unexpected topographical feature may show up and necessitate changing one or more terrace lines. After a reasonably satisfactory set of terrace lines is laid out, the setup should be examined to see if minor adjustments can improve farmability. Here, too, adjustments up- or downslope are limited by the resulting deeper cuts or higher ridges. The final terrace positions should be identified by plow furrows or other implement marks before construction begins.

Parallel Terraces. Farmers often object to terraces because they interfere with farming operations. This objection can be greatly reduced by building the terraces parallel to each other at spacings that are multiples of equipment widths. The objection is practically eliminated if the terraces can also be made either straight or gently curved and parallel to the edge of the field (sometimes field boundaries are relocated to make them parallel to the terraces). Parallel terraces are especially important to farmers using large equipment to grow row crops. The many point-rows between nonparallel terraces are an inconvenience that many farmers will not tolerate. Nearly all steep backslope terraces are laid out in parallel systems.

Parallel terraces are usually much more expensive to construct than nonparallel ones, because they require extra cutting and filling. This is especially true if they are much straighter than the contour lines. Many farmers who have soil deep enough to permit the required cutting and filling operations think they are worth the added expense.

Use of a contour map to plan the terrace layout before staking begins may save a lot of field work and reduce construction costs. The design can be transferred to the field after it has been worked out on paper. A guide terrace is staked out first, usually in the middle of the layout. The other terraces are then measured the specified distances above or below the guide terrace. Two or more sets of parallel terraces at different intervals are used in some fields where the slope changes too much for a single large set to be used.

Preliminary land smoothing may be required before parallel terraces are built. Even then, the terraces usually cross one or more swales. These swales must either be made into grassed waterways or underground outlets must be provided to remove the water. The modern trend in the U.S. Corn Belt is toward tile-outlet and cut-and-fill parallel terraces built straight across the landscape wherever possible. Long-radius curves are made where the topography will not permit straight terraces. The height of the terraces is varied so that the top is level even though they cross ridges and swales.

Construction. The field to be terraced should be cleared of trash, the dead furrows filled in, and small ridges leveled before construction is started. Soil productivity of the terrace channels is improved if topsoil is removed, stockpiled, and later spread over the terrace channel and ridge as construction is completed. This, however, increases construction costs so much that it is seldom practiced unless the exposed subsoils would be very unfavorable for plant growth. Conventional terraces can be built with bulldozers, motor patrol graders, carryall scrapers, elevating grader terracers, moldboard plows, disk tillers with 60-cm or larger disks, and with hand tools and baskets, headpans, or other carrying devices. Contractors using large-scale earth-moving equipment build most of the terraces in countries with a commercial agriculture where labor is expensive. Bulldozers are probably the most economical for moving soil short distances, as in Figure 10-5; graders do a better job of smoothing and packing the terrace. Carryall scrapers are needed for terraces involving much cutting and filling. Publications available from state extension services and from the Soil Conservation Service describe the building and maintenance of terraces. Blakely and others (1957) describe methods for building terraces with disk tiller, two-way moldboard plow, and motor grader, but these implements are not adapted for building steep-backslope terraces. Figure 10-6 shows a terrace being built by hand in a developing country, as it was done historically.

Regardless of the implements used to build terraces, the gradients of the completed channels and the height of the settled ridge top above the channel need to be checked to be sure that they meet specifications. High spots in the channels and low spots in the terrace ridges need to be corrected before heavy rains fall.

Terrace ridges wear down and the channels fill with sediment as the land is farmed. Consequently, maintenance procedures must be undertaken on a regular basis if the system is to be kept operating efficiently. Blakely and others (1957) described cultivation techniques with ordinary farm equipment that can be used to maintain terraces. Powell (1978) and Phillips and Beauchamp (1972) also give terrace maintenance hints.

10-1.5 Farming Terraced Fields

Seedbed preparation, planting, cultivating, and harvesting operations should be conducted parallel to terraces to minimize water and soil

a

b

Figure 10-5 Large equipment constructing a terrace in Kansas.
(a) A bulldozer pushing up the terrace ridge. (b) A motor patrol
grader smoothing and packing the terrace. (Courtesy USDA—Soil
Conservation Service.)

Figure 10-6 Tribal people in central India building terraces with village-made hand hoes and head baskets. The state ministries of agriculture lay out and supervise the construction. (Courtesy Roy L. Donahue.)

movement between terraces and to reduce tillage damage to the terrace ridges. But to which terrace should the short rows be parallel in nonparallel systems? Operations parallel to either terrace will mean working at least a little off contour. This will cause tillage marks and rows to have a gradient. Water may run down toward the terrace outlet, which is desirable if it is not too swift, but it may run back toward the upper end of the terrace, which is not desirable. Proper placement of the short rows assures that water flows toward the waterway or the lower end of the channel. Figure 10-7 shows a guide to planning cultivation patterns on terraced land. An explanation of field operations is given in Note 10-1.

NOTE 10-1 FARMING TERRACED LAND

The plan proposed in Note 9-2 in Chapter 9 for farming contoured fields may be followed between terraces also. Alternatively, terrace intervals can be farmed so that furrows always guide water to the waterway or to the terrace channels. The long rows or furrows *parallel to the upper terrace ridge* will all carry excess water toward

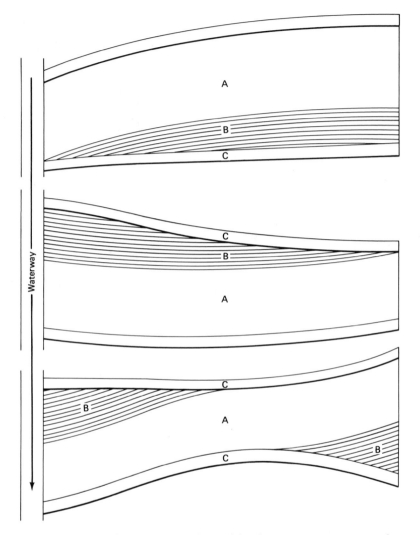

Figure 10-7 Guide to planning cultivation patterns on terraced land. In the diagrams the heavy lines represent terrace ridges and the lighter lines terrace channels. Unshaded sections represent long-row areas; shaded sections are short-row areas to be worked parallel to the shading lines.

the waterway where the terrace interval is narrowest as in the upper example in Figure 10-7. The short rows in section B will also guide the water toward the waterway side of the field, but will release it into the terrace channel short of the waterway. All furrows *parallel to the lower terrace* will carry excess water toward the waterway where the terrace interval is widest as in the middle example of Figure 10-7. The lower example illustrates a complex situation where the terrace interval is wide at both ends and narrow in the middle. The long rows will carry water all the way to the waterway if their upper parts are parallel to the upper terrace (as the interval gets narrower) and their lower parts are parallel to the lower terrace (as the interval widens). The short rows should be parallel to the long rows in their section of the field so they will guide water to the waterway or to the terrace channel.

Terrace intervals can be farmed in the field by working the long-row (A) areas first, then filling in the short-row (B) areas. The front slopes of the terrace ridges (C) are used for turn areas and are worked last. Plowed furrows should be turned uphill and up the front slope to oppose the downward movement of eroding soil and help maintain the height of the terrace ridge (Powell, 1978). Drilled crops in the terraced fields are often harvested as if there were no terraces on them, but with row crops the last rows planted (C) are harvested before the short rows (B).

10-1.6 Diversions

A diversion is a ditch or channel with an accompanying ridge on the downhill side that is designed to intercept runoff water and to carry it away at a nonerosive velocity. Diversions are usually constructed at the top or the foot of steep slopes or on property lines to protect productive soil that might otherwise be eroded or inundated. They are used to carry water away from the heads of gullies, away from roads (as shown in Figure 10-8), and around farmsteads. They are also built to carry water to ponds, to water spreading sites, and to special planting areas. In many erosion-control plans, a diversion is the first structure that intercepts runoff. For this reason, it must be well sited and carefully laid out and constructed. Many states have laws that control activities that change the flow path and the volume of water; these laws, where applicable, must be kept in mind when designing diversions.

Specifications. A diversion designed to conduct runoff from higher land around a cultivated area should have capacity sufficient to handle a ten-year-frequency storm. Diversions designed to protect houses, farmsteads, or expensive engineering works will need capacity to control more severe storms, at times as high as fifty-year storms.

The channels of diversions are vegetated and are designed to

Figure 10-8 A diversion ditch in Nigeria designed to carry water from a highway ditch safely away from the right-of-way. Spreading the water on naturally-vegetated sites dissipates its energy. (Courtesy J. A. Hobbs.)

carry water away more rapidly than terrace channels so sediment will not collect, but not fast enough to cause erosion in the channel. Permissible flow velocity depends in part on how thick the vegetative cover is in the diversion channel. Gradients are often as high as 0.5% and sometimes as high as 0.8%.

A diversion commonly has a flat bottom 1 to 6 m wide, and straight front and back slopes (trapezoidal shape). The sides often have slopes of about 4:1 although they may range from 2:1 to 6:1. The channel depth ranges from 35 to 100 cm. The actual size depends on the volume of water to be handled and the velocity of flow. Diversions, particularly those with steep side slopes, are difficult to construct with plows and disks or other farm implements, so the work is generally done by conservation contractors.

10-2 TERRACE OUTLET AND WATERWAY AND GULLY CONTROL STRUCTURES

A protected waterway is needed wherever runoff is discharged from terraces or diversions. Usually vegetated waterways such as those described in Chapter 12 are the cheapest and most effective structures for this purpose. There are conditions, however, that reduce the effectiveness of vegetation so much that special structures such as those used to control gullies are necesary in surface waterways to control erosion. Also, the waterways occupy valuable land, so it may be preferable to remove the water through underground outlets.

10-2.1 Underground Outlets

Underground outlets take runoff water from low points in terrace or diversion channels or from behind other forms of earthen embankments and carry it through a pipeline to a place of safe discharge. Underground outlets are used in preference to vegetated waterways because the possible waterway sites are too steep for nonerosive water movement, because the rate of peak runoff must be reduced for flood control, or because the cost in installing a system of underground pipe is less than that of forming the waterway *and* taking its area out of crop production. Outlets of this sort are not new, but they were not widely used until the concept of detention storage in the collecting system was introduced in the early 1960s.

There are four major parts to an underground water outlet system. The *inlet tube (riser)* is made of plastic, metal, or concrete. It rises from a pipeline below the soil and has holes or slots at intervals above the ground level. An *orifice plate* is located at the base of the inlet tube where it joins the horizontal conducting pipe. This plate regulates the rate of downward water movement and prevents water pressure from building up in the pipe and flooding the terraces lower in the field. The *conducting pipe* can be of plastic, metal, or concrete. It carries water from one or more inlet tubes down to the outlet. The *outlet,* which is the fourth essential component of the system, is usually located in a natural waterway with enough protection to handle the runoff water without excessive erosion.

Advantages and Disadvantages. Several distinct advantages are obtained by use of underground outlets, but there are also a number of disadvantages. A major advantage is that soil loss from the field is reduced because sediment settles out in the stored-water area and only suspended material travels to the outlet. Low sections in terrace channels in the vicinity of former gullies tend to fill up with the soil washed down from the land above the terrace. This sediment deposition levels the field. Peak runoff rates from terrace systems or diversions are reduced because of the detention storage built into the system. The fact that grassed waterways are not needed makes more land available for cultivated crop production. Escalating land values make this an increasingly important advantage.

One of the main disadvantages of underground outlets is that the cost of construction is usually higher than for vegetated waterways. The design and construction of a satisfactory underground outlet are much more critical than for a simple grassed waterway. Damage to crops may occur in the detention areas because of ponding during and after excessive storms. There is also a chance of damage to the system and to lower-lying fields if excess rainfall causes overtopping of the ridges. Crop and soil damage from standing water and from overtopping occur when the riser inlet holes or the orifice plate become plugged with trash.

Specifications. Underground outlets are usually designed so that the discharge rate and storage capacity of the terrace system can handle a ten-year-frequency storm and dispose of the accumulated runoff in less than forty-eight hours. Actual size of the inlet holes, orifice plates, conducting pipe, and outlet must be designed to meet this criterion. Slope of conduit pipe influences speed of discharge and must be considered also. Arriving at detailed specifications is a complicated procedure and is beyond the scope of this book. Griessel and Beasley (1971) describe methods using tables, complicated figures, and local hydrological information to arrive at specific design criteria. Farmers can obtain planning assistance from Soil Conservation Service technicians.

The inlet riser for an underground outlet should be approximately 7 to 10 cm higher than the adjacent terrace or diversion ridge. The riser should be equipped with a removable cap to prevent entry of debris and to permit the orifice plate to be taken out and cleaned if it becomes plugged. The orifice plate opening should be at least 4 cm in diameter to reduce danger of clogging. The terrace or diversion ridge must be level in the vicinity of the major storage area to minimize the chance of overtopping. Detention capacity of the system must be sufficient, together with the drawdown capacity of the inlets, to handle the runoff from normal storms without damage to the system or to the crops. Figure 10-9 shows a terrace system in Kansas with underground outlets.

Construction. Construction of an underground outlet system is similar to the installation of tile drain lines (Ch. 15). The construction procedure involves digging the trench, laying the conduit pipe, and fitting an inlet for the surface riser. The trench is then filled and compacted all the way to the surface. Next the diversion or the terraces are constructed with the ridges being well compacted, especially over the trench area. The conduit is then exposed again in the

Figure 10-9 A terrace system in Kansas with underground outlets. Water drains through the black riser pipes in the terrace channels. This area received 230 mm of rain in three hours the day before the photo was taken. (Courtesy USDA—Soil Conservation Service.)

center of each channel area, and each riser with its orifice plate is installed. The soil is again packed in place and the system is ready for use.

10-2.2 Artificial Mulch

Artificial mulches are often useful to control water erosion on newly formed waterways and other areas while a vegetative cover is being established. Burlap was one of the first materials used for this purpose but is too expensive to use at the present time. Several types of mulch mats consisting of shredded wood, paper, or plastic strips held in wide-mesh, fine-string envelopes 2 m or more wide by 15 m or more long are now available commercially in the United States. Envelopes are staked side by side over the shaped, seeded, and smoothed surface, as shown in Figure 10-10.

The mulch intercepts the erosive forces of the raindrops and the running water, thus reducing erosion until the seeding produces its own protective cover. These mulches maintain their integrity for two to six months depending on the material from which they are constructed and on the climate. Water from outside the protected area

Figure 10-10 A fibrous protective mulch placed over a shaped streambank in Virginia. The mulch will control erosion until the seeded vegetation is established. (Courtesy USDA—Soil Conservation Service.)

may need to be diverted by means of a berm. A berm consisting of a furrow turned onto the mulch nets serves the double purpose of diverting foreign water and preventing wind from getting under the nets and ripping them or blowing them away.

Asphalt, latex, and other synthetic mulches are also used to control both water and wind erosion in road cuts, ditches, and on other construction sites until vegetation can be established. Success of these materials is reviewed from time to time by the USDA Wind Erosion Laboratory (Armbrust and Lyles, 1973). They have so far proven too costly for use on agricultural soils. It is usually better to use a fast-growing companion crop or a preliminary cover crop that either freezes or is killed before the permanent cover is planted (Chs. 11 and 12).

10-2.3 Broken Rock for Erosion Control

Stone and broken-rock coverings are a simple and long-used technique to reduce erosion in waterways and gullies. *Rip-rap,* which is a loose covering of stone on the soil surface, has been widely employed for this purpose. It has also been used on the front slopes of earthen dams to prevent wave action from wearing the dam face. The stones have been sorted and placed by hand, but are now more likely to be dumped over the surface and smoothed by machine. More rock is required this way, but the amount of labor is markedly reduced.

The soil surface should be smoothed before rock is applied, otherwise water may still flow in the old channel below the stones. The nature of the eroding site and the velocity of the runoff water dictate the thickness of the protective stone layers. The material placed next to the soil is coarse sand or fine gravel that will prevent soil from washing through its pores. Each succeeding layer has larger particles but not large enough for the preceding layer to move through the holes. The top layer of stones must be too large for the stream to move.

Broken rock has become so expensive that it is no longer being used for rip-rap on the front slopes of the small dams constructed under the watershed district program in central United States. It is still a useful technique in many areas, though, because rock is a natural material, is widely available, and needs no special treatment except breaking and sorting into suitable sizes.

Rock Barriers. A barrier or a series of barriers is often needed to reduce the erosive power of the water in steeply sloping waterways and in many gullies so vegetation can be established. Piles of rocks can serve to accomplish this end, but the surface rocks must be too large and too carefully laid to be moved by the runoff water, and the soil must not be permitted to wash out from between them. Wire netting can be used as a fence to prevent the breakdown of a rock dam, or it may be used to form a basket (gabion). The netting is laid all the way across the channel and loose stones are placed on its upstream half. The remaining netting is folded over the rocks and is wired to the edge of the netting on the ground. These rock barriers slow water velocity and trap sediment. They are flexible enough to maintain contact with the soil even if the ground settles beneath them.

A stepped condition develops where several barriers are installed in a waterway or gully. Erosion is reduced by the flatter slope between barriers, and vegetation has a chance to grow on the more level areas (Ch. 12).

10–2.4 Brush, Log, or Timber Barriers

Temporary wooden structures were used to slow runoff and trap sediment in waterways and gullies during the early years of the conservation movement in the United States when labor was more plentiful than money. Wood and other natural materials are still recommended and used regularly in many developing countries (Kunkle and Harcharik, 1977).

Brush Barriers. Two rows of posts driven vertically into the soil across the waterway or gully bed are used to anchor brush barriers in place. Posts are spaced about a meter apart in each row and 50 cm between rows. Loose branches or small trees are packed tightly between the rows of posts. Care must be taken to insure that the bottom members make firm contact along the sides and bottom surface. The barrier must be sufficiently impermeable to prevent water from jetting through and undermining the structure. Protective aprons must be provided where water drops to the channel floor (Heede, 1976). The ends of the brush piles should be dug into the channel walls and the soil packed tightly around them. The top of the brush pile normally is low in the middle so no water will flow around the ends. The brush may be wired firmly to the posts or held in place by logs or small trees fastened to the upright posts.

Log Barriers. Logs may be used to form barriers in larger gullies. Sturdy posts are driven deeply into the channel sides and bottom as for brush barriers. The logs often must be dug into the bottom as well as the sides of the channel so they make firm contact with the soil. Logs are wedged and piled tightly between the upright posts and are held in place by cross pieces spiked or wired to the posts. A large flat notch should be left in the middle of the barrier so overflow water will be guided onto an apron and not wash away the banks.

Timber Barriers. Heavy-dimension lumber or timber, or a series of thick posts driven closely together, will also serve for barrier construction. Posts are driven vertically into the soil to support the barrier, or the timber itself may be driven vertically into the ground and reinforced with horizontal members. The vertical members should be driven deeper into the soil than the length of the exposed part aboveground so the force of the water cannot move the tops downstream. The effectiveness of the dam is greatly impaired if movement occurs and water flows between the upright members.

The larger or thicker the pieces of wood used in the barrier, the longer it should last. Selection of termite-resistant wood helps to guarantee longer life to the structure in areas where these pests occur. A rectangular notch invariably is used for a spillway where timber is employed.

10–2.5 Brick Barriers

Brick barriers can be used to stop gully erosion. Fired construction bricks can be purchased, but the cost is high unless bricks with blemishes (seconds) can be obtained. Sun-dried clay bricks are available in many developing countries, but these will not stand up well if they are continuously wet. Laterite blocks cut from the soil in some tropical areas and allowed to harden by desiccation also can serve. Sand-cement blocks can be used in place of bricks.

A good foundation such as poured concrete or layered rock is necessary for any barrier built with bricks or blocks. The ends of the barrier must penetrate the gully wall and be sealed in with soil material (not topsoil) packed tightly between the barrier ends and the excavated gully walls. Water must not be allowed to seep around the ends and wash out the barrier.

A straight wall of bricks and mortar can be pushed over by a mass of water. Buttresses supporting the wall on the downstream side will strengthen it, or the barrier may be built so it arches upstream. This structure passes the force of the water from the center toward the outer ends of the barrier, eventually to the point where the ends butt into the soil. This type of structure requires very strong resistance to compression where the barrier meets the gully wall.

All barriers built of bricks or blocks must have a notch large enough to pass the largest expected flood without overtopping the barrier at any other point. Otherwise, flood water will wash around the barrier at one or both ends and cut a new channel. The gully floor immediately below the notch must be protected so that the falling water cannot erode the gully surface and undercut the barrier. Loose stones are suitable for protection if they are large enough to resist movement by flood water. Smaller stones may be used, but they must be placed in gabions or anchored in some way to hold them in place on the gully floor.

10–2.6 Drop Structures and Chutes

The barrier structures discussed in the preceding sections are built to control erosion temporarily until vegetation can be established. There are situations, however, where the erosion-control structure will be needed for an indefinite period of time. Under these conditions, more durable structures and more expensive construction methods may have to be used. Most of these are made of poured concrete and some are steel-reinforced.

Drop Structures. Drop structures are small dams used to stabilize steep waterways and other channels, to level waterways so they need not be planted to perennial vegetation, to serve as outlets for highway culverts and ditches, and to serve as outlets for sediment traps. They can handle large volumes of runoff water and are effective where falls are less than 2.5 m.

A drop structure can be built of timber, sand-cement blocks, rubble masonry, poured concrete, or corrugated metal. As shown in Figure 10–11, its main wall is placed across the gully or channel and has cutoff walls extending into the banks of the channel to anchor the structure and insure that water will not cut around it. The main

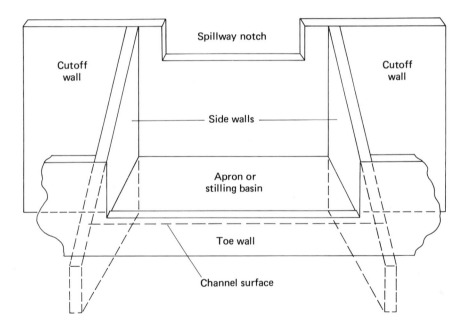

Figure 10-11 Diagram of a concrete drop structure. The side walls join the toe wall and extend sideways as indicated by the solid lines if the waterway below the structure is parallel to the to the toe wall. Where the waterway below the structure is perpendicular to the toe wall, the side walls extend down the waterway as indicated by the dotted lines.

wall has either a notch or a box inlet (for larger volumes of runoff) to serve as a spillway. A horizontal apron or stilling basin is provided below the spillway to absorb the energy of the falling water. The front of the apron is reinforced and stabilized by a toe wall that projects into the soil parallel to the main wall. Permanent side walls extend from the main wall to the end of the apron or beyond. Structures with long main walls may need one or more buttress supports between the side walls on the downstream face.

Failure of drop structures usually results from water washing away the soil at the structure-soil interfaces. For this reason, the cutoff walls and the toe wall must be long enough to protect against water undercutting the apron. Soil material must be packed very tightly against these elements to prevent water damage. The notch size required to pass the runoff from the maximum expected storms can be calculated from the weir formulas in Figure 16–8. A box inlet can be used where the channel is too narrow to allow a large enough straight notch to handle the expected runoff. Flow rate into a box inlet can be predicted from the combined length of the sides and end(s) of the open box and the depth of water flowing over the lip. Discharge rate is 12% greater for flows 0.3 m deep and about 16% greater for flows 1 m deep than for straight notches.

Chutes. Chute spillways collect runoff water at one elevation and carry it down a slope to a lower elevation, as shown in Figure 10–12. Chutes for short slopes and for small amounts of runoff (0.5 to 3.5 m^3/sec) may be built without forms by excavating the desired shapes in the surface of the ground. Mixed concrete is poured onto the prepared surface and smoothed in place. Wire mesh reinforcing is required in areas where large temperature variations are expected, but it may not be needed in many parts of the world.

Flat slab limestone and other rocks were used to form chute spillways in the early days of conservation work. Rocks were placed on the channel and the joints were filled with a sand-cement mixture. These structures were reasonably satisfactory, but they frequently cracked at the stone edges and deteriorated with time, especially where freezing and thawing occurred. Their main advantages are that less cement is needed and the chute surface is usually rough enough to reduce flow velocities.

The shapes of the inlet and outlet sections of chutes are very important. Some energy-dissipating structure must be provided at the outlet, because the water attains very high velocities on the smooth surfaces of these structures. Energy dissipators usually consist of a boxlike device that holds a pool of water and overflows at

Figure 10-12 A concrete chute designed to carry runoff water safely down a slope to the bottom of a road ditch. (Courtesy F. R. Troeh.)

ground level. Some of these boxes are partly filled with stones too large to be moved by the water velocities expected.

Formed sidewalls and cutoff walls are needed where larger amounts of water must be carried or where the drop is more than two meters. Formed wing walls may be required in addition to diversions to channel the runoff into the chute.

10-3 EARTHEN DAMS

Several types of earthen dams are used in conservation. The main reasons for building such dams are:

1. To trap sediment.
2. To stabilize drainage ways and reduce erosion.
3. To store excess water temporarily to reduce flood damage.
4. To store water for livestock, irrigation, household, or municipal use.

Dams for water storage will be discussed in Chapter 14. Dams with one or more of the other three objectives are described here.

Earthen dams are divided into three classes on the basis of the severity of the damage that might occur if the dam failed and the impounded water rushed downstream:

Class A dams are located in strictly rural or agricultural areas. Failure will cause water to inundate farm fields and may do damage to local (township or county) roads. Farm buildings, but not homes, may lie in the path of the flood waters.

Class B dams are located in predominantly rural and agricultural areas. Failure may cause damage to isolated homes, as well as to farm buildings, main (state and federal) highways, branch railroad lines, and public utilities.

Class C dams are located where failure would cause serious damage to homes, industrial and commercial buildings, main highways, and main railroad lines. Possible damage to utilities could cause serious interruptions of use or service.

The dam classification assignment is based not only on the type of damage than can occur with the present development, but also on the damage that will occur with possible expanded future development of the land area below the dam.

Most dams constructed for individual farmers belong to Class A. Most dams built in the small watershed program of the U.S. Soil Conservation Service also belong to Class A, but some are Class B, and a few near urban centers are Class C structures.

10–3.1 Soil-Saving Dams (Sediment-Storage Dams)

A soil-saving dam is designed to intercept and trap waterborne sediments. The dam usually has a principal spillway that passes the water off slowly enough to allow sediment to settle out. This spillway may be in the form of a notch or box inlet with sufficient freeboard so water will never overtop the dam.

10–3.2 Grade-Stabilization Dams

Grade-stabilization dams are used as shown in Figure 10–13 to prevent gullies from eating back into fields, to stabilize or raise gully channel floors, or to drop water from terraces, waterways, or diversions to stream channels at lower elevations. The rapid growth of gullies often makes installation of a dam an urgent matter. The size and cost of the required structure or set of structures increases rapidly as a gully grows. Gullies generally flow on rela-

Figure 10-13 A class B dam constructed to stop erosion in a gully and to provide a waterfront for recreation. (Courtesy USDA—Soil Conservation Service.)

tively flat gradients because the nonvegetated surfaces and relatively deep, narrow channels are conducive to high flow velocities or reduced slope gradients or both (Manning's formula, Note 4-2, can be used to evaluate these effects). Low slope gradients cause many gullies to become deeper as they eat their way back into landscapes.

The simplest way to stop a gully with a structure is to place the dam at the site of the overfall. Some dams are placed downstream because the site at the gully head is not suitable. A long gully is usually best stabilized by a set of small structures at intervals along its length. The need for land shaping above a dam depends primarily on the amount of previous cutting and the amount of sediment that will be trapped. High vertical walls should likely be pushed in, shaped, fertilized and revegetated, especially where further sloughing is expected. The water pool often will be filled with sediment as time passes.

10-3.3 Flood Control Dams

Flood control in the United States comes under the jurisdiction of two separate government agencies. Control of floods along the main rivers is the responsibility of the U.S. Army Corps of Engineers; control of flooding on small watersheds in the upper reaches of the rivers and streams was assigned to the USDA Soil Conservation Service by the Omnibus Flood Control Act of 1936. The 1947 federal Watershed Law made provision for watershed districts, set up under state laws, to obtain financial assistance from the federal treasury to build flood control structures. These funds paid all the design and construction costs and were separate from those paid for conservation work through the Agricultural Stabilization and Conservation Service of the USDA (Ch. 19). Accordingly, most of the small flood control dams in the United States have been designed, constructed, and paid for under the watershed program.

Most flood control dams in small watersheds serve two main purposes: flood control and grade stabilization. They also trap sediment, but this is not a major objective. A certain amount of sediment storage is designed into each flood storage reservoir so that its life expectancy is about fifty years.

Flood control dams are built with capacity to store the runoff from a ten- to fifty-year storm. This flood water passes from the storage pool by means of the principal spillway, usually a pipe through the dam, over a period of several days. Runoff in excess of that from the designed storm passes immediately over an emergency spillway—usually a grassed waterway.

Some flood control dams in arid regions seldom contain any water but must have large capacities to control flash floods. Figure 10-14 shows one of several structures built to protect Las Cruces, New Mexico. These structures impound large volumes of runoff water and release it at a controlled rate. They have handled all runoff since they were built with no flood damage to the city.

10-3.4 Design and Construction of Dams

A wide variety of detailed technical information is needed to select a suitable site, plan, justify, and build an earthen dam. The work is so specialized and the construction so critical that it should be done only by well-qualified and experienced people (Beasley, 1972). District conservationists in the U.S. Soil Conservation Service may plan small stock water dams, but plans must be developed by the SCS State Engineer if the product of the height of the dam crest above the spillway floor (m) times the dam capacity (ha · m) exceeds 115. The breakdown of responsibility is often made more simply on a watershed area basis—greater than 10 to 40 ha, depending on rainfall, being the responsibility of the State Engineer.

Figure 10-14 Flood-control dam protecting Las Cruces, New Mexico. This is one of several similar structures built to impound runoff water from heavy rainstorms in the hills above the city. This structure is about 1 km long and has a road along the top. (Courtesy F. R. Troeh.)

10-4 STREAMBANK EROSION-CONTROL STRUCTURES

Bank erosion in perennial streams is often severe. Not only is soil lost, but new channels meander across fields on alluvial plains. Severely eroding sections may migrate inland at a rate of 50 to 75 m/yr.

Vegetative and mechanical means of protecting streambanks have been developed. Vegetative control measures are presented in Chapter 12. The nonvegetative techniques can be divided into those that divert the faster-flowing water away from the bank and those that protect the erodible bank with mechanical covers.

In the United States it is necessary to obtain a federal permit, and in many states a state permit also, before the direction or volume of flow in a perennial stream can be changed. The permit will usually be issued if inspection by representatives of the U.S. Army Corps of Engineers (and of the state water resources protection agency, where necessary) shows that the planned work will not damage land across the channel or downstream.

10–4.1 Current Deflectors

Two main types of *dikes* are used to divert the faster-flowing water away from an eroding stream bank. Regular dikes consist of loose stone or rock piles that extend above the stream surface and are built out into the water at a slight angle downstream. These are probably the most reliable stream bank protection, but they are also the most expensive works to install. They may extend a meter or so above the low-flow water level or may go to full bank height. They are usually shorter in height farther from the bank. The stones and rock pieces used must be too large for flood currents to move. Similar dikes have been made of poles driven vertically into the streambed.

The other type is a *vane dike* placed out in the stream with no intimate contact with the bank. Vane dikes must be placed far enough upstream to deflect the current away from the bank needing protection. Vane dikes have not been as useful as dikes that extend from the bank.

10–4.2 Bank Protectors

Mechanical covers to protect eroding streambanks include toe protectors, hardpoints, and revetments.

Toe Protectors. The toe of a streambank is the part where the gradient of the relatively steeply sloping bank changes abruptly near the water line. Toe protectors cover the toe and part of the more steeply sloping bank with stones, rocks, or other protective material, as shown in Figure 10–15. The material can be hand placed or it can be dropped and spread by machine. Hand placing saves on material but requires much more labor. Usually the toe is protected intermittently along the eroding part of a bank at the more seriously eroding sites. The distance between areas of protection depends on the severity of the erosion hazard.

Hardpoints. Hardpoint protection usually consists of large stones or rocks dropped over the edge of the bank onto the toe of the slope. No attempt is made to place or spread the pieces. In general the height of the protection up the bank slope is limited, but the protected spots along the bank are closer together than in toe protection.

Revetments. A revetment is a retaining wall or facing consisting of protective material placed over and anchored to the soil. One of

Figure 10-15 A toe protector to stabilize a streambank. The rock covers the bank from the low water level to the height of normal flood stage. (Courtesy Kansas City District, Corps of Engineers, U.S. Army, Kansas City, Missouri.)

the longest-lasting types of revetments is a vertical stone wall shielding the land from the stream, as shown in Figure 10–16.

A windrow revetment is a pile of stone and rock placed on the surface of the soil at the upper edge of the bank, as shown in Figure 10–17. As the bank erodes, the rock drops down and lodges near the toe, thus forming a line of protection along the bank. A windrow revetment contains from 4.5 to 15 mt of rock per lineal meter of bank.

A tire revetment consists of used automobile tires placed on the bank both above and below the water line. Individual tires must be fastened to each adjacent tire and to the soil to hold the protection in place. Willow cuttings can be placed in the soil below the center of each tire. A very effective and permanent protective cover is provided when these cuttings take root and grow.

A car-body revetment is made of a series of car bodies, preferably flattened and freed of all glass and loose metal parts, placed tightly together along the eroding bank. They must be cabled together and anchored in place to form an effective shield from erosion.

Figure 10-16 Rock wall revetment protecting a cultivated field from floods of the Urubamba River near Machu Picchu, Peru. (Courtesy F. R. Troeh.)

A fence parallel to the shoreline at the base of the bank is another type of revetment. The fence often consists of a double row of posts driven vertically into the ground, cabled together, and filled with protective material such as stones, tires, or logs. This is probably the least permanent type of revetment because the posts will rot in time. Posts treated to delay decomposition will last longer, but the materials cost more.

Loose stone and rock pieces can also serve as a revetment. Rough stone placed along the bank over an extended distance is often called "rip-rap." Large stones and rock chunks must be used on top so they will not be washed away by the streams when they are in flood. Smaller stones and gravel are used underneath as described in Section 10-2.3. Broken concrete from old highways or building foundations serve effectively if slabs are laid flat on the sloping area needing protection. Gabions of smaller stones may be used if the shallow wire cages are placed side by side down the bank slope, loaded with stone, and wired shut, or if long wire baskets are filled and later laid in place up and down the bank by means of a crane.

Figure 10-17 A windrow revetment. The stones are piled in a windrow near the edge of the streambank. As the stream erodes the bank, the stones fall and protect the toe of the slope from further erosion. (Courtesy Kansas City District, Corps of Engineers, U.S. Army, Kansas City, Missouri.)

10-4.3 Floodways

Floodways are used to protect urban property from irregular flooding and erosion damage. These range in size and complexity depending on the nature of the hazard and the value of the property. The city of Winnipeg in western Canada has suffered from flooding caused by rapid snow melt and ice jams in the Assiniboine River and the Red River of the North ever since the settlement was established. A floodway was built east of the city after the very severe 1950 flood. The floodway consists of a very wide, shallow channel with broad, low levees on each side. It starts at the Red River some distance south of the built-up area, intercepts excessive water flow, carries it to the east and north, and dumps it back into the river about 25 km north of the city. The construction of this floodway involved more earth moving than accompanied the construction of the Panama Canal. No serious flooding has occurred in the city since the structure was completed.

10-5 WIND EROSION STRUCTURES

Soils that are too susceptible to wind erosion to be cultivated safely should be planted with perennial vegetation. Sometimes special protection must be provided while the perennial vegetation is being established. Occasionally an overwhelming need for food requires that highly erodible soils be used for cultivated crop production. These soils must be specially protected. Artificial wind barriers may be used in establishing perennial cover or for protecting the cultivated soil. The barriers reduce wind velocity for a combined windward-leeward distance thirty or more times the barrier height, but they control wind erosion for only about ten times their height. For most effective protection the barrier must be placed perpendicular to the direction of the erosive winds.

10-5.1 Woven Mat Barriers

Mats of woven plant materials are erected as barriers to erosive winds in many areas where land scarcity forces the use of erodible soils. Grasses, reeds, and crop stalks are all used. Sometimes the materials are woven into mats which are later erected at sites where they are needed. In other cases the barriers are constructed at the site and cannot be moved without being dismantled.

Figure 10-18 shows barriers of reeds used in the production of tomatoes along the Mediterranean Sea about 65 km west of Algiers. The principal barriers run perpendicular to the sea coast at intervals of about 10 to 15 m. The secondary barriers, perpendicular to the primary ones, are spaced about 0.75 m apart between tomato rows. These barriers control soil movement and also reduce desiccation damage in the hot, dry months.

10-5.2 Snow Fence and Other Wooden Barriers

Temporary snow fences are used in parts of the United States and in other countries to stop snow from drifting onto highways, airport runways, and other critical areas. The fences consist of strips of wood about 0.75 cm thick, 4 cm wide, and 120 cm long fastened together by wire so that the wood slats are separated by about 2.5 cm (approximately 40% porosity). The fencing is usually mounted on steel posts driven into the ground. When no longer needed, the fencing is removed from the posts, laid flat on the soil surface, and rolled up for storage. This commercially available fencing is often used where temporary wind protection is needed, such as stabilizing active

Figure 10-18 Woven-reed wind barriers in Algeria. The primary barriers are about 2 m tall, the secondary ones about 75 cm to 1 m tall. (Courtesy Mrs. A. W. Zingg.)

sand dunes or recently denuded, erosive land (Fig. 5-5). It is generally employed only until wind erosion can be brought under control by vegetative means (Ch. 12).

Wind barriers occasionally are constructed of wood boards nailed onto a framework between substantial posts driven into the ground. The boards are placed vertically with spaces between adjacent boards. A porous barrier does not reduce wind velocity as much as a solid barrier does, but the distance of wind reduction is greater with the porous fence, and the cost is lower when the boards are spaced.

Reducing wind velocity and erosion damage with fencing is expensive, so it cannot be used on a regular basis on any but very high value crops or in critical situations where an attempt is being made to revegetate eroding sites.

10-5.3 Dune-Leveling Devices

Crests of dunes often have to be reduced in height before the dunes can be stabilized. This was once accomplished by horse-drawn scrapers or by pulling drags along the crests. Modern earth-moving equipment also can perform this task and may be the cheapest way to do the job where labor is expensive. Where equipment is not available or where labor is plentiful and cheap, wind deflectors and barriers have been used to increase wind velocity and sweep the sharp crests off the active dunes.

The snow fencing described in Section 10-5.2 can be stretched across the dune crests so that the wind blows under as well as over the barrier. This funneling wind carries the sand down the leeward side. As the crest is lowered, the fence must also be lowered by driving the supporting posts farther into the remaining sandy soil. When the crest has been lowered sufficiently, the barrier is lowered so it contacts the surface of the soil to protect it from erosion while vegetation is established.

Sand-filled burlap sacks were placed at closely spaced intervals along dune crests in early years of the fight against encroaching dunes in the Great Plains and around the Great Lakes. The accelerated wind whipping between adjacent sacks swept away the exposed sand and reduced the bases on which the sacks rested. The sacks then settled down without attention by the farmers, except for occasional straightening. Some means of reducing wind velocity must be provided after the dune crests are reduced to prevent soil drifting while vegetation is being established on the flattened dunes.

SUMMARY

Crop and soil management practices do not always provide enough erosion control on cultivated land. Similarly, runoff and soil loss from watersheds in native vegetation may be excessive. Special conservation structures are needed in these situations to reduce erosion to tolerable levels.

Bench terraces are a very old means of controlling runoff and erosion and are still widely used in areas with large populations and limited areas of arable land. Graded terraces are used in areas with a commercial-type agriculture where machinery is available and labor costs are high. A graded terrace consists of a channel with a ridge on the downhill side. The channel slopes gently toward a protected outlet. Graded terraces reduce erosion because they shorten slope lengths and thereby reduce runoff volume and velocity. Parallel and steep backslope terraces are modifications that make farming terraced fields easier. Terraces need proper care to maintain adequate channel capacity and must be repaired when storms cause major damage.

Diversions serve many purposes ranging from diverting runoff water away from a gully or around a cultivated field to carrying runoff to ponds and storage reservoirs. The diversion channel is usually a high-capacity grassed waterway and is seldom cropped.

Diversions and nonlevel terraces must have protected outlets into which the accumulated runoff water is released. Grassed waterways are common outlets, but underground pipe outlets are becoming more popular because they release land for cultivated crop production.

Erosion sometimes occurs in the beds of vegetated waterways as well as in gullies on cultivated fields and on grass and timber lands. Structures needed to control this erosion may be either temporary or long-term. Temporary structures are often used to control erosion in waterways and gullies while perennial vegetation or other permanent control is being established. Temporary structures include artificial mulch in shaped and seeded waterways and barriers in channels. Artificial mulch may consist of burlap or specially prepared cloth, paper, plastic, or shredded wood mats staked to the soil. Barriers may be made of rock, wood (natural or dressed), or brick. They must make firm and intimate contact with both floor and walls of the waterway or gully so water cannot wash under or around the structure.

Concrete drop structures and chutes are permanent control devices used where it seems impractical to control erosion by vegetative means. Simple concrete chutes may be used for relatively small water volume and short water drops, but reinforced concrete is needed where the volume is large or the drop great. The most critical parts of drop structures and chutes are the inlets, outlets, and the aprons onto which the water falls and from which it flows onto the soil at a lower level.

Several types of storage dams are used in soil and water conservation activities. Dams may be built to trap sediments, to stabilize a gully or a channel grade, or to store runoff temporarily in order to reduce flooding, soil loss, and sedimentation.

Current deflectors, bank protectors, and floodways have been used with varying degrees of success in attempts to control streambank erosion. No such attempt can be undertaken in the United States, however, without first obtaining permission from the U.S. Army Corps of Engineers or the state water control agency or both.

Wind-erosion control structures are used to stabilize erosive soils that either must be or have been cropped. Woven mat barriers and snow fences have been used successfully to reduce wind velocities at ground level. Dune-leveling devices have been used to smooth dune topography to make it easier to establish vegetation.

QUESTIONS

1. What are the differences in purpose and in structure of graded terraces and diversions?
2. Describe the important elements involved in the construction of simple barriers in waterways and gullies. Why is each important?

3. What are the major differences in specifications for dams built to (a) trap sediment? (b) stabilize a gully that is cutting back into a field? (c) store flood water? Explain why these differences exist.

4. Describe the major conditions that dictate which technique (such as toe protectors, windrow revetments, tire revetments, or protective fence) will be chosen for reducing stream-bank erosion. Explain why each of these conditions is important in making the correct choice.

5. Under what conditions would you expect to find artificial wind barriers used in a country with a highly developed commercial agriculture?

REFERENCES

ARMBRUST, D. V., and LEON LYLES, 1975. Soil stabilizers to control wind erosion. In *Soil Conditioners.* Soil Sci. Soc. Amer. Spec. Publ. No. 7, p. 77–82.

BEASLEY, R. P., 1972, *Soil Erosion and Sediment Polution Control.* Iowa State University Press, Ames, Iowa, 320 p.

BENSALEM, B., 1977. Examples of soil and water conservation practices in North African countries, Algeria, Morocco, and Tunisia. In *Soil Conservation and Management in Developing Countries.* FAO, Rome, Italy, Soils Bull. 33, Paper No. 10, p. 151–160.

BLAKELY, B. D., J. J. COYLE, and J. G. STEELE, 1957. Erosion on cultivated land. In *Soil,* USDA Yearbook of Agriculture, Washington, D.C., p. 290–307.

GRIESSEL, OTTO, and R. P. BEASLEY, 1971. *Design Criteria for Underground Terrace Outlets.* Univ. Missouri Ext. Div. Sci. and Tech. Guide 1525.

HEEDE, B. H., 1976. *Gully Development and Control.* USDA Forest Service Research Paper RM–169.

KUNKLE, S. H., and D. A. HARCHARIK, 1977. Conservation of upland wildlands for downstream agriculture. In *Soil Conservation and Management in Developing Countries.* FAO, Rome, Italy. Soils Bull. 33, Paper No. 9, p. 133–149.

PHILLIPS, J. A., and E. J. KAMPRATH, 1973. Soil fertility problems associated with land forming in the Coastal Plains. *J. Soil Water Cons.* 28:69–73.

PHILLIPS, R. L., and V. W. BEAUCHAMP, 1972. Design, layout, construction and maintenance of terraces. ASAE recommendation R. 268.1. *Amer. Soc. Agric. Eng. Yearbook,* p. 491–495.

POWELL, G. M., 1978. *Terrace Maintenance.* Kansas State Univ. Coop. Extension Serv. LR–16.

WITTMUS, HOWARD, 1973. Construction requirements and cost analysis of grassed backslope terrace systems. *Trans. Amer. Soc. Agric. Eng.* 16:970–972.

11

Vegetating Mining and Construction Sites

Sites where the surface soil and underlying strata have been cut, filled, intermixed, and compacted by heavy machinery in mining and construction activities are often difficult to revegetate. Establishment problems result from inferior soil physical conditions, droughtiness, wetness, low or unbalanced fertility, excess acidity, alkalinity or salinity, steep erosive slopes, or disturbance of the newly established stands by people, animals, and machines.

Areas drastically disturbed by mining are an environmental menace because they are a source of large quantities of sediment, strongly acid and toxic seepage, and toxic heavy metals. Iron and coal tailings often contain iron pyrite, which can cause soil conditions too acid for plant growth. Acid mine waters may contain toxic quantities of copper, iron, aluminum, and manganese. In addition, the mine spoils may contain toxic heavy metals such as cadmium, copper, lead, and zinc. Most mine spoils have steep, unstable slopes; many are compact; some are excessively stony; some are deficient in silt and clay and hold little water; most are low in fertility. In arid regions mine spoils are too dry and may be too saline or sodic for satisfactory vegetation establishment. Some mine spoils have been reclaimed and revegetated, but a large proportion remains as the mining operation left it—bare, scarred by gullies, useless, and unsightly.

Soils drastically disturbed by construction activities are often difficult to revegetate also, because the soil material has been compacted so much by heavy machinery that plant roots cannot penetrate it. Land slopes are generally steeper than before construction was started. The texture of the exposed material on some sites may not permit storage and release of adequate amounts of water. Essential plant nutrients may not be present in the new surface material in available form or in balanced proportions. Nitrogen is invariably deficient; phosphorus is generally in short supply. The sites may be too wet because of a naturally high water table or because of an inflow of water. In spite of these problems, considerable success has been attained in vegetating soil along highways, around buildings, on airfields, and along pipelines. The task of revegetation is generally expensive per unit area of land, but the cost is small compared to the total cost of the project.

11-1 MINERAL SELF-SUFFICIENCY

Everyone wants a pleasant environment, and no one suggests that the environment is enhanced by mining dumps or by spoils being spread on the land surface. Yet minerals that come from the earth are essential to the industrial way of life, so minerals must either be purchased from other areas or obtained by disturbing and then reclaiming the nearby lands where minerals are found.

Actually, the decision has already been made that the United States will mine its large coal reserves and a wide variety of other mineral resources. However, some minerals must be supplemented from abroad. In fact, the United States is becoming increasingly dependent on foreign sources of ores for the nine metals shown in Table 11-1.

There are two general types of mining—*shaft* and *surface* or *strip* mining. Shaft mining consists of digging a vertical shaft a few hundred meters deep, blasting tunnels into the deposit, and hauling the ore to the surface. Surface or strip mining consists of removing the overburden from the mineral vein and removing the ore with large power shovels. Mine spoils from shaft mines originate from the interbedded rocks and soil material. Surface mine spoils come mainly from the overburden, but also contain interbedded rocks and earthy materials from below the surface. Whatever the source, mine spoils degrade the environment and must be stabilized by vegetation.

At present, surface mines such as that shown in Figure 11-1 account for slightly more than half of the coal produced in the United States. In addition, 90% of all copper ore, 94% of iron ore, and all of the phosphate ore are mined by surface techniques. Surface mining is expected to develop faster than shaft mining in the future. For each unit of mineral produced, surface mining disturbs more than ten times as much land as shaft mining.

Table 11-1 The increasing dependence of the United States on foreign sources of nine essential metals

Metals	Domestic mineral production (% of U.S. demand)	
	In 1971	In 2000 (estimated)
Aluminum	11.4	2.0
Copper	93.5	45.6
Gold	22.8	7.3
Iron	72.0	37.3
Lead	61.2	45.0
Silver	40.9	21.0
Tungsten	62.0	3.6
Uranium	96.9	39.5
Zinc	37.0	17.8

SOURCE: General Accounting Office, 1974.

Figure 11-1 A small-scale surface (strip) coal mine in Pennsylvania. The soil materials are drastically disturbed and may be difficult to revegetate, especially if they are mixed with the underlying rock. (Courtesy EPA-DOCUMERICA.)

11-2 SURFACE MINING LEGISLATION

A federal law of 1872 permitted any person to mine any "hard-rock" minerals such as gold, copper, lead, and zinc on federal lands. Recent U.S. laws, however, require permits for surface mining on certain environmentally sensitive federal lands. State and federal environmental laws place additional restrictions on some mining methods. No longer can a miner create ugly scars on the landscape without a planned program to revegetate the disturbed sites.

On August 3, 1977, the U.S. Congress passed Public Law 95-87, a law regulating surface mining of coal (U.S. Congress, 1977). This law seeks to:

1. Regulate surface mining of coal to assure adequate protection of the environment by requiring restoration of mined land to its original use or to an approved higher use.
2. Legislate criteria for reclamation and revegetation of all areas of soil disturbed by mining operations in the past, present, and future.
3. Assist involved states in implementing the law.
4. Sponsor research and demonstrations on improved surface coal mining technology, including techniques for minimizing damage to hydrologic systems, restoring mined land and spoils to nonerosive contours, stockpiling and replacing top-soil, and establishing perennial vegetation.

Each coal producer is required to pay into a fund for soil reclamation of newly disturbed areas as follows:

1. For surface-mined coal, $0.32/mt,
2. For underground-mined coal, $0.14/mt,
   or
3. 10% of the value of the coal at the mine, whichever is less.
4. For lignite (soft brown coal), $0.09/mt *or* 2% of the value of the coal at the mine, whichever is less.

This fund is administered by the Office of Surface Mining Reclamation and Enforcement in the U.S. Department of the Interior. The money is used to prevent damage to adjoining land during mining and to reclaim disturbed land.

Technical assistance in reclamation is provided by the USDA Soil Conservation Service under long-term agreements, not to exceed ten years. Cost-sharing with the land owner is permitted up to 80% of the cost of such reclamation for a maximum of 48 ha for each cooperator.

Other provisions in the law specify that the topsoil shall be placed in a separate pile and returned to the disturbed soil surface after mining operations have ceased. Protective vegetation must be established and maintained by appropriate means such as irrigating, liming, and fertilizing for a period of five years in humid areas and for ten years in regions where the mean annual precipitation is 660 mm or less.

11-3 AREAS DISTURBED BY MINING AND AREAS RECLAIMED

The Soil Conservation Service estimates that 69% of the spoils on abandoned mines in need of reclamation are located in Appalachia,

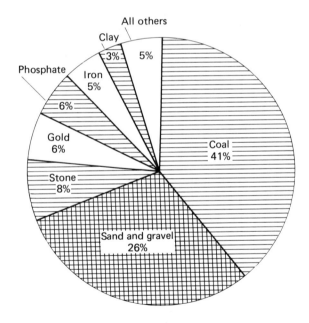

Figure 11-2 Land area disturbed by mining for various materials as percentages of the total mining disturbance in the United States. Coal plus sand and gravel account for two-thirds of the land disturbed by mining in the United States. (Courtesy EPA-DOCUMERICA, 1973.)

29% in the Midwest, and 2% in the Far West. Before the enactment of Public Law 95-87, there were thirty-one state laws mandating reclamation of both active and abandoned mine spoils. All states had started reclaiming mine spoils by July, 1978, including those from 450,000 ha of abandoned mines.

11-3.1 Location of Disturbed Areas

About 1.74 million hectares in the United States were drastically disturbed by the various mining activities indicated in Figure 11-2 up to 1974. This represents 0.16% of the total land area of the fifty states. It does not include areas disturbed by oil and gas exploration and extraction. During the same period, 43% of all areas disturbed by mining were reclaimed. However, the area reclaimed in 1971 was equal to 80% of the land disturbed by mining that year. Another 1 million hectares were expected to be reclaimed by 1985. A vivid portrayal of the state-by-state location of areas drastically disturbed by both surface and shaft coal mining is presented in Figure 11-3.

Surface (strip) coal mining increased faster than shaft mining in the 1970s, and all coal use was predicted to double from 1975 to

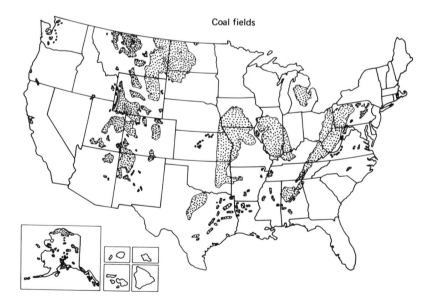

Coal fields

Figure 11-3 Disturbance of land by coal mining is a national problem. At least twenty-eight of the fifty states have significant coal fields and fifteen states have reported erosion, sedimentation, and toxic drainage as major problems. (Courtesy USDA, 1974.)

1985. The location of major strippable coal reserves (areas where minable coal is within 30 meters of the soil surface) is given in Table 11-2. Montana leads all states with 20.7 billion metric tons, representing 21% of all U.S. coal reserves listed as strippable.

11-3.2 Comparison of Disturbed and Reclaimed Areas

A summary of the total land area disturbed and reclaimed in the United States from 1930 to 1971, by class of mineral mined and type of mining disturbance, is presented in Table 11-3. These data indicate that mining for metals represented 14% of the total land disturbed and the rest was evenly divided between coal and the nonmetals (mostly sand and gravel). Disturbed land reclaimed was 64% for coal mining, 26% for the nonmetals, and 8% of the area mined for metals.

An indication of mining disturbance and reclamation in each state is shown by maps in Figure 11-4. Pennsylvania, West Virginia, Kentucky, the Corn Belt states, and California are the states with the largest areas of land disturbed by mining.

Table 11-2 Strippable coal in beds lying within about 30 meters of the soil surface

State	Strippable coal (billion metric tons)
Montana	20.7
Illinois	14.0
North Dakota	13.5
Wyoming	11.7
West Virginia	8.6
Pennsylvania	7.2
Kentucky	5.4
Ohio	4.5
Indiana	3.2
Texas	3.0
New Mexico	2.7
Alaska	1.8
Colorado	1.1
Virginia	0.9
Missouri	0.9
Total	99.2

SOURCE: Averitt, 1970.

Table 11-3 Areas disturbed and reclaimed by mining in the United States, 1930–1971[a]

| | Kind of mineral mined | | | | | |
| Type of disturbance | Coal | | Nonmetals | | Metals | |
	Area disturbed (ha)	Disturbed area reclaimed (%)	Area disturbed (ha)	Disturbed area reclaimed (%)	Area disturbed (ha)	Disturbed area reclaimed (%)
Surface mining excavation	391,000	74	429,000	24	59,000	12
Surface mining spoils	130,000	84	118,000	44	50,000	4
Underground mining spoils	67,000	12	1,000	9	9,000	7
Underground mining; surface subsidence	36,000	5	2,000	2	5,000	15
Both surface and underground mining; processing mill wastes	13,000	20	81,000	12	90,000	8
U.S. Total	637,000	64	631,000	26	213,000	8
% of U.S. Total	43		43		14	

[a]During the year 1971, reclamation equalled 80% of all areas disturbed by mining that year.

U.S. grand total area disturbed by mining—1,481,000 hectares; area reclaimed—591,300 hectares (40% reclaimed of area disturbed)

SOURCE: Paone and others, 1974.

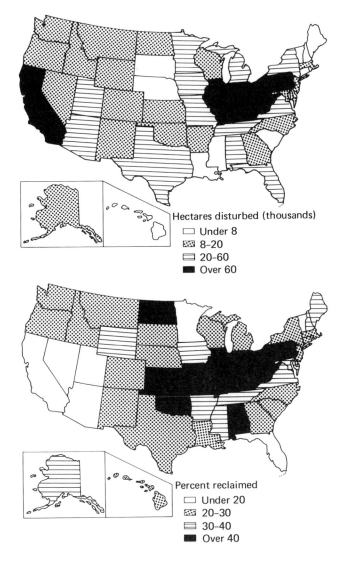

Figure 11-4 Every state has had some mining, but the land areas disturbed from 1930 to 1971 (above) and the percentages reclaimed (below) vary widely. (Source: Paone and others, 1974.)

11-4 ESTABLISHING VEGETATION
ON MINE SPOILS

Reclamation of mine spoils has different meanings for different people. In this discussion, the reclamation of mine spoils includes revegetation of mine dump sites and the control of acid waters and toxic materials such as heavy metals. Temporary mechanical techniques to retain mine spoils at the site include the use of sediment basins, terraces, berms, or diversion dams. Steep slopes must be graded, as shown in Figure 11-5, and the topsoil must be replaced after mining activities have ceased. The final step is the establishment of either perennial vegetation or cultivated crops.

Soil drastically disturbed by surface mining can be restored for successful crop production. Figure 11-6 shows an experiment estab-

Figure 11-5 The "highwall" labelled A in this mine in Montana resulted from strip mining before Montana law mandated highwall reduction and elimination of impoundments. The area labelled B was mined later and reduced to a 1:3 (33%) gradient to meet state and federal requirements. (Courtesy USDI—Bureau of Mines.)

Figure 11-6 This cornfield in Illinois was regraded for corn production after surface mining of coal. The area on the right was covered with 25 cm of topsoil that the area on the left did not receive. (Courtesy Alten F. Grandt, Peabody Coal Co.)

lished in Illinois in an area of Muscatine silt loam (an Aquic Argiudoll) to compare corn yield on (1) undisturbed soil, (2) topography regraded after mining but not topsoiled, and (3) topography regraded after mining and surfaced with 25 cm of topsoil. The plant population in all plots was about 50,000/ha. Comparative yields of corn for the four-year period, 1975–1978, were (personal communication from Alten F. Grandt):

	Yield of corn in kg/ha
Undisturbed Muscatine soil	8472
Soil disturbed by mining	
With topsoil	7248
Without topsoil	4760

11-4.1 Techniques for Establishing Vegetation

Materials that can produce extreme acidity or extreme alkalinity or that contain excessive soluble salts should be identified before mining begins. These adverse materials can be located by laboratory testing of core samples. All such materials should be kept separate during excavation and buried below plant root depth before the final grading of the surface.

Final reclamation of mine spoils consists of establishing perennial vegetation, cultivated crops, ponds, or lakes over the entire area. Sometimes temporary vegetation is used to stabilize the surface until perennial vegetation can be established to hold the soil against water and wind erosion. Management techniques for improving the productive capability of disturbed soil include topsoiling, liming (if acid), fertilizing, applying manure or sewage sludge, and mulching.

Topsoiling means to apply a productive surface soil to the final soil grade. Lime and fertilizers are usually applied on the basis of a soil test before planting vegetation. Each soil sample should represent a smaller area on mine spoils than on cropland because of the greater variability of the spoils. Czapowskyj (1973) reported the following variabilities in spoils from Kentucky, Indiana, and Pennsylvania:

$N = \, < 0.1$ to 0.2% $pH = 2.2$ to 7.3
$P = 6.6$ to 64.2 ppm $Ca = 1.0$ to 17.5 me/100 g spoil
$K = \, < 0.1$ to 0.8 me/100 g spoil $Mg = 0.3$ to 4.8 me/100 g spoil

A unique problem in many mine spoils of humid regions and in a few in arid regions is the presence of pyrite (FeS_2). Pyrite oxidizes to sulfuric acid when exposed to the atmosphere (Note 11-1) and may kill all vegetation. The acid is produced by bacterial action, and the process stops when the conditions become so acid that neither the bacteria nor any other living thing can tolerate it (a pH between 2 and 3). The acidity can be neutralized with lime, but the neutralization may last for only a few months until more sulfuric acid is formed. The best solution is to bury the spoils that contain pyrite; an expensive alternative is to apply lime whenever a soil test indicates a need for it, and to use acid-tolerant vegetation as described in Section 11-4.2.

NOTE 11-1 OXIDATION OF PYRITE

Pyrite (FeS_2) is a pale brass-yellow mineral known as "fool's gold" that commonly exists as impurities in coal deposits. Upon exposure to moist air, pyrite oxidizes to ferrous sulfate and sulfuric acid. This reaction is represented as follows:

$$2\,FeS_2 + 7\,O_2 + 2\,H_2O \longrightarrow 2\,FeSO_4 + 2\,H_2SO_4$$

A second reaction takes place when the *ferrous* sulfate is oxidized to *ferric* sulfate:

$$4\,FeSO_4 + O_2 + 2\,H_2SO_4 \longrightarrow 2\,Fe_2(SO_4)_3 + 2\,H_2O$$

The ferric sulfate then hydrolyzes to form colloidal ferric hydroxide (called "yellow-boy" by miners) and sulfuric acid:

$$Fe_2(SO_4)_3 + 6\,H_2O \longrightarrow 2\,Fe(OH)_3 + 3\,H_2SO_4$$

Mine spoils are ideal sites for heavy applications of manure and sewage sludge. Nearly all spoils are low in organic matter, droughty, and low in available plant nutrients. Furthermore, few mine spoil sites are used for food crops that might become contaminated with pathogens or toxic heavy metals from sewage sludge.

Numerous trials have shown that sewage sludge and wastewaters can be used to help revegetate acid mine spoils. An example from Ohio is shown in Figure 11-7. Another example occurred where digested sewage sludge from Chicago was applied on extremely variable coal mine spoils in Fulton County, Illinois. Rates as high as 1000 mt/ha (dry basis) were sprayed as a slurry. All application rates hastened the establishment of annual and perennial vegetation. Runoff was trapped by a levee built around the perimeter of the mine spoils.

Variable rates of municipal sewage sludge and wastewaters were applied to coal strip-mine spoils in Pennsylvania before seeding or planting perennial vegetation. Most species of grasses, legumes, and trees grew better on the areas treated with sewage (Sopper and others, 1970).

Surface mulching with organic wastes reduces splash erosion, surface puddling, and sealing of the soil. Mulches are usually applied immediately after seeding or planting, but they also may be applied earlier to protect the bare soil until the proper season for seeding or planting. The most common organic mulches are wood chips, wood fibers, grain straws, and hay. Amounts vary, but the materials should have a packed thickness of 3 to 6 cm over all disturbed soil surfaces.

11-4.2 Vegetating Mine Spoils in Humid Regions

Several soil-plant management principles must be applied to assure success in establishing vegetation on mine spoils in humid regions:

1. Spoil materials are extremely variable; a soil test for pH and plant nutrients is essential.

Plot A

Plot B

Plot C

Figure 11-7 A revegetation experiment on acid (pH 2.3) mine spoils in Ohio. The spoils were high in pyrite, and no vegetation grew without special treatment. A sparse stand of rye grew in Plot A, where 10 mt/ha of lime had raised the pH to 3.3 and 1000 kg/ha of 6-24-12 fertilizer was applied. A normal stand of rye was produced in Plot B, where 200 mt/ha of lime raised the pH to 5.8 and 1000 kg/ha of 6-24-12 was added. The best growth was obtained from Plot C, where 660 mt/ha of sewage sludge (air-dry weight) raised the pH to 5.8 and improved the fertility without any lime or mineral fertilizer being added. (Sutton and Vimmerstedt, 1973; photos courtesy Paul Sutton, Ohio State University.)

2. Either acid-tolerant vegetation must be used or heavy applications of lime or organic wastes must be applied where the soil
   pH is low. Both practices must be applied where the pH is
   below 3.5.
3. Forage legumes will not grow well if the pH is below 4.5.
4. A vegetative cover is crucial. Sometimes a fast-starting cereal
   grain and a slower-to-establish perennial are seeded together
   as companion crops. Or, the cereal may be grown alone and
   its residues used as a mulch for seeding perennial vegetation.
5. Various forage grasses and legumes, trees for lumber or pulp,
   and shrubs, vines, and brambles have different adaptations.
   The type and species of vegetation must be chosen to fit the
   climate and the soil conditions.

Grasses. Many common grasses have been tested on mine spoils
with widely varying results. The results depend greatly on the pH of
the spoil, as shown in Figure 11–8. Only deertongue, Korean lovegrass, weeping lovegrass, and switchgrass are recommended in humid
regions of the United States where the spoil pH is less than 4.0 (Soil
Conservation Service, 1978). Reed canarygrass, sand lovegrass, and
tall fescue are suited to a pH between 4.0 and 5.5. Chinese silvergrass, coastal panicgrass, orchardgrass, and perennial ryegrass do well
on spoils with pH above 5.5. All grasses grew better at the higher pH
values even if they did survive at a lower pH.

Cold hardiness must also be considered in selecting a grass
species. The three lovegrasses are cold-sensitive grasses that are restricted to warm climates; orchardgrass is adapted to cooler climates
such as northern United States. The remaining seven grasses recommended on spoil materials are adapted throughout the humid part of
the United States.

Legumes. Legumes are desirable on mine spoils because of their
ability to fix atmospheric nitrogen. Many legumes were tested on
acid mine spoils, but only seven gave good results, and none below
pH 4.0. Birdsfoot trefoil, crownvetch, flatpea, and sericea lespedeza
survived at pH 4.0 to 5.5; alfalfa and alsike clover did not do well in
southern United States (Soil Conservation Service, 1978). Legumes
may not fix appreciable quantities of N at a pH below 5.5. Legumes
are usually seeded with adapted grasses to increase the chances of a
successful stand.

Trees. Trees may be used to vegetate mine sites, but usually grass
is seeded between the tree seedlings to protect the soil until the

Figure 11-8 Selection of an adopted grass species is imperative for vegetating acid mine spoils. The upper photo shows that at pH 4.0, weeping lovegrass was the best of the five species shown (but it must be limited to warm climates because frost may kill it) and switchgrass was second. The lower photo shows that all five grasses grew satisfactorily on this spoil at pH 4.5. (Courtesy USDA—Forest Service.)

trees provide enough canopy and litter to do so. Only two tree species tested, black locust and European black alder, tolerated a pH less than 4.0. Black alder grows well even at pH 3.0. Black locust grew well from spoil pH less than 4.0 to above 8.0. American sycamore, eastern cottonwood, green ash, loblolly pine, northern red oak, Norway spruce, red maple, red pine, Scotch pine, silver maple, sweetgum, Virginia pine, and white pine were established on many sites with pH 4.0 to 5.5. Shortleaf pine such as that shown in Figure 11-9, can be used only when the pH is above 5.5. Other species tested were not adapted to mine spoils (Soil Conservation Service, 1978). Loblolly pine, shortleaf pine, and Virginia pine are adapted primarily to a warm climate such as that of the southern United States.

Shrubs, Vines, and Brambles. Nineteen fast-growing shrubs, vines, and brambles have been grown successfully on acid mine spoils.

Figure 11-9 Trees can be used to stabilize mine spoil with pH ranging from less than 4.0 to more than 8.0. This shortleaf pine planting on mine spoil in Kentucky is adapted to pH above 5.0. (Courtesy USDA—Soil Conservation Service.)

Most will tolerate pH 4.0 to 5.5, but bristly locust can tolerate a pH below 4.0 and kudzu requires a pH above 5.5. American cranberry; amur privet; autumn olive; Japanese flowering, Siberian, tea, and toringa crabapple; amur and tartarian honeysuckle; indigobush; bicolor and Japan lespedeza; memorial and multiflora rose; russet buffaloberry; and fragrant and shining sumac all tolerated pH 4.0 to 5.5. Autumn olive, bristly locust, bicolor lespedeza, indigobush, and multiflora rose gave the best results (Soil Conservation Service, 1978).

Multiflora rose presents a problem because of its very vigorous growth. It sometimes spreads to adjacent lands and crowds out other vegetation. It grows so thick and has thorns so sticky that it forms a living fence whether or not one is wanted.

11-4.3 Vegetating Mine Spoils in Arid and Semiarid Regions

Surface mining in arid and semiarid regions of the United States is expected to increase in the future, mainly because 90% of the low-sulfur coal is located there. Increased mining will be accompanied by a need for vegetating the area of mine spoils produced. However, even though the new federal mining laws require the topography to be smoothed and surface soil replaced, there are many difficulties in establishing vegetation under arid conditions:

1. Fewer plant species are adapted, and their density and productivity will always be much less than in humid areas because little water is available during the growing season.
2. Time of seeding or planting is more critical because of seasonality of available moisture.
3. Soils often contain toxic quantities of total soluble salts or boron. Some soils contain excessive molybdenum and selenium that are taken in by plants and are toxic to livestock. Plants that are selenium accumulators must be avoided in selecting vegetation for reclamation.
4. Some soils contain excessive sodium that causes a high pH and a dispersed physical condition unfavorable for plant growth.
5. As a general rule, a lower annual precipitation is also more variable from month to month, season to season, and year to year. During some entire years, soil moisture may be inadequate to establish a stand of perennial vegetation unless irrigation water is used.
6. Some mine spoils are too sandy, too stony, too salty, or too dry to support any plant growth.

Establishing vegetation on mine spoils in arid and semiarid regions is usually restricted more by low available soil moisture than by any other factor. A small amount of irrigation water can be very helpful for establishing newly planted vegetation. When water for irrigation is not available, plant species adapted to arid conditions must be chosen and planting should be at the beginning of the normal rainy season. Other useful practices include terracing, replacing surface soil, mulching, and planting vegetation on only the most suitable spots. Another popular technique is to plant a mixture of adapted species. Drastically disturbed mine sites are so variable that one species or cultivar may be adapted to one material and site ecology whereas another may grow better elsewhere, sometimes only a meter away.

Plants tolerant of drought, sodium, bicarbonates, alkalinity, and boron are generally also tolerant of total soluble salts. A list of plants moderately or highly tolerant of total soluble salts is given in Table 11-4. All of these plants have been used successfully to vegetate mine spoils in arid and semiarid regions. Ayers and Westcot (1976) have ranked several grasses according to their comparative resistance to total soluble salts as follows: wheatgrasses > barley > fescue > bermudagrass > perennial ryegrass. Selected drought-tolerant trees and shrubs are listed in Chapter 12.

Northern Great Plains. Most of the coal that occurs in the arid and semiarid regions of the United States is in the northern Great Plains. States in this region are ranked according to coal production as follows: Montana > Wyoming > North Dakota > Colorado > South Dakota (Averitt, 1975).

Most of the land containing recoverable coal in the northern Great Plains is used for range grazing of cattle and sheep. The percentage of land so used varies from 50% in North Dakota to 90% in Wyoming. Other uses include the production of wheat, barley, and oats. Annual precipitation in the region varies from 250 to 400 mm, with June the wettest month.

Table 11-4   Relative salt tolerance of plants used for vegetating mine spoils in arid and semiarid regions[a]

Relative salt tolerance	
Moderate *(4–8 mmhos/cm)*	*High* *(8–12 mmhos/cm)*
Alfalfa[b]	Alkali sacaton
Birdsfoot trefoil	Alkaligrass
Bromegrasses	Barley
Hardinggrass	Bermudagrass[b]
Oats	Fescue grasses[b]
Orchardgrass	Fourwing saltbush
Reed canarygrass[b]	Perennial ryegrass
Rye, cereal	Saltgrass[b]
Sorghum	Sweetclovers
Wheat	Switchgrass[b]
	Wheatgrass:
	Pubescent
	Crested
	Slender
	Tall
	Wildryegrass:
	Beardless
	Russian

[a]Relative salt content is measured by electrical conductivity in millimhos per centimeter at $25°C$ on a saturated soil extract.

[b]Salt-tolerant but not very drought-resistant.

SOURCE: Bernstein, 1964, and EPA, 1975.

The removal of thousands of tons of coal from a site requires deep trenches that may intercept and disrupt water-bearing strata and thereby lower water tables in wells. Furthermore, the inevitable intermixing of surface soil with subsoil and substrata nearly always results in a soil that is less productive than the original.

The productivity of the surface soil on the final grade after mining can be increased by tillage to a depth of two to three centimeters, adding gypsum if the exchangeable sodium is excessive, and applying nitrogen and phosphorus fertilizers according to a soil test. In general, the native species of vegetation are not used to reseed the disturbed site. Exotic species such as crested wheatgrass, intermediate wheatgrass, Russian wildrye, smooth bromegrass, sweetclover, and alfalfa are easier to establish by seeding. Sometimes wheat, oats, or barley can be grown on areas that are level enough to be harvested with a combine (Power, Ries, and Sandoval, 1978). A successful seeding of grain sorghum in Wyoming is shown in Figure 11-10. The sorghum residue helped stabilize the spoils until perennial vegetation was established.

Figure 11-10 Grain sorghum was seeded on raw coal mine spoil in Wyoming and grew as tall as 60 cm even though no irrigation water was applied. The average annual precipitation at the site is 350 mm. (Courtesy USDI—Bureau of Mines.)

Four techniques have been used to increase the chances of success in establishing vegetation:

1. Replace topsoil and apply soil amendments and fertilizer as needed.
2. Prepare a seedbed on the mine spoils similar to that prepared for seeding a cultivated crop. Drill or broadcast the seed just before the onset of the normal rainy season.
3. Apply a suitable organic mulch after seeding.
4. Consider the practice a success if a stand of vegetation is established on an average of once in four attempts. The odds can be improved by irrigating for a period of about two months or until the seeded vegetation has become well established.

Southwestern States. There is much less coal in the southwestern states than in the northern Great Plains, and reclamation of mine spoils is more difficult because of lower annual precipitation combined with higher temperatures and the resulting higher evaporation losses.

Most plant species used successfully to stabilize mine spoils in the southwestern states are native to the area. These include four-wing saltbush, western wheatgrass, alkali sacaton, and Indian rice-grass. Other native species used with some success are slender wheatgrass, sand dropseed, and yellow sweetclover. Exotic species sometimes successful are crested wheatgrass and Siberian wheatgrass. Nursery-grown transplants of pea-tree, Russian olive, New Mexico olive, and kochia have usually been the most successfully used shrubs for controlling wind and water erosion in the southwestern states.

Most seedings in the southwestern states are more successful when some kind of organic mulch is applied to the soil surface and stabilized by being rototilled, disked, or compressed by a sheepsfoot packer. The mulch may be grain straw or wild grass hay. Sawdust and tree bark are satisfactory except that they often blow or wash away. Animal manures and sewage sludges have also been used with success. Usually nitrogen and sometimes phosphorus fertilizers aid in rapid early growth. Irrigating until the plants become established is always helpful.

Mineral Mine Spoils. Much of the mine spoil in southwestern United States, and some in all regions, comes from mineral mines rather than coal mines. The problems and solutions are similar but not always the same as for coal mining. Many situations are unique because there may be only one or a few major mines for a particular mineral.

More than half of the U.S. production of copper ore and much of the production of several other minerals comes from arid portions of the country. An open-pit copper mine in Arizona will serve as an example of surface mining for mineral ore. This mine has been operated by the Pima Mining Company since 1957. Overburden and milling wastes cover several hundred hectares. Both water and wind erosion are problems despite efforts made to stabilize the spoils.

The spoils from the copper mine have a pH between 7.5 and 8.0 and require only N and P fertilizers to make them fertile. They are high in total Cu, Fe, and Mn, but these micronutrients are not available enough to be toxic to plants because the high pH reduces their solubilities. The organic-matter content is low, but the spoils are otherwise suitable for plant growth.

The Arizona climate near the Pima mine is warm and provides an average annual precipitation of only 300 mm. Only four months average more than 25 mm of precipitation—July, August, September, and December. The most favorable time for seeding or planting is therefore early July.

About 50 ha of the copper mine spoils have been successfully stabilized by vegetation by (1) grading the spoil material to the angle of repose (nonslumping slope) for each kind of spoil, (2) fertilizing according to a soil test, (3) planting adapted species just before rains in July, (4) applying grain straw or native hay mulch, (5) irrigating once or twice during the first season if water is available. A system of hydroseeding by which a mixture of seed, wood fiber, fertilizer, and water were sprayed on the area to be vegetated has also been successful.

Wastewaters from the Tucson, Arizona, sewage system were compared with well water as a source of 37 cm of irrigation water on some plantings on the copper tailings. For all plants, sewage wastewaters resulted in the best survival and growth (Ludeke, 1973; Verma and others, 1977).

11–5 CONSTRUCTION ACTIVITY
AND THE ENVIRONMENT

Construction activity takes place on a large area each year in the United States, but it is only a small fraction of the nation's total land. Existing roadways occupy 12.6 million hectares, about 1.4% of the land area. Urban areas occupy 14 million hectares, 1.5% of the United States. Each year an estimated 600,000 ha of land surface is drastically disturbed by construction of new urban areas and roads and highways. Other construction activities that disturb soil include pipeline burial, communication establishment, pond and lake development, and dredging and other water developments. These disturbances occupy a much smaller area than highway and urban developments.

All construction activities disturb the soil on which they occur and destroy the protective vegetative cover over much of the area. Exposure to beating raindrops together with compaction of the soil surface reduces soil infiltration and increases runoff and erosion, as shown in Figure 11-11. Subsoil covers or becomes mixed with topsoil in some construction areas, thus increasing the clay content of the new topsoil and reducing its fertility and productivity. Compacting fill sites and excavated areas with heavy earth-moving equip-

Figure 11-11 This construction site is an example of gross negligence. Erosion was measured and reported to be about 13,000 m^3/km of roadbed. The weather when the picture was taken was too cold to establish perennial vegetation, but annual vegetation plus mulch could have controlled most of the erosion and sedimentation. (Courtesy USDA—Soil Conservation Service.)

ment and packers may add to the soundness and safety of the structure being built, but it also reduces the infiltration rate of the soil and makes it a very unsuitable medium for establishing plant growth. The slope of the land is often increased by land forming that accompanies construction activity, again increasing the tendency for runoff and erosion. In many situations, surface waters concentrated in new watercourses cause gully erosion as shown in Figure 11-12. Even after the exposed area has been shaped and reseeded, runoff from the impervious structural surfaces may cause additional erosion.

The U.S. Geological Survey made a study of sediment yield from highway construction sites in Scott Run Basin near Washington, D.C. Although they occupied only 11% of the land area, highway construction activities were the source of 85% of the total sediment eroded and transported. Soil sediment yield each year from highway construction activity was 168 mt/ha under conditions of normal rainfall (Cywin and Hendricks, 1969). This was ten times as much as from cultivated land, 200 times as much as from grassland, and 2000 times as much as from forestland.

Construction sites should be stabilized by water-control structures and temporary cover while work is in progress. Terraces and diversion ditches that lead into a debris basin as in Figure 11-13 can retain most or all soil sediments originating on the site.

Figure 11-12 The vegetation held the soil in place here, until a highway was built and the diverted run-off water cut this gully through the trees and shrubs. Drop structures (Ch. 10) are now needed along with vegetation to stabilize the soil. (Courtesy USDA—Forest Service.)

Figure 11-13 A debris basin is often the only way to retain sediment from soil erosion on the site during construction activities. Sediment from this project in West Virginia would pollute stream waters if the basin were not used. (Courtesy USDA—Soil Conservation Service.)

11-6 VEGETATING CONSTRUCTION SITES

Reseeding grasses and legumes and planting seedling trees and shrubs on a prepared site are relatively straightforward and simple tasks. But preparing the site for seeding and protecting it until the planted vegetation can do so is complicated and requires that adapted techniques be chosen for different areas and sites.

11-6.1 General Site Preparation and Planting Technology

In general, topsoil from the site should be removed and stockpiled during the early stages of construction. This material should be spread over the surface of the exposed areas after construction is complete. Replacing topsoil is most important when the exposed material is unduly sandy, stony, or clayey, or contains toxic materials. Hard soil surfaces must be scarified, and heavily compacted areas must be loosened by ripping with a chisel device or similar implement (Ch. 9). On extremely steep slopes it may be necessary to loosen the soil by hand. Soil samples should be taken from the top 15 cm of the exposed areas and tested for lime requirement and available N, available P, and exchangeable K. The necessary lime and fertilizer applications for the site should be applied and worked into the soil. Steep exposed banks may have to be formed into benchlike terraces to prevent excess water from washing out the seeds and seedlings and causing excessive erosion.

The plant material for construction sites should be selected with great care, usually with professional guidance. Single species or complex mixtures may be needed to satisfy local conditions. Steeply sloping land should be seeded as soon after construction as possible. On less erodible sites, it may be possible to wait for the best time of year. Even on gentle slopes, it often pays to cover the surface with a mulch or to seed a temporary cover to hold the soil until it is time to seed the perennial crop. After seeding but before setting out seedling trees, the site should be mulched with suitable plant material such as straw or hay, wood chips, or an artificial mulch. It may be advisable to spray-seed some steep slopes with a mixture of seed and mulching material, using a blower designed for this purpose, as shown in Figure 11-14.

11-6.2 Specific Site Preparation and Planting Technology

Establishing vegetation is site-specific. Soil amelioration, selection of plant species, time of seeding or planting, kind and rate of fertilizer and lime applications, and maintenance are technical factors unique in combination to each construction site. For this reason, techniques will be presented that were used for establishing vegetation on specific construction sites in Alaska, California, Colorado, Mississippi, Montana, New Mexico, and Virginia (EPA, 1975).

Alaska. Vegetating soils disturbed in the process of laying the 1287-km Alaska oil pipeline (1974–1977) was hampered by inadequate research. In 1978 a 7723-km gas pipeline was approved for construction in the same tundra environment. The area is humid even though the average annual precipitation is only 250 mm. Soils are fine textured and belong mostly to the extensive Great Group of Cryaquepts. There are about one hundred freeze-free days per year.

Figure 11-14 The final slope for this roadcut has been chiseled; now cellulose mulch plus seed in a slurry are being blown on the cut surface. This technique of revegetating disturbed sites has proved successful and economic in humid but not arid regions. In arid regions the seed must be drilled and then mulched. (Courtesy USDA—Soil Conservation Service.)

Permafrost (permanently frozen layer) is common. Maintaining a continuous surface cover of some type of organic or inorganic insulating material is essential to prevent the ice lenses from melting and the surface soil from collapsing. The ecosystem (soil and vegetation) is so fragile that if a person walked across the landscape ten to twenty times in the same path, that path would be visible for twenty-five years or more. The tracks made by a caterpillar tractor pulling a cargo sled across the soil surface in 1945 appeared to be freshly made in 1978.

The following forage seeding mixture is recommended for drilling or broadcasting on disturbed soils in central Alaska:

Mixture	*Variety (cultivar)*
Fescue	Arctared
Creeping foxtail	Garrison
Kentucky bluegrass	Nugget, Merion
White Dutch or alsike clover	Use local source of seed
Bering hairgrass	Collect local seed of native species

Figure 11-15 A grass experiment in central Alaska not far from the Alaska oil pipeline. The grasses are fescue, arctared variety (left); Bering hairgrass (center); and Kentucky bluegrass, Nugget variety (right). The fescue and bluegrass were equally as vigorous as the hairgrass but were more palatable to herbivorous animals. (Courtesy W. W. Mitchell, Agricultural Experiment Station, University of Alaska.)

Figure 11-15 shows three grasses growing in the Alaskan environment. Woody plants adapted to wet soil in Alaska are bog rosemary and wintergreen. Woody plants adapted to drier sites in central Alaska include dwarf caragana, creeping juniper, cinquefoil, and Indian snowberry.

California. Research efforts to vegetate two contrasting construction sites in California will be described briefly, one in a subhumid mountainous area and one in the Mohave Desert.

The first site was a roadway cut slope near Lake Tahoe in the Sierra Nevada Mountains. The average annual precipitation at the site is 800 mm, received mostly in the winter. The soil is classified as a Meeks very stony loamy coarse sand in the Entic Cryumbrepts. It was successfully vegetated with these techniques:

1. A loose rock breast wall was built and willow cuttings were buried in it.

2. Bundles of woody brush (wattles) were buried across the slope on contour lines with a 1-m vertical interval.
3. Orchardgrass, big bluegrass, crested wheatgrass, pubescent wheatgrass, intermediate wheatgrass, and cicer milkvetch were seeded.
4. Big sagebrush, penstemon, squawcarpet, pinemat manzanita, and bitterbrush were planted.

The second research effort described here attempted to establish vegetation along the right-of-way of the second Los Angeles Aqueduct in the Mohave Desert. The mean annual precipitation is 200 mm. The soil is Arizo gravelly loamy sand, a member of the Typic Torripsamments. The vegetation used consisted of five native shrubs. Treatments included spot-seeding versus transplanting, and watering with 2 liters of water per planting site at seeding or transplanting versus not watering (Graves and others, 1978). The survival percentages after two years showed that 2 liters of water did not improve survival. The survival rates were 56% for seedings of fourwing saltbush, 6% for desert saltbush, 8% for scalebroom, and none for white bursage and creosote-bush. Transplanting improved the survival rate of white bursage to 44%, desert saltbush to 25%, and creosotebush to 12%, but did not help the fourwing saltbush and scalebroom.

Colorado. Cut-and-fill slopes on a 13-km section of Interstate 70 west of Denver were successfully vegetated by seeding a mixture of grasses, white clover, and ponderosa pine. The area receives an average annual precipitation of 450 mm. The soils are gravelly loams with the predominant soil, the Stecum series, classified in the Typic Cryorthents. Four years after seeding, the vegetation was dominated by crested wheatgrass, which constituted 75% to 80% of the soil cover. Intermediate wheatgrass and smooth bromegrass made up most of the remaining 20% to 25%.

Mississippi. Annual precipitation in Mississippi averages 1450 mm. Research on vegetating highway and other construction slopes was conducted there for soils classified in the Great Groups of Fragiudalfs and Paleudults. These soils are low in essential elements, have rolling topography, erode readily and produce much sediment, and are difficult to vegetate. Forage species combinations recommended statewide include:

Bahiagrass and sericea lespedeza;
Bermudagrass, annual lespedeza, and *Lespedeza vergata:*

Weeping lovegrass and sericea lespedeza, bahiagrass, vetch, and crownvetch.

Montana. Two techniques of establishing shrubs on construction slopes in Montana are reported by Hodder (1970). In areas receiving about 250 mm of annual precipitation, seeds of shrubs such as caragana were planted in a greenhouse in plastic tubes about 6 cm in diameter and 60 cm long. The tubes were filled with fine soil in the bottom and coarse soil on top. After the plants were well established in the tubes, they were planted on construction sites in holes made by a power-driven auger. Survival was satisfactory.

The second technique of planting shrubs on construction sites in arid areas consisted of the following. A pit about 25 cm in diameter and about 10 cm deep was dug for each shrub. The shrub was planted in the center of the pit on a mound of soil about 5 cm high. A clear plastic film with a slit for the shrub stem was laid over the entire pit, as shown in Figure 11-16. Moisture condensed on the bottom side of the plastic, soaked into the soil around the plant roots, and supplied adequate moisture for growth.

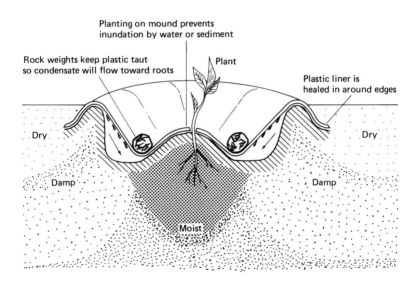

Figure 11-16 A plastic sheet can be used to concentrate soil moisture for establishing shrubs in arid regions. (Courtesy Richard L. Hodder, Montana State University.)

New Mexico. The successful establishment of roadside vegetation in southwestern New Mexico is representative of other southern desert areas in western United States, including parts of Texas, Arizona, California, Nevada, and Utah. Mean annual precipitation on the demonstration site is 250 mm, half of which is normally received during summer. The soil is fine textured and classified in the Great Group of Haplargids. The usually intense summer rainfall adds to the difficulty of soil stabilization. The relationship between soil textural class and the adaptability of six grasses in this arid region is shown in Figure 11–17. This figure indicates that on a sand soil, black gramagrass is best; on a loam soil, crested wheatgrass and sideoats gramagrass are both well adapted; and on a clay soil, western wheatgrass grows best (Currier, 1971). Other plants adapted to the southern desert include alkali sacaton, Lehmann lovegrass, blue gramagrass, and fourwing saltbush. Irrigation is usually necessary in establishing all vegetation.

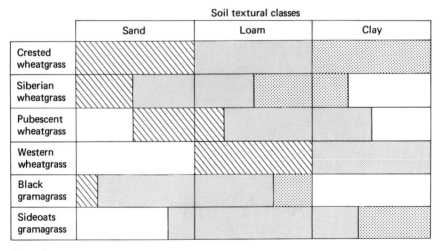

Figure 11-17 Relative adaptability of six grass species to sand, loam, and clay soils in southern desert areas of western United States. (Courtesy U.S. Forest Service, Region 3, Albuquerque, New Mexico.)

Virginia. Precipitation in the Piedmont Plateau on the vegetated site described here averages 1050 mm a year. Soils belong to the Cecil and Appling soil series, members of the Typic Hapludults. Usually lime, nitrogen, and phosphorus are necessary to assure the establishment of adapted vegetation on construction slopes; only by a soil test, however, can the needed rates be determined. The recommended grasses and legumes are:

Perennial grasses: tall fescue, redtop, and weeping lovegrass;
Annual grasses: rye, wheat, annual ryegrass, and German millet;
Legumes: crownvetch and sericea lespedeza.

SUMMARY

Mine spoils are refuse from both shaft and surface mining. Spoils consist of rock and soil materials in all degrees of coarseness and fineness. Some contain heavy metals in toxic concentrations and pyrite that oxidizes to toxic sulfuric acid. Some spoils and highwalls are steeper than the stable angle of repose for that material; this causes slumping and destruction of established vegetation.

Mining is necessary to obtain essential minerals. The spoils must be smoothed and vegetated to avoid serious environmental damage. Of all land disturbed by mining in the United States, 41% has been mined for coal, 26% for sand and gravel, and 33% for all other materials. The 1.74 million hectares in the United States disturbed by mining up to 1974 had been 43% reclaimed by that date. Reclamation is now taking place at a much faster rate. The U.S. surface mining law 95-87 of 1977 aids the states in enforcing environmentally acceptable reclamation standards for mine spoils. A tax on all coal mined is paid by coal companies into a reclamation fund in the Department of Interior. Technical assistance in reclamation is provided by the Soil Conservation Service.

Almost all mine spoils are deficient in nitrogen and phosphorus, and some require lime to enhance plant growth. Mulching is also generally helpful. Legumes seeded on mine spoils need more than the normally recommended *Rhizobium* inoculum because none are present and the spoil environment is not an ideal growth medium for them.

Many species of grasses, legumes, trees, shrubs, vines, and brambles tolerate acid spoils in humid regions. They should be used whenever feasible. Usually a different group of plants are adapted for mine spoil reclamation in arid and semi-arid regions. For the northern Great Plains, these are mostly introduced cool-season grasses that are salt-resistant and drought-resistant. For the southwestern United States, native warm-season plants are usually best adapted for reclamation.

Soils that are drastically disturbed by road and highway construction and urbanizing developments need to be stabilized by mechanical and vegetative techniques. Compacted materials need to be loosened and topsoil should be replaced, fertilized, and limed as needed. Adapted plant species must be chosen and planted at the right season. Companion crops and mulches are often useful to hold the soil until perennial vegetation can be established.

QUESTIONS

1. Explain why mine spoil reclamation is difficult and sometimes almost impossible.
2. What are the mandates of Public Law 95–87 on surface mining legislation?
3. Compare the percentage of land disturbed with kind of mineral mined. Which kind of disturbance is most extensive as well as most difficult to reclaim?
4. Name two grass and four tree species that can be used to reclaim mine spoils with a pH less than 4.0.
5. Discuss the principal differences encountered in reclaiming mine spoils in arid versus humid regions.
6. What principles are important for establishing and maintaining vegetation on all construction sites?

REFERENCES

ALDON, E. F., 1978. Reclamation of coal-mined land in the Southwest. *J. Soil Water Cons.* 33(2):75–79.

AVERITT, PAUL, 1970. *Stripping-Coal Resources of the United States— January 1, 1970.* U.S. Geological Survey Bull. 1322.

AVERITT, PAUL, 1975. *Coal Resources of the United States.* U.S. Geological Survey Bull. 1412.

AYERS, R. S., and D. W. WESTCOT, 1976. *Water Quality for Agriculture.* Food and Agriculture Organization of the United Nations, Irrigation-Drainage Paper No. 29, Rome, Italy.

BARKER, R. E., R. E. RIES, and P. E. NYREN, 1977. Forage species establishment and productivity on mined land. *North Dakota Farm Research* 34(6):8–12.

BENNETT, O. L., E. L. MATHIAS, W. H. ARMIGER, and J. N. JONES, JR., 1978. Plant materials and their requirements for growth in humid regions. In *Reclamation of Drastically Disturbed Lands,* American Society of Agronomy, Madison, Wisc., p. 285–306.

BERG, W. A., 1975. Revegetation of land disturbed by surface mining in Colorado. In MOHAN K. WALI (ed.), *Practices and Problems of Land Reclamation in Western North America.* University of North Dakota Press, Grand Forks, North Dakota, p. 78–89.

BERNSTEIN, LEON, 1964. *Salt Tolerance of Plants*, USDA Information Bull. No. 283, p. 10–12.

CARROLL, JAMES, 1978. New federal agency tackles surface mining problems. *J. Soil Water Cons.* 33:77–79.

CURRIER, W. F., 1971. Basic principles of seeding critical areas. In *Proceedings, Critical Area Stabilization Workshop*, Report 7, New Mexico Inter-Agency Range Committee, Albuquerque, New Mexico, p. 106–111.

CYWIN, A., and E. L. HENDRICKS, 1969. An overview of USDI's role in sediment control. *Proceedings, National Conference on Sediment Control, Washington, D.C.*, U.S. Department of Housing and Urban Development.

CZAPOWSKYJ, M. M., 1973. Establishing forest on surface-mined land as related to fertility and fertilization. *Forest Fertilization Symposium Proceedings.* USDA–Forest Service, General Technical Report NE-3, p. 132–139.

ENVIRONMENTAL PROTECTION AGENCY, 1975. *Methods of Quickly Vegetating Soils of Low Productivity, Construction Activities.* EPA-440/9-75-006, Washington, D.C., p. 149–166.

GENERAL ACCOUNTING OFFICE, 1974. *Report to Congress: Modernization of the 1872 Mining Law Needed to Encourage Domestic Mineral Production, Protect the Environment, and Improve Public Land Management.* Report No. B-118678. Washington, D.C., p. 7.

GRAVES, W. L., B. L. KAY, and W. A. WILLIAMS, 1978. Revegetation of disturbed sites in the Mohave Desert with native shrubs. *California Agriculture* 32:4–5.

HODDER, R. L., 1970. *Roadside Dry-Land Planting Research in Montana.* Montana State University.

LUDEKE, K. L., 1973. Soil properties of materials in copper mine tailing dikes. *Mining Congress Journal* 59:30–37.

PAONE, JAMES, J. L. MORNING, and LEO GIORGETTE, 1974. *Land Utilization and Reclamation in the Mining Industry, 1930–1971.* USDI, Bureau of Mines, Information Cir. 8642.

PAONE, JAMES, PAUL STRUTHERS, and WILTON JOHNSON, 1978. Extent of disturbed lands and major reclamation problems in the United States. In *Reclamation of Drastically Disturbed Lands*, American Society of Agronomy, Madison, Wisc., p. 11–22.

POWER, J. F., R. E. RIES, and F. M. SANDOVAL, 1978. Reclamation of coal-mined land in the Great Plains. *J. Soil Water Cons.* 33:69–74.

SOIL CONSERVATION SERVICE, 1978. *Plant Performance on Surface Coal Mine Spoil in Eastern United States.* SCS-TP-155, 76 p.

SOPPER, W. E., J. A. DICKERSON, C. F. HUNT, and L. T. KARDOS, 1970. *Revegetation of Strip Mine Spoil Banks Through Irrigation with Municipal Sewage Effluent and Sludge.* Series No. 20, Institute for Research on Land and Water Resources, Pennsylvania State Univ., University Park.

SUTTON, PAUL, and J. P. VIMMERSTEDT, 1973. *Treat Stripmine Spoils with Sewage Sludge.* Ohio Report 58:121-123. Ohio Agricultural Research and Development Center, Wooster, Ohio.

THAMES, J. L. (ed.), 1977. *Reclamation and Use of Disturbed Land in the Southwest.* Univ. of Arizona Press, Tucson, 362 p.

U.S. CONGRESS, 1977. *Surface Mining Control and Reclamation Act of 1977.* Public Law 95-87, Washington, D.C.

U.S. DEPARTMENT OF AGRICULTURE, 1974. *Our Land and Water Resources,* May, p. 14.

VERMA, T. R., K. L. LUDEKE, and A. D. DAY, 1977. Rehabilitation of copper mine tailings slopes using municipal sewage effluent. In *Proceedings of the Arizona Academy of Science,* Las Vegas, Nevada, April, 15, 16.

VERMA, T. R., and J. L. THAMES, 1975. Rehabilitation of land disturbed by surface mining coal in Arizona. *J. Soil Water Cons.* 30:129-131.

12

Vegetating Other Areas of High Erosion Hazard

The actions of water and wind are so concentrated in certain areas that they cause intense erosion hazards. These areas are usually small, but they are the source of large quantities of sediment. This eroded soil is more concentrated than that from other areas and therefore more likely to cause serious sedimentation problems.

Soil particles in transport augment the erosion process by making air and water more abrasive. Wind has to be strong enough to break off large pieces of plants or structures before the air flow can do much damage, but wind carrying soil particles causes damage at much lower velocities. The sandblast effect can erode the stems of plants and wear away fenceposts as well as take the paint off buildings and machines. Soil particles in streams of water also serve as gouging tools that help the stream erode its banks and wear away its bed even where it flows on solid rock.

Concentrated erosion commonly leads to concentrated pollution problems as well. The soil particles in transit produce muddy water and dusty air. When deposited, they fill ponds and lakes by their sheer bulk and contribute plant nutrients that cause unwanted algae to grow in the water (Ch. 17). Floods and wind both deposit thick layers of sediment on land where it can smother plants, cover productive soil, and damage structures and machines.

Concentrated erosion, abrasion, and deposition problems are best controlled at the source by protecting the areas of high erosion hazard. This chapter deals particularly with waterways and areas subject to wind erosion.

12-1 WATERWAYS

Runoff water concentrates in waterways that may or may not be stable against erosion. Unstable waterways produce gullies and eroding streambanks that often call for drastic measures to prevent severe damage. Protective action may be needed to slow down runoff from the fields above a waterway as well as in the immediate area. Cropping systems, tillage methods, and structures that hold more of the water in the fields are discussed in Chapters 8, 9, and 10. This section deals with measures applicable to the area of a waterway or the banks of a pond.

12-1.1 Gully Control

Gullies are distinguished from rills by size—the gullies are too large to be crossed and smoothed by normal farming operations. Gullies grow toward the source of runoff water by the eroding action of water falling into them and are deepened by the abrasive action of sediment in the water flowing through them. Some gullies, such as the one shown in Figure 12-1, grow extremely large. Gully control is expensive and becomes even more so when the gully is allowed to grow larger and more complex.

The following procedures are useful for controlling erosion and healing a gully:

1. Diverting water from the head of the gully. This is usually done by constructing a diversion terrace above the head of the gully and diverting the water into a dense forest, a luxuriant pasture, or a constructed, vegetated waterway. The diversion terrace should be removed after vegetation in the gully is well established. Sometimes the establishment of a terrace system on a field above the gully is more desirable than construction of a single diversion terrace.
2. Grading the head and both sides of the gully to a slope no steeper than the angle of repose for the particular soil. The stable angle is commonly between a 2:1 (26.5° or 50%) and a 3:1 (18.5° or 33%) slope.
3. Building temporary dams across the gully, starting at the head. Any trash or debris in the gully should be removed before dams are built. Each dam of a series constructed down the gully should have the top of the spillway on the same level as (or so the slope is no steeper than 0.5% to) the toe of the dam above it (like stair steps). Temporary check dams can be made

Figure 12-1 Part of a gully near Lumpkin, Georgia that was ne-glected and continued to grow for over one hundred years until it became several kilometers long and 15 to 60 m deep and affected an area of over 40,000 ha. (Courtesy USDA—Soil Conservation Service.)

of loose rock, lumber, logs, or brush laid between posts (Ch. 10). It is very important to extend the bottom and sides of all dams about 15 cm into undisturbed soil, leave the center low for water to flow over, and to construct an apron on the downhill side of the dam to reduce the velocity of the over-flow water and thereby reduce the hazard of water undercut-ting the dam. The gully may be gradually filled by building new check dams at higher elevations when sediment has filled the space behind the old check dams.

4. Establishing adapted perennial vegetation using some combina-tion of grasses, legumes, trees, and shrubs. The selection of species, varieties, and cultivars is determined by climate, soils, and personal desire of the decision-maker.

5. Fencing the entire area around gullies in pasture or range to exclude domestic animals until the vegetation has become established. Fencing is also necessary when trees and shrubs

are grazed (browsed) by herbivorous wild animals such as deer.

The five-step control of gullies may be modified on large watersheds (more than 20 ha) by building permanent check dams in the gullies. The materials may be concrete or rock masonry. Sometimes loose rock dams are superior because hydrostatic pressure is not as great behind them, nor do freezing and thawing and the burrowing of wild animals disrupt them as much as concrete or rock masonry dams. Regardless of the type of dam constructed, perennial vegetation should be established around it to deal with the shifting of erosive forces over time. Rigid dams in a dynamic environment are usually not as long-lasting as adapted perennial vegetation.

Some gullies may be controlled by constructing a drop inlet at the head, sloping the banks, installing flumes as shown in Figure 12-2, or converting the eroding gully into a noneroding grassed waterway.

12-1.2 Establishing Vegetated Waterways

Vegetated waterways are natural or constructed channels that have been shaped to transport water at a nonerosive velocity from fields, diversions, terraces, and road ditches. Essential steps in establishing waterways include the following:

1. Divert all surface and subsurface flow of water by a diversion terrace or berm before establishing the waterway.
2. Design the size, shape, length, and gradient of the waterway according to the area of watershed, type of vegetation to be used, and maximum 10-year, 24-hour runoff or perhaps 25-year, 24-hour runoff.
3. Construct the waterway and establish erosion-resisting vegetation before constructing terraces or other water-concentrating facilities, as shown in Figure 12-3.
4. The cross section of the waterway may be V-shaped, parabolic, or trapezoidal, as shown in Figure 12-4. If a spring causes continuous wetness in the waterway and stones are readily available, parabolic and open V-shaped waterways should be lined with stone for greater erosion control, as shown in Figure 12-5. An alternative is to place a drain tile line beneath the waterway as described in Chapter 15.

Establishing and maintaining vegetation in the waterway channel requires the application of engineering and agronomic principles

a

b

Figure 12-2 (a) A large active gully in Alabama. (b) The gully was healed by grading and installing a flume with a drop structure at each end. (Courtesy USDA—Soil Conservation Service.)

Figure 12-3 This V-shaped grassed waterway in North Carolina was vegetated with tall fescue in preparation for terracing the field. It provides a safe channel to guide runoff water to a permanent stream. (Courtesy USDA—Soil Conservation Service.)

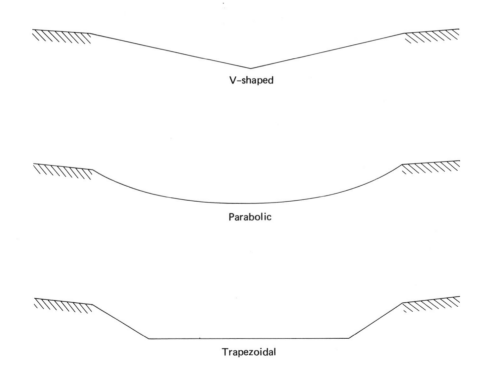

V-shaped

Parabolic

Trapezoidal

Figure 12-4 The cross sections of most grassed waterways are V-shaped, parabolic, or trapezoidal.

Figure 12-5 Waterways constructed where there is prolonged wetness may need to be drained with a tile line (Ch. 15) or lined with stone, as indicated here, for greater erosion resistance. Stone linings work well with either the V-shape (above) or the parabolic shape (below). (Courtesy USDA—Soil Conservation Service.)

and practices. The waterway must be designed with a suitable channel gradient and a large enough cross section to carry the runoff water at a nonerosive velocity. Agronomic factors include plant selection, seedbed preparation, soil testing to diagnose lime and fertilizer needs, time and rate of seeding or planting, the use of an appropriate mulch to hasten plant establishment, the ability to determine relative soil erodibility, and proper maintenance of vegetation. Figure 12–6 shows a well-designed and vegetated waterway. Table 12–1 indicates maximum permissible water velocities for specified conditions. Probable velocities for different slope, depth, and surface conditions can be estimated using Manning's formula (Note 4–2).

Following is a brief description of eight grasses used extensively in the areas of their adaptation for vegetating waterways.

Bermudagrass is ideal for use in vegetating constructed waterways in southern, central, and southwestern United States. It is a tough, vigorous, sod-forming, perennial grass that tolerates both wet and dry soils, as well as acid and alkaline soils. Bermudagrass grows best on fertile fine-textured soils. It propagates by aboveground stolons, belowground rhizomes, and by seed.

Italian ryegrass is a cool-season annual bunchgrass that is adapted to the Pacific Coast states west of the Cascade Mountains and as a winter-season grass in the south. It has a special function on disturbed soils as a rapidly established grass that will stabilize erosion

Figure 12-6 A well-designed and vegetated waterway with a concrete drop outlet to reduce erosion and sedimentation and a tile drain to reduce the time the channel stays wet (note outlet into structure). (Courtesy USDA—Soil Conservation Service.)

and sedimentation until the proper season for establishing perennial vegetation.

Kentucky bluegrass is a cool-season, sod-forming, long-lived perennial that spreads by underground rhizomes. It grows throughout the humid and irrigated regions of the United States except the lower part of the Gulf Coast states. It can survive at a soil pH of 6.0 but grows best in the limestone regions where the pH may approach 8.0.

Reed canarygrass is noted for its ability to grow on poorly drained soils and even in standing water. It will grow throughout the United States on acid soils (pH 5.0) and on alkaline soils (pH 8.0). Although a cool-season bunchgrass, when growing in wet soils, it forms a sodlike surface mass of erosion-resisting adventitious roots.

Redtop is a cool-season perennial grass that grows well in northern humid areas on poorly drained soils as acid as pH 4.0. It reproduces by underground rhizomes and tolerates low soil fertility.

Smooth bromegrass is a widely used, cool-season, sod-forming perennial grass that grows best in soils of very high fertility. It is used in soil erosion and sediment control plantings. Two distinct

Table 12-1 Grasses and legumes recommended for seeding or planting in constructed waterway channels throughout the United States, slope range of the channel gradient, and permissible (non-erosive) velocities on soils of two erodibilities

Grass or legume	Slope range (%)	Permissible water velocity (m/sec)	
		Erosion-resistant soils	Easily eroded soils
Bermudagrass	0–5	2.4	1.8
	5–10	2.1	1.5
	> 10	1.8	1.2
Bahiagrass Buffalograss Kentucky bluegrass Smooth bromegrass Blue gramagrass Tall fescue	0–5 5–10 > 10	2.1 1.8 1.5	1.5 1.2 0.9
Grass mixtures Reed canarygrass	0–5 5–10	1.5 1.2	1.2 0.9
Sericea lespedeza Weeping lovegrass Yellow bluestem Redtop Alfalfa Red fescue Common lespedeza Sudangrass	0–5	1.1	0.8

SOURCE: Adapted from USDA–Soil Conservation Service.

types are identified: *Northern,* adapted to western Canada and the northern Great Plains, and *Southern,* adapted to the Corn Belt and the central Great Plains.

Tall fescue is a vigorous-growing, cool-season, perennial bunchgrass that forms a sodlike cover when seeded heavily. It grows in humid and irrigated areas of the United States except on the lower Gulf Coast. Tall fescue will grow satisfactorily on soils of low fertility. It does better on fine-textured than on coarse-textured soils. Its pH tolerance extends to as low as 5.0 and as high as 8.0.

Western wheatgrass is a cool-season, sod-forming, perennial grass that grows from Wisconsin south to Texas and west to the Pacific Ocean. It is drought-resistant and tolerates high soil alkalinity and high sodium.

All of these grasses need to be carefully managed to maintain vigorous stands in vegetated waterways. They should be mowed and fertilized regularly. Both animal and vehicular traffic should be kept off them when they are wet enough to be damaged.

12-1.3 Pond Bank Stabilization

Sometimes a gully is controlled by building an earthen dam across the lower end. The pond thus formed may be cheaper than an excavated or embankment pond of the same volume, but it is likely to have steep banks. Most small farm ponds, however, are formed by excavation in a location where the watershed is large enough to provide the amount of water needed. Water control is important because fluctuating water levels make it difficult to maintain vegetation on the banks. The proper number of hectares of watershed to furnish a specific amount of runoff water for the proper depth and surface area of a pond can be obtained from the regional engineering handbooks of the USDA—Soil Conservation Service.

Specific techniques for establishing adapted vegetation on critical areas around newly constructed ponds, such as that shown in Figure 12-7, are similar to those for stabilizing gullies (Section 12-1.1) and for vegetating construction sites (Ch. 11). However, one special practice may be needed on pond banks subject to wave action caused by high winds. Until the vegetation is well established on such sites, wave energy may be dissipated by floating logs anchored near the shore or by bales of straw anchored in the shallow water.

12-1.4 Streambank Stabilization

Streambank erosion is a major problem. Land owners who can control gullies, stabilize pond banks, and establish effective vegetated waterways often believe that streambank erosion cannot be prevented because it is a form of natural geologic erosion. Whether perceived as geologic or anthropic, streambank erosion cannot be stopped but it can be controlled. Work on navigable streams in the United States is the responsibility of the Army Corps of Engineers. Hydraulic engineers and agronomists with the Soil Conservation Service have a mandate from the United States Congress to assist land owners in applying streambank erosion control and other conservation activities to smaller streams. The Soil Conservation

Figure 12-7 The banks are being stabilized with adapted vegetation around this well-constructed pond in Minnesota. It is a part of the West Willow Creek Watershed project and is designed to store 250,000 m³ of water from an 800-ha drainage area. (Courtesy USDA—Soil Conservation Service.)

Service estimates that there are 480,000 km of streambanks in the United States that yield 450 million metric tons of sediment each year.

The following practices help to control streambank erosion:

1. Clearing the stream channel of all trees, shrubs, brush, stumps, and debris drifts.
2. Fencing the critical areas to exclude all livestock until the control measures are firmly established.
3. Establishing one or more of the following mechanical or combination mechanical-vegetative devices according to size of watershed, ten-year maximum flow, and available materials.
   a. A willow jetty can be made by driving willow poles (large end down so they will sprout and grow) into the stream channel adjacent to the eroding bank. The poles should be about 1

meter apart, staggered, and wired together so they support
each other. Willow cuttings are then placed between the upper
row of poles and the eroding bank with their base ends in the
soil. The poles and cuttings should grow into a dense thicket
of willows to stabilize the eroding bank, as shown in Figure
12–8.

b. A tree revetment can be made by laying entire trees against
an eroding bank in a wide stream channel. The butts of the
trees should point upstream to slow the water as it flows past
the tree branches. Each tree should be held in place by a log
buried horizontally as a "deadman" or driven vertically as a

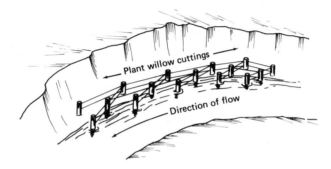

Figure 12-8 A jetty made of willow poles driven into the bank
above and below the water line, then wired together, plus willow
cuttings above the poles, should grow into a dense thicket and
stabilize the bank. (Courtesy USDA–Soil Conservation Service.)

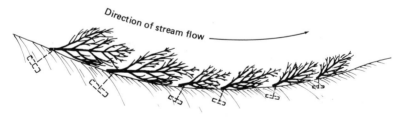

Eroding streambank planted with willow cuttings

Figure 12-9 A tree revetment to control streambank erosion
showing these features: (1) tree butts are next to the bank and
point upstream, (2) "deadmen" (logs at least 20 cm in diameter
and 1 m long) are buried in the bank, and (3) each tree is tied to
a "deadman" by a cable at least 1 cm in diameter. (Courtesy
USDA–Soil Conservation Service.)

pile. The arrangement is shown in Figure 12-9. The adjoining bank should be sloped and planted with willow cuttings. Tree revetments should not be used in narrow channels; to do so would make the channel so narrow that stream velocity would be increased and erosion accelerated.

c. Mechanical structures such as dikes, toe and hardpoint protectors, revetments, and riprap (Ch. 10) are used if vegetation alone will not provide enough protection. Riprap is illustrated in Figure 12-10.

12-2 WINDBREAKS AND SHELTERBELTS

Windbreaks and shelterbelts are groups of trees and shrubs planted at right angles to the prevailing winds for the purpose of moderating the winds, reducing wind erosion, trapping dust and snow, reducing evaporation, increasing relative humidity, ameliorating the environment for livestock and wildlife, reducing fuel costs in heating and cooling a home, and enhancing the environment for people. *Wind-*

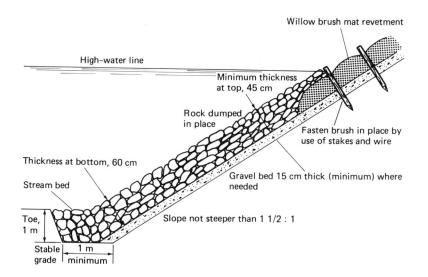

Figure 12-10 Riprap stabilizes a streambank with stones too large for the stream to move. The stones are underlain by gravel so neither soil nor gravel can be washed away. The upper bank is protected by willows. (Courtesy USDA—Soil Conservation Service.)

Figure 12-11 Windbreaks around homes and farmsteads ameliorate the weather for people and livestock, and shelterbelts along field borders protect crops against wind erosion in North Dakota (above) and on the High Plains of Texas (below). (Courtesy USDA—Soil Conservation Service.)

breaks are small groups of trees and shrubs planted to protect live-stock and people. *Shelterbelts* are extensive groups of trees and shrubs planted primarily to protect fields from erosive winds. Wind-breaks and shelterbelts can be seen in Figure 12-11.

12-2.1 Wind Erosion

Wind erosion on the Great Plains damaged 2 million hectares or more each year during 1938, 1939, 1953-1957, and 1975. As recently as the winter of 1976-1977, more than 3 million hectares of land were severely damaged in the Great Plains. This is more wind damage than during any winter since the mid-1930s, except for the years 1954–1957. Hectares of land damaged annually by wind erosion in each of the ten states in the Great Plains and the cropland percentage of the total area damaged are portrayed in Table 12-2.

12-2.2 Windbreak Effectiveness

Windbreaks reduce winter fuel bills, protect cattle and other live-stock, and reduce wind erosion. They also provide food and habitat for wildlife.

Table 12-2 Mean annual hectares of land seriously eroded by wind in the Great Plains, by states, 1956-1975

	Mean annual area damaged by wind	
State (principal area of wind erosion)	*Total land damaged (ha)*	*Cropland (% of total land damaged)*
Colorado (eastern)	197,000	74
Kansas (western)	147,000	97
Montana (eastern)	120,000	97
Nebraska (western)	52,000	84
New Mexico (northeastern)	48,000	74
North Dakota (western)	169,000	99
Oklahoma (western)	42,000	94
South Dakota (southwestern)	45,000	96
Texas (northwestern)	411,000	88
Wyoming (southeastern)	12,000	43
Total	1,243,000	Average = 88

SOURCE: Lyles, 1976.

During the early days of the promotion of windbreaks, the Lake States Forest Experiment Station conducted an experiment at Holdrege, Nebraska, on the home fuel saved by the proper establishment of a windbreak. Two identical homes were selected, one with a windbreak and one without. The home with a windbreak used about 23% less fuel (Stoeckeler and Williams, 1949).

Windbreaks and shelterbelts are desirable and almost necessary for economical production of range livestock in northern states. The University of Montana researched this relationship and reported that during a mild winter, tree-protected cattle gained 16 kg more and during a severe winter lost nearly 5 kg less than cattle without protection from a windbreak or shelterbelt (Stoeckeler and Williams, 1949).

A windbreak or shelterbelt that is well designed and properly oriented will reduce wind speed to less than half of that in the open, as shown in Figure 12-12. Windbreak effectiveness extends as far leeward as fifteen or twenty times the height of the windbreak and windward for about twice its height. Dense windbreaks give the most reduction in wind velocity near the windbreak, but more open ones are effective for a greater distance downwind. The most effective windbreaks have porosities of about 50%. Any reduction in wind speed is important in decreasing wind erosion because the amount of

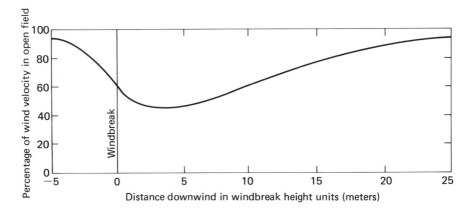

Figure 12-12 Wind velocities about 40 cm above ground level in the vicinity of a windbreak as percentages of what they would be without the windbreak. The curve represents average results of data from several sources. Many data vary ±10% from the curve depending on width, height, and porosity of the windbreak, wind velocity, and topographic features.

soil eroded is proportional to the fifth power of the wind speed (Ch. 5). Thus, the amount of wind erosion is approximately halved when the wind velocity is reduced to 87% of what it would have been without the windbreak.

12-2.3 Trees and Shrubs for Windbreaks

Suitable trees and shrubs for windbreak and shelterbelt plantings adapted to conditions in the northern Great Plains are listed in Table 12-3 and those for the southern Great Plains in Table 12-4. Selection of the most appropriate species depends partly on the number of rows to be included in the windbreak. Traditional windbreaks have had seven rows, with the tallest trees flanked by shorter

Table 12-3 Tree and shrub species adapted for planting windbreaks and shelterbelts in the Northern Great Plains

Trees	*Shrubs*
American elm	American plum
Austrian pine	Amur maple
Black Hills spruce	Arnold hawthorn
Boxelder	Buffaloberry
Bur oak	Caragana (Siberian peashrub)
Chinese elm	Common chokecherry
Chinkota elm	Cotoneaster
Colorado spruce	Diamond willow
Cottonwood	Golden currant
Green ash	Hanson hedgerose
Hackberry	Late lilac
Harbin pear	Laurel willow
Jack pine	Manchurian apricot
Manchurian crabapple	Nanking cherry
Northwest poplar	Redosier dogwood
Norway poplar	Russian mulberry
Robusta poplar	Saskatoon serviceberry
Rocky Mountain juniper	Siberian apricot
Siberian crabapple	Silverberry
Siberian larch	Skunk bush sumac
Silver poplar	Tartarian honeysuckle
Scotch pine	Western sandcherry
White spruce	
White willow	

SOURCE: Suedkamp, 1976.

Table 12-4   Tree and shrub species adapted for planting for windbreaks and shelterbelts in the Southern Great Plains

Trees	*Shrubs*
American elm	Buckthorn
Chinese elm	Caragana (Siberian peashrub)
Crack willow	Chickasaw plum
Desert willow	Cotoneaster
Eastern redcedar	Lilac
Hackberry	Redbud
Honeylocust (thornless)	Soapberry
Kentucky coffeetree	
Mulberry	
One-seed juniper	
Osage-orange	
Pecan	
Russian olive	
Shortleaf pine	
Sycamore	

SOURCE: USDA—Forest Service, 1949.

trees and shrubs. One row of trees should be evergreens for winter protection.

The seven-row windbreak effectively diverts the wind upward but it occupies a lot of land area. This may be justified if the trees chosen can be marketed for wood products when they mature. Otherwise, a smaller windbreak with fewer rows may be preferred. The most effective wind diversion with three-, five-, and seven-row windbreaks occurs with the tallest trees in the second, fourth, or fifth row downwind, respectively (Woodruff and Zingg, 1953). The most efficient use of land for windbreaks is achieved with single-row windbreaks. These are usually composed of evergreens so they will provide winter protection, and they must have branches near the ground so the wind cannot blow under them.

Tree spacing is also important and should be proportioned to the size of the trees. The mature windbreak should still be open enough to permit some air movement through the windbreak, but there must be no major gaps. Missing trees should be replaced promptly because wind speeds through a gap are likely to be about 120% of what they would be without the windbreak. Also, windbreaks should end in sheltered or vegetated areas because wind velocities reach about 120% of normal around the ends. Windbreaks should be fenced to keep livestock from eating the vegetation needed to form a good barrier near the ground.

12-2.4 Prairie States Forestry Project

The U.S. Congress authorized the establishment of the Prairie States Forestry Project in 1934 following the drought and dust-storm years of the early 1930s. During the years from 1935 to 1942, 218 million trees and shrubs were planted on 31,000 farms and ranches to establish 32,180 km of windbreaks and shelterbelts in the ten Great Plains states from Texas to the Canadian border.

Farmers and ranchers in the Great Plains were pleased to have the new plantings of trees and shrubs because it seemed a sign of government concern during the crisis years of drought and economic depression. Since then, however, farms and ranches have been bought by people from other regions. To operate more efficiently in "normal years," farms have become larger, tractors and equipment larger and more powerful, and large center-pivot irrigation systems are being used in many areas.

12-2.5 Recent Trends

Many farmers, most economists, and some technical agriculturists claim that soil management systems such as strip cropping, stubble mulching, minimum tillage, and clod tillage eliminate the need for windbreaks and shelterbelts. Many existing tree belts are being destroyed, mostly by newcomers to the Great Plains. They refuse to believe that wind erosion and dust storms are hard facts of life in the area (McMartin, Frank, and Heintz, 1974).

Many conservationists, however, believe that the new soil management practices are necessary and, furthermore, that plantings of trees and shrubs as windbreaks should be increased tenfold. So, while some windbreaks and shelterbelts in the Great Plains are being destroyed, new ones are being planted. The Forest Service and the Soil Conservation Service offer assistance in establishing trees and shrubs. Recent soil survey reports list the tree and shrub species recommended for planting as windbreaks and shelterbelts on each soil map unit. Cost-sharing for planting trees in the Great Plains is available through the Agricultural Stabilization and Conservation Service. Twenty-two plant materials centers operated throughout the United States by the USDA—Soil Conservation Service are constantly searching for and testing new plants for use as windbreaks and shelterbelts in arid and semiarid regions and for water erosion control in humid regions.

12–2.6 Irrigation and Windbreaks

Thousands of windbreaks and shelterbelts have been removed because they interfered with the establishment of large center-pivot irrigation systems. These systems are carried by wheels traveling in concentric circles as described in Chapter 16. The tracks for the wheels must be smooth and nothing should obstruct the moving irrigation pipe; hence, no shelterbelts. However, windbreaks are needed to calm the winds to assure even application of irrigation water.

An example of a compromise solution to the irrigation-windbreak dilemma is presented in Figure 12–13. Four of the usual 54-ha irrigation circles can be arranged in one section (259 ha) of land and still have a windbreak located every 0.8 km. The nine odd-shaped areas outside the circles can also be planted to trees or they may be seeded to grass or nonirrigated crops.

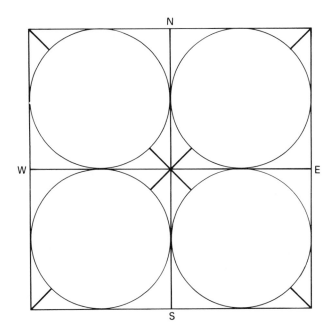

Figure 12-13 A section of land in the United States (1 square mile, 640 acres, or 259 hectares) has room for four standard center-pivot irrigation systems. Each circle irrigates about 54 ha of land. Shelterbelts can be planted around the outside and across the middle of the section and, if necessary, along the diagonals. Such shelterbelts reduce wind velocities and improve the distribution of the irrigation water.

12-3 SAND DUNES

Conditions are conducive to the formation of sand dunes on about 1.45 billion hectares or 11% of the total world land area. Most sand dunes occur in areas of Psamments astride the Tropics of Cancer and Capricorn (23½° north and south latitude). In the United States, sand dunes occur on many sandy soils in windy areas adjacent to the Atlantic Ocean, the Gulf of Mexico, the Pacific Ocean, and around the Great Lakes. Sand dunes also occur on sandy areas in the interior, such as in Idaho and Nebraska.

Stabilization techniques vary widely, but the principles include reducing wind velocity and establishing a vegetative cover. Dunes in dry climates need irrigation and mechanical obstructions such as a lath "snow" fence to reduce wind velocity and the abrasive action of moving sand while vegetation is becoming established. A surface covering of brush, hay, gravel, clay, oil, or emulsified asphalt can also be used on critical areas. All plants selected should be resistant to damage by grazing and browsing animals. Salt-tolerant plants must be used to vegetate dunes next to salt water.

The first mechanical structure or vegetation established must be on the windward side to reduce wind velocity and thus decrease the amount of moving sand. The entire dune can then be vegetated in stages. Stabilization is more effective and of longer duration when bands of adapted herbaceous plants are planted at right angles to the prevailing winds on the windward side, then a band of shrubs, and finally a band of trees.

12-3.1 Stabilizing Coastal Dunes

Sand dunes are very active along the coastlines of the Pacific and Atlantic Oceans and the Gulf of Mexico. Shifting sands can be stabilized by planting adapted vegetation, starting at the high water-line of the ocean. Recommended plants to establish first along the Atlantic Coast from Maine to North Carolina are American beach-grass, European beachgrass, and Volga wildrye. From North Carolina southward to Florida and westward along the Gulf of Mexico, sea-oats and sea panicgrass are favored along with broomsedge bluestem, hoary milkpea, and trailing wildbean. On the Texas Gulf Coast, sand dunes have been partially controlled by seacoast bluestem, weeping lovegrass, and veldtgrass. On the Pacific Coast, tall fescue, clatsop fescue (red fescue), hairy vetch, and beachpea have been used successfully.

Grass should be planted rather than seeded for stabilizing dunes because strong winds along the coasts blow the seed away and sand-blast young seedlings. A complete fertilizer should be broadcast over the plantings as soon as growth starts in the spring. Brush is some-times laid over the plantings to prevent them from blowing out in critical areas.

Adapted shrubs and trees should be interplanted among the grasses to further stabilize the sand. Along the northern part of the Atlantic Coast, native shrubs recommended for planting are beach plum and bayberry. Tree species used successfully include Scotch pine, mugho pine, Austrian pine, and pitch pine. Trees used suc-cessfully from North Carolina to Texas to interplant among herba-ceous plants include sand pine, Virginia pine, loblolly pine, sweetgum, and several local species of willows. On the Pacific Coast, Scotch-broom (a shrub), Monterey pine, and shore pine are planted among the grasses to further stabilize sand dunes.

12-3.2 Stabilizing Inland Dunes

Sand dunes in the interior of the United States have been stabilized by two contrasting techniques, one without irrigation water and one using irrigation.

The nonirrigation system of stabilization consists of first estab-lishing drought-resistant annual plants such as grain sorghum, sundan-grass, or rye. Adapted grasses such as sand bluestem, side-oats grama, Indiangrass, switchgrass, and Canada wildrye are seeded in the resi-dues of the annual plants just prior to the next rainy season.

When irrigation water is available, the sand dunes can be leveled to slope gradients less than 5%, fertilized according to soil test, and planted to alfalfa, wheat, corn, Irish potatoes, or other field or forage crop.

12-3.3 Stabilizing Great Lakes Dunes

The Great Lakes region has more than 216,000 ha of sand dunes. Some of the early practical but scholarly work on sand-dune stabiliza-tion was done around the Great Lakes by Michigan State University (Sanford, 1916). It was confirmed by field tests that the proper place to start control was on the windward side of dunes. A typical planting of vegetation to stabilize sand dunes consisted of several rows each of:

1. European beachgrass, American beachgrass, and/or Volga wildryegrass at the windward edge of the shifting sands.

2. Beach pea, wild lupine, sandgrass, wildryegrass, or a combination of these herbaceous plants.
3. Wild rose, ground hemlock, wax myrtle (bayberry), sweetgale, wild red cherry, Virginia creeper, redosier dogwood, snowberry, or a combination of these shrubs.
4. Willow cuttings from any local willow species.
5. A mixture of adapted fast-growing hardwoods and slower-growing conifers. Recommended hardwoods include cottonwood, white poplar, trembling aspen, white birch, red oak, sassafras, silver maple, and black locust. Approved conifers include jack pine, Scotch pine, white spruce, hemlock, and white cedar.

12-3.4 Managing Stabilized Dunes

Good management is essential to prevent deterioration after sand dunes have been stabilized by perennial vegetation. Sand may start blowing again when the vegetation is destroyed along recreation trails of off-road vehicles. Even a foot path may be enough to destroy the protective vegetation. Overgrazing is a common cause of damage; some vegetation is destroyed by fire. Homesites or commercial buildings located on stabilized sand dunes can easily kill enough vegetation to permit the sands to become mobile again.

Persons managing stabilized sand dunes must be alert to all of the preceding hazards. Prompt action must be taken whenever the vegetation is damaged and the soil exposed to the wind. Traffic should be diverted from such areas and steps taken to revegetate them as soon as possible. Mechanical wind barriers may be used either temporarily or permanently in critical areas.

SUMMARY

Soils in areas of high erosion hazard such as waterways and sites subject to wind erosion need to be stabilized by vegetation. On some sites, the vegetation must be accompanied by mechanical structures. Almost every barren area can be successfully vegetated by using proper agronomic and engineering practices. Good management is needed to maintain the vegetation after it is established.

Gullies are controlled by diverting water from them, grading the banks to stable slopes, building temporary dams, and establishing vegetation. Vegetated waterways can prevent the formation of gullies if they are properly maintained. Pond banks and streambanks need protection from waves and running water.

Windbreaks are established primarily to enhance the ecological environment for people and domestic livestock. Shelterbelts are established for the purpose of reducing wind velocity and wind erosion on cropland. Massive efforts have been expended to establish shelterbelts and windbreaks in the Great Plains where wind erosion and dust storms are a threat during every season of low rainfall.

Sand dunes occur around ocean and lake shorelines and inland in arid and sandy regions. They can be stabilized with vegetation, but several years may be required to establish vegetation on them. Careful management is essential even after the dunes have been stabilized.

QUESTIONS

1. Explain how to control a gully.
2. Why shouldn't waterway channels be allowed to stay wet all the time? How can they be drained?
3. Name three techniques for controlling erosion along streambanks.
4. What are the recent trends in the use of windbreaks and shelterbelts?
5. Explain how to stabilize sand dunes.

REFERENCES

BAILEY, R. G., 1974. *Land-Capability Classification of the Lake Tahoe Basin, California-Nevada—A Guide for Planning.* USDA—Forest Service in cooperation with the Tahoe Regional Planning Agency.

COUNCIL FOR AGRICULTURAL SCIENCE AND TECHNOLOGY, 1976. *Application of Sewage Sludge to Cropland: Appraisal of Potential Hazards of the Heavy Metals to Plants and Animals.* CAST Report No. 64, EPA-430/19-76-013.

ENVIRONMENTAL PROTECTION AGENCY, 1975. *Methods of Quickly Vegetating Soils of Low Productivity, Construction Activities.* EPA-440/9-75-006, 467 p.

ENVIRONMENTAL PROTECTION AGENCY, U.S. Army Corps of Engineers, and USDA, 1977. *Process Design Manual for Land Treatment of Municipal Wastewater.* EPA 625/1-77-008 and COE EM 1110-1-501, Oct.

LYLES, LEON, 1976. Wind patterns and soil erosion on the Great Plains. In *Shelterbelts on the Great Plains, Proceedings of the Symposium,* Denver, Colorado, April 20-22. Great Plains Agricultural Council Pub. No. 78, p. 22-30.

McMARTIN, WALLACE, A. B. FRANK, and R. H. HEINTZ, 1974. Economics of shelterbelt influence on wheat yields in North Dakota. *J. Soil Water Cons.* 29:87-90.

SANFORD, F. H., 1916. *Michigan's Shifting Sands: Their Control and Better Utilization.* Michigan Agr. Expt. Sta. Spec. Bull. No. 79, 31 p.

SOIL CONSERVATION SERVICE, 1973. *How to Control a Gully.* Farmers Bull. No. 2171. USDA—Soil Conservation Service.

STOECKELER, J. H., and R. A. WILLIAMS, 1949. Windbreaks and shelterbelts. In *Trees,* Yearbook of Agriculture, 1949, p. 191–199.

SUEDKAMP, J. F., 1976. Tree and shrub species for conservation use in the northern Great Plains. In *Shelterbelts on the Great Plains, Proceedings of the Symposium,* Denver, Colorado, April 20-22. Great Plains Agricultural Council Pub. No. 78, p. 130–133.

U.S. DEPARTMENT OF COMMERCE, 1968. *Climatic Atlas of the United States,* Environmental Science Services Administration, U.S. Dept. of Commerce, p. 73–77.

WOODRUFF, N. P., and A. W. ZINGG, 1953. Wind tunnel studies of shelterbelt models. *J. Forestry* 51:173–178.

WRIGHT, D. L., H. D. PERRY, and R. E. BLASER, 1978. Persistent low-maintenance vegetation for erosion control and aesthetics in highway corridors. In *Reclamation of Drastically Disturbed Lands.* American Society of Agronomy, Madison, Wisc., p. 553–583.

13

Pasture, Range, and Forest Management

There are no better soil stabilizers than luxuriant pasture grasses and legumes, range grasses, and forest trees and shrubs. Close-growing perennial vegetation cushions the impact of raindrops on bare soil and thereby decreases soil dispersion and sheet erosion. The velocity of surface water flow is reduced by contact with plant stems and residues. The result is clean water flowing slowly along the soil surface, more and faster infiltration of water into deep soil horizons, and less soil erosion and sediment. Vegetation also stabilizes soil against wind erosion by the "holding" action of plant roots and by decreasing wind velocity at the soil-atmosphere interface.

An example of the effectiveness of vegetation in increasing infiltration of rainfall, and therefore decreasing runoff and potential water erosion, is reported by Hart, 1974, as shown in Figure 13–1. Soils used for pastures and meadows permit more rapid infiltration than soils used for clean-tilled crops. Heavy grazing in pastures and bare areas in cropland reduced the infiltration rates.

In humid areas, soils subject to wind erosion, such as sand dunes along the shores of the Great Lakes and most oceans, are relatively easy to stabilize. Salt-resistant perennial vegetation can be established even near an ocean. Wind erosion in arid and semiarid areas is much more difficult to control because there is seldom enough water to support close-growing vegetation.

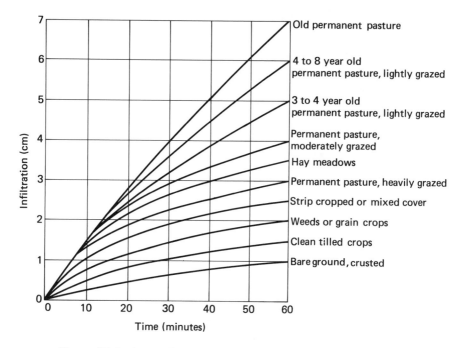

Figure 13-1 Increasing intensity of use reduces the rate of water infiltration into soil. (Courtesy USDA—Agricultural Research Service [now Science and Education Administration].)

13-1 PASTURELAND, RANGELAND, AND FORESTLAND

Pastureland usually refers to an intensively managed humid area that supports forage such as improved grasses or a mixture of grasses and legumes. Pastureland is usually plowed and fertilized every few years. Pastures in arid and semiarid areas are often irrigated.

Rangeland refers to unplowed areas where native grasses, forbs, shrubs, and trees are used for forage. Some ranges may be fertilized and reseeded to native or exotic grasses; they are seldom plowed.

Forestland is an area of growing trees or of soil capable of supporting trees. A tree is any woody plant at least 4.5 m high supported by a single stem.

The land area of the United States is classified as 23.9% pasture, 12.8% range, and 25.8% forest (Table 13-1). Additionally, about 10% of the forestland (woodland) is grazed by domestic livestock.

Table 13-1   Pastureland, rangeland, and forestland in the fifty United States

Land use	Total area (million hectares)	Percentage of total U.S. land area
Pastureland:		
Pastureland used only for pasture	183	20.0
Cropland used only for pasture	36	3.9
Total pastureland	219	23.9
Rangeland:		
Humid, semiarid, and arid woodland, shrub-		
land, and grassland—all grazed	117	12.8
Total rangeland	117	12.8
Forestland:		
Farm woodland:		
Pastured	25	2.7
Not pastured	20	2.2
Nonfarm forestland, some grazed	192	20.9
Total forestland	237	25.8
Total pasture-, range-, and forestland	537	62.5

SOURCE: USDA—Agricultural Statistics, 1976.

The relationship between the present pastureland, rangeland, and forestland can be inferred from a map of the native vegetation of the conterminous forty-eight states shown in Figure 13-2. Most of the pastures are in areas that originally grew either forests or tall grasses. Present rangeland for domestic livestock includes most of the areas shown as shortgrass, mesquitegrass, sagebrush, creosote bush, and arid woodland. A large percentage of the forests of southeastern United States is also used as rangeland. Most forestlands occupy parts of the areas identified in the map as forest vegetation.

13-2 PASTURE MANAGEMENT

The approach of the pasture manager should be agronomic; that is, the manager uses pasture species suited to the soil and climate of the area. Lime and fertilizers are applied according to soil test recommendations that are correlated with field plot responses. Tillage

Native vegetation

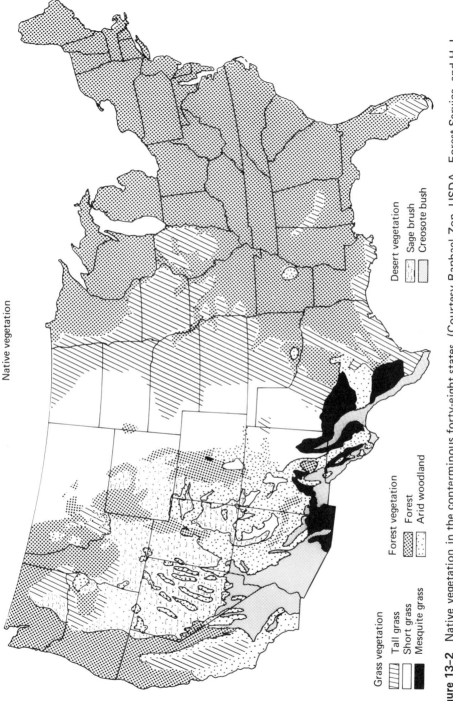

Grass vegetation   Forest vegetation   Desert vegetation

Tall grass   Forest   Sage brush

Short grass   Arid woodland   Creosote bush

Mesquite grass

Figure 13-2 Native vegetation in the conterminous forty-eight states. (Courtesy Raphael Zon, USDA—Forest Service, and H. L. Shantz, Bureau of Plant Industry.)

Table 13-2 Erosion resisting pasture grasses and their ecological adaptation to regions in the United States shown in Figure 13-3

Pasture grass	Ecological adaptation
Bahiagrass	Region 3. Florida and lower Costal Plains. Sandy, medium-acid, droughty soils.
Bermudagrass, common and coastal	Region 1. Southern U.S. from Maryland to Texas, southern Arizona, and southern California where rainfall or irrigation water is adequate. Well-drained, medium-textured soils of high fertility.
Bromegrasses; smooth, mountain, and California	Regions: Smooth, 1, 2, and 5 (irrigated); California and mountain, 6. Smooth bromegrass grows best on well-drained, deep, fertile, slightly acid soils. California and mountain bromegrasses are tolerant of droughty soils, of low fertility, and of cold soils.
Fescue, tall	Regions 1, 2, 4, and 5. Northern, southern, central, and intermountain areas where precipitation or irrigation water is adequate. Well-drained, medium- and fine-textured soils of medium to low fertility (but not coarse sands).
Johnsongrass	Regions 2 and 3. The southern and southwestern U.S. where moisture is adequate. Well-drained, fine-textured soils of high fertility.
Kentucky bluegrass	Regions 1, 4, and 5. Northern two-thirds of the U.S. and northwestern U.S. where moisture is adequate. Slightly acid to neutral, sandy loams to clay soils.
Reed canarygrass	Regions 1, 4, and 6. Adapted to areas with high precipitation or adequate irrigation water in the northeastern U.S., north central Great Plains, and humid Pacific Coast areas. Thrives on moist or marshy, fertile soils as well as well-drained, productive soils.
Redtop	Region 1. Humid northern areas. Well-drained to poorly drained, acid soils of fine texture.
Timothy	Region 1. Cool and humid climate of the northern and northeastern U.S. Well-drained to somewhat poorly drained, fine-textured soils (not on sands).
Weeping lovegrass	Regions 2 and 3. Southern U.S. Not winter-hardy. Well-drained soils of low fertility, including sands.

operations are used when needed to improve the quality of the pasture. All of these activities are coordinated with the livestock specialist for the ultimate benefit of the livestock producer.

13-2.1 Erosion-Resisting Pasture Grasses

Several productive pasture grasses that resist erosion because of their vigorous growth or tolerance to wet, droughty, acid, clayey, or sandy soils are listed in Table 13-2. The principal areas in the United States where each grass is adapted are shown in the table and in Figure 13-3.

13-2.2 Erosion-Resisting Pasture Legumes

Legumes are desirable in seeding mixtures with pasture grasses because of their ability to serve as the host for *Rhizobium* bacteria that biologically fix atmospheric N_2. Additionally, legumes are usually rich in minerals essential for livestock. In most situations, however, the grasses persist longer and often crowd out the companion legumes.

The need to reestablish legumes is the most common reason for renovating pastures (Section 13-2.5). A list of vigorous erosion-resisting pasture legumes is presented in Table 13-3. Ecological regions of their adaptation are shown in Figure 13-4. Adapted cultivars selected for a particular farm will persist longer than most

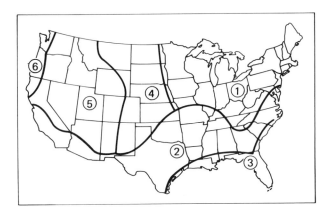

Figure 13-3 Ecological regions for pasture and range grasses in the United States. Irrigation must be used to supplement natural precipitation for some of the grasses in the western United States. (Courtesy U.S. Department of Agriculture.)

Table 13-3   Erosion-resisting pasture legumes and their ecological adaptation to regions shown in Figure 13-4

Legume	*Ecological adaptation*
Alfalfa	All regions except Florida and the lower Gulf Coast. Very fertile, neutral soils with good drainage for at least 2 m. Irrigated especially in Regions 5, 6, 7, and 10.
Alsike clover	Regions 1, 7, and 9. Northeastern, north central, intermountain areas and on the humid western slopes of the Cascade and Olympic Mountains. Tolerates most soils except coarse sands, poorly drained, and acid soils. Irrigated in Region 7.
Birdsfoot trefoil	Regions 1, 9, and 10. Northeastern, north central, humid Washington and Oregon, and irrigated California. Well-drained and moderately well-drained, medium- to fine-textured soils of low fertility. (The forage will not bloat livestock.)
Crownvetch	Regions 1, 2, and 3. All of humid eastern U.S. except Florida and the lower Gulf Coast. Tolerant of low fertility and soil pH as low as 5.0. Grows best on well-drained soils of medium texture such as loam.
Lespedezas, annual	Regions 2, 3, and 4. Southern part of the north central states and all of the humid southern U.S. Best adapted to well-drained, medium- to fine-textured soils with a pH of 6.5. Tolerates infertile, droughty soils of low pH.
Sainfoin	Regions 5 and 7. Northern Great Plains and intermountain regions. Tolerates a high soil pH, droughtiness, and low soil N and P. Grows best on well-drained soils. (The forage will not bloat livestock.)
Sweetclover	Regions 1, 2, 3, 4, 5, and 6. All of the eastern two-thirds of the U.S. Must be irrigated in areas with less than 40 cm of annual precipitation. Adapted only to well-drained, neutral to alkaline, medium- to fine-textured soils high in fertility.
White clover	Regions 1, 2, 3, 4, 7, 8, 9, and 10. Must be irrigated in semiarid and arid regions. Adapted to well-drained to poorly drained soils of medium to high fertility and medium to fine texture.

because of strong seedling vigor or tolerance to droughtiness, wetness, acidity, alkalinity, or low soil fertility.

13-2.3 Fertility Management

Soil tests can identify needs for fertilizers and soil amendments. However, fertilizers cannot be utilized efficiently by plants when the soil is too acid or toxins are present in lethal quantities. The application of lime will reduce acidity, lower the exchangeable aluminum, and make soil phosphorus more readily available. Excessive sodium and alkalinity may be corrected with gypsum.

Nitrogen is the nutrient most likely to limit the growth of pasture grasses. However, excessive applications cause luxury consumption which leads to a large increase in top growth but not in root growth. High rates of nitrogen fertilizers favor grasses in a legume-grass mixture and decrease atmospheric nitrogen fixation by legume *Rhizobium.*

Phosphorus is often the second most critical nutrient in pasture production and, indirectly, in soil erosion and sediment stabilization. Phosphorus fertilizer is most efficiently applied before or at the time of seeding. As much as a three-year supply of phosphorus can often be applied at this time because very little will leach from the soil.

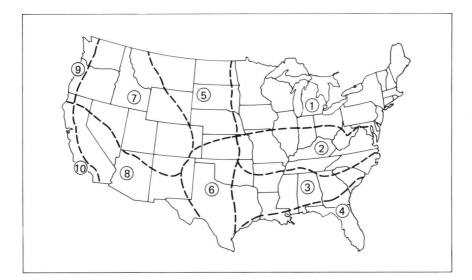

Figure 13-4 Ecological regions for pasture legumes in the United States. (Courtesy U.S. Department of Agriculture.)

Topdressing a pasture with phosphorus fertilizer is less efficient because the phosphorus moves downward very slowly.

Potassium is required on pastures, especially in humid regions and on sandy soils in semiarid areas. Plants will absorb more potassium than they need (luxury consumption) when it is applied in surplus. Low available soil magnesium or surplus plant absorption of K^+ or NH_4^+ may cause a decrease in plant uptake of magnesium. When forages contain less than 0.20% magnesium (Mg) and cattle blood serum is less than 1.5 mg/100 ml, grass tetany (hypomagnesemia) usually results. This nutritional disease is often fatal to cattle.

Animal manures and sewage sludges are effective fertilizers on pastures. The amounts and the times of application, however, must be reasonable to comply with pasture plant requirements as well as to insure environmental integrity (Ch. 17).

13-2.4 Grazing Management

Grazing management is one of the most neglected pasture practices. The principal management systems are: (1) continuous, (2) rotational, and (3) deferred grazing.

Continuous grazing means placing livestock on a large pasture and allowing them to graze there until the end of the grazing season. When the stocking rate is moderate, this system is suitable for such grass species as bermudagrass, Kentucky bluegrass, pangolagrass, perennial ryegrass, and tall fescue. There is a tendency, however, to graze the pasture with the same stocking rate throughout the grazing season with the result that it is underused during the spring flush of growth and overgrazed during dry weather and dormant periods. Consequently, pasture productivity may decrease and soil erosion and sediment yield may take place if the land is sloping.

Rotational grazing means placing cross fences in the pasture so the livestock can graze only part of the pasture at a time. This grazing system is best adapted to grasses such as bromegrass and intermediate wheatgrass. Such grasses should not be grazed closer to the ground than about 10 cm. This system has the potential of producing more total pasturage per unit of land by permitting the seeding of each subdivision to grasses or grass mixtures with different seasons of growth. For example, tall fescue, a cool-season grass, can be seeded in one pasture subdivision and grazed early in the spring. Another subdivision could be seeded to bermudagrass which produces most abundantly in midsummer.

Some pastures are rotated on a daily basis by means of movable electric fences. Daily pastures with many animals in a small area cause the livestock to utilize the vegetation more completely rather than choosing only the most succulent growth. This technique reduces the bloat hazard of grazing legumes such as alfalfa.

Deferred grazing means delaying the grazing period either to permit the most desirable grass species to become more vigorous or produce seed or both, or until a freeze has stopped growth of leaves and stems. Such "frosted pasturage" is often ideal when other forage is scarce or expensive. Deferred grazing and rotational grazing work well in combination. The livestock can graze in one pasture while another is being deferred. Different pastures can be deferred each year in a rotation sequence that maintains productive vegetation in all of them.

13-2.5 Renovation

Most perennial pastures deteriorate at times because of overgrazing, soil compaction, drought, insects, diseases, a decrease in percentage of legumes, or a depletion of one or more essential plant nutrients. On sloping pastures, such deterioration is usually accompanied by soil erosion and sediment transport that pollutes surface waters. The solution is pasture renovation.

Pastures should be renovated when their productivity declines to between 50% and 75% of their potential. A small-grain crop is sometimes grown before reseeding pasture if the soil is suitable, but pasture is reseeded immediately where the erosion hazard is high. Either way, a suitable seedbed must be prepared, preferably with crop residues left as a protective mulch.

Renovation of a pasture is usually accomplished by chiseling or disking on the contour, sometimes applying herbicides to kill existing vegetation, adding lime and fertilizers as indicated by soil tests, then reseeding with the pasture mixture recommended for that specific soil series and season. Livestock must be kept off the renovated pasture until the new vegetation is well established.

A newer technique of pasture renovation to reduce soil erosion includes heavy grazing of the existing forage followed by the use of a contact herbicide and then seeding the pasture mixture directly into the dead sod. A modification of this system uses a special implement that tills the dead sod down to mineral soil in bands about 10 cm wide in which the seeds are planted. In the southern United States, cool-season legumes such as crimson clover may be seeded into a warm-season grass pasture. In the northern United States, legumes such as white clover, alfalfa, birdsfoot trefoil, and crown-vetch are seeded in this manner.

13-3 RANGE MANAGEMENT

Any wild land grazed by domestic livestock is called *rangeland*. There are 117 million hectares of humid, semiarid, and arid woodlands, shrublands, and grasslands used as rangeland in the United States. This is 12.8% of the land area of the fifty states (Table 13-1 and Figure 13-2).

The range manager should take an ecological approach; that is, the use of mostly native plants, soils, climate, and kinds and numbers of livestock to encourage the growth of the most desirable forage species. The control of soil erosion and sedimentation is of immediate concern to the range manager because sheet and gully erosion and active sand dunes reduce the forage produced for the range livestock. Sedimentation cannot be ignored because it reduces the storage capacity of watering ponds after each heavy rain. Since the range manager usually cannot directly control erosion, the best recourse is to prevent it by limiting the rate of stocking. Reasonable stocking rates reduce erosion and sedimentation and maintain the most palatable and desirable erosion-resisting grasses by natural regeneration, as shown in Figure 13-5.

The general condition of ranges in the United States and many other countries is not good. There are several reasons for this. Unpredictable drought and related overgrazing are partly at fault. Lack of adequate research and extension efforts certainly contribute. Also, stocking rates are too high on much rangeland.

The Forest Service in the U.S. Department of Agriculture and the Bureau of Land Management and the Bureau of Indian Affairs in the U.S. Department of Interior are responsible for nearly all of the publicly owned U.S. rangeland. They lease grazing rights to private livestock owners. The USDA—Forest Service made a study of the condition of the range on 20 million hectares under their management and concluded that 20% was productive up to its potential, 40% to 60% was only 40% as productive as it could be, and 37% had a productivity less than 40% of its potential (USDA—Forest Service, 1972).

A similar study was made of the range condition of all 66 million hectares under the management of the Bureau of Land Management. The results were: 2% excellent, 15% good, 50% fair, 28% poor, and 5% bad. No comparable study has been made of the condition of

a

b

Figure 13-5 Good grazing management is the only practical way to keep rangeland continuously productive and environmentally safe. These two ranges in Wyoming are both on sandy soils receiving about 400 mm of annual precipitation. (a) Overgrazing has caused severe range deterioration and wind and water erosion. (b) Good grazing management has resulted in productive range that controls wind and water erosion. (Courtesy USDA—Soil Conservation Service.)

privately owned rangelands, but the conventional wisdom is that they average about the same or a little better than publicly owned ranges. The effects of grazing management can be seen in Figure 13-6.

13-3.1 Erosion-Resisting Range Grasses

Eleven erosion-resisting species of range grasses have been selected for more study. All of these grasses are palatable to livestock and have one or more other characteristics that make them desirable range grasses. These characteristics include excellent seedling vigor, good tolerance to drought, tolerance to sodicity, and/or quick recovery when grazed. None of the species requires irrigation for successful establishment except in rare instances (Table 13-4).

There is a renewed research effort to find native legumes (or to develop legumes by breeding) that can withstand competition from range grasses and the harsh environment of the range. Some success has been achieved in semiarid regions with subterranean clover, yellow-flowered alfalfa, cicer milkvetch, birdsfoot trefoil, and sainfoin.

Figure 13-6 Highly productive bluestem grasses on alkaline soils in Texas rangeland managed by the U.S. Forest Service (right) and deteriorated private rangeland (left) where a sparse growth of buffalograss has replaced the bluestems in this 800-mm precipitation zone. (Courtesy USDA—Soil Conservation Service.)

Table 13-4 Erosion-resisting range grasses and their ecological adaptation to regions shown in Figure 13-3

Range grass	*Ecological adaptation*
Bluestem grasses: big, little, sand	Regions: *Big bluestem,* Regions 1 and 4—the midwest and the eastern Great Plains. Well-drained loam soils. *Little bluestem,* Regions 1, 4, and 5—the northeast, midwest, and intermountain regions. Well-drained loams. *Sand bluestem,* Region 4 from Nebraska south. Deep sandy soils.
Buffalograss	Region 4 and eastern part of Region 5. Adapted to silty and clayey soils, locally known as "hard lands." Tolerates soil alkalinity.
Grama grasses: black, blue, sideoats	*Black gramagrass,* Region 5. One of the most drought-resistant of all grasses. *Blue gramagrass,* Regions 4 and 5. More extensive but less drought-resistant than black gramagrass. *Sideoats gramagrass,* Regions 1, 2, 4, and 5. Extensive in distribution but the least drought-resistant.
Wheatgrasses: crested, slender, western	All three species adapted to Region 4 and northern part of Region 5. *Crested wheatgrass* is drought- and cold-resistant but not tolerant of sodic soil. *Slender wheatgrass* is highly tolerant of sodic soils but less drought-tolerant. *Western wheatgrass* is very tolerant of droughty and sodic soils. The three species grow well on most soil textures except deep sands.
Wildryegrass, Russian	Region 4 and western Canada. Tolerant of most soil textures and droughty soils.

13-3.2 Grazing Management

Although rangelands include much of the open pine and hardwood lands of humid regions, the principal areas are in the arid and semi-arid regions. Rangelands in these drier regions include tall grass prairies, short grass plains, and semidesert areas supporting sparse bunchgrasses, forbs (broad-leaved, herbaceous plants), and woody shrubs.

The following range management practices increase the amount and efficiency of use of range forage as well as protect the soil against erosion, as shown in Figure 13-7.

a

b

Figure 13-7 Stocking rates must be adjusted to the season of growth of the grass and to the precipitation, as shown by these semiarid rangelands in California. (a) Overgrazed rangeland with benchlike slumping caused by cattle trails and weakened grasses. (b) Well-managed rangeland with abundant grass and stable soils. (Courtesy Agricultural Experiment Station, University of California.)

1. Seeding of improved grass cultivars such as crested wheat-grass.
2. Fertilizing the range with about 45 kg/ha of nitrogen fertilizer.
3. Delaying spring grazing until the grasses have a good start and the soil is dry enough to avoid trampling damage.
4. Grazing the range simultaneously with cattle and sheep.
5. Adjusting the rate of stocking to the season of growth of grass and to precipitation.
6. Leaving about 50% of all range forage for reserve and residue, as in Figure 13-8. In the words of the best ranchers, "graze half and leave half."
7. Integrating range grazing with the grazing of irrigated pastures.
8. Practicing rotational and deferred grazing. This usually requires building more cross fences, establishing more water facilities as in Figure 13-9, and adding more salt boxes.

Figure 13-8 Cattle on rangeland in Kenya (eastern Africa). More than 44 million hectares, or about 80% of the country, is rangeland. Experts from the Food and Agriculture Organization of the United Nations helped the Kenyans improve the range and stock it with the proper number of cattle so they "graze half and leave half." (Courtesy N. Nagata, Food and Agriculture Organization of the United Nations.)

Figure 13-9 Good grazing management includes establishment of enough fences and water facilities to permit rotational and deferred grazing. A cowboy noticed wild iris growing here and realized it meant wetness. This small pond dug with a bulldozer provides livestock water throughout the grazing season. (USDA— Farmers' Bulletin 2212.)

9. Moving salt periodically to undergrazed areas away from the water so cattle will graze the range as uniformly as possible. Cattle need both salt and water, but not together. Beef cattle can walk a kilometer or more for a drink, and need only one drink every second day.
10. Clearing brush from ranges to encourage the growth of desirable forage grasses.

13-3.3 Burning Bluestem Ranges

In the Great Plains, annual burning of the little bluestem and big bluestem range increases the quality of forage for livestock. Reasons cited in favor of burning include weed control, insect control, earlier growth, more total growth, and improved forage quality. Opponents of range burning claim it increases air pollution and soil erosion and is poor aesthetically.

Hyde and Owensby (1970) cite results of range burning in the 760-mm annual precipitation belt in Kansas for a twenty-year period. They concluded that burning a bluestem range at the same time the bluestem grasses start to grow, usually about May 1, results in the greatest gain of yearling beef cattle. This is true in spite of the fact that the nonburned range produced more total forage (Table 13-5). Damage to the environment from range burning must be weighed against the 12 kg/ha additional gain in beef each year. The conflict can be solved only by further research that measures aesthetics, air pollution, and soil erosion against range condition and beef production.

13-4 FOREST MANAGEMENT

Forests grow mostly in humid regions; however, the term "forest-lands" includes many semiarid areas. The definition of forestland requires only 10% of the area to be occupied by trees. Total area in the United States so classified is 237 million hectares distributed as shown in Figure 13-10. About 85% of the forestland is commercial forest, of which 73% is privately owned. By definition, commercial forestland must produce, or be capable of producing, at least 1.4 m³/ha of wood products per year.

The U.S. government, recognizing that forests are excellent protectors of watersheds and that forests supply essential products, assists private forest landowners in making their forests more pro-

Table 13-5 A comparison of forage yield and beef cattle gain on bluestem ranges not burned and burned on different dates

	Total forage produced annually (kg/ha)	*Total gain in yearling beef cattle annually (kg/ha)*
Not burned	3629	105
Burned about March 10	2647	107
Burned about April 10	3180	115
Burned about May 1	3506	117

SOURCE: Hyde and Owensby, 1970.

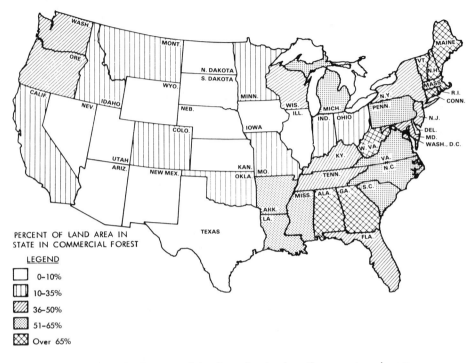

Figure 13-10 Commercial forestland in the conterminous United States. (Courtesy USDA—Forest Service.)

ductive. Such assistance is provided under three laws: the Clarke-McNary Act of 1924, the Cooperative Forest Management Act of 1950, and the Forestry Incentives Act of 1973.

Federal and state agencies have cooperated to grow and sell at concessional rates more than 500 million forest trees for planting each year since 1959. Millions more have been produced in private forest nurseries. In addition to planting nursery-grown forest tree seedlings, new forests are established on thousands of hectares by direct seeding of the most desirable forest tree species. Further assistance has been given to private forest landowners in forest fire protection, estimating the merchantable volume of timber ready for harvest, the best harvest methods, and finding alternative market outlets.

13-4.1 Forests and Watersheds

Well-managed forests are unsurpassed as a vegetative cover for watersheds. Leaves, branches, and the leafy organic layer on the forest floor break the velocity of falling raindrops. Rain may slowly infiltrate layers such as that in Figure 13-11 or be held by the spongy leaf litter and fine roots. Some water moves down branches and trunks and infiltrates into the soil along root channels. The net result is that a properly managed forest has more infiltration and less runoff, erosion, and sedimentation than it would have as cropland. Furthermore, slow, deep seepage gives rise to many springs and to a three- to five-day delay in flood crests.

Because of higher precipitation and denser vegetation, eastern forests yield more runoff water and a lower sediment concentration than western forests.

Water yields on western ranges are less than from forests but more than from ranges on the Great Plains. Sediment yields are greatest on western ranges (Table 13-6).

In forested areas with a mixed land use pattern of trees, farms, and urban areas, such as those in eastern United States, sediment yields decrease with increasing percentage of the land area covered with trees (Table 13-7).

Figure 13-11 The leafy organic layer on the forest floor absorbs the energy of falling raindrops, increases infiltration, and decreases runoff, erosion, and sedimentation. This picture was taken in a ninety-five-year-old red pine plantation in Minnesota. (Courtesy USDA—Forest Service.)

Table 13-6   Runoff water and sediment yield in relation to land use in the United States

Land use	Runoff water yield (ha-cm/yr)	Soil erosion sediment yield (mt/ha-yr)
Forest:		
Eastern	15.30	0.96
Western	13.57	1.17
Range:		
Western	2.96	6.14
Great Plains	0.99	2.50

SOURCE: USDA—Forest Service, 1972.

Table 13-7   Influence of forest cover on control of sediment yield from soil erosion on subbasins of the Potomac River

Land area with forest cover (%)	Sediment yield (mt/ha-yr)
20	4.00
40	2.00
60	0.90
80	0.45
100	0.22

SOURCE: Lull and Reinhart, 1972.

Forest trees are excellent protectors of the watershed but only after a uniform cover of at least 5 cm of surface leaves or needles has accumulated and remains throughout the year, as shown in Figure 13-12. A new pine plantation on severely eroded and eroding soils in northern Mississippi, for example, effectively controlled erosion and sediment yield only after a period of about four to five years (Ursic and Dendy, 1963). In similar studies in Tennessee, sediment loads from an eroded watershed were reduced by 96% in about the same length of time (Tennessee Valley Authority, 1962). The time necessary to produce sufficient leaves or needles on the soil surface to control erosion can be reduced by one to two years with fertilizer applications based on a soil test (Duffy, 1977).

Figure 13-12 This ten-year-old slash pine plantation in Oklahoma was established on abandoned, eroded cropland. These trees and their thick needle layer have been fully protecting the area against erosion and sedimentation for at least five years. (Courtesy USDA—Soil Conservation Service.)

McClurkin (1970) showed that most forest trees increase the infiltration of water. Starting with bare soil, the infiltration rate under most forest tree species and mixtures of species was higher after fifteen years of growth than it was before. Increasing the infiltration reduces the surface flow, erosion, and sedimentation (Table 13-8). However, infiltration was not increased when red cedar was planted alone or in mixture with shortleaf pine. A logical explanation is that layers of red cedar needles tend to "waterproof" the soil surface by their resin coating.

The selection of forest tree species that are adapted to the soil is an important matter in reforestation, whether done primarily to grow commercial forests or to reduce soil-erosion sediments. Guidance is given by several agencies, but the reports and maps of the National Cooperative Soil Survey are the most site-specific. The soil interpretations for woodland use are based upon 22,000 plots of trees planted or managed on representative soil series throughout the United States where climate and soils favor tree growth. The site index (height at a specified age such as fifty or one hundred years), soil-erosion hazard, equipment limitations, wind-

Table 13-8 Water infiltration rates in surface soils before and after fifteen years of tree growth

	Infiltration rates (mm/hr)	
Species planted	1951	1966
Red–cedar plus loblolly pine	42	132
Shortleaf pine	38	141
Loblolly pine	85	187
Red–cedar plus shortleaf pine	43	43
Red–cedar	133	84

SOURCE: McClurkin, 1970.

throw hazard (likelihood of trees being blown down), and annual growth rate in volume of wood are measured on the test plots. Information on woodland suitability groups of soils is incorporated in individual farm and ranch conservation plans and also is included for all forested soil map units in published soil survey reports.

An example of how to use the woodland suitability groups of soils is presented in a published soil survey report of Chilton County, Alabama. The report indicates that 26,325 ha of land in Chilton County are in need of tree planting for one or more reasons, including soil sediment control for the enhancement of water quality. All soil map units in the county are placed in one of fifteen woodland suitability groups, based on their ecological similarities, to assist in selecting the most suitable tree species for planting. Each of the fifteen woodland groups is assigned a corresponding group of adapted trees of high commercial value with predicted site index and volume of annual growth (McNutt and others, 1972).

13-4.2 Harvesting Methods and Erosion Potentials

The timber harvesting method that causes the least soil disturbance should be favored for maintaining a productive forest. Trade-offs must always be made, however, because the harvesting method causing the least soil disturbance is nearly always the most expensive.

Road building is the cause of most soil loss and sediment yield from forests. Erosion and sloughing result when fill slopes are greater than the angle of repose. The angle of repose is about 34° for many fills for logging roads in northwestern United States. Cut slopes are also sources of sediment when excessively long and steep in relation to soil stability. The most common erosion-control techniques for forest roads include the seeding of adapted grasses, legumes, and shrubs during the next suitable planting season after road construction. After logging is completed, the road bed should be abandoned and seeded to grasses and legumes.

There are four principal methods of harvesting trees: selection, shelterwood, seed-tree, and clearcutting. Each method has a different effect on erosion potential, as follows. (Environmental Protection Agency, 1973).

Selection. The selection system of silvicultural harvest consists of removing individual trees or small groups of trees as they mature. The selection system results in an all-age stand. It is adapted to tolerant species that will reproduce satisfactorily under severe competition for soil moisture, soil nutrients, and light. Such species include redwood on the Pacific Coast in California; white fir and incense cedar in California; ponderosa pine on the eastern slope of the Sierra Nevada and Cascade Mountains; Engelmann spruce, alpine fir, and western larch in the Rocky Mountains; sugar maple and beech in the northern hardwoods; and most of the white and red oaks in the central states.

The most tolerant forest tree species will reproduce satisfactorily following the single-tree selection method, but less tolerant trees reproduce better where larger openings are made by the group selection method. the only significant erosion potential resulting from the selection harvesting method is that associated with the traffic to remove the trees.

Shelterwood. The shelterwood system of tree harvest removes all mature trees in a series of several harvests with enough years between to leave adequate overstory to shelter the site. The protective shelter is aesthetically appealing and provides partial shade for reproduction of forest species that require it. Heavy-seeded species such as oaks usually reproduce well under this system.

The shelterwood system of harvest is well adapted to the Appalachian mixed hardwood forest type, including species such as northern red oak, yellow poplar, basswood, hickories, and white ash. Eastern white pine and red pine also are well adapted to this system. A continuous shelterwood system of harvest results in forest stands that are essentially even-aged. Very little erosion and sedimentation result from the shelterwood method.

Seed-Tree. The seed-tree method leaves only enough trees to bear seed for natural regeneration. The system is applicable to light seed that can be borne by the wind. The seed trees may be harvested after a new forest is reseeded. The new forest is therefore even-aged. The four southern pines (loblolly, longleaf, shortleaf, and slash) are the principal species that are adapted to the seed-tree method of silvicultural harvest. The potential for soil erosion and sediment pollution is great for a few years.

Clearcutting. Clearcutting removes all the trees from the logged area. The purpose is to clear the area to establish a new, even-aged stand, usually of a valuable fast-growing species that will not reproduce satisfactorily in the shade of other trees. The area clearcut may consist of patches, strips, or an entire watershed. Regeneration may be achieved through established reproduction, natural seeding before cutting, artificial seeding after cutting, sprouts from stumps (coppice), or planting.

Clearcutting as in Figure 13-13 is used to achieve satisfactory reproduction of Douglas-fir in the Pacific Northwest, western white

Figure 13-13 Clearcutting Douglas-fir in patches in a national forest in Oregon. The open patches are needed because Douglas-fir seedlings will not tolerate shade. Solid blocks are left standing to reduce windthrow hazard. (Courtesy USDA—Forest Service.)

pine in northern Idaho, jack pine near the Great Lakes, loblolly pine in the southeastern United States, lodgepole pine in the Rocky Mountains, and black cherry in the Allegheny Mountains.

Clearcutting is a standard practice to permit efficient use of high-lead, skyline, balloon, or helicopter logging systems. Because of the great erosion hazard and the continuous public outcry of environmentalists, the advantages and disadvantages of clearcutting are given in Note 13-1.

NOTE 13-1 ADVANTAGES AND DISADVANTAGES OF HARVESTING A FOREST BY CLEARCUTTING

Advantages	Disadvantages
1. Creates good growing conditions for shade-intolerant tree species (e.g., Douglas-fir, noble fir).	1. Exposes seedlings to injury from temperature extremes.
2. Eliminates danger of wind damage or disease infection to residual trees in the cutover area.	2. Increases risk of windthrow or heat damage to trees bordering the cutover area.
3. Improves forage for many game animals (e.g., deer, elk) and provides habitat for many animals not present before logging.	3. May increase stream temperature, debris jams, and sedimentation (effect on fish population) and reduce habitat of some animals (e.g., woodpeckers, tree squirrels).
4. Increases water yield during low-flow periods.	4. Elevates water table in swampy areas.
5. Permits harvesting on slopes too steep for ground equipment.	5. May reduce protection against erosion and landslides.
6. Minimizes road construction and increases logging efficiency.	6. Is conspicuous and unattractive during the harvest stage.
7. Facilitates administration in that it limits tree mar-	7. Magnifies need for proper harvest boundary layout.

NOTE 13-1   (CONTINUED)

Advantages	Disadvantages
keting to definition of boundaries.	
8. Facilitates slash disposal and site preparation.	8. Increases quantity of debris (and fire hazard) to eliminate at one time.
9. Usually maximizes the immediate financial return.	9. Eliminates merchantable timber from the small landowners' cutover area for many years.
10. Permits the use of genetically improved tree planting stock.	10. Creates good growing conditions for many unwanted brush species, which compete with the young seedlings of commercial species.

Source: Archie and Baumgartner (undated).

13-4.3 Log Transport Systems and Soil Disturbance

The principal log transport systems include logging by tractor, high-lead cable, skyline cable, balloon cable, and helicopter as shown in Figure 13-14. In general, the systems that cause the least soil disturbance are the most expensive.

Tractor Logging. Tractor logging is the most popular system of moving logs to the log yard. Forests on slopes of less than about 30% are usually logged by tractors; on slopes of more than 30% and on very fragile soils, the skyline, balloon, and helicopter systems of transport are less injurious to the environment.

Tractor logging is substantially less expensive than other log transport systems. Soil disturbance, however, is greater than for any other log transport system because the tractors and logs make erodible skid trails as they are dragged across the forest floor.

High-Lead Cable. The high-lead system of logging uses a mobile spar and yarder with mounted engine and winches to drag logs toward a loading yard. Only the front ends of the logs are lifted to

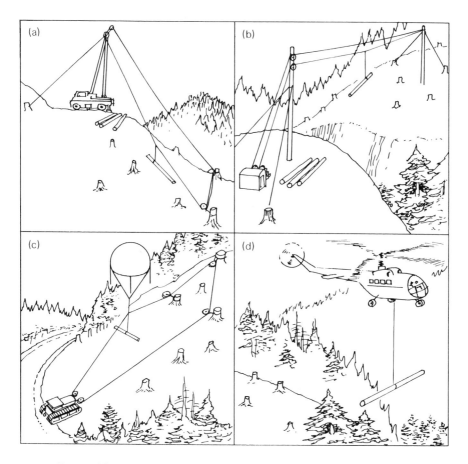

Figure 13-14 The principal log transport systems used to remove logs from a forest being harvested are (a) high-lead cable, (b) skyline cable, (c) balloon cable, (d) helicopter, and (e) tractor logging (not shown).

clear obstacles or to reduce soil disturbance. The logs make skid trails as they are moved to the yarding area. Each skid trail could be the beginning of a gully.

Skyline Cable. As early as 1915, skyline cable logging was tried as a method adaptable to remote areas, steep slopes, and unstable soils where road building creates excessive erosion from landslides and exposed cuts and fills. When operated skillfully, skyline cable logging does not produce skid trails because the entire log is lifted in transport. Erosion is therefore minimal.

Balloon Cable. This system uses a balloon to lift and transport logs. It is well adapted to steep slopes (up to 90%) and shallow or fragile soils, where only helicopter logging or skyline logging may compete. The system is also adapted to selective logging where the minimum harvest is about 70 m^3/ha.

Balloon logging causes soil disturbance only at the yarding areas, from which trucks haul the logs to the mill. Yarding areas can be as far as 900 m apart, but they must be downhill from the logged areas and therefore may be a hazard to streams. Balloon logging is more expensive than all other logging systems except helicopter logging.

Helicopter Logging. Logging by large helicopter so minimizes erosion that it is the apparent answer to the fondest dreams of concerned environmentalists. Logging by helicopter requires fewer access roads (and therefore results in minimized sediment pollution of streams) and is the most versatile system of moving logs from where they are cut to a yarding area for truck loading and hauling, but it costs more per cubic meter of lumber. A weakness in the helicopter system is the need to enter the forest on the ground to replant, thin trees, and take out the commercial thinning (poles) and for fire control.

Typical soil disturbance caused by each of the log transport systems, except helicopter, in the northwestern United States is presented in Table 13-9. Tractor logging causes more bare soil and more soil compaction than any other log transport system. Logging by

Table 13-9   Effects of log transport systems on soil disturbance

Log transport system	Soil disturbance[a]	
	Logged watershed with bare soil (%)	Logged watershed with compacted soil (%)
Tractor	35.1	26.4
High-lead	14.8	9.1
Skyline cable	12.1	3.4
Balloon cable	6.0	1.7

[a]Compacted soil averaged about 40 to 50% higher in bulk density than uncompacted soil. Actual values of the 0–5 cm depth of the latter were between 0.6 and 0.7 g/cm^3.

SOURCE: Rice, Rothacher, and Megahan, 1972.

balloon causes the least soil disturbance. Balloon logging causes 83% less bare soil and 94% less compacted soil than tractor logging. Soil disturbance by the helicopter system would be about the same as that for balloon logging.

13-4.4 Grazing

About half of all forestlands are grazed by domestic livestock. The percentage varies from 41% in the northeastern to 83% in the western United States. Forest range as a percentage of all land is depicted by states and regions in Figure 13-15.

The results of livestock grazing farm woodlands are nearly always detrimental to tree reproduction and growth. Animals trample and compact the soil (especially fine-textured soil), injure shallow roots, and browse on tree seedlings and sprouts.

Grazing of nonfarm forestlands is usually not as destructive as grazing of farm woodlands because of fewer cattle per unit area of forest, more coarse-textured and stony soils, less soil compaction by trampling, and more conifers that are not browsed as much as hardwoods. In addition, the pinelands of the southern and western states include many open forests with areas of forage grasses. The

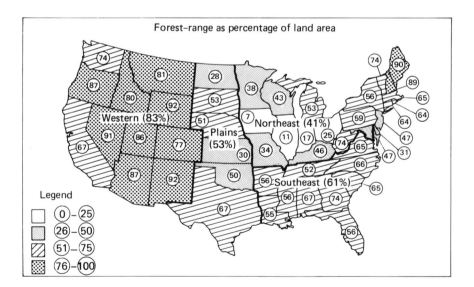

Figure 13-15 Forestland grazed by domestic livestock as a percentage of the total land area by states and regions in the United States. (Source: U.S. Department of Agriculture, 1974.)

grasses, forbs, and hardwood seedlings and sprouts make fair to good forage during the months of April through July. Supplemental forage can be supplied by establishing improved pasture on all fire lanes and forest roads. When livestock graze these fire lanes, forest roads, and the forestlands in general, they reduce the fire hazard by removing vegetation that is flammable when dry.

13-4.5 Fertilization

The use of chemical fertilizers on forests has been increasing along with the value of forest products. The present fertilizer used on forest is mostly nitrogen; its use is centered on the Douglas-fir region of the Pacific Northwest and in the southern pine region. In addition, young stands of commercial redwood in northern California and the western hemlock-sitka spruce forest type along the coasts of Alaska, Washington, and Oregon are judged to have a potential for responding economically to the application of fertilizer.

Forest fertilization with nitrogen in the Pacific Northwest started in 1965, reached a level of 48,165 ha in 1970, and averaged about 100,000 ha per year from 1975 to 1980. Douglas-fir has responded to nitrogen fertilization with about 30% faster growth during a five- to seven-year period; trees as old as 300 years have shown growth acceleration.

Southern pines on well-drained soils respond well to fertilization. Nitrogen alone is expected to enhance their growth by about 5% a year. A second area of present and predicted future response is in the flatwoods coastal plains where both nitrogen and phosphorus give increased growth of pines. Forest fertilization in the southern states started on a commercial basis in 1963 and reached an estimated 44,500 ha in 1971.

Helicopters are preferred for use in fertilizing forests. They are environmentally safer than fixed-wing aircraft because they can fly slower, spread fertilizer more accurately on the land intended, and avoid streams and lakes.

Guidelines for environmentally safe application of fertilizers to forests include the following (Environmental Protection Agency, 1973):

1. Fertilize only when a soil test indicates that benefits are expected to be economically worthwhile.
2. Fertilize at rates which do not exceed the adsorption capacity of the soil and the uptake capability of timber stands.

3. Frequent fertilization at low rates is environmentally safer than infrequent application at high rates.
4. Do not fertilize water courses; leave buffer strips between streams and fertilized areas.
5. Apply fertilizers when wind drift is minimal.
6. Avoid fertilization just prior to periods of anticipated heavy rainfall.
7. Coarse-pelleted fertilizers are environmentally safer than fine pellets or dusts; liquid fertilizers have the greatest fugitive loss potential and the greatest water-pollution hazard.

SUMMARY

Pasture, range, and forest should be managed to obtain continuous high productivity combined with minimum soil erosion and polluting sediment. Pastures usually are in humid regions or are irrigated, are seeded to improved grass plus legume cultivars, and are limed (if acid) and fertilized. Ranges normally are in semiarid and arid regions or are a secondary use of land such as open forest in humid or semiarid regions. Native species are used for grazing, although some exotic species have been used to reseed the range. Forests, by definition, must have 10% of the area covered by trees, and a tree is a woody plant at least 4.5 m high.

There are many erosion-resisting pasture grasses, pasture legumes, and range grasses, and each one has its own area of adaptation. Nitrogen fertilizer makes grasses more productive but may cause them to crowd out legumes. Pastures should be renovated when their productivity declines to 50% to 75% of its potential. Rotational and deferred grazing are good management techniques to improve pasture and range productivity.

Forest cover usually keeps erosion to very low levels except when roads are built and trees are logged. Trees are harvested by the selection, shelterwood, seed-tree, or clearcutting methods. Log removal is by tractor, high-lead cable, skyline cable, balloon cable, or helicopter. About half of all forest land is grazed by livestock; the percentage is highest in the south and west where there are open areas with grass vegetation in the forest. Forest fertilization is increasing now along with the value of forest products.

QUESTIONS

1. Define: pastureland, rangeland, forestland. Compare and contrast wind and water erosion potentials on pasturelands, rangelands, and forestlands.

2. Name a representative productive and erosion-resisting pasture grass and explain why it is so classified.
3. What is meant by "fertility management" of a pasture?
4. Why is grazing management the key to successful range management?
5. Describe a timber harvesting method and a log transport system that minimize soil erosion and sediment yield. Why aren't these two methods used universally?

REFERENCES

ANDERSON, D. A., and W. A. SMITH, 1970. *Forest and Forestry.* The Interstate Printers and Publishers, Danville, Illinois, 357 p.

ARCHIE, STEVE, and D. M. BAUMGARTNER (undated). *Clearcutting in the Douglas-Fir Region of the Pacific Northwest.* Washington Woodland Council, 17 p.

DUFFY, PAUL, 1977. *Fertilization to Accelerate Loblolly Pine Foliage Growth for Erosion Control.* USDA—Forest Service Research Note SO-230.

DYRNESS, C. T., 1972. *Soil Surface Conditions Following Balloon Logging.* USDA—Forest Service Research Note PNW-182, 7 p.

ENVIRONMENTAL PROTECTION AGENCY, 1973. *Process, Procedures, and Methods to Control Pollution from Silvicultural Activities.* EPA 430/9-73-010, 91 p.

FOOD AND AGRICULTURE ORGANIZATION, 1976. *Conservation in Arid and Semiarid Zones.* FAO Conservation Guide 3, Rome, Italy, 125 p.

FOOD AND AGRICULTURE ORGANIZATION, 1978. *Special Readings in Conservation.* FAO Conservation Guide 4, Rome, Italy, 101 p.

GROMAN, W. A., 1972. *Forest Fertilization: A State-of-the-Art Review and Description of Environmental Effects.* U.S. Environmental Protection Agency, EPA-R2-72-016, 57 p.

HART, R. H., 1974. Crop selection and management. In *Factors Involved in Land Application of Agricultural and Municipal Wastes,* Agr. Res. Service, USDA, Beltsville, Maryland, p. 178-200.

HYDE, R. M., and C. E. OWENSBY, 1970. *Burning Bluestem Range.* L-277, Kansas State University.

LULL, H. W., and K. G. REINHART, 1972. *Forests and Floods in the Eastern United States,* USDA—Forest Service Research Paper NE-266, p. 72-73.

McCLURKIN, D. C. 1970. Site rehabilitation under planted red cedar and pine. In *Tree Growth and Forest Soils.* Proceedings, Third North American Forest Soils Conference, North Carolina State University, p. 339-345.

McNUIT, R. B., AND OTHERS, 1972. *Soil Survey of Chilton County, Alabama.* USDA—Soil Conservation Service and USDA—Forest Service, in cooperation with the Alabama Agr. Expt. Sta. and Alabama Dept. of Agriculture and Industries, 82 p. and 47 soil maps.

McVICKAR, M. H., 1974. *Approved Practices in Pasture Management.* Interstate Printers and Publishers, 400 p.

PATRIC, J. H., 1973. *Deforestation Effects on Soil Moisture, Streamflow, and Water Balance in the Central Appalachians.* USDA—Forest Service Research Paper NE-259. Upper Darby, Pennsylvania.

RICE, R. M., J. S. ROTHACHER, and W. F. MEGAHAN, 1972. *Erosional Consequences of Timber Harvest: An Appraisal.* Proceedings of a Symposium on Watershed in Transition held at Ft. Collins, Colorado, June 19-22, 1972, p. 321-329.

SANDER, I. L., 1977. *Oaks in the North Central States.* General Tech. Report NC-37, USDA—Forest Service, 35 p.

SWANSTON, D. N., 1974. *Slope Stability Problems Associated with Timber Harvest in Mountainous Regions of the Western United States.* General Technical Report PNW 21, USDA—Forest Service.

TENNESSEE VALLEY AUTHORITY, 1962. *Reforestation and Erosion Control Influences Upon the Hydrology of the Pine Tree Branch Watershed, 1941 to 1961.* Div. of Water Control Planning. Unnumbered.

URSIC, S. J., and F. E. DENDY, 1963. *Sediment Yields From Small Watersheds Under Various Land Uses and Forest Covers.* Misc. Pub. 970, USDA.

U.S. DEPARTMENT OF AGRICULTURE, 1974. *Land Use Planning Through the United States Department of Agriculture,* 54 p.

U.S. DEPARTMENT OF AGRICULTURE, 1976. *Agricultural Statistics.*

USDA—ARS, 1976. *Improved Vegetation and Management Practices for Range.* USDA—Agr. Research Service, ARS—NRP No. 20110, USDA Program, 22-677, 45 p.

USDA—FOREST SERVICE, 1972. *The Nation's Range Resources: A Forest-Range Environmental Study.* Forest Resources Report No. 19.

USDA—FOREST SERVICE, 1973. *The Outlook for Timber in the United States.* FRR-20, USDA, 367 p.

WEBER, F. R., 1977 *Reforestation in Arid Lands.* Action/Peace Corps, Washington, D.C., and VITA (Volunteers in Technical Assistance), Mt. Rainier, Maryland, 248 p.

14

Water

Conservation

Average annual precipitation in the United States ranges from less than 125 mm in parts of the desert southwest to over 2500 mm west of the Olympic Mountains in western Washington State on the mainland, and to 16,680 mm at one location in Hawaii. The range over the world is from almost zero in the deserts of Africa and central Asia to the high figure for Hawaii. Precipitation fluctuates widely both above and below average at all locations.

People have learned to exist in all but the most extreme ecological conditions and have devised methods of coping with minor changes in the environment; serious problems arise only when a major change occurs, such as a drastic reduction in rainfall over several years. Great suffering occurs and many may die when the traditional methods of living fail to support them during a catastrophe.

Dry weather is most significant when it occurs at an unexpected time. Dry winters in the central United States or dry seasons in areas with a monsoon type of rainfall pattern present no serious problems. But problems develop quickly if the dry conditions extend into what should be a rainy season.

Crop damage from dry weather during the growing season can be reduced by irrigation or by conserving as much water in the soil as possible beforehand. Irrigation is discussed in Chapter 16; water conservation is the subject of this chapter.

14-1 WHAT IS DROUGHT?

The terms *dryland* and *drought* are associated in the minds of many people, but they are not synonymous. A dryland area is one in which the major factor limiting plant growth is shortage of water. A specific average annual rainfall cannot serve to distinguish between drylands and humid areas because other factors such as rainfall distribution and reliability, humidity, temperature, rate of evaporation, and soil characteristics all determine whether a given amount of rainfall will be sufficient for or will limit plant growth. Droughts of varying severity and duration are common in drylands, but they also occur in more humid areas.

14–1.1 Definition of Drought

Many attempts have been made to define drought in terms of precipitation, but rainfall alone is not a good criterion. Temperature and wind also affect plant needs for water. The evapotranspiration concept of Penman (1948) and Thornthwaite (1948) provides a sound basis for describing sufficiency or deficiency of rainfall in an area, but these methods describe normal or average conditions, not the weather at a specific time.

Climatic conditions alone cannot define drought either. Soil properties and crop and soil management practices also influence plant survival. Crops may survive a relatively long dry period without serious damage if the soil initially contains an abundance of stored water within the root zone.

For purposes of this discussion, drought will be defined as a period in which lack of water reduces growth and final yield of the staple crops of a region. The staple crops of the central Great Plains in the United States are grain sorghum and winter wheat. Those of the adjacent Corn Belt are corn and soybeans with wheat grown on a much smaller area. Drought, in terms of wheat production, is relatively common in the Great Plains, but is rare in the Corn Belt. However, drought occurs more frequently in the Corn Belt if it is assessed in terms of corn growth.

There are two types of drought—atmospheric drought, caused by high temperature, high wind velocity, or low humidity, and soil drought, caused by low soil moisture, the result of low precipitation, slow soil permeability, or low soil storage capacity. Either type of drought causes plant stress. The severity and duration of the stress determine the amount of plant damage that results. A plant can develop and grow normally on stored soil water through a short rainless period. Plant stress develops as the dry period continues—first on soils with limited stored water, but eventually on all soils. Short periods of stress damage the plants and reduce their potential for growth but do not kill them. Extended stress increases the damage and eventually kills the plants.

14-1.2 Effect of Drought on Plants, Animals, and People

A plant's ability to survive dry conditions depends on the severity of the drought and on the plant's characteristics. Some plants are in a race with drought. The annuals that have very short growing periods (desert ephemerals) *escape* drought by germinating, growing, and producing flowers and seeds in a very brief life span. These plants usually can mature if there is enough moisture to germinate the seed. Some plants *evade* drought by large absorbing systems (roots) or by restricting water loss by low transpiration rates or by adjusting to the dry conditions by reducing leaf area or closing stomata. A third group *endures* drought by means of massive water-storage organs (cacti) or by shedding leaves and becoming dormant (mesquite).

Crops for an intensive type of agriculture must come from the drought-evading group. The drought escapers have too limited production; the drought endurers grow too slowly. Actually, a cultivated crop's ability to survive drought is less important than its ability to produce the greatest possible amount of grain or forage in spite of dry conditions. In this respect, the cereal grains are pre-eminent despite their relatively rapid collapse under severe drought stress (Barnes, 1938).

Animals are affected by drought in two major ways. They run short of food and they run short of water. Animals can migrate to areas where dry conditions are less severe, but often drought occurs over such wide areas that migration to better pasturage and more water is impossible. Without adequate food, and especially without water, animal condition deteriorates rapidly and death occurs.

Humans also suffer from drought. They must eat and drink. When plants and animals die, there is no food for humans. In addition, people suffer as soon as or sooner than animals when water supply fails. Humans could migrate, but distance to less droughty areas often is excessive and attachment to animals and home often makes flight difficult to contemplate.

The inhabitants of most large, developed countries can survive a drought. Crops may fail, livestock may die, farmers will be financially hurt, but people will not starve or die of thirst because food and finances from outside the drought area will be made available. In many developing countries with dense populations and poor transport systems, drought can cause starvation because there is no quick way for people to seek outside help or for food to be taken to them. Massive famines have occurred regularly in the developing world, as for example in the Sahel region of western and central Africa in the early 1970s.

14-2 COMBATING DROUGHT

Combating drought is one of the primary objectives of successful dryland farming and ranching and may be important in more humid areas. It is a many-faceted war. Every effort must be made to conserve rainfall, to store it in the soil, and to use it wisely.

Crops need to be adapted to the area. Many experiment stations evaluate common crop hybrid and variety performance annually. Best-adapted varieties commonly outyield poorer ones by 50% to 75% or more (Walters, 1978). Farming and ranching success is not assured even by efficient water use. Several drought years often succeed one another in dryland areas and reduce current production and income below that necessary to meet even minimum living requirements and farm expenses. Accordingly, dryland farmers must accumulate reserves during favorable years.

Farmers with livestock face additional difficult problems. Water supplies in some areas are adequate in favorable years but deficient in dry periods. In other areas, water is a perennial problem. Extra effort to obtain and store water is needed. Deeper wells may solve the problem, or ponds and dugouts to store runoff water and snow melt may help. Reserve feed is more difficult and often more expensive to accumulate and store, especially in hotter climatic areas. Planting a crop on a fallowed field each year specifically for animal forage has much to commend it in the higher latitudes of temperate regions where summer fallow is common. This is especially true if cereal grains are used that can be harvested as grain if not needed for forage.

Drought continued for four to seven consecutive years in parts of the Great Plains and Canadian Prairies during the 1930s and 1950s. This suggests that the best livestock venture for a dryland farm is one that can be cut back quickly when a drought occurs and can be built up speedily when more normal weather returns.

14-3 WHAT HAPPENS TO RAINFALL?

Estimates of the water used (transpired) by a wheat crop at Akron, Colorado, range from about 17% of the 419 mm of annual precipitation based on Briggs and Shantz (1914) data to about 40% based on evapotranspiration studies (Note 14-1). What happens to the rest of the rainfall? Why isn't more used by the crop? Answers to these questions will suggest ways to improve conservation and wise use of the rain that falls on the soil both in drylands and in humid areas.

NOTE 14-1 WATER TRANSPIRED BY WHEAT

The water requirement (transpiration ratio) of winter wheat is 481 kg water/kg dry matter (Briggs and Shantz, 1914). The average annual precipitation at Akron, Colorado is 419 mm and the average yield of continuous wheat is 497 kg/ha (Greb and others, 1974). Assuming that 1119 kg of straw was produced (2.23 kg of straw for each kg of grain) and that the grain was 88% and the straw 90% dry matter, the total dry matter production is 1445 kg/ha.

Calculated water requirement for the wheat crop then is 695,045 kg/ha (1445 × 481) or the equivalent of 70 mm of rainfall. This means that nearly 350 mm, or over 83%, of the average annual precipitation at Akron is not "used" by the crop.

The plants in these early studies were grown without water stress, so they probably used less water to produce each gram of dry matter than plants growing in the field under normal conditions. It seems likely that the higher values calculated from evapotranspiration results from field trials are more accurate estimates of transpiration by wheat.

Precipitation (P) is lost to crop plant use because it is intercepted (I), runs off (R), evaporates (E), is transpired by weeds or volunteer plants (T), or percolates below root depth (D). The amount of water available for use by the crop or for storage in the soil (A) may be expressed as

$$A = P - (I \pm R + E + T + D)$$

14-3.1 Interception

Vegetation intercepts and holds some rain during each storm. This water evaporates into the air without ever touching the ground, but it has little effect on water availability for crop use because the energy used to evaporate free water from the surface of plants is not available to evaporate water from the plant or from the soil.

14-3.2 Runoff

Some of the rain that penetrates the vegetative canopy runs off the land instead of soaking into the soil. Runoff from individual sites ranges from zero on highly permeable, level, and vegetated soils to over 75% of the rain on impermeable, steeply sloping, poorly vegetated sites. Runoff from watersheds (including both surface runoff and subsurface flow) in the continental United States ranges from more than 50% in some humid areas (57% in the Middle Branch of the Westfield River watershed in Massachusetts) to less than 5% in the drylands (2.4% for the Smoky Hill River watershed in Kansas). Runoff is affected by soil properties, rainfall intensity, soil configuration, and vegetative cover.

Coarse-textured and well-aggregated soils have high infiltration rates; fine-textured, poorly aggregated soils have low infiltration rates. Runoff rates are therefore higher from fine-textured, poorly aggregated soils than from coarse-textured or well-aggregated soils. Infiltration rates are usually higher at the beginning of a storm, when the soil is dry, but they drop off quickly as the soils become wet.

Increasing slope gradient increases the amount and velocity of runoff; surface soil depressions hold water and permit local water, and even runoff from other areas, to be absorbed. Vegetation, both living plants and dead crop residues, reduces the number of raindrops that hit the soil directly. This reduces soil compaction and helps keep the infiltration rate high.

14-3.3 Evaporation

A saturated soil loses water by evaporation as fast as a free water surface. Soil water evaporates whenever the relative humidity is less than 100%. Losses by evaporation often exceed 50% of the annual rainfall in dryland areas. Hot areas have greater evaporation losses than cold areas. The world's drylands with their low relative humidities and high wind velocities lose a larger proportion of rainfall by evaporation than do humid regions. Dark-colored soils absorb more heat than light soils, so they are hotter and lose more water by evaporation. When the surface soil is dry, evaporation is reduced to the rate that water vapor moves upward through the dry layer. South-facing slopes in the northern hemisphere are warmer and have higher evaporation rates than north-facing slopes. Living and dead vegetation reduces evaporation because it acts as an insulator to heat change and a barrier to wind.

14-3.4 Transpiration

Transpiration by a crop cannot be measured or predicted accurately, but estimates range from about 70 mm to produce a crop of dryland wheat to 400 mm for the growth of corn in a humid region. Transpiration by crop plants is not really a "loss" of water, because it is being used to grow the crop. Transpiration losses from weeds and volunteer grains are unnecessary, however. Whether they occur from soil being fallowed for water storage, from land being prepared for immediate seeding, or from fields currently in crop, they are more completely under the control of the farmer than almost any other type of moisture loss.

14–3.5 Deep Percolation

Water that percolates deeper into soils than roots penetrate is lost to plants. Plant roots can penetrate as deep as 9 m (taprooted crops such as alfalfa) into permeable, moist but not wet soils. Usual root penetration, though, is no more than 125 to 150 cm in the case of annual spring-seeded cereals, 150 to 180 cm for winter cereals, and 250 cm or so for some fibrous-rooted perennial grasses.

The limited rainfall in dryland areas seldom penetrates below root depth in medium- and fine-textured soil, even when the land is summer fallowed; in humid regions, considerable water is lost for plant growth by deep percolation.

14–3.6 Storage

Rainfall not lost by one of the foregoing processes is used by crops or is stored in the soil. Stored water is the key to survival in dryland areas. It is the cushion that smooths the effect on plants of the excesses and deficiencies of rainfall. Rains rarely fall regularly enough to constantly provide plants with the water they need; dry periods of a week or more between rains occur in most areas. The more arid the region, the longer these dry periods are likely to be and the longer plants have to depend on stored water to supply their needs. Water-conservation methods, water-storage techniques, and efficient use of stored water all help increase or maintain the supply of stored water in the soil.

Three of the five avenues of moisture loss—runoff, evaporation, and transpiration by weeds—cause losses that can be significantly reduced in dry areas. Water loss by deep percolation is important on specific sites in humid areas and on very coarse-textured soils in dryland regions. Water conservation must include management methods that (1) decrease runoff, (2) reduce evaporation, (3) reduce deep percolation, and (4) prevent losses from storage.

14–4 DECREASING RUNOFF LOSSES

Special conservation practices reduce runoff losses but some runoff will always occur except on level permeable soils. Contour cultivation, level terraces, and other water-spreading devices help hold rain water on the soil and give it time to infiltrate. Tillage that retains crop residue on the surface rather than burying it, application of vegetative and other mulches, and the use of soil-conserving cropping systems increase infiltration and reduce runoff by maintaining or increasing soil permeability.

Runoff is a water loss to upland farmers, especially those in dryland areas, but to farmers downstream who depend on a river impoundment for irrigation water, that same runoff is a source of water. Where farmers reduce runoff by applying conservation practices, they reduce inflow into storage reservoirs. One farmer's gain may be another farmer's loss. Reduced runoff from cultivated watersheds is already posing problems in some irrigated areas east of the Rocky Mountains in the United States.

14-4.1 Contour Cultivation

Contour cultivation, as shown in Figure 14-1, is defined and described in Chapter 9. It produces miniature furrows and ridges across the slope that trap rainwater and give it more time to infiltrate. Water storage is largest when furrows are exactly on the contour because water moves across the slope when there is even a slight gradient. More water is conserved by contouring on gentle than on steep slopes, because the effective capacity of channels decreases as the slopes become progressively steeper. Large ridges, like those produced by a lister, trap more water than the small ridges thrown up by a disk, chisel implement, or cultivator.

Figure 14-1 Contour cultivation on broad gentle slopes in the central Great Plains in a crop system of alternate wheat and fallow. (Courtesy USDA—Soil Conservation Service.)

Furrows left by tillage and planting implements are seldom exactly on the contour over an entire field. A *damming* or *basin lister* was developed in the United States in the early years of the conservation movement to improve water distribution over fields by preventing surplus water movement from flowing along lister furrows. These implements reduced lateral water movement, but the dams made tractor travel so rough and uncomfortable that few mechanized farmers accepted the practice. A similar system called *tie-ridging* has been successful in countries where hand tillage is used.

Many studies show that contouring reduces runoff. A study at Ottawa, Canada, showed that loss was reduced from 38 to 16 mm by contour cultivation of a corn field on Rideau clay soil. Runoff was reduced from 8.7% to 3.6% of the rain falling on the growing crop (Ripley and others, 1961). A classic study on a 0.5% slope at Spur, Texas, showed that farming cotton up and down the slope permitted 70 mm of runoff compared to 50 mm from contour-cultivated land. Water loss was reduced from 13.7 to 9.7% of the annual rainfall (Fisher and Burnett, 1953).

Not all the "saved" runoff that enters the soil is stored there, but some extra water usually is available for crop use, and crop yields invariably are higher on the contoured plots. At Spur, Texas, lint cotton yields were 25% higher on the contoured plots (168 kg to 134 kg/ha).

14-4.2 Terracing

Graded terraces do not increase soil water storage. Terraces that are designed to conserve runoff must hold the water on the soil surface until it soaks in. Therefore, the channel must be level to be effective. There are two major types of level terraces: level ridge-type terraces and conservation-bench terraces.

Level Ridge-Type Terraces. These are combination channel and ridge structures similar in appearance to the broad-based terraces described in Chapter 10 except that the channels are level. Consequently, runoff water ponds in the channels as shown in Figure 14-2. They are used for both water-erosion control and water conservation. The design criteria for these terraces are different from those of the graded terraces described in Chapter 10. Level terraces should be constructed only on deep soils that have large water-storage capacity. Soils on which they are placed must be permeable so water will not pond in the channel area long enough to damage

Figure 14-2 A level-terraced field with water ponded in the terrace channels after a heavy rain. (Courtesy USDA—Soil Conservation Service.)

crops. Land slope needs to be gentle so that trapped runoff can be spread over the greatest possible area, and so that front and back terrace slopes can be crossed easily with tillage implements. These terraces are generally used in fields with slopes less than 5%.

The first experiments to study the effect of level terraces on water conservation in the United States were started at Spur, Texas, and at Goodwell, Oklahoma, in 1926. Some of the terraces had partly closed ends, so that water could not escape. The end closure and periodic blocks along the terrace channel were not as high as the terrace ridge. This design allowed excessive rain to run off, but held all the water from less intense storms. These experimental terraces reduced runoff losses and improved water-conservation efficiency. At Spur, Texas, terraces supported by contour cultivation increased lint cotton yield 40 kg/ha over contouring alone.

Level terrace spacing can be determined by using the vertical and horizontal interval equations for regular terraces (Ch. 10) by using a value of 0.24 for X in the vertical-interval equation in all regions. The soil-loss prediction equation (Ch. 6) can also be used to calculate a slope length that will keep erosion below the tolerable limit. Under no circumstances should the horizontal spacing exceed 122 meters. Level terraces usually are designed to cope with the runoff from ten-year-frequency 24-hour storms, but channel capacity is generally somewhat larger than for graded terraces on comparable slopes.

Terrace length may be up to 1000 meters. It can be even longer if the terrace channel is blocked at intervals along its length. Level terrace channels may be blocked and may have closed or partially closed ends to prevent water from moving laterally. These blocks enhance water storage and guard against excessive damage if the structures overtop in intense storms, but the blocks should be used only on permeable soils so standing water will not damage crops.

Outlets should be provided where level terraces have open or only partly closed ends. The outlets may be natural waterways, grassed areas, shaped and vegetated waterways, or underground outlets. Excess runoff water must be conducted to a safe discharge point. Waterways must be ready to carry runoff before terrace construction is started.

Three general designs of level ridge-type terraces are shown in Figure 14–3: the normal ridge-and-channel terraces, steep-backslope terraces, and flat-channel terraces. Normal ridge-and-channel terraces can be used anywhere that level terraces can. Steep-backslope terraces can be used only on deep loess or other permeable soils and must be provided with outlets. They can be used on slopes up to

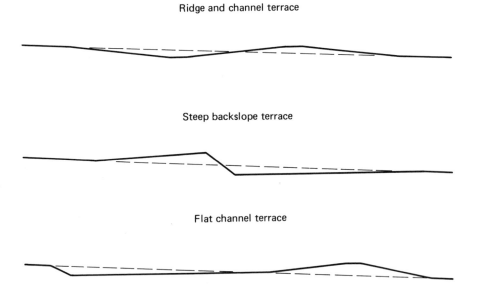

Ridge and channel terrace

Steep backslope terrace

Flat channel terrace

Figure 14–3 Types of level ridge-type terraces.

20%, but the structures on steep slopes must be so massive and close together that construction costs are very high. Flat-channel terraces can be used where regular level terraces are suited, with two additional requirements: all soil exposed in the cut area must be permeable, and the slope must be between 0.5% and 4%. Flat-channel terraces are best adapted to fields with uniform slopes. The greatest permissible variation in slope along each terrace site is one-fifth of the average slope for that particular terrace. The less the slope variation, the easier it is to design and build the terrace system. The width of the flat channel is 29 m on a 0.5% slope with a ridge height of 0.5 m; narrower channels are used on steeper slopes.

Conservation-Bench (Zingg) Terraces. Zingg and Hauser (1959) reported the development of a series of level benches for catching runoff water. These benches were separated from each other by unleveled, runoff-contributing areas, as shown in Figure 14–4. The first set of structures was built at the U.S. Agricultural Research Station at Bushland, Texas. The level benched areas occupied 5.25 ha in a 16-ha field. The benches varied in length from 335 to 425 m and in width from 24 to 44 m. Maximum cut-and-fill depth employed while leveling the land was about 30 cm. The proportion of contributing area to leveled area in the experimental setup was 2:1. The original land slope ranged from 1% to 1.8%. Each bench was equipped with a lip on the downhill side to prevent trapped water from flowing off the front of the benched area. Similar level bench studies were established at Akron, Colorado; Hays, Kansas; Newell, South Dakota; and Spur, Texas. Contributing area to benched area in these studies ranged from 1:1 to 3:1. Contributing areas are used for production of crops in the normal cropping systems of the area, invariably including summer fallow. The benched areas have been seeded each year to an adapted crop, often grain sorghum, that can tolerate standing water for short periods.

The results with Zingg terraces have not been totally favorable. Water ponding in more humid regions and in wetter-than-normal years in drier areas has caused occasional crop damage. Corn yields on the excavated sections of the benches were lower than on the built-up areas, but this can be remedied over time by good manage-

Figure 14-4 Diagram of a conservation-bench (Zingg) terrace.

ment including fertilizer and manure applications and crop-residue incorporation. Under conditions favorable for runoff production, water losses have been markedly reduced and yields on leveled areas have been nearly doubled (Black, 1968; Cox, 1968; Hauser, 1968; Mickelson, 1968).

Conservation-bench terraces are spreading from experiment stations to production farms. One farmer in Kansas started to replace regular level terraces with conservation benches in 1969. He claims that no runoff water has left the benched area since then. Crop yields on the benches are as high each year as yields on untreated land that is fallowed every second year. The lips on the downhill side of the benches have outlets so that excessive collected water can be released to reduce crop damage.

14-4.3 Water Spreading

Methods of channeling and concentrating runoff and trapping it in prepared sites is an ancient art practiced by stone-age civilizations in the arid sections of the Negev and Sinai Deserts. These early catchment structures and channels, often covered with flat stone flakes, diverted runoff from winter rainstorms down hillsides and onto prepared, permeable sites in the valleys. The valley sites were crisscrossed with stone fences that trapped soil and water so that each unit of soil was moistened to capacity to considerable depths. The moistened sites were then used to produce the food needed by the relatively large population. Crop production would have been impossible without these structures.

Runoff concentration on a small scale was accomplished by constructing individual microwatersheds, each of which delivered runoff toward its center where a single fruit tree or a small patch of vegetables or vine crops was located. The contributing land, which was as much as twenty to twenty-five times the area of the cultivated site, was usually kept free of vegetation and was compacted so it would shed as much water as possible. This technique accumulated water to produce crops in areas too dry for normal crop production methods to be effective (Medina, 1976). Modern Israeli farmers have rediscovered this technique and are using it to expand crop production in the part of Israel that receives less than 200 mm of rainfall annually.

The "syrup pan" system of water spreading was developed in the southern Great Plains of the United States. For example, the runoff from a 485-ha, sloping, native grassland area at Spur, Texas, was diverted back and forth across a 50-ha cultivated field, as shown in

Figure 14–5. The water flow was controlled by a series of thirteen diversions 75 to 100 cm high with vertical intervals of about 45 cm. This system added an average of 100 mm of water to the cultivated field. This is equivalent to increasing the rainfall on the field by 20%. Similar systems have been developed on other research stations, but they seem not to have spread to private farms to any extent.

Lagoon-leveling is another special water-spreading practice that has increased the efficiency of runoff use. A lagoon (pot-hole, slough, or swale) is a small depression that collects runoff water from the surrounding land and remains wet or ponded for extended periods. Lagoons in pastures serve as temporary water supplies, but in cultivated fields the wet spots are a nuisance and rarely produce a good crop.

The water in a lagoon can be spread over a wider area by moving soil from the land above normal water level to the center of the depression. Water buildup is then shallower and may be absorbed more quickly over a broader area, thus improving both convenience and crop production.

Several lagoons were leveled at Akron, Colorado. One 0.8-ha lagoon was leveled to a 1.6-ha area by backsloping the lagoon walls to a 5% slope and using the excavated material to fill the center of the depressed area. Maximum cuts were about 60 cm; maximum fills were 25 cm. Cost of leveling was considerably less than the price of productive land. Annual forage yields on the leveled area are not greatly superior to those on unleveled upland sites, but the lagoon can now be cultivated successfully and is no longer a hindrance to field operations (Mickelson and Greb, 1970).

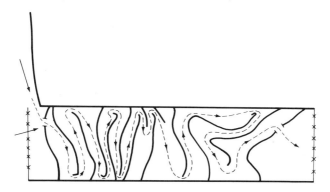

Figure 14–5 Syrup-pan water-spreading system at Spur, Texas. The water entering the system from the left is passed from side to side of the spreading area by diversions until it soaks in or exits on the right. (Courtesy Texas Agricultural Experiment Station.)

Polyethylene film and similar impermeable materials have been used to waterproof soils and cause 100% runoff from some areas. The extra water makes crop production possible every year on half the land instead of alternating fallow and crop every other year on all the land. The cost of the film and its short life in windy climates, however, make the practice uneconomical.

Mehdizadeh and others, (1978) describe a method of spraying microwatersheds in Iran with an impermeable asphalt formulation and using the runoff water produced to supplement rainfall in the production of trees. The contributing area was 1.5 times as large as the cultivated area. Over a five-year period, the soil on the collecting area below the asphalt microwatersheds received an extra 487 mm of runoff water, or 35% of the total 1409 mm of rainfall. These runoff contributions appeared to be an attractive alternative to providing irrigation water for tree growth under the conditions of this study.

Recharging underground aquifers by spreading runoff water on soil is an important practice where water is available and where the surface conditions and the underlying geological formations are suitable. The usefulness of this practice and some of the available techniques are being researched.

14-4.4 Use of Chemical Wetting Agents

Chemical wetting agents (surfactants) were first recommended for increasing water infiltration into dryland soils in the early 1950s. Several materials have been developed and recommended for this use, but none has shown practical promise with normal dryland soils.

More recently, wetting agents have been recommended as additives for use in sprinkler irrigation systems. Farmers are apparently using some of these materials, but there is no clear proof that they increase water intake rates on normal irrigated soils.

Letey (1975) demonstrated that surfactants increase infiltration rate in water-repellant soils in California, but questions the effectiveness of these materials on normal soils (Note 14-2).

NOTE 14-2 EFFECT OF SURFACTANTS ON INFILTRATION

The major force moving water into and through soils during rainfall is capillary force. Capillary attraction is equal to twice the product of the surface tension of water and the cosine of the wetting angle, divided by the radius of curvature ($2 \gamma \cdot \cos \theta / r$). A surfactant (wetting agent) added to water reduces both the surface tension of the water and the wetting angle between water and the solid it contacts. Effective wetting agents decrease surface tension in laboratory systems by over 50%. In order for the capillary attraction to be increased (to increase infiltration), the wetting angle must be decreased enough so that the cosine of the angle is increased more than the surface tension is decreased.

The wetting angle between normal soil and water is generally $10°$ or less (cos $10°$ = 0.985). It is impossible therefore to decrease this angle enough to increase cos θ by 50%. Accordingly, it appears impossible for wetting agents to increase infiltration in normal soils by capillarity.

Nonwetting soils, on the other hand, have wetting angles much greater than those for normal soils. In many cases the angle may exceed $90°$. This gives the cosine a negative value and means that the soils are truly water repelling. Capillary force will be greater and infiltration may be increased if this angle can be reduced sufficiently by surfactant addition (Letey, 1975).

14-4.5 Use of Surface Crop Residues

The best way to maintain a high water-infiltration rate and to reduce runoff is to use vegetation and vegetative residues. Standing crop residues also add to soil water by trapping snow that might otherwise blow off the field. The effect of vegetation, both living crops and dead residues, on runoff and erosion is discussed in Chapters 8, 9, 11, and 12. It is only necessary here to point out that soil water storage is increased by stubble mulch tillage (Greb and others, 1970).

Three ways to get the greatest possible benefit from vegetation are: (1) Use crop rotations, cropping systems, and crop management practices that keep the soil well covered for as long as possible each year (Ch. 8). (2) Leave as much of the crop residue on the soil surface as practical, particularly between crops. Tillage and planting equipment that can work through trash and effective herbicides that supplement or replace tillage help to bring this about (Ch. 9). (3) Apply crop residue to fields that would otherwise be bare and unprotected. Applications of hay or straw to reduce erosion also reduce runoff. (See Chapters 11 and 12.)

14-4.6 Improving Soil Structure

Runoff is inversely related to the infiltration rate and permeability of the soil. Soil texture and soil structure determine the rate of water movement into and through soil. Nothing practical can be done to change soil texture, but soil structure can be altered by management practices including the use of sod crops, crop and animal residues and mulches, reduced tillage, and addition of chemical soil conditioners.

Cropping Systems and Soil Structure. The crops raised and the practices used in their culture affect soil structure. In drylands, where moisture conservation is most important, there are few adapted crops and few cropping systems that are practical. Sod crops are impractical in cultivated cropping sequences because of the difficulties of getting stands and the slow rate of establishment.

Crop and Animal Residues and Organic Mulches. Crop residues incorporated into the soil contribute part of the beneficial effect of crops on soil structure. Leaving residues on or adding an organic mulch to the soil surface helps maintain a better and more stable structure. Annual applications up to 55 mt/ha of manure or sewage sludge improve soil structure and increase soil productivity if the supplement contains no harmful chemicals. Manure and sewage sludge applications to dryland soils also improve structure, but often upset soil moisture relations and reduce crop yields.

Tillage. The immediate effect of tillage on soil permeability is often beneficial. A recently plowed field is much more permeable than a firm, unplowed soil. Postplanting cultivation of fine-textured, low-organic-matter soils improves permeability temporarily and reduces runoff.

The long-term effect of tillage, however, usually reduces soil permeability. The more tillage a soil receives, the denser it becomes, the lower its infiltration rate, and the slower its permeability. Even the large ripping machines used to tear up indurated subsurface layers (Ch. 9) do not improve infiltration rate or soil permeability permanently.

Chemical Conditioners. Chemicals added to soils to improve soil structure and permeability may reduce runoff losses also.

Sodic soils have deflocculated clay and poor structure. If the exchangeable sodium in these soils can be replaced by calcium (by the application of gypsum—$CaSO_4 \cdot 2H_2O$), the colloid will flocculate and desirable structure will regenerate. This improves soil permeability, as discussed in Chapter 16. Sodic soils generally are found in dryland regions where water is most important.

Several synthetic organic chemicals have been promoted as soil conditioners. One of the earliest of these, hydrolyzed polyacrylonitrile (HPAN), was developed and promoted under the trade name of Krilium by Monsanto Chemical Company in 1950. Several research articles on Krilium and other synthetic soil conditioners appeared in the June 1952 issue of *Soil Science*. Since that time, claims have been made for soil-conditioning properties of many additional materials. Investigations have regularly shown that some materials improve soil structure or increase aggregate stability, but only at such high rates that they are economically impractical. For example, Duley (1956) reported that applications of 1.1 to 4.4 mt HPAN/ha increased the size of aggregates and also increased infiltration rate. This same study showed that applications of 5.6 mt of straw/ha had about twice as much effect on infiltration as HPAN. The chemical then sold for \$2.25 to \$3.50/kg, so the cost of Duley's applications was from \$2475 to \$15,400/ha. So far no synthetic material has been found that improves soil structure and permeability at rates that are economical for use on agricultured soils.

14-4.7 Water-Storage Structures

Methods for reducing runoff losses described so far all involve water storage in the soil. Aboveground storage in ponds, lakes, and reservoirs is also common. Water stored in these structures is used to meet irrigation, livestock, industrial, or human needs.

Farm Ponds and Dugouts. Trapping surface runoff behind small earthen dams is a common way to provide water for livestock in areas where well water is scarce or unavailable, or where additional watering sites are needed to insure better use of pasture or range. Stock water dams are usually sited on small watercourses that drain 10- to 40-ha grassed watersheds. The dams are relatively simple structures with a grassed spillway at one end about a meter lower than the crest of the dam. These dams are seldom fitted with a pipe drawdown device. A farm pond is shown in Figure 14-6.

Dugouts, rather than dams, may be used to store water on more level land, especially in higher latitudes where snow accumulates over the winter and melts during a short spring thaw. Dugouts that intercept snow melt should be large and deep to hold enough water for the entire summer season. An example of a dugout is shown in Figure 14-7.

The bottoms and sides of reservoirs must be impermeable to retain stored water. Dams also must be impermeable to prevent seepage. Therefore subsoil material at the site of a dam or dugout should

Figure 14-6 A farm pond in Kansas that combines catfish production with water storage for irrigation. (Courtesy USDA— Soil Conservation Service.)

Figure 14-7 A dugout excavated in glacial till to impound water for livestock. A pump is located in the far corner. (Courtesy Canada-Manitoba Soil Survey.)

be impermeable or slowly permeable. Construction material for dams is obtained most conveniently and economically from the site of the reservoir. This minimizes hauling distance and makes the reservoir deeper—a factor that reduces the proportion of stored water lost by evaporation. Accordingly, sites for both dams and dugouts must be selected carefully. If a water storage structure is needed at a site where impermeable soil is not available, bentonite, a swelling clay, may be purchased and spread over the floor of the reservoir at a rate of 5 to 15 kg/m^2 and mixed with the top 15 cm of soil. This will add materially to the cost of the structure.

The bed of the reservoir and the dam itself should be compacted as much as possible during construction. This can be accomplished by rolling with a sheepsfoot packer. Herding cattle, hogs, or other animals in the basin after completion and before water is too deep will help to seal the bed.

Plastic film, butyl rubber, or a thin asphalt layer may be placed over the entire bed of a reservoir to seal the surface completely. The film or layer must be applied very carefully to insure complete coverage with no breaks, and the film must be protected with a cover of 15 cm or more of fine (not cloddy or stony) soil. Where these materials are used it is absolutely essential that the reservoir be fenced to prevent livestock from punching holes in the film.

Small dams and dugouts can be constructed by individual farmers, but many will want to have the work done by a competent conservation contractor with large earth-moving equipment. Construction specifications for both dams and dugouts should be obtained from the Soil Conservation Service or from a competent engineering consultant.

Ponds should be fenced to reduce bank trampling and to reduce eutrophication. A pipe should be installed to carry water to a trough or tank below the dam. Dugouts must also be fenced to keep livestock away from the steeply sloping sides. Animals may be permitted access to the water by way of the ramp used by the earth-moving equipment during construction, but it is preferable to keep them out and pump water to a tank above the dugout. A reservoir providing water for home use must be fenced; in fact, animals should be kept out of the entire watershed to reduce the possibility of water pollution.

Municipal Water Supply Reservoirs. Many small- to medium-sized dams have been built to trap streamflow (runoff) for use in municipal water systems. Many more reservoirs will be required as population increases.

Large Irrigation-Water Reservoirs. Flow in the major rivers of most countries is seasonally greater than the needs of downstream users. Where irrigation water can be used effectively, the seasonal surplus can be stored for use during the growing season. Many reservoirs such as the one shown in Figure 14-8 have been built in the western half of the United States and in dryland areas of other countries. Since more surplus water flows in the rivers and streams of humid areas than in most dryland rivers, storage for use in the short dry periods in humid regions may be a reasonable project of the future.

14-5 REDUCING EVAPORATION LOSSES

The quantity of water lost from soils by evaporation may exceed 70% of the annual precipitation in dryland regions. In subhumid areas the loss probably amounts to 30% to 50%. Reducing this loss, especially in drylands, would significantly increase the water supply for crop production.

Figure 14-8 Lovewell Dam and Reservoir in north central Kansas was built by the Bureau of Reclamation as an irrigation storage reservoir. The irrigation-water discharge outlet and canal are in the foreground beside the spillway. Water was being discharged from the spillway when the picture was taken. (Courtesy USDA—Soil Conservation Service.)

The earliest recommended method for reducing evaporation from soil was to use a *dust mulch*—a thin dry layer produced by cultivating the soil after every rain. This technique was suggested by experiments conducted by Professor King at the University of Wisconsin around 1900. It has since been abandoned because it was never successful in increasing available moisture in the dryland regions, and it produced an extremely erodible soil surface. Using vegetative mulches and other mulching materials, and forcing water to percolate deeper, are the methods presently used to reduce evaporation from soil.

14-5.1 Vegetative Mulches

Mulches of crop residue, forest litter, sawdust, and wood chips greatly reduce evaporation by reducing soil temperature and wind velocity near the soil. The German investigator Eser (1884) first showed the effects of mulches on evaporation. In his month-long study, evaporation was reduced from 5739 g/1000 cm² on bare soil to 621 g/1000 cm² from a soil mulched with 5 cm of fir needles. Subsequent studies show that a reduction of this magnitude occurs only as long as the soil surface remains moist. Subsequent evaporation losses from dry soil are too slow for mulches to influence water loss greatly. Mulches appreciably reduce water loss by evaporation only in years or in regions in which rain wets the soil frequently.

14-5.2 Other Mulches

Nonvegetative mulches applied to soils also reduce evaporation loss. Stones and gravel added to, or not removed from, surface soil increase infiltration and reduce water loss. Fairbourn and Gardner (1975) coated natural soil aggregates with water-repellent materials and applied the treated aggregates as mulches with reasonable success. Tar-paper caps placed on ridges between sorghum rows to cover six-sevenths of the soil area increased yields from 38% to 240% according to the 1937 to 1940 annual reports of the Garden City and Fort Hays (Kansas) Branch Agricultural Experiment Stations. The investigators credited yield increases to three effects of the mulch: (1) evaporation was reduced because a smaller surface area was exposed to sun and wind, (2) rainfall was concentrated onto smaller areas so it percolated deeper into the soil and was less subject to evaporative forces, and (3) the cover maintained faster water absorption by preventing raindrops from compacting a large part of the soil surface.

Shaw (1959) grew corn to maturity on plots covered with black plastic film. The plastic stopped rainfall from entering the soil and also greatly reduced evaporation. Corn on the plastic-covered plot, with only the water in the soil at seeding time, produced a yield nearly as high as the adjacent unmulched plot that received normal rainfall supplemented by several irrigations (75.9 to 80.9 q/ha). In an Arizona study, asphalt sprayed on the soil immediately after cotton and sorghum seeding held more moisture in the seed zone and improved germination and early growth. Good results were obtained on some soils, but the surface had to be smooth to minimize the quantity of asphalt required. If soil shrinkage occurred, the film cracked and was useless.

Plastic film is the only material tested that has been used commercially. Black polyethylene film has been used in humid parts of the United States to produce high-value vegetable crops. Actually, the yield increases obtained with plastic do not arise from evaporation control alone. Weeds are controlled by the cover, and the greenhouse effect raises soil temperature and increases early growth.

14-5.3 Forcing Deeper Water Penetration

Water close to the soil surface is more subject to evaporation than water deeper in the profile. Consequently, the proportion of water evaporated is smaller where water is forced to percolate more deeply. Extra water that stays in the root zone should increase dryland crop yield. The Kansas study using tar-paper caps caused deeper percolation because runoff water was concentrated on a smaller area of soil. Fairbourn and Gardner (1974) used this technique in an experiment at Akron, Colorado. The soil surface was formed into beds 2 m wide. Each bed had two 75-cm sloping (3:1) contributing areas leading down from each side onto a 50-cm flat collecting area. The flat area had a 15-cm deep vertical mulch slot running down the middle with two rows of sorghum 15 cm on either side. The slopes were treated with a hydrophobic material to further reduce water penetration on the sloping shoulders. Check dams were constructed at intervals across the flat furrows to prevent lateral movement of water. The bedded, mulched, and vertical-mulched plots saved 41% more rainfall and produced from 37% to 150% more sorghum grain than did regular flat-planted, unmulched land.

14-5.4 Reducing Losses from Reservoirs

Much of the runoff water stored in reservoirs is lost by evaporation. Annual evaporation from open water surfaces in agricultural regions ranges from about 350 mm in north central Canada (54°N latitude) to over 2000 mm in northern Nigeria (13°N). Hot desert areas suffer even larger losses. Actual evaporation rates are directly related to temperature and wind velocity, and inversely related to relative humidity. Evaporation losses from small reservoirs may exceed livestock or household use.

Better methods for reducing evaporation losses from reservoirs are constantly being sought. For example, a field shelterbelt planted around a reservoir site reduces evaporation losses by reducing wind velocity over the water. At the same time, it beautifies the site and makes a useful recreational area and wildlife sanctuary. Shelterbelts also trap snow for dugout recharge. Trees should be at least 30 m from the water to reduce transpiration losses from the reservoir.

Materials such as hexadecanol and other long-chain fatty alcohols reduce evaporation about 20% by forming monomolecular films over the water surface. Because they are biodegradable, however, the area covered decreases with time. Furthermore, even gentle winds can blow the films toward the pond or reservoir shore and leave the water surface unprotected. Nicholaichuk (1978) describes rafts made of inexpensive, lightweight concrete that are as effective as monomolecular films and much more durable.

14-6 REDUCING DEEP PERCOLATION LOSSES

Deep percolation losses are of little significance in nonirrigated dryland areas because the limited rainfall can usually be trapped in the root zone, except possibly in sands that are rarely cropped. Percolation losses do occur, however, in humid or irrigated areas (Ch. 16).

Deep percolation is a common avenue of water loss in humid regions, but this loss does not seriously reduce the amount of water available to plants unless the soil has a low water-holding capacity. Most deep medium- and fine-textured soils hold 150 to 300 mm of available water before water moves below the plant root zone. This is usually sufficient to last the crop through a short dry period. Sandy soils lose large amounts of water through percolation because some of them hold less than 50 mm of available water in the root zone. Reducing deep percolation losses in sands could increase water available to crops and might increase crop yields.

Erickson and others (1968) demonstrated in Michigan that horizontal asphalt barriers 55 to 60 cm below the soil surface in Bridgman fine sand (unclassified) and Grayling loamy sand (Typic Udipsamment) appreciably increased the water available to plants. Vegetable crop yields were increased by 35% to 40% on the fine sand, but only small increases occurred on the loamy sand soil. A trial in Taiwan with paddy rice on a sand soil showed yields were increased ten- to fourteen-fold with barriers placed at depths of 20 to 60 cm. Material costs have increased greatly since 1968, but there are situations where the technique may still be usefully employed (Erickson, 1972).

Another approach that may eventually prove useful for holding more water in sands is to add a chemical that absorbs water. A copolymer of starch and acrylonitrile called "super slurper" has been reported to absorb up to 1400 times its weight of distilled water (Agricultural Research Service, 1976). This material has been tested on sandy soils, and preliminary reports indicate that it increases the water available for plant growth. Further trials are needed to reveal whether the material does enough good and lasts long enough to be worth its cost.

Deep percolation through soils is important in another way. Plant nutrients are leached and soils are rendered more acid by the percolating water. Controlled runoff (without serious erosion) in humid regions may be less damaging than deep percolation, particularly in areas where production inputs such as fertilizers and lime are expensive and hard to obtain. In much of the tropical world with monsoon rainfall, water conservation is important mainly at the beginning and toward the end of the rains. In the heart of the rainy season, good water management should emphasize controlled surface drainage rather than surface detention and infiltration.

14-7 STORING WATER IN SOIL

Soil is an effective reservoir for water. The soil in humid regions is usually wet to field capacity beyond rooting depth at least once each year. Water stored over winter in the subhumid sections of north central United States makes high corn and soybean yields possible the following summer even though these crops need much more water in July and August than normally falls as rain during those months. Winter moisture storage can be equally beneficial in sections of the intermountain valleys and the Pacific Northwest. It is important in dryland areas of the Great Plains but is limited because winter precipitation is usually meager. Crop production under these conditions may not be possible every year, even when all practical water-conservation measures are used.

Water can be stored in the soil if plant growth is prevented during a growing season. This water will supplement rainfall the next growing season. The practice of preventing plant growth and of storing water in the soil during one crop growing season for use by a crop planted in the next season is called *summer fallow*. This must be distinguished from the term *fallow* used to designate the period of soil recuperation under several years of forest or grass regrowth in a shifting cultivation system (Ch. 20).

Summer fallow has been used in various parts of the world for several centuries, including extensive use in England during and after the Roman occupation. It was first used in North America in the early 1850s by the Selkirk settlers in the area north of Winnipeg, Canada, but it was not widely used in dryland regions until the 1880s, shortly after the Great Plains area of the United States was first settled. The area of land that is summer fallowed each year in the United States west of the Mississippi River is currently a little less than 15 million hectares. Summer fallow is also common in western Canada, over vast areas of the USSR, in Australia, and in many of the wheat-growing areas in the southern part of South America.

14-7.1 Objectives of Summer Fallow

The major objective of summer fallowing is to store water in the soil for subsequent crop use. No other objective is of much consequence in dryland areas of summer-type rainfall, such as the central and northern Great Plains of the United States and the western prairies of Canada. However, weed control, release of extra nitrogen for the use of a succeeding crop, and spreading the workload of seedbed preparation over a longer period may be important reasons for using summer fallow in some areas.

14-7.2 Efficiency of Water Storage

Twenty-three federally supported experiment stations were organized in the drylands of the United States between 1905 and 1918. These stations and several state stations studied moisture storage in fallow-crop and continuous-crop systems until the late 1940s. The average amount of rainfall stored during a fifteen- to nineteen-month fallow period ranged from 38 mm (6%) at Dalhart, Texas, to 157 mm (40%) at Sheridan, Wyoming, in the summer rainfall area. Over the same period moisture stored between harvest and planting in continuous-crop systems ranged from 19 mm (10%) at Dalhart to 99 mm (40%) at Sheridan (Mathews and Army, 1960). Fallow storage efficiency at Swift Current in western Canada was nearly 27% (Doughty and others, 1949). These results explain why summer fallow is used less commonly in hot drylands such as the southern Great Plains of the United States. More recent studies in the central Great Plains quoted by Greb and others (1974) show increasing efficiency of soil storage with improvement in cultivation methods (Table 14-1).

Water-storage efficiency of summer fallow in the winter rainfall area of the United States is usually greater than 30%. More than 60% of the precipitation was stored in the soil during the early winter period when temperature was low and precipitation relatively abundant.

Soil permeability also affects the efficiency of water storage in fallowed land. Sandy soils are permeable and absorb rainfall readily. Percolating water goes deeper into a sandy soil with a low water-holding capacity than it would into a finer-textured soil and is less likely to be lost by evaporation. Consequently, sandier soils store rainfall more efficiently as long as they have sufficient storage capacity to hold the percolating water in the root zone. Probably the best soils for efficient water storage are those with sandy surface layers overlying medium-textured subsoils.

14-7.3 Cultivating Fallow Land

Efficient storage of moisture in fallowed land depends on successful weed control and on maintaining crop residues on the soil surface. Weeds must be killed in a timely way by undercutting implements or by chemicals, but tillage should not be performed more often than necessary to control weeds. Extra tillage dissipates moisture, costs money, buries residues, and does not increase crop yields.

Frequency of fallow in a cropping system should be governed by soil moisture and by climatic conditions at the time. A dryland

Table 14-1 Increasing water-storage efficiency in the central Great Plains with improving technology

Years	Stage of technology	Average soil storage efficiency (% of precipitation)
1911–30	Shallow operating plows	19
1931–46	Introduction of small one-way disk	23
1947–58	Introduction of rod weeder	26
1959–66	Modern stubble mulch with large sweeps and rod weeder with tongs	32
1967–70	Fall weed control in combination with stubble mulch	38

SOURCE: Greb and others, 1974.

soil should be fallowed when its moisture content just before seeding is insufficient to assure a reasonable yield. Medium- and fine-textured soils in dryland regions are generally fallowed once in two, three, or four years. Government restrictions on crop production in the United States have forced farmers to cut back on cash-crop area, which in dryland areas has meant more land is summer fallowed. More land is being fallowed in many areas than agricultural efficiency requires.

14-7.4 Crop Response to Summer Fallow

Crop yields on summer fallow in dryland areas are higher than yields on land that produces a crop each year. The more favorable the condition for extra moisture storage by fallowing, the larger are the increases in yields. Average wheat yield increases up to the early 1950s ranged from a low 13 kg/ha (4.4%) at Big Spring, Texas, to 7.2 q/ha (120%) at Colby, Kansas, in the Great Plains, to 20.3 q/ha (153%) at Moscow, Idaho, in the winter rainfall area of the intermountain valleys.

Other adapted crops respond to summer fallow about the same as wheat does. Percent yield increases of oats and barley are as great as those of wheat in the northern Great Plains. Percent yield increases of sorghum are as great as, or greater than, those of wheat in the southern Plains. Corn is not well adapted to most dryland areas, and its response to fallow is small and erratic. Yield increases indicate, as does water-storage efficiency, that summer fallow is most useful in dryland areas with cool temperatures where evaporation losses during storage are small.

14-7.5 Summer Fallow and Saline Seeps

Opportunity for water losses from fallowed soils by deep percolation increases as efficiency of moisture storage increases. Stored water may move downward in the soil beyond the reach of crop roots and be lost for crop production. It also carries dissolved salts from the soil and causes a loss of plant nutrients. These percolating waters may resurface farther down the slope and provide plants there with extra water and nutrients. The salts in excess of those used by the plants are left in the soil and in time may produce *saline seeps*. Considerable areas of saline seeps are developing, particularly in the northern Great Plains.

One obvious method of reducing the magnitude of saline seeps is to restrict fallowing to areas where the water that can be saved in the soil will not exceed the amount that can be stored in the root zone. This would mean a shift from alternate fallow and crop to less frequent fallow or to continuous cropping when water losses are reduced.

14-8 EFFICIENT USE OF STORED SOIL WATER

The storage of water in a soil is not an efficient process, but stored water is as useful for crop production as an equal amount of rain that falls on the growing crop. The stored water must be husbanded carefully if it is to serve the crop and the farmer well.

There are several ways to reduce unnecessary loss of stored soil water: (1) plant crops only when there is enough water for a reasonable chance of successful production, (2) grow efficient crops, (3) plant and cultivate with timeliness and precision, (4) plant at the proper seeding rate, (5) control weeds and volunteer crop plants, (6) use windbreaks to reduce transpiration, and (7) use antitranspirants.

14-8.1 Predicting Successful Crop Production

Water stored in a soil will be wasted if a planted crop fails to mature. A technique for predicting cropping success can help reduce unnecessary water loss. Hallsted and Mathews (1936), Thomson (1947), and Fisher and Burnett (1953) developed relationships between soil moisture at seeding time and yield of winter wheat, spring wheat, and cotton, respectively. Each expressed available moisture in terms of depth of wet soil and pointed out how a knowledge of depth of wet soil at seeding time could be used to estimate the likelihood of successful crop production.

A crop should not be planted when chances for successful crop growth are low and chances of failure are great, as when 30 cm or less of wet soil is available. Rather, the land should be set aside and kept free of weeds so that additional water can be stored for growing a crop at the next planting season. Hallsted and Mathews also recommended that soil moisture content be used to make the decision on whether to abandon a winter wheat crop. Early abandonment (April) permits the saving of some soil moisture for the next crop.

Wise postponement of planting and judicious use of abandonment permit farmers to obtain the advantages of summer fallow in many places without specifically setting aside large areas of land for this purpose every year. It gives them more flexibility. This technique has never been widely used by United States or Canadian farmers because government controls on planting area or on marketing have reduced cropped area and increased land in fallow.

14-8.2 Growing Efficient Crops

Crop plants use (transpire) 15% to 30% of the rainfall each year. The amount used depends on the type of crop, the climate, and on crop and soil management. Water-requirement studies at Akron, Colorado (Briggs and Shantz, 1914) show that the transpiration ratio (kilograms of water transpired per kilogram of dry matter produced) is 298 for sorghum, 368 for corn, 481 for wheat, and over 1000 for some grasses. This suggests that sorghum should perform better on limited water than the other crops and that sorghum and corn should produce more than wheat on a specified amount of water. These three crops, however, use almost identical amounts of water in the Great Plains, drying the soil to the wilting point to the depth of rooting and using all the available water each year. Accordingly, it seems that crop selection for dryland areas should be based on performance under stressful conditions rather than on transpiration ratios. Many developing countries use mixtures of varieties and even of species, seeding drought-tolerant and water-loving types together so that the chance of crop failure is reduced in drier years without losing productive potential in more humid periods.

In less arid areas, selecting crop varieties on the number of days required to reach maturity permits partial control of the amount of soil water that remains at harvest and the time that will be available for water recharge between harvest and the next seeding.

14-8.3 Timeliness of Operations

As seeding time approaches, it often happens that the surface soil dries out and a rain is needed to insure seed germination and seedling emergence. After a rain, seeding can start as soon as the surface soil dries enough for traffic if the seedbed is free of weeds and ready for planting. Seed planted immediately after a rain has an excellent chance of germinating and establishing a vigorous root system before the moisture in the surface layer of soil is lost by evaporation. If, on the other hand, the land needs cultivation to control a crop of weeds or to fit it for planting when a rain is received, the surface moisture may be dissipated by the tillage and seeding operations. It may then be necessary to wait for another rain before planting.

Seeding either too early or too late reduces yields. Planting in dryland areas is often dictated by the climate of the particular year. An early rain moistening the surface soil may cause farmers to plant even though they know a later planting date is better. This is particularly true of farmers planting winter wheat in a rainfall area where rains at planting time in the autumn are scarce and another rain may not come in time for best planting success. However, the early-planted crop uses extra moisture in the fall. Moisture reserves may be so depleted by spring that the crop is entirely dependent on current rainfall for its needs. This crop will die if timely rains do not fall.

Some of the detrimental effects of early seeding and excess early growth of winter wheat can be counteracted by judicious pasturing of the fall and early spring herbage. The pastured crop does not deplete the moisture reserves as much as unpastured early-planted crops. It protects the soil from wind erosion and often yields more than a similar unpastured crop.

Delayed planting may allow too much water to be lost from the soil by evaporation and leave too little for the crop. Timing is especially important in tropical areas with wet-dry seasons where delayed seeding after the end of the monsoon rains wastes stored water.

14-8.4 Rate of Seeding

The amount of water available for crop production dictates the number of plants that can be supported. Thick stands do well where stored water and rainfall are abundant, but population density must be restricted where moisture is limited or all plants will suffer moisture stress. Corn, soybeans, and other crops that do not tiller must be planted at the population dictated by the climate, soil fertility, and other factors. Widely spaced corn plants (low populations) may produce bigger ears, or in some varieties more than one ear per plant, but yield per hectare will not reach the potential for that set of ecological conditions. Wheat, other small grains, and sorghum often counteract low seeding rates by tillering profusely under favorable conditions. Thus wheat yield may not be greatly different whether seeded at a rate of 35 or 75 kg/ha because the thin crop will tiller to fill the space. If too much seed is planted, though, the plants compete for water and space so that no individual plant grows well; in extreme cases, water is insufficient to bring the crop to maturity. A thinner stand under the same moisture regime can survive and produce a harvestable crop.

Studies were conducted in the drylands of North America to find out if planting crops in widely spaced rows would reduce water use enough to increase the growth of wheat the following year. Moisture use was reduced by this technique and yields of the succeeding wheat crops were increased. The yields of the widely spaced row crops, however, were reduced by wide spacing, and the total production per unit area (row crop plus wheat) was always less on the widely spaced plots. For example, at Colby, Kansas, wheat yields averaged 260 kg/ha more on the 2-m row-spaced corn land than on the 1-m spacing, but the corn in wide rows yielded 340 kg/ha less. Nor did the use of widely spaced corn insure against wheat failure. Only once in thirty-one years was a wheat crop obtained on the 2-m row area when no crop was harvested on the 1-m row plot (Kuska and Mathews, 1956).

14-8.5 Controlling Weeds and Volunteer Plants

All plants, whether seeded crops, volunteer plants, weeds, or native plants, absorb and transpire water. Weeds and other unwanted plants use moisture from seedbeds, from summer fallow, and from fields in crop. One Russian thistle plant uses about as much water as three sorghum plants, and two wild sunflowers use as much as five corn plants. Studies in western Canada showed that widely spaced Russian thistle plants (9 m^2 per plant) use over 560,000 kg water per hectare. This is enough to produce 4 to 4.5 q/ha of wheat or 5 q/ha of sorghum grain. Weed and volunteer plant growth must be prevented if maximum conservation of available water is to be achieved and maximum crop yields obtained. Transpiration by weeds and volunteer crop plants is the largest single cause of stored water loss. It is especially costly under dryland farming where every drop of water is precious.

14-8.6 Windbreaks and Field Shelterbelts

Barriers perpendicular to the wind reduce wind velocity and affect air temperature near the ground. Potential transpiration close to the barrier is reduced. Reductions in transpiration of 10% or more are obtained for as far as fifteen to twenty times the height of the barrier to leeward. Greatest reductions are at night, with the maximum, about 30%, being found at a point twice the windbreak height to leeward. At midday greatest reduction, about 20%, is attained about eight times the windbreak height to leeward (Woodruff and others, 1959). (See Chapters 5 and 13.)

Changes in transpiration are sufficient at times to prevent desiccation of plants in the shelter of the windbreaks and to reduce the effect of drought on yield. Unfortunately, reductions in crop transpiration are offset in part by use of water by the trees, reducing crop yields next to the windbreak unless the tree roots are severely pruned.

14-8.7 Antitranspirants

Long-chain fatty alcohols and some long-chain fatty acids are known to reduce transpiration by plants. Wilting of transplanted tree seedlings and other plants has been reduced by spraying leaves with octadecanol and hexadecanol. Trials with field crops also show reduced transpiration, but plant growth is reduced also. Similar applications to soils rather than to plants have no significant effect on water use (Peters and Roberts, 1963).

Fuehring (1973) reports reductions in water use and significant increases in crop growth from small applications of phenylmercuric acetate (PMA), atrazine, and Folicote (a wax antitranspirant manufactured by Sun Oil Co.) to sorghum just before the boot stage. An earlier study by Brengle (1968) showed that, although PMA reduced water use when applied to spring wheat at heading or flowering, plant growth also was reduced. Use of PMA on crops is now banned. Interest in antitranspirants remains high, and materials may yet be found that can be used to decrease transpiration losses and increase yield.

14-8.8 Controlling Irrigation Losses

Water used for irrigation of crops is always "stored" water. It comes either from aboveground (surface) storage or from belowground (groundwater) storage. Consequently, any careless or wasteful practices in irrigation constitute inefficient use of stored water. Conservation practices in irrigation are discussed in Chapter 16.

SUMMARY

Dry periods of varying length cause problems for crops, livestock, and people all over the world. Problems are most severe in the areas with the driest climates. Without irrigation, the only way to meet the challenge of dry weather and droughts is to conserve and use wisely the water that is received. Good water management prevents damage from nearly all water shortages in humid regions; the use of all practical conservation measures prevents damage and hardship in only the least severe dry periods in arid regions.

Water from precipitation is lost for economic use by plant interception, runoff, evaporation, transpiration, and deep percolation. The greatest losses in humid areas are from runoff and deep percolation. Evaporation and unnecessary transpiration are the most serious in dryland regions.

The principal means of reducing runoff are to increase the soil's infiltration rate, to hold the water on the soil surface longer so that it may infiltrate, and to trap runoff in dugouts, ponds, and reservoirs. Dams and reservoirs must be built of properly compacted material containing enough clay to control seepage losses.

Evaporation losses are hard to control. Some loss reduction results from use of crop residues and other mulches. Soil bedding designed to concentrate water in the crop row area has increased yields, but the technique is too complicated and too costly for common field use. Use of chemical monolayer and other surface evaporation barriers is not yet economically feasible.

Crops in dryland areas generally use all the water that is available each year, so crop selection and population density have little effect on water use. Weed and volunteer crop plant control reduces unnecessary transpiration loss. Windbreaks have some effect over a limited area. Antitranspirants have not proved effective in reducing loss in the field.

Summer fallow is often a useful practice where sufficient water cannot be stored for profitable annual crop production. Water stored during one crop growing season is thus held over and used along with current rainfall in the next crop season. Efficiency of fallow storage was originally low but has been increased by better weed-control and residue-management procedures. Fallow is used successfully for wheat and other small grains and for sorghum production. Increased moisture-storage efficiency is the cause of some saline seeps in the northern Great Plains.

The precious water that has been stored in the soil must be guarded zealously. Great care must be taken to grow the right crops in the right way so that water is used efficiently and crops are grown successfully.

QUESTIONS

1. Describe the five avenues by which precipitation is lost from soils and the factors that influence each.
2. Describe the water-control structures needed in dryland areas.
3. What are the principal mechanisms by which surface crop residue increases the amount of soil water available for crop use in dryland areas? What is the relative effectiveness of each mechanism?
4. List the approaches that have been used to try to reduce water losses from soils and explain how each one works.
5. How efficient is moisture storage by summer fallowing? Where is summer fallow recommended for regular use?

REFERENCES

AGRICULTURAL RESEARCH SERVICE, 1976. An honor for super slurper. *Agric. Res.* 24(7):12-13.

BARNES, S., 1938. *Soil Moisture and Crop Production Under Dry Land Conditions in Western Canada.* Canada Dept. Agric. Publ. 595.

BLACK, A. L., 1968. Conservation bench terraces in Montana. *Trans. Amer. Soc. Agric. Eng.* 11:393-395.

BRENGLE, K. G., 1968. Effect of phenylmercuric acetate on growth and water use by spring wheat. *Agron. J.* 60:246-247.

BRIGGS, L. J., and H. L. SHANTZ, 1914. Relative water requirements of plants. *J. Agric. Research* 3:1-63.

COX, M. B., 1968. Conservation bench terraces in Kansas. *Trans. Amer. Soc. Agric. Eng.* 11:387-388.

DOUGHTY, J. L., W. J. STAPLE, J. J. LEHANE, F. G. WARDER, and F. BISAL, 1949. *Soil Moisture, Wind Erosion, and Fertility on some Canadian Prairie Soils.* Canada Dept. Agric. Publ. 819 (Tech. Bull. 71).

DULEY, F. L., 1956. The effect of a synthetic soil conditioner (HPAN) on intake, runoff, and erosion. *Soil Sci. Soc. Amer. Proc.* 20:420-422.

ERICKSON, A. E., 1972. Improving the water properties of sand soil. In DANIEL HILLEL (ed.), *Optimizing the Soil Physical Environment Toward Greater Crop Yields.* Academic Press, New York, p. 35-41.

ERICKSON, A. E., C. M. HANSEN, and A. J. M. SMUCKER, 1968. The influence of subsurface asphalt barriers on the water properties and the productivity of sand soils. *Trans. 9th Intern. Cong. Soil Sci.,* Adelaide, Australia, Vol. 1, p. 331-337.

ESER, C., 1884. Investigations on the influence of the physical and chemical properties of the soil on the evaporation potential. *Forsch. Gebeite Agric. -Phys.* 7:1-124.

FAIRBOURN, M. L., and H. R. GARDNER, 1974. Field use of microwatershed with vertical mulch, *Agron. J.* 66:741-744.

FAIRBOURN, M. L., and H. R. GARDNER, 1975. Water-repellant soil clods and pellets as mulch. *Agron. J.* 67:377-380.

FISHER, C. E., and EARL BURNETT, 1953. *Conservation and Utilization of Soil Moisture.* Texas Agric. Exp. Sta. Bull. 767.

FUEHRING, H. D., 1973. Effect of antitranspirants on yield of grain sorghum under limited irrigation. *Agron. J.* 65:348-351.

GREB, B. W., D. E. SMIKA, and A. L. BLACK, 1970. Water conservation with stubble mulch fallow. *J. Soil Water Cons.* 25:58-62.

GREB, B. W., D. E. SMIKA, N. P. WOODRUFF, and C. J. WHITFIELD, 1974. Summer fallow in the central Great Plains. In *Summer Fallow in the Western United States,* U.S. Dept. Agric. Conserv. Res. Report No. 17.

HALLSTED, A. L., and O. R. MATHEWS, 1936. *Soil Moisture and Winter Wheat with Suggestions on Abandonment.* Kansas Agric. Exp. Sta. Bull. 273.

HAUSER, V. L., 1968. Conservation bench terraces in Texas. *Trans. Amer. Soc. Agric. Eng.* 11:385-386, 392.

KUSKA, J. B., and O. R. MATHEWS, 1956. *Dryland Crop-Rotations and Tillage Experiments at the Colby (Kansas) Branch Experiment Station.* U.S. Dept. Agric. Circ. 979.

LETEY, J., 1975. The use of nonionic surfactants on soils. In *Soil Conditioners*. Soil Sci. Soc. Amer. Spec. Publ. No. 7, Madison, Wisc., p. 145–154.

MATHEWS, O. R., and T. J. ARMY, 1960. Moisture storage on fallowed wheatland in the Great Plains. *Soil Sci. Soc. Amer. Proc.* 24:414–418.

MEDINA, JORGE, 1976. Harvesting surface runoff and ephemeral streamflow in arid zones. In *Conservation in Arid and Semi-Arid Zones*. FAO Conserv. Guide 3, Food and Agriculture Organization, Rome, Italy, p. 61–73.

MEHDIZADEH, P., A. KOWSAR, E. VAZIRI, and L. BOERSMA, 1978. Water harvesting for afforestation: I. Efficiency and life span of asphalt cover. *Soil Sci. Soc. Amer. J.* 42:644–649.

MICKELSON, R. H., 1968. Conservation bench terraces in eastern Colorado. *Trans. Amer. Soc. Agric. Eng.* 11:389–392.

MICKELSON, R. H., and B. W. GREB, 1970. Lagoon levelling to permit annual cropping in semiarid areas. *J. Soil Water Cons.* 25:13–16.

NICHOLAICHUK, W., 1978. Evaporation control on farm-size reservoirs. *J. Soil Water Cons.* 33:185–188.

PENMAN, H. L., 1948. Natural evaporation from open water, bare soil, and grass. *Proc. Roy. Soc.*, Ser. A. 193:120–145.

PETERS, D. B., and W. J. ROBERTS, 1963. Use of octa-hexadecanol as a transpiration suppressant. *Agron. J.* 55:79.

RIPLEY, P. O., WILLIAM KABBFLEISCH, S. J. BOURGET, and D. J. COOPER, 1961. *Soil Erosion by Water.* Canada Dept. Agric. Publ. 1083.

SHAW, R. H., 1959. Water use from plastic-covered and uncovered corn plots. *Agron. J.* 51:172–173.

THOMSON, L. B., 1947. *Progress Report 1937-47*, Dominion Exp. Sta., Swift Current, Saskatchewan. Canada Dept. Agric., Ottawa.

THORNTHWAITE, C. W., 1948. An approach toward a rational classification of climate. *Geog. Rev.* 38:55–94.

WALTERS, TED, 1978. *1977 Kansas Sorghum Performance Tests. Kansas Agric. Exp. Sta. Report of Progress*, 321.

WOODRUFF, N. P., R. A. READ, and W. S. CHEPIL, 1959. *Influence of a Field Windbreak on Summer Wind Movement and Air Temperature*. Kansas Agric. Exp. Sta. Tech. Bull. 100.

ZINGG, A. W., and V. L. HAUSER, 1959. Terrace benching to save potential runoff for semiarid land. *Agron. J.* 51:289–292.

15

Drainage
of Cropland

Terms such as well drained, moderately well drained, and poorly drained are used to describe the degree to which excess water limits the use of soil for crop growth. Well-drained soils have no excess water limitations, and moderately well-drained soils have only minor ones. Somewhat poorly drained soils have high water tables long enough to cause problems and delays in planting, tillage operations, or other practices, but not to prevent cropping. Poorly drained soils usually cannot be cropped without artificial drainage, and very poorly drained soils are, or at least were, saturated with water most of the time.

Artificial drainage is appropriate for some land but should not be used on other land for a variety of reasons. Land that has adequate natural drainage receives no benefit if more water is removed. Some land should not be drained because its wet condition benefits its most appropriate use. Swamps and marshes may, for example, be more valuable for wildlife and recreation than they would be as cropland or pasture. And some drained land becomes so alkaline from sodic conditions (Ch. 16) or so acid from the oxidation of sulfides (Ch. 11) that nothing will grow on it. Artificial drainage should be provided only where soil conditions are suitable and the land use will benefit.

15-1 OCCURRENCE OF WET LANDS

Depressional areas can be poorly drained in arid as well as humid regions. Wetness occurs whenever the water supply by precipitation,

490

overland flow, and seepage into the area exceeds the water loss by outward flow, seepage, and evapotranspiration. Extremely low areas, such as the valley of the Dead Sea and Death Valley, accumulate salt water at their lowest points because there is no place else for the water to go. It must accumulate until a large enough area is wet enough for all the water to be removed by evapotranspiration. Salt accumulates because it is left behind when the water evaporates.

Wet seep spots occur in many footslopes and hillsides because water flows above impermeable strata. The water may have infiltrated from a depression, a level area on top of a hill in a humid region, or it may have entered the soil and rock layers in the hills or mountains and passed through several kilometers of rock before reaching the surface again in an arid valley. Such water can be under considerable pressure as it passes through its aquifer, as shown in Figure 15-1. A hole from the aquifer to the land surface becomes an artesian well if the pressure is high enough to make water flow at the surface. The water flow through an aquifer varies from slight seepage to voluminous springs. At the largest springs in the world, near Thousand Springs, Idaho, water flows from basalt cliffs in such volume that Idaho Power Company has built a concrete structure along the cliff to use the water for producing electricity, as shown in Figure 15-2. Much of this water is believed to have entered the basalt layers 200 km away where Big Lost River, Little Lost River, and some smaller streams disappear into openings in the rock.

Not suprisingly, wet lands are more abundant in humid regions than in arid ones. Zwerman (1969) estimated that one-fourth of the cropland in New York state needs drainage. The situation is similar

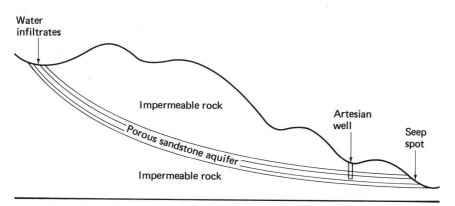

Figure 15-1 A cross section of a landscape showing an aquifer carrying water to an artesian well and a seep spot.

a

b

Figure 15-2 Electric power is produced from the water emerging from the canyon wall near Thousand Springs, Idaho. (a) The springs as they once appeared. (b) The power plant. (Courtesy S. Z. Thayer.)

in many other states. Any broad flat area underlain by a layer with low permeability is likely to have wet soil when precipitation exceeds evapotranspiration. Often there is an excess of water during part of the year and a deficit at other times. Thus the soil is wet only part of the year. The limitations imposed by wetness depend on how wet, how long, and when. Wetness during winter may not impose any limitations, wetness in spring often means a delay in cropping, and wetness in fall interferes with harvest of many crops.

15-2 CHARACTERISTICS OF WET SOILS

Several distinctive characteristics result from soil wetness. Some have strong positive or negative effects on soil productivity either in its wet state or in an artificially drained condition. These conditions should be identified before any action is taken to drain a wet area. Important properties to be considered include the vegetation and soil color patterns that reveal the degree of wetness, the organic-matter content, clay type and amount, soil pH, and related chemical factors.

Somewhat poorly drained soil may have similar vegetation to the well-drained soils in the vicinity but poorly and very poorly drained soils have sedges, reeds, and other water-loving vegetation. The difference is usually noticeable even during dry seasons and in areas that have no ponds on the surface.

15-2.1 Colors of Wet Soils

A pit dug in a wet soil reveals characteristic colors and color patterns even during dry periods. The colors involved are black, rust, bluish-gray, and white. The surface color of most poorly and very poorly drained soils is dark, often black, because of high organic-matter content. These dark A1 (surface) horizons are usually thicker than those of well-drained soils. The subsoil is normally grayer than the brighter colors common in drier soils, though there may be rust mottles in parts of the soil that sometimes receive oxygen. Mottles give a clue as to how much the water table fluctuates. The permanently wet part is the bluish-gray material sometimes called "blue clay" even though its texture may be almost anything from sand to clay. White colors result from salt accumulations on the surface of arid-region soils that have water movement upward from a water table.

15-2.2 Organic Matter in Wet Soils

The soil organic-matter content increases progressively from the driest to the wettest soils of an area. The driest soils usually have the least plant growth to produce organic matter and lose much of their organic matter by erosion and oxidation. The wet soils accumulate organic matter, not only because they receive organic matter eroded from dry soils above them, but also their limited oxygen supply slows decomposition and preserves their organic matter.

Organic-matter accumulation contributes to the high fertility of many artificially drained soils. It also contributes to a generally favorable soil structure. However, the organic-matter content gradually declines after aeration is increased by drainage, and the fertility and structural conditions move toward the norms for cropped soils of the area.

The loss of organic matter is most serious in peat and muck soils that are mostly organic matter. Losses by wind erosion and oxidation cause many of these soils to subside at rates between 2 and 5 cm per year when they are drained and cropped. The organic soil may be completely lost in a few decades or, at most, a few centuries. These soils are highly productive while they last, but there is no known way to crop them without losing them. The rate of loss can be minimized by keeping the water table as high as possible while crops are growing and saturating the soil when there are no crops.

15-2.3 Clay in Wet Soils

Many wet soils have higher clay contents than their drier neighbors. Erosion and weathering both influence clay content. Erosion sorts out the finer particles from soils on slopes and deposits some of them on flat areas below. Thus the sloping soils become coarser, and the flat soils become finer textured. This mechanism is most effective in materials that contain a wide range of particle sizes (are well graded). It has little effect on a well-sorted material such as many loess deposits.

Weathering requires water and is likely to progress faster where the soil stays moist. Poorly drained soils therefore form more clay than drier soils. This difference is more noticeable in old soils than in young soils.

Wetness influences the type as well as the amount of clay in old soils. Most soils of warm climates are dominated by kaolinite and oxide clays representing advanced stages of weathering and removal of silica. However, the wet soils retain their silica and enough bases to form montmorillonitic clay instead. The higher cation-exchange capacity of the montmorillonite clay contributes to higher fertility in areas where the drier soils have very low fertility.

15-2.4 Reducing Conditions in Wet Soils

A small proportion of wet soils have a moving water table that carries a fair supply of oxygen. Most, however, have stagnant water in their saturated zones. Decomposable organic matter in the presence of stagnant water produces reducing conditions. Microbial activity is slowed by the lack of oxygen. Some microbes reduce nitrates to N_2, N_2O, or NO gases under reducing conditions. Others reduce ferric iron to ferrous iron and thus produce bluish-gray colors. Rust mottles contain ferric iron resulting from the oxidation of ferrous iron.

Certain wet soil and rock materials, especially those associated with coal deposits, contain significant amounts of iron pyrite (FeS_2, otherwise known as "fool's gold" or ferrous disulfide). Like most sulfide minerals, this material has very low solubility and causes no problem in a wet soil. It can even be present in the nodular concretions known as "cat-clay" without causing trouble. However, drainage can ruin such a soil by permitting the sulfide to be oxidized to sulfate:

$$2 \, FeS_2 + 7 \, O_2 + 2 \, H_2O \xrightarrow[\text{bacteria}]{\text{sulfur}} 2 \, FeSO_4 + 2 \, H_2SO_4$$

The sulfuric acid formed by this and subsequent reactions (see Note 11-1) causes the soil pH to drop to between 2 and 3. The reaction then stops because nothing will grow, not even the sulfur bacteria.

Neutralization of sulfuric acid produced by oxidation of sulfides requires very large amounts of lime, because the oxidation process continues until either the sulfide or the lime is gone. It is usually better to avoid draining such soils. Material containing sulfides is sometimes drained, however, when someone fails to recognize cat-clay (a costly oversight) or when coal mine spoil is left in a heap (an old practice that is now illegal in most states). Acidity from coal mine spoil is especially objectionable because it is likely to acidify nearby bodies of water.

15-2.5 Alkalinity in Wet Soils

Some soils in low areas in arid regions have excess water in their subsoils or substratum at least part of the year. These soils are likely to be alkaline because soluble salts accumulate when water moves upward from a saturated zone. Such salts commonly include carbonates that cause alkaline reactions. The amount of water is important and depends greatly on the depth of the saturated zone as well as the nature of the soil material. Types of soils influenced by water tables are shown in Figure 15-3. The "water table" may or may not be broad and continuous. In many places it is a temporary perched water table or merely a saturated zone with only a few meters of lateral continuity.

Water moves upward from a water table by capillary action. A few centimeters of soil above the water table, known as the capillary fringe, are saturated with water. The capillary fringe may be as thick as 15 or 20 cm where all the pores are small but is thinner where larger pores are present. However, the soil to a height of 30 or 40 cm above the water table is usually poorly aerated and preserves enough organic matter to be black. Salts do not accumulate here because they diffuse back down through the moist soil.

Soils with white salt crusts occur where water moves upward to a dry surface. The water table commonly occurs at depths between 40 and 100 cm, depending on the size of the pores in the soil. The white crust disappears during a rain or when irrigation water is applied but reappears when the soil is dry again. These soils, known as saline soils, develop high osmotic concentrations when dry. Lowering the water table makes them drier and less suitable for plant growth unless proper treatment for the salt content is also applied. This process, known as soil reclamation, is discussed in Chapter 16. It is important to realize that although saline-sodic soils look the same as saline soils, they will become sodic if they are drained and leached. Proper reclamation technique is especially important for saline-sodic soils.

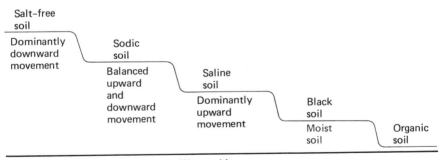

Figure 15-3 Soils developing in uniform material above a water table in an arid region.

Enough sodium ions may accumulate to produce a sodic soil when upward and downward movement of water and dissolved salts are nearly balanced. This typically happens in an arid region where the water table is between 100 and 150 cm below the surface of the soil. The sodium component becomes larger than usual because its salts are so soluble that they keep moving back to the surface. Other factors such as the salt content of the water table, the sodium content of the parent material, and the rate of release of sodium and other ions by weathering also have significant effects on the formation of sodic soils. Sodic soils have over 15% exchangeable sodium, but the salt content is low. The sodium concentration causes dispersed clay, shrinkage and cracking when dry, and very low permeability when wet. High sodium concentrations accompanied by carbonate anions cause the soil pH to rise above 8.5. The organic-matter contents are normally low, and what little there is dissolves at the high pH and moves with the soil water. The thin black organic coating that forms at the soil surface has caused sodic soils to be given the name "black alkali." Water seeping from a sodic soil into a drainage ditch or other outlet appears brown and oily with dissolved organic matter. Nothing grows on such soils, and they are very difficult to reclaim. Reclamation techniques are discussed in Chapter 16.

Saline, sodic, and salt-free soils are often mixed in the same landscape. These are usually alluvial bottomlands that have spots and lenses of gravel, sand, silt, and clay in unpredictable patterns. The variations in texture cause variations in capillary rise that produce the soil differences. Salt-free soils occur, for example, where a gravel lens interrupts the capillary rise.

15-3 LIMITATIONS RESULTING FROM WETNESS

The original land survey maps for some of the flatter parts of the U.S. Corn Belt labeled whole counties as "unfit for agricultural use" because the soils were poorly drained. The rolling land was considered best because excess water could escape. Erosion on the hills and drainage on the flats have since reversed the ratings. The flat land now produces significantly higher yields than the hills.

The surveyors were undoubtedly concerned with the physical problems of wet soils—especially the lack of support for animals and vehicles and the stickiness of soils with high clay contents. Mosquitoes and flies would also have been significant to them. These factors are still important along with other physical and chemical limitations.

15-3.1 Physical Limitations of Wet Soils

Wetness interacting with texture has a strong influence on soil strength. Water weakens the bonds between clay particles and makes it easier for them to shift under a load. A wet clay soil becomes very weak, especially for supporting a load concentrated on a small area.

A pure sand behaves quite differently than a clay, as a sandy beach will illustrate. Dry sand is easily displaced by anything that moves. It will form dunes or cones up to the slope at which the grains cease to interlock. Moistening the sand increases its strength. Sand castles with vertical walls can be built with moist sand because the water films bind the particles together. Vehicles travel easily on the moist sand a few meters inland from the water line. However, the vehicles are likely to sink and get stuck if they stray into the dry sand above or the wet sand below the water line. Saturated sand loses the binding effect of water films because there are no air-water interfaces to produce surface tension. Also, the water provides buoyancy that makes the particles easier to move than dry sand. An upward flow of water can provide enough added buoyancy to separate the sand particles from each other and produce the extreme lack of support known as quicksand.

Most soils contain enough clay to provide binding strength to support a load when dry, but neither clay nor sand provides much

Figure 15-4 Cattle trampled this pasture when it was wet, killed about half of the grass, and produced a rough surface. (Courtesy F. R. Troeh.)

498

strength under very wet conditions. Also, thick films of water make clay particles sticky, causing soil to adhere to feet, wheels, and other objects.

Traffic across a wet soil causes soil damage like that shown in Figure 15-4. The soil that shifts out of the way or is compacted under feet and wheels is often converted into a puddled mass that dries to a smooth, hard surface that may resist later penetration by plant roots. Animal and vehicular traffic should therefore be kept away from wet soils for the sake of both soil and traffic.

Wetness often postpones tilling and planting for several days. The more clay the soil contains, the longer the delay. Soil wetness in temperate climates is usually accompanied by low soil temperatures in the spring (Note 15-1). The coldness contributes to planting delay because the seed might rot and not germinate. Even a few wet spots in a field create a problem. The farmer must either wait for them to dry before working the whole field or work around them and leave them until later.

NOTE 15-1 EFFECT OF WETNESS ON SOIL TEMPERATURE

Wetness lowers the temperature of soil in two ways—by evaporation and by the heat capacity of the water. Each gram of water evaporating requires 585 cal of heat to change from liquid to vapor at $20°C$ (539 cal at $100°C$). More water evaporates and therefore more heat is withdrawn from a wet soil than from a dry one. This cooling effect increases as the soil temperature rises because water evaporates faster from a warmer surface. Cooling by evaporation remains significant until the soil surface becomes dry.

The heat capacity of water does not actually cool the soil but it does increase the amount of heat required to raise the temperature. The heat capacity of water is 1.0 cal/g whereas that of dry soil is about 0.2 cal/g. A comparison of a representative dry soil and a similar wet soil will illustrate the effect of heat capacity:

	Soil near wilting point	*Saturated soil*
Percent H_2O by weight	20%	60%
Heat capacity per gram of solid:		
From solids	0.2 cal	0.2 cal
From water	0.2 cal	0.6 cal
Total heat capacity	0.4 cal	0.8 cal

Heat applied to the saturated soil in this example would raise its temperature only half as fast as it would raise the temperature of the dry soil, even without allowing for evaporation.

The actual temperature difference between wet and dry soils is limited by the tendency of cool soil to absorb more heat and lose less than warm soil. Wesseling (1974) cites data from researchers who either measured temperature differences in drained and undrained soils or calculated theoretical differences. Most differences ranged from 2° to 4°C between drained and undrained sandy soils and from 0.5° to 1°C in clay soils. The clay soils showed less difference because they retained more water when they were drained.

The importance of differences in soil temperature was demonstrated by Walker (1969). He found that 1°C difference in temperature could make as much as 50% difference in initial growth rates of early-planted corn.

A rain heavy enough to produce runoff often causes ponds to form in low spots even after a crop has been planted. Sometimes the crop is drowned and the wet spot remains bare or becomes a weed patch unless it is retilled and replanted. Another problem may occur if the crop has been planted but not yet germinated when a heavy rain falls. The pounding by raindrops followed by silt settling out of standing water produces a puddled surface that dries into a crust too hard for seedlings to penetrate.

15-3.2 Chemical Effects of Wetness

Most chemical effects of wetness are related to the shortage of oxygen that results when a soil is saturated with water. Oxygen concentrations influence plant growth and seed production (Hardy and Quebedeaux, 1974). Plant roots need oxygen for respiration to provide energy for growth, nutrient absorption, and other life processes. Small amounts of oxygen may be obtained from water as in solution culture, but this source requires frequent replenishment. Rice and a number of other water-loving plants have mechanisms for absorption of oxygen by the upper part of the plant and transport within the plant to the roots. But most plants lack such mechanisms and rely on oxygen absorbed from soil air. Their roots will not grow into saturated soil or even into soil that has isolated pockets of air in its larger pores. There must be enough interchange with the atmosphere to replenish the oxygen supply in the soil and exhaust carbon dioxide.

Research by several workers has indicated that minimum oxygen diffusion rates between 5 and 25×10^{-8} g of O_2/cm^2 per minute are needed for the root growth of a wide variety of plants. On a volume basis, Patt, Carmeli, and Safrir (1966) reported that citrus trees need 8% to 10% air space at field capacity in the 25- to 75-cm layer to produce an adequate root density. The effective depth of many soils is limited by excess water causing poor aeration rather than by an unfavorable physical layer.

Certain plant nutrient deficiencies can be attributed to soil wetness. Two of these will be discussed here—potassium and nitrogen. Several others could be added, especially if the effects of pH changes produced by draining wet soils, as discussed in Section 15-2, were considered.

A given content of soil potassium is less adequate in a wet soil than in one that has better aeration. The potassium is said to be physiologically unavailable because the plant roots are less able to absorb it from a soil that is too wet. Plants normally absorb so much potassium that it is much more concentrated inside the roots than in the soil water. Such absorption requires energy derived from root respiration and is therefore slowed by the shortage of oxygen in wet soil.

Nitrogen deficiencies are most likely to result in soils that are alternately saturated and unsaturated for a few days at a time, as was the soil shown in Figure 15-5. Nitrifying bacteria convert ammonium ions to nitrates during the periods when oxygen is available. Other microbes reduce the nitrates to gaseous N_2, N_2O, and NO during the saturated periods. This denitrification process can use up large quantities of available nitrogen and produce a deficiency whether the nitrogen came from soil sources or from fertilizer.

Another kind of chemical problem results where metal pipelines cross both wet and dry soils. The difference in redox potential causes an electrolytic action that ionizes metal, creating pits in the pipe that may become holes in one-fourth to half of its normal life expectancy. Saline soils make the problem worse because dissolved salts increase the electrical conductivity of the water.

15-4 WATER REMOVED BY DRAINAGE

Soil water is commonly classified as unavailable, available, and gravitational, according to how tightly it is held in the soil. The line between unavailable and available water is known as the wilting point and is usually assumed to be at either 15 bars or 15 atmospheres (1 atm = 1.0127 bars) of soil moisture tension. Actually, the change

Figure 15-5 This corn is pale green as a result of nitrogen deficiency caused by denitrification in this intermittently wet area. The cracked and curled soil surface is another result of ponding. (Courtesy F. R. Troeh.)

is gradational and varies a few bars according to the plant, soil, and atmospheric conditions. The line between available and gravitational water is called field capacity and is commonly taken to be one-third bar. It, too, is gradational and varies from values as low as one-tenth bar for very sandy soils to as high as one-half bar for clay soils. These fractional changes in soil moisture tension near field capacity influence the amount of available water as much as variations of several bars near the wilting point, as shown by the soil moisture retention curve in Figure 15-6.

Field capacity is defined in terms of water movement rather than soil-moisture tension. It is the amount of water retained by the soil when downward movement into dry soil below nearly ceases. The time required varies from about a day for sandy soils to three or four days for soils with low permeability. The dry soil below is an important factor because the soil-moisture tension of a loamy soil exerts as much force on the water as about 3 m of gravitational head. Sandy soils exert 1 or 2 m of tension and clay soils as much as 5 m.

Soils with water tables obviously do not have dry soil below to

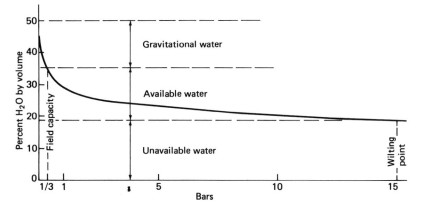

Figure 15-6 A soil-moisture-retention curve showing water relationships in a representative loamy soil with 50% pore space.

exert soil-moisture tension. The gravitational force can be taken as the only force on the soil water if salt concentrations and temperature conditions are equal throughout the soil.

A subsurface drainage system would theoretically have to lower the water table to a depth of 3.4 m to produce a tension of one-third bar at the soil surface. Because few drains are placed that deep, most do not remove all of the gravitational water even from the upper part of the soil. Figure 15-7 shows the amount of air space resulting from a drain at a depth of 2 m in a soil like that of Figure 15-6.

15-5 SURFACE VERSUS SUBSURFACE DRAINAGE

Drainage systems can be described and classified in several ways. This section will consider the removal of water either before it has entered the soil (surface drainage) or after (subsurface drainage). Later sections will consider ditches, tile, and other mechanisms of water removal and the various layout patterns of drainage systems.

The natural development of stream systems (Ch. 3) provides surface drainage for most sloping land. Areas that need artificial surface drainage are either nearly level or depressional. The excess water to be removed has not had time to infiltrate and therefore has probably not moved very far. Most of it comes from precipitation either directly on the wet land or on the watershed above it. Surface

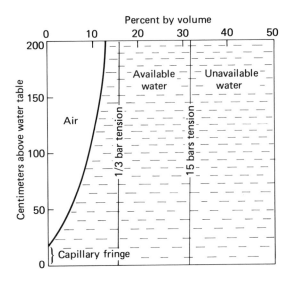

Figure 15-7 Air and water held by a soil like that of Figure 15-6 above a water table at 2 m.

drainage is most useful where slowly permeable soils occur in level or depressional areas in humid climates.

Subsurface drainage is used where sufficient water has entered the soil to cause a high watertable. The water may have come from precipitation on the land, surface flow, seepage from nearby land, or from seeping through an aquifer from a long distance. Irrigation water also contributes to the need for subsurface drainage in irrigated areas. Whatever the source, the water is already in the soil and must be removed.

15-6 METHODS OF REMOVING WATER

Ditches are often used for surface drainage and tile for subsurface drainage, but there are exceptions. It is possible to use ditches for subsurface drainage and tile lines can have surface inlets. Several other drainage methods are also available including land smoothing, wells, bedding systems, mole drains, and other types of subsurface channels. The preferred method of drainage depends on the amount of water to be removed, soil characteristics, cost and convenience factors, availability of equipment and materials, and personal preferences.

15-6.1 Land Smoothing

Filling the low places in a field is called land smoothing or, in irrigated areas, land leveling. Irrigation-land leveling improves both the irrigation and the drainage of the land. Actually, the leveled land usually has a gentle slope that is as uniform as possible rather than being absolutely level. Elimination of high and low areas in a field is costly, but it makes it much easier for an irrigator to obtain uniform water application with a surface irrigation system.

Land smoothing for drainage purposes can improve both surface and subsurface drainage. The surface drainage is improved by eliminating depressions so that water can flow across the area without being trapped. Subsurface drainage is improved because the soil surface of the former low area is raised higher above the water table.

The drainage improvement achieved by land smoothing makes the field more uniform in its drainage characteristics. This is likely to be the only drainage practice needed in fields like the one shown in Figure 15-8 where only the depressions are too wet. Land smoothing may also be used in other fields to make a ditch or tile drainage system function better. An important advantage of land smoothing is that it usually requires no maintenance.

15-6.2 Drainage Ditches

Cato discussed Roman methods of farm drainage by ditches as an established practice in 200 B.C. (King, 1931). The Egyptians, Baby-

Figure 15-8 Land smoothing to allow water to escape would have saved the crop in this depression in an Iowa corn field. (Courtesy F. R. Troeh.)

lonians, and perhaps others evidently practiced drainage centuries before Cato's time. Ditches can be used for either surface or subsurface drainage or for both at the same time. They offer high capacity, even with nearly level channels. Installation costs are usually less than those for a covered drain installed at the same depth. Ditches often require more maintenance than covered drains to remove sediment and unwanted vegetation that inhibit the water flow, but they are easy to check and it is easy to see when maintenance is needed. Ditches such as that shown in Figure 15-9 are often used for main drains and as outlets for tile and other covered drains.

The principal disadvantages of ditches relate to the land area occupied by the channel and the banks that often accompany it. This land would probably be good cropland if a covered drain were there. In addition, the ditch is an obstacle and may be a hazard to the movement of people, animals, and machines. These disadvantages are usually least serious along a fence or other field boundary.

Minor variations in ditch gradient cause variability of water depth but are much less serious than similar variations in covered drains. Ditches are therefore preferred for draining land that is unstable and may settle unevenly. Sometimes an area is drained initially by ditches that are later replaced by covered drains after settling has ceased.

Figure 15-9 This 6-m-deep ditch in Idaho serves as an overflow for irrigation water if the canal above gets too full, as an interceptor for seepage water, and as a drainage outlet for drainage systems in the valley. (Courtesy F. R. Troeh.)

The ditch gradient is sometimes controlled by a small elevation difference between the wet land and the outlet. The steepest gradient used should produce a nonerosive velocity of no more than 0.2 to 0.8 m/sec, depending on the erosiveness of the soil.

Ditches are usually widely spaced—hundreds of meters apart where possible—to minimize the obstacle problem and the amount of land removed from crop production. Ditches for surface drainage vary in size according to the amount of water they must carry. They should be designed to carry the maximum anticipated flow when filled to 80% of their depth. Their capacities can be calculated by Manning's formula, as explained in Note 4-2.

Ditches for subsurface drainage are usually dug considerably deeper than tile drains would be placed. Depths of 2 to 3 m permit ditches to provide drainage in many soils even though they are spaced 100 to 200 m or more apart. Soils that need more drainage may have tile lines between ditches that are 400 m or more apart. These ditches, too, need to be 2 to 3 m deep to serve as outlets for the tile.

The slope of the ditch banks is an important design factor. Often the steepest stable slope (the angle of repose) is sought in order to minimize the amount of soil to be moved and the land area occupied. A safety margin should be allowed, and maintenance requirements need to be considered. Donnan and Schwab (1974) indicate that common side slopes in clay soils range from 0.5:1 (0.5 m horizontal to 1 m vertical) to 1.5:1 and that side slopes for coarser-textured soils are between 1:1 and 2:1, with some very sandy soils needing slopes of 3:1. Cleaning by dragline requires side slopes no steeper than 1:1, grazing by livestock requires slopes of 2:1 or flatter, and banks to be crossed by machinery or mowed should have slopes no steeper than 3:1 (Soil Conservation Service, 1973).

Vegetation is both a help and a detriment to drainage ditches, as shown in Figure 15-10. Vegetation on the banks helps stabilize them against slumping and erosion and may be of value for wildlife. Vegetation such as water lilies, cattails, and other water plants, however, slows the water flow, raises the water level, and reduces the effectiveness of the drain. The effectiveness of a ditch for subsurface drainage is, after all, limited by its water level regardless of how deep the ditch may be. Major maintenance costs are often incurred to keep vegetation from plugging drainage ditches.

15-6.3 Tile Drainage

Tile lines are the method usually chosen when a drainage system must extend into the interior of a field. They are especially common

Figure 15-10 Vegetation is helping stabilize the banks of this drainage ditch, but the vegetation growing in the water slows the flow and raises the water level. (Courtesy F. R. Troeh.)

for subsurface drainage and are also used with surface inlets to drain depressions and low areas above terraces. This last use has developed mostly in recent years as a means of making terraces as straight and parallel to one another as possible (Ch. 10) and to eliminate the grassed waterways previously used.

Tile drainage has been practiced in flat croplands for hundreds of years. The oldest tile, known as horseshoe tile, were made of baked clay with a U-shaped cross section. They were placed with the open side down in the bottom of a trench, sometimes with a flat clay pallet beneath them. These tile were invented in France about the fourteenth or fifteenth century, then forgotten and later re-invented in England in the seventeenth or eighteenth century (King, 1931). The practice of tiling was brought from Scotland to the United States in 1835 (Wooten and Jones, 1955). All tile were made by hand until a tile-making machine was invented in England in 1841. All tile were placed in hand-dug trenches until about 1883, when a steam-powered trenching machine was first marketed. Almost all tile are now placed by wheel-type or bucket-ladder-type trenching machines, most of which can dig as deep as 1.8 m. Cuts deeper than 1.8 m are dug with special large trenchers, backhoes, or draglines and are considerably more expensive.

The advantages of tile for drainage include a smooth land surface that permits normal equipment and livestock traffic across the field. A good system should function for hundreds of years with relatively minor maintenance (some sewer tile thousands of years old are still serviceable). The biggest disadvantage is cost—unless, of course, something prevents tile drainage from working. Conditions that limit the use of tile include shallow soil, excessive stoniness that interferes with installation, and soils with hydraulic conductivities below 0.5 to 1 cm/hr.

Types of Tile. Three types of tile are now in common use—clay, concrete, and plastic. All three types have round cross sections in preference to the original horseshoe tile. Clay tile are the traditional type, made by forming moist clay into short lengths of pipe (usually 30 cm long) and baking them until they are dry and hard. They are available with inside diameters ranging from 10 to 30 cm. The walls are usually between 12 and 15 mm thick. Clay tile are brittle and will deteriorate if subjected to freezing and thawing but are otherwise very durable. Cracked clay tile lack the characteristic ring of good tile and should be rejected.

Concrete tile are similar to clay tile except that they are usually longer (60 or 90 cm) and are available in larger sizes (up to 90 cm diameter). Concrete tile resist freezing and thawing and are therefore better than clay tile for lines that are above the frost line. Concrete is subject to attack by acids and therefore should not be used in extremely acid soils (Soil Conservation Service, 1973).

The newest type of tile is made of either polyvinylchloride or polyethylene plastic and began to be marketed in the 1960s. It is a thin-walled plastic with a corrugated form that adds to its strength and makes it flexible. As shown in Figure 15-11, it comes in rolls 70 to 90 m long and is slotted so water can enter. Diameters range from 7.5 to 25 cm. Plastic resists damage by both freezing and acids but there have been reports of rodents chewing holes in it. It is less rigid than clay or concrete and relies more on proper packing of soil around it for support to keep it from collapsing. The continuity and easy joining of lengths of plastic tile eliminate the misalignment problems that can occur with clay or concrete.

Several types of pipe, including steel, aluminum, rigid plastic, and fiber, are used where strength or rigidity are needed in a drainage system. Most of these are not true tile because they have no holes for water to enter. A 6-m length of corrugated steel is especially common at the outlet of a tile line. Rigid pipe may also be needed where a tile line passes under a road, through a very deep cut where

Figure 15-11 The newest type of tile is made of corrugated plastic, comes in rolls, and has slots sawed in it for water to enter. (Courtesy F. R. Troeh.)

the overburden is heavy, or through an organic soil that may shrink and settle unevenly.

Depth and Spacing of Tile Lines. Old hand-dug tile lines were often placed at depths of about 50 or 60 cm. The shallow lines had to be spaced only 5 or 6 m apart in some fields. Most lines are now placed at depths between 70 and 130 cm in humid regions and about 200 cm in arid regions. The greater depths give protection from frost, heavy vehicles, and plant roots and permit a wider spacing between lines. The 2-m depth for arid regions is to prevent capillary movement from carrying salts to the soil surface. Many tiling contractors charge extra for placing tile deeper than 120 cm. Tile lines are now commonly placed between 10 and 40 m apart depending on the soil and the depth of placement.

Soil permeability is a factor in determining the depth and spacing of tile lines. Less permeable soils need closer-spaced, shallower lines to remove the water within a reasonable time. The horizontal permeability is more important than the vertical permeability for determining rate of drainage because most of the water has to move farther horizontally than vertically. Basak (1972) found that soil structure tends to cause the hydraulic conductivity in the horizontal direction to be 1.0 to 1.6 times as high as in the vertical direction. The variation in permeability from one soil horizon to another should also be considered. Increased depth of penetration into a less permeable horizon may not affect water removal, although equal penetration into a more permeable layer may be very beneficial.

Tile lines can rarely be placed at a uniform depth throughout their length because they must also have suitable slope gradients for water flow. Donnan and Schwab (1974) suggest a minimum gradient of 0.1% for 10-cm drain lines and 0.05% for 15-cm lines. Beauchamp (1955) suggests that even large tile lines should have gradients of at least 0.05% and that special practices are needed where gradients are steeper than 1%. Steeper line gradients require that tile joints be wrapped with tar-impregnated paper or other durable material and packed tightly with soil to keep the tile properly aligned and on grade. Or, sewer tile with sealed joints can be used where the line must pass through steeper areas that do not need drainage. Breathers (vents) to allow air entrance are sometimes needed at the top of a slope, and relief wells at the bottom, to prevent pressure buildup and to facilitate the flow of water.

Laying Tile. Tile were laid with tiling hooks as shown in Figure 15–12 long after trenching machines were developed. Some machines made a wide enough trench for a worker to ride inside a trailing shield in the trench and place the tile by hand. New machines provide a tile chute that automatically guides tile from an aboveground loading point down into place in the trench. Nearly all plastic tile is placed automatically as shown in Figure 15–13. Such machines can lay tile at rates up to about 40 m per minute (Fouss, 1971).

The depth of tile placement by trenching machines is usually controlled by a guide line or a laser beam. Either method requires a survey of the area so that depths and gradients can be planned. The guide-line method involves setting stakes to hold a line at a specified height above the level of the tile line. The machine operator then keeps a pointer on the machine at the level of the guide line.

The laser method is an example of new technology applied to an old problem. The laser beam is aimed parallel to the desired grade line in place of the staked guide line. A photo sensor on the tiling machine detects the laser beam and controls a hydraulic unit that raises or lowers the machine to keep it on grade. The laser unit can control the depth for distances up to 500 m with a vertical accuracy of 1 cm (Agricultural Research Service, 1967).

Figure 15-12 Concrete tile being placed with tiling hooks behind a trenching machine. (Courtesy W. H. Lathrop.)

Figure 15-13 Plastic tile being installed by a tiling machine. (Courtesy USDA—Soil Conservation Service.)

Plastic tile has slots for water to enter, but clay and concrete tile allow water entrance only at the joints. Rough ends on the tile may keep them far enough apart to permit water to enter freely, but many tile are so smooth that they can fit too tightly together. Openings of 2 or 3 mm are recommended for most soils. Larger openings, such as those resulting from changes in direction, should be covered to keep soil from entering the tile.

The nature of the soil or other material next to the tile is important. It needs to be permeable to water, stable enough to stay out of the tile and not plug the entrances, and shaped to contact the tile and give support on all sides. Some soil can meet these requirements, but some will not. Some surface soils have a stable granular structure and will serve for *blinding* (surrounding and covering) the tile. A sand and gravel mixture can be used for blinding if suitable soil is not available.

15–6.4 Other Closed Drains

Drains that are covered and concealed are called closed drains. Tile lines are the leading type, but several others have been used including box drains, rock drains, and mole drains. The mole drain is the only one of these latter types currently used to drain anything but very small areas.

Box drains consist of three or four boards made into a box with triangular or rectangular cross section and buried in a trench. They have a short life expectancy unless treated with a wood preservative to keep them from rotting. They and rock drains are usually homemade and were most common in pioneer times.

Rock drains are constructed by placing several layers of rocks in the bottom of a trench and covering them with soil. The capacity is low and becomes even lower if soil fills the space between the rocks.

Mole drains are drawn rather than laid. A torpedo-shaped "mole" attached to the bottom of a long plow shank is pulled through the soil to create an unlined channel about 10 cm in diameter. Mole drains are commonly made at depths of 50 to 75 cm and spaced 3 to 5 m apart. The close spacing and the fracturing produced by the plow shank help make mole drains effective. Any open slots left by the shank should be closed as soon as possible by tillage to prevent surface soil from being washed into the mole channel by the next rain.

Mole drains are relatively inexpensive and can be quickly made when the soil is dry on top and moist at the depth of the mole. They should be drawn more slowly if the soil is wet because a vacuum can form and cause the channel to close behind the mole. The lift expectancy of mole drains depends on the stability of the soil. Sandy soils are too unstable for their use. Properly constructed moles in clay subsoils will probably last from three to fifteen years; those in organic soils may last three to five years. If necessary, a new set can be drawn when the old set becomes ineffective. Mole drains are best suited for temporary drainage of an area where the need may disappear (as for the removal of excess salts from a saline soil) or where a more permanent drainage system will be installed later (as for an organic soil that will settle unevenly when it is first drained).

15–6.5 Bedding Systems

Surface drainage on land with slope gradient less than 1% is sometimes accomplished by a bedding system. These systems are most often used in humid regions on soils whose slow permeability and moderate depth prevent the use of most other types of drainage. They are the most common type of surface drainage in Europe. The crops are often grasses and legumes used for pasture or hay, although some row crops and truck crops are grown on bedded land.

Bedding is also called crowning because the areas between drains are usually graded into a raised convex shape. The grading is sometimes accomplished by always plowing in the same direction, but it is much faster to use earth-moving equipment. Shallow grassed waterways about 0.5 m deep with about 8:1 side slopes are located between the crowned areas. These should be oriented with the natural slope of the land so they will have enough gradient for water to flow. Row crops may be grown on the crowned areas but not in the waterways. The rows run the length of the crowned areas, parallel to the waterways. The crowned areas are usually about 20 m wide, their exact width being a multiple of the width of the equipment used to crop them.

15–6.6 Vertical Drainage

Both pumped wells and dry wells are used for drainage. Pumped wells lower the water table in places where highly permeable material occurs at a suitable depth. Pumped wells are relatively expensive to install and operate, but they can reduce the water table to lower levels than other drainage methods and the pumped water may be useful for irrigation or livestock. Pumped wells may also be used to remove water from aquifers and thus reduce their contribution to water tables and springs.

Dry wells, otherwise known as drainage wells or vertical drains, act as wells in reverse. Either surface or subsurface water from a depressional area is permitted to run into the well and down to an absorbing layer below. This apparently happy solution to a drainage problem entails some hazards that limit its use. One is that sediment carried into the well may plug the pores in the absorbing layer. Sediment can be reduced by filtering the water before it enters the well. Another peril is the pollution potential of draining surface water into an underground aquifer. Most states have laws restricting or prohibiting the use of dry wells for public health reasons.

15-7 RANDOM, REGULAR, AND INTERCEPTOR DRAINS

The layout of a drainage system may or may not show a regular pattern. The topography of the area, source of the water, and pattern of wetness are important factors in determining whether a drainage system will be random, regular, or interceptor.

Random drains are used where small wet areas are separated by higher, drier land. The drains go through one wet area and on to the next, usually through the lowest connecting areas. The layout of the ditches or tile lines is determined by the locations of the wet spots.

Regular drainage systems drain broad flat areas where several parallel ditches or tile lines are needed. A variety of patterns are possible, including two basic ones known as parallel and herringbone, as shown in Figure 15-14. Laterals may enter the main drain from one or both sides in either system, but the angle of the herringbone pattern allows both the laterals and the main line to flow down the general slope of the area rather than directly across it.

Interceptor drains are placed between the source of the water and the area needing drainage so the water can be led away. The drain must be deep enough to catch the main flow of water and must run across that flow. The water being intercepted in humid regions comes from natural precipitation whereas in arid regions it may come from an irrigation canal.

15-8 DESIGN FACTORS FOR DRAINAGE SYSTEMS

The first factor to be considered in the design of a drainage system is what land should be drained. The area that will be benefited and

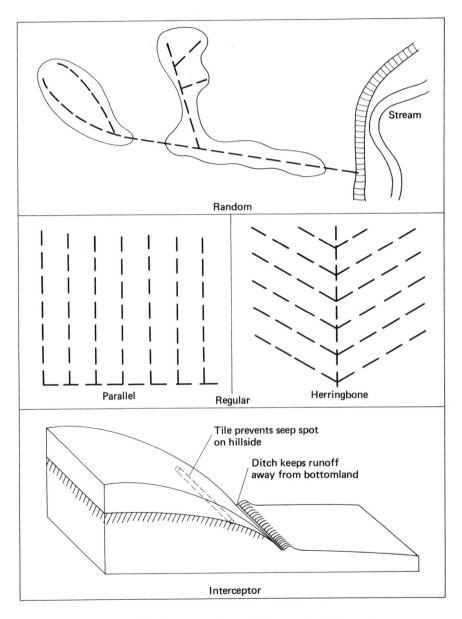

Random

Parallel

Regular

Herringbone

Tile prevents seep spot
on hillside

Ditch keeps runoff
away from bottomland

Interceptor

Stream

Figure 15-14 Random, regular, and interceptor drainage systems each have their own distinctive layout patterns.

nearby areas that might be harmed by removal of water should be identified and mapped. Then the nature of all of the land involved must be considered. Soil maps, topographic maps, geologic maps, and hydrologic maps are all useful and may need to be obtained if they are not already available.

A soil survey can be helpful for identifying both problems and potentials. It shows where the wet soils are and which soils are clay soils, organic soils, sodic soils, or soils with impermeable layers within or beneath them. Soils shallow to bedrock are identified on soil maps. Soil surveys also show which soils are permeable enough to drain easily or are already well enough drained for their intended purpose.

Soil maps show some topographic information such as soil slope, but more precise information is needed for drainage design. The elevations of the outlet and of high and low points throughout the system must be known. Often a full topographic survey showing contour lines and elevations of critical points is worthwhile. Some elevations may need to be measured even if a topographic map is already available.

Geologic maps tell what underlies the soil to a greater depth than soil maps. Permeable layers that can carry water either in or out of the area are identified, and the nature and locations of impermeable rock layers are revealed.

Hydrologic maps show the source of the water, the direction of its movement, and the depth of the water table at various points. They help identify places where an interceptor drain can be used instead of placing ditches or tile in the field being drained.

A combination of all of these types of maps plus field observation is ideal and may be necessary for a complex project. However, many projects are simple enough to be designed from available maps plus some field observations to supply any missing information. Aerial photographs are often very helpful. For example, a strip of sandy soil that conducted water into the corner of an orchard in Idaho was much easier to see on an aerial photograph than on the ground.

15-8.1 Choosing the Type of System

Decisions regarding drainage systems are based on information from the maps and other sources discussed in the preceding paragraphs and the choices of the persons involved. Some choices become obvious as information is gathered. The Idaho orchard mentioned in the last paragraph should be drained by an interceptor system. Rolling land with several low wet areas needs a random system, whereas a large uniformly wet area calls for a regular system (parallel or herringbone).

Surface drainage works where water stays on the land surface long enough to be gathered and carried away. Subsurface drainage is the only choice when the water enters the soil rapidly or as artesian water from beneath. Sometimes a combination system is best, with some water being removed from the surface and some from beneath.

The decision to use ditches, tile lines, wells, or some other method to remove excess water is strongly influenced by economics and convenience factors that relate to the amount of water involved and the use of the land; preferences and customs are also factors. Tile lines are advantageous in fields where ditches would be in the way. Ditches, on the other hand, are often used for main outlets where the high volume would require very large tile that might be too expensive. The special adaptations of other types of systems were explained in Section 15-6.

15-8.2 Layout of a Drainage System

The outlet is one of the most important parts of a drainage system and is a natural beginning point for a design. Its location and elevation are both significant to the placement of ditches and tile lines. Also, the outlet must have adequate capacity to handle the added water and be legally accessible for that purpose.

Figure 15-15 shows the layout of three different kinds of drainage systems on a farm in a humid region. The water from all three systems is drained into a main ditch beside the road along one side of the farm. This ditch was built and is managed by a drainage company. The smaller ditches and the tile lines belong to the farm owner.

The bottomland in the southwest corner of Figure 15-15 is surrounded by ditches on all sides. The main ditch is about 2.5-m deep across this bottomland and the two farm ditches have gradients of about 0.1%, so the water flows at nonerosive velocities into the main ditch. All three ditches have side slopes of 1.5:1. The soil in this bottomland is sufficiently permeable that these three ditches provide adequate drainage, especially since the ditch next to the slope intercepts both surface and subsurface water. Like many ditches, these all have so much surplus capacity that no calculation is required. Where needed, ditch capacities can be calculated by Manning's formula as explained in Note 4-2. If it had been needed, additional surface drainage for the bottomland could have been pro-

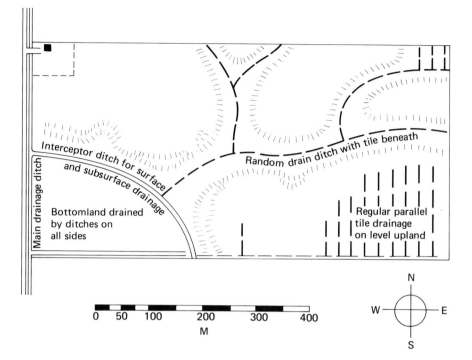

Figure 15–15 The drainage systems on this 32-ha area include a bottomland surrounded by drainage ditches, a level upland with a regular parallel tile drainage system, and a random system of ditches with tile beneath. The single branch tile line near bottom center of the map allows air to enter the line at the top of the slope.

vided by a few field ditches or a bedding system, and subsurface drainage could have been supplemented by tile lines.

The level upland in the southeast corner of Figure 15–15 is drained by a regular parallel tile drainage system. The most important design factors for a system such as this are the depth, spacing, gradient, and size of the tile lines. These are placed approximately 1.2 m deep at the main line and as shallow as 0.9 m at the upper ends of the laterals. A spacing of 25 m between lines was chosen for this moderately permeable soil. Each lateral is made of 10-cm clay tile and is placed on a controlled gradient of 0.2%. The upper end of each lateral is closed to keep out soil and animals.

The laterals in most tile drainage systems have more than adequate capacity, but appropriate calculations must be made to determine the size of main line required. A *drainage coefficient* telling how much water must be removed in twenty-four hours must be assumed. For the tile drainage system shown in Figure 15–15, the drainage coefficient is taken as 1.0 cm/24 hr. For other places it might range from about 0.3 to 4 cm/24 hr (Table 15–1). The drained area is equivalent to a rectangle 150 m wide by 250 m long, so the amount of water to be removed is

$$150 \text{ m} \times 250 \text{ m} \times 1.0 \text{ cm/24 hr} \times 1 \text{ m/100 cm} = 375 \text{ m}^3/24 \text{ hr}$$

The main line in Figure 15–15 has a slope gradient of 0.1% through most of its length and needs a 15-cm tile to transport this quantity of water (Table 15–2). A 20-cm tile would have been needed if there had been surface inlets into the line.

The gradient of the main line increases to about 1% for the last 100 m before it empties into the ditch. This change in gradient could produce a vacuum that would draw soil into the lines. Two methods are available to avoid this problem. One is to install a surface inlet so air can enter the line at the top of the slope. The other is to use a short branch line as shown in Figure 15–15 to allow air to enter through dry soil. The bottom of the main line is protected by a 6-m length of corrugated steel pipe that spills the water into the middle of the drainage ditch. This pipe prevents the water from producing a gully by undercutting tile. Three rods inserted through holes in the end of the pipe prevent animals from entering. Many tile lines have been plugged by animals that crawled as far into a tile line as they could and died there because they could not turn around.

The random drains shown in Figure 15–15 are a combination of field ditches and tile. These ditches range from 0.5 to 1 m in depth, have bottom widths of 0 to 2 m and side slopes between 3:1 and

Table 15–1 Drainage coefficients for subsurface tile drainage[a]

	Field crops (cm/24 hr)	Truck crops (cm/24 hr)
Arid regions (irrigated):	0.3–0.6	0.6–1.2
Humid regions:		
Mineral soils	0.6–1.2	1.2–1.8
Organic soils	1.2–1.8	1.8–4.0

[a]These values should be doubled or a known amount added where surface drainage is also carried by the tile.

SOURCE: Based on Soil Conservation Service, 1973, and Donnan and Schwab, 1974.

Table 15-2 Flow velocities[a] and carrying capacities[b] of well-aligned clay or concrete tile[c]

	Tile gradient				
	0.05%	*0.1%*	*0.2%*	*0.5%*	*1.0%*
10-cm tile:					
Velocity of flow, m/sec	[d]	0.25	0.36	0.56	0.79
Capacity m^3/24 hr	—	171	241	381	539
12.5-cm tile:					
Velocity of flow	0.21	0.29	0.41	0.65	0.92
Capacity	219	309	437	692	978
15-cm tile:					
Velocity of flow	0.23	0.33	0.47	0.74	1.04
Capacity	356	503	711	1120	1590
20-cm tile:					
Velocity of flow	0.28	0.40	0.56	0.89	1.26
Capacity	766	1080	1530	2420	3420
25-cm tile:					
Velocity of flow	0.33	0.46	0.65	1.04	1.46
Capacity	1390	1960	2780	4390	6210
30-cm tile:					
Velocity of flow	0.37	0.52	0.74	1.17	1.65
Capacity	2260	3190	4510	7140	10100

[a]Velocity based on Manning's formula adapted to pipe diameter in meters and slope as a decimal = $36.9D^{2/3}S^{1/2}$.

[b]Capacity = $\pi r^2 \cdot$ velocity $\cdot$ time

[c]The corresponding values for corrugated plastic drain tubing are about two-thirds as large.

[d]Ten-cm tile is not recommended on 0.05% slope.

4:1. They are about 6 m wide and are crossable with farm machinery. These have a cover of smooth bromegrass to prevent erosion. Other sod-forming grasses such as Kentucky bluegrass, tall fescue, bermudagrass, and dallisgrass can be used, each in its own appropriate climatic zone. Reed canarygrass in cool climates and bahiagrass in warm climates offer tough sods that resist gully formation even in severe conditions. Switchgrass has become important for field ditches in recent years because it resists grass-control herbicides such as the triazines that have killed the grass in many waterways.

Tile lines are located under one side of the field ditches to provide subsurface drainage so the waterway will dry between rains. These are 10- or 15-cm tile, with the larger size being used for the lower part of the main line because it carries the most water. They are located at the side of the ditch area to reduce the likelihood of surface water entering through cracks and washing holes down to the tile line. The upper ends of the lines are closed and the lower end is protected by a steel pipe the same way as the regular tile drain already described. The three short lines in the northeast corner of Figure 15-15 constitute a small regular tile drainage system that drains through the random tile line.

15-8.3 Installing a Drainage System

The installation of a drainage system begins at the outlet and moves toward the upper end. Moving constantly upward permits water to escape so that no pond is formed. In fact, the gradient of some systems has been controlled without surveying by watching how fast the water flowed away while the ditch or trench was being dug. Surveying is strongly recommended, though, to allow planning of the system and more accurate control of the installation.

Junctions involve special techniques in both ditch and tile systems. Branch ditches are often given a short length of steeper gradient near the junction so their water level will be at least as high as the deeper water in the larger ditch. This prevents water from backing up and depositing sediment in the branch ditch.

Tile joints need to fit together as tightly at junctions as anywhere else to keep out soil. Many lines have been installed by "chipping tile" (breaking out pieces to make them fit), but the use of manufactured junction tile is recommended for a faster and better installation. Special junction tile are available for branches, corners, and size changes. These and the pipe needed for the outlet and perhaps for road crossings or other vulnerable areas should be on hand when the job begins.

Installing surface inlets to tile lines involves special techniques. Inlets need to be located in the lowest point on the land surface to completely drain the area, though some land smoothing can be done, if necessary, to move the low point. Surface inlets need protection from being hit by machinery. Many are installed in fencelines or enclosed in a small area. Others are made either tall and conspicuous or else low enough to permit traffic to cross them. The tall types have holes or slots that control entrance; the low types are covered by gratings. These should be checked frequently to remove any trash that may have accumulated. Another variation, the "blind inlet," consists of tile placed in the bottom of a pit filled with gravel or small stones.

Any type of inlet should have openings small enough to keep out animals and trash. Also, surface inlets should enter a branch line about 5 m long rather than going directly into a main tile line. The main line will then function even when the inlet line is plugged.

Occasionally a drain is needed in an area that stays too wet for drainage equipment to operate. Dynamite has been used successfully to open drains in some such areas. This method works where the soil is cohesive but is not satisfactory for gravel or loose dry soils. Bennett (1947) gave suggestions for the procedure involving charges placed about 50 to 75 cm apart and 75 cm deep. Some trial dynamite charges should be set off first to determine the optimum placement and size of charge.

15–8.4 Maintenance of Drainage Systems

Drainage ditches need to be kept clean and free of excess vegetation and debris. Sometimes enough sediment accumulates in them to require removal. Field ditches may fill up as high as the land alongside them in a few years time. They must then be completely re-excavated. Regular maintenance is essential to keep any ditch functioning properly.

Grass growing on ditch banks is usually desirable for erosion control, but reeds and cattails in the water slow the flow and raise the water level, making the ditch less effective. Some ditches become so clogged with vegetation that they lose all effectiveness. Several techniques including mowing, burning, use of herbicides, and hand removal of vegetation, are used to limit the amount of growth in ditches, but none gives a permanent remedy.

Tile lines also need maintenance, though less frequently than ditches. Sometimes the tile outlet is covered by debris or by high water in an outlet ditch. The covered outlet may cause water to deposit sediment in the line and thus reduce its capacity. Also, pressure builds up in the line and water may flow out into the soil, washing out a hole into which the tile falls. The resulting misalignment allows soil to enter and block the line. Similar problems result when a heavy load crushes one or more tile.

Problem spots in tile lines show themselves either as wet spots or as holes in the field. Either of these conditions should be checked promptly by digging a hole to expose the tile. The damage can then be repaired and the hole refilled. Excessive delay permits more soil to be washed into the line; sometimes sections of the line become so blocked by sediment that they have to be dug up, cleaned, and relaid.

15-8.5 Inadequate Drainage Systems

Sometimes a drainage system becomes inadequate either because the soil conditions change or because a new crop with stricter requirements is grown or planned. It may then be necessary to add to the system so it will again function adequately. The procedure for a ditch system is simplified because the existing ditches are easily located. The planning may proceed the same as for an original system.

A need for additional tile lines may be noticed when the area midway between lines stays wet too long after a rain. Unfortunately, this wetness does not reveal the exact location of the tile lines and therefore does not tell exactly where new tile should be placed. If available, a well-made map of the original system can be very helpful. Sometimes the old lines can be seen faintly on an aerial photo or located by watching for tile chips or different-colored soil in the field. The fastest-drying soil and the earliest-maturing crops may also help identify the approximate locations of tile lines. Precise locations can then be determined with a probe and suitable plans made for enlarging the system.

SUMMARY

Wet lands occur in arid as well as in humid climates wherever more water enters an area than can exit conveniently. Wet soils are identified by black, rust, bluish-gray, and white colors. They usually have higher organic-matter contents and often have more montmorillonitic clay than neighboring soils. Reducing conditions occur in wet soils and influence their chemical behavior. Wet soils containing sulfides can become extremely acid when drained, and those with excess sodium salts can become extremely alkaline.

The limitations resulting from wetness depend on how wet the land is, when the wetness occurs, and how long it stays wet. Clay soils become sticky when wet and may become too weak to support a load. Sandy soils are strongest when moist but not wet. Traffic on wet clay soil can puddle it and make it hard when it dries. Wet soil delays planting because of coldness as well as wetness. Lack of oxygen prevents root growth of most plants and results in denitrification and reduced availability of potassium.

Surface drainage removes water before it enters the soil. Subsurface drainage removes part of the gravitational water after an excess accumulates in the soil. Either surface or subsurface water can be removed by ditches, tile, or any of several other methods. Land smoothing and bedding systems are additional means of surface drainage. Mole drains are the least expensive and shortest-lived means of subsurface drainage. Both pumped wells and dry wells are sometimes used for drainage.

Ditches offer high capacity and are less expensive than tile, but they occupy significant land areas and are inconvenient to have in fields. Tile cost more, especially in large sizes, but allow traffic to move unrestricted and require less maintenance than ditches. Tile are available in clay, concrete, and plastic and are usually placed at depths between 70 and 130 cm in humid regions or about 2 m in arid regions.

Drainage systems are designed in random, regular, or interceptor patterns. Soil maps, topographic maps, geologic maps, and hydrologic maps are all helpful for design purposes. The outlet is a very important feature of a drainage system and is the beginning point for installation. A drainage coefficient must be assumed in calculating how much capacity is needed before minimum tile or ditch sizes and gradients can be determined. After a drainage system is installed, it needs to be checked occasionally and given proper maintenance to keep it functioning properly.

QUESTIONS

1. Explain how well-drained, somewhat poorly drained, and poorly drained soils are identified in the field.
2. What causes some wet soils to become extremely acid when drained and others to become extremely alkaline?
3. What factors determine whether a drainage system should be surface or subsurface, ditch or tile, and random or regular?
4. Describe a circumstance where an interceptor drain would be useful and explain how it would be installed.
5. How does land smoothing improve drainage?
6. What special precautions are needed for locating and installing a tile drainage outlet?

REFERENCES

AGRICULTURAL RESEARCH SERVICE, 1967. Laser beam controls pipe depth. *Agr. Research*, USDA, Apr., p. 8–9.

BASAK, P., 1972. Soil structure and its effects on hydraulic conductivity. *Soil Sci.* 114:417–422.

BEAUCHAMP, K. H., 1955. Tile drainage—Its installation and upkeep. In *Water*, USDA Yearbook of Agriculture, U.S. Govt. Printing Office, p. 508–520.

BENNETT, H. H., 1947. *Elements of Soil Conservation.* McGraw-Hill, New York, 406 p.

DONNAN, W. W., and G. O. SCHWAB, 1974. Current drainage methods in the U.S.A. In *Drainage for Agriculture,* Agronomy No. 17, American Society of Agronomy, Madison, Wisc., p. 93-114.

FAUSEY, N. R., and G. O. SCHWAB, 1969. Soil moisture content, tilth, and soybean (*Glycine max.*) response with surface and subsurface drainage. *Agron. J.* 61:554-557.

FOLLETT, R. F., R. R. ALLMARAS, and G. A. REICHMAN, 1974. Distribution of corn roots in sandy soil with a declining water table. *Agron. J.* 66: 288-292.

FOUSS, J. L., 1971. Tomorrow's drainage systems today. *Crops and Soils* 23(7): 12-14.

GRASS, L. B., A. J. MACKENZIE, B. D. MEEK, and W. F. SPENCER, 1973. Manganese and iron solubility changes as a factor in tile drain clogging: II. Observations during the growth of cotton. *Soil Sci. Soc. Am. Proc.* 37:17-21.

HARDY, R. W. F., and B. QUEBEDEAUX, 1974. Oxygen—A key growth regulator. *Crops and Soils* 26(4):10-13.

KING, J. A., 1931. *Tile Drainage.* Mason City Brick and Tile Co., Mason City, Iowa, 108 p.

PATT, J., D. CARMELI, and I. SAFRIR, 1966. Influence of soil physical conditions on root development and on productivity of citrus trees. *Soil Sci.* 102:82-84.

RYCROFT, D. W., and A. A. THORBURN, 1974. Water stability tests on clay soils in relation to mole draining. *Soil Sci.* 117:306-310.

SOIL CONSERVATION SERVICE, 1973. *Drainage of Agricultural Land.* Water Information Center, Inc., Port Washington, New York, 430 p.

VOORHEES, W. B., D. A. FARRELL, and W. E. LARSON, 1975. Soil strength and aeration effects on root elongation. *Soil Sci. Soc. Am. Proc.* 39:948-953.

WALKER, J. M., 1969. One degree increments in soil temperatures affect maize seedling behavior. *Soil Sci. Soc. Am. Proc.* 33:729-736.

WESSELING, JANS, 1974. Crop growth and wet soils. In *Drainage for Agriculture,* Agronomy No. 17, American Society of Agronomy, Madison, Wisc., p. 7-90.

WOOTEN, H. H., and L. A. JONES, 1955. The history of our drainage enterprises. In *Water,* USDA Yearbook of Agriculture, U.S. Govt. Printing Office, p. 478-491.

ZWERMAN, P. J., 1969. *Land Smoothing and Surface Drainage.* Cornell Extension Bull. 1214, Cornell Univ., Ithaca, New York.

16

Irrigation
and Reclamation

Irrigation and reclamation are powerful means of increasing land productivity. Irrigation, the addition of water to meet plant needs, overcomes drought limitations and improves both the quality and the quantity of crop production. Reclamation, the irrigation, drainage, salt removal, or other amelioration of soils so that better crops can be grown on them, expands the land base for crop production. Both irrigation and reclamation are needed to supply the food and fiber needs of the world's growing population.

Irrigation and reclamation are obviously significant in arid regions (Note 16-1). Most land reclamation by addition of water is limited to arid and semiarid conditions, but supplemental irrigation to meet special or occasional needs is used in subhumid and even humid climates.

NOTE 16-1 ARID CLIMATES AND ARID REGIONS

An arid climate is defined in *Soil* (the 1957 Yearbook of Agriculture, p. 752) as "A very dry climate like that of desert or semidesert regions where there is only enough water for widely spaced desert plants." Arid regions are defined as "Areas where the potential water losses by evaporation and transpiration are greater than the amount of water supplied by precipitation." The arid-region definition encompasses the areas of arid climates plus large additional areas classified as semiarid climates.

The maximum precipitation for arid climates and arid regions depends on temperature and, to some extent, on the season during which most of the precipitation occurs. It is suggested in *Soil* that the upper limit of precipitation for arid climates is about 250 mm per year in cool regions and about 500 mm per year in tropical regions. The upper limit of precipitation for an arid region is two to three times as high as for an arid climate.

The precipitation in arid climates is seasonal and erratic as well as limited in amount. Plants must either grow during short periods of favorable moisture or rely on irrigation. The erratic nature of the precipitation adds to the difficulty of growing crops.

Some wet soils occur within and near arid regions and even in arid climates. Many of these regions are hilly or mountainous and have much more precipitation at the higher elevations. Water flows or seeps down to the lower elevations where some of it saturates the soil in low areas. Some runoff and seepage occur and create local wet spots even from the limited precipitation within an arid area. These wet spots can often be used as sources of water for household or livestock needs. Some of the larger ones fed by water from higher elevations can be developed for irrigation water sources.

Irrigation is practiced in many countries. Every continent has some irrigation, but Asia has about three times as much as all other continents combined. China is in first place with about 76 million hectares of irrigated land followed by India with 27.5 million (Table 16-1).

16-1 EFFECTS OF IRRIGATION

Irrigation has a great impact on the agriculture of an area. It changes low-priced grazing land into expensive cropland. New crops can be grown and much of the risk taken out of growing established crops, even in humid regions. Farming systems, including field arrangements, crops, tillage, and fertilization are adjusted to work with the irrigation system. All operations depend on the irrigation schedule. Costs and returns are both increased, and better management is needed to take advantage of the opportunities while avoiding the pitfalls.

16-1.1 Increased Production with Irrigation

The low level of food production under arid conditions can be increased manyfold if irrigation water is available for land reclamation. Land that formerly supported only a few grazing animals per square

Table 16-1 Irrigated land in the major irrigating countries of the world (data mostly for the years 1968 to 1971)

Country	Irrigated area (millions of hectares)	Cultivated area (millions of hectares)	Percentage of cultivated land irrigated
1. China	76.0	110.3	68.9
2. India	27.5	164.6	16.7
3. United States	15.8	192.3	8.2
4. Pakistan	12.5	19.2	65.0
5. USSR	11.1	232.8	4.8
6. Indonesia	6.8	18.0	37.8
7. Iran	5.3	16.7	31.4
8. Mexico	4.2	23.8	17.6
9. Iraq	3.7	10.2	36.2
10. Egypt	2.9	2.9	100.0
11. Japan	2.8	5.5	51.5
12. Italy	2.4	12.4	19.7
13. Spain	2.4	20.6	11.8
14. Thailand	1.8	11.4	16.0
15. Argentina	1.6	26.0	6.0
16. Turkey	1.5	27.4	5.7
17. Australia	1.5	44.6	3.3
18. Chile	1.1	4.6	23.6
19. Peru	1.1	3.0	37.5
20. Bulgaria	1.0	4.5	22.6
Total	203.6	1457.0	14.0

SOURCE: Economic Research Service, 1974.

kilometer has been converted to high production of a wide variety of crops. The change requires many more workers to manage the land.

Irrigation in humid regions does not necessarily change the crop to be grown, but it does increase production. Irrigation can increase yields even in humid areas when the time between rains is too long for the available water in the soil to adequately meet crop needs. A surplus of water at another time is of no use if it is lost by runoff or deep percolation. The available water-holding capacity of the soil is therefore significant in determining irrigation needs. A deep loamy soil able to store 25 or 30 cm of water for plant growth can support a crop through a much longer dry period than a shallow or sandy soil storing only 10 cm.

A reliable water supply increases yields so much that 30% to 40% of world agricultural production comes from the 14% of cropland that is irrigated (Booher, 1974). Adequate water often improves the crop quality as well as increasing the quantity. Drought can cause problems in nutrient absorption, cell development, fruit production, and other growth factors that affect crop quality.

Irrigation systems offer some protection from crop hazards other than drought. For example, sprinkler systems have been turned on to protect sensitive fruit crops from frost damage. The heat released by freezing water holds the temperature near 0°C rather than letting it drop low enough to freeze plant tissue. Similarly, warm temperatures can be cooled a few degrees by frequent light irrigation to increase evaporation for protection against hot summer periods.

16-1.2 Hazards of Irrigation

Hazards as well as benefits are associated with irrigation and reclamation. For example, the high costs create an economic hazard. Also, excess salts accumulating from improper use of water can ruin soil productivity, as shown in Figure 16-1. Some such soils can be reclaimed, as will be discussed later in this chapter, but the effort is not always economical.

Erosion hazards are often increased by irrigation. In some fields, every irrigation forms rills and removes large amounts of soil. The cumulative effects of many such irrigations can be ruinous. Deposition of sediment can also lead to staggering costs that make continued irrigation impractical. The best cure for such problems is a well-designed program of soil and water conservation. The conservation potential is so great in some places that the thicker vegetative cover produced with irrigation can reduce erosion to below the natural rate. More commonly, however, erosion increases with irrigation but can be held to tolerable rates.

The hazards associated with irrigation have led some observers to suggest that all irrigation systems are temporary. In fact, some irrigation systems have never produced a marketable crop. Others have failed after a few years, decades, or centuries of use. Sodic soils that will not produce a crop can cause early failure. Erosion and sedimentation cause longer-term problems. Even so, it is unfair to suggest that the failure of some irrigation systems means that all will fail.

Gulhati and Smith (1967) enumerate many examples of long-lasting irrigation systems. Egyptians have been practicing basin irrigation for more than 5000 years. Iranians are still using *kanat* (tunnels)

Figure 16-1 Excess salts prevent crop growth in this spot in a barley field in California. Similar bare spots can result from sodic conditions or high concentrations of boron. (Courtesy U.S. Department of Agriculture.)

that are 2500 years old to supply irrigation water, as shown in Figure 16-2. Japanese paddy fields have been irrigated for more than 2500 years. Irrigation works in Peru appear to have been built before the time of Christ. Other ancient irrigation works occur in India, Pakistan, China, Central America, southwestern United States, and in other arid regions. Some of these have been abandoned, but many are still in use. Some have been resurrected when modern surveyors laying out a new system discovered they were following the precise course of a long-lost, sediment-filled canal.

16-2 SELECTING LAND FOR IRRIGATION

Several factors must be favorable for irrigation to be practical. Soil factors will be considered in this section and water in the next. Other important factors such as climate, suitable crops, roads, and markets will be assumed to be favorable.

Important soil factors that can make the land difficult and unprofitable to irrigate include depth, texture, slope, and salt content.

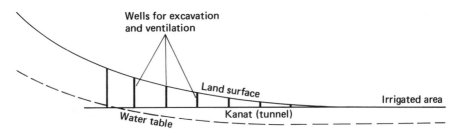

Figure 16-2 Kanat are used in several Asian countries to tap the water table under higher land and carry it out onto the lower land.

Many of these factors are already known for land that has previously been cropped either with or without irrigation. A preliminary evaluation of uncropped land can be made visually by observing the topography and vegetation of the area (more vegetative cover than average usually means better than average soil). Soil maps and topographic maps are very helpful.

The minimum depth of soil for irrigation varies with other soil properties, the crop, and the irrigator. Any soil less than 150 cm deep may limit yields to some degree, and less than 100 cm is often considered a limiting factor. Nevertheless, some soils that are only 30 cm deep to hard bedrock are used for irrigated cropland. Such shallow soils require frequent light irrigation because their water-holding capacity is low, the plant root zone is limited, and deep tillage is out of the question. The topography must be left unchanged because little or no land leveling can be done on these shallow soils. Erosion control is vital to retain what little soil there is.

A loamy soil texture throughout the solum is desirable for most purposes, though sandy loam is sometimes preferred for ease of tillage, faster infiltration rate, and easy harvesting of root crops. Extremely sandy soils have low water-holding and nutrient-storage capacities and are easily eroded by surface irrigation. Wind erosion becomes a serious factor with fine sand. Clay soils have some of the opposite problems—low infiltration rate, waterlogging, and stickiness. A clay subsoil can cause infiltration and waterlogging problems even if the surface soil is favorable. Nearly pure silt, as found in some loess or alluvial deposits, can have moderately low infiltration rates and is the easiest texture of all to erode by running water. Stony conditions cause tillage difficulties, and any kind of coarse fragments reduces the water-holding capacity of the soil.

A slope gradient of about 0.5% is ideal for surface irrigation. Slopes flatter than 0.2% are difficult to irrigate by surface methods because of the depth of water required to make it flow fast enough to irrigate long rows uniformly. Such problems can be solved by using basin, trickle, or sprinkler irrigation or by "leveling" the field into segments that have enough slope for the desired method of irrigation. The problems are more serious where slopes are too steep or irregular. Trickle, sprinkler, or contour irrigation offer only limited solutions. Large elevation differences make uniform water application more difficult no matter what method is used. Variable soils and slow infiltration rates that make it difficult to avoid runoff are common complications.

Erosion is a potential problem wherever surface irrigation is practiced on slopes steeper than 2%. In the United States, the usual maximum slope for irrigation varies from 3% in the Gulf Coastal Plain to 6% in the central Great Plains to 20% for pasture and hay in Colorado, to 35% with good cover in the Pacific Northwest (Maletic and Hutchings, 1967). Irregularities in slope gradient and direction make irrigation more difficult than uniform slopes.

Salt content may be the easiest soil limitation to overlook, yet it may make the soil barren, as shown in Figure 16-1. Salt problems vary from minor and easily remedied to severe and not worth reclaiming. Reclamation techniques are discussed later in this chapter. The main items to be noted here are that excess salts, high percentages of sodium, and boron concentrations are hazards to plant growth.

16-3 WATER FOR IRRIGATION

The water supply for irrigation is usually more limiting than the area of suitable soil. Most of the water available in arid regions is already in use. Humid regions have more water available, but not always at the right place and time. Water supplies tend to be deficient when they are most needed.

Inadequate supplies of water result in competition among irrigators, would-be irrigators, and other types of users such as cities and factories. Furthermore, streams and lakes need to have water left in them for fish, wildlife, recreational, and navigational use. No single need can supersede all the others.

16-3.1 Water Rights

Both economic and legal aspects are involved in water usage. The simplest application of economics would be to sell the water to the highest bidder. A more complex analysis is needed, however, to allow for the interaction between water and land values—often the water is not for sale apart from the land. Laws regulating the use of water also have considerable impact on its economic value.

Legal water rights in the United States are underlain by two doctrines known as *riparian rights* and *prior appropriations*. The riparian rights doctrine is based on old English law and is used in the eastern part of the United States, as shown in Figure 16-3. Riparian rights are related to ownership of land along a stream or lake. Nobody owns the water, but land owners own the right to use it in certain ways (Busby, 1955). The water can be used for domestic needs including household, livestock, garden, and lawn, regardless of the effect on stream flow. Other uses are allowed if they do not diminish downstream flow or if they are within the land owners' reasonable share of the water remaining after all domestic needs are satisfied. Riparian rights give a low priority to the use of water for irrigation.

The prior appropriations doctrine used in western United States is based on beneficial use of water. A potential user must apply to the state for a permit to divert and use a certain amount of water from a certain place (Busby, 1955). The permit is granted if the water has not previously been granted to someone else. The water can then be diverted to the land where it is to be used even if the land is not adjacent to the water source. A license is granted after the water is diverted and put to beneficial use. This license is renewable as long as the beneficial use continues uninterrupted; it is treated as real property that can be bought and sold. Irrigation and other nondomestic water rights are given higher priority under the prior appropriations doctrine than under riparian rights.

Other laws can modify or supplement the riparian rights and prior appropriations doctrines. In some states, for example, municipalities and some other organizations can obtain water by condemnation proceedings. Under other circumstances, a use that has continued for at least twenty years (or some other specified legal period) may attain legal status.

Many recent laws designed to maintain water quality place limitations on the sewage, chemicals, and other pollutants that can be emptied into streams or lakes. Also, water used for cooling a power or manufacturing plant must not be warm enough to damage aquatic life when it is returned to the stream.

16-3.2 Surface Water

Water supplies in streams and lakes are used for irrigation on both small and large scales. Irrigation began thousands of years ago with

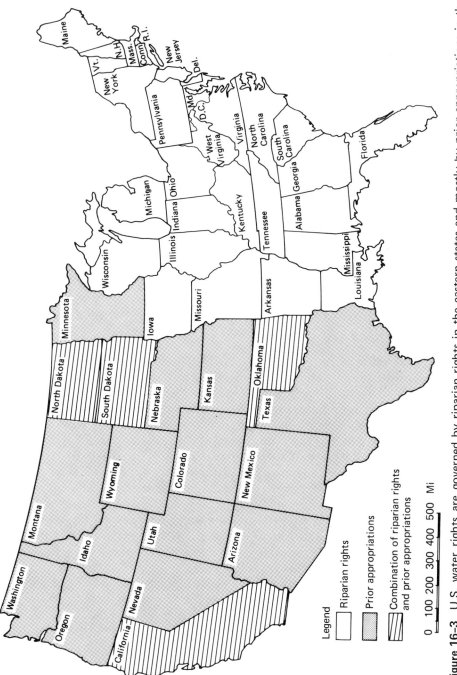

Figure 16-3 U.S. water rights are governed by riparian rights in the eastern states and mostly by prior appropriations in the western states. A few states use both.

Legend

☐ Riparian rights

▦ Prior appropriations

▨ Combination of riparian rights and prior appropriations

0 100 200 300 400 500 Mi

simple diversions of stream water through a ditch onto nearby bottomland. Large diversions are now distributed to many users by canal and ditch systems.

Bottomland is usually irrigated first because a diversion a short distance upstream is high enough for the water to reach the land by gravity flow. Higher land requires either a long canal to carry water diverted far upstream, a high dam, or a means of lifting the water. Many lifting devices have been used, including water wheels, Archimedean screws, and various types of pumps. Pumps were once powered by people or animals but in developed countries are now driven by engines or electric motors. These ancient methods are still common in developing countries.

Irrigation by diversions is limited by low stream flow during dry seasons. An upstream reservoir can increase the water supply and make it more reliable. Such reservoirs are often best placed on a small tributary rather than on the main stream. A diversion from the main stream can be used to help fill the reservoir without requiring the reservoir to accept all the flood waters and sediment carried by the main stream.

16-3.3 Harvesting Rainwater

The amount of runoff water available for irrigation and other uses is sometimes increased by treating the land surface to produce more runoff. The runoff can be stored in a reservoir and used as a water supply for households, livestock, gardens, small fields, and wildlife. Rainwater harvest has been practiced for thousands of years and can be used where average annual rainfall is as low as 50 to 80 mm (Council on International Relations, 1974).

Ditches were used in ancient times to harvest rainwater from hillsides or from gentle slopes where the natural soil permeability was slow. Newer practices include treating soils with sodium salts to decrease soil permeability and using water-repellant compounds such as asphalt, paraffin, or silicone to make the soil surface impermeable. Some projects have used large sheets of plastic covered with a layer of gravel for their runoff-producing area.

Harvested rainwater may be guided directly to a field or garden and distributed through some form of irrigation system. A simple water-spreading system can be very helpful in places where the climate is too arid for the desired crops but the soil is deep enough to store enough additional water.

Storage reservoirs are needed when collected water is to be saved for later use. Evaporation is an important consideration because the air is usually very dry in areas where this kind of water storage is needed. A deep reservoir with minimum surface area helps to reduce evaporation. Still less evaporation occurs from an oversize reservoir filled with stones, gravel, and sand as shown in Figure 16–4. The sand filters the water and thus improves its quality. Water is removed from such reservoirs through a well shaft.

16–3.4 Underground Water

Far more fresh water is stored underground than aboveground. It has been estimated that there is enough underground water to cover the land surface to a depth of about 30 m (Thomas and Peterson, 1967). Much of this water is unobtainable because it is locked into small pores or occurs at great depth. Also, much of it occurs in humid regions where not all of it is needed. Still, there is much underground water that could be used for irrigation, as shown in Figure 16–5.

Good supplies of groundwater depend on porous rock layers that are permeable enough to release water and well enough connected to the surface to be recharged. Gravel and sand layers beneath valleys are usually good sources; sandstone, limestone, and some basalt flows are also potential sources. Most other rocks are too dense to release water at a significant rate.

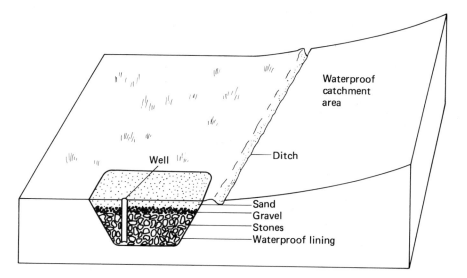

Figure 16–4 A landscape cross section showing a catchment area and storage basin for harvesting rainwater.

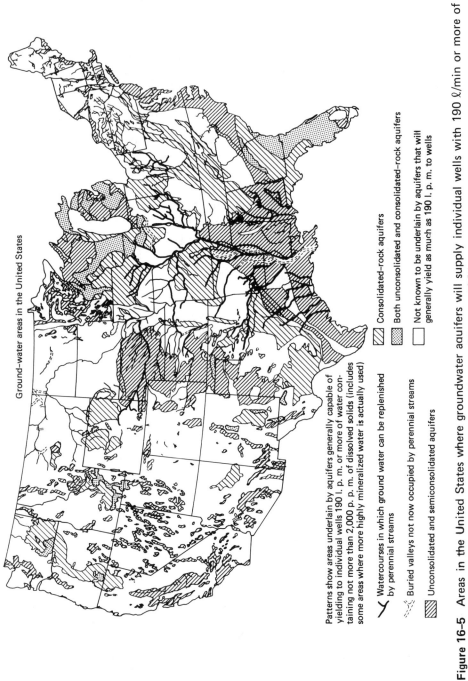

Ground-water areas in the United States

Patterns show areas underlain by aquifers generally capable of
yielding to individual wells 190 l. p. m. or more of water containing not more than 2,000 p. p. m. of dissolved solids (includes
some areas where more highly mineralized water is actually used)

Y   Watercourses in which ground water can be replenished
    by perennial streams

    Buried valleys not now occupied by perennial streams

    Unconsolidated and semiconsolidated aquifers

    Consolidated-rock aquifers

    Both unconsolidated and consolidated-rock aquifers

    Not known to be underlain by aquifers that will
    generally yield as much as 190 l. p. m. to wells

Figure 16-5 Areas in the United States where groundwater aquifers will supply individual wells with 190 ℓ/min or more of
water containing less than 2000 ppm dissolved solids. (Source: Thomas, 1955.)

Groundwater has several advantages over surface water: (1) The soil and rock layers serve as a reservoir that minimize yield fluctuations from wet to dry periods. (2) The temperature, salt content, and other quality factors are relatively constant and favorable in most places. (3) A well near where the water is to be used makes long conveyor systems and the attendant rights-of-way unnecessary. (4) Land that has no rights to surface water under the riparian rights doctrine may still be irrigated with groundwater (but the prior appropriations doctrine often applies to groundwater as well as surface water).

Long-term groundwater use must be based on recharge rates rather than on the amount present. The old system of *kanat* shown in Figure 16-2 lasted for centuries because it could withdraw water only from the upper part of the water table. Some wells are pumped until the water table is lowered to where they no longer supply adequate water, then drilled deeper and pumped some more. Some wells in southwestern United States are now pumping water from depths of 300 m. In a few decades, the wells have removed "fossil water" that took many centuries to accumulate. Such wells will eventually be abandoned and cropping discontinued on the land they irrigate.

Sometimes there are two water tables under the same land—a perched water table near the surface and a permanent or main water table below, as shown in Figure 16-6. Persons seeking a reliable water supply should not be misled by the perched water table. It will usually disappear during dry seasons.

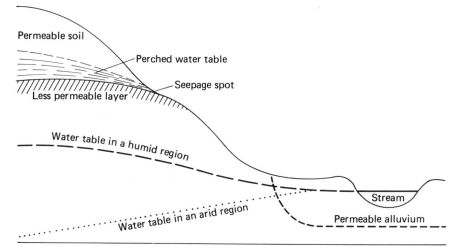

Figure 16-6 Representative forms of a perched water table and permanent water tables in humid and arid regions.

Another significant factor shown in Figure 16-6 is the difference between permanent water tables in humid and arid regions. Water percolates through humid region soils into the substratum and down to the water table. The water table is therefore high enough at all points for water to flow toward an escape point such as a stream or spring. In an arid region, evaporation and plant growth use all of the available water; the substratum stays dry, and most of the soils have no permanent water table. Percolation forming a water table in an arid region occurs only where water is concentrated as in a stream or in a wet soil in a low place. Consequently, the water table slopes away from these water sources.

Although underground water is most often obtained from wells, other possibilities should not be overlooked. Some springs are large enough and reliable enough to be used for irrigation. A spring is especially convenient when its elevation is high enough to supply the needed water without pumping. Other good sources of underground water occur where gravel pits, rock quarries, or other excavations reach below the water table.

16-3.5 Icebergs

Glacial ice contains about three-fourths of the world supply of fresh water. Snow adds to the ice every year as it moves slowly but steadily toward the ocean. Some glacial ice melts before it reaches the ocean, but much of it breaks off and floats away as icebergs. Many icebergs are huge—many kilometers across and hundreds of meters thick. They melt and break apart as they float in the ocean.

The idea of using icebergs as sources of fresh water was seriously explored in a conference at Ames, Iowa, in 1977. Some of the countries occupying desert lands of southeastern Asia are most interested in icebergs as a potential source of fresh water. Technical problems of navigating the icebergs, controlling their melting, containing the meltwater, and distributing the water are still unsolved.

16-3.6 Desalinized Water

Oceans contain 97% of the water on earth, but it is too salty for most uses. Ocean water and brackish water can be desalinized by various techniques including several forms of distillation, electric membrane processes, and ion-exchange resins. Some of these methods are useful for modest needs such as supplying water for a ship at sea or even for city water supplies, but all are too expensive for irrigation purposes. Furthermore, transportation and lifting costs would be expensive additions to the desalinization costs if the water were to be used anywhere except at low elevations near a coast.

16-3.7 Water Quality

Water falling as rain or snow is nearly pure H_2O. The initial runoff into a nearby stream is still relatively pure unless it erodes enough soil to pick up a significant sediment load. Water that seeps through soil and rock layers, however, dissolves various materials. Water containing more than 50 parts per million (ppm) calcium and magnesium salts is considered medium hard, and more than 100 ppm causes it to be classified as hard water because much soap is required for cleaning purposes. These limits are still far below the acceptable amount of salt for irrigation water.

Streams pick up more and more seepage water and dissolved salts as they flow into flatter areas and lower elevations. The salt content increases more rapidly in arid regions than in humid regions because the dilution factor is smaller. In addition, the water in arid regions is likely to have been diverted, used for irrigation, and returned to the stream several times. The salt concentration increases each time this cycle is repeated, as less water and more salt returns to the stream. The highest concentrations occur in arid regions because arid soils contain the most salt to be leached, and in the lower parts of long small rivers because the length permits several leaching cycles to occur and the small water volume gives minimum dilution.

Four factors should be considered for predicting the effect of a particular kind of irrigation water on soils and crops: (1) total salt concentration, (2) the proportion of Na^+ to Ca^{++} and Mg^{++} ions, (3) toxic ions, and (4) solid matter such as weed seeds and sediment.

High salt concentrations make it difficult for plants to absorb water. The soil must therefore be kept at a high moisture content for the sake of plant growth. Additional water is needed to leach the salts from the soil so it will not become saline. The traditional leaching requirement has been based on salt concentrations in the irrigation and drainage waters:

$$\text{leaching water} = \frac{\text{salt conc. in irrigation water}}{\text{salt conc. in drainage water}} \times \begin{array}{l} \text{amount of} \\ \text{irrigation} \\ \text{water} \end{array}$$

The salt concentration in drainage water is often taken as the concentration that would cause a 50% decrease in yield in uniformly saline soil. Some researchers have maintained that a smaller amount of leaching water will suffice if salts are allowed to precipitate outside the root zone with trickle irrigation or in the lower part of the root zone with surface irrigation (Agricultural Research Service, 1974).

Total salt concentration can be evaluated on any of several scales. Electrical conductivity in mmhos/cm has been widely used because it is easily, quickly, and reliably measured with a conductivity meter. Other measures of concentration can be estimated by these approximations:

$$1 \text{ mmho/cm} \cong 750 \text{ ppm} \cong 0.075\% \cong 10 \text{ meq/liter} \cong 0.01 \, N$$

Water quality classes for salt concentration as used by the U.S. Department of Agriculture are shown on the horizontal scale in Figure 16-7.

The sodium hazard of irrigation water is evaluated by the sodium adsorption ratio (SAR) shown as the vertical scale in Figure 16-7. The SAR value is calculated as:

$$\text{SAR} = \frac{\text{Na}^+}{\sqrt{(\text{Ca}^{++} + \text{Mg}^{++})/2}}$$

where the ion concentrations are expressed in milliequivalents per liter. High SAR values are hazardous because such water tends to produce the high exchangeable sodium percentages (ESP) that characterize saline-sodic and sodic soils. High proportions of bicarbonate ions in the water increase the tendency to produce sodic soils because HCO_3^- reacts with Ca^{++} and Mg^{++} and causes CaCO_3 and MgCO_3 to precipitate. This removal of Ca^{++} and Mg^{++} from the system increases the SAR and ESP values.

Borate ions are the most common toxic ions in irrigation water. Apples, cherries, grapes, and several other fruit and nut crops are sensitive to boron concentrations as low as 1 ppm. Boron-tolerant crops such as alfalfa, asparagus, and date palms tolerate boron concentrations up to 3 or 4 ppm. Chlorides and some other ions may occur in water in concentrations high enough to be detrimental to plant growth but are seldom toxic to plants. Several ions, however, can be toxic to animals without injuring plant growth. These include ions of arsenic, fluorine, lithium, nitrogen (nitrate), selenium, and several heavy metals when they are present at concentrations much above normal.

Solid matter in irrigation water can cause a variety of problems or, occasionally, be helpful. Sediment can block irrigation furrows and smother young plants. Smaller quantities of sediment can plug soil pores and thus reduce permeability. Reduced permeability might be good for a very porous soil, but it is detrimental to most soils. Sediment may also carry pesticides and other chemicals from the soil where they were applied to other crop areas or bodies of water where they are not wanted. Various soil conservation techniques are the best solution to sediment problems.

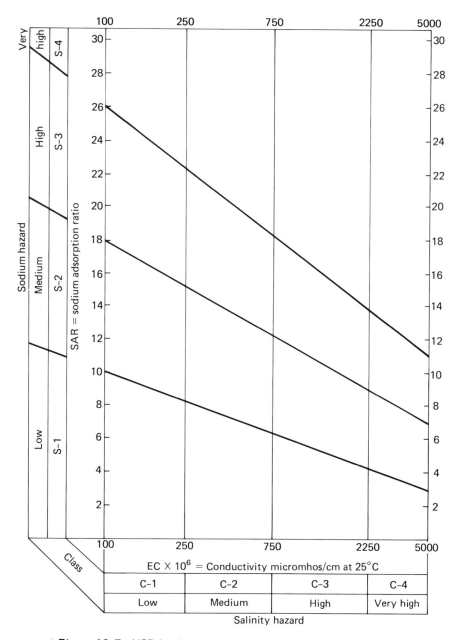

Figure 16-7 USDA classes of salinity and sodium hazard for irrigation water. (Source: *Diagnosis and Improvement of Saline and Alkali Soils,* USDA Agr. Handbook 60, 1954.)

Weed seeds are another form of solid matter that can cause problems. Too many irrigation reservoirs and ditch systems are lined with weeds. The irrigation system is a ready-made conveyor for distributing weed seeds through the fields.

16-4 DISTRIBUTING WATER

Canals and ditches are generally used to distribute water for surface and subsurface irrigation; pipelines are needed for sprinkler and trickle irrigation. Canal systems are operated by irrigation districts, companies, or cooperatives that sell water to individual farmers. Sometimes a government agency such as the U.S. Bureau of Reclamation is involved in building the reservoirs, diversions, canals, and main ditches to deliver the water to users.

Canals normally flow on a flatter gradient than the rivers from which they were diverted. Thus they gradually reach a position along the side of the valley and some distance above the river. Several hazards exist where they cross permeable alluvial fans, go around or through hills, and cross the valleys of tributary streams. Large water losses on the alluvial fans produce seepage spots below the canal—the canal needs a clay or concrete lining through such areas. Landslides and sediment eroded from an overgrazed hillside may obstruct the canal—upland drainage and reduced grazing are needed to stabilize the hillside. Often the canal must cross tributary streams in a flume, on a fill, or through a large pipeline. The valleys are expensive to cross even if the streams are dry during the irrigation season.

Water from a canal is often subdivided three or four times on its way to the fields. First, a main ditch or lateral is led away from the canal, often down the divide between two tributaries to the river from which the canal was diverted. Smaller ditches that serve a few farms branch from the lateral. Even after the water reaches the individual users, it may be divided into still more parts to irrigate individual fields and parts of fields.

16-4.1 Measuring Water Flow

Each division point requires a metering device to control the flow of water. These may be adjustable metal gates that partially cover a submerged opening, or an adjustable opening for the water to spill over. Most division points also involve a device to measure how much water is being delivered. Weirs are the most common measuring devices; they are relatively inexpensive and a good installation has an accuracy of ±2%. Three styles of weirs are shown in Figure 16-8.

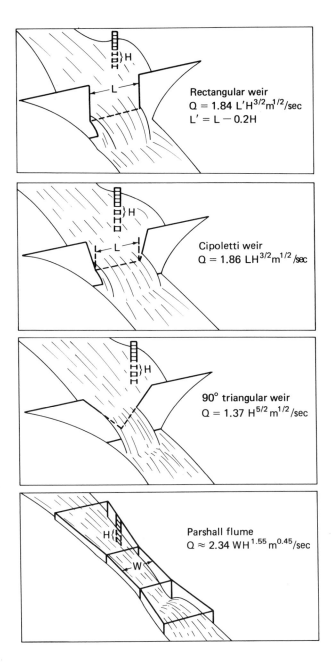

Figure 16-8 Water-measuring devices and equations for calculating their flow. The $m^{1/2}$ in the equations completes the cubic form of the units. The constant must be adjusted if the $m^{1/2}$ is changed to anything other than meters.

Rectangular weirs are simple to build, but the flow constriction below the notch requires extra arithmetic to calculate how much water is being delivered. The Cipoletti weir has a trapezoidal shape with a 1:4 side slope that offsets the constriction tendency and simplifies the calculations. Triangular weirs have a wide range of capacity with good percentage accuracy at small flows as well as large, but they require the most head loss between the water levels above and below the weir.

Weirs need a pool of quiet water above them so water will not approach at a velocity high enough to increase their flow. The head measurement should be made in the level surface of the pool at least four times as far from the notch as the head (depth) of water flowing over the notch. Undersize or sediment-filled pools can cause the discharge to increase by as much as 10% or 15% above the calculated values. Weirs also need a sharp edge at the notch to cut the water cleanly and a free fall below the notch so the water escape is unrestricted.

Parshall flumes (lower part of Figure 16-8) are often used where the land is too flat to allow the head loss required for free flow over a weir. Parshall flumes cause the water to flow at a high velocity through a narrow steep passage, then back up nearly as high as its original elevation. A good installation should measure water flow with an accuracy of ±3%, but a faulty one might be ±10% (Robinson and Humphreys, 1967). Excessive flow that submerges the drop and rise characteristics of a Parshall flume may reduce delivery by 25% or more.

The delivery equation for Parshall flumes given in Figure 16-8 is only approximate. Robinson and Humphreys (1967) list values of coefficients and exponents that vary by about ±3% from those given depending on the size of the flume. They also discuss a newer style flume with trapezoidal cross section instead of vertical walls. Several other measurement devices such as submerged orifices and current meters can be used for measuring water but are less common than weirs and flumes.

16-4.2 Water-Control Structures

Canals are usually placed on a constant nonerosive grade that requires few structures other than outlets to laterals. An emergency spillway is sometimes needed because cost factors require the canal to be built with little spare capacity; a heavy rain or damage to the canal or its laterals could require rapid diversion of a large volume of water.

Laterals and other ditches often must flow down slopes that are steep enough to require erosion control. Drop structures like the one diagrammed in Figure 10-11 are used to absorb enough elevation change to keep this flow from eroding the ditch. Often they are placed like a series of stairsteps with the apron of each drop structure at the same elevation as the notch of the one below it, as in Figure 16-9. Large drop structures are usually made of poured concrete. Smaller ones may be poured or made of concrete blocks with their cores filled with concrete.

Check structures are used to raise the flow of water in a ditch, perhaps to irrigate the field next to it. A drop structure can also be used as a check by placing boards in its notch. A simple check structure consists of the main wall and notch of the drop structure but without the apron and its side walls.

A division box such as that shown in Figure 16-10 allows water to be directed in any of two or three directions. Boards dropped in slots close one channel while another is opened. Division boxes take various forms according to the ditch pattern and topography. Some are made of wood, but those made from poured concrete or concrete blocks are more durable. Special concrete blocks are available with slots cast in them to hold the control boards.

16-4.3 Distributing Water from Ditches

When water finally reaches the field to be irrigated, it must somehow be taken out of the ditch and applied to the land. Usually the water

Figure 16-9 A series of drop structures protecting a ditch in Idaho. (Courtesy USDA—Soil Conservation Service.)

Figure 16-10 A division box for diverting water in any of three directions. (Courtesy F. R. Troeh.)

has been flowing below ground level and must be raised by blocking the ditch. Boards may be placed in a check for this purpose, or a temporary blockage such as a canvas dam or a sod dam may be used. A canvas dam is a canvas rectangle attached to a pole long enough to reach across the ditch. The canvas lies in the ditch upstream from the pole and is held there by water pressure. A sod dam is constructed of pieces of sod taken from the ditchbank with a shovel.

Turnouts (notches through the ditch bank) are the simplest way to allow water to escape onto the field, but other methods offer more precise control. Siphon tubes as shown in Figure 16-11 are a popular means of irrigating. They come in several sizes and their flow can be adjusted by raising or lowering the outlet end. One type has a water trap on each end to keep the tube from emptying when the ditch is dry. Spiles (tubes permanently installed at ground level through the ditch bank) are another means of removing water from ditches. Spiles usually have adjustable gates on their lower ends.

16-4.4 Irrigation Pipelines

Metal pipelines are required to sustain the pressure of most sprinkler irrigation systems. The main lines are often buried if the system is considered permanent. Portable branch lines are attached to risers

Figure 16–11 Siphon tubes conducting water from an irrigation ditch in Idaho. (Courtesy F. R. Troeh.)

on the main lines. Temporary installations use portable pipe for the entire system.

Metal pipe is expensive whether it is made of steel for maximum strength or of a lightweight metal such as aluminum for portability. Systems are therefore designed to use minimum sizes and amounts of metal pipe. Engineers qualified to design irrigation systems have flow-rate tables to calculate required pipe sizes and friction losses for a particular system.

Often a pipeline is used as an inverted siphon where water must be carried from a high point across a low area to another high point. A fill or a flume could serve the same purpose but would be a barrier to traffic and would occupy land area that can be cropped if a buried pipeline is used. Concrete pipe is usually used for such lines because it is the least expensive type generally available that meets the strength and durability requirements. Ordinary concrete pipe is usually adequate for pressure heads up to 5 or 6 m of water. Elevation differences that produce higher heads require the use of reinforced concrete, steel, or other high-pressure pipe.

Carrying capacities of inverted siphons and other concrete pipelines can be estimated from Table 15–2 by calculating the average slope from the inlet to the outlet. An intervening low area has no effect on carrying capacity as long as no air is trapped in the pipeline. Air entrapment is avoided by having only one low point in the line.

Pipelines hold water for extended periods and should therefore be installed below frost depth. They should usually have a concrete structure at each end to protect these points from erosion. Sometimes they are built into a division box at one or both ends. Properly installed pipelines should last for many decades and nearly eliminate water losses by seepage and evaporation.

16-5 IRRIGATION METHODS

Irrigation methods can be divided into four main types—surface, subsurface, sprinkler, and trickle irrigation—and many subtypes. Surface irrigation is the oldest type and still accounts for about three-fourths of all irrigation. Subsurface irrigation is limited in its adaptation. Sprinkler irrigation can be used in any climate, is the most popular method in humid regions, and is still expanding in use. Trickle irrigation, the newest type, makes the most efficient use of water.

16-5.1 Surface Irrigation

Surface irrigation includes both furrow and flood types. Furrow irrigation is used with row crops by running water in the cultivated channel between the rows. The rows can be fed with siphon tubes or with spiles or in groups from ditch turnouts.

Furrow Irrigation. Furrow irrigation creates a serious erosion hazard because the water flows in the unprotected area between the rows where the soil has been loosened by cultivation. The maximum nonerosive stream flow in liters per second can be estimated from the equation:

$$Q_{max} = \frac{0.6 \text{ liters/sec}}{\text{percent slope}}$$

This equation should be used only for slopes of more than 0.3% because the flow on flatter slopes is usually limited by the furrow capacity rather than by erosion. The 0.6 factor should be decreased if the soil is known to be more erodible than average.

Irrigation furrows with slope gradients steeper than 2% are difficult to irrigate without erosion. Large streams would erode the soil and small streams will only flow a short distance before all the water infiltrates. Contour furrows overcome this problem because they are placed on a gradient of about 0.5% across the main slope. Extra care must be taken to be sure that water does not cut through any of the ridges between contour furrows. The resulting overload on the lower furrow could cause it to overtop and begin a chain reaction that would likely produce a gully.

The length of irrigation furrows is limited by the distance irrigation streams will flow during an irrigation period. Uniform irrigation requires that this period of time be no longer than one-fourth of the total irrigation period. For example, the irrigation water should reach the end of the rows in two hours out of an eight-hour irrigation period or three hours out of a twelve-hour period. The maximum length of irrigation rows therefore depends on the infiltration rate and erodibility of the soil, the slope, and the amount (depth) of water to be applied. Table 16-2 contains estimates of the appropriate lengths of rows for various conditions.

Irrigation according to the principles outlined in the preceding paragraphs can achieve about 60% efficiency in the application of water. The other 40% is lost by evaporation, deep percolation in the upper ends of the rows and in the most permeable soil, and in waste water from the lower end of the rows. The waste water loss can be lessened if the irrigator will reduce the size of the irrigation streams when they approach the lower end of the rows. The extra water can then be used elsewhere, perhaps on a pasture that needs a short irrigation period.

Principles similar to those outlined for furrow irrigation apply to related methods of irrigation. Small furrows known as corrugations are used for noncultivated grain and forage crops. Such vegetation protects the soil better than row crops, but corrugations are too small to carry large streams of water. The row lengths are therefore similar to those for furrow irrigation.

Flood Irrigation. The three main types of flood irrigation are basin irrigation, border irrigation, and wild flooding. Basin irrigation is probably the oldest method of all. It was practiced in Egypt more than 5000 years ago (Gulhati and Smith, 1967). It is a simple method that is still widely used to keep land flooded for long periods for paddy rice production or for shorter periods for many other crops.

Land preparation for basin irrigation is accomplished by forming a narrow ridge between 15 and 50 cm high on all sides of each area to be flooded. The elevations within any one basin should be as uni-

Table 16-2 Suggested maximum lengths in meters of cultivated furrows for different soils, slopes, and depths of water in cm to be applied

Furrow slope (%)	Clays				Loams				Sands			
	Average depth of water applied (cm)											
	7.5	15	22.5	30	5	10	15	20	5	7.5	10	12.5
0.05	300	400	400	400	120	270	400	400	60	90	150	190
0.1	340	440	470	500	180	340	440	470	90	120	190	220
0.2	370	470	530	620	220	370	470	530	120	190	250	300
0.3	400	500	620	800	280	400	500	600	150	220	280	400
0.5	400	500	560	750	280	370	470	530	120	190	250	300
1.0	280	400	500	600	250	300	370	470	90	150	220	250
1.5	250	340	430	500	220	280	340	400	80	120	190	220
2.0	220	270	340	400	180	250	300	340	60	90	150	190

SOURCE: Booher, 1974. Courtesy Food and Agriculture Organization of the United Nations.

form as possible—certainly within a range of 5 or 10 cm. The area of a basin may be limited by elevation changes, by the size that can be covered uniformly by the available water supply on permeable soils, or by cropping factors. Basins range in size from those designed to irrigate individual trees or small areas of vegetable crops to rice paddies occupying several hectares.

A ditch or other water supply large enough to flood the basin must be available on one side. Water is turned in until the desired depth is reached, then cut back to just enough to hold a constant depth of about 10 cm for paddy rice or shut off completely for other crops. The water in the basin may be allowed to completely infiltrate or, in some low-permeability soils, the excess may be drained onto a lower basin after a specified time.

Border irrigation can be described as elongated basins with a gentle slope in the long direction. Water is turned in at the upper end of the border and allowed to flow down its length as though it were a very wide furrow, as shown in Figure 16–12. Borders range from 3 to 30 m wide and must be nearly level across their width so the entire area will be irrigated uniformly. Their lengths are similar to the lengths of furrows on comparable soils and slope gradients shown in Table 16–2.

Border irrigation can be used with slope gradients between 0.2% and 2% for cultivated crops, up to 4% or 5% for small grain or hay crops, and up to about 8% for pastures. Extensive land leveling is

Figure 16–12 Border irrigation in California. (Courtesy F. R. Troeh.)

often required because the topography must be smoother than for furrow irrigation. The cost of land leveling is offset by the low labor requirement for turning water into a few borders rather than into many furrows or corrugations. The smooth topography is easy to work across at harvest time.

Several variations of border irrigation have been devised. Irrigation terraces made with surfaces that either slope like borders or are level like basins are one example. In another variation, ditches replace the ridges between borders and the area between is irrigated by blocking the ditches so they flood the border. Unfortunately, erosion can be a problem in the ditches, and uniform water application is often difficult to attain with this method.

Wild flooding is used to irrigate forage crops and sometimes small grains on uneven topography. Water flows down the ridges in ditches and is diverted to flood across the land. It is often necessary to have small spreader ditches to redistribute water that naturally accumulates in swales. The irrigator uses a shovel to make small furrows and ridges to guide water to any areas that would otherwise remain dry.

Wild flooding is inefficient in use of water and labor, but it irrigates land that cannot be managed by other methods of surface irrigation. The soil may be too shallow or stony to have its surface smoothed by land leveling, and it may not be used intensely enough to justify a large investment. Rolling topography with slope gradients up to about 10% can be irrigated by wild flooding with permanent close-growing vegetation.

16-5.2 Subsurface Irrigation

Subsurface irrigation, also called subirrigation, can be considered as a controlled drainage system. Ditches are usually used, but some systems use tile lines. The systems remove water during wet seasons and add it during dry seasons so the water table is always at a controlled depth. That depth might be as little as 30 cm for shallow-rooted vegetation in a coarse sandy soil or as great as 120 cm in some loamy soils. The surface soil should be dry but most of the root zone should be moist. The field can even be cultivated and irrigated at the same time.

The required conditions for subsurface irrigation are so stringent that relatively little land is subirrigated. The land surface must be quite smooth and have a slope gradient of less than 0.5%. The subsoil must be highly permeable, but it must have a shallow water table or be underlain by an impermeable layer that permits a perched water table to be maintained. Both the soil and the irrigation water must be low in salts to avoid the formation of saline and sodic soils. Suitable conditions for subsurface irrigation most often occur on glacial outwash plains, terraces, or deltas in humid or subhumid areas.

16–5.3 Sprinkler Irrigation

Large-scale sprinkler irrigation is much newer than surface and subsurface irrigation because the necessary pipes, pumps, and power supply were not available until comparatively recent times. Advantages such as portability, adaptability to a wide range of soil and topographic conditions with little or no land preparation, and good control of water application have made sprinkler irrigation popular. High efficiency of water application may result in energy savings and help avoid erosion and leaching nitrates from the soil. Disadvantages limiting its use include high equipment and operating costs, the need to move lines in muddy conditions, salt damage to some plants if poor-quality water is used, and disease problems with some plants.

Most field sprinklers use a rotating sprinkler head of the general type shown in Figure 16–13. Although the sprinklers may be fixed in permanent locations for limited areas of high-value crops, they are usually mounted on either moving or movable lines. Sprinkler systems using portable lines, rolling lines, and center-pivot systems will be considered here.

Portable Lines. Hand-moved sprinkler lines are conventional in most areas. They may be used throughout the growing season in arid climates, but in humid climates they are often kept in storage except during periods of drought. Occasional use is adjusted to the needs of the time. Regular use is usually scheduled as outlined in the following paragraphs.

Irrigation once every seven to ten days with applications of 7 to 10 cm of water each time is common. The application rate should be slower than the soil infiltration rate to avoid runoff. Sprinklers are available to apply water at rates as slow as 3 or 4 mm/hr, but faster rates are usually more efficient. Rates that result in irrigation sets of 8 or 12 hr are convenient for work schedules.

The number of irrigation lines needed depends on the area in the field, the irrigation period and frequency, and the area irrigated by each line. A field 400 m square (16 ha) might be irrigated from a main line through the middle of the field as shown in Figure 16–14. Each irrigation line could be composed of nineteen sprinkler pipes, each 10 m long, plus a 5-m coupling to the main line. Outlets every

Figure 16-13 A sprinkler at the top of a riser attached to portable lines in a potato field. Water strikes the protruding arm and makes it work back and forth against a spring. This action makes the sprinkler rotate and helps distribute the water. (Courtesy F. R. Troeh.)

10 m along the main line would irrigate an area 200 m by 10 m (or 0.2 ha) at any one time. Complete irrigation of 16 ha with 0.2-ha sets requires eighty sets. An irrigation period of 8 hr (three per day) and a frequency of once every nine days would result in twenty-seven irrigation periods. Such a system requires three lines (80 ÷ 27). Four lines would probably be used so there could always be three lines operating and still allow the soil to dry before a line is moved.

The system described in the preceding paragraph and illustrated in Figure 16-14 is designated as a 10-m by 10-m system because it uses 10-m pipe lengths and 10 m between lines. Other sizes are available, with pipe lengths from 6 to 12 m and line spacings from 9 to 18 m being most common.

Each length of irrigation pipe has a quick-coupling device at the end permitting it to be uncoupled, carried to its next position, and reconnected. Each length has a sprinkler attached to the reinforced area near the coupling. The sprinklers usually spray water to about the next sprinkler position and thus provide overlap for complete coverage. Sprinkler irrigation is usually about 75% efficient in use of

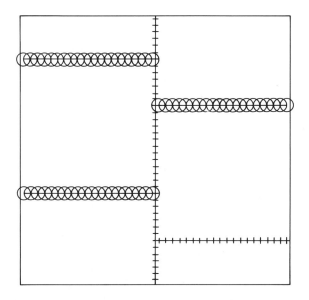

Figure 16–14 A hand-moved sprinkler irrigation system for a field 400 m square using four lines with three operating at any one time. The lines are spaced around the field so the moving distance is only from one position to the next.

water—the other 25% is lost by evaporation and by deep percolation where the overlapping circles result in heavier-than-average water application. Excess wind causes a poor irrigation pattern and reduces the efficiency.

Moving sprinkler lines is muddy work even when there is a drying time. One way to avoid the mud is to use a tractor to tow the line across the main line to the other side of the field and alternate the two sides.

Rolling Lines. Another way to make sprinkler lines easier to move is to mount them on wheels. Some lines run through the hubs of large wheels. Other systems use small wheels on each side of the line. Some rolling lines have long flexible supply lines so they can be motor-driven to roll during the irrigation period. Others are detached, moved, and reconnected much like a hand-moved line.

Center-Pivot Systems. Center-pivot irrigation systems are the most convenient and the most expensive movable systems. They are designed to move slowly and continuously around a central pivot point. Either a well or a buried main line or, occasionally, a line with crossing ramps supplies water to the pivot point. The sprinkler line is supported at about 30-m intervals by two-wheeled, motor-driven towers that carry it at a height of about 2 or 3 m, as shown in Figure 16–15. Either hydraulic or electric power is used to move the towers at a rate proportional to their distance from the pivot point. The number and size of sprinklers varies along the line so that the water applied is proportional to distance from the center pivot.

The most common size of center-pivot system is a line 400 m long that traverses a 50-ha circular area in a 64-ha square. Water spraying beyond the end of the line will cover another 2 or 3 ha. The corners may be left unirrigated, or special provisions may be made for them. Some lines have an extension that swings out into the corners but turns off and trails behind where it is not needed. Another method uses a very large sprinkler known as a "big gun" at the end of the line to irrigate the corners.

The use of center-pivot systems has increased rapidly in recent years, especially in the Great Plains and the southwestern parts of the United States. The high cost of installing such systems is offset by their convenience and the low labor requirement of their automated operation.

16–5.4 Trickle Irrigation

Trickle irrigation, also called drip irrigation, is the newest method and the one that achieves the highest irrigation efficiency: about 90%

Figure 16–15 A center-pivot irrigation line in Texas. (Courtesy F. R. Troeh.)

of the applied water is available to the plants. High efficiency is achieved by supplying water to individual plants through small plastic lines. Water is supplied either continuously or so frequently that the plant roots grow in constantly moist soil.

Trickle irrigation is especially suitable for watering trees or other large plants. Much of its use has been in orchards and vineyards but it has also been used to irrigate a variety of row crops including several kinds of vegetables and fruits. Its advantages are greatest where areas between plants can be left dry. It has no advantage for close-growing vegetation such as lawns, pastures, or small grain crops.

An Israeli engineer named Symcha Blass developed the idea of trickle irrigation in the 1930s (Shoji, 1977), but it had to wait until plastic tubing was available to make a practical system. Trickle irrigation in the United States increased from 40 ha in 1960 to over 50,000 ha in 1976 out of a worldwide total of about 160,000 ha. Nearly half of the trickle irrigation in the United States is in California, some of it in avocado orchards with slopes up to 50% or 60%. Erosion is not a problem because there is no runoff.

A bonus with trickle irrigation is its ability to use water with a higher salt content than any other method—up to about 2500 mg/liter. The constant flow of water from the trickle emitter toward the outer edges of the plant root zone carries the salt along with it. Salt concentrations become very high in the dry areas between plants but not in the actual root zone.

Trickle irrigation saves water, is able to use water high in salt, functions well in all but the extremes of coarse- and fine-textured soils, works on almost any topography without causing erosion, and requires little labor. The disadvantages are mainly high equipment costs and plugging of the lines by sediment, salt encrustation, or algae.

A trickle irrigation system normally includes a control box that regulates the water pressure, filters the water, and provides for the addition of fertilizers and herbicides. Chlorine may be added to eliminate algal growth. The water pressure for trickle irrigation is normally 0.4 to 1 kg/cm^2 (Shoji, 1977) as compared to 1 to 8 kg/cm^2 for sprinkler irrigation. Some trickle controls are set to increase the pressure periodically and flush the lines to reduce clogging.

Trickle irrigation lines branch into several parts at three or four stages to provide the many outlets required. The last stage is a flexible plastic lateral line 12 to 32 mm in diameter that lies either on or just below the soil surface and applies the water either through small holes in the line or through emitter nozzles. Emitter nozzles lead the water through a long spiral path that slows the flow and permits a larger emission hole to be used. The larger hole is less subject to plugging.

16-6 LAND RECLAMATION

Reclamation in its broad sense means modifying land to make it suitable for cropping. Vegetating mine spoils and construction sites (Ch. 11), drainage of wet lands (Ch. 15), and irrigation of arid lands are reclamation processes that have already been discussed. The reclamation of saline and sodic soils will be considered in this section.

The formation of saline and sodic soils and the significant effects of water moving upward from a watertable were discussed in Section 15-2.5. Saline soils form where upward water movement is dominant; sodic soils form where upward and downward water movements are approximately equal. Saline and sodic soils can be defined as follows:

Saline soils have electrical conductivities of saturation extracts higher than 4 mmhos/cm. A determination is made by saturating a soil sample with water, extracting the water by vacuum, and measuring the conductivity. They contain less than 15% exchangeable Na^+.

Sodic soils have more than 15% of their cation-exchange capacity occupied by exchangeable Na^+. They are low in total salt content and electrical conductivity.

Saline-sodic soils have electrical conductivities higher than 4 mmhos/cm and have more than 15% exchangeable Na^+.

The only important difference between saline-sodic and saline soils is that leaching changes saline-sodic soils into sodic soils.

Both saline and saline-sodic conditions are called white alkali because the soluble salts form a white deposit on dry soil. The soluble salts make it more difficult for plant roots to absorb water. Plants vary widely in salt tolerance as shown by the figures in Table 16-3. Electrical conductivity of 4 mmhos/cm represents an arbitrary division point that sometimes needs to be lowered or raised according to the kind of crop being grown. The stage of growth is also important—plants are more sensitive to salinity during the germination and seedling stages than they are during the rapid growth period.

Very few soils are as unproductive and as difficult to reclaim as sodic soils. The high Na^+ percentage causes the soil colloids to dis-

Table 16-3 Salt tolerance of crops during their rapid growth period in terms of electrical conductivities of saturated soil extracts

	Conductivity in mmhos/cm at 25°C causing yield reductions of		
	10%	*25%*	*50%*
Forage crops:			
Bermudagrass	13	16	18
Tall wheatgrass	11	15	18
Crested wheatgrass	6	11	18
Tall fescue	7	10	15
Perennial ryegrass	8	10	13
Bird's-foot trefoil	6	8	10
Beardless wildrye	4	7	11
Alfalfa	3	5	8
Orchardgrass	2	4	8
Alsike clover, red clover	2	3	4
Field crops:			
Barley	12	16	18
Sugar beets, cotton	10	12	16
Wheat, safflower	7	10	14
Sorghum	6	9	12
Soybeans	6	7	9
Corn, paddy rice	5	6	7
Flax	3	4	6
Field beans	1	2	3
Vegetable crops:			
Beets	8	10	12
Spinach	6	7	8
Tomatoes, broccoli	4	6	8
Cabbage	2	4	7
Potatoes, corn, sweet potatoes	2	4	6
Lettuce, bell pepper	2	3	5
Onions	2	3	4
Carrots	1	3	4
Beans	1	2	3

SOURCE: Bernstein, 1964.

perse and the pH to rise above 8.5 (often to about 10) when the Na^+ is not masked by a high salt concentration. The dispersed colloids reduce the permeability of very sandy soils to 1 or 2 mm/hr and make silty or clayey soils essentially impermeable. A smooth, crusted, barren surface forms that is so slippery when wet that sodic soils are commonly called "slick spots." The organic-matter content of sodic soils is usually less than 1%, and what organic matter there is becomes soluble in the alkaline conditions and moves with the soil water. Some moves to the soil surface where it forms a thin black covering that is the basis for the common name "black alkali." Some organic matter is dissolved in drainage water seeping from the sodic soil and gives the water a brown, oily appearance.

16-6.1 Reclaiming Saline Soils

Suitable irrigation water, appropriate means of application, and good drainage are required for reclaiming saline soils. Large quantities of water are needed with low enough salt content to leach salts from the soil and leave it sufficiently low in salinity for the desired purpose. Flood irrigation is usually preferred because the entire soil surface needs to be covered, often for two or three days or longer. Methods such as furrow and trickle irrigation would reclaim part of the soil at the expense of the rest by causing much of the salt to accumulate in the drier parts of the soil.

Salt-tolerant vegetation helps reclaim saline soils, especially those that are fine textured. Plant roots help keep the soil permeable and the top growth helps prevent erosion. A study by Reeve, Pillsbury, and Wilcox (1955) established a basis for determining how much water is needed. A depth of water equal to half the depth of the soil will remove about 50% of the salts from the soil profile. A water depth equal to the soil depth will remove about 80% of the salts; 1.5 times the soil depth removes about 90% of the salts.

A good drainage system is required to remove the leaching water fast enough to keep the water table from rising while a saline soil is being reclaimed. Sometimes the leaching is done intermittently both to save water and to give more time for drainage. Intermittent leaching requires only about 70% as much leaching water as continuous leaching if the time intervals are long enough to dissolve more salts but short enough to avoid large evaporation losses (a day or two is usually appropriate).

Reclamation is futile unless the land is well managed afterwards. The water table should be kept low enough to prevent upward movement of water from making the soil saline again, and enough irrigation water should be applied for drainage to remove the salts brought in by the irrigation water. The amount of drainage water needed is calculated as explained in Section 16-3.7.

16–6.2 Reclaiming Saline-Sodic Soils

Saline-sodic soils require that a soil amendment to replace Na^+ be applied prior to the leaching process described for saline soils. The amount of amendment can be calculated as shown in Note 16–2 when the required chemical data are available. The gypsum requirement may also be measured directly by mixing a soil sample with a saturated solution of $CaSO_4$ and determining how much Ca^{++} is adsorbed by the soil. This amount is adjusted by the proportionate weights involved to determine the soil-amendment requirements. The gypsum in this test reacts with both the exchangeable Na^+ and the Na_2CO_3 because Ca^{++} is adsorbed more strongly than Na^+, and insoluble $CaCO_3$ precipitates.

NOTE 16–2 SOIL-AMENDMENT CALCULATIONS

Problem: A saline-sodic soil contains 9 meq exchangeable Na^+/100 g plus 0.5% soluble Na_2CO_3 by weight. Calculate the amounts of soil amendment needed per hectare if gypsum, sulfur, or calcium chloride is used to reclaim the soil to a depth of 50 cm.

Solution:

1. The weight of soil can be calculated by assuming an average bulk density of 1.3 g/cm^3:

$$1 \text{ ha} = 10^4 \text{ m}^2 = 10^8 \text{ cm}^2$$

$$10^8 \text{ cm}^2 \times 50 \text{ cm} \times 1.3 \text{ g/cm}^3 = 6.5 \times 10^9 \text{ g}$$

2. Each 100 g of soil contains:
   (a) 9 meq $\times$ 23 mg/meq = 207 mg = 0.207 g of exchangeable Na^+
   (b) 0.005 $\times$ 100 g $\times$ (46/106) = 0.217 g of soluble Na
       (0.5%) (wt of 2 Na/Na_2CO_3) _____

       0.424 g Na/100 g of soil

3. Each hectare of soil 50 cm deep contains:

   6.5 $\times$ 10^9 g $\times$ 0.424 g Na/100 g = 2.76 $\times$ 10^7 g of Na
   = 27.6 mt of Na

4. The required amounts of each amendment can be calculated from the equivalent weights of each material divided by that of Na:

(a) $CaSO_4 \cdot 2H_2O$ 27.6 mt $\times$ 86/23 = 103 mt
     $(172/2 = 86)$

(b) S   27.6 mt $\times$ 16/23 = 19 mt
     $(32/2 = 16)$

(c) $CaCl_2$ 27.6 mt $\times$ 55.5/23 = 67 mt
     $(111/2 = 55.5)$

Step 2 shows that approximately half of the soil amendment required for this soil is needed for replacing exchangeable Na^+ and the
other half for the soluble Na_2CO_3. Actually, the replacement would
not be complete because the process is not 100% efficient, but any
of the suggested amendment applications should reduce the sodium
content to a safe level.

The amount of soil amendment required varies according to its
equivalent weight, as illustrated in Note 16–2. Gypsum is often used
because it is cheap or even free, but the amount required is large and
the process is slow. Gypsum is sometimes added to the irrigation
water, but it takes 5 to 10 ha-cm of irrigation water to dissolve 1 mt
of gypsum. Mixing the gypsum into the soil helps, but the reclamation process may still take months or years.

Less sulfur is required to replace sodium than is required of other
amendments because sulfur has a low equivalent weight. Reclamation
with sulfur is usually less expensive than with anything except gypsum. However, sulfur has its own limitations. Soil bacteria must first
oxidize the sulfur to sulfuric acid. This may take months or years.
The H^+ of the acid must then react with soil lime to release Ca^{++},
which in turn exchanges for the soil-adsorbed Na^+. Only then is the
Na^+ ready for leaching. Lime is common in saline-sodic soils but its
presence should be verified rather than assumed.

High solubility in water makes calcium chloride a fast-acting soil
amendment. It can be applied to the soil surface or added to the
irrigation water. Reclamation of a saline-sodic soil treated with calcium chloride proceeds in the same manner and at the same rate as
if it were a saline soil. The main problem is high cost.

The amount of soil amendment needed to reclaim a saline-sodic
soil can often be greatly reduced if salty irrigation water is available.
The soil must not be leached with pure water because that would
make it sodic, but salty water can be used as a preliminary treatment.
Water containing mostly calcium salts is best, but even sea water has
been used with a degree of success. After the soil is partially re-

claimed, a new soil test should indicate a reasonable amendment requirement to complete the reclamation process.

16-6.3 Reclaiming Sodic Soils

Sodic soils are difficult to reclaim because their permeability is too slow for water to carry soil amendments to the soil colloids. Mechanical mixing helps because it gets the amendment into the soil and it opens up some passages for water percolation. Unfortunately, deep plowing may not provide enough mixing and any other method is usually too expensive for large areas. However, sodic soils often occur as small spots mixed with more productive soils. Some such spots have been improved by mixing the soil with a backhoe. Many sodic soils have layers containing concentrations of gypsum and lime underlying the soil. Mixing should incorporate these free soil amendments into the soil.

A sodic soil contains negligible soluble salts and therefore requires less soil amendment than a saline-sodic soil. The soil in Note 16-2 would have required only half as much amendment if it had been sodic instead of saline-sodic. However, slow permeability makes sodic soils slow to reclaim. Few plants will grow on them until some reclamation has been achieved. Even weeds should be encouraged because their roots open channels that improve soil permeability. Permitting the soil to dry and crack open occasionally is also helpful (sodic soils shrink and swell more than other soils of similar clay content).

Salty water is much better than pure water for the initial stages of sodic soil reclamation because salts help flocculate the soil colloids and increase the soil permeability, often by one or two orders of magnitude. Calcium ions in the water are especially helpful because they replace exchangeable Na^+.

16-7 CONSERVATION IRRIGATION

An irrigator can either waste or conserve large amounts of soil and water. Attitude is important because the easiest way to irrigate is often not the best way and the best methods of irrigation are often more costly than other methods. One interaction is usually favorable —irrigation methods that conserve water also conserve soil.

The method of irrigation influences how much soil and water are wasted. Most surface irrigation methods require careful management to achieve 60% efficiency in water use; sprinkler irrigation systems are commonly about 75% efficient; and trickle irrigation should be about 90% efficient. Subsurface irrigation efficiency depends on the amount of seepage loss.

Subsurface, sprinkler, and trickle irrigation should not produce any runoff and therefore should not cause erosion. In fact, the improved vegetative cover should reduce both wind and water erosion. Sprinkler and trickle irrigation are sometimes used on steep slopes that need both vegetative and mechanical erosion-control practices. These needs result from natural erosive forces rather than from irrigation.

Surface irrigation can be a significant cause of erosion because large amounts of water flow across the land. The worst case results when preirrigation is used to fill the soil profile with water before a crop is planted. The hazards of preirrigation are reduced if residues from the previous crop still remain on the soil. Irrigation frequency is also important, especially where row crops are cultivated between irrigations. Most of the erosion occurs during the first hour or two of irrigation while the soil is still loose. Longer but less frequent irrigations therefore erode less soil than an equal amount of water applied in several shorter irrigations.

The length of irrigation furrows, corrugations, and borders is frequently a problem. Long rows are convenient because it takes fewer rows and less work to cover the same area. The problem is that longer rows require larger, more erosive streams of water and make it more difficult to irrigate to a uniform depth. Rows that are too long therefore waste both soil and water. One solution to some long-row problems is to place portable gated pipe such as that shown in Figure 16–16 across the middle of the rows. The lower half of the field is irrigated first and the upper half is irrigated after the pipe has been removed. All tillage, planting, and harvesting operations run the full length of the rows.

Variations in soil permeability and slope gradient both cause water to be wasted because it cannot be applied uniformly. Soil erosion is also likely to result on the steeper parts. Variable soil permeability usually cannot be corrected, but variable slope gradient often can be smoothed by land leveling. Major land leveling requires staking the field on a grid pattern, surveying the elevations of the stakes, and preparing a leveling plan to balance the cuts and fills. The elevation change is then marked on each stake and large earth-moving equipment is used to level the land to the prescribed uniform slope gradient. Carryalls such as those used for building roads are used for major leveling. Lighter smoothing work is done with a land plane such as that shown in Figure 16–17. A smooth field with uniform

Figure 16-16 Gated pipe being used in Iowa for furrow irrigation. Each opening in the pipe has an adjustable gate to control the water flow. (Courtesy USDA—Soil Conservation Service.)

Figure 16-17 A land plane is used to smooth land surfaces for more uniform surface irrigation. (Courtesy F. R. Troeh.)

slopes contributes greatly to the ease and uniformity of surface irrigation and to reduced erosion.

Ditch erosion is another irrigation hazard. Farm ditches placed on an ideal gradient of about 0.15% seldom cause much problem (larger ditches need to be flatter). But, water must often go down a steeper slope where it can easily cause erosion. Drop structures, concrete-lined ditches, and irrigation pipelines are all used to avoid ditch erosion. Lined ditches and pipelines are also good ways to minimize seepage losses.

SUMMARY

Irrigation and reclamation are used to increase the productivity of land. Irrigation is practiced on every continent, but about three-fourths of the world's irrigation is in Asia. Irrigation has a large impact on the agriculture of an area and causes changes in both crop and soil management. Average worldwide yields with irrigation are over twice as high as those without; crop quality may be improved as well. However, irrigation costs are high and erosion and sedimentation may result.

Soil suitable for irrigation must have satisfactory depth, texture, structure, and topography. Maximum slope gradients for irrigation vary from 3% to over 35%, depending on soil, climate, crop, and type of irrigation system. Good water is needed, because salts in either the soil or the water can produce saline and sodic soils. Water rights are an important issue for irrigators and are usually based on either riparian rights or prior appropriations. Water for irrigation comes from surface water diverted from streams, harvested rainwater, and underground water. Water quality depends on salt content, sodium adsorption ratio, toxic ions, and solid matter such as sediment and weed seeds.

Water for small projects is distributed through ditches or pipelines. Large projects require canal systems that branch into laterals and ditches for individual users. Water flow is measured by weirs or flumes. Drop structures, checks, and division boxes are used to control water flow. Water flow in ditches is blocked by checks, canvas dams, or sod dams and delivered to fields through turnouts, siphon tubes, or spiles. Pipelines are used for sprinkler irrigation and for problem spots in ditch systems.

Irrigation is divided into surface, subsurface, sprinkler, and trickle methods. Surface methods include furrow irrigation, corrugation irrigation, basic irrigation, border irrigation, and wild flooding. Subsurface irrigation can be considered as a controlled drainage system and is limited to specific conditions. Most sprinkler irrigation uses movable lines, rolling lines, or center-pivot systems. Trickle irrigation is the newest method and the most efficient of all for watering individual plants. It can use water containing more salt than the other methods.

Land reclamation includes drainage of wet lands, irrigation of arid lands, and correction of saline and sodic conditions. Salinity can be leached from a soil, but sodium replacement requires a soil amendment such as gypsum or sulfur.

Water-use efficiency depends upon the type of system and on how it is managed. Sprinkler irrigation usually applies water more uniformly than surface methods and trickle irrigation supplies the water directly to the plant root zone for maximum efficiency. Erosion from surface irrigation is reduced by limiting lengths of irrigation runs, using less frequent but longer irrigation periods, and careful land leveling. The other methods of irrigation should not produce runoff and therefore do not cause much erosion.

QUESTIONS

1. Irrigation would improve crop yields in most humid regions. Why is it not used more there?
2. What difference does it make to an irrigator whether water rights are based on the riparian doctrine or on prior appropriations?
3. How is water delivered from a ditch onto a field?
4. What happens to the salt contained in irrigation water applied by surface irrigation? by trickle irrigation?
5. Why is a sodic soil worse than a saline-sodic soil?
6. What erosion problems may be caused by irrigation?

REFERENCES

AGRICULTURAL RESEARCH SERVICE, 1974. Attacking salinity on irrigated lands. *Agr. Res.* 23(6):7–10.

BERNSTEIN, LEON, 1964. *Salt Tolerance of Plants.* USDA Agric. Inf. Bull. No. 283, 24 p.

BERNSTEIN, LEON, and L. E. FRANCOIS, 1973. Comparisons of drip, furrow, and sprinkler irrigation. *Soil Sci.* 115:73–86.

BOOHER, L. J., 1974. *Surface Irrigation.* FAO Agricultural Development Paper No. 95, Food and Agriculture Organization of the United Nations, Rome, Italy, 160 p.

BORDOVSKY, D. G., W. R. JORDAN, E. A. HILER, and T. A. HOWELL, 1974. Choice of irrigation timing indicator for narrow row cotton. *Agron. J.* 66: 88–91.

BUCKS, D. A., L. J. ERIE, and O. F. FRENCH, 1974. Quantity and frequency of trickle and furrow irrigation for efficient cabbage production. *Agron. J.* 66:53–57.

BUSBY, C. E., 1955. Regulation and economic expansion. In *Water*, USDA Yearbook of Agriculture, U.S. Government Printing Office, p. 666–676.

COMMISSION ON INTERNATIONAL RELATIONS (JH 215), 1974. *More Water for Arid Lands.* National Academy of Sciences, Washington, D.C., 154 p.

CRIDDLE, W. D., and CORNELIS KALISVAART, 1967. Subirrigation systems. In *Irrigation of Agricultural Lands,* Agronomy No. 11, American Society of Agronomy, Madison, Wisc., p. 905-921.

DOLAN, JEANIE, 1972. The impact of center pivot irrigation on dryland farming. *Crops Soils* 25(3):9-11.

ECONOMIC RESEARCH SERVICE, 1974. *The World Food Situation and Prospects to 1985.* USDA Foreign Agricultural Economic Report No. 98, 90 p.

FRANÇOIS, L. I., 1975. Effects of frequency of sprinkling with saline waters compared with daily drip irrigation. *Agron. J.* 67:185-190.

GULHATI, N. D., and W. C. SMITH, 1967. Irrigation agriculture: An historical review. In *Irrigation of Agricultural Lands,* Agronomy No. 11, American Society of Agronomy, Madison, Wisc., p. 3-11.

MALATIC, J. T., and T. B. HUTCHINGS, 1967. Selection and classification of irrigable land. In *Irrigation of Agricultural Lands,* Agronomy No. 11, American Society of Agronomy, Madison, Wisc., p. 125-173.

OSBORNE, DENNIS, 1973. Combine drainage and subirrigation to crop wetlands. *Crops Soils* 25(5):18-19.

RAUSCHKOLB, R. S., D. E. ROLSTON, R. J. MILLER, A. B. CARLTON, and R. G. BURAU, 1976. Phosphorus fertilization with drip irrigation. *Soil Sci. Soc. Am. J.* 40:68-72.

REEVE, R. C., A. F. PILLSBURY, and L. V. WILCOX, 1955. Reclamation of a saline and high boron soil in the Coachella Valley of California. *Hilgardia* 24:69-91.

ROBINSON, A. R., and A. S. HUMPHREYS, 1967. Water control and measurement on the farm. In *Irrigation of Agricultural Lands,* Agronomy No. 11, American Society of Agronomy, Madison, Wisc., p. 828-864.

ROBINSON, E. E., O. D. McCOY, G. F. WORKER, JR., and W. F. LEHMAN, 1968. Sprinkler and surface irrigation of vegetable and field crops in an arid environment. *Agron. J.* 60:696-700.

SHOJI, KOBE, 1977. Drip irrigation. *Sci. Am.* 237(5):62-68.

TADMOR, N. H., M. EVENARI, and L. SHANAN, 1970. Runoff farming in the desert. IV. Survival and yields of perennial range plants. *Agron. J.* 62:695-699.

THOMAS, H. E., 1955. Underground sources of our water. In *Water,* USDA Yearbook of Agriculture, U.S. Government Printing Office, p. 62-78.

THOMAS, H. E., and D. F. PETERSON, JR., 1967. Groundwater supply and development. In *Irrigation of Agricultural Lands,* Agronomy No. 11, American Society of Agronomy, Madison, Wisc., p. 70-91.

17

Soil and Water Pollution

Pollution contaminates things and makes them unclean or impure. Soil and water are polluted in many ways. Physical degradation results when eroded soil becomes a water pollutant or buries a fertile soil beneath unproductive sediment. Soil may be covered by discarded trash or ruined chemically by contamination with heavy metals or other toxic materials. Poisons sometimes escape from soil or trash into streams and lakes where they kill fish and perhaps birds and animals that live on the fish. The soil may be biologically degraded either by toxic materials or by poor management that exhausts its fertility, depletes its organic matter, and changes its soil structure to crusts and clods that restrict air and water movement.

The current rapid increase in world population, as shown in Figure 17-1, increases the value of productive soil and clean water. The pollution problem can no longer be ignored because there is no fresh desirable frontier land to replace that which is "worn out." Earth's resources are now recognized as being a closed system of limited size that is much easier to damage than to improve. Soil and water pollution squander the resources that support life.

17-1 RECENT CONCERN ABOUT POLLUTION

People have caused pollution for as long as their history can be traced. In fact, the careless discards of bygone civilizations have yielded much of the available information about ancient people. There was relatively little concern about pollution until recent times,

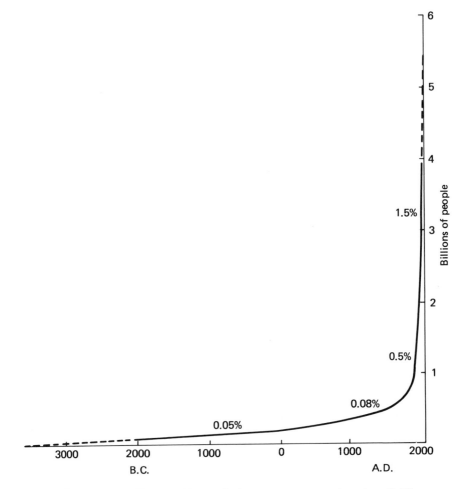

Figure 17-1 The world population grew at a rate less than 0.1% per year until about 1600 A.D.; since then the growth rate has increased to about 1.5% per year. The numbers beside the population curve tell the approximate annual increase in population.

however, because the population was only a fraction of its present size. There was plenty of room for both the people and the pollution they caused. The earth is now so fully populated that space restrictions limit the standard of living in many areas. Reducing productivity by soil pollution further decreases the standard of living. Water pollution, as shown in Figure 17-2, likewise has many unpleasant effects including aesthetic, health, and productivity problems.

Figure 17-2 Polluted water is both a hazard and a disappointment for these children. (Courtesy EPA-DOCUMERICA.)

The damage caused by pollution is difficult to evaluate accurately but some estimates are available. Shaw, Heggestad, and Heck (1971) state that pollution damage in the United States adds up to many billions of dollars each year. They indicate that air pollution alone causes more than half a billion dollars of damage to agricultural crops annually. That loss might double by the year 2000 because increased crop production will be required. Pollution itself will increase unless billions of dollars are spent to control it.

Another reason for increased concern about pollution is the variety of new types of pollutants. Items made of wood and other plant materials and those composed of animal products cause little pollution. The smelting of ores for metal products has caused some pollution for a long time and a growing amount since the industrial revolution. The wide variety of useful products coming from chemical industries in recent decades has been accompanied by an equal variety of pollutants. The more exotic materials are more likely to become pollutants rather than decompose into harmless chemicals. Fortunately the trend toward more serious chemical pollution is now being slowed or reversed by considering decomposition rates when new products are developed.

Nuclear wastes are the newest major class of pollutants and the cause of much concern. Part of the problem is the very long lifespan of many radioactive wastes and the extreme toxicity of some materials, especially plutonium. Safe disposal of such materials is a difficult problem that has not yet been solved on a long-term basis. Also, what should be done with the power plants when they are worn out or obsolete?

The increasing concern about pollution has been accompanied by more sensitive means of detecting pollutants and measuring their concentrations. Parts per trillion are measured as routinely now as parts per billion were measured a generation ago and as parts per million were before that. This increased sensitivity identifies pollutants that would have escaped notice before and raises the question of how much hazard such tiny amounts can cause. The current standard of zero tolerance imposed by the Delaney clause on any chemical that causes cancer in laboratory animals is being questioned by increasing numbers of people. Tolerable levels may need to be defined in some way other than the minimum detectable concentrations.

17-2 SOURCES OF POLLUTANTS

A pollutant is sometimes defined as a resource out of place—much like dirt is soil out of place or a weed is a plant out of place. Most pollutants either were once useful but have outlasted their useful stage or are produced as by-products of something useful. The problem is to eliminate the pollution without losing the useful products.

The sources of pollutants can be divided into many types, but only three will be used here: (1) people-related sources, (2) industrial sources, and (3) agricultural sources. People-related sources are produced from residences and the associated offices and businesses and are proportional to the number of people involved. For example, the amount of sewage produced daily by a city can be estimated by multiplying 0.38 m³ by the population (Thomas and Law, 1977). Industrial wastes are related to products and outputs rather than to the number of people. Agricultural sources are related to land areas, crop production, and livestock numbers. Each of these sources produces its own unique pollutants and needs its own kind of management to control pollution.

17-3 PEOPLE-RELATED WASTES

Population centers must provide means for disposal of solid and liquid wastes. Gaseous wastes are also produced, especially by burning solid wastes, but the resulting air pollution is outside the scope of this book. The solid and liquid wastes will be considered because they are significant pollutants of soil and water.

17-3.1 Solid Wastes

Objects composed of metal, wood, paper, plastic, glass, and other materials (Table 17-1) are dumped into trash cans and then into trucks to be hauled away. The disposal site used to be the city dump where piles of trash accumulated and scavengers searched for usable items in the debris. Open dumps fostered air pollution, especially when fires smoldered in them; many were havens for rats and other pests and created health hazards. Dumps were replaced by sanitary landfills where the trash is covered by a layer of soil the same day it is dumped. Sanitation was thereby improved and the hazards re-

Table 17-1 Percentage composition of solid waste from two cities and two nearby counties

	City		County	
Solid Waste	Oakland, Calif.	Phoenix, Ariz.	Sacramento Co., Calif.	Pima Co., Ariz.
Cans and metals	7.4	7.1	6.4	8.0
Glass	10.0	8.9	9.8	9.7
Paper	38.0	42.5	26.0	39.2
Organics and yard trim	31.0	27.2	29.0	28.5
Plastics	5.0	6.2	1.3	4.8
Textiles (rags)	2.5	3.1	1.1	1.6
Wood	2.5	1.2	0.8	1.0
Tires	2.2	1.0	1.0	1.0
Other (ashes, dirt, etc.)	1.4	2.8	24.6	6.2

SOURCE: Reproduced from *Soil for Management of Organic Wastes and Waste Waters,* Chapter 18, Fuller and Tucker, 1977, pp. 472–489 by permission of the American Society of Agronomy, Crop Science Society of America, and Soil Science Society of America; data credited to Benjamin Petrucci, Sacramento, California, and W. H. Fuller, University of Arizona, Tucson.

duced, but satisfactory landfill sites are scarce. Possible pollution of percolating water is a significant factor, and sight and odor pollution problems still cause people to protest the location of a landfill site near their residences.

Solid-waste recovery plants are the newest approach to solid-waste disposal. The first municipally owned plant of this type began operation at Ames, Iowa, in 1975. The Ames plant shreds the waste into small pieces and sorts it into combustible material, ferrous metal, aluminum, other metals, and reject material, as shown in Figure 17-3. The metals are sold and the combustible material is mixed with coal for electric power production. According to A. O. Chantland, Ames Director of Public Works, the plant processed 41,000 mt of waste during its first year of operation and recovered 93% of the materials as salable products. Research is underway to see if some of the remaining glass and other mineral matter can be used in paving or some other way rather than being buried.

Ames recovered nearly $11 worth of marketable products per ton of waste in 1976, nearly enough to cover operating costs but not depreciation on the plant. The cost-return ratio has since improved and should eventually reach the break-even point on total expenses if the waste volume approaches plant capacity. An extra benefit to the city is the low sulfur content of the combustible portion of the waste.

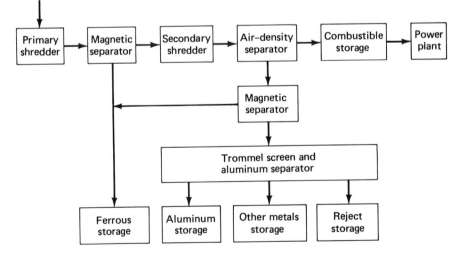

Figure 17-3 A flow diagram for the solid-waste recovery system at Ames, Iowa.

17-3.2 Liquid Wastes

Sewer systems transport liquid wastes to sewage plants for treatment. At least, the sewage should be treated. Garman (1971) indicates that 1300 cities and towns in the United States empty raw sewage into streams without any treatment and another 1300 do so after minimal treatment. *Primary treatment,* removing materials that will either float or settle out of quiet water, is all that is provided by about half of the sewage treatment plants in the United States. The effluent passed on to a nearby stream still carries about two-thirds of the biological oxygen demand (BOD) of the sewage along with dissolved materials and suspended solids.

The sewage treatment plants of most cities also provide *secondary treatment* which allows bacteria to act on the effluent of primary treatment. The bacteria work either in an activated sludge tank through which air is blown to promote bacterial growth, or on the surface of stones about 10 cm in diameter that fill trickling-filter tanks. Secondary treatment should remove at least 90% of the solid matter and BOD from the sewage. The effluent from secondary treatment is usually chlorinated to kill harmful bacteria and then discharged into a stream.

The water pollution from sewage effluent is much less serious than it would be without treatment, but the effluent still causes eutrophication because it contains plant nutrients. Nitrogen and phosphorus are the most important nutrients because they are the most likely to be deficient enough in water to prevent algal growth. Algae form an unsightly scum on water and then die. Decomposition of the algal mass depletes the water of dissolved O_2 and produces a rotten odor. This type of water pollution can be avoided or controlled if either nitrogen or phosphorus can be held to low enough concentrations in the water.

Laundry detergents and other cleaning agents are the source of most of the phosphorus in sewage effluent. The phosphorus content of streams increases dramatically below sewer outlets and commonly results in large masses of algal growth. One way to reduce such pollution is to reduce the phosphorus content of detergents. Researchers are seeking alternate ways of producing effective cleaning agents. One reason for optimism is the earlier success in changing detergents from the hard type that produced foam in streams, as shown in Figure 17-4, to the present soft type that is biodegradable.

Sludge is the solid material removed by primary and secondary treatment of sewage. The amount is significant even though it is only about 0.1% of the total volume of the sewage. The wet sludge is

Figure 17-4 Hard detergents once produced masses of foam in streams and even in drinking water. The change from hard to biodegradable detergents in the United States was completed in 1965. (Courtesy USDA—Office of Information.)

usually dried on a sand bed. The dried sludge is a mellow material of variable composition averaging about 4% N, 3% P, and 0.3% K (Sommers, 1977). It is sometimes used to loosen and fertilize garden soils, or it can be applied to fields when the supply is large. Sometimes it is finely ground and mixed with effluent for distribution through a sprinkler irrigation system.

Relatively few sewage plants provide *tertiary treatment*, but the number is increasing as a result of pollution-control requirements. Tertiary treatment removes dissolved materials from the effluent of secondary treatment. Two methods are used—chemical treatment and disposal on land by sprinkler irrigation. The large quantities of resins required to absorb anions and cations usually make the cost of chemical treatment prohibitive. Most of the interest in tertiary treatment is therefore directed toward disposal on land.

The soil to be used for tertiary sewage treatment must be permeable and well drained. High rates of disposal are usually desired to minimize the land area and the size of the irrigation system required. High rates usually require a tile drainage system to prevent waterlogging. A forage crop should be grown on the land to protect the soil from the relatively large droplets resulting from the large sprinkler nozzles required to avoid clogging problems. The forage should be harvested to remove plant nutrients so they will not build up to high concentrations in the soil.

Waste disposal on land usually results in application of water and nutrients at much higher rates than are needed for plant growth. Management should therefore be directed toward disposal of nutrients. Nitrogen loss by denitrification can be promoted by keeping the soil wet for about six days and then allowing it to dry for about five (Lance, Whisler, and Bauwer, 1973). Phosphorus will form insoluble compounds with calcium or iron and aluminum. Excess potassium may be held on cation-exchange sites unless it is removed by the crop by luxury consumption or leached from the soil.

Heavy-metal ions contained in the sewage are usually the factor that limits application amounts. The metallic ions are held in the soil by cation exchange and are difficult to remove. Some heavy metals are quite toxic to plant growth and their toxicity may persist for decades. In order to monitor the problem, the zinc equivalent has been defined as the zinc concentration plus double the copper concentration and eight times the nickel concentration. According to Larson, Gilley, and Linden (1975), the zinc equivalent added to agricultural soils should not exceed 5% to 10% of the soil's cation-exchange capacity. Typically, a soil with a cation-exchange capacity of 20 meq/100 g can probably accept 500 to 1500 mt of average sewage sludge (a depth of about 5 to 15 cm) before being limited by the zinc equivalent. Much larger amounts of effluent can be applied, because the metals tend to be concentrated in the sludge rather than in the effluent.

17-3.3 Rural Home Wastes

Rural homes and others not connected to sewer systems still have to dispose of both solid and liquid wastes. Residents of many such homes use their own small version of the old city dump, often by discarding their trash in a gully or on a stony area as shown in Figure 17-5. One advantage many rural homes have is that garbage can be fed to livestock and therefore need not be included with the other solid waste.

Septic tanks are used to dispose of liquid wastes apart from sewer systems. They provide both settling and bacterial action in the tank, followed by disposal by subirrigation through a tile drain field. A system that functions properly provides the equivalent of primary and secondary sewage treatment in the tank and tertiary treatment in the soil. Problems arise when the tank fills with sediment (in which

Figure 17-5 Trash discarded in a gully is unsightly, may harbor mice and rats, can cause water pollution, and must be removed before the gully can be repaired. (Courtesy F. R. Troeh.)

case it needs to be pumped out) or when the drain field will not accept all of the effluent. Bacterial products often clog the pores of the soil around the drain lines and thus reduce the permeability. Septic tank effluent that reaches the surface from faulty operation causes unpleasant odors and can cause a health hazard.

17-3.4 Litter

People have a distressing habit of littering wherever they go. Wrappers, containers, worn-out items, and other discards fall by the wayside and clutter the landscape. Some of these items injure only the appearance of the area. Others stifle plant growth by cutting off air, water, and light. Still other items such as broken glass and sharp pieces of metal can inflict wounds on persons or animals, and some discarded poison containers can be deadly. A small percentage of the population undoubtedly produces most of the litter—those with the attitude "I don't care." The problem seems to be worst when leisure time is involved and people are relaxing.

Cities, towns, national parks, and other public bodies spend large sums cleaning up litter. Fines may be levied on those who litter, but it seems that few are ever caught. A newer approach of outlawing disposable bottles and cans (major litter items) and requiring a deposit on all beverage containers has been more successful but cannot solve the whole problem. Changes in attitudes and habits are needed.

17-4 INDUSTRIAL WASTES

There are many kinds of industries producing a wide variety of wastes. The wastes may be solids, liquids, or gases, and they often carry heat with them. The solid wastes include slag from smelters, gypsum from phosphate fertilizer plants, sawdust from sawmills, and scrap pieces or remnants of almost anything that is made. The material may be wood, metal, cloth, paper, glass, rubber, plastic, or almost anything else. Reactive chemicals are important concerns, especially if they are toxic to people, animals, or plants. Some wastes are dense and some are bulky; some are combustible whereas others are inert and resistant to decomposition.

17-4.1 Solid Industrial Wastes

Disposal methods for solid industrial wastes depend on the nature and amount of the waste. Municipal solid waste disposal systems accept some industrial wastes; some large industries manage their own landfills. Much combustible waste is burned in high-temperature incinerators. These means dispose of part of the waste, but there is still much that accumulates and pollutes land near factories.

Scrap metal and some other materials can often be kept separate from other wastes and recycled. Proper planning coupled with attitude changes could result in much more recycling than is now occurring. Recycling reduces both the waste disposal problem and the consumption of raw materials.

17-4.2 Liquid Industrial Wastes

Most liquid industrial wastes are either water or water-based; petroleum materials are a distant second. According to Shaw, Heggestad, and Heck (1971), there are more than 300,000 factories in the United States and they discharge three to four times as much BOD into streams as the human wastes carried by sewers. The water may be acid or alkaline and often absorbs chemicals as it serves as a transporting agent or a medium in which materials interact or chemicals react. The water may be hot from chemical reactions or from serving as a coolant.

Petroleum products, toxic chemicals, and hot water pose diffi-cult waste disposal problems. Dilution and natural stream processes will purify the water only when the waste flow is small relative to the stream flow. Environmental protection frequently requires that chemicals be removed from water or the water be cooled before it can be emptied into a stream. Sometimes a closed system is required in which the used water is purified and reused so pollutants cannot reach the stream. Of course, some provision must be made to reuse, market, or dispose of the materials removed from the water.

17-4.3 Air Pollution

Air pollution will be mentioned briefly here as it relates to soil and water pollution. Sometimes the atmosphere becomes the preferred waste disposal site, as when heat is exhausted through a radiator or a cooling tower. Carbon dioxide and water vapor are expelled to the atmosphere along with heat when materials are burned. Un-fortunately, burning may produce gaseous oxides of sulfur and nitro-gen plus fine particles of solid matter that pollute the atmosphere. Such materials often concentrate in droplets of rain, mist, or fog and sometimes react to produce smog. The droplets become soil and water pollutants when they fall.

Sulfur dioxide dissolved in water produces sulfurous acid that may be oxidized to sulfuric acid. These acids can produce rainwater with a pH as low as 2 (Likens and Bormann, 1974). Acid rain is corrosive to metals and concrete and virtually eliminates the growth of flowers and many other plants in industrial centers where much coal is burned. Pollution-control efforts are making slow progress in solving the acid-rain problem. There is some concern, however, about tendencies to apply pollution-control requirements universally. The soil in areas away from industrial centers commonly receives free fertilizer benefits amounting to 10 to 15 kg/ha of available N and 15 to 20 kg/ha of available S annually.

17-4.4 Nuclear Wastes

Atomic bombs, nuclear-powered ships, and nuclear reactors for generating electricity inevitably produce nuclear wastes. These wastes are so hazardous and so long-lived that no means of disposal has yet proved to be satisfactory for the long run. The disposal hazard, the remote but frightening possibility of a nuclear accident, the fearsome prospects of nuclear warfare or nuclear blackmail, and the limited supply of uranium have raised strong opposition to the use of nuclear energy. Equally strong support is based on energy needs and the military potency of atomic power.

A nuclear reactor uses only a few thousand tons of uranium oxide during its entire lifetime. The amount of radioactive wastes produced is comparatively small. But the twin hazards of long-lasting radioactivity and extreme toxicity of waste components such as plutonium make the storage and disposal methods very important. Corrosion-resistant steel tanks embedded in thick concrete have been used to contain the wastes. Some of these containers rest on the ocean floor where they were dumped several years ago; they are now regarded as potential hazards to fish and other life because the projected lifespan of the wastes may be 1000 times as long as that of the containers.

Consideration is being given to disposal of atomic wastes in deep rock formations. The formations need to be dense and free of earthquake faults and other fractures that would permit water flow. There must be a way to form a cavity, place a waste capsule in it, and seal the hole. Preferably, the capsule should be retrievable if the need should arise. Certain salt deposits are regarded as best fulfilling the requirements, but it is difficult to be sure that nothing would ever leak out even from them.

Another problem is what to do with an obsolete or worn-out nuclear reactor. Some are now reaching this stage, but none has yet been dismantled and removed from its site. The process will have to be accomplished in a way that protects the workers from radioactivity and leaves the site uncontaminated. The radioactive parts of the plant present a disposal problem similar to that of the spent fuel. Until the problem is solved, old power plants will have to be sealed and guarded to keep out people and animals.

17-5 AGRICULTURAL WASTES

Livestock in the United States produce between 1.5 and 2 million metric tons of waste per year. Plant residues total hundreds of millions of tons. These materials are generally beneficial when returned to the soil, but not all of them go there. Some get into streams, ponds, and lakes where they cause pollution. In addition, agriculture uses many chemicals, containers, and other items that can become either soil or water pollutants.

The task of reducing agricultural pollution is complicated by the diffuse or nonpoint nature of the sources. Livestock wastes may be deposited anywhere and may later be washed into a nearby stream. Similarly, persistent chemicals applied to either soil or plants can be carried into streams by runoff water. Pollution-control efforts must be applied to large areas to significantly reduce the effects of nonpoint sources.

17-5.1 Livestock Wastes

The handling of livestock wastes varies widely. Cattle droppings in India may be dried and used to fuel a fire. Such fuel is prized because none other is affordable. However, the manure from a large feedlot in western United States accumulates in mammoth piles and is a serious disposal problem. Operations that feed tens of thousands of animals seldom have access to enough land to make beneficial use of the manure produced. Smaller operations can use their manure as fertilizer on nearby land, but the hauling distance becomes too great for the large operations. Attitude is also important—many livestock managers of both large and small operations think of the manure as a nuisance rather than as a resource. In fact, in years past, many feedlots such as the one shown in Figure 17-6 were deliberately placed on sloping land next to a stream so the manure would be washed away.

Much manure has been carelessly handled or ignored because its fertilizer value was deemed to be too low to pay the handling costs.

Figure 17-6 Many feedlots are located next to a stream because it was formerly thought to be desirable to let the stream carry the wastes away. (Courtesy USDA—Office of Information.)

The composition varies with types of livestock and management, but an average ton of wet cattle manure contains about 6 kg of N, 1.5 kg of P, and 5 kg of K (Table 17-2). The commercial fertilizer value of these nutrients was about $2 in 1970, $4 in 1975, and $3.50 in 1978. The cost of loading, hauling, and spreading the manure is approximately the same as its fertilizer value. Given this equal cost option, many people have preferred to handle a small bag of commercial fertilizer instead of a ton of manure. This reasoning overlooks three significant factors: (1) cleanup costs should be charged to the livestock operation rather than to fertilizer value; (2) manure contains other valuable nutrients in addition to N, P, and K; (3) manure applications usually improve soil structure. These factors added to the value of the N, P, and K make a ton of manure worth much more than its handling cost. Furthermore, manure management would be important to control pollution even if it had no value for crop production.

Much manure has accumulated in piles behind barns until there was a convenient time to haul and spread it. Such manure usually contains straw or hay used as bedding for the animals. Bedding helps absorb the liquid excrement and the nutrients it contains and thereby increases the tonnage without diluting the nutrient content. Odors from manure piles indicate that volatilization is occurring; nitrogen is being lost as ammonia, and sulfur as hydrogen sulfide (Mosier, Morrison, and Elmund, 1977). Ammonia and hydrogen sulfide accumulate in the atmosphere around feedlots. Some volatil-

Table 17-2 Average water and nutrient contents of animal manures

Animal	H_2O (%)	Nutrients (kg/mt)					
		N	P	K	S	Ca	Mg
Dairy cattle	79	5.6	1.0	5.0	0.5	2.8	1.1
Fattening cattle	80	7.0	2.0	4.5	0.85	1.2	1.0
Hogs	75	5.0	1.4	3.8	1.35	5.7	0.8
Horse	60	6.9	1.0	6.0	0.7	7.85	1.4
Sheep	65	14.0	2.1	10.0	0.9	5.85	1.85
Broiler	25	17.0	8.1	12.5	—	—	—
Hen	37	13.0	12.0	11.4	—	—	—

SOURCE: Reproduced from *Soils for Management of Organic Wastes and Waste Waters,* Chapter 8, Olsen and Barber, 1977, pp. 197–215 by permission of the American Society of Agronomy, Crop Science Society of America, and Soil Science Society of America; data credited to R. C. Loehr.

ized nitrogen and sulfur may be absorbed by soil or water in the downwind area, but some circulates in the atmosphere until it is brought down by rain. The Agricultural Research Service (1970a) reported that more nitrogen from cattle feedlots may reach nearby lakes and rivers as airborne ammonia than as dissolved nitrogen in runoff and drainage water. Volatilization losses can be minimized by compacting the manure to keep it anaerobic and by getting the manure to the field and into the soil as soon as possible. Plowing or disking it into the soil is important, because volatilization losses are faster under aerobic conditions in the field than under anaerobic conditions in a pile. Lauer, Bouldin, and Klausner (1976) found ammonia losses ranging from 61% to 99% during five to twenty-five days after surface applications.

Manure piles should have a roof over them to keep out rain. A covered area in a feedlot works well because trampling by the animals compacts the manure and helps make the pile anaerobic. Piles that must be in the open should be tall and rounded to shed water as well as possible. Any water that leaches through a pile will carry nutrients away.

Lagoons have become an alternate means of handling livestock wastes. The wastes are often washed to the lagoon through a pipeline since water must be added anyway to dilute the wastes. Most lagoons are anaerobic and therefore produce some odors. Most of the solid matter in the waste eventually liquefies by anaerobic digestion; the remainder settles as sludge on the bottom of the lagoon. Much of the organic matter is decomposed to CO_2 and H_2O. Half or more of the nitrogen and sulfur may be volatilized when long-term retention is practiced. The effluent from a lagoon can be applied to land by a sprinkler system or a spray truck but should not be emptied into a stream. It still contains much organic matter and many plant nutrients that would contribute to water pollution.

Manure rates up to about 20 mt/ha properly applied and incorporated into the soil are effective for fertilizer purposes and cause little or no pollution. Such applications can be supplemented by commercial fertilizers to meet any remaining fertility requirements. Numerous trials have indicated that combinations of organic and mineral fertilizers are equal to or better than other means of fertilizing. Although they represent inefficient use of the nutrients in the manure, rates up to 70 mt/ha have been used in humid regions for as long as forty years without causing harmful buildups of nutrients or soluble salts in the soil (Sommerfeldt, Pittman, and Milne, 1973).

Manure is sometimes applied to land at rates of 100 to 200 mt/ha to minimize the amount of land area required for disposal purposes.

Such high rates can cause pollution because the crops growing on the land cannot use all of the available nutrients. Nitrates and other soluble salts accumulate in the soil and in drainage water. Runoff water, too, may be contaminated, especially if the manure has been left on the soil surface. The best way to use manure without causing pollution is to spread it at lower rates across more land. The added hauling costs are offset by the increased fertilizer value obtained from the manure. If high rates must be used, luxury consumption and denitrification should be encouraged as discussed for sewage applications in Section 17-3.2.

17-5.2 Plant Residues

Plant residues seldom cause serious pollution. In fact, plant residues are usually an asset for controlling soil erosion, retaining plant nutrients, and producing beneficial effects in the soil. Nevertheless, plant residues can cause problems by accumulating as debris either on land or in water. The debris is unsightly and it may block a watercourse or plug a screen. Sometimes the residues smother vegetation. Sometimes they cause odors as they rot or produce smoke and soot as they burn.

Tumbleweeds are a common source of debris in arid regions. They accumulate in fences and ditches and against buildings where they may obstruct passage and increase the fire hazard. Broken tree branches and fallen trees also produce litter that can block pathways and even roads, or they and other debris may fall into a stream and accumulate in areas of quiet water or next to a dam. The decomposing debris adds to the biological oxygen demand along with other waste that may be in the water.

It is fortunate that pollution problems from plant residues are usually minor. Plant residues are too abundant for all such problems to be avoided. The usual approach is simply to clean up the offending residues.

17-5.3 Agricultural Chemicals

Thousands of different chemicals are used for agricultural purposes. Many chemicals are used in very large quantities to cover the immense areas involved in growing various crops and livestock. There would certainly be some problems even under ideal conditions. Actually, conditions are far from ideal. Weather, soil, and animal interactions with chemicals are often unpredictable. Chemical users and their equipment are fallible and may apply too much chemical in one place and not enough elsewhere. Not all users are well trained;

some are inclined to experiment even in adverse circumstances. A pessimist could easily predict that problems with agricultural chemicals would be much more common and more severe than they actually are.

Most of the concern about agricultural chemicals has involved either fertilizers or pesticides. There have been other concerns such as the use of nitrates and nitrites as food preservatives and the use of growth stimulants, but only the fertilizers and pesticides will be emphasized in this section.

Fertilizers. Over 80 million mt of fertilizer N, P, and K are now being applied annually in the world as mineral fertilizers and the rate is increasing steadily. About 20% of this fertilizer use is in the United States. Fertilizer application rates range from zero to several hundred kilograms of nutrients per hectare. High value horticultural crops tend to receive the highest fertilizer rates, but fields of agronomic crops such as corn, cotton, and tobacco also receive more N, P, and K than is being removed in harvested crops. An illustration of the effects of changing cropping and fertilizer practices on soil fertility is shown in Figure 17–7.

Fertilizer use is increasing because fertilizers are very potent means of increasing crop production. Supplying a deficient nutrient improves both the quality and the quantity of the crop. Few people who have studied the matter believe that the food and other needs of the human population could be properly met without increasing the use of fertilizer as the population grows. Nevertheless, several environmental charges made against fertilizers need to be taken seri-

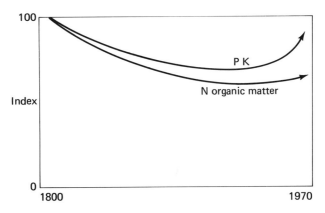

Figure 17-7 A schematic illustration of the general trends of soil fertility in Illinois from 1800 to 1970.

ously. Three such concerns will be considered here—the effects of fertilizers on water pollution, the effect of denitrification on the ozone layer, and the effects of fertilizers on soil microbes.

Plant nutrients can be carried to a stream either by overland flow or in drainage water. Overland flow can carry nutrients in solution or attached to soil particles carried in suspension whereas subsurface drainage water carries only dissolved nutrients. The nutrients attached to eroding soil particles constitute by far the largest of these losses and will be considered in Section 17-6.

Solution losses are proportional to the concentration of the plant nutrients in the runoff or drainage water. Nitrate nitrogen (NO_3^-) is one of the prime concerns because it is highly soluble and it is very weakly held in the soil. In contrast, both ammonium and potassium ions $(NH_4^+$ and $K^+)$ are held by cation exchange, and phosphates $(H_2PO_4^-$ and $HPO_4^{--})$ have both low solubility and strong attraction to anion-exchange sites. Organic forms are mostly held against loss unless the organic material itself is washed away.

Leaching losses of nitrate nitrogen are usually small but can be large under certain conditions. Data from a nearly level Minnesota soil with tile drainage are shown in Table 17-3. The recommended rate for fertilizer nitrogen in this area is about 200 kg N/ha for continuous corn. About one-fourth of that amount would have been lost by leaching in this study. Increasing the fertilizer rate increased the leaching loss; decreasing the rate decreased but did not eliminate the loss. Between 15 and 20 kg/ha of nitrate nitrogen would have been leached into the tile drains even without any fertilizer, because the normal decomposition of organic matter produces nitrates that can be leached. A thirty-year study by the Agricultural Research Service (1970b) showed that the nitrate content of the Rio Grande River had not increased although there were large increases in fertilizer use on nearby land.

The Webster soil represented by the data in Table 17-3 must have drainage if it is to be cropped. Unfortunately, drainage systems make leaching possible. Without drainage there would be no escape

Table 17-3 Nitrate nitrogen loss in tile drainage water from various rates of nitrogen applications to continuous corn on fine-textured Webster soil in Minnesota

N fertilizer rates (kg/ha)	20	112	224	448
NO_3-N in tile drainage water (kg/ha)	19	25	59	120

SOURCE: Gast, Nelson, and Randall, 1978.

point for the water and its solutes. The loss rate by leaching from better-drained soils in humid regions is usually slower than that indicated in Table 17-3, because the water has farther to go. Deep-rooted plants use more of the nitrogen and reduce the loss when the percolation time is longer. Denitrifying microbes also consume more nitrate and reduce its concentration in the deeper soils. Nitrate leaching is therefore greatest in permeable soils that are shallow to tile drainage or to a gravel layer that drains the water. No leaching occurs from soils of arid regions unless they are irrigated or located in wet positions on the landscape.

Fertilizer rates influence nitrate leaching if the fertilizer increases the nitrate concentration in solution at times when leaching losses occur. The losses can be reduced by applying only as much nitrogen as necessary and putting it on as late as possible to meet the crop needs.

The form of nitrogen fertilizer also makes a difference in leaching rates, especially when the weather is cool. Ammonium and organic forms of nitrogen must be oxidized to nitrate before much leaching loss can occur from soils that have significant cation-exchange capacities. The process is called nitrification; it proceeds slowly at soil temperatures below $10°C$ and stops when the soil freezes. The nitrification rate increases when the soil warms up in the spring, but plant growth should begin to use the nitrate nitrogen at that time.

Runoff losses of nitrogen fertilizer range from none to a few percent, rarely exceeding 10% of the amount applied. Dunigan, Phelan, and Mondart (1976) fertilized a silt loam soil on a 5% slope in Louisiana and measured the runoff loss. The nitrogen in the runoff was less than 3% of that applied, except for one treatment when a heavy rain on the third day after fertilization carried away 9.5% of the nitrogen. Phosphorus and potassium losses were less than 1% of the amounts applied.

Runoff losses of surface-applied fertilizer are usually small be-cause most rains have a significant wetting period before runoff begins. The soluble fertilizer is carried down into the soil during these first few minutes. Little fertilizer remains on the surface to be lost in the runoff. Exceptional losses can occur if intense rain strikes very suddenly or if the soil is frozen or otherwise imperme-able so the rain cannot infiltrate.

Denitrification and ammonia volatilization cause nitrogen to be lost from the soil to the atmosphere. *Ammonia volatilization* can become significant when urea from either commercial fertilizer or manure is used as a nitrogen source and left on the soil surface, especially if the soil is alkaline. The urea reacts with water to form ammonium carbonate:

$$CO(NH_2)_2 + 2 H_2O \longrightarrow (NH_4)_2CO_3$$

Reaction with any base under alkaline conditions can then volatilize ammonia:

$$(NH_4)_2CO_3 + 2 NaOH \longrightarrow Na_2CO_3 + 2 H_2O + 2 NH_3 \uparrow$$

Much of the volatilized ammonia is probably carried back to the soil somewhere in rainwater, although some may be oxidized to the same gaseous nitrogen compounds produced by denitrification.

Denitrification occurs when a soil with anaerobic conditions contains nitrates. The nitrates may have been applied as fertilizer or they may have been formed by nitrification in an aerated part of the soil or during a time when the soil was dry enough to allow air to enter. A wetter time or the movement of nitrate ions to a wetter part of the soil causes anaerobic bacteria to take oxygen from nitrate ions and produce N_2, N_2O, and NO. The molecular nitrogen is harmless, but the oxides may be a threat to the ozone layer. Small quantities of these oxides in the atmosphere are normal since they are formed by lightning and rise from the soil and other sources. The concern is whether increased fertilization might increase denitrification and its products enough to decompose too much ozone. The same concern applies to nitrogen oxides from automobile exhausts and other sources.

The amounts of nitrogen oxides produced by denitrification are largest where soils having alternate wet and dry conditions receive large amounts of available nitrogen. This situation is sometimes deliberately created for waste disposal as described in Section 17-3.2. However, the loss by denitrification of fertilizer nitrogen and nitrates formed by decomposition of organic matter is undesirable because it decreases the nitrogen supply for plant growth. The best remedy for these losses is to drain the wet spots and thus improve aeration and reduce losses of available nitrogen. Undrained wet spots usually should not be cropped and fertilized. Some denitrification occurs naturally in wet spots, and fertilization would increase the amount.

Van Cleemput (1971) showed that under denitrifying conditions an acid medium evolved nitrogen oxides but an alkaline medium produced N_2. Proper liming of soils that are sometimes wet enough for denitrification should therefore reduce the output of nitrogen oxides. Another approach is indicated by the work of Bollag and Henninger (1976). They found that fungicides such as captan, maneb, and nabam inhibited denitrification and that the herbicide 2,4-D had a lesser but significant inhibitory effect.

Chemical changes resulting from fertilization can have considerable impact on the microbial population. The effect may show within a few days, as when the addition of a nitrogen source speeds up the decomposition of plant residues in the soil. Long-term effects may develop over periods of years, as when the microbial population changes in response to gradual acidification resulting from nitrification of ammonium fertilizers. Fortunately, these changes are normal and reversible. The microbial population is versatile and able to adjust to the changing conditions.

Conditions vary from one part of a soil to another as well as from one time to another. Banded fertilizer applications concentrate the fertilizer effect in a part of the soil and therefore have an increased impact on that part. The salt effect may dehydrate and kill microbes in a fertilizer band. Even when this happens, there is a zone around the band where the added nutrients cause microbes to multiply and give a larger total population than the soil would have without the band. Similar effects result from ammonia injection into soil. The pH in the injection zone rises to about 10 and stops all microbial activity, but microbes thrive on the margin of the zone and gradually work their way through it, reaching the center and acidifying the soil in a few weeks (Frederick, Openshaw, and Thorup, 1968).

Fertilizers, like most other things, can be misused. Low to moderate fertilizer rates cause little or no environmental damage because the nutrients are used by growing plants. In fact, the improved plant growth often reduces pollution by reducing erosion. However, fertilizer rates above the amounts that can be used by plants can contribute to pollution. The excess nutrients may be held by the soil for a while, but eventually they must move into either water or air.

Nitrogen is usually the main nutrient of concern in fertilizer pollution studies. Phosphorus and potassium are held more firmly against loss. Table 17-4 shows what happened to the nitrogen applied to two soils on the North Carolina coastal plain. About half of the nitrogen applied was used by the crops. Surface runoff removed more than is usually expected, especially from the poorly drained soil where the runoff amount was small but the nitrogen concentration was high. The unmeasured nitrogen loss would have included denitrification and deep percolation losses that bypassed the tile drains.

Two indirect forms of fertilizer pollution should be mentioned here. One is by their manufacture. The processing plants necessarily produce by-products such as gypsum and other materials that may become pollutants. The second form results when fertilizers are sub-

Table 17–4 Nitrogen inputs and removals from two fertilized coastal plain soils in North Carolina (kg/ha-yr; two-year field averages)

	Field 1 (moderately well-drained soil)	Field 2 (poorly-drained soil)
Nitrogen input—fertilizer	160	196
Nitrogen removal:		
Grain harvested	92	91
Surface runoff	22	29
Subsurface drains	26	16
Total removal measured	140	136
Nitrogen not measured	20	60

SOURCE: Reproduced from *Journal of Environmental Quality*, Volume 4, No. 3, Gambrell, Gilliam, and Weed, 1975, pp. 317–323 by permission of the American Society of Agronomy, Crop Science Society of America, and Soil Science Society of America.

stituted for animal wastes. The unused animal wastes cause much more pollution than those that are properly handled and used for fertilizer.

Pesticides. The combined impact of weeds, insects, and plant diseases commonly limits yields to a fraction of plant potentials. Farmers and gardeners have fought pests with tillage practices, crop rotations, and selections of resistant crops. Some have even gone out to battle insects in person against hopeless odds. The pests may be small but they are exceedingly numerous. A single field may harbor more insects than the human population of the entire nation. The soil in the field almost always holds more weed seed than the farmer would ever plant of crop seeds.

Chemical warfare against agricultural pests is a relatively recent innovation. Some of the earliest pesticides were Paris green—a mixture containing arsenic trioxide and copper acetate used as an insecticide since about 1870, and bordeaux mixture—a copper sulfate and lime mixture used as a fungicide since the 1880s. Bordeaux mixture was originally applied to grape vines to make them look poisonous so schoolboys would not steal them. Paris green may have been a by-product of political intrigue, since arsenic compounds were favorite poisons during the Middle Ages.

Highly toxic materials such as arsenic compounds and heavy metals such as copper present environmental problems that can hardly be overlooked. These problems are amplified by the relatively high application rates required for these materials and the unde-composable nature of their active elements. Furthermore, the heavy metals are strongly held by cation exchange in the soil. Aerial photos show poor crop growth where the spray drippings from former trees and vines were most concentrated, even though the orchards and vineyards have been gone for decades.

The development of DDT as an insecticide in 1940 and of 2,4-D as an herbicide in 1941 along with many other less well known com-pounds led to the replacement of the metallic compounds with organic materials. The organic pesticides have several advantages—lower rates and fewer applications are needed, they are more selec-tive in their toxicity than the metals, and they can be decomposed into simple harmless compounds. Their use, especially that of DDT, expanded rapidly until it was realized that they could create prob-lems. DDT became the subject of much controversy and was banned after the discovery that it threatened unintended victims by bioac-cumulation. Metcalf (1971) cites data from Lake Michigan showing DDT concentrations of 2 parts per trillion in the water increasing progressively through the food chain to 99 parts per million in herring gulls.

Pesticides now go through an elaborate testing procedure to prove that they will control the target pests and will not harm the environment. Their effects on many different forms of life are deter-mined, their decomposition rates and tendencies to be adsorbed by soil components are measured, and the specific conditions under which they may be used are defined. Thousands of chemicals are screened to find a few that can be used.

There are still problems with pesticides in spite of all the pre-cautions. Some of them don't last long enough and have to be ap-plied again and again the same season; others last too long and damage the next year's crop. Some are quite sensitive to soil condi-tions such as organic-matter content, cation-exchange capacity, and pH, so they need to be applied at different rates on different soils. Some chemicals are carried by runoff water into places where they are not wanted. Many grassed waterways, for example, have been killed by atrazine washed from a corn field. Another problem is the tendency of the pests to adapt and develop resistance. New materials are needed to maintain control when the old materials become ineffective.

Pesticides, especially insecticides, applied to the soil can have a significant impact on soil animals ranging in size from earthworms to protozoa. The impact depends on both the toxicity and the persistence of the chemical and is stronger if the chemical is mixed into the soil than if it remains on the surface (Edwards, 1969). The soil animals are normally able to adjust to the effects of applied chemicals and repopulate the soil within a few months. Edwards concluded that the ecological effects of soil pollution are less serious than those of water pollution.

Despite the remaining problems, modern pesticides are making possible several agricultural improvements. They are a significant factor in increased crop production during recent decades and are needed to continue that trend in the future. Herbicides save time and energy by reducing or even eliminating the need for cultivation of row crops. No-till farming would be impossible without effective herbicides to control weeds. Erosion control and energy conservation are important benefits from reducing tillage.

Work is still underway to develop better pesticides and pesticide alternatives. Several biological control methods are favored in specific circumstances. Crop breeding to develop improved resistance to pests is old enough to be considered standard practice and yet current enough for workers to still be searching all over the world for native plants that might carry significant genetic material. Similar searches are conducted for natural predators that can control insect pests. Other biological control methods that have been effective against certain insects are the release of large numbers of sterile male insects to interfere with normal insect breeding and the use of synthetic sex attractant compounds to confuse the insects. Such methods are laborious because every situation must be handled separately, but they provide means of controlling pests without harming the environment.

17–6 ERODED SOIL AS A POLLUTANT

No other pollutant occurs in amounts comparable to sediment. Streams in the United States carry over 700 times as much eroded soil as sewage. Soil is an important factor in water pollution because of the large volume it occupies, the murkiness it produces, the plant nutrients, pesticides, and other polluting chemicals it carries, and the microbes that may be present.

17–6.1 Sediment

A thin layer of loamy sediment rich in organic matter often has a beneficial effect on the soil it covers. Fertile bottomlands are built of such sediments. But sediment deposition also occurs in detrimental forms. Some sediment has much lower fertility than the soil it covers. Other sediment is so high in clay that it is unfavorable for plant growth and for tillage operations. Sediment is frequently deposited in such thick layers that plants are smothered and killed, as shown in Figure 17-8. Similar problems can occur with sediment from wind erosion. Sedimentation problems can be considered as a form of land pollution; they have already been discussed in Chapters 4 and 5.

Sediment problems usually last longer in water than on land. Much of the sedimentation damage on land is temporary because new crops can be planted on the sediment or other vegetation will grow and the land may become as productive as it was before. Sediment deposited in streams, ponds, lakes, and oceans displaces water in ways that can be quite detrimental. Sediment-filled reservoirs no longer serve well for flood control, electric power production, and recreation. Sediment on deltas and riverbeds raises water levels and increases flood hazards. Sediment in canal and ditch systems requires costly clean-out operations. The progressive and recurring nature of sedimentation problems makes them particularly bothersome in bodies of water.

Figure 17-8 A heavy spring rain deposited about 45 cm of silt on this Iowa pasture, killing the grass and half burying the fence. (Courtesy USDA—Soil Conservation Service.)

17-6.2 Muddy Water

Only a small amount of clay and organic matter is required to make water cloudy, and some of this effect is natural. Even so, agricultural soil erosion contributes greatly to the opacity of streams and lakes. The nickname "The Big Muddy" given to the Mississippi River indicates what has happened to it. Other human activities also contribute to muddy waters. For example, the Clearwater River in Idaho is fed mostly from forest lands but has nevertheless become cloudy rather than clear, largely because of mining operations.

Murky water is obviously objectionable for drinking and cleaning purposes. It may be acceptable for swimming and fishing, but clear water is certainly preferred. The effects on aquatic life are also significant; fewer plant and animal species thrive in muddy water than in clear water, partly because of the dimmer light. The influence of other factors such as oxygen and nutrient concentrations also varies with the murkiness of the water.

17-6.3 Plant Nutrients in Sediment

Plant nutrients and other chemicals associated with soil colloids are important parts of sediment pollution in water. Sediment carries much larger quantities of nutrients than are dissolved in the water. An Alabama study (Bradford, 1974), for example, showed that most of the nitrogen and over 95% of the phosphorus losses from cotton, corn, and soybean plots were associated with the sediment. Alberts, Schuman, and Burwell (1978) cited several studies showing that losses of nitrogen and phosphorus were mostly associated with sediment. Their own study conducted in Iowa showed that over 90% of both nitrogen and phosphorus losses were carried by sediment and that most of the loss occurred during the corn crop establishment period from April through June.

The phosphorus content of surface waters is important because it is usually the easiest nutrient to control adequately to prevent eutrophication. Sediment and sewage are the two principal sources of phosphorus in water. A combination of soil-conserving practices and sewage treatment therefore can effectively control eutrophication. A significant aspect of erosion control is that the proper use of fertilizers can reduce pollution by increasing plant growth enough to reduce erosion and the associated nutrient losses.

17-6.4 Pesticides Carried by Sediment

Chemical analyses of water, fish, and other aquatic life reveal that pesticide residues are widely distributed in streams, lakes, and oceans

(Nicholson, 1969). The concentrations are usually low, but the occurrence is widespread and many different pesticides are represented either in their original forms or as metabolites. Some pesticides are dissolved in water, but many are adsorbed by soil colloids and are carried mostly by the sediment. The sediment gradually releases adsorbed pesticides to the water, thus maintaining a low but significant concentration for months or years.

Insecticides are usually the cause of more concern than other pesticides because they are most likely to be harmful to animals and humans. One exception was the implication of the herbicide 2,4,5-T as a cause of birth defects after it was widely used to kill trees and brush in Viet Nam. The most troublesome insecticides have been the chlorinated hydrocarbons (DDT and its relatives) because they combine high potency with long persistence and a tendency to accumulate in living things.

Nicholson (1969) lists the principal sources of water pollution by pesticides as (1) runoff from land that has been treated to control pests, (2) industrial wastes from plants that either produce pesticides or use them in producing textiles, (3) accidents and carelessness in using chemicals or disposing of remnants and containers, and (4) the use of pesticides to control aquatic life. Erosion-control practices can reduce the sediment carried in runoff; holding ponds and other waste-treatment practices can reduce the industrial source; and educational and licensing programs are currently aimed at reducing the careless and improper use of pesticides.

SUMMARY

Pollutants contaminate and degrade the environment. People have always caused pollution, but significant concern about pollution problems is a recent development as a result of increasing population, new types of pollutants, and increasingly sensitive techniques for detecting pollutants.

People-related wastes are directly related to population. Solid waste has been discarded in open city dumps or buried in sanitary landfills but is beginning to be viewed as a resource containing reusable materials. The treatment of sewage wastes varies from none to tertiary. Primary treatment removes materials that float or sink, secondary treatment allows bacteria to decompose organic materials, and tertiary treatment removes dissolved ions. Disposal by sprinkler irrigation on land is the favored method of tertiary treatment, but heavy-metal ions can be a problem.

Industrial wastes include a wide variety of scrap and by-product materials, some of which are highly toxic. Solid materials are often placed in landfills but recycling is preferable where it is feasible. Liquid industrial wastes include chemicals that must be removed and water that must be cooled before it can be returned to a stream or recycled in a closed system. Air pollution also pollute soil and water because rain brings sulfur dioxide, nitrogen oxides, and solid particles back to land or water. Nuclear wastes present the most difficult disposal problem of all.

Agricultural waste disposal is complicated by the large amounts of wastes and the large areas involved. Manure has fertilizer value but is often ignored or poorly handled. Losses can be minimized by keeping the manure anaerobic, protecting it from leaching, and working it into the soil as soon as applied. Manure application rates up to 20 mt/ha make effective use of its fertilizer value. Higher rates can be applied for disposal purposes but pollution problems can arise.

Some producers apply excessive amounts of fertilizers that raise the nutrient content of both runoff and drainage water above natural levels. Nitrate nitrogen is the nutrient most likely to be lost in large amounts in water. Nitrates are also subject to loss from wet soil by denitrification. Denitrification can be reduced by draining wet spots or by using certain chemicals.

Pesticides are chemicals used to combat weeds, insects, and plant diseases. Copper and other heavy metals used in early pesticides accumulate in the soil and are hard to remove. Organic pesticides developed since the 1940s are applied at lower rates than the metal-based materials and have more selective toxicity, but some, such as DDT, cause trouble by bioaccumulation. Some pests can be controlled by biological methods including crop breeding, natural predators, and sterile males.

Sediment is the bulkiest pollutant of all. It pollutes land by covering plants and fertile soil. It produces murky water, fills reservoirs, and raises the beds of rivers. Plant nutrients carried by sediment commonly produce low but long-lasting contents of nutrients and pesticides in bodies of water.

QUESTIONS

1. What is a pollutant?
2. Why weren't people concerned about pollution centuries ago?
3. How is it possible to dispose of liquid wastes without polluting a stream?
4. What air pollutants can be either helpful or harmful to plant growth?
5. Why is the fertilizer value of manure often ignored?
6. How should manure be handled for maximum benefit and minimum pollution?
7. How can denitrification be reduced?
8. What pollution problems are caused by sediment?

REFERENCES

AGRICULTURAL RESEARCH SERVICE, 1970a. Airborne ammonia eutrophies lakes. *Agr. Res.* 19(2):8-9.

AGRICULTURAL RESEARCH SERVICE, 1970b. Farm nitrates: No menace to the Rio Grande. *Agr. Res.* 18(10):3-4.

ALBERTS, E. E., G. E. SCHUMAN, and R. E. BURWELL, 1978. Seasonal runoff losses of nitrogen and phosphorus from Missouri Valley loess watersheds. *J. Environ. Qual.* 7:203-208.

ALDRICH, S. R., 1972. Fertilizing for optimum yields will give you minimum pollution. *Crops Soils* 24(5):17-18.

ANONYMOUS, 1969. A story of growth—Pesticides. *Farm Tech.* 25:12-16.

BOLLAG, JEAN-MARC, and N. M. HENNINGER, 1976. Influence of pesticides on denitrification in soil and with an isolated bacterium. *J. Environ. Qual.* 5:15-18.

BRADFORD, R. R., 1974. *Nitrogen and Phosphorus Losses from Agronomy Plots in North Alabama.* EPA-660/2-74-033, Office of Research and Development, U.S. Environmental Protection Agency, Washington, D.C.

BREMNER, J. M., and A. M. BLACKMER, 1978. Nitrous oxide: Emission from soils during nitrification of fertilizer nitrogen. *Science* 199:295-296.

DUNIGAN. E. P., R. A. PHELAN, and C. L. MONDART, JR., 1976. Surface runoff losses of fertilizer elements. *J. Environ. Qual.* 5:339-342.

EDWARDS, C. A., 1969. Soil pollutants and soil animals. *Scientific American* 220:89-99.

FREDERICK, L. R., M. D. OPENSHAW, and R. M. THORUP, 1968. Patterns of ammonia distribution in the soil. *Proc. Agron. Workshops on Anhydrous Ammonia. Agri. Nitrogen Inst.*, Memphis, Tenn., p. 17-23.

FULLER, W. H., and T. C. TUCKER, 1977. Land utilization and disposal of organic wastes in arid regions. In *Soils for Management of Organic Wastes and Waste Waters,* Soil Science Society of America, American Society of Agronomy, and Crop Science Society of America, Madison, Wisc., p. 471-489.

GAMBRELL, R. P., J. W. GILLIAM, and S. B. WEED, 1975a. Denitrification in subsoils of the North Carolina Coastal Plain as affected by soil drainage. *J. Environ. Qual.* 4:311-316.

GAMBRELL, R. P., J. W. GILLIAM, and S. B. WEED, 1975b. Nitrogen losses from soils of the North Carolina Coastal Plain. *J. Environ. Qual.* 4:317-323.

GAST, R. G., W. W. NELSON, and G. W. RANDALL, 1978. Nitrate accumulation in soils and loss in tile drainage following nitrogen applications to continuous corn. *J. Environ. Qual.* 7:258-261.

GHASSEMI, MASOOD, S. C. QUINLIVAN, and H. R. DAY, 1976. Landfills for pesticide waste disposal. *Environ. Sci. Tech.* 10:1209-1214.

HEALD, W. R., and R. C. LOEHR, 1971. Utilizing agricultural wastes. In *A Good Life for More People,* USDA Yearbook of Agriculture, p. 299-304.

KEENEY, DENNIS, 1978. Can nitrogen fertilizers harm our atmosphere? *Crops Soils* 30(4):9-10.

LANCE, J. C., F. D. WHISLER, and H. BOUWER, 1973. Oxygen utilization in soils flooded with sewage water. *J. Environ. Qual.* 2:345-350.

LARSON, W. E., J. R. GILLEY, and D. R. LINDEN, 1975. Consequences of waste disposal on land. *J. Soil Water Cons.* 30:68-71.

LAUER, D. A., D. R. BOULDIN, and S. D. KLAUSNER, 1976. Ammonia volatilization from dairy manure spread on the soil surface. *J. Environ. Qual.* 5:134-141.

LIKENS, G. E., and F. H. BORMANN, 1974. Acid rain: A serious regional environmental problem. *Science* 184:1176-1179.

METCALF, R. L., 1971. Pesticides. *J. Soil Water Cons.* 26:57-60.

MOSIER, A. R., S. M. MORRISON, and G. K. ELMUND, 1977. Odors and emissions from organic wastes. In *Soils for Management of Organic Wastes and Waste Waters,* Soil Science Society of America, American Society of Agronomy, and Crop Science Society of America, Madison, Wisc., p. 529-571.

NICHOLSON, H. P., 1969. Occurrence and significance of pesticide residues in water. *J. Wash. Acad. Sci.* 59(4-5):75-85.

OLSEN, S. R., and S. A. BARBER, 1977. Effect of waste application on soil phosphorus and potassium. In *Soils for Management of Organic Wastes and Waste Waters,* Soil Science Society of America, American Society of Agronomy, and Crop Science Society of America, Madison, Wisc., p. 195-215.

SHAW, W. C., H. E. HEGGESTAD, and W. W. HECK, 1971. Pollution poses threat to man, farms, nature. In *A Good Life for More People,* USDA Yearbook of Agriculture, p. 293-299.

SOMMERFELDT, T. G., U. J. PITTMAN, and R. A. MILNE, 1973. Effect of feedlot manure on soil and water quality. *J. Environ. Qual.* 2:423-427.

SOMMERS, L. E., 1977. Chemical composition of sewage sludges and analysis of their potential use as fertilizers. *J. Environ. Qual.* 6:225-232.

STALL, J. B., 1972. Effects of sediment on water quality. *J. Environ. Qual.* 1:353-360.

TABATABAI, M. A., and J. M. LAFLEN, 1976. Nitrogen and sulfur content and pH of precipitation in Iowa. *J. Environ. Qual.* 5:108-112.

THOMAS, RICHARD, and J. P. LAW, 1977. Properties of waste waters. In *Soils for Management of Organic Wastes and Waste Waters,* Soil Science Society of America, American Society of Agronomy, and Crop Science Society of America, Madison, Wisc., p. 45-72.

VAN CLEEMPUT, O., 1971. Etude de la denitrification dans le sol. *Pedologie* 21:367-376.

18

Economics
of Soil Conservation

The costs of soil conservation are usually obvious and therefore seldom overlooked. The returns are less identifiable, especially where conserving the soil merely preserves the status quo of productive potential that would otherwise be slowly eroded away. Lowered potential is easily overlooked as it may be masked by weather variations, more fertilizer, new crop varieties, and improved crop management. It takes a perceptive person to understand the balance that needs to be struck between the obscure costs of inaction and the obvious costs of acting to conserve soil. Perception must be followed by decisive action if the soil is to be saved.

Soil-conserving practices often provide long-term benefits in exchange for immediate costs. However, when the relative merits of present versus future values are weighed, the balancing must be done by the people presently involved. It is unfortunate but not surprising that the pressing needs of the present often win over more important but indefinite needs of the future. Conservation practices that include short-term benefits are therefore easier to promote than those that are strictly long term. Even so, some practices such as terracing are used even though it usually takes a long time to recover their costs. Changes in tillage including contour tillage, reduced tillage, and no-till systems are usually profitable, but their adoption has been slow because of appearance and convenience factors and pest problems.

The benefits of conservation often accrue to many people besides the land owner. For example, soil that is held on a field neither muddies the water of a stream nor becomes sediment on other land. People living downstream therefore have an economic interest in the use of soil conservation practices upstream. In a broader sense, all the people of the nation and even of the world have a stake in the productive potential of the land. Such diffuse interest is represented to some degree by governmental participation in soil conservation through research, education, cost sharing, tax benefits, and legal actions. Such participation is justified because the productive potential of its land is a very important asset of a nation. Reduced productive potential is the most serious long-term effect of erosion.

Economic emphases of soil conservation have shifted considerably in the last twenty years from the value of tons of soil to farmers to the cost of tons of sediment to the public. Both aspects are important, but the sediment problem was largely ignored until environmental concerns became a public issue.

18-1 BENEFITS FROM SOIL CONSERVATION

Soil conservation yields several different types of benefits. Some are uniquely attributable to conservation practices, but others are strongly influenced by practices that influence plant growth. Some benefits can be evaluated monetarily, some are difficult to quantify, and some benefits are aesthetic. Benefits to be considered in this section include increases in net returns from land, retention of the productive potential of land, reductions in erosion losses and sediment damage, and environmental benefits.

18-1.1 Increases in Net Returns

Some conservation practices produce an immediate profit, some lead to a delayed profit, and some produce no monetary profit but are used for aesthetic or other nonmonetary reasons. Some profitable practices are usually considered under the heading of good management rather than conservation because many people use them primarily because they are profitable. Fertilization according to soil tests is such a practice. The recommended rate of fertilizer application is usually based on an economic optimum with little thought for the reduced soil loss resulting from the improved plant growth. Fertilization is actually a very important soil conservation practice that happens also to be profitable.

Conservation Tillage. The various forms of conservation tillage discussed in Chapter 9 are distinctive conservation practices that often increase net returns. Most conservation tillage systems reduce

Table 18-1 Energy required in diesel fuel equivalent (liters/ha) to produce corn in Nebraska by four types of tillage under dryland and irrigated agriculture

	Dryland				Irrigated			
Input	Conventional	Disk and plant	Till-plant	Slot-plant	Conventional	Disk and plant	Till-plant	Slot-plant
Machinery	23.9	21.6	20.5	19.7	57.4	55.1	53.9	53.1
Fuel	48.2	25.6	24.3	17.5	48.2	25.6	24.3	17.5
Transport grain	16.9	16.9	16.9	16.9	28.2	28.2	28.2	28.2
Fertilizer	202.8	202.8	202.8	202.8	282.8	282.8	282.8	282.8
Pesticides	10.6	10.6	10.6	13.4	10.6	10.6	10.6	13.4
Drying	77.0	77.0	77.0	77.0	128.2	128.2	128.2	128.2
Irrigation	—	—	—	—	288.9	288.9	288.9	288.9
Total	379.4	354.5	352.1	347.3	844.3	819.4	816.9	812.1

SOURCE: Calculated from data of Wittmus, Olson, and Lane, 1975.

the energy input used for tillage and thereby reduce costs. Table 18-1 shows savings of 18% for machinery and 64% for fuel when slot-planted corn was compared to conventionally tilled dryland corn. There was a small increase in pesticide input but it equalled only a fraction of the machinery and fuel savings. This was a study of average energy requirements for growing corn in Nebraska; yield data were not included. Similar fuel savings are indicated in data from Ohio, as shown in Figure 18-1. The Ohio data showed equal average corn yields whether conventional tillage or no-tillage planting was used (Triplett and Van Doren, 1977). There were, however, differences between soils. The well-drained Wooster silt loam yielded more with no tillage than with conventional tillage but the reverse was true of the less well-drained Hoytville silty clay loam.

Several studies have shown that average corn yields are insensitive to tillage practices as long as comparable stands and adequate weed control are obtained (Van Doren, Triplett, and Henry, 1976). Minimum tillage usually shows an advantage on sloping land where it helps conserve soil and water. No-tillage corn yields are usually less than those from conventional tillage where continuous corn is grown on land wet enough to be conducive to root disease. Results with wheat and some other crops have generally been less favorable to no tillage than corn yields have been.

Producers that can save fuel and machinery costs and still produce equal yields by using less tillage make larger profits even if they

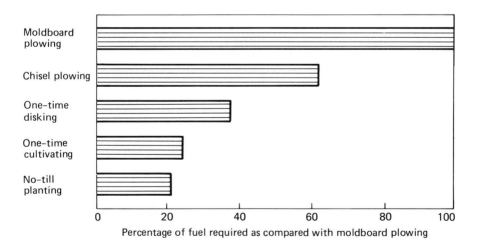

Percentage of fuel required as compared with moldboard plowing

Figure 18-1 Relative fuel requirements for growing corn with five different tillage systems. (Triplett and Van Doren, 1977.)

have to increase their use of pesticides. Such profits combined with rising energy costs and new types of herbicides, insecticides, and fungicides have led to a marked increase in the use of minimum tillage in recent years. Estimates indicate that minimum tillage was used on 1.54 million hectares in the United States in 1963, 13.4 million hectares in 1974, and will be used on 120 million hectares by 1990 (Allen, Stewart, and Unger, 1977). The fuel savings from such changes could well be $100 million per year by 1990.

Water Conservation. The importance of water conservation depends on the amount of water already in the soil, the weather following the time it is conserved, and the plant needs at the time. Water conserved before a dry period can make the difference between success and failure for a growing crop. Excess water retained during a wet period can damage the crop and reduce yields, especially in low spots. Good water control sometimes helps even in wet periods, though, by holding the water on drier sloping land rather than letting it run onto level areas below.

Times when water conservation will increase yield are common in semiarid climates but are not limited to such areas. Subhumid and even humid climates have dry periods during which plant growth may suffer. Periods of water deficit are especially common during the warmest months, as illustrated in Figure 18-2, because potential water use is highest then.

Contour tillage and other water conservation practices described in Chapter 14 might typically make an additional 50 mm of water available for plant growth on sloping lands during the growing season. On an average, this amount of water could be expected to increase yields of small grains or soybeans by 5 q/ha, of corn by 15 q/ha, or of lint cotton by 50 kg/ha.

Water conservation on irrigated land is also profitable but in a different way than in dryland agriculture. Any irrigation water conserved can ultimately be used to irrigate additional land and thereby increase profits. Individuals who do not have additional land available can either purchase less water or spend less for pumping water and thus leave more water available for other persons or for a later time.

Soil Drainage Profits. Soil drainage is another profitable practice that is associated with soil conservation, especially in humid and irrigated areas. Situations vary but drainage is seldom used where it is not profitable as well as convenient to have the land drained. As an example, Bornstein and Fife (1973) calculated 13% and 19% annual

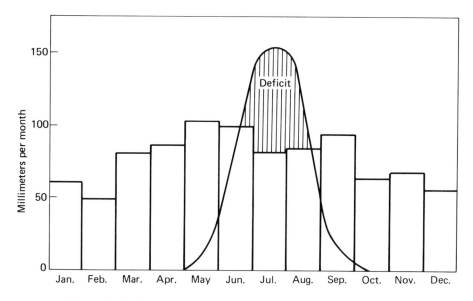

Figure 18-2 Average monthly precipitation in Illinois as compared to the water needs of corn.

returns on the investment in drains spaced 30 m and 60 m apart on poorly drained soils in Vermont.

Irrigation Profits. Irrigation can be used in ways that either increase or decrease soil loss. In either case, it normally increases both inputs and yields. The main reason that irrigation is used, of course, is to increase profits. Bitney (1974) calculated corn prices needed to make irrigation profitable over a ten-year period to be equivalent to about $7.50 per quintal. Sanghi and Klepper (1977) concluded that the short-term profit from exploiting underground water for irrigation is too large to leave groundwater conservation to market forces alone. Social costs and future water needs should also be considered.

Pest-Control Profits. Weeds, insects, and plant diseases can cause increased erosion by reducing the stand of the crop. Controlling these pests can reduce erosion and increase profits at the same time. The possible savings depend on how much loss is being suffered. As an example, Peters (1975) showed that use of aldrin or heptachlor to control insects on Iowa corn increased yields an average of 5 to 6 q/ha over a twenty-year period. Insecticide treatment increased yields over those on untreated fields whether the comparisons were made on the best or the poorest soils.

Deferred Profits. Fertilizer, tillage, water management, and pest-control practices can be expected to increase income the same year they are applied. Several years may be required to repay the investment costs of drainage, irrigation, and new machinery but the required returns usually begin with the next crop harvested. The returns may be slower in coming when practices such as terracing, revegetating land for grazing use, replanting forests, or soil reclamation are used. These practices must therefore be considered as long-term investments.

Terracing is a very effective means of conserving soil but it is also expensive. However, the fact that it permits yields to be maintained on a long-term basis under more intensive use than would otherwise be feasible makes it economical in many places. Nonetheless, yields may be reduced for the first few years on the parts of the field where topsoil has been removed to build the terraces. The yield reduction can be minimized by stockpiling the topsoil and replacing it after the terraces are built from the subsoil, but this adds to the cost. Sometimes it is more practical to use fertilizers, manure, green manure, and tillage practices to improve the exposed subsoil than to replace topsoil. The reduced soil loss should result eventually in higher yields than would have been obtained without the terraces.

Forage crops and trees are also effective for conserving soil but they take time to grow. Range management may require several years of less than normal use or possibly no use to let desirable grasses become well established. A few years later they will make up for the decreased use by producing more usable forage. A grazing program that maintains their productivity should then be established (see Ch. 13). Trees take even longer to grow and become marketable. The value is there, however, as a part of the land value. The market price of the land increases as the trees grow and approach marketable size.

Reclamation of sodic soils often takes years to accomplish and thus is another example of delayed profits. Sodic spots are often so unproductive that *any* plant growth is an improvement. Improving them to where they will not only grow something but will produce a profitable crop takes time as well as investment (see Ch. 16).

Deferred profits often create a conflict between long-term and short-term values. The need for short-term income can lead to an exploitation of soil and water with as much as possible being removed and as little as possible being replaced. Soil is eroded, vegetative cover is degraded, and serious long-term loss can occur under short-term exploitation of land.

18–1.2 Retaining Productive Potential

Nutrient losses and flood damage cause decreases in production for the year in which they occur but they do not always reduce the future productivity of the land. In fact, a flood often deposits a thin layer of sediment that may improve the soil's productive potential. However, the area that lost the soil almost surely lost productive potential. The loss is often overlooked because crop yields may be maintained or even increased by the use of fertilizer, new crop varieties, and improved management practices even while the yield potential is dropping.

Soil loss usually reduces yield potential; the amount of the reduction ranges all the way from 0% to 100%. The amount depends greatly on the nature and thickness of the topsoil, subsoil, and soil parent material. A loss of 5 cm from the top of a deep uniform soil may have little long-term impact. A 5-cm loss from another soil may mean that clayey subsoil will become a part of the plow layer and productive potential may drop by 10% to 25%. An equal soil loss from a soil that is shallow to bedrock might make the soil so droughty that a complete crop failure could occur. The most unfortunate feature of such losses is their permanence. The yields of the future are decreased along with those of the year when the damage occurs.

Soil erosion is seldom uniform across any large area of land. The value of soil conservation for preserving productive potential must therefore be considered on the basis of areas within a field. The most eroded spots are usually easily detected by the subsoil color and by the sparse vegetation on them. The field as a whole may be producing reasonably well, but these spots are not. Calculation of costs and returns on the eroded spots will frequently show a loss from cropping that reduces the profit obtained from the rest of the field. The damaging effect is sometimes increased by the lost soil becoming sediment that destroys the crop in low areas.

Severely eroded spots in productive fields pose difficult management problems. Using the field intensively causes more erosion and sedimentation damage. Limiting the land use to a system suitable for the problem spots produces little income and fails to use the capability of the rest of the field. Sometimes the spots can be protected with contouring or by building terraces or by using minimum tillage on them. Sometimes it is best to exclude the spots from the field either by going around them or by relocating the field boundary. Permanent vegetation on the eroded spots and appropriate crops on the rest may maximize the productivity of the field as a whole. The permanent vegetation may be useful for wildlife or for the forage crop produced on it as well as for conserving soil.

18–1.3 Reduced Erosion Losses

The value of lost soil is an obvious cost of soil erosion. Reductions in soil loss are obvious benefits from soil conservation. The value of each ton of eroded soil varies according to its clay, organic-matter, and nutrient contents plus other properties of both the eroded soil and the soil left behind. The sorting action of both wind and water causes fine particles to be removed while coarse particles are left behind. Textural sorting combined with the effects of organic-matter accumulation, fertilization, and liming being concentrated in the upper part of the soil usually makes a ton of eroded soil more fertile and therefore more valuable than a ton of average soil.

An approximation of the gross value of the plant nutrients in eroded soil can be based on the following assumptions:

1. The commonly accepted estimate of 3.6 billion metric tons of detrimental soil erosion occurring annually from land in the United States is correct (about 2.7 billion metric tons coming from cropland).
2. Each ton of soil has a total nutrient value of $5, totaling $18 billion each year (see Note 18-1).

NOTE 18-1 FERTILITY VALUE OF A TON OF SOIL

The fertility value of a ton of eroded soil can be calculated by using the following assumed values:

1. An average temperate-region topsoil contains about 3% organic matter, but an average ton of sediment contains more colloids so it has about 6% organic matter.
2. The soil organic matter is about 5% N, 0.5% P, and little K apart from that held by cation exchange. The mineral matter contains little N, about as much total P as the organic matter, and about 1.5% K.
3. The amounts of these nutrients that will become available annually in a temperate region can be estimated as 3% of the N, 5% of the P, and 1% of the K (these percentages might be as

high as 25% of the N in a tropical climate and as low as 1% of the N in a cold climate with the other nutrients in proportion).

Using the above figures and 1975 prices in the United States, an average metric ton of eroded temperate-region soil has the following fertility value:

	Total content		Available in 1 year	
	Amount (kg/mt)	*Value (1975)*	*Amount (kg/mt)*	*Value (1975)*
Nitrogen	3	$1.20	0.1	$0.04
Phosphorus	0.6	0.30	0.03	0.015
Potassium	14	2.70	0.14	0.025
Other nutrients		0.80		0.02
Total value		$5.00		$0.10

The calculated total fertility value of soil eroded in the United States thus comes to approximately $18 billion per year—an amount that exceeds the value of all the fertilizer marketed in the country. The 3.6 billion metric tons of eroded soil contains about the same amount of N and P and more than ten times as much total K as the annual application of commercial fertilizer. A more realistic but considerably more complex value can be obtained by basing the calculations on available nutrients. This calculation requires computation of a discounted value for all nutrients that will be released in future years. The total K value would be discounted most because only about 1% of it becomes available each year. The $5 figure will be used here both for simplicity and because the discount might well be offset by the value of soil components other than plant nutrients.

Soil erosion cannot be completely stopped. Part of it is natural geologic erosion and part of the accelerated erosion is unavoidable when land is cropped. Much land, however, is being eroded at excessive rates. Limiting erosion on all lands in the United States to the tolerable rates specified in Chapter 6 would probably reduce the sediment load of streams by 0.5 to 1.0 billion metric tons of soil annually and keep $5 billion worth of plant nutrients from leaving the fields each year.

18-1.4 Reduced Sedimentation Damage

Soil eroded from one place is deposited elsewhere as sediment. Rapid erosion is accompanied by rapid deposition and significant damage in both places. Part of the sedimentation damage occurs in the fields near the source of the sediment and part of it occurs in downstream areas. The soil and water damage caused by floods are inseparable. Estimated amounts of various types of flood damage are shown in Table 18-2. The total flood damage in the United States is approximately $3 billion per year. Some damage is unavoidable, but hundreds of millions of dollars per year could be saved through flood-prevention efforts.

About 60% of the flood damage shown in Table 18-2 occurs along small and moderate-sized streams in *upstream areas* where the drainage area above the site is less than 100,000 ha. One implication of this is that flood control applied in the upstream areas can do more good than large downstream structures. The upstream floods typically result from intense rainfall of limited duration. Terraces, contour tillage, and small upstream reservoirs are most effective means of reducing the magnitude of upstream floods. Protective vegetation and allowing no buildings on the floodplains are further means of reducing losses.

Table 18-2   Estimated average annual flood damage in the United States (excluding Alaska and Hawaii)

Type of damage	Annual cost (1975 dollars)	Percentage of total cost
Upstream damage (from drainages < 100,000 ha):		
Crops and pasture	$800,000,000	27.0
Other agricultural	355,000,000	12.0
Sediment	153,000,000	5.2
Nonagricultural	318,000,000	10.7
Indirect	157,000,000	5.3
Total upstream damage	$1,783,000,000	60.2
Downstream damage:		
Metropolitan areas	$708,000,000	23.9
Agricultural	380,000,000	13.1
Other	83,000,000	2.8
Total downstream damage	$1,180,000,000	39.8
Total flood damage	$2,963,000,000	100.0

SOURCE: Calculated from data of Ford, 1964, Ford, Cowan, and Holtan, 1955, and others, adjusted by the authors to 1975 dollars.

Downstream floods result from more widespread and longer-lasting storm systems than upstream floods. The downstream damage is more spectacular because it is concentrated in occasional large events. Usually there is some advanced warning that a flood crest is coming. Sandbag levees may be erected and people evacuated from their homes. Sometimes the damage is averted but other times the dikes fail and major damage occurs. There is no known way to permanently control large rivers so they cannot flood. Levees provide some containment but they also cause the river to deposit sediment in its bed and thus raise its level to a more hazardous position. The lower reaches of rivers such as the Yellow River in China and the Mississippi River in the United States now flow several meters above their floodplains for long distances because efforts have been made to control them. Unfortunately, many people live on the floodplains where they can be instantly inundated by a breach in a levee. The resulting loss of life cannot be evaluated in economic terms. The surest way to reduce downstream flood disasters is to avoid building structures in floodplains.

Agriculture sustains over half of the flood damage, as shown in Table 18-2. Most of the land involved in practices to prevent or reduce flooding is used for agricultural purposes. Flood control is therefore even more significant to farmers and ranchers than it is to the rest of the population. Fortunately, many of the same practices that conserve soil and water on farms and ranches are also helpful for reducing flooding.

18-1.5 Environmental Benefits from Conservation

The soil conservation movement began primarily out of concern for land that was suffering from erosion. The emphasis from the 1930s to the 1960s was on productivity losses caused by erosion. The effects on the total environment, including the polluting aspects of sediment, began to be emphasized in the 1960s. It is now realized that soil erosion damages the land and water where the soil goes as well as where the erosion occurred. The entire process is an environmental concern.

Several types of soil and water pollution that can be reduced by using soil conservation practices are discussed in Chapter 17. Sediment and the chemicals often associated with it are prime examples. Soil conservation practices can keep most of the soil and chemicals in the fields where they are useful. Stabilizing soil returns benefits to the land and its owner equal to the productive value of the soil that is conserved. Other benefits occur in down-stream areas where sedimentation, eutrophication, and chemical toxicity problems are reduced. Most of these benefits accrue to other landowners and to the general public rather than to the person who built the terraces, changed tillage practices, or planted protective vegetation.

Dollar values can be attached to some but not all of the environmental benefits from conservation. How much is it worth to be able to swim in clean water such as that shown in Figure 18-3?

18-2 COSTS OF CONSERVATION PRACTICES

The costs of conservation practices are almost as hard to evaluate as the benefits. Even the direct payments made for particular practices are variable enough to make it difficult to obtain accurate average prices. Furthermore, direct payments do not reflect the management

Figure 18-3 Swimming in Lake Washington after new sewage treatment plants were built and other pollution-control practices established at a cost of $121,000,000. This beach is shown in its earlier, polluted condition in Figure 17-2. (Courtesy EPA-DOCUMERICA.)

input of the land owner and other persons who may have provided the required technology. A lot of experience and probably some research work were needed to provide the knowledge that made the practice feasible.

Opportunity costs are another means of considering many of the less obvious costs of conservation. For example, one must forego the opportunity to grow a profitable crop on the area where a grassed waterway is planted. The opportunity to make a profit is real, even though a gully might form a year or two later.

The costs of conservation do not stop when a practice is installed. Opportunity costs will usually remain like a ghost in the background. Someone will surely be tempted to plow up the waterways, fencerows, odd corners, and steep slopes even if the erosion hazard is great. Educational programs are needed to train new land owners and operators; there is always a new generation to learn what their predecessors already knew. The cost of the educational programs is also chargeable to conservation.

Maintenance is usually the most obvious continuing cost of conservation. Terrace channels and grassed waterways need to be cleaned and occasionally reshaped. Drainage systems must be kept open. Vegetation must be fertilized, mowed, reestablished, or otherwise tended. Nothing lasts forever without attention.

18-2.1 Direct and Indirect Costs

Most conservation practices involve both out-of-pocket *direct costs* and less tangible *indirect costs*. The relative proportion of direct and indirect costs varies considerably from one practice to another. Building terraces involves large direct costs, usually in expectation that increased profits resulting from more intensive use will repay the costs. The alternative of less intensive land use involves little or no direct costs but usually leads to indirect costs in the form of lower gross returns from the land.

Practices that involve less intensive cropping tend to be used only where necessary because crop output and income are reduced. Establishing permanent forage crops or other protective vegetation drastically reduces erosion but does not usually produce a high-value crop. Strip cropping and crop rotations have intermediate effects on both erosion and income. None of these practices is too costly to install, but each one has indirect costs that sometimes prevent its use. Many such costs become large in the long run because they reduce income year after year.

Large direct costs do not necessarily prevent a conservation practice from being extensively used. The direct cost of installing a relatively permanent practice can be spread over many years. The profit, convenience, and other benefits may more than compensate for the investment in a practice that is costly to install but inexpensive to maintain.

Typical direct costs of several conservation practices are shown in Table 18-3. The costs are presented as ranges to allow for variations in the work done and in local charges. Indirect costs are too variable

Table 18-3 Direct costs of selected conservation practices

Practices that produce a net short-term profit	
(direct costs compensated within a year):	
Basic good management:	
Good varieties and high-quality seed	
Proper timing of operations	
Optimum plant populations and spacings	
Fertilizing and liming as needed	
Conservation tillage:	
Contour tillage	
Reduced tillage	
No tillage	
Practices with indirect costs but little or no direct costs:	
Land retirement	
Less intensive cropping:	
Crop rotations	
Strip cropping	
Practices with large direct costs:	
Water management practices:	
Land smoothing	$200– 600/ha
Tile drainage	500–1000/ha
Irrigation	1000–2000/ha
Land reclamation:	
Saline soils	$100– 300/ha
Sodic soils	500–5000/ha
Sulfuric soils	500–5000/ha
Smoothing spoil heaps	500–1000/ha
Establishing vegetation:	
Cover crops	$100– 300/ha
Grassed waterways	200– 600/ha
Woodland or wildlife plantings	200– 600/ha
Terracing	$500–5000/km
Fencing	$500–2000/km

to be generalized in a table such as this and can be estimated only when the circumstances of a specific situation are known.

18-2.2 Conservation Practices as Investments

The long-term nature of some conservation practices makes it logical to consider them as investments. A drainage project, for example, usually is not expected to repay its total cost the first year. Sometimes the installation cost exceeds the gross returns from any crop that may be grown on the land in a year. It may take several years to repay the cost and make a net profit.

A conservation practice can be justified as an investment if it produces a satisfactory rate of return over a long enough lifetime. For example, an irrigation system with a projected lifetime of twenty years could be considered a good investment if the profits resulting from its use were as high as the annual payments on a twenty-year mortgage with the same principal amount. A system costing $1500/ ha would need to increase the annual profit by about $153/ha to yield an 8% return on the investment and repay its costs in twenty years. Another way to analyze such investments is to calculate their *net present value (NPV)* for comparison to their costs (Note 18-2).

NOTE 18-2 CALCULATION OF NET PRESENT VALUE

A given amount of present benefits is generally preferred over an equal amount of future benefits. This preference is quantified in interest rates showing how much more a person is willing to pay at a future time for a present benefit. Interest rates can also be used to determine the present value of future benefits. The general formula for calculating the present value as a fraction of the future value is

$$\frac{1}{(1+x)^t}$$

where x is the interest rate in decimal form and t is the number of interest periods (usually years).

A practice with a projected lifetime of ten years with anticipated benefits worth $100 per year for each of the ten years will serve as an example. An interest rate of 10% per year will be assumed with remaining returns discounted at the end of each year:

Year	$1/(1 + x)^t$	Anticipated benefits	Net present value of anticipated benefits
0	1.00	$100	$100
1	0.91	100	91
2	0.83	100	83
3	0.75	100	75
4	0.68	100	68
5	0.62	100	62
6	0.56	100	56
7	0.51	100	51
8	0.47	100	47
9	0.43	100	43
Totals		$1000	$676

The percentage of total returns counted as net present value is sensitive to both the interest rate and the time span involved. The above method can be used to calculate the following net present values as percentages of total returns:

Time periods	Interest rates					
	4%	6%	8%	10%	12%	15%
5 years	92.6	89.3	86.2	83.4	80.7	77.1
10 years	84.4	78.0	72.5	67.6	63.3	57.7
20 years	70.7	60.8	53.0	46.8	41.8	36.0

Any future costs involved can be discounted and summed in the same manner. When both costs and returns are anticipated, they may be handled separately or the differences may be calculated for each time period and discounted to obtain the net present value.

Most water management, land reclamation, and terracing projects are installed in anticipation of long-term profits. The costs shown for these practices can therefore be justified as good investments from economic considerations alone. Some other practices, such as plantings that provide good cover but little income, must be justified on the basis of nonmonetary values such as aesthetic considerations.

18-2.3 Costs of Soil-Loss Restraints

The Iowa legislature passed a conservancy law in 1971 to protect the soil and water resources of the state. The legislature also authorized Iowa soil conservation districts to establish legal limits for rates of soil loss from each type of soil in the state. The U.S. Congress passed the Federal Water Pollution Control Act Amendments in 1972 with the objective of making all possible streams in the nation clean enough for swimming and fishing by 1983. Both of these laws and several others passed more recently in other states place restraints on rates of soil loss. Large direct-cost expenditures plus indirect costs resulting from changes in land use will be required to meet the legal standards limiting soil loss. Some of these costs are borne by land owners, some by taxpayers, and some by consumers of agricultural products.

Some estimates have been made of the effects soil loss restraints would have on erosion, crop prices, and farm income. Heady and Nicol (1974) used a computer analysis to estimate the effects of a soil-loss limit of 11.2 mt/ha on prices in the year 2000. They concluded that such a limit would reduce the average annual soil loss from U.S. cropland from 22.2 mt/ha without the limit to 6.3 mt/ha with the limit (Table 18-4). Crop prices under the 11.2 mt/ha limit in the year 2000 were estimated to be 7% higher for corn, 3%

Table 18-4 Estimated average soil loss in regions of the United States in the year 2000 (soil loss restriction to be met by practices such as contouring, strip cropping, terracing, and reduced tillage, with changes in land use where required)

	Estimated average soil loss (mt/ha)	
Region	Where loss is unrestricted	Where loss is limited to 11.2 mt/ha
National	22.2	6.3
North Atlantic	20.2	7.8
South Atlantic	48.2	7.4
North Central	20.6	6.3
South Central	33.8	8.1
Great Plains	7.2	3.4
Northwest	5.2	3.8
Southwest	7.4	5.8

SOURCE: Calculated from Heady and Nicol, 1974.

higher for hay, 4% higher for cattle, and 5% higher for hogs. Milk prices were projected to be unchanged by the limit on soil loss.

The income effects of soil-loss restrictions depend greatly on how they are achieved and to what area they are applied. Some alternative approaches for reducing soil loss are subsidies for the use of conservation practices, taxes on soil loss, and enforced legal limits on soil-loss rates. Taylor (1977) considered the effects that each of these approaches would have on farm income in the High Plains and in the Rolling Plains of Texas. He concluded that terrace subsidies would increase farm income and reduce soil loss but not enough to meet tolerance limits. A tax on each ton of soil loss would reduce both net returns and soil loss. Legal limits were the only approach that was projected to reduce soil loss below tolerance value in all places. Such limits would cause much land in the Rolling Plains to be idled. The number of hectares of cotton and wheat in that area would be reduced by 56% and net returns would be reduced by 63%. The effects in the High Plains were less severe, as much grain sorghum would be replaced by wheat, and net returns would be reduced by 15%.

Soil-loss limitations applied to certain areas or states place them at an economic disadvantage relative to others that are not restricted. Broader limits that restrict soil loss in the entire nation are likely to increase prices for the crops and may increase the net returns to the producers.

18-3 PAYING FOR SOIL CONSERVATION

Willingness to pay for a conservation practice often depends on the benefits associated with the practice. The practices that produce short-term profits are adopted most readily. Other practices that require long terms to produce profits are adopted more cautiously, especially if large investments are required. The person paying for the practice must be confident that conditions will remain stable long enough for the expected benefits to be worth more than the expected costs. An owner-operator is more likely to invest in such practices than an operator with a short-term lease.

Practices that are not profitable or practical for individuals may nevertheless be worthwhile. Sometimes a group such as a drainage district or an irrigation district can be formed to handle such practices. State or federal government may become involved through subsidies or other incentives. Careful planning may be required and detailed analyses made, but the practices may still be justified economically.

Some practices are used for reasons other than economics. Aesthetic, legal, and moral considerations may motivate their use in spite of the net costs involved. Some land owners may pay for such practices but group or public action is more common. A park, for example, might be supported by a community and made available to the public at little or no charge.

18-3.1 Payments by Land Owners and Operators

Owners and operators pay most of the direct costs of practices that increase profits on their land. Most crop management practices are included—the use of clean, viable seed of good crop varieties, optimum plant populations and spacings, and proper timing of operations. Costs of conservation tillage and of fertilizing and liming also are usually paid by land owners and operators.

Investments in practices with large direct costs that require long terms to become profitable may be shared between land owners and public groups or government agencies. Operators with long-term leases might pay part of the costs, but those with annual or other short-term leases usually are not expected to pay for long-term investments. Irrigation and drainage systems, land reclamation, and terracing are examples of practices that usually require several years to repay their costs.

The division of costs between owners and operators varies widely according to lease arrangements. In general, owners and operators often share the costs of short-term practices in the same proportion that they share the profits resulting from those practices. Owners pay a larger share of the entire cost of long-term practices because these are investments that increase the value of their land.

Practices that require large investments often require borrowed money. Sometimes the money can be obtained from traditional lending institutions such as banks. Other sources are Production Credit Associations and the Farmers Home Administration.

18-3.2 Payments by Groups

Many soil and water problems extend across property lines and involve several or many people. Flood control, drainage projects, and irrigation developments are examples of practices that commonly require group action. Typically, all of the people involved form a district or other legal entity that can act in their behalf. The district authority varies according to how and where it is established. It can include the right to design and apply needed practices, assess the costs to the individual members, obtain assistance from various agencies, borrow money to accomplish its purposes, and, in some cases, levy taxes. Counties or municipalities sometimes act in similar manners.

Groups are sometimes able to obtain assistance that would not be available to the individual members. For example, an irrigation district needing to improve its water supply might obtain help from the Bureau of Reclamation. Or, a flood-control district might obtain both technical assistance and payment of part of the costs from the small watershed program of the Soil Conservation Service.

Payments made by groups are much like those made by individual land owners but on a larger scale. Usually the costs must be recovered from the land owners by assessments, taxes, or selling of the group services.

18-3.3 Government Participation in Soil Conservation

The various districts, counties, and municipalities discussed in the preceding section are actually local units of government. State and federal governments represent broader areas and more people. These larger governmental units may want to encourage the application of conservation projects, especially when the projects provide benefits to large numbers of people. The benefits from some projects are so diffuse that they would not likely be installed by individuals or small groups but they may be feasible as government projects. Parks and preserves are examples.

Government has several ways of encouraging the application of soil conservation practices. It can choose to pay part or all of the costs. It can provide technical assistance. It can allow tax credits or other benefits to those who apply the practices. It can provide low-interest loans to finance the practices. It also has the option of passing conservancy laws and enforcing them through the court system. Some of these approaches operate by modifying the economic incentives to individuals; others bypass economics by establishing legal requirements.

The United States government pays part of the cost of selected conservation practices through the Agricultural Conservation Program administered by the Agricultural Stabilization and Conservation Service (ASCS) and the Soil Conservation Service (SCS). Payment is made by the ASCS after the SCS has verified that the practice was needed, practical, and properly installed. Government payments for group projects, however, are funded through the small watershed program administered by the Soil Conservation Service.

The Soil Conservation Service provides technical assistance without charge to farmers and others. This program is designed to conserve soil and water by helping people install conservation practices on their land. The technicians are paid by federal funds that are supplemented in some states by state and local funds.

Environmental concerns have resulted in the passing of several federal and state laws in recent years. The 1972 Federal Water Pollution Control Act, as amended, for example, include provisions in Section 208 for reducing the sediment load in runoff water. Federal cost sharing is being made available through the Agricultural Conservation Program and other programs. A loan program is being handled by the Small Business Administration. Supplemental programs are being developed by various states to help keep pollutants out of streams and lakes.

Some state laws are more stringent than the federal laws. The Iowa Soil Conservation Districts Law was amended in 1971 to establish means by which erosion can be declared a "nuisance" and land owners can be required to limit soil loss to tolerable rates. It also required that 75% cost sharing be available before soil conservation practices could be mandatory and provided a state fund to pay 25% of the cost of required practices in addition to the 50% available from the U.S. Rural Environmental Conservation Program.

18–3.4 Conservation Research and Education

Conservation practices must be developed and the information disseminated before the practices can be widely used. The research and educational expenditures are important indirect costs of conservation. Most of the research is done through government agencies and universities with government support. Foundations, companies, and individuals also are involved in some research projects. The Science and Education Administration is the principal federal agency involved, and the Hatch Act is one of the main federal sources of agricultural research funds in the universities. State governments also provide substantial funding for research.

Educational activities dealing with soil conservation are part of the curricula of many schools at various grade levels. The educational effort is extended to farmers and others through the Extension Service in each state. The Extension Service is funded from federal, state, and sometimes county sources and works as an extension of the land-grant universities to disseminate agricultural research findings. Educational work is also accomplished by the Soil Conservation Service as a part of its technical assistance program and by such groups as the Soil Conservation Society of America. Various equipment, agricultural chemical, and other agri-business companies also have programs that include aspects of conservation education. The largest expenditures for educational activities, however, are funded by the federal and state governments.

18-4 CONSERVATION INCENTIVES

People use conservation practices for various monetary, legal, aesthetic, moral, and other reasons. The relative importance of each factor varies from one person and situation to another.

The relationship between monetary effects and soil conservation is usually considered even when other factors influence the decision to install a practice. The results of an economic analysis are sometimes expressed as a *benefit/cost ratio* by dividing probable benefits by estimated costs. A benefit/cost ratio of 1.0 or larger is favorable and may suffice to cause a practice to be installed. A benefit/cost ratio smaller than 1.0 is likely to end consideration of a project unless there are strong nonmonetary incentives to continue it.

Nonmonetary incentives for soil conservation are important and often strongly influence decision making. They are needed because the economic benefit/cost ratios of conservation practices are often less than 1.0.

Legal requirements may leave the individual no choice about whether or not to install a conservation practice. The choice has already been made by a governmental body. Usually such laws reflect some background consideration related to one of the other factors. The legislators believe that important public benefits are involved—benefits that are more decisive for the public interest than to the individual decision makers. The polluting effects of soil erosion, for example, are often ignored by the persons losing the soil and have been the basis for the passage of several recent laws. The public benefits might be monetary savings such as not having to remove sediment and other pollutants from water, they might be aesthetic reasons such as the prevention of eutrophication, or they might be based on moral principles.

Convenience factors enter into many decisions. It is, for example, inconvenient to go around a wet spot or other obstacle. Eventually the owner may drain the spot even if there is no hope that the profit will repay the cost. Rock outcrops have been blown out with dynamite at great expense for the sake of convenience. Sometimes convenience is a secondary factor influencing the nature of the practice after the need has been established. For example, expensive parallel terraces might be installed for convenience even though cheaper nonparallel terraces could hold the soil equally well.

Aesthetic impressions vary from person to person. Some aesthetic considerations have negative effects on conservation. The feeling that crop residues left on the surface appear "trashy" is an example. The desire for straight rows where contour practices are needed is another aesthetic problem. However, many people see beauty in the patterns of contour strip cropping or in the uniform growth of crops on a field where the soil has been reclaimed. Ponds and wildlife plantings are aesthetically appealing to many people and may be built or planted for that reason.

Moral reasons are another incentive for action. It is right to conserve soil rather than let it erode away. It is right to stop pollution even if it is expensive. It is right to provide some areas for wildlife even if crops could be grown there. Soil stewardship programs emphasize the moral aspects of conservation by suggesting that soil should be conserved for the sake of future generations. The word "conservation" has a strong moral tone that helps to promote its cause.

SUMMARY

Soil conservation costs are usually immediate and obvious whereas the benefits are often delayed, obscure, and dispersed. Government participation in soil conservation is justified to protect the productive potential of land and to represent the interests of the many people who are affected by the way each land owner treats the soil. Soil conservation emphases have shifted in recent years to include the effects of sediment deposition along with soil erosion.

Some soil conservation practices produce an immediate profit. Fertilization is so profitable that its conservation effects are often overlooked. Conservation tillage reduces energy input costs. Water conservation can result in significantly increased yields on sloping land. Drainage of wet land produces a high return on the investment; irrigation gives high returns on dry land. Effective pest control can also increase yields and reduce erosion.

Practices such as terracing, planting of forage crops and trees, and reclamation of problem soils result in deferred profits. A conflict may develop between the need for short-term income and the need for long-term protection of the land. Environmental concerns also often conflict with practices that would maximize income.

Eroded soil has a total plant nutrient value of about $5 per ton. Effective soil conservation might save $18 billion worth of plant nutrients each year in the United States. The same conservation practices would reduce flood damage by hundreds of millions of dollars per year. Soil loss reduces yield potential by amounts ranging from 0% to 100% depending on the amount of soil lost and the nature of the soil and its underlying material. Eroded spots in a field pose difficult management problems about how to use the field without further rapid erosion on the spots.

The direct costs of installing conservation practices represent only part of the total costs. Indirect costs such as research and education provide needed background. Often there are opportunity costs in the form of a profitable crop that could have been grown. And many practices entail costly periodic maintenance. Indirect costs such as reduced income from less intensive cropping are often stronger deterrents than are large direct costs. Conservation practices can be justified on an investment basis if they produce an adequate annual return over a period of years.

Legal limits on soil-loss rates first became law in the United States in the 1970s. Such laws reduce the income from the affected land if they apply to only part of the crop-producing area. Applied to the entire nation, these laws tend to raise prices and are likely to increase the producers' income. Subsidies that pay much of the cost of installing conservation practices increase net farm income whereas taxes on excessive soil loss would reduce it.

Conservation practices may be worthwhile even if they are not profitable or practical for individuals. Owners and operators may share the costs of practices that produce short-term profits. Owners pay most or all of the costs when long-term profit is anticipated. Groups such as districts or other legal entities become involved when projects are too large for individuals. Governments can encourage the application of soil conservation practices by paying for them directly; by providing technical assistance, low-interest loans, tax credits, or other benefits; by taxing soil loss; or by passing conservancy laws. Governments can also help by providing good research and education programs.

There are several different kinds of incentives for installing conservation practices. A benefit/cost ratio larger than 1.0 represents a positive economic incentive. Legal requirements represent situations where a governmental body has made choices on behalf of the public to require action by individuals. Convenience may be an incentive either to install a practice or to choose one practice over another. Aesthetic appeal and moral considerations also provide strong incentives for conservation.

QUESTIONS

1. What are the costs of erosion to a nation?
2. Who suffers most from flood damage?
3. What are the effects of conservation tillage on income and expense for a particular crop?

4. How do direct and indirect costs influence the economic desirability of a conservation practice to a land owner?
5. Which conservation practices are likely to be evaluated on the basis of their suitability as investments?
6. What economic effects would mandatory soil conservation on farms have on a nonfarm family?
7. What conservation costs should be paid by land owners? by operators? by groups? by the general public?

REFERENCES

ALLEN, R. R., B. A. STEWART, and P. W. UNGER, 1977. Conservation tillage and energy. *J. Soil Water Cons.* 32:84-87.

BITNEY, L. L., 1974. Can you afford to irrigate? *Crops Soils* 27(1):7-9.

BOCK, C. A., 1974. The expanding public interest in private property. *J. Soil Water Cons.* 29:109-113.

BORNSTEIN, J., and C. L. FIFE, 1973. Economic aspects of sloping land drainage. *J. Soil Water Cons.* 28:76-79.

DOREMAN, ROBERT, and N. S. DOREMAN, ed., 1977. *Economics of the Environment.* 2nd ed., W. W. Norton & Co., Inc., New York, 494 p.

FORD, E. C., 1964. Upstream flood damage. *J. Soil Water Cons.* 19:231-234.

FORD, E. C., W. L. COWAN, and H. N. HOLTAN, 1955. Floods—and a program to alleviate them. In *Water,* USDA Yearbook of Agriculture, U.S. Government Printing Office, p. 171-176.

FOUND, W. C., A. R. HILL, and E. S. SPENCE, 1976. Economic and environmental impacts of agricultural land drainage in Ontario. *J. Soil Water Cons.* 31:20-24.

GRANT, LINDSEY, 1979. Speculators in the cornfield. *J. Soil Water Cons.* 34: 50-53.

HEADY, E. O., and V. S. S. V. NAGADEVARA, 1975. Economic impacts of state environmental programs in a national framework: The Iowa conservancy law. *J. Soil Water Cons.* 30:272-278.

HEADY, E. O., and K. J. NICOL, 1974. Models and projected results of soil loss restraints for environmental improvement through U.S. agriculture. *Agr. and Environ.* 1:355-371.

JACOBS, J. J., and J. F. TIMMONS, 1974. An economic analysis of agricultural land use practices to control water quality. *Am. J. Agr. Econ.* 56:791-798.

LACEWELL, R. D., and J. G. McNEELY, 1976. Flood insurance as a component of land use management. *S. J. of Agr. Econ.* 8(1):175-180.

McMARTIN, WALLACE, H. J. HAAS, and W. C. WILLIS, 1970. Economics of forage production on level benches in the Northern Plains. *J. Soil Water Cons.* 25:185-189.

MOORE, C. V., 1970. Economics of water quality control. *W. Agr. Econ. Assoc. Proc.* 43:288-294.

MOORE, I. C., B. M. H. SHARP, S. J. BERKOWITZ, and R. R. SCHNEIDER, 1979. Financial incentives to control agricultural nonpoint-source pollution. *J. Soil Water Cons.* 34:60–64.

MUTHOO, M. K., 1976. Economic evaluation of the environmental effects of erosion. *Agr. and Environ.* 3:21–29.

NAGADEVARA, V. S., E. O. HEADY, and K. J. NICOL, 1975. *Implications of Application of Soil Conservancy and Environmental Regulations in Iowa Within a National Framework.* CARD Report 57, Center for Agricultural and Rural Development, Ames, Iowa, 152 p.

PETERS, D. C., 1975. The value of soil insect control in Iowa corn, 1951–70. *J. Econ. Ent.* 68:483–486.

PIPER, D. G., 1975. Using linear programming to evaluate agricultural flood control projects. *J. Soil Water Cons.* 30:227–230.

SANGHI, A. K., and ROBERT KLEPPER, 1977. Economic impact of diminishing groundwater reserves on corn production under center-pivot irrigation. *J. Soil Water Cons.* 32:282–285.

SENECA, J. J., and M. K. TAUSSIG, 1974. *Environmental Economics.* Prentice-Hall, Inc., Englewood Cliffs, New Jersey, 354 p.

SWANSON, E. R., and D. E. MACCALLUM, 1969. Income effects of rainfall erosion control. *J. Soil Water Cons.* 24:56–59.

TAYLOR, C. R., 1977. An analysis of some erosion control policies for the high and rolling plains of Texas. *J. Am. Soc. Farm Mgrs. and Rur. Appr.* 41(1): 49–52.

TRIPLETT, G. B., JR., and D. M. VAN DOREN, JR., 1977. Agriculture without tillage. *Sci. Am.* 236:28–33.

VAN DOREN, D. M., JR., G. B. TRIPLETT, JR., and J. E. HENRY, 1976. Influence of long term tillage, crop rotation, and soil type combinations on corn yield. *Soil Sci. Soc. Am. J.* 40:100–105.

WADE, J. C., and E. O. HEADY, 1977. Controlling nonpoint sediment sources with cropland management: A national economic assessment. *Am. J. Agr. Econ.* 59:13–24.

WADE, J. C., K. J. NICOL, and E. O. HEADY, 1976. Income effects of reducing agricultural pollution. *S. J. Agr. Econ.* 8(2):65–72.

WITTMUS, HOWARD, LARRY OLSON, and DELBERT LANE, 1975. Energy requirements for conventional versus minimum tillage. *J. Soil Water Cons.* 30:72–75.

19

Soil and Water
Conservation Agencies

Soil erosion became a matter of national concern in the United States in the 1930s. Four main factors were responsible for this widespread awareness of the erosion problem: results from early field research, a worldwide depression, dust storms, and a dedicated leader. The response of Congress and the people led to the development of a system of soil and water conservation that became a model for countries around the world.

19-1 FIRST FIELD RESEARCH ON SOIL AND WATER CONSERVATION

The first field research on soil and water conservation in the United States was established on the plots shown in Figure 19-1 by M. F. Miller and F. L. Duley at the University of Missouri. They wanted to discover the reasons for declining soil productivity. (Note 19-1.)

NOTE 19-1 FIRST FIELD RESEARCH

Inscription on the Monument at the University of Missouri, Columbia, commemorating the first field research plots for studying soil and water conservation:

SITE OF FIRST PLOTS IN THE UNITED STATES FOR MEASURING RUNOFF AND EROSION AS INFLUENCED BY DIFFERENT CROPS

The study was started in 1917. The first results were published in 1923. They provided the foundation for the Soil Conservation movement. The design

629

Figure 19-1 The first soil and water conservation field research plots in the United States were established by M. F. Miller and F. L. Duley on land that is now part of the campus of the University of Missouri at Columbia. The sign reads "Soil Erosion Experiment—Comparison of Different Crops and Methods of Tillage for Preventing Soil Washing. Begun May 1, 1917." The site is now a Registered National Historic Landmark. (Courtesy C. M. Woodruff, University of Missouri.)

of the Experiment served as the prototype for future experiments by the U.S.D.A. throughout the United States.

The investigations were initiated by M. F. Miller and F. L. Duley in their search for the causes of declining soil productivity. The original plots are being used now to investigate the renovation of eroded soil through the use of legumes, grass, and corn with treatments to supply the nutrients lost through erosion.

In 1965 the plots were designated by the National Park Service as a Registered National Historic Landmark. The first fourteen-year summary of the soil and water losses from the research plots was presented in Table 4-3. The table shows that the number of years required to erode an average 17-cm plow depth of soil varies from twenty-four years under fallow to 3214 years with continuous bluegrass. In 1941, twenty-four years after the erosion plots had been established, the level of the continuous bluegrass plot was 20 cm higher than the continuous fallow.

The Missouri research plots were all desurfaced in 1941 to the level of the continuous fallow. Several different crops have been grown in various combinations on the research plots since that time. The general conclusions in 1978 were as follows (personal communication from C. M. Woodruff):

1. Alfalfa, fescue, and orchardgrass do not yield satisfactorily unless potassium fertilizer is added after each cutting.
2. Corn, even with adequate fertilization, has been a failure because of excessive cracking of the soil during dry weather. Supplemental irrigation in addition to fertilization has been necessary for successful corn yields.
3. Fescue is crowding out lespedeza.

19-2 BUCHANAN AMENDMENT

Congress officially recognized soil erosion as a problem when it passed the Buchanan Amendment to the Agricultural Appropriation Bill for fiscal year 1930 (Public Law 70-769, February 16, 1929). The amendment provided $160,000 for establishing ten soil erosion experiment stations and ten plant nurseries throughout the United States (Note 19-2). These were administered by the Bureau of Chemistry and Soils and the Bureau of Agricultural Engineering in the U.S. Department of Agriculture.

NOTE 19-2 EROSION EXPERIMENT STATIONS AND PLANT NURSERIES

The ten erosion experiment stations were located at Guthrie, Oklahoma; Temple, Texas; Tyler, Texas; Hays, Kansas; Bethany, Missouri; Statesville, North Carolina; Pullman, Washington; Clarinda, Iowa; LaCrosse, Wisconsin; and Zanesville, Ohio.

The ten plant nurseries were at Mandan, North Dakota; Stillwater, Oklahoma; Cheyenne, Wyoming; Elsberry, Missouri; San Antonio, Texas; Shreveport, Louisiana; Ames, Iowa; Pullman, Washington; Belle Mina, Alabama; and Safford, Arizona.

19-3 CIVILIAN CONSERVATION CORPS

The decade of the 1930s was a period of worldwide depression. Millions of people were unemployed and desperate for work. Seeking election as President of the United States, Franklin D. Roosevelt promised to do something about the job situation. He was inaugurated March 4, 1933, and instituted a large government spending program that same month. A law establishing the Emergency Conservation Work Agency was passed by Congress and signed by Roosevelt on March 31, 1933. The name of this agency was changed to the Civilian Conservation Corps in 1937.

About three million persons, mostly young men such as those shown in Figure 19-2, were employed in government work programs from the time the Emergency Conservation Work Agency was established until the Civilian Conservation Corps ceased activities in 1942. They were stationed in camps throughout the nation and assigned to work for various government agencies. Many of them worked on soil and water conservation projects.

19-4 SOIL EROSION SERVICE

The Soil Erosion Service was established in the U.S. Department of the Interior as a temporary public works program by a resolution of Congress adopted July 17, 1933. Hugh Hammond Bennett was its director. Five million dollars were appropriated for soil erosion control on both public and private lands. Contracts were signed with local governments and individual land owners that permitted persons employed by the Emergency Conservation Work Agency to plant

Figure 19-2 Millions of young men were employed by the Civilian Conservation Corps during the 1930s. Many of them did soil and water conservation work. This group from the Knoxville, Iowa CCC camp is on its way to winter work in a quarry. (Courtesy USDA—Soil Conservation Service.)

trees, grasses, and legumes on eroding lands and to construct erosion-control dams in gullies and in other drainageways, as shown in Figure 19-3.

Forty soil-erosion-control projects were established throughout the United States as part of the growing conservation movement. Each project included an entire watershed for the purpose of making the public aware of soil erosion and how to control it. Land owners signed agreements with the Soil Erosion Service permitting the service to apply soil erosion technology on their lands. All labor, machinery costs, materials costs, and technical assistance were supplied free to the land owners.

The Soil Erosion Service had only a two-year life span before it was replaced by the Soil Conservation Service. Considering that the primary objective was to provide work for the unemployed, it had a tremendous impact on public awareness of the evils of erosion, as well as on erosion-control technology.

19-5 SOIL CONSERVATION SERVICE

Severe droughts during the years 1931 to 1938 coincided with the Great Depression and made the Great Plains of the United States a disaster area. Two giant dust storms made history on May 11, 1934,

Figure 19-3 A masonry drop structure and tile outlet built by the Civilian Conservation Corps to prevent a gully from advancing up this Iowa waterway. (Courtesy USDA—Soil Conservation Service.)

and March 6, 1935. These storms started in the powder-dry Great Plains, and for several days clouds of dust obscured the sun eastward for a distance of 2500 km. Total silt and clay as particulates in the air masses were estimated at 185 million metric tons. Dust from the Great Plains filtered into the offices and onto the desks of U.S. senators and representatives in Washington, D.C.

At this time Hugh Bennett, Director of the Soil Erosion Service, was trying to have the Service transferred from the Department of Interior to the Department of Agriculture and changed from a temporary works program into a permanent soil conservation agency. Two bills were introduced in Congress to make these changes. The first bill, the National Soil Conservation Act, transferred all funds, personnel, and property of the Soil Erosion Service from the U.S. Department of the Interior to the U.S. Department of Agriculture. This act was signed by President Roosevelt on March 25, 1935. On March 27 the Secretary of Agriculture assigned all soil erosion activities to the Soil Erosion Service. The law establishing the Soil Conservation Service was passed on April 27, 1935, fifty-two days after the start of the second disastrous dust storm, without a dissenting vote. What senator or representative could vote against Public Law 74-46 while brushing the Great Plains dust from his desk? Bennett had won his political battle. He became the chief of the new agency and spent the rest of his professional career as its head.

19-5.1 Legal Mandates

The National Soil Conservation Act of 1935, Public Law 74-46, establishing the Soil Conservation Service, states in its preamble:

> That it is hereby recognized that the wastage of soil and moisture resources on farms, grazing and forestlands of the Nation, resulting from soil erosion, is a menace to the national welfare and that it is hereby declared to be the policy of Congress to provide permanently for the control and prevention of soil erosion and thereby to preserve natural resources, control floods, prevent impairment of reservoirs, and maintain the navigability of rivers and harbors, protect public health, public lands and relieve unemployment, and the Secretary of Agriculture, from now on, shall coordinate and direct all activities with relation to soil erosion: . . . (Soil Conservation Service, 1977).

The broad mandates listed by this law, together with subsequent amendments and laws, define the present activities of the Soil Conservation Service. These mandates are:

1. Public Law 74-46 in 1935, as amended. This basic law authorized technical assistance to cooperators for carrying out soil
and water conservation practices in all fifty states, Puerto
Rico, and the Virgin Islands. Cooperators include conservation districts as well as individuals, communities, watershed
groups, counties, and state and federal agencies.
2. Public Law 78-534 in 1944 authorized watershed protection and flood prevention programs on eleven designated
watersheds.
3. Public Law 81-516 in 1950 provided for emergency flood
control.
4. Public Law 83-156 in 1954 established the pilot watershed
program.
5. Public Law 83-566 in 1954 broadened watershed protection
and flood prevention programs and was extended in 1970
to include 1000 watersheds.
6. Public Law 84-1021 in 1956 set up the Great Plains Conservation Program.
7. Public Law 87-703 in 1962 established the resource conservation development program.
8. Public Law 95-92 in 1977 emphasized soil and water resources.

In the process of administering these legal mandates, the Soil
Conservation Service provides direct formal national and indirect
informal international leadership in soil and water conservation.
Technical assistance on wise land use is given at no charge to individuals, groups, organizations, cities, towns, churches, schools, or
county and state governments. The breadth of the assistance given
can be judged by the kinds of specialists working for the Soil Conservation Service. These include soil surveyors, soil scientists, soil
conservationists, agronomists, foresters, plant materials specialists,
land use specialists, biologists, range management specialists, wildlife
specialists, geologists, economists, landscape architects, recreation
specialists, ecologists, environmentalists, and the following kinds of
engineers: agricultural, irrigation, hydraulic, civil, design, drainage,
sanitary, and cartographic.

19-5.2 Assistance to Conservation Districts

Under Public Law 74-46 of 1935 and amendments, the Soil Conservation Service administers a broad program of assistance in soil
and water conservation on the land in cooperation with Conservation

Districts (Section 19-6). Through district organizations, the Soil Conservation Service provides these kinds of assistance at the request of farmers, ranchers, and other land owners:

1. Determining soil suitability guidelines based on soil surveys for agriculture, housing, recreation, waste disposal, and road construction.
2. Recommending the best management practices for soil erosion control (Figure 19-4).
3. Designing sediment interception systems.
4. Designing water facilities such as farm ponds.
5. Planning recreational facilities.
6. Designing terrace, irrigation, and drainage systems.
7. Developing cropping systems, such as that in Figure 19-5, to reduce erosion.
8. Recommending pasture plantings.

Figure 19-4 Minimum tillage makes erosion nearly zero in this Illinois field. Weeds were killed by a contact herbicide at the time the corn was seeded in the wheat stubble. (Courtesy USDA—Soil Conservation Service.)

9. Developing range management guidelines.
10. Promoting wildlife conservation.
11. Promoting woodland conservation.
12. Supplying adapted plant materials for conservation plantings.
13. Promoting surface mine reclamation guidelines.
14. Providing expertise on land use planning.

The Soil Conservation Service now has more than 15,000 career employees who provide on-the-land service in stabilizing the soil and water environment for the public good. Most of this service is provided through Conservation Districts.

19–5.3 Assistance to Individual Land Owners and Operators

Individual land owners or operators can obtain assistance from Soil Conservation Service personnel by signing an agreement with the local Conservation District. Land use plans and designs for conservation practices recommended by the soil conservation technicians are based on soil maps interpreted according to the information in soil survey reports described in Chapter 7. Plans are made according to the choices made by the cooperating land owner or operator in harmony with the capabilities and needs of the soils.

Figure 19-5 Terracing, contour strip cropping (eight rows of peanuts alternating with two rows of grain sorghum), winter cover crops, and subsoiling are used in combination to control erosion in this Texas field. (Courtesy USDA—Soil Conservation Service.)

Soil Conservation Service personnel make agronomic and engineering recommendations for each of the thousands of soil series and map units recognized in the United States. Appropriate combinations of practices are recommended for the particular conditions existing at a specific site. The intent is to conserve soil and water and protect the environment while using the land for the purposes desired by the owner or operator. The Soil Conservation Service provides the technical assistance needed for planning, designing, and guiding the application of conservation practices.

Selected soil and water conservation practices completed in 1977 and cumulatively through 1977 are given in Table 19-1. These data indicate the amount of conservation work done by farmers, ranchers, and others in cooperation with conservation districts.

Table 19-1 Selected soil and water conservation practices completed in 1977 and cumulative completions through 1977

	Completed on the land	
Practice	During fiscal 1977	Cumulative through 1977
Minimum tillage	1,560,647 ha	19,205,735 ha
Strip cropping	184,803 ha	8,977,929 ha
Terraces	33,678 km	2,013,586 km
Contour farming	5,265 ha	56,638,845 ha
Drainage:		
Surface	12,122 km	633,280 km
Subsurface	46,308 km	1,695,953 km
Farm ponds (no.)	45,147	2,186,934
Grassed waterways	30,689 ha	917,858 ha
Irrigation systems:		
Number	14,474	376,862
Area	575,980 ha	15,440,670 ha
Field windbreaks	4,740 km	174,566 km
Brush management pastures and ranges	1,044,819 ha	23,896,620 ha
Planning grazing systems for pastures and ranges	3,141,546 ha	30,976,770 ha
Pasture and hay land seedings	763,590 ha	30,293,797 ha
Range reseeding	139,413 ha	7,038,321 ha
Improved tree harvesting	385,275 ha	15,640,016 ha
Tree planting	153,612 ha	10,141,630 ha
Windbreak renovation	10,999 ha	58,009 ha

SOURCE: USDA — Soil Conservation Service, 1978.

Many types of assistance are available to Conservation District cooperators without charge. Soil and crop specialists will develop cropping- and pasture- management systems to reduce erosion and sedimentation. Engineers design conservation structures including terraces, diversions, waterways, ponds, irrigation systems, drainage systems, and waste disposal systems. Range conservationists assist ranchers with grazing management techniques for maximizing production with minimum erosion. Foresters recommend tree species and planting and harvesting techniques for woodlands and windbreaks. Plant materials specialists recommend special plant species for use in unusual sites such as acid mine spoils (Ch. 11). Many such plants are distributed each year from the twenty-one plant materials centers operated in the United States by the Soil Conservation Service. About 8 million seedlings, nearly 6 million kilograms of seed, and millions of cuttings and shoots for conservation plantings are distributed annually.

19-5.4 Surface Mine Spoils Reclamation

Agronomists, soil scientists, plant materials specialists, and engineers work through Soil Conservation Districts to help stabilize mine spoils. The help is available to mine operators, individuals, groups, or any governmental unit. Four phases of surface mine reclamation are assisted by personnel of the Soil Conservation Service:

1. Planning before mining, including the making of a soil survey.
2. Applying conservation practices during mining.
3. Applying soil and water conservation practices after mining.
4. Assistance in reclaiming abandoned mine spoils.

During fiscal year 1977, 13,623 hectares of land disturbed by mining were reclaimed, as shown in Figure 19-6. The total cumulative area reclaimed, to September 30, 1977, was 766,902 hectares.

19-5.5 Water Resources

Under Public Laws 78-534 passed in 1944 and 83-566 in 1954, the Soil Conservation Service offers assistance to cities, towns, and rural areas in flood reduction, erosion control, reduced siltation, and lower maintenance costs for roads, bridges, and housing developments.

During fiscal year 1974, conservation work on twenty-four small watersheds was completed, making a total of 450 watersheds completed since 1954. Water impounded in reservoirs provides multiple use options such as a municipal water supply, fire protection, irriga-

Figure 19-6 This area of coal mine spoils in Kentucky has been vegetated with shortleaf pine and wildlife-food plants such as black cherry. (Courtesy USDA—Soil Conservation Service.)

tion, and recreation. River basin studies are also conducted in co-operation with state and other federal agencies. These investigations include flood-hazard analyses of selected streams and salinity-control studies on 220,000 hectares of land in the Colorado River Basin.

19-5.6 Resource Conservation

Public Law 87-703 of 1962 authorizes the Soil Conservation Service to assist regional (multicounty) areas in aspects of physical resource development. The term "resource conservation" includes conventional soil and water conservation activities plus the development of recreation facilities, fish and wildlife conservation, and the reduction of air and water pollution. Assistance is also offered in land use planning, preservation of scenic and historical sites, and industrial expansion. The goal is to improve the environment, economy, and living standards of people in selected areas. The program involves 1196 counties in all states except Alaska.

19-5.7 Great Plains Conservation Program

As mandated by Public Law 84-1021 in 1956, the Soil Conservation Service administers the Great Plains Conservation Program. This region is subject to severe climatic hazards such as periodic droughts and extremes in temperature. As a consequence, during periods of favorable weather, farmers and ranchers tend to cultivate marginal soils and to overstock ranges that, during dry years, are subject to devastating wind and water erosion. During fiscal year 1977, 1904 farmers and ranchers signed long-term agreements to apply permanent conservation practices on 1.8 million hectares. Since the passage of the law in 1956, over 40 million hectares managed by 54,000 farmers and ranchers have been assisted in the program.

Additional funds are set aside by Congress for exclusive use in the Great Plains to help intensify and accelerate the normal soil and water conservation activities of the Soil Conservation Service. Special emphasis is being given to making a soils map of the entire Great Plains, converting marginal cropland to permanent pasture and range, and improving rangelands by encouraging more rational grazing management as shown in Figure 19-7.

Figure 19-7 Controlled grazing is emphasized in the Great Plains conservation program. The tobosa grass in this Texas range shows the effects of severe overgrazing on the left and less severe grazing on the right. (Courtesy USDA—Soil Conservation Service.)

19-5.8 Land Use Conversions

Based upon a soil survey, soils are classified into Land Use Capability classes identified by Roman numerals I through VIII. Class I land has the fewest hazards associated with use and Class VIII the greatest (Ch. 7). This system helps to identify land that is suffering excessive erosion because of use beyond its long-term capability. For example, the only practical way to reduce erosion and sedimentation on very erosive sloping soils used for continuous row crops is to convert the land use to permanent grassland or woodland, as shown in Figure 19-8. For this reason, the Soil Conservation Service program includes land use conversion. This means persuading thousands of farmers, ranchers, and other land managers to make changes toward less intensive land use. It is also true that smaller but still significant areas of grassland and woodland on Class I and II land could be converted to cropland with little erosion hazard.

Figure 19-8 An example of land use conversion. This former wheat field in Wyoming was subject to severe wind erosion until it was seeded to crested wheatgrass and converted to rangeland. (Courtesy USDA—Soil Conservation Service.)

19-5.9 International Assistance

About 400 foreign nationals come each year to the United States to study the organization and field operations of the Soil Conservation Service. These educational experiences are usually financed by the U.S. Agency for International Development or by the Food and Agriculture Organization of the United Nations. Furthermore, many overseas governments request the on-site services of an experienced person from the Soil Conservation Service for two or more years. An erosion control project in Nicaragua is shown in Figure 19-9.

While studying the program of the Soil Conservation Service, foreign nationals are invariably surprised to learn that much of its success is credited to the service-oriented technique of unpaid farm and ranch officials of the Conversation Districts and other volunteers.

Figure 19-9 A request from the Government of Nicaragua through the U.S. Agency for International Development brought technical assistance from the Soil Conservation Service for controlling wind erosion in cotton fields. Windbreaks consisting of eucalyptus (in the photo) flanked by leadtree (upwind) and cassia were established to control the erosion. (Courtesy USDA—Soil Conservation Service.)

19-6 CONSERVATION DISTRICTS

When the Soil Conservation Service was established in 1935, its chief, H. H. Bennett, quickly realized that it was a long distance from Washington, D.C. to farmers and ranchers, both geographically and psychologically. Bennett had been raised on a farm in the red Piedmont hills of Anson County, North Carolina. He had witnessed serious sheet and gully erosion and the resultant widespread poverty and decline in crop yields. He became a professional soil scientist and for many years mapped soils in both southern and northern states. This background provided a rare but broad insight. He realized that no agricultural bureaucracy can be effective without major input from farmers and ranchers. As a consequence, he led the development of "A Standard State Soil Conservation Districts Law" to authorize the establishment of districts throughout the United States. For maximum acceptance among the states, Bennett persuaded President Roosevelt to send this model law to all state governors on February 27, 1937. Four days later the first Soil Conservation District law was enacted in the state of Arkansas. The first Soil Conservation District actually organized was Brown Creek Soil Conservation District in North Carolina; it was approved on August 4, 1937.

Twenty-two states had passed Soil Conservation District laws by the end of 1937, and ten years later all the states plus Puerto Rico and the Virgin Islands had enacted such legislation. Each state modified the model law to fit its land and the wishes of the people, but all these laws included the principle that local citizens have the authority to establish policy and the mandate to accept responsibility for soil and water conservation in each district. During the 1960s several states changed the names of their districts to "Soil and Water Conservation Districts" in recognition of the importance of water management in their programs. More recently, many of the names have been shortened to "Conservation Districts."

19-6.1 Present Scope

As of 1977 there were 2950 conservation districts in all fifty states, Puerto Rico, and the Virgin Islands. As shown in Figure 19–10, these districts comprise 99% of all farms and ranches, 2.3 million cooperators, and 8.91 million hectares.

A typical conservation district coincides with the boundaries of one of the 3097 counties. Each district has an elected governing board of three to five persons who serve without salary. In each

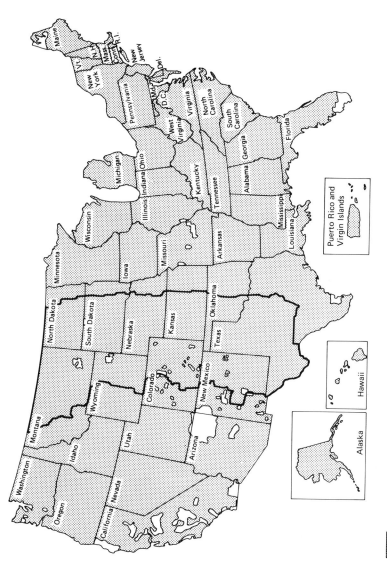

Figure 19-10 The 2950 Soil Conservation Districts in the United States comprise 99% of the farms and ranches in all fifty states, Puerto Rico, and the Virgin Islands. (Courtesy USDA—Soil Conservation Service.)

Area in soil conservation districts

Great Plains Conservation program boundary

Puerto Rico and Virgin Islands

Hawaii

Alaska

state, a board or commission controls state appropriations and serves the conservation districts of the state in administrative, legal, and financial matters. Nationwide, about 18,000 men and women serve on the district governing boards. The National Association of Conservation Districts was organized in 1946; its permanent headquarters is in Washington, D.C.

Although the elected conservation district officials serve without pay, the states appropriate funds to be used for official travel, establishing an office, and employing a secretary. During the year 1977, fourteen states had appropriated from $3 million to nearly $11 million. The mean appropriation for the fifty states was $2.3 million per state (U.S. Department of Agriculture, 1977).

19-6.2 Traditional Activities

Conservation districts are managed by private citizens elected by the residents of the district. Duties of the district supervisors (directors, board members, or commissioners) include the planning and directing of the soil and water conservation program in the district. This involves the request for use of professional assistance from the USDA—Soil Conservation Service, the USDA—Forest Service, the Land-Grant University Cooperative Extension Service, the Land-Grant Agricultural Experiment Station, the USDA—Bureau of Land Management, the USDA—Science and Education Administration, and other federal and state agencies.

Although conservation districts have been organized for many years, changes have been taking place in most of them. The trends of change have included (National Association of Conservation Districts, 1974):

1. The incorporation of more business and professional members on the boards.
2. The broadening of authority to control soil erosion on urban as well as on farm and ranch lands.
3. The inclusion of pollution control and environmental enhancement.
4. The reclamation of surface-mined sites.
5. More land use planning.
6. A trend toward mandatory rather than voluntary compliance when neglect would mean public disaster. An example is the law in New York State requiring every occupier of land to request a conservation plan from the soil and water conservation district by January 1, 1980.

19-7 AGRICULTURAL STABILIZATION AND CONSERVATION SERVICE

The present Agricultural Stabilization and Conservation Service had its origin in the Agricultural Adjustment Administration (AAA), established in 1933, early in Roosevelt's term of office. Its purpose was to control agricultural production so farmers would receive a fair price, or parity, for their products. Overproduction was a problem because great effort had been made to increase farm production during World War I, and that level of production was too high after the war. Farm bankruptcies resulted and were a leading factor in the Great Depression.

The Agricultural Adjustment Administration was empowered to reduce the glut of farm products through marketing quotas, establishment of reserves, and benefit payments for reduced production. The form and emphasis of production controls have varied with changing administrations and economic conditions, but the program remains as the "stabilization" part of the Agricultural Stabilization and Conservation Service. A part of the changing emphasis is revealed in the name changes of this organization. During World War II it became the Agricultural Adjustment Agency to increase the production of food. After the war the name was changed to the Production and Marketing Administration, then to the Commodity Stabilization Service, and finally to the Agricultural Stabilization and Conservation Service.

In 1936 the U.S. Supreme Court invalidated the part of the Agricultural Adjustment Act of 1933 that provided for direct cash benefit payments to farmers. Congress responded by promptly passing the Soil Conservation and Domestic Allotment Act of 1936, which changed the emphasis of the payments program to soil conserving practices, including land use changes that served the original purpose of reducing surplus crop production. The Agricultural Conservation Program was established to manage cost-sharing payments for soil and water conservation and was administered through the Agricultural Adjustment Administration and its successor agencies.

The Soil Conservation Service became a partner in the handling of the Agricultural Conservation Program in 1951 and has been responsible for the technical part of the program since that time. Soil Conservation Service technicians must certify that a practice is needed and practical before funds are allocated and that it has been properly installed before payment is made by the Agricultural Stabilization and Conservation Service. A fee usually amounting to 5% of the Agricultural Conservation Program funds is paid to the Soil

Conservation Service to compensate for their technical supervision of the practices installed under this program.

The word "service" was added to the names of several agencies in 1953 and the Agricultural Conservation Program Service became a separate agency at the national level from then until 1961. Little was changed in the handling of cost sharing at the local level, however, except for some name changes in the 1970s. The name was changed to Rural Environmental Assistance Program, then to Rural Environmental Conservation Program, and then back to Agricultural Conservation Program.

The various acts relating to the Agricultural Conservation Program made financing soil and water conservation a joint responsibility of government and land owners. The cost-sharing function is used to encourage both Conservation District cooperators and others to establish soil and water conservation practices on their land. The federal cost share often pays for about half of the cost of a conservation practice but may pay more or less, depending on the need to encourage the practice. This program provides a means for public funds to pay for public benefits resulting from soil and water conservation.

Many revisions have been made in the Soil Conservation and Domestic Allotment Act. Provisions that directly relate to soil and water conservation and that are currently available for cost-sharing include:

1. Restoring conservation structures under the Emergency (natural disaster) Conservation measure.
2. Planting trees under the Forestry Incentives Program.
3. Maintaining privately owned wetland for migratory waterfowl in the Water Bank Program.
4. Establishing soil and water conservation practices under the Agricultural Conservation Program, authorized by the Agricultural Stabilization and Conservation Act of 1961, as amended.

In this program three million farmers received $148 million as cost sharing during 1976 for applying soil and water conservation practices on 4.7 million hectares (U.S. Department of Agriculture, 1977).

The Agricultural Stabilization and Conservation Service is entirely a service and action agency. Rather than employing its own technical staff, it seeks and uses the advice of staff of other agencies in the U.S. Department of Agriculture. Most often used are personnel of the U.S. Soil Conservation Service and the U.S. Forest Service in providing technical program guidance and on-farm assistance. Technical advice is also supplied by the State Agricultural Extension Service, the State Agricultural Experiment Station, the State Forester, and the personnel of the Farmers Home Administration.

19-8 SCIENCE AND EDUCATION ADMINISTRATION

Three federal agencies involved in soil and water conservation were combined in 1978 and given the name of Science and Education Administration (SEA). These were:

1. SEA–Extension (formerly Cooperative Extension Service).
2. SEA–Cooperative Research (formerly Cooperative State Research Service).
3. SEA–Agricultural Research (formerly Agricultural Research Service).

19-8.1 SEA–Extension

SEA–Extension traces its beginning to the Smith-Lever Extension Act passed on May 8, 1914. This and supplementary amendments and acts have been the legal and partial-funding basis for the federal-state-county system of nonformal education for farmers, ranchers, homemakers, and 4-H Clubs. The system includes a small technical and administrative federal staff in Washington, D.C., a large technical staff at each of the land-grant universities, and a still larger staff of County Agricultural Agents, County Home Demonstration Agents, and County 4-H Club Leaders. The Extension work varies by states, but the County Agricultural Agent is designated by law to be the director of all county agricultural education, including leadership in educational programs of soil and water conservation.

19-8.2 SEA–Cooperative Research

This agency administers federal research grant funds to all state agricultural and forestry experiment stations in the fifty states, Puerto Rico, the Virgin Islands, and Guam. In recent years, grants for research have also been made to organizations that are not members of the land-grant system. SEA-Cooperative Research is involved presently with more than one hundred state institutions, six federal agencies, and about 12,000 scientists who are conducting research on approximately 24,000 projects. The problem areas recognized in these massive research programs that are related to soil and water conservation are: appraisal of soil resources; soil, plant, water, and nutrient relationships; management of saline and sodic soils and salinity; alternative uses of land; efficient drainage and irrigation systems; watershed protection and management; and conservation and efficient use of water (Cooperative State Research Service, 1977).

19-8.3 SEA—Agricultural Research

SEA—Agricultural Research is a federal agency with a central national research laboratory at Beltsville, Maryland, where its National Program Staff is located. However, most of its research personnel are located at agricultural universities and their field experiment stations.

As of September 1, 1976, all of the National and Special Research Programs were concerned either primarily or occasionally with research on soil and water conservation. These programs, called National Research Programs (NRP), had the following titles (Agricultural Research Service, 1976):

NRP 20730—Reduction of Salt Damage to Crops, Soils and Waters.

NRP 20740—Improvement of Irrigation and Drainage of Agricultural Land.

NRP 20750—Tillage Practices for Improving Soil Properties and Crop Growth.

NRP 20760—Management and Use of Precipitation and Solar Energy for Crop Production.

NRP 20770—Reclamation and Revegetation of Land Areas Disturbed by Man.

NRP 20780—Utilize, Manage, and Conserve Soil Fertility for Increased Production and Nutritional Quality of Plants and Animals.

NRP 20790—Preventing Pollution of and Improving the Quality of Soil, Water, and Air.

NRP 20800—Control of Water Erosion, Wind Erosion, and Sedimentation.

NRP 20810—Conserve and Manage Agricultural Water Resources.

Special Research Program—Remote Sensing.

Most of the field research of the SEA—Agricultural Research is conducted in cooperation with the Agricultural Experiment Stations, which are an integral part of all land-grant agricultural universities.

19-9 UNIVERSITIES AND COLLEGES

The U.S. Congress passed the first Morrill Act in 1862 to assist the states in establishing land-grant colleges to teach agriculture and applied science. Research at these and other institutions was assisted by the Hatch Act of 1887 and the Second Morrill Act of 1890. Statewide informal education from the colleges was authorized and assisted by the Smith-Lever Extension Act of 1914. These agricultural universities and colleges are all intimately involved in soil and water conservation. They conduct research such as that shown in Figures 19-11 and 19-12, teach, and extend knowledge of soil and water conservation throughout each respective state. Recently, increasing amounts of soil and water conservation research have been conducted at non-land-grant universities and colleges.

Figure 19-11 Field research by the University of Alaska to find grass species with sufficient vigor to stabilize construction slopes disturbed by the laying of the Alaska pipeline. The most promising species are selections of fescue, Kentucky bluegrass, bromegrass, timothy, and foxtail (Courtesy W. W. Mitchell, Agricultural Experiment Station, University of Alaska.)

a

b

c

Figure 19-12 Research on the use of an aerated pond for cattle waste disposal conducted by Purdue University to minimize air and water pollution while using the waste for pasture production: (a) aeration pond, (b) close-up of floating aerator in operation, (c) effluent being sprayed on pasture. (Courtesy A. C. Dale, Purdue University.)

Many students are taught principles of soil and water conservation in the agricultural universities before they are employed by such agencies as the USDA—Soil Conservation Service. Research at the universities serves as the basis for the soil and water management practices taught in classes and promoted throughout each state by SEA—Extension and the Soil Conservation Service. Furthermore, the National Cooperative Soil Survey is usually conducted in cooperation with the Soil Conservation Service and the respective state agricultural university's agricultural experiment station. All twenty-one Plant Material Centers supervised by the Soil Conservation Service are managed in close cooperation with the agricultural universities.

Many of the agricultural universities teach and conduct research in forestry. Some of this research is conducted in cooperation with the USDA—Forest Service and some of the state forestry agencies.

19-10 U.S. FOREST SERVICE AND STATE FORESTRY AGENCIES

The United States Forest Service has responsibility for managing the 73 million hectares in the 150 National Forests and the 1.5 million hectares of National Grasslands. It also cooperates with agricultural universities and state forestry agencies in tree planting, fire protection, and other activities related to soil and water conservation. The Forest Service contact with private land management is usually through cooperative programs with the state forestry agencies and the conservation districts. Federal and state forest nurseries supply forest tree seedlings to plant on eroded and other lands.

The USDA—Forest Service is the principal agency in the United States conducting research on trees-soil-water relationships. This research applies to the 203 million hectares of commercial forests—over 20% of the area of the United States.

Research relevant to this chapter includes that on the relationship between trees and water yield and erosion. Some precipitation is intercepted by trees and evaporated into the atmosphere without reaching the soil. Another fraction infiltrates the soil, is absorbed by roots, and is transpired into the atmosphere through stomata of the leaves. A third segment becomes surface or subsurface runoff; a final fraction moves downward to replenish the water table.

The Forest Service has established a research project to find ways to increase runoff water yield from a forested watershed. Treatments have included clearcutting the trees and establishing grass as compared to cutting varying percentages of the trees. On some watersheds, an open stand of trees was found to yield more water than an all-grass watershed because the trees held additional snow. The open stand is also better than a clearcut watershed for erosion control.

Research on trees and watershed protection is continuing, especially that in relationship to establishing a reasonable balance between maximum water runoff for irrigation and soil-erosion losses. Another aspect of research, forest harvest methods and their relationship to erosion, is discussed in Chapter 13.

Criteria for maximum permissible erosion on construction activities in the Appalachian Region and minimum ground cover needed

Table 19-2   Ground cover needed to limit soil loss to permissible erosion rates on construction activities in the Appalachian region[a]

Rooting depth of trees (cm)	Maximum permissible erosion from all sources (mt/ha-year)	Slope of land (%)	Minimum ground cover needed to control erosion (%)
25–50	4.5	5	40
		10	75
		15	80
		20	90
		25	100
50–100	7	5	35
		10	70
		15	75
		20	85
		25	95
100–150	9	5	30
		10	60
		15	70
		20	80
		25	90
>150	11	5	25
		10	50
		15	65
		20	75
		25	85

[a]Based on slope length of 22 m and a moderately erodible soil with a K factor of 0.38 (Ch. 6).

SOURCE: Davey, 1977.

to control erosion are given in Table 19-2. At any given slope percentage, a greater rooting depth increases the permissible erosion and reduces the ground cover needed to stabilize the soil.

19-11 OTHER FEDERAL CONSERVATION AGENCIES

Almost all federal agencies have relevance to soil and water conservation; the agencies listed below are statutorily involved (National Wildlife Federation, 1978).

Corps of Engineers, U.S. Department of the Army. The "Corps" manages navigable surface waters and recreation facilities adjacent to public reservoirs, builds dams for water conservation and power generation, conducts research on erosion and sedimentation, and dredges sediment-laden channels.

Bureau of Land Management, U.S. Department of Interior. This agency administers 190 million hectares of U.S. public lands, mostly in the west. This is about 60% of all public lands. Much of it is in small tracts of 16 to 65 hectares. The principle of management is multiple-use, including livestock grazing, timber production, watershed protection, industrial mineral development, and outdoor recreation.

Bureau of Reclamation, U.S. Department of Interior. The Bureau of Reclamation builds dams on federal lands in western states for power generation, irrigation, flood control, industrial development, fish and wildlife, and recreation, as shown in Figure 19-13.

Bureau of Indian Affairs, U.S. Department of Interior. The Bureau of Indian Affairs is responsible for soil and water conservation on all Indian lands. Personnel of this Bureau advise the Indian land operators on useful and necessary conservation practices. When land is leased to nonreservation operators, the lease contains provisions for the conservation practices required of the lessees.

Environmental Protection Agency. This agency was established to reduce pollution of water and air by solid and liquid residues, toxic substances, pesticides, radiation, and noise. It is an independent agency functioning separately from major departments such as Agriculture and Interior. When eroded soil becomes a sediment

Figure 19-13 This swimming facility in California was established and is managed by the U.S. Bureau of Reclamation. It is part of a multiple use reservoir providing irrigation water and outdoor recreation. (Courtesy USDI—Bureau of Reclamation.)

pollutant of water or a particulate (dust) pollutant of air, its control is the official concern of this agency. The EPA administers the Water Pollution Control Act of 1972, Public Law 92-500 and amendments.

Tennessee Valley Authority. The Tennessee Valley Authority is an independent agency with headquarters in Knoxville, Tennessee. It was established as an areawide organization to develop the natural and human resources of parts of seven states in the watershed of the Tennessee River, an area of 106 million hectares. It conducts research and demonstration projects to reduce erosion and sedimentation by applying all practical conservation measures. This includes a research and demonstration national laboratory for formulating new fertilizers and testing them in the Tennessee Valley and elsewhere, establishing model dams with hydroelectric generation, flood control techniques, and navigation development. Recreation has become one of its most popular uses of water and adjacent lands.

19-12 FOOD AND AGRICULTURE ORGANIZATION

The Food and Agriculture Organization (FAO) is an agency of the United Nations with permanent headquarters in Rome, Italy. The FAO works worldwide, but concentrates on helping the developing countries.

Soil and water conservation activities of the FAO include:

1. Helping governments establish a viable organization to apply erosion- and water-control practices in each country that requests it.
2. Giving technical training and education to selected staff.
3. Encouraging governments to adequately finance the programs.
4. Helping to establish pilot watersheds to serve as a research and demonstration program.
5. Assisting local country staff in helping farmers to apply suitable soil and water conservation practices on their farms.

Specific projects of the Food and Agriculture Organization include (Hauck, 1974):

1. Sending consultants on soil and water conservation for specific work in response to government requests.
2. Conducting seminars on a regional or country basis.
3. Publishing bulletins on soil and water conservation.
4. Conducting specific programs as requested in several countries. Recent studies on soil and water conservation have been made in Argentina, Botswana, Ghana, Korea, Malaysia, and Morocco.

SUMMARY

In early 1929 the U.S. Congress passed the Buchanan Amendment establishing erosion experiment stations and plant nurseries, in recognition of critical soil erosion. This was followed in 1933 by the establishment of the Soil Erosion Service, a public works program to provide employment during the Great Depression. Through the effective leadership of H. H. Bennett, assisted by two dust storm episodes, the permanent Soil Conservation Service was established in 1935. The Soil Conservation Service has taken the national and international leadership in all phases of soil and water conservation.

Conservation Districts are nationwide. They are legal subdivisions of state governments and are managed by a governing board elected by private citizens.

They call for assistance from technical and other agencies, especially the Soil Conservation Service.

The Agricultural Stabilization and Conservation Service has many functions, one of which is to administer a cost-sharing program for soil and water conservation practices adopted by farmers and ranchers.

The Science and Education Administration (SEA) has three branches. Their assistance to states includes grants to the State Extension Services and to the State Agricultural Experiment Stations through SEA—Cooperative Research for the conduct of research, mostly in cooperation with the Land-Grant Universities. Some of the extension and research grants to the states are used to further soil and water conservation. Nearly all federally funded research is administered by SEA—Agricultural Research, known before 1978 as the USDA—Agricultural Research Service.

Teaching of soil and water conservation in colleges is largely the province of the state agricultural universities. State funds are also used to support off-campus extension teaching and research on soil and water conservation.

The USDA—Forest Service practices and researches soil and water conservation on its National Forests and National Grasslands and offers management advice for private lands. It and the state forestry agencies promote conservation by supplying forest tree seedlings at concessional rates for planting on eroded soils.

Other federal agencies that practice conservation include the Corps of Engineers, Bureau of Land Management, Bureau of Reclamation, Bureau of Indian Affairs, Environmental Protection Agency, and the Tennessee Valley Authority.

The agency with worldwide jurisdiction in soil and water conservation is the Food and Agriculture Organization of the United Nations.

QUESTIONS

1. Explain the factors that led to national awareness of soil erosion in the United States.
2. List the major mandates of the Soil Conservation Service.
3. Enumerate the principal practices promoted by the Soil Conservation Service.
4. Describe the origin and functions of Conservation Districts.
5. Explain cost-sharing by the Agricultural Stabilization and Conservation Service.
6. Agricultural universities have three main functions involved in soil and water conservation. Identify and explain their relevant work.
7. Name the other federal agencies that work in soil and water conservation.
8. How does the Food and Agriculture Organization function in soil and water conservation activities?

REFERENCES

AGRICULTURAL RESEARCH SERVICE, 1976. *Soil, Water, Air Sciences Programs.* USDA Agricultural Research Service, 63 p.

BENNETT, H. H., 1955. *Elements of Soil Conservation,* 2nd ed. McGraw-Hill, New York, 358 p.

CLAWSON, MARION, and BURNELL HELD, 1957. *The Federal Lands: Their Use and Management.* Johns Hopkins Press, Baltimore, 498 p.

COOPERATIVE STATE RESEARCH SERVICE, 1977. *Inventory of Agricultural Research FY 1976, Research Program Summary.* Vol. III, Table V CSRS-30-77, USDA, 124 p.

DAVEY, W. B., 1977. *Conservation Districts and 208 Water Quality Management.* U.S. Environmental Protection Agency and National Association of Soil Conservation Districts, Washington, D.C.

HAUCK, F. W., 1974. Possibilities for assistance by FAO. In *Shifting Cultivation and Soil Conservation in Africa.* Soils Bull. 24. Swedish International Development Authority and Food and Agriculture Organization of the United Nations, p. 245-247.

MILLER, M. F., and H. H. KRUSEKOPF, 1932. *The Influence of Systems of Cropping and Methods of Culture on Surface Runoff and Soil Erosion.* Missouri Agr. Expt. Sta. Bull. 177, 22 p.

MORGAN, R. J., 1965. *Governing Soil Conservation.* Johns Hopkins Press, Baltimore, 399 p.

NATIONAL ASSOCIATION OF CONSERVATION DISTRICTS, 1974. *Conservation Districts in the Decade Ahead, 1975-1985.* Washington, D.C., 10 p.

NATIONAL ASSOCIATION OF CONSERVATION DISTRICTS, 1977. *Proceedings of the 31st Annual Convention, Atlanta, Georgia, Feb. 6-11,* League City, Texas.

NATIONAL WILDLIFE FEDERATION, 1978. *Conservation Directory,* Washington, D.C., 264 p.

SIMMS, D. H., 1970. *The Soil Conservation Service.* Praeger Publishers, New York, 238 p.

SOIL CONSERVATION SERVICE, 1977. *Employee Handbook.* SCS-PERS-750 (SI), USDA, unpaged.

SOIL CONSERVATION SERVICE, 1978. 1977 Conservation Highlights. *Soil Conservation* 43:17-22.

SOIL SURVEY STAFF, 1975. *Soil Taxonomy: A Basic System of Soil Classification for Making and Interpreting Soil Surveys.* Agriculture Handbook 436, USDA, Washington, D.C., 754 p.

U.S. DEPARTMENT OF AGRICULTURE, 1977. *Agricultural Statistics,* U.S. Government Printing Office, 614 p.

20

Soil and Water Conservation Around the World

There always has been erosion and always will be. Overcutting of trees, overgrazing of pastures and ranges, and overplowing of fields accelerate it. Accelerated soil erosion diminishes the ability of farmers around the world to produce satisfactory yields and thereby maintain a satisfying standard of living. Tillage agriculture is especially conducive to the acceleration of water- and wind-erosion processes.

For survival and well-being, governments throughout the world have responded to the challenge of stabilizing erosive soils. Many countries have adopted techniques of organization and practices patterned after those of the USDA—Soil Conservation Service. Most countries have made an effort, however uneven, to conserve soil and water, as shown in Figure 20-1.

20-1 TRANSFER OF CONSERVATION TECHNOLOGY

Some of the most difficult problems facing world development are the geographic and cultural impediments resulting from the efforts to transfer technology from one region to another. The majority of people in developed countries are willing but unable to help people in other countries conserve soil and water. Even the technicians of the USDA—Soil Conservation Service have difficulty adapting effective techniques from the United States to other cultures, especially to situations as different as those in the tropics. The transfer of technology to the tropics will be emphasized because the greatest

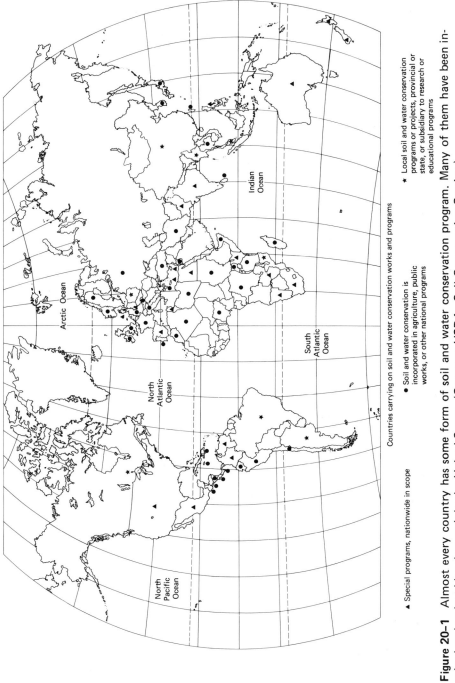

▲ Special programs, nationwide in scope

● Soil and water conservation is incorporated in agriculture, public works, or other national programs

Countries carrying on soil and water conservation works and programs

★ Local soil and water conservation programs or projects, provincial or state, or subsidiary to research or educational programs

Figure 20-1 Almost every country has some form of soil and water conservation program. Many of them have been inspired and assisted by the work in the United States. (Courtesy USDA—Soil Conservation Service.)

unsolved problems of soil and water conservation are in this half of the world, where people are in dire need of greater productivity to keep pace with population growth.

Nearly all regions of the world have failed in some conservation efforts, and most countries offering assistance have made many mistakes. Some of the most serious mistakes in technology transfer have involved soil management and have resulted in accelerated erosion, surface crusting, and rapid decline in crop production.

Several years ago, large mechanization projects based on soil-management techniques of continuous cropping were tried in Ghana and Tanzania. Both projects led to a rapid decline in crop yields, owing to irregular topography, small farms, plinthite (laterite) or otherwise fragile soils, crusting of the soil surface, and serious wind and water erosion. The traditional shifting cultivation was a much more satisfactory cropping system than the substitutes that were instituted. More viable alternatives to shifting cultivation have been found since then, as will be discussed later.

Modern western techniques of crop production were tried in 1974 in tropical southern Tanzania (eastern Africa) at the Kilombero Agricultural Training and Research Institute, Ifakara, Tanzania. Here the elevation is 250 to 300 m, the mean annual temperature is 26°C, and the mean annual rainfall is about 1300 mm. The dry season lasts for six months. The soils have an ironstone layer at about 80 cm. The vegetation consists of trees and grasses (savanna). The traditional agriculture is hand-hoe shifting cultivation, with the cropping period lasting from three to five years and the forest-grass fallow lasting from ten to twenty. Density of population is about twenty persons per square kilometer and is increasing.

The modern western management techniques applied to about 30 ha of land included clearing the land, plowing with a tractor and disk plow, and growing fertilized crops every year. Corn, rice, soybeans, and sesame were among the crops grown. All crops were fertilized with about 20 kg/ha of N as ammonium sulfate, 26 kg/ha of P as triple superphosphate, and 40 kg/ha of K as potassium chloride. The fields were cropped continuously for six years, and the yields decreased each year. The soil pH during this period decreased from 5.4 to 4.1, mostly as a result of acidification by the ammonium sulfate fertilizer. Lime was applied to raise the pH to 4.9, but wild animals destroyed the following rice crop. Animal manures increased yields slightly, but there were very few livestock in the area. The last statement in the report says: "At the present early stages of investigation, no improvement can be suggested on the customary method of shifting cultivation as practiced by farmers on soils of this type" (Vieweg and Wilms, 1974).

Failure of a mechanization project, as illustrated in Figure 20-2, does not mean that the soil is useless for agriculture. Shifting cultivation is one answer. Until recently it was the only one available to subsistence farmers with almost no capital, few advisory services, few productive inputs, and a surplus of forested land. Mulching with crop residues combined with minimum tillage now shows promise as an alternative for tropical soils where population pressure has increased. These practices are also excellent soil and water conservation techniques.

Figure 20-2 Many developing countries have machinery graveyards like this one in Ghana. The machinery was purchased in a mechanization program about 1960, but most of it was never used because the technology was inappropriate for the situation. (Courtesy C. K. Kline, Michigan State University, East Lansing, Michigan.)

20-2 THE TROPICS AND TROPICAL SOILS

Because of its variability, the area of the world known as the tropics is difficult to define. It will be identified here as the equatorial zone that consists of about half of the world's land area and lies between the Tropic of Cancer at 23½° north latitude and the Tropic of Capricorn at 23½° south latitude. *Lowland* tropics are the warm areas below 1500 m at the equator and below 300 m at the north and south limits of the tropics; *highland* tropics are above these levels.

Lowland tropics usually have mean monthly temperatures above 10°C, mean annual temperatures of more than 25°C, and no freezes. The humid tropics have an annual precipitation in excess of 750 mm; evaporation is so high that any month with less than 100 mm of precipitation is considered a drought month. Another characteristic of tropical climate is that daily fluctuations in air temperatures are greater than those of the means of the coldest and warmest days of the year. Another way of saying this is: "Night is the winter of the tropics."

An increase in altitude in the tropics results in a temperature decrease of about 2°C for each 300 m in elevation. Areas at higher latitudes also are cooler and tend to have longer dry seasons as a result of being farther from the equator.

Soils of the tropics vary greatly in their properties because of great spans of geologic age, extremes of climate, and wide differences in parent materials. The greatest contrasts are in humid tropical regions. Soils in high rainfall areas in the tropics have much deeper profiles than counterpart soils in temperate areas. Tropical weathering of parent materials and soils continues uninterrupted every day in the year. On old land surfaces, this environment produces soils low in weatherable minerals and low in the basic cations, Na, Ca, Mg, and K. However, in low-rainfall tropical regions, soils are similar to those in the temperate zones. The tropics have both the highest and lowest rainfall in the world, ranging from nearly 16,700 mm a year on the Island of Kauai in Hawaii and Cherrapunji, Assam, in northeastern India, to a low of less than 20 mm in the Sahara Desert of northern Africa. Parent materials of tropical soils include continuously shifting sand dunes, wind-deposited silts, fresh volcanic ash, river flood plains of variable textures, lake-laid clays, and many kinds of rocks.

Desert soils are mostly in the tropics and subtropics and cover nearly one-third of the earth's land surface. The principal deserts are the Sahara Desert in northern Africa; the Arabian Desert in the

Middle East; the Victoria Desert of Australia; the Kalahari Desert in southwestern Africa; the Sonora Desert in northwestern Mexico, southern Arizona, and southern California; the Atacama Desert in Peru and Chile; and the deserts of Afghanistan, Baluchistan, and northwestern India. A smaller desert also exists in eastern Africa.

About one-fourth of the area of the tropics has soils that are reasonably fertile because they are only slightly or moderately weathered and leached. Almost all such soils are dry part or all of the year (Table 20-1). Some of the dry soils can be irrigated; these and the few soils in the humid tropics that are fairly young, medium- to fine-textured, developed from high-calcium parent materials, and on slopes of less than about 2% can be cultivated continuously if the following practices are adopted:

1. Apply minimum tillage.
2. Practice surface mulch residue management.
3. Lime to a pH of about 5.5 (not to 6.0 or above as in temperate regions).
4. Where toxic concentrations of soluble or exchangeable aluminum are present in the soil, select crops that are less sensitive to them such as peanuts, pearl millet, bermudagrass, napiergrass, and stargrass.
5. Test the soil every one to three years and apply the NPK fertilizer recommended, plus any needed secondary and micronutrients.

About half of the soils of the tropics are highly weathered and leached and are classified mostly as Ultisols and Oxisols. These soils tend to be deep and low in fertility, having low cation-exchange capacities because their clay consists of kaolinite and oxides of iron and aluminum. The clay tends to be aggregated into silt-sized granules so the soil is friable, but the organic-matter content is low and the granules are often not stable enough to resist dispersion and crusting when exposed to raindrop impact. Table 20-1 shows that 42% of such soils are potentially arable (able to be cultivated) but their fertility and productivity usually drop rapidly when they are cropped, and the rate of erosion increases. Shifting cultivation is successful on them because it allows the jungle to return after two or three years of cropping.

Some of the highly weathered soils of the tropics have a *plinthite* (laterite) layer that will crystallize into *ironstone* if the surface cover is removed and the soil becomes completely dry between wet periods. Ironstone at a shallow depth ruins the soil because the hardening is irreversible.

Table 20-1 Kinds of soils in the tropics and their potential arability[a]

Soil classification	Moisture conditions (area in millions of hectares)						Potentially arable	
	Wet all months	Wet most months	Wet-dry	Dry most months	Semi-desert and desert	Total	Million hectares	Percentage of total
Light-colored, base-rich (mostly Aridisols)	4	7	98	378	211	698	134	19
Dark-colored, base-rich (mostly Vertisols, some Mollisols and Inceptisols)	23	56	119	93	2	293	140	48
Moderately weathered and leached (mostly Alfisols and Inceptisols)	4	34	90	75	6	209	77	37
Highly weathered and leached (mostly Ultisols and Oxisols)	931	1084	474	49	2	2540	1071	42
Shallow soils and deep sands (Entisols and shallow families of most soil orders)	81	105	170	153	336	845	77	9
Alluvium (mostly Entisols and Mollisols)	146	124	71	24	5	370	174	47
Total	1189	1410	1022	772	562	4955	1673	34

[a]Technology, farm inputs, relative prices, and irrigation water are assumed to be equal to those in the United States in 1967.
SOURCE: President's Advisory Committee Panel on World Food Supply, 1967.

20-3 SHIFTING CULTIVATION AND CONSERVATION

Two contrasting kinds of shifting cultivation are used, depending on the soil and its vegetation. The most common type is practiced on humid, forested soils of low fertility on steep slopes with high erodibility. The other type is conducted on humid, grassed, high-based, clay soils with gentle topography and moderate erosion hazard.

20-3.1 Forested Soils

About 250 million farmers in the humid tropical world produce a subsistence living by shifting cultivation. This kind of agriculture is common and sometimes dominant in parts of Asia, Africa, Central America, and South America. The soils are generally permeable, are leached of essential plant nutrients, and are commonly classified as Oxisols or Ultisols.

Shifting cultivation means partially clearing and burning a patch in a forest as shown in Figure 20-3, raising crops mostly by hoe-culture and to a lesser extent by animal-powered farming methods for a period of two to three years, then allowing the patch to revert to forest trees for ten to twenty years. After this decade or two of soil rejuvenation, the same patch is again cleared and cropped. The cropping period is usually extended for as long as the farmer considers crop yields satisfactory or until there are excessive infestations of weeds, insects, or disease, but this period seldom exceeds five years. Likewise, the period that forest trees are allowed to grow depends on how rapidly and completely trees occupy the cleared patches and how soon the farmer needs the area again for cropping.

Trees are essential during the soil-rejuvenation stage to accelerate the weathering of essential soil minerals, to add organic matter, and to break the cycle of insects, disease, and weeds. Soil productivity is renewed less rapidly where grasses dominate the vegetation during the rejuvenation cycle. This is especially true on soils with low-base status and plinthite. Trees maintain more uniform soil water and temperature conditions, which reduce crystallization of iron and aluminum in plinthite.

Hardened plinthite becomes almost waterproof. The few centimeters to a meter or more of soil above the plinthite become saturated and easily eroded during heavy rains. Another condition conducive to soil erosion exists on steep slopes when a patch for cropping is cleared and burned. Most soils of the tropics are less fertile, residual organic matter decomposes faster, and precipitation

Figure 20-3 Shifting cultivation on forested soils requires that a dense stand of trees be cut down and burned. Bulldozers may be used but much of the work is done with an axe, as in this scene in Ivory Coast. (Courtesy Roy L. Donahue.)

is usually more intense than in temperate regions. The resulting erosion is therefore more rapid than it would be in temperate regions.

An example of high rainfall intensity causing severe erosion on low-base forested soils used for shifting cultivation in the tropics is cited by Rapp (1977). On February 23, 1970, 100 mm of rain fell in two hours and caused more than 1000 landslides and mudflows that moved about 400,000 mt of sediment into the Morogoro River and its tributaries in southern Tanzania. In April 1973, another heavy rain in the same watershed resulted in a 26,000-mt mudflow that blocked the water supply of the town of Morogoro for several weeks. During the years 1966 to 1970, the suspended soil sediment load in the Morogoro River averaged 7500 mt/year.

It is unfortunate that a viable alternative to shifting cultivation was not developed until recently. That alternative is the use of fertilizers and pesticides combined with minimum tillage to leave organic residues on the surface of the soil. Such a system was researched at Ibadan, Nigeria, by the International Institute of Tropical Agriculture (IITA, 1975). This is a humid forested area and the dominant soils are high in plinthite and ironstone. Traditional shifting cultivation is the predominant cropping system. Research personnel at the Institute hypothesized that modern scientific agriculture could replace shifting cultivation successfully if the new system:

1. Reduced excessive wetting and drying and warming and cooling of the soil and reduced soil erosion.
2. Broke the insect, disease, and weed cycle.
3. Rejuvenated soil fertility by hastening the release of essential plant nutrients from slowly weatherable soil minerals.

Field research the Institute used to test this hypothesis included:

1. A surface mulch of crop residues and no-till cultivation to reduce extremes of soil moisture and soil temperature and to control soil erosion.
2. Modern insecticides, fungicides, and herbicides to control pests.
3. Chemical fertilizers to increase soil fertility and crop productivity.

Soybeans grown in this research lost only 1% of the precipitation received, and no soil was eroded. Plowed and cultivated soybeans caused a 15% loss of precipitation and 38 mt/ha of soil loss per year (Table 20-2). Loss of water and soil from other crops was much higher.

Table 20-2 Effects of cropping systems on runoff water and soil erosion sediment loss under tropical conditions in Nigeria

	Runoff water lost		*Annual soil loss (mt/ha)*
Treatment	*Loss in cm/yr*	*Percentage of total received*	
No-till soybeans	1.3	1	0
Plowed soybeans	17.3	15	38
Corn plus cassava	24.1	21	69
Cassava	32.1	28	109

SOURCE: International Institute of Tropical Agriculture, 1975.

20-3.2 Grassland Soils in Humid Tropics and Subtropics

Vertisols are the most abundant grassland soils in humid tropical areas. The 2,340,000 ha or 1.8% of the land surface of the earth that they occupy is mostly in tropical or subtropical areas with wet and dry seasons. They commonly occur where the annual rainfall is 600 to 1000 mm—enough to support forest vegetation on other soils, but the Vertisols grow grasses. Two factors favor the grasses— the high base saturation and the high content of montmorillonite clay (at least 30% clay to a depth of 50 cm) that gives Vertisols their self-swallowing action. The shrink-swell potential of the montmorillonite causes deep cracks to open in these soils during dry seasons, as shown in Figure 20-4. Granular surface soil falls into these cracks and causes the soil to shift and "churn" when it gets wet. The churning action distributes organic matter throughout the soil and produces a deep, dark-colored soil. It also can break deep roots of perennial plants and the foundations of buildings.

Traditional crop culture on Vertisols in Ethiopia includes cotton, grain sorghum, and sesame in a shifting cultivation that involves burning the soil. Only Vertisols are burned—never the adjoining red

Figure 20-4 A Vertisol in northwestern Ethiopia. This soil developed on high-lime materials, is dark colored, has a high percentage of montmorillonite clay, and has wide deep cracks for at least ninety consecutive days a year. (Courtesy Roy L. Donahue.)

clay soils. The native tall-grass prairie is plowed with a village-made, tongue-type plow pulled by oxen (bullocks). The plowed rows are crooked, and the seedbed is always cloddy and full of large sod pieces with soil attached. The farmer gathers these sod pieces, puts them in piles, and adds cattle manure in the center of each pile, as shown in Figure 20-5. When the soil and sod pieces have dried, each pile is set on fire and may smolder for several days. Upon cooling, the residues from each burned pile are spread over the field. The soil has improved tilth after burning. After further plowings, seeds of cotton, grain sorghum, or sesame are sown. Field crops are then grown for a period of three to five years, after which the land is abandoned. During abandonment, weeds, annual grasses, and finally perennial native grasses grow over a fallow period of ten to twenty years until the burning and cropping cycle is repeated.

During the cropping cycle, the soil becomes weedy, insect and disease populations build up, and soil tilth decreases. Soil fertility is decreased by crop removal; soil crust formation becomes more serious; and sheet and gully erosion are increased. By contrast, during the fallow cycle, the grasses improve the physical condition of the soil, pests decrease, fertility increases by weathering of minerals, and erosion is controlled. The native grasses help to develop a fine crumb structure that makes a desirable physical, chemical, and biological seedbed. Burning the black clay soil inside each pile of sod pieces destroys pests, eliminates cloddiness, and transforms the montmoril-lonitic clay into nonswelling particles that resemble brick dust. The surface soil that was a clay loam now tests a loamy sand. The burning also increases soil pH, available phosphorus, and total carbonates but decreases organic carbon (Donahue, 1972).

Shifting cultivation on burned Vertisols supporting native grasses is a soil conserving practice but is an inefficient land use that will not support rising populations with their increasing demand for land. Replacement of this traditional system awaits field research solutions. Perhaps a solution will be found that is comparable to that for forested areas using minimum tillage, organic surface-residue management, pesticides, and chemical fertilizers. In the meantime, Ethiopian farmers are using a system with no modern inputs that maintains yields and stabilizes the soil against excessive erosion.

20-4 EROSION AND ITS CONTROL IN THE TROPICS

In the tropics, soil erosion increases with increasing annual rainfall up to about 1000 mm, but usually decreases at higher rainfalls be-

a

b

Figure 20-5 Traditional shifting cultivation on Vertisols in Ethiopia involves (a) plowing the grassland several times with a village-made plow and then (b) gathering sod pieces into piles. Cattle manure is added to the piles and they are allowed to dry; then they are burned and spread back over the field. (Courtesy Roy L. Donahue.)

cause trees are the usual vegetation in the higher-rainfall areas, and they are more protective than grasses that thrive under lower rainfall. Rains usually come with greater intensity in the tropics than in temperate regions, and high rates of erosion are common on cleared land. Lal (1974) measured soil erosion losses in the tropics on bare slopes varying from 1% to 15%. The rates were 3, 37, 50, and 115 mt/ha on 1%, 5%, 10% and 15% slopes, respectively.

Many sloping soils are used in shifting cultivation, and changes in soil characteristics during the cropping cycle are often catastrophic. Two years after cutting the trees, for example, as much as 30% of the soil organic matter and 70% of the soil nitrogen may be gone.

Clearing the soil also results in higher soil temperatures, slower water infiltration, and greater erosion (Lal, 1974).

Techniques of soil-erosion control commonly used in temperate regions have been tried in the tropics with only partial success. These have included terracing, contour ridging, strip cropping, and the use of cover crops. Some success has been reported when cereal crops are minimum-till planted into herbicide-killed vegetation of selected perennial grasses and legumes that were used as cover or rotational crops.

Terracing and contour ridging have failed in many tropical areas because of torrential rains, frequent overtopping of structures, surface sealing such as that shown in Figure 20-6, and a rapid decline in infiltration. Furthermore, subsoils exposed in the process of constructing terraces are often very infertile and difficult to stabilize with vegetation. Strip cropping with annual crops only, such as alternate strips of broadcast cowpeas and corn, is rarely successful in the tropics. Soil erosion is reduced when a dense perennial sod crop is alternated with an intertilled crop on slopes less than about 10%. Selected shrubs and several perennial tropical grasses have been used effectively in strip cropping.

Figure 20-6 Contour ridging of cotton in tropical northern Nigeria was only moderately successful. The ridges shown did not overtop during the last rain, but the soil is badly puddled. (Courtesy Roy L. Donahue.)

Annual cover crops seldom conserve soil in the tropics because additional tillage is necessary to establish them and to incorporate them into the soil. A successful modification of this system known as *mixed cropping* is commonly used in the tropics. This system consists of establishing and maintaining several crops at the same time on the same field. Examples of mixed cropping include corn and peas; banana, cassava (tapioca) and rice; and peanuts and grain sorghum. A mixed crop of cowpeas and corn increased the infiltration rate of the soil on a 10% slope by more than 40% as compared with corn alone (Lal, 1974).

Besides the use of mixed cropping to conserve soil, the most promising technique for erosion control on land cultivated continuously is to use an organic surface mulch in a minimum-tillage system. This method was proved a success at the International Institute of Tropical Agriculture at Ibadan, Nigeria (Lal, 1974). Infiltration rates with no tillage were more than 50% higher than on the plowed fields. Runoff losses from 295 mm of rainfall during the season on 5% to 10% slopes were about 120 mm (40%) from unmulched corn, 20 mm (7%) from mulched corn, and 5 mm from forest. Corn yields were consistently increased in another no-tillage experiment in Nigeria (Table 20-3).

Soils and agriculture similar to those in Africa also occur in tropical Central and South America, but very little research on soil and water conservation has been conducted in the latter regions. However, until such time as reliable field research is available, the

Table 20-3   Comparison of corn yields on conventional and no-tillage for the years 1975–1977 in Nigeria

| | | Yield (mt/ha) | | |
| | | Conventional tillage | No tillage | Ratio, no-tillage: conventional |
Year	Season			
1975	1	1.5	1.6	1.07:1
	2	1.1	1.2	1.09:1
1976	1	2.8	2.9	1.04:1
	2	1.2	1.6	1.33:1
1977	1	2.3	3.1	1.35:1
	2	1.6	1.7	1.06:1

SOURCE: IITA, 1978.

results from Africa should be useful. As a Latin American authority writes (Sanchez, 1973, p. 59): "The soil should be covered by crops at all times to prevent possible physical damage and excessive increases in soil temperature. Multiple cropping could not only decrease compaction, erosion, and runoff, but also reduce weed control efforts."

20-4.1 Coffee Plantations

Coffee is a large shrub or small tree, as shown in Figure 20-7, that grows wild in the highlands of southeastern Ethiopia in Kaffa Province (hence, the name "coffee"). It is a major export crop in tropical Ethiopia. Kenya, Tanzania, and Uganda, but Brazil now produces most of the world's coffee. Two distinct species supply the bulk of coffee grown: arabica coffee and robusta coffee. Arabica coffee at low latitudes grows best at about 1500 m, where air temperature stays between 15° and 20°C, annual rainfall is between 1500 and 1900 mm, and the soil is deep, well drained, and has a pH of about 6.5. Robusta coffee is best adapted to areas with an elevation around 1000 m, air temperature about 25°C, annual rainfall around 1500 mm, and well-drained soils with a pH of about 6.0.

Figure 20-7 A small coffee tree with green fruit at the Jimma Research Station in southern Ethiopia. The rolling topography provides needed air drainage but makes soil erosion a hazard on coffee plantations. (Courtesy Food and Agriculture Organization of the United Nations.)

Topography for both arabica and robusta coffee plantations is typically rolling, resulting in good air drainage without frost pockets. The rolling topography and cultivation necessary to establish a coffee plantation are conducive to surface crusting and erosion. Field research in eastern Africa has resulted in a mulching recommendation for reducing the erosion hazard. Mulches made with cut wild grasses or banana leaves applied immediately after cultivation and fertilization have been used successfully to reduce erosion, protect the soil against high soil temperatures, and increase yields of coffee by 22% to 93%. Living legumes and grasses cannot be substituted for a dead mulch of plant residues (Donahue, 1969).

20-4.2 Tea Plantations

Tea comes from fast-growing, newly formed leaves of a genus of *Camellia,* an evergreen shrub or small tree native to eastern Asia. There are at least eighty species of *Camellia,* and several are used in plantations to produce commercial tea.

The ideal conditions for growing tea are tropical and subtropical latitudes, high elevations, and sloping topography, such as the area in Figure 20-8. In general, higher-quality tea is produced at higher elevations. Elevations of 750 to 1500 m along with slopes that permit good air drainage are considered ideal (the ideal elevation is highest near the equator). The most suitable precipitation is in the range of 1500 to 2000 mm a year, and there should be no dry months. A mean annual temperature of 20°C is considered ideal, with a daily minimum of 10°C and a maximum of 35°C. The tea plant can withstand moderate amounts of frost and snow.

Soils for tea should be sloping for good air drainage, freely permeable for good aeration, of medium texture for favorable plant nutrient and available water capacity, and at least 2 m deep. Ideal soil pH is about 5.5, with an acceptable range of 4.5 to 6.0. As much as 100 kg/ha of N fertilizer is generally recommended to be applied annually in early spring.

Rolling topography and high rainfall can cause serious erosion in tea plantations. Erosion-control techniques include planting tea bushes on the contour and mulching all exposed soils with organic residues. Terraces and grassed waterways are sometimes established on the steepest slopes before tea seedlings are planted in rows parallel to the terraces. Trees interplanted with well-managed tea bushes provide shade and also help to control soil erosion. A tea plantation may be productive for one hundred years, so soil and site selection, terracing, and contour planting should be given serious consideration before establishment (Chinzei and others, 1967).

Figure 20-8 Tea comes from the leaves of *Camellia* bushes grown on rolling topography at high elevations in the tropics. *Camellia* needs high rainfall, but this causes an erosion hazard. This plantation in eastern Africa was therefore terraced and planted on the contour. (Courtesy Roy L. Donahue.)

20-4.3 Pineapple Plantations

Pineapples are a tropical crop with unique soil requirements. Erosion is controlled by selecting fairly level soils as shown in Figure 20-9, by terracing more sloping fields, or by mulching. Any soil loss results in a shallower root system because the roots seem never to develop below the A or Ap horizon. Sandy soils are preferred because the soil must be well drained. Pineapples are sometimes grown in beds raised 30 to 50 cm above adjoining channels to improve the drainage.

The soil pH for pineapples should be between 4.5 and 5.5, though some varieties have been grown in Hawaii at pH 7 or above by spraying the plants with a solution containing iron. Pineapples are so sensitive to iron deficiency resulting from high soil pH that dust from a road surfaced with limestone fragments caused a crop failure in a pineapple plantation in Okinawa. The farmer solved the problem by planting a strip of vegetables where the limestone dust settled along the road.

Erosion control is not much of a problem on level plantations or where level terraces are constructed. Mulching has been an effective

Figure 20-9 A pineapple plantation on level land in Puerto Rico. (Courtesy Department of Agriculture, Puerto Rico.)

means of erosion control on some sloping plantations. Chinzei and others (1967) report an annual soil loss of only about 1 mt/ha from a mulched pineapple plantation on a 45° (100%) slope where an unmulched plantation lost about 80 mt/ha.

20-4.4 Wheat in the Tropics

The U.S. Agricultural Trade Development and Assistance Act of 1954 and the Act for International Development of 1962 permitted the export of surplus foods in the United States to friendly but dollar-short countries. As a consequence, much surplus wheat and wheat flour was sent to countries in the tropics that had never used food products made from wheat. Bread made from wheat became very popular with the people. These countries soon tried to raise wheat themselves, but few succeeded.

Wheat can be grown successfully near the equator at elevations between 1500 and 2500 m with annual rainfall of about 800 to 1600 mm or with irrigation. Wheat is grown in Kenya on fine-textured soils plowed out of virgin grassland. However, no more than two to three years of continuous wheat can be raised because of soil structural deterioration, severe surface and gully erosion on sloping lands, and a decrease in wheat yields. Temperate-region agronomists usually think first of maintaining yields of wheat with chemical fertilizers, but fertilizers alone are not very effective. Selection of suitable soils that are not too steep, rotation of wheat with perennial grasses such as rhodesgrass, and then using nitrogen and phosphorus fertilizers appear to be the modern solution to economic yields of wheat (Donahue, 1969).

The first attempt to raise wheat in Kenya was in 1966 on 300 ha of virgin Vertisols at elevations above 1500 m; the crop failed. It was concluded that the soil must be prepared during the dry season and the wheat planted in a dry seedbed at a depth of 5 cm (wet Vertisols are too sticky to work). Seedbed preparation on dry Vertisols requires tractor power and takes many passes over the field before proper tilth can be achieved. This results in a high potential for surface crust formation, sheet erosion, and gully erosion.

During the first trial year, wheat was planted on level-contoured land, and the soil became waterlogged. During subsequent years the soil was laid out in lands 15 m wide with a grade of one-half to one percent to improve surface drainage. Dead furrows were left along the sides of each section of land to further improve drainage. Even with these techniques, wheat yields were satisfactory for only three years; then the land was abandoned and a new virgin area was plowed and planted to wheat.

20-5 SOIL AND WATER CONSERVATION IN SELECTED AREAS

Specific examples of soil and water conservation are cited here for arid northern Africa and the Middle East, Ghana, Liberia, Greece, the USSR, India, Pakistan, the humid Amazon Jungles of Peru, Brazil, and Nicaragua.

20-5.1 Arid Tropical and Subtropical Africa and the Middle East

Soil and water conservation is especially difficult in arid regions. Aridity is common at latitudes between about 15° and 30° north and south of the equator. At these latitudes air masses usually descend, become warmer, and increase their capacity to hold moisture. The result is low precipitation and little plant growth to protect the soil against both water and wind erosion. Also, in areas receiving low precipitation, the annual rain may be received in one or a few storms. The combination of torrential rain and scant vegetation results in excessive erosion.

Desert is commonly defined as an area that receives about 100 mm or less of annual precipitation—not enough to support protective vegetation. However, at an annual precipitation of 150 to 250 mm, many plants can be established to stabilize the soil as well as to supply some forage, firewood, and construction materials.

Special studies of techniques for successful establishment of productive and protective vegetation have been made by the Food and Agriculture Organization of the United Nations (Bensalem, 1977). These activities have been conducted in Tunisia, Morocco, and Algeria. However, the results are considered to be equally applicable to many other countries. Greater success is assured if the site selected for establishing vegetation is in a swale where additional rainwater collects or if the soils are deep sands where all rainwater infiltrates and plants root deeply.

About 50,000 ha of spineless cactus have been planted in Tunisia to stabilize the soil and to provide forage for livestock. Also in Tunisia during a recent five-year period, about 1000 ha/yr of spineless acacia have been established. Windbreaks have been successfully established on fine-textured soil in Tunisia and Algeria by planting native acacia species in mixture with eucalyptus trees from Australia. Two species of pines have proved satisfactory on deep sands— stone pine and cluster pine. New plantations must not be grazed by livestock for a period of two to five years. This restriction requires rigid enforcement by the local government.

Trees and shrubs that have been successfully established in the arid and semiarid tropical and subtropical regions as windbreaks or woodlots are listed in Table 20-4.

20-5.2 Ghana and Liberia

Ghana and Liberia are located in the humid part of western Africa about 5° to 10° north of the equator. The Soil Research Institute at Kwadaso-Kumasi in central Ghana has conducted outstanding work relating soils, mechanization, erosion, and soil productivity. The Institute made a soil survey of an area where attempts to use mechanized agriculture on soils with plinthite had failed. The survey identified the problem soils and it was recommended that all soils with plinthite be seeded to perennial pasture. Soils without plinthite were recommended for continuous mechanized cultivation. More detailed soil surveys were made after this experience and were used

Table 20-4 Tree and shrub species recommended for planting as woodlots, windbreaks, or shelterbelts in tropical and subtropical regions with annual precipitation of 150 to 250 mm[a]

Common English names[b]	
Acacia	Mesquite tree
African locust	Mulga
Aleppo pine	Neem tree
Argan tree	Olive tree
Calligonum	Russian olive
Carob tree	Shinus
Eucalyptus	Siris tree
Fourwing saltbush	Sissoo
Horsetail tree	Salsola shrub
Jerusalem thorn	Tamarix
Kassod tree	Tassili cypress

[a]Plants will grow in areas of the lower range of precipitation in swales and on sandy soils.
[b]Scientific names are given in Appendix B.

to make a map of Ghana delineating areas suitable for the three kinds of cultivation: tractors, oxen, and hand-hoes such as those shown in Figure 20-10).

Liberian agriculture consists mostly of shifting cultivation, with vegetables, upland rainfed rice, and cassava (tapioca) as the main crops. Many viable commercial rubber, cocoa, coffee, and oil palm plantations also exist. Erosion is serious on sloping croplands during extended periods of cropping, especially near large centers of population. Some soils apparently can be cropped without deterioration for five or more years, whereas others cannot support more than two or three crops without a serious decline in yields. To determine suitable soils for the most feasible land resettlement, the government of Liberia requested assistance in establishing a nationwide soil survey.

For three and a half years the U.S. Agency for International Development financed a soil surveyor from the USDA—Soil Conservation Service to help establish a soil survey in Liberia. The survey is used to aid in scientific land use decisions, including practices to maximize production and minimize erosion and sedimentation (Geiger, 1978).

20-5.3 Greece

Greece has a mean annual temperature ranging from 15° to 20°C and mean monthly temperatures from 6° to 27°C. Oranges are grown

Figure 20-10 Two kinds of tillage implements used in equatorial Africa. The village-made hoe commonly used in subsistence agriculture seldom disturbs the soil enough to cause serious soil erosion. The disk plow makes it possible to use tractor power in commercial farming and also increases the potential for soil erosion. (Courtesy Roy L. Donahue.)

in the warmer parts of the country and olives are grown over a more extensive area. Mean annual precipitation varies from 400 mm at Athens to 850 mm at Kalmia in the Peloponnesus. The dry season, ranging from about one month on the island of Crete to about four months at Athens, is a constraint on production of warm-season plants.

The soils of Greece are dominantly shallow over highly weathered limestone. Nearly all of the topography is hilly to mountainous. Shallow soils on steep slopes are conducive to erosion even though the rains are usually gentle. Soil erosion is a serious handicap to the country because a deep soil is needed to hold sufficient available water for plant growth during the dry summers when temperatures are most favorable for plant growth.

According to a twenty-year study by the Athens Soils Institute, serious erosion had occurred on 45,000 ha in the Peloponnesus. In another study made by the Land and Water Reclamation Service in two states in northern Greece, Thrace and Macedonia, the loss of agricultural production due to erosion was valued to $8 million per year.

Action programs to control erosion in Greece have consisted of terracing, contour farming, strip cropping, subsoiling, tree planting, grazing control, and gully reclamation (personal communication from B. Moussouros). Terraces have been built to protect 9000 ha of land, as shown in Figure 20-11.

20-5.4 USSR (Soviet Union)

The Union of Soviet Socialist Republics (Soviet Union) with a land area of 2227 million hectares is the largest country in the world.

Figure 20-11 Olive trees planted on some of the 9000 ha of land protected by terraces in Greece. This hillside has a slope gradient of 15% to 25%. (Courtesy K. Karoyannakis, Land Reclamation Service, Greece.)

Its geographic location is analogous to that of Canada and northern United States. The USSR cropland has a climate as variable as that from northern Alaska to southern California (Central Intelligence Agency, 1974).

Approximately 27% of the land area of the Soviet Union is classified as agricultural and about one-third of the agricultural land is arable. Almost all of the 224 million hectares of arable land in the USSR was sown to crops in 1972. This compares with 186 million hectares of arable land in the United States, of which less than 75% is sown annually. Cropland in the USSR has been increased by 43 million hectares since 1950, including 29 million during the 1953 to 1958 period in the "New Lands Program." This program included marginal areas (cold and dry) in southern Siberia and northern Kazakhstan. Because of intense cold and too little moisture, several million hectares of New Lands had to be abandoned for crops. Many such areas were devastated by wind and water erosion and salinization because the former protective grasses and shrubs had been destroyed.

A major part of the 224 million hectares of arable Soviet farmland is subject to severe wind and water erosion. These natural processes have been accelerated in many areas by traditional farming practices stressing production rather than conservation. Plowing of steep slopes, overgrazing, overcutting of trees, and other practices that remove vegetative cover have been particularly damaging in the forest-steppe and forest zones of the European USSR and in the Transcaucasus and central region. In the dry steppe and semidesert, bare ground is exposed frequently to wind erosion by strong, dry winds.

Dust storms are becoming more frequent each year, even though erosion-control measures have been applied. In the grain-growing Kuban and southern Volga regions, for example, dust storms occurred in 1960, 1964, and 1965; and in the winter of 1969 a storm completely destroyed crops on 820,000 ha and severely damaged crops on 634,000 ha in a period of only five days.

Thick loess deposits lead to another problem. Loess is very susceptible to deep gullying even on gentle slopes. Occasional downpours of summer rain produce vast networks of gullies and ravines, particularly in the deep loess deposits that occupy large areas of the Ukraine.

Hundreds of millions of tons of grain and several million tons of fodder are lost annually in the USSR because yields are reduced by wind and water erosion. Soviet estimates indicate that the control of erosion on arable land would result in an annual increase in national income of about $6 billion.

The severity of the erosion problem was acknowledged in a 1967 joint resolution of the USSR Communist Party and the Council of Ministers. The resolution called for increased contour plowing, crop rotation, strip cropping, and sowing grass on steep slopes; the planting and cultivation of forest belts; afforestation of gullies, ravines, and shorelines of rivers and reservoirs; and the construction of erosion-control and flood-control structures.

Many Soviet organizations, including the Ministry of Agriculture of the USSR and the corresponding ministries in the respective republics (states), are concerned with soil and water conservation. Also involved are the USSR and republic ministries of Land Reclamation and Water Resources, the State Forestry Committee, several research organizations, and all of the *sovkhozes* (rural industries) and *kolkhozes* (collective farms).

Windbreaks and shelterbelts are prominent among measures designed to combat both wind and water erosion. Concentrated on the steppe and forest-steppe of European USSR, these forest belts protect against wind erosion, increase the accumulation of snow, check the erosive action of surface water, and raise the water table. In addition to the local windbreaks maintained by forestry farms, *kolkhozes,* and *sovkhozes,* a series of major shelterbelts some 30 to 100 m wide and hundreds of kilometers long were established in the Volga-Don region as a result of a 1948 state decree. Altogether, about 2 million hectares of land have been planted to windbreaks and shelterbelts. Unfortunately, about two-thirds of the total area planted to shelterbelts before 1956 has been lost because of improper planning or subsequent neglect.

Contour plowing, crop rotations, fallowing, stubble-mulching, and terracing are used in many areas. Stubble-mulch tillage is a necessity for adequate erosion control in the New Lands area of western Siberia and northern Kazakhstan and in other moisture-deficient areas. Also called trashy fallow, this practice protects the soil from baking, contributes to lower soil temperatures in hot summer weather, decreases the depth of freezing, impedes runoff and evaporation, and enables the soil to absorb more rainfall.

Various types of terraces are used in hilly terrain to reduce the slope gradient. Found primarily in the mountains of Moldavia, the Caucasus, and Soviet Central Asia, terracing was once considered the basis for mountain agriculture; however, recent research has shown that some mountain soils, slopes, and crops do not need terraces.

20-5.5 India

Cropping in India is becoming more intensive with increasing population, and water and wind erosion are becoming more serious. Of the 305 million hectares in India, 150 million (49%) are subject to deterioration by water and wind erosion, as shown in Figure 20-12. About 16.5% of the land area of India has extremely low produc-

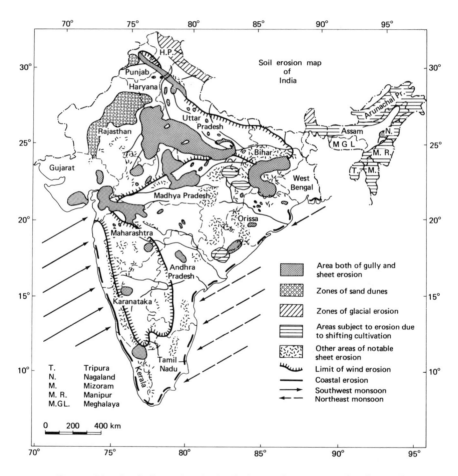

Figure 20-12 Soil erosion in India is a serious constraint for agricultural production. There are large areas of sheet, gully, and wind erosion plus areas of glacial erosion and erosion related to shifting cultivation. (Source: Food and Agriculture Organization of the United Nations, *FAO Soils Bulletin* No. 33, D.C. Das, 1977.)

tivity because of the following problems (National Commission on Agriculture, India, 1976, and Das, 1977):

Cause of low productivity	Hectares (million)
Deserts	14.2
Ironstone (hardened plinthite)	12.0
Sandy coastal land	7.5
Saline, sodic soils	7.0
Waterlogged soils	6.0
Riverine gullies	3.7
Total	50.4 (16.5% of India)

Practices used to control erosion in India include contour cultivation, terracing, and the establishment of protective vegetation. Most of the soil and water conservation works have been concentrated to stabilize shifting sands or to reduce erosion and sedimentation on the watershed of the reservoirs used for hydroelectric power generation and irrigation.

An example of techniques to stabilize dunes occurred in northwestern India where 14 million hectares of land receive less than 60 mm of precipitation annually. Soils are mostly sandy and move with moderate winds. The most successful technique for controlling wind erosion has been to plant trees and shrubs as windbreaks and shelterbelts according to the following guidelines (Arakeri and others, 1962):

1. Select adapted species of trees and shrubs (Table 20-5).
2. Plant at least three rows of trees and shrubs at right angles to the prevailing erosive winds. Plant a row of taller trees in the center and a row of shrubs on each side in staggered positions about 2 m apart.
3. Protect from cattle and people.
4. Irrigate when possible until the plants are well established.

20-5.6 Pakistan

Pakistan needs an organization capable of supplying on-farm service on a multidisciplinary basis to permit farmers to achieve higher crop yields. Specific recommendations made for improving this service to farmers include the following (Cox, 1977):

Table 20-5 Trees and shrubs recommended for sand-dune control in north-western India[a]

Trees	Shrubs
Babul	Assyrian plum
Cashew	Caper bush
Casuarina	Century plant
Fig	Glyricidia
Gum arabic	Jerusalem thorn
Horseradish tree	Jujube
Kanju	Mesquite
Kassod tree	Munj
Khejri	Phog
Madras thorn	Salvadora
Neem	Tarwar
Redgum	Vitex
Safed kikar	
Salt cedar	
Sausage tree	
Siris	
Sissoo	
Tamarind	

[a]See Appendix B for scientific names.
SOURCE: Arakeri and others, 1962.

1. Lining irrigation canals with brick or other suitable material to reduce water-delivery losses. In one study on sandy soils, water-delivery efficiency varied from 5% to 50%.
2. Technical on-farm assistance in precision leveling of fields to be irrigated, including a tractor and landplane rental service.
3. Technical on-farm assistance in water application methods and cultural practices.
4. A cost-sharing (subsidy) system for farmers, similar to that of the USDA—Agricultural Stabilization and Conservation Service.
5. A long-term assistance and training program to establish these recommendations.

The application of individual production practices such as improved varieties, proper fertilization, pest control, and improved water management can be expected to increase yields by 10% to 70%. However, the use of improved practices in one complementary "package" could result in a doubling or tripling of crop yields.

Research results on wheat yields are given to illustrate the effect of positive interaction of practices. On irrigated wheat, no land leveling and no fertilizer resulted in a yield of 1624 kg/ha. Land leveling alone increased yields by 17% and fertilizing alone by 67%; however, combining land leveling and fertilizing increased yields by 180% to 4510 kg/ha.

20-5.7 Amazon Jungles of Peru

Research on intensive cropping of corn, peanuts, cowpeas, rice, soybeans, and cassava has been conducted at Yurimaguas, Peru, since 1969 (North Carolina State University, 1976). The soil is classified as a Typic Paleudult, a highly leached, acid soil typical of the humid, lowland, forested tropics in the Amazon River Valley. Shifting cultivation is the dominant kind of traditional agriculture. The research treatments included NPK fertilizers and lime, mulching with kudzu (surface applied versus incorporated). The results are shown in Table 20-6 and can be summarized in this way:

1. Mulching increased yields of all crops by lowering soil temperatures, lowering bulk density, reducing surface crust formation, controlling weeds, and increasing available soil moisture.

Table 20-6 Yields of rough rice (in metric tons per hectare) in relation to mulching, liming, and fertilizing at Yurimaguas, Peru, in 1975

	No organic matter added	Surface mulching		Incorporation of mulch in soil		Mean fertility level
		Guinea-grass[a]	Kudzu	Guinea-grass	Kudzu	
Unfertilized	1.76	2.94	2.50	2.05	2.39	2.34
Lime + rock phosphate[b]	0.74	2.57	2.48	2.58	2.70	2.21
Low NPKL[c]	2.67	2.41	2.09	2.43	1.84	2.29
High NPKL[d]	2.74	2.31	2.28	1.75	2.12	2.24

[a]Organic matter was applied at the rate of 8 mt/ha (green weight).

[b]Residual effect of 2 mt/ha of lime plus 400 kg/ha of P as rock phosphate.

[c]Low: 60 kg of N/ha per year as urea for nonlegumes, 25 kg of P/ha per year as single superphosphate, 60 kg of K/ha per crop, plus residual effect of 1 mt lime/ha, plus B and Mo applied the previous year.

[d]High: twice the low rate.

SOURCE: North Carolina State University, 1976.

2. Fertilizing with 120 + 50 + 120 kg/ha of NPK, plus liming, resulting in yields equal to those of the mulched plots.
3. Leaving the grass and kudzu mulch *on the soil surface* resulted in higher yields of all crops than when the mulches were incorporated into the soil.

The researchers were not able to explain how the use of mulch alone gave crop-yield increases equal to the best chemical fertilizing and liming practices. The grass contained the equivalent of 22 + 8 + 21 and the Kudzu 45 + 3 + 30 of NPK fertilizer. Perhaps the chemical fertilizer and lime contained an excess of nutrients or some of the nutrients were not available to the current crops. Another explanation may be that the mulch supplied secondary and micronutrients and stimulated soil organisms to decompose soil minerals and bring slowly available plant nutrients into solution. Whatever the cause, mulching was very effective for maintaining crop yields. Also, the mulching would increase infiltration for cultivated crops and be an effective soil and water conservation practice (Lal, 1974).

The temperate region technique of clearing forested land with a bulldozer was tried and declared a failure in tropical Peru. The bulldozer scraped off too much of the most productive topsoil and compacted the remaining soil. The technique of clearing tropical jungle with hand tools and burning was far superior.

An update on research in the Amazon Jungles at Yurimaguas, Peru, has been favorable toward the use of lime and chemical fertilizers on corn and soybeans. Satisfactory crop yields of corn and soybeans were achieved continuously with lime and fertilizers for three crops a year for six years. Lime treatment consisted of 4.5 mt/ha every three years. Fertilizer treatment for corn was 117 kg N, 70 kg P, 110 kg K, and 45 kg Mg per crop and 3 kg each of B, Cu, and Zn and 0.3 kg Mo/ha each year. Soybeans received the same treatment but without N. Yields of corn were about 4000 kg/ha; and of soybeans 2550 kg/ha for each crop. This may be the first reported success of producing continuous crops in the lowland humid tropics with practices similar to those used in temperate regions.

20-5.8 Brazil

A soil survey of 82 million hectares in the principal cropped areas in humid southern and western Brazil classified the soils as Oxisols, Ultisols, and Mollisols (Bloomfield, 1977). It was found that erosion had been accelerated by the rapid increase in soybean production on slopes up to 12%. Soybeans in Brazil had increased 385% from 1.3 to 6.3 million hectares during the period from 1970 to 1976, mostly on land formerly planted to coffee and pasture grasses. Annual precipitation in the region varies from about 1200 to 1500 mm, with a dry season from April to August.

The survey also showed that 52% of the land in the 82 million hectares area had suffered moderate or severe erosion. The severity of past erosion indicated a need for an effective soil and water conservation program in Brazil. A proposal was made that soil and water conservation and soil survey be combined in an organization similar to that of the USDA—Soil Conservation Service.

One study indicated that a soybean field averaged about 20 mt/ha of soil loss annually and water runoff loss was about 7% of the precipitation received. This compared with about 42 mt/ha and 12% of the precipitation for castor beans and 7 mt/ha and 4% for a field planted to sweet potatoes. Fields in ten other crops had soil and water losses between these extremes.

20–5.9 Nicaragua

Nicaragua is located in Central America between 11° and 15° north latitude. Elevations range from sea level to several thousand meters. The northeast trade winds bring moist air from the Caribbean Sea from December through February, and the southeast trade winds bring moist air from the Pacific Ocean from June to August.

Temperatures are warm and rainfall throughout Nicaragua is heavy and variable, depending on the direction of the air masses as deflected and modified by mountains. On the western Pacific Coast, Managua, the capitol, receives about 1200 mm of annual precipitation but has a dry season from December to February because the mountains intercept a large part of the rainfall from the northeast trade winds. The wet season is from June through August because the moist southeast trade winds drop moisture as they rise over the mountains. Mean annual precipitation at other stations in the country varies from about 1000 mm to 4370 mm, but all stations have several dry months. Water erosion from heavy rains is a hazard during the wet season, and serious wind erosion occurs during the dry season.

Cotton has been grown for many years on productive, fine-textured, well-drained, fairly level soils that are dry during summer months. The seedbed is usually prepared in June by moldboard plowing and many harrowings. Cotton is usually planted in July or August and emerges in late August. The soil is dry, loose, and unprotected during this period. Strong southeasterly winds cause severe wind erosion, seedings are often blown out, and dust storms degrade the air environment for many kilometers.

Some cotton growers use windbreaks to protect their cotton fields. Preparations for a windbreak are shown in Figure 20-13. These windbreaks have consisted of the following (Darby, 1978):

1. Border windbreaks on the windward side of the field, consisting of a row of eucalyptus trees in the center, a row of leadtrees on the windward side, and a row of cassia trees on the leeward side. The rows of trees are 3 m apart and trees are 2.5 m apart in each row.
2. Barrier strips (field windbreaks) consisting of two rows of napiergrass, four rows of corn, or two rows of tall sorghum between every twelve rows of cotton. Other wind-erosion control practices recommended include the use of a lister to prepare the seedbed, a disk plow instead of a moldboard plow, fewer harrowings, and minimum tillage.

20-6 ONLY A SAMPLING

This is not the end of the story. Erosion and pollution problems exist in every country, and each country has its own approach to

Figure 20-13 Site preparation for a windbreak to be planted at the edge of a cotton field in Nicaragua. (Courtesy USDA—Soil Conservation Service.)

managing and conserving soil and water. This book has sampled only a few of the many examples that could have been cited. Many other problems and solutions could have served as well, but those chosen will convey something of the breadth and magnitude of the need for soil and water conservation in the United States and around the world.

Many things change with time, and the conservation story is no exception. People come and go and they change their ways of doing things. Even small changes may have great impact on the soil and water resources on which everyone depends. Governments and their programs are always limited by earth's finite land base. The human population, however, has never stopped increasing. The pressure on soil and water resources increases with the population. The need to protect the environment and the productivity of the earth is already great and is becoming greater. Everyone's life depends on these resources. Soil and water conservation is everybody's business.

SUMMARY

Soil and water conservation practices are essential around the world to retain the productive base of agriculture needed to support a rapidly increasing population. Most countries have established some kind of conservation agency, often based on the model of the USDA—Soil Conservation Service. Progress to date, however, has been uneven, partly because the differences in culture, soil, and agriculture are so great that adaptation is necessary but usually has been inadequate. Massive mechanization schemes, as well as most temperate-region techniques of soil management, have failed in the tropics. One reason is that most soils in the tropics, when cropped continuously, form surface crusts and become cloddy, and crop yields soon decline below economic levels.

Shifting cultivation is the traditional technique used in forested tropics to maintain yields and control the loss of soil and water. This consists of two to three years of cultivated crops followed by ten to twenty years of wild trees and shrubs. Some Vertisols in the tropics are burned and cropped until yields decline, then are "rested in native grass" to rejuvenate them.

Terracing and ridging on the contour have failed in many tropical and subtropical regions because of physical deterioration of the soil. The use of annual cover crops has also failed because the additional tillage they require is conducive to erosion. Perennial crops in rotation with cultivated crops are satisfactory if the perennial crop is killed with an herbicide and the following crop is planted in the crop residue.

The most successful techniques of continuous cropping in the tropics have been these two soil-management systems:

1. Maintain an organic surface mulch at all times (no-tillage), or
2. Scientifically determine the major and minor nutrients required for each crop grown and supply them in the amounts needed at the times when the plants can absorb them. This approach must also include the incorporation of enough plant and animal residues to maintain suitable soil tilth.

QUESTIONS

1. Why doesn't the technology of the U.S. Corn Belt work for raising corn in Nigeria?
2. Defend these statements: "Shifting cultivation is a successful technique of agricultural production." "Shifting cultivation is a failure and must be replaced by a more efficient system."
3. Explain how to stabilize the soil in the arid tropics against water and wind and at the same time keep it productive for agriculture.
4. Tell how to control erosion in the humid forested tropics while harvesting continuous agricultural crops.
5. Why does the USSR have so many windbreaks and shelterbelts?

REFERENCES

ARAKERI, H. R., G. V. CHALAM, P. SATAYARANAYA, and R. L. DONAHUE, 1962. *Soil Management in India,* 2d ed., Asia Publishing House, Bombay, India, 609 p.

BENSALEM, B., 1977. Examples of soil and water conservation practices in North African Countries, Algeria, Morocco, and Tunisia. In *Soil Conservation and Management in Developing Countries.* Soil Bull. 33, Food and Agriculture Organization of the United Nations, Rome, Italy, p. 151-160.

BLOOMFIELD, N. J., 1977. *An Evaluation of Soil Erosion in Southern Brazil, and a Proposal for an Integrated National Program of Soil Conservation and Soil Survey.* M. S. Thesis, University of Wisconsin, Madison.

CENTRAL INTELLIGENCE AGENCY, 1974. *USSR Agriculture Atlas.* U.S. Supt. of Documents, Government Printing Office, Washington, D.C.

CHINZEI, T., K. OYA, Z. KOJA, R. L. DONAHUE, and J. C. SHICKLUNA, 1967. *Soils and Land Use in the Ryukyu Islands.* University of the Ryukyus, Naha, Okinawa, 187 p. (In English and Japanese.)

CONSTANTINESCO, I., 1976. *Soil Conservation for Developing Countries.* Soils Bull. 30, Food and Agriculture Organization of the United Nations, Rome, Italy, 92 p.

COX, M. P., 1977. *On-Farm Management at the Field Level in Pakistan.* Unpublished paper presented at the Seminar on Water Management, Lahore, Pakistan, Nov. 15-17, 1977, 12 p.

DARBY, G. M., 1978. Controlling wind erosion in Nicaragua. *Soil Conservation* 43(11):18-19.

DAS, D.C., 1977. Soil conservation practices and erosion control in India—A case study. In *Soil Conservation and Management in Developing Countries,* FAO Soils Bull. 33, Food and Agriculture Organization of the United Nations, Rome, Italy, p. 11-50.

DONAHUE, R. L., 1969. *Mechanization as an Essential Factor for Increasing Agricultural Productivity in Equatorial Africa.* Terminal Report for the period October 1, 1967 to March 31, 1969. Michigan State University—United States Agency for International Development.

DONAHUE, R. L., 1972. *Ethiopia: Taxonomy, Cartography, and Ecology of Soils.* Monograph No. 1, African Studies Center and the Institute of International Agriculture, Michigan State University, 44 p.

GEIGER, L. C., 1978. Soil survey in Liberia. *Soil Conservation* 43(11):16-17.

IITA, 1975. *Annual Report.* International Institute of Tropical Agriculture, Ibadan, Nigeria, 219 p.

IITA, 1978. *IITA Research Highlights, 1977.* International Institute of Tropical Agriculture, Ibadan, Nigeria, 72 p.

LAL, RATTAN, 1974. Soil erosion and shifting agriculture. In *Shifting Cultivation and Soil Conservation in Africa*, Soil Bull. 24, Swedish International Development Authority and Food and Agriculture Organization of the United Nations, Rome, Italy, p. 48-71.

LE HOUÉROU, H. N., 1976. Can desertization be halted? In *Conservation in Arid and Semiarid Zones*, FAO Conservation Guide 3, Food and Agriculture Organization of the United Nations, Rome, Italy, p. 1-15.

NATIONAL COMMISSION ON AGRICULTURE, INDIA, 1976. *Report of the National Commission on Agriculture*, Part V, Resource Development, Government of India Press, New Delhi, p. 177-322.

NORTH CAROLINA STATE UNIVERSITY, 1976. *Tropical Soils Research Program, Annual Report for 1975*, Raleigh, North Carolina, 312 p.

OTHIENO, C. O., and D. H. LAYCOCK, 1977. Factors affecting soil erosion within tea fields. *Trop. Agric.* 54: 323-330.

PRESIDENT'S ADVISORY COMMITTEE ON WORLD FOOD SUPPLY, 1967. *The World Food Problem*, Vol. II, Washington, D.C., p. 471-500.

RAPP, ANDERS, 1977. Soil erosion and reservoir sedimentation—Case studies in Tanzania. In *Soil Conservation and Management in Developing Countries*. Soils Bull. 33, Food and Agriculture Organization of the United Nations, Rome, Italy, p. 123-131.

SANCHEZ, P. A. (ed.), 1973. *A Review of Soils Research in Tropical Latin America.* North Carolina Agr. Expt. Sta. in cooperation with the U.S. Agency for International Development, 197 p.

SEUBERT, C. E., P. A. SANCHEZ, and C. VALVERDE, 1977. Effects of land clearing methods on soil properties of an Ultisol and crop performance in the Amazon jungle of Peru. *Trop. Agric.* 54:307-321.

VIEWEG, G., and W. WILMS, 1974. Problems associated with a change from shifting cultivation to permanent cultivation of a light soil in the Kilombero

Valley, Tanzania. In *Shifting Cultivation and Soil Conservation in Africa*. Soils Bull. 24, Swedish International Development Authority and Food and Agriculture Organization of the United Nations, Rome, Italy, p. 228-229.

WILKINSON, G. E., 1975. Canopy characteristics of maize and the effect on soil erosion in western Nigeria. *Trop. Agric.* 52:289-297.

Appendix A
Conversion Factors

Most of the units of measurement in this book are part of the metric system of SI (from the French title "Le Système International d' Unités). The SI system, with some variations, is in nearly universal use around the world. Its use in the United States is growing, having been authorized or promoted by acts of Congress such as the act in 1866 authorizing the use of both metric units and foot-pound-second units. In 1975 U.S. Public Law 94–168 authorized the establishment of a seventeen-member board to plan for voluntary conversion to metric units by 1985.

The SI system uses six basic units of measurement. These are metre (m) for length, kilogramme (kg) for mass, second (s) for time, degrees Kelvin (K) for temperature, ampere (A) for electric current, and candela (cda) for luminous intensity. The first three of these are used in this book (with the American spellings of meter and kilogram) along with the prefixes kilo- (10^3), hecto- (10^2), centi- (10^{-2}), and milli- (10^{-3}). Degrees Celsius (°C) is generally used instead of degrees Kelvin for temperature. The required units are used in various combinations to produce units for area (m^2), volume (m^3), velocity (m/s), and other measurements as needed. Certain combinations have been named and symbolized to shorten the notations; for example, joules (j) are used for kg m^2/s^2. A few nonrelated units such as atmospheres have been used for convenience. Occasionally, units related to the foot-pound-second system have been mentioned where essential for the material being discussed.

The following list of conversion factors is intended to relate the units used in this book to each other and to significant units from the foot-pound-second system. Some combination units are included

in the list; the others can be derived from those shown. For convenience, the units are grouped according to function.

Length, distance, depth, height (meter and its derivatives)
    1 km = 1000 m = 100,000 cm = 1,000,000 mm = 0.6214 miles
        = 3281 ft
    1 m = 100 cm = 1000 mm = 1.094 yd = 3.281 ft = 39.37 in.
    1 cm = 10 mm = 0.3937 in.

Area ($meter^2$ and derivatives, hectare)
    1 km^2 = 100 ha = 0.3861 $mile^2$ = 247.1 acres
    1 ha = 10,000 m^2 = 2.471 acres

Volume ($meter^3$, liter, milliliter, $centimeter^3$, hectare-meter, hectare-
        centimeter)
    1 m^3 = 1000 ℓ = 1,000,000 ml = 35.32 ft^3 = 264.2 gal (U.S.)
    1 ℓ = 1000 ml = 1000 cm^3 = 1.057 qt (U.S.) = 61.02 $in.^3$
    1 ha-m = 10,000 m^3 = 8.107 acre-ft
    1 ha-cm = 100 m^3 = 0.9728 acre-in.

Weight (metric ton, gram and its derivatives, quintal)
    1 mt = 1000 kg = 1,000,000 g = 1.102 short tons = 0.984 long tons
        = 2204.6 lb
    1 q = 100 kg = 100,000 g = 220.5 lb = 2.205 hundredweight (cwt)
    (US)
    1 kg = 1000 g = 2.2046 lb
    1 g = 1000 mg = 0.03527 oz (avoirdupois)

Yield (weight per hectare)
    1 mt/ha = 10 q/ha = 1000 kg/ha = 0.446 short tons/acre =
        892 lb/acre
    1 q/ha = 100 kg/ha = 1.49 bu/ac (wheat at 60 lb/bu)
                        = 1.59 bu/ac (corn at 56 lb/bu)
                        = 1.59 bu/ac (sorghum at 56 lb/bu)
    1 kg/ha = 0.892 lb/ac

Density (weight per unit volume)
    1 g/cm^3 = 62.4 lb/ft^3

Pressure, tension (weight per unit area)
    1 kg/cm^2 = 10 m of H_2O = 14.22 $lb/in.^2$ = 0.968 atm = 0.981 bar
    1 atm = 1.013 bar = 1.033 kg/cm^2 = 14.7 $lb/in.^2$

Force (newton)
    1 N = 1 kg m/sec^2 = 100,000 dynes

Energy, work (joule)
    1 j = 1 kg m^2/sec^2 = 10,000,000 ergs = 0.2387 cal = 0.7377 ft-lb

Velocity, permeability (distance per second, minute, or hour)
1 m/sec = 100 cm/sec = 3.6 km/hr = 2.237 miles/hr
1 cm/sec = 0.3937 in./sec = 1.969 ft/min
1 km/hr = 1000 m/hr = 100,000 cm/hr = 0.6214 miles/hr
1 cm/hr = 10 mm/hr = 0.3937 in./hr

Flow rates (volume per second or hour)
1 m^3/sec = 1000 ℓ/sec = 3600 m^3/hr = 35.32 feet^3/sec

Viscosity (poise)
1 p = 0.1 kg/m-sec

Temperature (degrees Celsius, Kelvin)
°C = °K - 273.15 = (°F - 32) /1.8

Chemical concentrations (normal, gram-equivalent)
1 N = 1 g-eq/ℓ = 1000 meq/ℓ
1 g-eq = gram-weight of 1 mole/valence
1 meq/100 g = 1 mg-eq/100 g

Electrical conductivity (millimho/cm)
1 mmho/cm = 0.001 mho/cm = 0.001 siemen/cm

Ratios (percent, parts per million)
1/1 = 100% = 1,000,000 ppm

Appendix B
Common and Scientific Names of Plants Mentioned in the Text

The common English names of plants vary widely from one place to another. The following list is supplied to remove any ambiguity that would otherwise arise from the common names used in this book. The equivalent scientific names listed here should have worldwide meaning. The names were selected from the following six standard references:

ANDERSON, K. L., and C. E. OWENSBY, 1969. *Common Names of a Selected List of Plants*, Tech. Bull. No. 117, Kansas State University, 62 p.

BAILEY, L. H., and ETHEL ZOE BAILEY, 1976. *Hortus Third: A Concise Dictionary of Plants Cultivated in the United States and Canada*. Macmillan, New York, 1290 p.

HALLS, L. K., ed. 1977. *Southern Fruit-producing Woody Plants Used by Wildlife*. General Tech. Report SO-16, USDA—Forest Service, 235 p.

HANSON, A. A., 1972. *Grass Varieties in the United States*. Agriculture Handbook No. 170, ARS, U.S. Dept. of Agriculture, 124 p.

SOIL CONSERVATION SERVICE, 1978. *Plant Performance on Surface Coal Mine Spoil in Eastern United States*. TP-155, U.S. Dept. of Agriculture, 76 p.

TERRELL, E. E., 1977. *A Checklist of Names for 3000 Vascular Plants of Economic Importance*. Agriculture Handbook No. 505. ARS, U.S. Dept. of Agriculture, 201 p.

Acacia—*Acacia farnesiana*
Alder, European black—*Alnus glutinosa*
Alfalfa—*Medicago sativa*
Alkaligrass, nuttall—*Puccinellia airoides*
Alkali sacaton—*Sporobolus airoides*

American cranberrybush—*Viburnum trilobum*
Apple—*Malus* species
Apricot:
　Manchurian—*Prunus* species
　Siberian—*Prunus* species
Argan tree—*Argania spinosa*

Ash:
    green—*Fraxinus pennsylvanica*
    white—*Fraxinus americana*
Asparagus—*Asparagus officinalis*
Aspen, trembling—*Populus tremu-loides*

Babul—*Acacia arabica*
Bahiagrass—*Paspalum notatum*
Banana—*Musa* species
Barley—*Hordeum vulgare*
Basswood—*Tilia americana*
Bayberry—*Myrica cerifera*
Beachgrass:
    American—*Ammophila breviligulata*
    European—*Ammophila arenaria*
Beachpea—*Lathyrus japonicus*
Bean (bush, climbing, wild)—*Phaseolus* species
    field—*Phaseolus vulgaris*
Beech, American—*Fagus grandifolia*
Beets, red (garden)—*Beta vulgaris*
Bermudagrass:
    (common and coastal)—*Cynodon dactylon*
    African—*Cynodon transvaalensis*
Birch, white—*Betula alba*
Birch, yellow—*Betula allegheniensis*
Birdsfoot trefoil—*Lotus corniculatus*
Bitterbrush:
    antelope—*Purshia tridentata*
    desert—*Purshia glandulosa*
Blueberry—*Vaccinium* species
Bluegrass:
    big—*Poa ampla*
    Kentucky—*Poa pratensis*
Bluestem:
    big—*Andropogon gerardi*
    broomsedge—*Andropogon virginicus*
    little—*Andropogon scoparius*
    sand—*Andropogon hallii*
    seacoast—*Andropogon littoralis*
    yellow—*Andropogon ischaemum*
Boxelder—*Acer negundo*
Bromegrass:
    California—*Bromus carinatus*

mountain—*Bromus marginatus*
smooth—*Bromus inermis*
Buckthorn—*Rhamnus* species
Buckwheat—*Fagopyrum esculentum*
Buffaloberry, russet—*Shepherdia argentea*
Buffalograss—*Buchloe dactyloides*

Cabbage—*Brassica oleracea*
Cactus—*Cactaea* species
Calligonum—*Calligonum arich*
Camellia—*Camellis japonica*
Caper bush—*Capparis spinosa*
Caragana—*Caragana arborescens*
Carob tree—*Ceratonia siliqua*
Carrot—*Daucus carota*
Cashew—*Anacardium occidentale*
Cassava (tapioca)—*Manihot esculenta*
Cassia—*Cassia* species
Cattail, common—*Typha latafolia*
Cedar:
    incense—*Calocedrus decurrens*
    red- —*Juniperus virginiana*
    salt—*Tamarix articulata*
    white—*Thuja occidentalis*
Century plant—*Agave* species
Cherry:
    black—*Prunus serotina*
    Nanking—*Prunus tomentosa*
Chinese silvergrass—*Miscanthus sinensis*
Chokecherry, common—*Prunus virginiana*
Cinquefoil—*Potentilla fruticosa*
Clover:
    alsike—*Trifolium hybridum*
    crimson—*Trifolium incarnatum*
    ladino—*Trifolium repens*
    red—*Trifolium pratense*
    white (Dutch)—*Trifolium repens*
Coffee:
    arabica—*Coffea arabica*
    robusta—*Coffea robusta*
Corn, field, pop, or sweet—*Zea mays*
Cotoneaster—*Cotoneaster apiculata*
Cotton, American, Egyptian—*Gossypium barbadense*

Cottonwood—*Populus deltoides*
Cowpea—*Vigna unguiculata*
Crabapple:
    Japanese flowering—*Malus floribunda*
    Manchurian—*Malus sylvestris*
    Siberian—*Malus baccata*
    tea—*Malus hupenhensis*
    toringo—*Malus sieboldi*
Cranberry—*Vaccinium macrocarpon*
Creosotebush—*Larrea tridentata*
Crownvetch—*Coronilla varia*
Currant, golden—*Ribes* species
Cypress, bald—*Taxodium distichum*

Dallisgrass—*Paspalum dilatatum*
Deertongue—*Panicum clandestinum*
Desert saltbush—*Atriplex polycarpa*
Dogwood:
    flowering—*Cornus florida*
    redosier—*Cornus stolonifera*

Elm:
    American—*Ulmus americana*
    Chinese—*Ulmus parvifolia*
    chinkota—*Ulmus* species
Eucalyptus—*Eucalyptus brockwayi*

Fescue:
    red and Arctared—*Festuca rubra*
    tall—*Festuca arundinacea*
Fig—*Ficus* species
Fir:
    Alpine—*Abies lasciocarpa*
    Douglas—*Pseudotsuga menziesii*
    white—*Abies concolor*
Flatpea—*Lathyrus sylvestris*
Flax—*Linum usitatissimum*
Fourwing saltbush—*Atriplex canescens*
Foxtail, creeping—*Alopecurus arundinaceus*

Glyricidia—*Glyricidia maculata*
Grama:
    black—*Bouteloua eripoda*

    blue—*Bouteloua gracilis*
    sideoats—*Bouteloua curtipendula*
Grape—*Vitus* species
Guineagrass—*Panicum maximum*
Gum arabic—*Acacia senegal*

Hackberry—*Celtis* species
Hairgrass, Bering tufted—*Deschampsia caespitosa*
Hanson hedgerose—*Rosa* species
Harbin pear—*Pyrus communis*
Hardinggrass—*Phalaris tuberosa*
Hawthorne, Arnold—*Crataegus* species
Hemlock:
    eastern—*Tsuga canadensis*
    ground—*Taxus canadensis*
    western—*Tsuga heterophylla*
Hickory—*Carya* species
Hoary milkpea—*Galactia mollis*
Honeylocust, thornless—*Gleditsia triacanthos*
Honeysuckle:
    amur—*Lonicera maackii*
    tartarian—*Lonicera tartarica*
Horseradish tree—*Moringa pterygosperma*
Horsetail tree (casuarina)—*Casuarina cunninghamia*

Indiangrass—*Sorghastrum nutans*
Indigobush—*Amorpha fruiticosa*
Iris, wild—*Iris pseudacorus*

Jerusalem thorn—*Parkinsonia aculeata*
Johnsongrass—*Sorghum halepense*
Jujube—*Zizyphus* species
Juniper:
    creeping—*Juniperus horizontalis*
    one-seed—*Juniperus monosperma*
    Rocky Mountain—*Juniperus scopulorum*

Kanju—*Holoptelia integrifolia*
Kassod tree—*Cassia siamea*
Kelp, giant—*Macrocystis pyrifera*

Kentucky coffeetree—*Gymnocladus dioica*
Khejri—*Prosopis specigera*
Kochia—*Kochia prostrata*
Kudzu—*Pueraria lobata*

Larch:
    Siberian—*Larix* species
    western—*Larix occidentalis*
Leadplant—*Amorpha canescens*
Leadtree—*Leucaena leucocephala*
Lespedeza:
    bicolor—*Lespedeza bicolor*
    common (annual)—*Lespedeza striata*
    Japan (Japanese)—*Lespedeza japonica*
    sericea—*Lespedeza cuneata*
Lilac—*Syringa vulgaris*
    late—*Syringa villosa*
Locust:
    African—*Parkia clappertoniana*
    black—*Robinia pseudoacacia*
    bristly—*Robinia fertilis, R. hispida*
Lovegrass:
    Korean—*Eragrostis ferruginea*
    Lehmann—*Eragrostis lehmanniana*
    sand—*Eragrostis trichodes*
    weeping—*Eragrostis curvula*
Lupine:
    blue—*Lupinus augustifolius*
    wild—*Lupinus perennis*

Madras thorn—*Inga dulcis*
Maple:
    amur—*Acer ginnala*
    red—*Acer rubrum*
    silver (white)—*Acer saccharinum*
    sugar—*Acer saccharum*
Manzanita, pinemat—*Archtostaphylos* species
Mesquitegrass, vine—*Panicum obtusum*
Mesquite tree—*Prosopis chilensis*
Milkvetch—*Astralagus cicer*
    cicer—*Astragalus cicer*
Mulberry, red—*Morus rubra*

Mulga—*Acacia aneura*
Munj—*Saccharum munja*

Napiergrass—*Pennisetum purpureum*
Neem tree—*Azadirachta indica*

Oak:
    bur—*Quercus macrocarpa*
    northern red—*Quercus rubra*
    silk—*Grevillea robusta*
    southern red—*Quercus falcata*
    white—*Quercus alba*
Oat, common—*Avena sativa*
Olive:
    autumn—*Elaegnus umbellata*
    Russian—*Elaegnus angustifolia*
    tree—*Olea europaea*
Onion—*Allium cepa*
Orange—*Citrus sinensis*
Orchardgrass—*Dactylis glomerata*
Osage-orange—*Maclura pomifera*

Palm:
    date—*Phoenix dactylifera*
    oil—*Elaeis guineensis*
Pangolagrass—*Digitaria decumbens*
Panicgrass, coastal—*Panicum amarulum*
Pea, Austrian winter—*Lathyrus hirsutus*
Peanut—*Arachis hypogaea*
Pearl millet—*Pennisetum americanum*
Pea-tree, Siberian—*Caragana arborescens*
Pecan—*Carya illinoensis*
Penstemon—*Penstemon fruticosus*
Pepper, bell—*Capsicum annuum*
Phog—*Calligonum polygonoides*
Pineapple—*Ananas comosus*
Pine:
    Aleppo—*Pinus halepensis*
    Austrian—*Pinus nigra*
    eastern white—*Pinus strobus*
    jack—*Pinus banksiana*
    loblolly—*Pinus taeda*
    lodgepole—*Pinus contorta*
    longleaf—*Pinus palustris*

Monterey—*Pinus radiata*
mugho—*Pinus mugo*
pitch—*Pinus rigida*
ponderosa—*Pinus ponderosa*
red—*Pinus resinosa*
sand—*Pinus clausa*
Scotch (Scots)—*Pinus sylvestris*
shore—*Pinus contorta*
shortleaf—*Pinus echinata*
slash—*Pinus elliottii*
Virginia—*Pinus virginiana*
western white—*Pinus monticola*
Plum:
American—*Prunus americana*
Assyrian—*Cordia myxa*
beach—*Prunus maritima*
chickasaw—*Prunus angustifolia*
Poplar:
curly—*Populus canescens*
northwest, Norway (hybrid)—
Populus sargentii
robusta (hybrid)—*Populus robusta*
white (silver)—*Populus alba*
yellow (tulip)—*Liriodendron
tulipifera*
Potato:
Irish (white)—*Solanum tuberosum*
sweet—*Ipomoea batatas*
Privet, amur—*Ligustrum amurense*

Rape—*Brassica napus*
Redbud—*Cercis canadensis*
Redgum—*Eucalyptus rostrata*
Redtop grass—*Agrostis alba*
Redwood—*Sequoia sempervirens*
Reed canarygrass—*Phalaris arundi-
nacea*
Rhodesgrass—*Chloris gayana*
Rice—*Oryza sativa*
Ricegrass, Mandan (Indian)—*Oryzopsis
hymenoides*
Rosemary—*Rosmarinus officinalis*
Rose:
memorial—*Rosa wichuraiana*
multiflora—*Rosa multiflora*
wild—*Rosa blanda*

Rubber—*Hevea braziliensis*
Ryegrass:
Italian—*Lolium multiflorum*
perennial—*Lolium perenne*

Safed kikar—*Acacia leucophlces*
Safflower—*Carthamus tinctorius*
Sagebrush—*Artemisia* species
Sainfoin—*Onobrychis biciaefolia*
Salsola shrub—*Salsola paletskiana, S.
richteri*
Saltgrass, seashore—*Distichlis spicata*
Salvadora—*Salvadora persica, S.
oloides*
Sand dropseed—*Sporobolus cryptan-
drus*
Sandgrass—*Triplasis purpurea*
Saskatoon serviceberry—*Amelanchier
alnifolia*
Sassafras—*Sassafras albidum*
Sausage tree—*Kigelia pinnata*
Scalebroom—*Lepidospartum squam-
tum*
Scotch-broom—*Cytisus scoparius*
Sea-oats grass—*Uniola paniculata*
Sesame—*Sesamum indicum*
Shinus—*Shinus terebinthifolius, S.
molle*
Silverberry—*Elaeagnus argentea, E.
commutata*
Siris—*Albizzia lebbek*
Sissoo—*Dalbergia sissoo*
Snowberry—*Symphoricarpus
racemosus*
Soapberry—*Sapindus saponaria*
Sorghum, grain—*Sorghum bicolor*
Soybean—*Glycine max*
Spruce:
black—*Picea mariana*
Black Hills—*Picea glauca*
Colorado—*Picea pungens*
Engelmann—*Picea engelmanii*
Norway—*Picea abies*
white—*Picea glauca, P. canadensis*
Squawcarpet—*Ceanothus prostratus*
Stargrass—*Cynodon plectostachyum*
Strawberry—*Fragaria* species

Sudangrass—*Sorghum sudanense*
Sugarcane—*Saccharum officinarum*
Sumac:
  fragrant—*Rhus aramatica*
  shining—*Rhus copallina*
Sunflower—*Helianthus annuus*
Sweetclover:
  white—*Melilotus alba*
  yellow—*Melilotus officinalis*
Sweetgale—*Myrica gale*
Sweetgum—*Liquidambar styraciflua*
Switchgrass—*Panicum virgatum*
Sycamore (American)—*Platanus occidentalis*

Tamarind—*Tamarindus indica*
Tamarix (tamarisk)—*Tamarix aphylla, T. nilotica*
Tapioca (cassava)—*Manihot esculenta*
Tarwar—*Cassia auriculata*
Tassili cypress—*Cupressus dupreziana*
Tea—*Camellia theifera, C. sinensis*
Thistle, Russian—*Salsola kali*
Timothy—*Phleum pratense*
Tobosagrass—*Hilaria mutica*
Tomato—*Lycopersicon esculentum*
Tumbleweed—*Amaranthus albus*

Veldtgrass—*Ehrharta calycina*
Vetch:
  hairy—*Vicia villosa*
  reseeding—*Vicia* species

Virginia-creeper—*Parthanocissus quinquefolia*
Vitex—*Vitex negundo*

Water lily, fragrant—*Nymphaea odorato*
Wax myrtle—*Myrica cerifera*
Western sandcherry—*Prunus besseyi*
Wheat, common—*Triticum aestivum*
Wheatgrass:
  crested—*Agropyron desertorum*
  intermediate—*Agropyron intermedium*
  pubescent—*Agropyron trichophorum*
  Siberian—*Agropyron sibiricum*
  slender—*Agropyron trachycaulum*
  tall—*Agropyron elongatum*
  western—*Agropyron smithii*
Wildbean, trailing—*Strophostyles helvola*
Wildrye:
  beardless—*Elymus triticoides*
  Canada—*Elymus canadensis*
  Russian—*Elymus junceus*
  Volga—*Elymus giganteus*
Willow:
  crack—*Salix fragilis*
  desert—*Chilopsis linearis*
  diamond—*Salix euriocephala*
  laurel—*Salix pentandra*
Wintergreen—*Gaultheria procumbens*

Appendix C
Suggested Laboratory Exercises

1. *Soil-Loss Calculations.* The amounts of soil removed by specified amounts of sheet, rill, gully, and wind erosion can be calculated.
2. *Velocity and Energy of Water.* An eaves trough can be used to make an inexpensive water-flow channel. Equipped with an adjustable support, it can be used to measure water velocity on different slope gradients. The water volume can be measured by timing how long it takes to fill a container. Kinetic energy can then be calculated. The data can be graphed against slope gradient.
3. *Transporting Power of Water.* Sand grains of a particular size can be placed in an eaves trough and the velocity of water flow increased gradually until the grains begin to move. The water velocity can then be measured. Several sizes can be used and a graph prepared to relate velocity to grain size.
4. *Soil Permeability and Runoff.* Glass tubes a few centimeters in diameter and perhaps 20 cm long can be used to measure soil permeability and how it changes with time in various soils. The data can be used to calculate how much runoff would occur from a rainstorm of specified intensity and duration on a field of 10 ha.
5. *Rainfall and Erosion.* Artificial rainfall can be applied to a tray filled with soil. The time required to produce runoff, the rate of runoff, and the sediment contained in the run-off can all be measured. The type of soil can be varied and the experiment can be done with and without a mulch of plant residues.

6. *Wind Erosion.* An electric fan blowing across a bare sandy soil will produce wind erosion, especially if a small wind tunnel is used to guide the air flow. Saltation height and distance, relative amounts of deposition at various distances, and segregation of particle sizes can be studied with and without wind deflectors (windbreaks).

7. *Soil-Loss Prediction.* The water- and wind-erosion equations can be used to estimate soil loss under various defined circumstances. Alternatives can then be chosen to reduce erosion to specified tolerable levels. The water-erosion equation can also be used to estimate the amount of soil being carried into a stream or reservoir.

8. *Use of Soil Survey Reports.* An exercise sheet calling for a wide variety of types of soil information on erosion can be used for this exercise. The students obtain the answers from soil survey reports.

9. *Land Use Capabilities.* Classification theory and soil information can be combined in an exercise to assign land use capabilities to a group of soils. Each student can be assigned a land use capability unit to name and describe.

10. *Preparing Interpretive Maps.* A soil map can be used as a base to prepare interpretive maps for land use capabilities, suitability for various types of land use, and usefulness or limitations for various engineering practices.

11. *Planning Land Use and Management.* A soil map of a specific farm or other problem area can be used as a basis for planning the arrangements of field boundaries, lanes, cropping systems, and other land use and management decisions.

12. *Design and Layout.* Topographic maps and soil maps can be used for designing the layout of conservation practices such as strip cropping, terracing, shelterbelt plantings, drainage systems, and irrigation systems.

13. *Calculating Costs and Returns.* An economic analysis can be made of various land use and management alternatives. The costs and returns for each may be related to soil-loss predictions.

14. *Field Trips.* Field trips give the class an opportunity to see various erosion problems and the practices used to control them.

15. *Term Problem.* Several of the preceding exercises can be combined into a comprehensive term problem on soil and water conservation involving the use and management of a specific tract of land.

Index